WILLS & ADMINISTRATIONS

in the

Prerogative Court of Canterbury,

1610–1857

WILLS & ADMINISTRATIONS

in the

Prerogative Court of Canterbury,

1610–1857

Compiled by

Peter Wilson Coldham

Genealogical Publishing Co., Inc.

Copyright © 1989 by
Peter Wilson Coldham
Surrey, England
All Rights Reserved
Published by Genealogical Publishing Co., Inc.
1001 N. Calvert St., Baltimore, Md. 21202
Library of Congress Catalogue Card Number 88-83613
International Standard Book Number 0-8063-1235-1
Made in the United States of America

*Extracts from Crown Copyright Documents
are published by permission of
Her Majesty's Stationery Office*

Introduction

From mediaeval times until 1858 the proving of wills and the granting of administrations in England and Wales were matters falling almost exclusively to the ecclesiastical authorities who acted through any one of the 300 probate courts operating throughout the country.[1] The principal such court was the Prerogative Court of Canterbury (PCC), so called because its jurisdiction was exercised on behalf of the Archbishop of Canterbury, the Primate of All England. It was the PCC which handled all matters of probate affecting the personal estates remaining in England and Wales of subjects dying abroad or at sea, and its records are therefore of close genealogical interest to the descendants of those who chose, or were compelled, to emigrate to the American colonies.

During the past century and a half many abstracts and listings of American wills and administrations registered in the PCC have appeared in print, and spasmodic attempts have been made to provide finding aids. Such efforts have concentrated on the period prior to 1700, for which a variety of printed indexes are available, to the neglect of subsequent years for which the means of reference remain so inadequate as to present an almost insuperable barrier for those with limited time and funds at their disposal. This volume aims to bridge that gap and to bring together the many references scattered among other printed works.

A brief note on how the material for this volume has been assembled may be found useful. Summary notes of all grants of probate and administration registered in the PCC were recorded month by month in the Act Books (PROB 8 and PROB 6) now housed in the Public Record Office, Chancery Lane, London. (Until 1733 all entries in the Act Books were written in Latin.) Each Act Book covers a full year reckoned according to the modern calendar and is divided into sections called *Seats* or *Walks*, each covering a different territorial area. The Acts are consequently grouped according to the locality in which the testator or intestate resided or died. The so-called *Register Walk* catered for those areas falling outside the Province of Canterbury (the southern half of Britain), for all overseas territories, and for grants made following litigation. The Probate and Administration Act Books for 1609-1730 inclusive have been examined in their entirety in order to obtain abstracts of grants of American interest; thereafter, because of the dramatically increased volume of business being transacted by the PCC, only the *Register Walk* sections were scanned.

One advantage which derives from this approach is that many details not included in a will, such as the testator's relationships and place of death, and the record of subsequent disputes and grants, are revealed. Since executors and administrators tended to be closely related by blood or profession to those whose estates were entrusted to them, genealogical research relies heavily on these details.

It has been estimated that during the eighteenth century and earlier fewer than one person in ten in England died testate or had a personal estate of a sufficient value to warrant attention by one or other of the probate courts. The same pattern is discernible in the probate records of the colonial courts. Furthermore, throughout the colonial period there was a pronounced reluctance, for whatever reason, by those making wills both in England and America to refer to their transatlantic relatives. Added to these factors was the noticeable difficulty of the PCC clerks in absorbing the geographical complexities of a rapidly expanding colonial empire. Thus, for much of the seventeenth century they usually found it expedient to make notations such as "died in parts over the seas" rather than attempt any differentiation between Virginia, Africa or India. For this reason alone the names of a substantial number of early emigrants to Virginia and New England must be presumed "lost" from the record.

The principal reasons which determined the recording in the PCC of the will or administration of an English emigrant appear to have been:

a) Prestige and security. Throughout Britain and her possessions there was no higher probate court than the PCC. Its officials were not only efficient and thorough, they were well versed in conducting an international correspondence. The writ of the PCC ran wherever Britain ruled.

b) Necessity. The only safe way of protecting and controlling any assets remaining in England to the credit of a person who died overseas was through the agency of the PCC. Many residents in America during and after the colonial period were recruited to the Army and Navy and, when they died, it was often necessary for attornies to be appointed through the PCC to collect and distribute their wages.

c) Litigation. Claims against the estates of deceased persons and disputes about the validity and interpretation of wills, especially where these involved overseas claimants, were customarily heard in the PCC as the court of first instance, even when the aggrieved parties had little or no money. In support of such claims and disputes colonial wills were often brought in and re-proved in the PCC. A good example of such a process appears with the disputed estate of Bushrod Carpenter of Cornwall, p. 52.

The PCC registers therefore contain a large number of American wills previously proved in one or other of the colonial probate courts, the originals of some of which may have perished because of subsequent mishaps and hostilities.

It should be noted that the ecclesiastical courts of probate, including the PCC, had no jurisdiction over bequests of real estate and that, when such a bequest was disputed, it was necessary for the parties to resort to a court of common law. There are many such cases to be found amongst the records of the Chancery Court. Although freehold estate theoretically descended to the heir-at-law, this was not always the case. It may be noted, in passing, that slaves were regarded as personal property rather than real estate. When the PCC itself acted as a court of first instance where the validity of a will or grant of administration was disputed, depositions, affidavits and exhibits were assembled, and these documents now form a large part of the archives of this Court. Appeals against decisions reached by the PCC lay with the Court of Arches, whose records are kept in the Lambeth Palace Library, or with the High Court of Delegates, whose records are held by the Public Record Office. Appeals will also be found amongst the records of the Chancery Court.

The diversity of the documentary resources of the PCC has only recently been fully revealed and many classes of documents are still being calendared or indexed.[2] Of particular interest is the collection of warrants for administration or probate after 1666 (**PROB** 14), which usually state the place and date of the deceased's death. Since PCC grants could be made several years after a death in America, these documents have a special value.

An attempt has been made in this work to bring together a comprehensive calendar of American probates and administrations granted in the PCC from the earliest mention of Virginia to the demise of the Court in 1858. This volume includes all the material previously published,[3] but it has now been considerably expanded by the incorporation of grants discovered as the result of recent researches. Where wills of American interest have appeared in print or where additional information has been published, an attempt has been made to indicate this fact by the inclusion of abbreviations as follows:

American Colonists in English Records, by George Sherwood. 2 vols. London, 1932-1933. Abbreviated as **Sh**.

Genealogical Gleanings in England, by Henry FitzGilbert Waters. 2 vols. Boston: New England Historic Genealogical Society, 1901. Abbreviated as **Wa**.

Virginia Gleanings in England, by Lothrop Withington. Baltimore: Genealogical Publishing Co., Inc., 1980. Abbreviated as **Wi**.

National Genealogical Society Quarterly, Washington, D.C.: articles by Peter Wilson Coldham. Abbreviated as **NGSQ**.

American Loyalist Claims, by Peter Wilson Coldham. Washington, D.C.: National Genealogical Society, 1980. Abbreviated as **ALC**.

The following notes provide a brief description of the types of grant to be found in the PCC Act Books:

PROBATES

a. *Probate* was normally granted after an executor had submitted the original will to the PCC and when it had been found to be in order and subscribed by at least two witnesses. Executors could either attend the Court in person or be sworn by two local clergymen of the established church. Where one or more of the executors were unable to join in the swearing of probate, perhaps because they were overseas, the Probate Act would reserve powers to them to prove the will when they were able to attend and swear out *double probate*. A nuncupative will, i.e. a death-bed statement, was acceptable for probate provided it had been attested by three witnesses and the testator had been resident for ten days or more in the place where he died.

b. *Administration with will* annexed. A grant was made in this form when, for whatever reason, probate could not be granted to the executor(s) named or when the testator had omitted to include the name of an executor. In the case of American wills, grants were often made in this form because the named executors were unable to attend in person.

c. *Limited probate* empowered the executor(s) to act in the distribution of a testator's effects within defined limits of time or place, or portion of the estate. Grants of limited probate were usually accompanied by a lengthy legal disquisition in the appropriate Act Book.

d. *Limited administration with will* annexed. A grant of this kind, similar in form to c., was often made when the executor(s) was abroad for a period exceeding a year. After an American will had been probated in one of the colonial courts a copy could be transmitted to the PCC which would then empower a representative of the deceased to administer his effects in England and collect any debts owing to him.

Grants of probate and administrations with wills annexed (a. and b.) have been abstracted in abbreviated form so as to include all relevant information given in the Act Books; but limited grants (c. and d.), being usually lengthy and filled with legal jargon, have been only partially abstracted. Register copies of all wills noted in this volume are available for consultation in class PROB 11 at the Public Record Office in Chancery Lane, London. The means of reference to wills and probate acts are as follows:

Printed Indexes: 1385-1700; 1750-1800, A-G only (*in progress*).

Manuscript Calendars of Register Copies of Wills: PROB 12.

Probate Act Books: PROB 8. (Volumes for 1650, 1653, 1654 and 1662 wanting.)

Limited Probate Act Books: 1781 and 1800-1858. PROB 9.

Original Wills: PROB 10. (No index or calendar.)

ADMINISTRATIONS

a. *Administration*. Letters of administration were usually granted to the widow, next-of-kin, or principal creditor of a person who died without making a will, authorising the named administrator(s) to distribute the effects of the deceased.

b. *Limited administration* was granted when some limitation of time or place was imposed. In the case of Americans dying intestate such grants were usually limited to the administration of his effects in England. As with limited probates, the text of such grants tended to be lengthy and only the salient details are recorded in this volume.

Means of reference to grants of administration are as follows:

Administration Act Books: PROB 6. (Feb. 1643 to Apr. 1644 wanting.)

Limited Administration Act Books: 1810-1858. PROB 7.

[1] An account of these courts and their individual jurisdictions will be found in *Wills and Their Whereabouts* by Anthony J. Camp, London, 1974.

[2] A full description of the various classes of PCC documents appears in a publication of the Public Record Office, Chancery Lane, London WC2A 1LR, entitled *The Records of the Prerogative Court of Canterbury - A Provisional Guide*.

[3] *English Estates of American Colonists 1610-1699*; *English Estates of American Colonists 1700-1799*; and *English Estates of American Settlers 1800-1858*. (Baltimore: Genealogical Publishing Co., 1980-1981).

Peter Wilson Coldham
Purley, Surrey, England

October 1988
AMDG

A

Abbes, Edward, who died in Virginia. Probate to the relict, Sarah Abbes. (May 1637). Sh.Wi.

Abbott, James, of Charles Town, South Carolina, who died at sea. Administration to the sister, Mary Abbott. (May 1720).

Abbott, John, of St. Saviour, Southwark, Surrey, whose son, Josiah Abbott, was in New England. Probate to Sampson Eyton and Mary Eyton. (July 1693). Wa.

Abbott, Thomas, of H.M. ship *Russell*, bachelor. Administration to Jeremiah Jones, attorney for the father, Robert Abbott, now in Massachusetts Bay. (Jan. 1747).

Abbott, William, formerly of St. James' Street, Middlesex, but late of New York City. Administration to the relict, Eliza Abbott. (Aug. 1844).

Abdy, Roger, of London, merchant, who died overseas, bachelor, and who left a bequest to send vagrants to New England or Virginia. Probate to the brothers, Sir Thomas Abdy and Robert Abdy. (Sep.1642). Wi.

Abell, George, of Charles Town, South Carolina, widower. Probate to the brother, Thomas Abell. (Mar. 1742).

Abercrombie, James, of Philadelphia. Probate to William Neate, attorney for Charles and Alexander Stedman and Samuel McCall the younger in Philadelphia. (July 1761).

Abercrombie, James, Lieutenant-General of the 22nd Regiment, who died in Boston, New England. Administration with will to Arthur Mair, attorney for Lieutenant-General James Abercrombie, now in Glassaugh, Banffshire, Scotland. (Oct. 1775).

Abington, John, of St. Faith the Virgin, London, who had lands in Maryland. Administration with will to the sister, Muriel Parney, and to the niece by a brother, Muriel Abington; John Abington renouncing. (July 1694). Revoked and granted to William Isatt, guardian of John and Charles Nelmes. (Apr. 1698). Wa.

Ablett, Thomas, of Maryland, bachelor. Administration to Edward Parker, sole executor of the brother and next-of-kin, William Ablett, who died before administering. (Feb. 1755).

Aborn, Anne, of Providence, Rhode Island. Administration to Melvil Wilson, attorney for the husband, Peleg Aborn, in Providence. (May 1828).

Aborn, William Wellington, of Cranston, Rhode Island, bachelor. Administration to the father, Peleg Aborn. (June 1839).

Abrahams, Benjamin, formerly of Sheerness, Kent, but late of New Orleans, bachelor. Administration to the brother, Lawrence Abrahams; the mother, Rachel Abrahams, having died. (June 1857).

Achley, John, of London, merchant, who died in Virginia, bachelor. Probate to Dr. John Dolman of Stepney, Middlesex. (Nov. 1666). *See* NGSQ 67/61.

Acrod, Benjamin, of Hackney, Middlesex, who died in Pennsylvania. Administration to the relict, Sarah Acrod. (July 1684). Revoked and

Acrod, *(contd)* granted to John Acrod after sentence for validity of will, with similar powers reserved to Richard White. (Dec. 1684).

Acworth, John, of Philadelphia, merchant. Special administration with will to Abraham Acworth. (July 1746).

Adams, Elizabeth, of Rotherhithe, Surrey, widow, whose son was in Virginia. Probate to the daughter, Mary Adams. (Dec. 1660). Wa.

Adams, Henry, formerly of Loughton, Essex, bricklayer, but late of New York City, widower. Administration to the son, Charles Adams. (July 1848).

Adams, Henry the younger, of New York City, bachelor. Administration to Charles Adams, son and executor of the father, Henry Adams deceased. (July 1848).

Adams, James, of North Carolina, clerk, bachelor. Administration to Alexander Junes, attorney for the sisters and next-of-kin, Jannett and Elizabeth Adams, now in Aberdeen, Scotland. (Sep. 1711).

Addams, John, of St. Botolph Aldgate, London, who died in Virginia, bachelor. Administration to the mother, Anne Addams. (Aug. 1688).

Adams, Joseph, of York Town, Virginia, formerly of H.M. ship *Wolf* and late purser of H.M. ship *Fox*. Administration with will to Daniel Walton, attorney for the relict, Ann Adams, in York Town. (June 1758).

Adams, Robert, of Pennsylvania. Administration to the son and next heir, William Adams. (Nov. 1700).

Adams, William, of St. Ann, Limehouse, Middlesex, who died in Philadelphia, bachelor. Administration to the sister and only next-of-kin, Sarah, wife of Absalom Wood. (July 1756).

Addison, Anthony, of Prince George County, Maryland. Probate to the nephew, Henry Addison Callis. (Feb. 1838).

Aderne. *See* **Arderne**.

Adler, Joseph, marine of H.M. ship *Glasgow* who died in South Carolina. Administration to the father, Joseph Adler. (Aug. 1775).

Agar, Margaret, formerly Margaret Hayward, of New Orleans, widow. Administration to the sister, Ann, wife of John Saunderson. (Mar. 1827).

Aglionby, William, of Savannah, Georgia. Probate to William Bradley. (May 1745).

Agnew, James, Brigadier-General of St. Andrew, Auckland, Co. Durham, Lieutenant-General of the 44th Regiment, who died in German Town, North America. Probate to the relict, Elizabeth Agnew. (Feb. 1778).

Aire, Robert, purser of H.M. ship *Deal*, who died in New York, bachelor. Administration to the sisters, Jane, wife of Thomas Morland, and Mary, wife of Richard Thompson; the father, Thomas Aire, having renounced. (Dec. 1771).

Arey, John, of North Carolina, bachelor. Probate to Henry Trenchard Goodenough. (Nov. 1771).

Airey, Joseph, of York County, New York, Lieutenant of an Independent Company. Administration to James Goldtrap, attorney for the relict,

Airey, *(contd)*
Mary Airey, in New York. (May 1764).

Aishley. *See* **Ashley**.

Albin, Catherine. *See* **King**.

Albro, Maturian, of West Greenwich, Kent County, Rhode Island, belonging to Lieutenant-Colonel Christopher Hargill's Company in the Rhode Island Regiment of Foot, who died in Havanna, bachelor. Administration by his solemn declaration to Joseph Sherwood, attorney for the brother and next-of-kin, John Albro, in West Greenwich. (Dec. 1765).

Alcock, George, of St. Katherine Creechurch, London, who had lands in New England. Probate to Benjamin Walker and Peter Thatcher with similar powers reserved to Zachariah Whitman. (Mar. 1677). Wa.

Alcock, William, of Mollington, Oxfordshire, whose brother, George Elkington, was in New Jersey. Probate to Francis Abbitts. (Jan. 1738).

Alderne, Thomas, of Hackney, Middlesex, who had lands in New England. Probate to the relict, Dorothy Alderne, with similar powers reserved to Owen Row, Thomas Ludington and John Greene. (June 1657). Revoked on the death of the relict and administration granted to Edward Alderne, doctor of laws, uncle and guardian of the testator's children, Thomas, Owen, Edward and Dorothy Alderne. (Dec. 1660). Wa.

Alderson, Robert, formerly of Stockton-on-Tees, Durham, but late of Hopkins Creek, California, bachelor. Administration to the brother and sisters, Daniel Forsick Alderson, Elizabeth Hill, widow, and Martha Alderson. (May 1857).

Alexander, David, of Glasgow, Scotland, who died in Maryland, bachelor. Administration to the brother, James Alexander. (Apr. 1757).

Alexander, Isabella, formerly of Londonderry, Ireland, but late of Baltimore, United States of America, spinster. Administration to the nephew, James McClintock. (June 1839).

Alexander, James, formerly of Maidstone, Kent, but late of New York and East Florida. Limited administration to Edward Wildes, attorney for George Burr of Maidstone. (Dec. 1826). Revoked and granted to James George Langham. (Dec. 1832). Revoked and granted to Henry Atkinson Wildes. (Oct. 1840).

Alexander, John, of St. Olave, Southwark, Surrey, (bound for Carolina). Probate to the relict, Jane Alexander. (July 1700).

Alexander, Robert, of Kentucky, United States of America. Probate to the son, Robert Alexander, with similar powers reserved to Jacob Swigert, Joseph Weisiger, and John Hoard Slaughter. (June 1841).

Alexander, Thomas, formerly of Boston, New England, but late of Shelburne, Nova Scotia, widower. Administration to Lewis Wolfe, attorney for the son, Charles Alexander, now in Liverpool, Lancashire. (Apr. 1789).

Alexander, William, of St. Gregory, London, who died in Philadelphia. Probate to the relict, Mary Alexander. (Oct. 1727).

Alexon alias Ellixon, Jasper, of the merchant ship *Preservation*, who died in Virginia. Probate to the relict, Mary Alexon alias Ellixon. (Dec. 1706).

Aley, John, of Philadelphia, widower. Administration to the brother and next-of-kin, Robert Aley. (Dec. 1783).

Algeo. *See* **Allgeo**.

Alleine, Josias, of New England, bachelor. Administration to the brother, Jonathan Alleine. (June 1678).

Allen, Aaron, of Nether Providence, Delaware County, Pennsylvania. Administration with will to Nathaniel Mason, attorney for the son, Thomas Bidmead Allen, in Ridley, Delaware County; the surviving executor, Henry Forrest, renouncing. (July 1837).

Allen, Abijah, Daniel and Elizabeth, of Pennsylvania, bachelors and spinster. Administration to Elizabeth, wife of James Bottomley, administratrix with will to the mother, Sarah Allen, widow deceased; the brother, Aaron Allen, and the sister, Sarah, wife of Peter Heacock, having also died. (Apr. 1836).

Allen, Daniel. *See* **Allen, Abijah**.

Allen, Elizabeth. *See* **Allen, Abijah**.

Allen, George, of Queen's Ferry, Scotland, who died at sea near Virginia, bachelor. Administration to William Leget, attorney for the sisters, Isabel, Elizabeth and Merian Allen alias Orie. (Jan. 1673).

Allen, James, of Kempston, Bedfordshire, whose son, Roger Allen, was in New England. Probate to the son, John Allen. (Jan. 1658). Sh.Wa.

Allen, James, of Boston, New England. Administration to Barlow Trevethick, John Apthorp and John Thomlinson, attornies for the relict Martha, now wife of William Brattle, residing in Cambridge, New England. (Apr. 1763).

Allen, John, of Holborn, Middlesex, who died in Maryland. Probate to the relict, Elizabeth Allen. (Jan. 1675). Revoked on her death and administration granted to William Harmer, brother and administrator of the executor, Timothy Harmer deceased; the other executor, Paul Wheeler, having also died. (June 1688). Wi.

Allen, John the elder of the Island of New Jersey. Administration to the son, John Allen the younger. (Apr. 1685).

Allen, John, of Colonel Holt's Regiment, bachelor. Administration by decree to the principal creditor, Elizabeth Jennings, widow. Marked "pauper." (July 1722).

Allen, John, of H.M. ship *Roebuck*, who died in Philadelphia. Limited administration with will to Eleanor Brown, administratrix with will of the legatee, John Allen deceased. (July 1779).

Allen, Samuel, of Boston, New England, mariner, formerly of H.M. ship *Kent* but late of H.M. ship *Maidstone*. Probate to Daniel Gunn. (June 1747).

Allen, Samuel, of Saluda Mills, South Carolina, bachelor. Administration to Joseph Jeffries Evans, attorney for the father, Samuel Allen, in Saluda Mills. (Apr. 1800).

Allen, Sarah, of Craven County, North Carolina, widow. Administration to

Allen, *(contd)*
Malcolm Ross, attorney for the son, Whichcote White, in Craven County. (Mar. 1805).

Allen, Sarah, of Ridley, Delaware County, Pennsylvania, widow. Administration with will to the granddaughter, Elizabeth, wife of James Bottomley. (Apr. 1836).

Allin, Silvester, of Tower Precinct, London, who died abroad (on passage to Virginia). Probate to the relict, Elizabeth Allin. (Mar. 1636). Sh.Wi.

Allen, Thomas, of the City of London, whose brother, Bozonne [Allen], was in New England. Probate to the brother, William Allen. (Feb. 1647). Sh.Wa.

Allen, Thomas, of the merchant ship *Medway*, who died in South Carolina. Administration to Diana, wife of the father, George Allen, now at sea. Marked "pauper." (Feb. 1729).

Allenby, William Charles, of Baltimore, Maryland. Probate to the brother, George Allenby. (June 1801).

Allford, Dorothy, of Pennsylvania, spinster. Administration to the sister and next-of-kin Mary, wife of Joseph Little. (Nov. 1718).

Allgeo, John, formerly of Quebec but late of North Carolina, bachelor. Administration to Peter Ogden, attorney for the father, David Allgeo, in Quebec. (Dec. 1788).

Algeo, Margaret, of New York City, widow. Administration to Barnardus La Grange, attorney for the only child, David Algeo, now in Quebec. (Nov. 1792).

Allison, John, formerly of Bradfield, Norfolk, miller, but late of Berry, Dane County, [Wisconsin], widower. Administration to the father, James Allison. (May 1855).

Allman, Susanna, formerly Susanna Douglas, of New York City, widow. Limited administration with will to Howard Douglas, attorney for the only child, Louisa Douglas, during her minority. (Nov. 1807). Revoked and granted to John Philpot. (Feb. 1812).

Allright, William, of Arborfield, Berkshire, whose daughter, Margaret Avery, was in New England. Probate to the son, William Allright. (May 1667).

Allsopp, John, of Bonsall, Derbyshire, whose brothers and sister were in New England. Probate to Roger Jackson with similar powers reserved to Dorothy Hopkinson. (Feb. 1647). Wa.

Alsopp, Rev. Josias, of Combe Nevell, Kingston, Surrey, whose sister, Elizabeth Rosseter, was in New England. Probate to John Bestwood. (Oct. 1666). Wa.

Alsop, Timothy, of St. Mary Somerset, London, whose sister was in New England. Administration with will to the relict, Martha Alsop. (Aug. 1664). Wa.

Allwood, Hon. Robert, formerly of St. Catherine, Jamaica, but late of New York. Probate to the son, Rev. Robert Allwood, with similar powers reserved to John Gale Vidal and the son, James Allwood. (Jan. 1839).

Allwood, Richard, of New Sarum, Wiltshire, whose brother, Edmond

Allwood, *(contd)*
Batter, was in New England. Probate to the relict, Elizabeth Allwood. (Mar. 1645). Wa.

Alston, David, Captain on half pay of the New Jersey Volunteers, who died in Staten Island, New York. Administration with will to David Davies, attorney for the sons, Warren and Japhet Alston, in New York. (July 1806).

Altham, Emmanuel, who died abroad, bachelor, who made a bequest to Mrs. Thomasin in New England. Administration with will to the nephew, John Altham; the brother, Sir Edward Altham, having died. (Nov. 1638). Sh.

Amar, John, of Pensacola but late of New York City. Administration with will to James Dewey, attorney for the relict, Sarah Amar, and for Thomas Austen, now in New York. (Oct. 1782).

Ambrose, Isabella, of Newport, Rhode Island. Administration to James Cockburn, attorney for the husband, Robert M. Ambrose, in Newport. (Feb. 1802).

Ambrose, Peter, of Toxteth, Lancashire, who made a bequest to Joshua and Daniel Henshawe in New England. Probate to the relict, Judith Ambrose, with similar powers reserved to Nehemiah Ambrose. (Jan. 1653). Wa.

Amias, Francis, of Goosnargh, Lancashire, adventurer to Virginia. Probate to the brother, Paul Amias. (July 1622). Wi.

Amory, Simon, of Pensacola, West Florida. Limited special probate to the brother, Thomas Amory, clerk. (Nov. 1766).

Amphlett, William, Lieutenant of the Royal Navy, who died in St. Louis, Missouri. Probate to the brother, Richard Paul Amphlett, with similar powers reserved to the brother, Samuel Holmden Amphlett. (July 1852).

Amsed, James, of Virginia. Administration the to principal creditor, Rebecca Anyon. (Dec. 1696).

Amyand, Isaac, of Charles Town, South Carolina, gent. Special administration with will to Claudius Amyand. (Dec. 1739).

Anderson, Andrew, of H.M. ship *La Fortune*, who died in Long Island, bachelor. Administration to the brother and next-of-kin, James Anderson. (Oct. 1785).

Anderson, David, of Boston, New England, who died at sea. Administration to the principal creditor, Robert Thomson. (Jan. 1678). Revoked and granted to John Phillipps, attorney for the relict, Catherine Anderson, of Charles Town, New England. (Feb. 1678).

Anderson, George, of the Town of Georgia *(sic)*, Captain of the *Georgia Packet*, who died at sea. Administration to the principal creditor, James Gusthart; the relict Deborah Anderson and the only children, John, Mary and George Anderson, having been cited but not having appeared. (Nov. 1777).

Anderson, Henry, of Bantam, East Indies. Probate to the brother, David Anderson, with similar powers reserved to the father, John Anderson, of Boston, New England. (Feb. 1676). Wa.

Anderson, James, of George Town District, South Carolina, planter. Probate to the son, Richard Oswald Anderson. (Aug. 1821).

Anderson, James, of New York, merchant. Limited administration with will to the sons, Andrew, Smith Weeks, and Abel Tyler Anderson, with similar powers reserved to the relict, Hannah Anderson. (Oct. 1832).

Anderson, John, of New England. Probate to John Phillips with similar powers reserved to the relict, Mary Anderson. (Feb. 1678). Wa.

Anderson, Julia Ann, of Detroit, Wayne County, Michigan, widow. Limited administration with will to Henry Barkly and Henry John Lias. (Feb. 1845).

Anderson, Lauchlan, of Detroit, Canada, bachelor. Administration to John Anderson, attorney for the mother, Margaret Mongrief alias Moncrief, widow, now in Fifeshire, Scotland. (Mar. 1785).

Anderson, William, of Shadwell, Middlesex, who died in Virginia, bachelor. Administration to the principal creditrix, Anne Allen. (Sep. 1680).

Anderson, William, of the merchant ship *Herbert*, who died in Maryland, bachelor. Administration to the principal creditor, John Thompson. (Feb. 1734).

Anderson, William, formerly of Virginia but late of Vauxhall, Lambeth, Surrey. Probate to the relict, Mary Anderson, and Samuel Gist, William Fowke and John Anderson, with similar powers reserved to the nephew Overton Anderson. (Jan. 1796). Wi.

Andrade alias Andrada, Abraham, of Ohio, bachelor. Administration to the brother and only next-of-kin, Moses Andrade. (Nov. 1826).

Andre, John, Major and Adjutant-General of the Army in North America, Captain of the 54th Regiment, who died in Tappan. Probate to the uncles David Andre, Andrew Girardot and John Lewis, with similar powers reserved to the mother, Mary Louisa Andre. (Jan. 1781).

Andrews, Abraham, formerly of Hertford, Hertfordshire, but late of Baltimore, Virginia *(sic)*. Probate to the son, Samuel Andrews. (Oct. 1801).

Andrewes, John, of Cambridge, merchant, whose son, John Andrewes, was in Virginia. Probate to the relict, Hester Andrewes. (June 1616). Wi.

Andrewes, John, of Barbados, whose sister, Deborah, wife of Robert Fenn, was in Boston, New England. Administration to William Creeke. (Mar. 1649). Revoked and administration with will granted to Samuel Wild during the minority of the brother, Samuel Andrewes, and during the absence abroad of Morgan Powell and Thomas Sprigg. (Feb. 1650). Sh.Wa.

Andrews, John, formerly of Diss, Norfolk, afterwards of Beulah Cottages, Clifton Street, Wandsworth Road, Surrey, but late of New York, bachelor. Administration to the sister, Mary Andrews. (Sep. 1852).

Andrews, William, of Cote, Bishops Canning, Wiltshire, who died in Virginia, bachelor. Probate to Hester Brown alias Nash, sole legatee of the estate unadministered by the named executor, Nicholas Nash. (Aug. 1726).

Andrus, David, of Farmington, Hartford County, Connecticut, Lieutenant

Andrus, *(contd)* of the First Connecticut Regiment, who died in Havana. Administration to Phineas Lyman, attorney for the relict, Mary Andrus, now in Farmington. (Nov. 1764).

Angell, William, of St. Bartholomew by the Exchange, London, whose friend, Henry Kersey, was in Virginia. Probate to the relict, Anne Angell, and to Richard Angell. (Feb. 1637). Wi.

Angier, Bezaliel, of Dedham, Essex, whose brother, Edmund Angier, was in New England. Probate to the relict, Anne Angier. (Nov. 1678). Wa.

Angier, Samuel, of Dordrecht, Holland, whose brother, Edmund Angier, was in New England. Probate to Sir Richard Ford, alderman of London, attorney for the relict, Barbara Angier, during her absence abroad. (May 1667). Wa.

Annely, Richard, of New York. Probate to Thomas Annely. (Oct. 1750).

Anthonye, Charles, of St. John Zachary, London, adventurer to Virginia. Probate to the son, Thomas Anthonye. (Nov. 1615). Revoked on his death and administration granted to the relict, Elizabeth Anthonye. (Sep. 1623). Sh.Wi.

Anthony, David, of Virginia, bachelor. Administration with will to Margaret, wife of the executor, James Dicks, during his absence overseas. (July 1676).

Anthony, Francis, of St. Bartholomew the Great, London, doctor of medicine, who had goods in Virginia. Probate to the relict with similar powers reserved to Stephen Losure. (June 1623). Wa.

Anthony, John, of Rhode Island, mariner. Probate by her solemn affirmation to Elianor Potts with similar powers reserved to Richard Potts. (Dec. 1703).

Anthony, John, surgeon of H.M. fireship *Strombole*, who died in New York. Administration with will to William Palmer, attorney for the mother and sole executrix, Elinor Anthony, widow, now in Ballimahon, Co. Longford, Ireland. (Mar. 1778). Revoked on the death of William Palmer and granted to the mother. (Nov. 1781).

Antill, John, of New Burgh, Orange County, New York, Major of the 2nd Batallion of the late New Jersey Regiment of Volunteers. Administration with will to William Young, attorney for the relict, Jane Antill, in New York. (Apr. 1819).

Antill, Lewis, of New York, widower. Administration to the brother, John Antill; the mother, Ann Antill, having died before administering. (Feb. 1786).

Antram, William, of H.M. ship *Mermaid*, who died in South Carolina, bachelor. Probate to the mother, Mary, wife of Jacob Minor. (Feb. 1752).

Applebee, Benjamin, of New York who died in Dorset. Administration to William Bryant, attorney for the relict, Frances Applebee, now in New York. (Mar. 1744).

Appleton, John, of H.M. ships *Glasgow*, *Romney* and *Boston*, who died in Boston Hospital, bachelor. Administration to the creditor, Roger Dawson. (Feb. 1773 & June 1775).

Appleton, Samuel, of Boston, New England, who died in St. Andrew Undershaft, London. Limited administration to Jasper Waters, Thompson Hayne and Samuel Southouse. (Jan. 1729).

Appy, John, Secretary and Judge-Advocate of H.M. Forces in North America. Administration with will to the father, Peter Appy. (May 1763).

Apthorp, Charles, of Boston, Massachusetts. Administration to the son, Thomas Apthorp; the relict, Grizzell Apthorp, having been cited but not having appeared. (May 1784).

Apthorp, John, of Cambridge, Massachusetts. Probate to the brother, George Apthorp, with similar powers reserved to the relict, Hannah Apthorp, and to Barlow Trecothick, the brother, Thomas Apthorp, and to Martin Howard. (Feb. 1773). Double probate to the brother, Thomas Apthorp. (Nov. 1783).

Apthorp, William Rice, formerly of Boston, North America, who died on the Island of St. Thomas in the West Indies. Probate to the brother, Charles Ward Apthorp. (Feb. 1800).

Archbell, John, of the ship *Ephraim*, who died in Virginia. Probate by decree to Hannah, wife of Alexander Tompson, with similar powers reserved to the said Alexander. (Nov. 1692).

Archdeacon, James, of Norfolk, Virginia. Administration to the creditor, Robert Gilmour; the relict, Parnell Archdeacon, and the only child, John Archdeacon, having been cited but not having appeared. (Aug. 1784).

Archer, Henry, of St. John, Hereford, who left a bequest to George and Sarah Maynard in Virginia. Administration with will to William Burton, executor of the surviving executor, James Mailes deceased. (Nov. 1748). Wi.

Archer, John, clerk, who died abroad and whose brother was in New England. Administration with will to the relict, Susan Archer; no executor having been named. (Mar. 1649). Sh.

Archer, Robert, of St. Dunstan in the West, London, who died in Carolina. Administration to the sister, Elizabeth Cave, widow; the relict, Mary Archer, renouncing. (Dec. 1691).

Archer, Roger, of Virginia. Administration to the principal creditor, John Pennell. (Mar. 1642).

Aderne, John, of Carolina. Probate to Edward Warren. (Apr. 1715).

Arderne, John, of North Carolina. Probate to William Dunkinfield. (Sep. 1720).

Arey. *See* **Airey**.

Argall, Sir Samuel, who died overseas having lands in Virginia. Probate to Richard Hanes with similar powers reserved to the brother, John Argall. (Mar. 1626). Double probate to John Argall. (May 1626). Wa.

Argent, George, of Hoxton, Middlesex, whose daughter, Anne Ivey, was in Virginia. Probate to the cousins, John Langley and John Glascock. (Apr. 1654). Wi.

Arking, Robert, of St. Botolph Aldgate, London, who died in New York.

Arking, *(contd)*
Administration to the relict, Lilias alias Lillas Arking alias Arken alias Brown. (Mar. 1735).

Arlington, Michael, of Stepney, Middlesex, who died on H.M. ship *Lyme* in Virginia. Probate to Nathan Movelty with similar powers reserved to his wife, Sarah Movelty. (Aug. 1719).

Armistead, Henry, of Caroline County, Virginia, widower. Administration to Edward Hunt, attorney for the son, William Armistead, in Virginia. (Dec. 1748).

Armstrong, George, of the merchant ship *Concord*, who died in Maryland. Probate to Robert Pitt. (Dec. 1735).

Armstrong, Thomas, master of the merchant ship *Peggy*, who died in Philadelphia, bachelor. Administration to George Armstrong, attorney for the father, William Armstrong, now in Holy Island, Co. Durham. (July 1769).

Arnall, Thomas, of Whitechapel, who died at sea on a voyage to Virginia. Probate to the relict, Katherine Arnall. (Nov. 1694). *See* NGSQ 70/41.

Arnold, Edward, of Virginia, widower. Administration to the principal creditor, Thomas Allen. (May 1672).

Arnold, Henry, of New York City, Lieutenant in H.M. Service. Administration with will to Pownal Phipps, attorney for the relict, Hannah Arnold, and the daughter, Sophia Matilda Arnold, in New York. (July 1827).

Arnold, Henry, formerly of Uttoxeter, Staffordshire, but late of the Republic of Texas. Administration to the father, William Arnold the elder. (Jan. 1843).

Arnold, Mary Anne, of Union Township, Bush County, Indiana. Administration to Andrew Arnold, attorney for the husband, John Arnold, in Union Township. (Aug. 1830).

Arnold, Richard, citizen and goldsmith of London, whose nephew, Thomas Arnold, was in New England. Probate to Thomas Lofty. (Nov. 1644). Wa.

Arnold, Sarah, formerly of Paddington Street, St. Marylebone, Middlesex, but late of Philadelphia, spinster. Administration to the sister, Jemima, wife of Christopher Gartland. (Apr. 1798). Copy of will made in Philadelphia on 13 October 1797 appointing William Murray as executor. (PROB 20/63).

Arnold, Thomas, of St. Sepulchre, London, who died in Carolina. Administration to the sister, Elizabeth Arnold; the father, Jeremiah Arnold, renouncing. (Nov. 1688).

Arnot, Robert, of the merchant ship *Davy*, who died in Carolina, bachelor. Administration to the sister, Jane, wife of James Anderson. (May 1739).

Arrowsmith, Hugh, of the ship *Edgar* and of New York, who died at sea. Administration with will to Thomas Anger, attorney for Thomas Bishop and John Tongue during their absence abroad; no executor having been named. (Sep. 1691).

Arrowsmith, John, of Virginia, bachelor, who died overseas. Administration

Arrowsmith, *(contd)* to Dorcas, wife of the principal creditor, Gerrard Dobson, now overseas. (July 1688). Revoked and granted to Gerrard Dobson. (Oct. 1688).

Arthington, Robert, of London, (intending a voyage to Virginia), who died abroad. Probate to the sister, Mary Eldred. (May 1651). Sh.

Arthur, Christopher, of Sypryss Barony, South Carolina, who died in St. Dunstan, Stepney, Middlesex. Probate to Patrick Roche. (Dec. 1724).

Arthur, John, formerly of 42 North Street, Pentonville, Middlesex, but late of San Francisco, California, engraver. Probate to the mother, Mary Arthur, widow. (July 1856).

Arthur, William, of H.M. ship *Apollo*, who died in New York Hospital. Probate to Elizabeth, wife of William Sutherland, with similar powers reserved to the said William Sutherland. (Jan. 1781).

Arundell, Robert, of Ottery St. Mary, Devon, who died in Annapolis Royal. Administration to James Channon, guardian of Rebecca Channon, the niece by a daughter. (Nov. 1725).

Ash, Anne. *See* **Livingston**.

Ash, Francis, of Charleston, Philadelphia, cabinet maker. Administration to the brother and sister and only next-of-kin, James and Elizabeth Ash. (May 1839).

Ash, John, of Danho, Carolina. Probate to William Methuen, attorney for the relict, Mary Ash, in Carolina. (Jan. 1706).

Ash, John, of Westfield, Colleton County, South Carolina, who died in Wiltshire. Probate by decree to William Livingston, husband and administrator of the relict, Ann Livingston alias Ash, who died before administering. (Aug. 1721).

Ashe alias Batt, Mary, widow, lately wife of John Ashe of Danhoe, Colleton County, South Carolina. Administration by decree to William Ashe; all others with an interest having been cited but not having appeared. (Feb. 1719).

Aishley, Edward, of Ratcliffe, Middlesex, who died in Virginia. Administration to James Shaw, guardian of the only child, Elizabeth Aishley, during her minority. (Aug. 1656).

Ashley, John, of Virginia. Administration to Christopher Rowe, grandfather and guardian of the only child, Joane Ashley. (May 1657).

Ashley, John, formerly of Barbados but late of Blackheath, Kent, who had lands in Pennsylvania. Administration with will to the creditor, George Prescott; James Theobald, Solomon Ashley and William Whitaker renouncing; the relict, Mary Ashley, and the only children, John Ashley and Elizabeth Aynsworth Ashley, having been cited but not having appeared. (Oct. 1751) *See* NGSQ 63/40.

Ashlin, William, formerly of Boston, Lincolnshire, but late of Philadelphia, bachelor. Administration to the sister, Mary Anne, wife of Valentine Mantz Close. (Sep. 1828).

Ashton, James, of Stafford County, Virginia. Probate to John Foster with similar powers reserved to John Ashton. (July 1687). Wi.

Ashton, Anne, of Virginia. Administration to the husband, Charles Ashton. (Aug. 1704).

Ashton, John, of New York, widower. Administration to the son, George Ashton. (Nov. 1704).

Ashwood, Mary Ann, of Adams County, Illinois. Administration to Nathaniel Hollingsworth, attorney for the husband, Joseph Ashwood, in Illinois. (Jan. 1857).

Askew, Leonard, [formerly of South Carolina] but late of Bridgefield, Coulton, Lancashire. Probate to Joseph Penny and John Kendal with similar powers reserved to John Drinkall. (Sep. 1789). ALC.

Aslat, Edward, formerly of Vale Place, Hammersmith, Middlesex, but late of Galveston, North America, bricklayer. Probate to the sister, Elizabeth Aslat. (June 1840).

Aspitall, William, soldier of the 22nd Regiment of Foot in Captain Rawlin Hillman's Company, who died in Mobile, West Florida, bachelor. Probate to Thomas Levingston. (Aug. 1766).

Astbury, Thomas, Major of the 33rd Company of Marines on H.M. ship *Cornwall*, who died in New York, bachelor. Probate to Ann Lane, spinster. (Mar. 1779).

Astwood, John, of Milford, New England. Probate to the son, Samuel Astwood. (Aug. 1654). Wa.

Atchison, George, of Charles Town, South Carolina, who died in Islington, Middlesex, bachelor. Probate to David Atchison with similar powers reserved to James Pain. (Sep. 1728).

Atherstone, William, formerly of Leicester but late of the United States of America. Probate to Hannah Brown, spinster. (Feb. 1836).

Atkins, Edward, of Chard, Somerset, who died in Virginia or parts overseas. Administration to the son, Richard Atkins. (Sep. 1652).

Atkins, John, of Virginia, bachelor. Administration with will to the brother, William Atkins; no executor having been named. (Oct. 1624). Revoked on his death and granted to the brother, Richard Atkins, guardian of the children, Elizabeth, George, Anne and Lee Atkins, during their minority. (Aug. 1626). Revoked on his death and granted to the brother, Humfrey Atkins. (June 1627). Wi.

Atkins, John the elder of Chard, Somerset, whose grandchild was born in Virginia. Probate to the relict, Katherine Atkins. (Nov. 1636). Wi.

Atkins, Mary. *See* **Wade**.

Atkins, Richard, of Maryland, bachelor. Administration to the principal creditor, Thomas Ellis. (June 1669).

Atkyns, Ringrose, formerly of Devonshire Street, Portland Place, Middlesex, but late of Kanion, California, bachelor. Administration to the brother, Rev. Walter Baker Atkyns; the mother and next-of-kin, Sarah Atkyns, widow, having died. (July 1855).

Atkins, Samuel, of Warren Herkimer, New York. Administration to the brother, James Atkins; the relict, Margaret Atkins, renouncing. (Dec. 1842).

Atkins, Sarah, of New England, widow. Administration to the principal creditor, Sir Charles Hobby. (Sep. 1707).

Atkinson, Francis, of H.M. ship *Deptford* who died in Virginia. Probate to James Bowerman. (Dec. 1695).

Atkinson, George, of Charles Town, South Carolina, who died in Islington, Middlesex, bachelor. Double probate to James Pain. (Oct. 1729). [*Appears to be the same as George Atchison, q.v.*].

Atkinson, Theodore, of Portsmouth, New Hampshire. Administration with will to Thomas Dickason, attorney for George King, now George Atkinson, in Portsmouth, New Hampshire. (Oct. 1783).

Atkinson, William the younger, of St. Vedast, Foster Lane, London, (intending for Virginia). Probate to the father, William Atkinson, with similar powers reserved to Thomas and Ralph Atkinson. (Aug. 1613). Sh.Wi.

Atkinson, William, of West River, Maryland, Lieutenant on half pay. Administration with will to John Clapham, attorney for Frederick Green and Jonas Clapham, now in Maryland. (July 1795).

Atterbury, Richard, of London but resident in Virginia who died abroad, bachelor. Probate to the brother, William Atterbury. (June 1638). Wi.

Atwood, Anthony, of Newport, Rhode Island, sergeant in Lieutenant-Colonel Christopher Hargill's Company of the Rhode Island Regiment of Foot, who died in Havana, bachelor. Administration by his solemn declaration to Joseph Sherwood, attorney for the father, Joseph Atwood, in Newport. (Dec. 1765).

Attwood, Isaac, of Perth Amboy, North America, Captain in Colonel Fanning's late Regiment of the King's Americans. Administration to David Thomas, attorney for the relict, Elizabeth Attwood, in Perth Amboy. (Aug. 1795).

Augur, Margery, of St. Andrew Hubbard, London, widow, whose son, Nicholas Augur, was in New England. Probate to the daughter, Hester Augur. (Oct. 1658). Wa.

Aungier, John, of Drome Derrick, Cavan County, Ireland, clerk, who died in St. Clement Danes, Middlesex, or in Virginia. Probate to the relict, Anne Aungier. (Apr. 1692).

Austell, Joseph, of Boston, New England. Special limited probate to the cousin, Moses Austell. (Sep. 1748).

Austin, John, of New York City, M.D. Administration with will to Charles Dean, attorney for the relict, Mary Austin, the son, John Austin, and John Parkinson, John Singleton, Copley Greene and William Joseph Hubbard in the United States of America. (July 1839).

Austin, Joseph, of Shadwell, Middlesex, and late of New England. Probate to Mary Yems. (Sep. 1679).

Austin, Matt, unchristened black slave of H.M. ship *Winchelsea*, bachelor. Administration to William White, attorney for the owner, Mary Austin, widow, in Charles Town, South Carolina. (June 1762).

Austin, Sarah, of Philadelphia, widow. Administration to the son, William Austin. (Aug. 1786).

Austin, Thomas, of H.M. ship *Richmond*, who died in New York. Probate to Thomas Frampton. (June 1694).

Austin, William, surgeon's mate of H.M. Hospital in North America, who died in Albany, New York, bachelor. Administration to Kenneth Mackenzie, attorney for the father, Joseph Austin, in Kilspindie, Perthshire, Scotland. (Dec. 1764).

Avery, John, of Dorchester County, Maryland. Administration with will to Cuthbert Haslewood, brother of John Haslewood now overseas, husband of the relict, Anne Haslewood alias Avery, now deceased. (Aug. 1683).

Avery, Joseph, formerly of Connecticut, New England, but late of the City of Bristol. Probate to Jane Day, spinster. (July 1746).

Avory alias Avera, Mary, of Prince George County, Virginia, widow. Probate to the son, Charles Avera, and the daughter, Molly, wife of Amos Elliott. (Dec. 1769).

Avery, Richard, of Stepney, Middlesex, who died in New England, widower. Administration to the son, Richard Avery. (Apr. 1743).

Axby, Thomas. *See* **Haxby**.

Axtell, Daniel, of Stoke Newington, Middlesex, who died in Carolina. Administration with will to Walter Needham, doctor of medicine, attorney for the relict, Rebecca Axtell, now in Carolina. (July 1687).

Axtell, Nathaniel, of St. Peter's, St. Albans, Hertfordshire, but intending for New England. Probate to the brother, Daniel Axtell. (June 1640). Wi.

Aylward, William, formerly of Virginia but late of London, who died in France, bachelor. Probate to Robert Cary of London. (Feb. 1707).

Ayres, Thomas, of Carolina, bachelor. Administration to the brother, John Ayres. (June 1691).

Ayscough, Richard, of New York City. Probate to Rev. Francis Ayscough with similar powers reserved to the relict, Anne Ayscough, and to Charles Williams. (Nov. 1760). Administration of estate unadministered by Francis Ayscough granted to William Moore, husband of the relict Anne; the surviving executors, Anne Moore and Charles Williams, and the minor children, Richard Maximilian Ayscough and Ann Ayscough, having been cited but not having appeared. (Jan. 1768)

B

Babb, Thomas, of Stepney, Middlesex, who died in Virginia. Administration to the relict, Eleanor Babb. (July 1646). Revoked on her death and granted to the only child, Mary Babb. (July 1655).

Babb, Thomas, of New York City. Administration to William Babb, the uncle and guardian of the children, Julia and Thomas Sherry Babb, during their minority. (Mar. 1800).

Baber, Charles, of Tazwell County, Illinois. Administration to James Baber, attorney for the relict, Mary Ann Baber, in Tazwell County. (Aug. 1855).

Bache, Thomas, of Over Pen, Staffordshire, whose nephew, Peter Buck, was in Virginia. Administration with will to the daughter, Mary Dyson; no executor having been named. (July 1674). NGSQ 62/273.

Backman, Catherine, formerly of Easter, Northampton County, Pennsylvania, but late of St. Louis, Missouri, widow. Administration to George Cox, attorney for the son, William Shurlock Backman, in St. Louis. (Feb. 1857). New grant in May 1879.

Bacon, Anthony, of Cyfartha, Glamorgan, who bequeathed lands in Virginia to his half-brother, William Bacon. Probate to Thomas Harrison with similar powers reserved to Rev. Samuel Glasse, William Stevens and Richard Hill. (Feb. 1786). Wi.

Bacon, Butts, of Piscataway, New England, bachelor. Administration to the brother, Sir Edward Bacon. (May 1726).

Bacon, Richard, of Stepney, Middlesex, (bound for Virginia). Probate to William Chalke. (Dec. 1687).

Badenhop, Jesse, of South Carolina, bachelor. Administration to the uncle and next-of-kin, James Payzant. (Oct. 1740).

Badnadge, Thomas, of the ship *Honor* bound for Virginia, who died at sea. Administration to the relict, Abigall Badnadge. (June 1659).

Bagg alias Butler, Mary, of Washington, Westmoreland County, Virginia. Administration to the husband, John Bagg, clerk. (Sep. 1717).

Bagshaw, Joseph, formerly of Newcastle, Staffordshire, but late of Philadelphia. Probate to Samuel Worthington. (Nov. 1797).

Bayley, Barnard, of New York City. Probate to Edward Dry with similar powers reserved to the father, Thomas Bayley, and to Robert Henderson and Joseph Jennings. (June 1833).

Bayley, James Augustus, of Dexter, New York, merchant. Administration to the relict, Martha Washington Bayley. (Mar. 1855).

Bailley alias Bayley, John, of Philadelphia who died on H.M. ship *Jersey*. Probate to Hugh Higins alias Hogan. (Oct. 1748).

Bayly, Melchizideck, of Boston, New England, bachelor. Administration to the brother and next-of-kin, Benjamin Bayly. (Sep. 1720).

Baily, Richard, of Stoughton, Suffolk County, Massachusetts. Probate to the son, Henry Baily. (Nov. 1786).

Baily, Robert Nalder, of New York City. Administration to George Dibley, attorney for the only child, Sarah, wife of George Henry Geib, in New

Baily, *(contd)*
York; the relict, Sally Baily, having died. (Nov. 1847).

Bailey, Sarah, of St. James, Westminster, Middlesex, who died in Maryland, spinster. Administration to the father, Thomas Bailey. (Jan. 1751).

Baillie, William, of Maryland, bachelor. Probate to James Pitts. (Jan. 1703).

Bayly, William, of the Liberty of the Tower, London, who died in Virginia. Administration to the relict, Isabel Bayly. (Nov. 1727).

Baillie, William, Lieutenant of the Royal Regiment of Highlanders, who died in North America, bachelor. Administration to John Ogilvie, attorney for the sister, Mary, wife of William Duff, in Scotland. (July 1759).

Bailey, William Hyde, of Southfield, Richmond County, New York. Probate to the relict, Ann, now wife of John Taylor, with similar powers reserved to Hyde Williams. (May 1850).

Baird, Archibald, of South Carolina, who died in Plymouth, Devon. Limited administration with will to William Greenwood. (July 1777). Revoked and limited probate granted to James Cassels with similar powers reserved to James Gordon; the relict, Winifred, having now married John Wilson. (Mar. 1788).

Baker, John, of St. Bride's, London, whose sister, Jane Gilbert, was in New England. Probate to the relict, Jane Baker. (June 1664). Wa.

Baker, John, of Stepney, Middlesex, who died in New England. Probate to the relict, Sarah Baker. (Oct. 1678).

Baker, John, of Fairlight, Sussex, who died in East Jersey. Probate to Joseph Wakenham. (June 1709).

Baker, John, of Bristol, merchant, whose brother, Ebenezer Baker, was in South Carolina. Probate to the son, Stephen Baker. (Jan. 1736).

Baker, John, formerly of Bristol but late of Charles Town, South Carolina. Probate to Stephen Baker with similar powers reserved to Francis Baker, Paul Fisher and James Pearce. (Feb. 1737).

Baker, John, of New York. Administration to the son, Alfred Edward Baker. (Feb. 1845).

Baker, Nicholas, of St. George's, Maryland, widower. Administration with will to the universal legatee, Elizabeth, wife of George Pell, formerly Elizabeth Baker; no executor having been named and the brother, John Baker, having died before administering. (Jan. 1766).

Baker, Richard, of Stonedeane, Chalfont, Buckinghamshire, who had lands in Pennsylvania. Probate by her solemn affirmation to Rebecca Baker with similar powers reserved to Winifred Baker. (Nov. 1697).

Baker, Roger, of Wapping, Middlesex, who had lands in Maryland and died overseas. Administration with will to the daughter, Mary, wife of Thomas Johnson; the executor, Abraham Hughes, renouncing. (Jan. 1688). Wa.

Baker, Stephen, formerly of Dungarvon, Waterford County, Ireland, but late of Oxford, Indiana, widower. Administration to the creditor, John Sparkes Dalton; the son, Stephen Edward Baker, having renounced for himself and as guardian of the only other children, William,

Baker, *(contd)* Robert, Roger and Samuel Baker. (June 1851).

Baker, Thomas, citizen and apothecary of London, whose brother, Richard Baker, was in Virginia. Probate to the relict, Sarah Baker; the son, Thomas Baker, renouncing. (May 1654). Wi.

Baker, Thomas, of the ship *Elizabeth*, who died in Virginia. Probate to the sister, Mary Bennett alias Baker, with similar powers reserved to John Bennett. (Aug. 1698).

Balfoure, William, of Virginia. Probate to Alexander Blair. (Sep. 1686).

Balgay, Frances, formerly Frances Wright, of St. Paul Covent Garden, Middlesex, whose nieces, Elizabeth Gordon and Sarah Hassell, were in South Carolina. Probate to William Thompson and William Frankcombe with similar powers reserved to John Gordon. (Mar. 1764). Double probate to John Gordon. (Feb. 1774). *See* NGSQ 65/142.

Ball, James, of Waterton near Boston in parts overseas, bachelor. Administration to Joane Ball, mother of the niece and next-of-kin, Anne Ball. (Apr. 1672).

Ball, Mary, formerly Mary Chichester, of Stafford County, North America. Administration to Thomas Blane, attorney for the husband, Burgess Ball, now in Stafford County. (Jan. 1790).

Ballantyne, Hugh, of Henrico County, James River, Virginia, bachelor. Administration to the brother, George Ballantyne. (Jan. 1736).

Ballard, William, of Charleston, South Carolina, bachelor. Administration to the brother, Samuel James Ballard. (Feb. 1812).

Ballew, Abraham, of the merchant ship *Robert*, who died in Virginia. Probate to the relict, Mary Ballew alias Bellew. (Jan. 1709).

Balmain, William, of George Town, Potomac River, Maryland. Probate to George Steele. (Sep. 1784).

Balsley, Priscilla, formerly Priscilla Jope, of Pittsburgh, Allegheny County, Pennsylvania. Administration to George Cox, attorney for the husband, John Balsley, in Pittsburgh. (May 1837).

Bamber, William, of the merchant ship, *Bugill*, who died in New York, bachelor. Probate to Thomas Scott. (Dec. 1731).

Banford, Charles, of Boston, New England, who died on H.M. ship *Nonsuch*. Administration to Anne Gibbons, the wife and attorney of the principal creditor, William Gibbons, in New England. (Apr. 1695).

Bancks, Richard, of Carolina. Administration to the mother, Joane Bancks, during the absence abroad of the relict, Mary Bancks. (May 1682).

Bannister, William, formerly of Tutbury, Staffordshire, farmer, but late of the United States of America. Probate to Jenny Hall and to the son, Luke Bannister, with similar powers reserved to William Riley. (Apr. 1832).

Banyar, William, of Albany City, North America, bachelor. Administration to George Clarke, attorney for the uncle, Goldsbroro *(sic)* Banyar, in Albany. (May 1798).

Barber, Mary, of Amonia, Duchess County, New York, spinster.

Barber, *(contd)*
Administration to the father, Henry Barber. (Sep. 1849).

Barbot, Francis, of South Carolina, bachelor. Administration to the mother, Susanna Barbot, widow. (Dec. 1739).

Barbet, George, of Warton, Maryland, bachelor. Administration to the brother, John Barbet. (Dec. 1739).

Barbot, James, of St. Margaret, Westminster, Middlesex, who died in Maryland. Probate to the relict, Mary Barbot. (Apr. 1719).

Barbut, Theodore, of Boston, New England, Captain-Lieutenant of the 48th Regiment of Foot, who died in Quebec. Administration to the relict, Sarah Barbut. (June 1763).

Barclay, John, of New York City, seaman of H.M. ship *Emerald*. Probate to the relict, Ann, now wife of James Thain. (July 1779).

Barclay, Thomas, H.M. Consul for the Eastern States of America. Limited administration with will to John Brodribb Bergne, attorney for the relict, Susan Barclay, and for the sons, Thomas, George and Anthony Barclay, in the United States. (May 1831).

Barclay, William, formerly of Fenchurch Buildings, London, but late of Baltimore, United Staes of America. Probate to Robert Barclay. (Aug. 1814).

Barham, Anne, of Canterbury, Kent, widow, whose kinsman, Anthony Barham, was in Virginia. Probate to Thomas Lyne. (July 1640). Wi.

Barham, Anthony, of Mulberry Island, Virginia. Probate to Edward Major and William Butler. (Sep. 1641). Sh.Wa.

Barker, Nathaniel, of H.M. ship *Glasgow*. Administration to James Gibson, attorney for the brother, Jacob Barker, in Massachusetts. (Aug. 1750).

Barker, Robert, Collector of Customs in West New Jersey. Probate to the sister, Mary, wife of Francis Hurdd; the executors, Nathaniel Hurdd and Jane Worthington, having renounced, and the mother, Mary Barker, having died. (Dec. 1735).

Barker, Thomas, of Stepney, Middlesex, who died in Maryland. Administration to the relict, Mary Barker. (Sep. 1698).

Barling, Aaron, of Baltimore, North America. Probate to the relict, Sarah Barling. (July 1810).

Barlow, Jane, of Nottingham County, Virginia. Administration to Samuel Gist, administrator to the husband, Thomas Barlow deceased, for the benefit of the daughter, Elizabeth, wife of Thomas Kendall, now in Nottingham County. (Nov. 1797).

Barlow, Rev. John, formerly of Saxby, Leicestershire, but late of Rochester, Munroe County, New York, widower. Administration to the daughter, Charlotte Barlow. (Jan. 1841).

Barlow, Samuel, of H.M. ship *Shoreham*, who died in Virginia. Probate to the relict, Elizabeth Barlow. (June 1716).

Barlow, Thomas, of Nottingham County, Virginia, widower. Administration to Samuel Gist, attorney for the daughter, Elizabeth, wife of Thomas Kendall, now in Nottingham County. (Nov. 1797)

Barmby, Ellen, of Lee, Oneida County, New York, spinster. Administration

Barmby, *(contd)* to Elizabeth Risque, administratrix of the father, Henry Barmby deceased. (Feb. 1846).

Barnabe, Richard, of All Hallows, Lombard Street, London, whose brother, John Barnabe, was in Virginia. Administration with will to the sister, Elizabeth, wife of George Rookes, during the minority of the children, Elizabeth and Mary Barnabe. (July 1636). Wi.

Barnard, Anna, of Hendon, Middlesex, widow, whose sister was wife of Job Goodson in Pennsylvania. Probate to William Dolley. (Nov. 1741).

Barnes, Charles, formerly of Carshalton, Surrey, but late of Springfield, Washington County, Kentucky. Administration with will to Ann, wife of Robert Gumbrell, executrix of the mother, Ann Barnes, widow deceased. (Aug. 1809).

Barnes, John, of Christ Church, Surrey, who died in Georgia, widower. Probate to William Graves. (Oct. 1740).

Barnes, Mary, of Trenton, North America, widow. Administration with will to Daniel Coxe, attorney for Sarah Barnes Hooton and Mary Barnes, spinster, in Trenton. (June 1808).

Barnes, Thomas, of H.M. ship *Rose*, who died near New England. Administration with will to Susan Harbison, daughter of the relict, Elizabeth Barnes alias Harbison, who died before administering. (Nov. 1690).

Barnier, Peter, of St. Ann, Westminster, Middlesex, who died in Philadelphia, bachelor. Administration with will to the mother, Ann Barnier, now in Geneva. (June 1770).

Barnsley, Thomas, of Bensalem, Bucks County, Pennsylvania. Probate by their solemn affirmation to the surviving executors, William Redman and Gilbert Hicks. (Sep. 1774).

Barrack alias Benack, William, of Shadwell, Middlesex, who died in Staten Island. Administration with will to Adam Cromey; the sole executor, Robert Manley, having died. (Jan. 1777)

Barrell, Theodore, of Saugerties, Ulster County, New York. Administration with will to Thomas Boosey, attorney for the relict, Elizabeth Beckles Barrell, the daughter, Charlotte Barrell, and Isaac Winslow, in Saugerties. (Aug. 1847).

Barrett, Ann. *See* **Rimus**.

Barritt, Joanna, formerly Joanna Scantlebury, of Charlton, New York. Administration to the husband, William Barritt. (July 1854).

Barrett, Robert, of Christ Church, Surrey, who died in Virginia. Administration to the relict, Sarah Barrett. (Nov. 1698).

Barron, Charlotte, wife of Thomas Barron of Charles Town, South Carolina, formerly Charlotte Keith. Limited administration to John Tunno, attorney for the brother, John Keith. (Aug. 1807).

Barrow, Thomas, of Elswick Lodge, Lancashire, whose brother, John Barrow, was in New York. Probate by their solemn affirmation to the brother, William Barrow, the nephew, Corbyn Barrow, and to John Wadkin, John King the elder and John King the younger. (Oct. 1843). *See* NGSQ 60/90.

Barry, Edward, of New York, who died at sea, bachelor. Administration to the brother and next-of-kin, Timothy Barry. (Nov. 1841).

Barrie, Robert, Assistant Surgeon to H.M. Hospital in St. Augustine, East Florida, who died at sea. Limited administration with will to the relict, Dolly alias Dorothy Barrie. (Aug. 1775).

Bartlett, George, of St. Mary Somerset, London, whose daughter-in-law, Elizabeth Westcoate, was in Virginia. Probate to Elizabeth Ambler, widow. (Mar. 1660). Wi.

Bartlett, Rachel, formerly Rachel Pheasant, of Powis Place, Great Ormond Street, St. George the Martyr, Middlesex, but late of Maryland. Administration to the husband, John Bartlett. (Jan. 1798).

Bartlett, Sarah. *See* **Batson**.

Barton, Henry Lane, of Sussex, New Jersey, Lieutenant of the First Batallion of New Jersey Volunteers. Administration to David Thomas, attorney for the relict, Mary, now wife of Eben Owen, in Sussex. (Oct. 1801).

Barton, Joshua Joseph, of New Orleans, bachelor. Administration to the brother, Philip Henry Barton; the mother, Sarah Elizabeth Barton, having died. (Dec. 1849).

Barton, Thomas, of Berkeley County, South Carolina. Administration with will to Samuel Wragg, attorney for the sons, William and John Barton, in South Carolina. (Jan. 1735).

Barton, William, of H.M. ship *Play's* prize, who had children in Pennsylvania. Administration with will to John Bunce, attorney for Matthew Butts and Robert Walker, now at sea or abroad, no executor having been named. (Oct. 1697).

Barziza, Count Antonio; and

Barziza, Countess Lucia Paradine, both of Venice, and having property in Williamsburg, Virginia. Limited administration with wills to Count Giovanni Alvise Barziza. (Oct. 1815).

Baskerville, Henry, citizen and fishmonger of London, whose brother, John Baskerville, was in Virginia. Probate to the brother, Lawrence Baskerville. (May 1676). Wi.

Bassindine, Charles Boyle, of Virginia, bachelor. Administration to the brother, William Bassindine. (Jan. 1740).

Batchelder, Rev. William, of Haverhill, Essex County, Massachusetts. Administration to the relict, Huldah Batchelder. (Oct. 1819).

Batchelor, Elizabeth, of 233 Broadway, New York City. Administration to the husband, Charles Batchelor. (Dec. 1857).

Bate, Richard, of Lydd, Kent, whose mother, Alice Bate, was in New England. Probate to the son, James Bate. (Apr. 1657). Sh.Wa.

Bateman, Robert, of Charles Town, South Carolina, bachelor. Administration by his solemn affirmation to the father, George Bateman. (July 1728).

Bates, James, formerly of Holbeach. Lincolnshire, but late of Cincinnati, bachelor. Administration to Edward Key, attorney for the brothers, John and Richard Bates, in Cincinnati; the mother, Susanna Bates, widow, having died. (Nov. 1851).

Bates, Joseph, Captain's clerk of H.M. ship *Mercury*, who died in Boston, New England. Probate to Samuel Durham. (Nov. 1776).

Batley, John, formerly of Portland Street, Middlesex, but late of Norwalk, Connecticut, widower. Administration to the son, William Batley. (Mar. 1851).

Batson alias Bartlett, Sarah, of New England, widow. Administration to the aunt and next-of-kin, Benedicta, wife of William Nesbitt. (Nov. 1728).

Batt, Mary. *See* **Ashe**.

Battersbye, James, of Flushing, New York, bachelor. Administration to Thomas Prickman, guardian of Hester Prickman, a niece by a sister. (Feb. 1717).

Baugh alias Bough, Thomas, of H.M. ship *Nonsuch*, who died in Rhode Island. Administration to the daughter and next-of-kin, Jane Baugh. (Jan. 1781).

Bawdon, Sir John, of All Hallows the Great, London, who had lands in New England. Probate to the relict, Dame Letitia Bawdon. (Jan. 1689). Revoked on her death and administration granted to Robert Thornhill, guardian of the niece by a daughter and next-of-kin, Letitia Thornhill. (Nov. 1720). Sh.

Baxter, Benjamin, formerly of Wapping, Middlesex, but late of Nantucket. Administration to Thomas Dickason, attorney for the relict, Lydia Baxter, in Nantucket. (June 1801).

Baxter, John Exall, of Petersburgh, Virginia, bachelor. Administration to Rev. George Guildford Exall, attorney for the father, Thomas Baxter, in Petersburgh. (June 1846).

Bayley. *See* **Bailey**.

Bayliff, Featherston, surgeon's mate in General Oglethorpe's Regiment in Georgia, bachelor. Probate to James Mackay alias McKoy with similar powers reserved to Thomas Goldsmith. (Sep. 1750).

Bayliss, Joseph, soldier of the 15th Regiment of Foot, who died in Boston, New England. Administration to the brother, William Bayliss. (Apr. 1776).

Bayly. *See* **Bailey**.

Baynes, Henry, of the ship *Postillion*, who died in Virginia, bachelor. Administration to the brother, James Baynes. (Apr. 1705).

Baynton, John, of Bristol (bound for Virginia). Administration with will to Charles Harford and William Bathe, guardians of the son, Benjamin Baynton. (Jan. 1690). Wi.

Baytop, Thomas the elder, of Virginia, widower. Administration to Daniel Baytop, guardian of the only child, Thomas Baytop. (Jan. 1692). Revoked and granted to the said Thomas Baytop on his coming of age. (Sep. 1699).

Bayzand, William Seddon, of Baltimore, North America, who died at sea. Administration to the son, William Henry Bayzand; the relict, Susanna Asquith Bayzand, having died. (Oct. 1827).

Beadle, Robert, formerly of Salem, New England, but late of London, mariner. Probate to Joanna Mann of Bermondsey, Surrey, widow. (Sep. 1710).

Beale, Christopher, of East Farleigh, Kent, whose daughter, Margaret, was in New England. Probate to the son, Christopher Beale. (June 1651). Wa.

Beale, Elizabeth, of East Florida, spinster. Administration to the brother, Richard Beale; the mother, Elizabeth Beale, renouncing. (Nov. 1772).

Beale, Richard, formerly of Newport, North America, but late of Newark, Nottinghamshire. Administration to the relict, Mary Beale. (Jan. 1789).

Bean, Caleb, of Boston, New England, who died in the Bay of Honduras, widower. Administration to William Hodshon, attorney for the daughter, Ann Bean, in Boston. (Jan. 1753).

Beans, William, of Salem, New England, and of H.M. ship *Otter*. Administration to Thomas Dixey, attorney for the relict, Rachel Beans, in Salem. (Aug. 1754).

Beard, William, of Virginia. Probate to Alexander Chill. (Oct. 1646). Sh.Wi.

Beasant, Richard, formerly of Wolverton, Buckinghamshire, but late of New York, merchant. Limited administration to Campbell Hobson. (May 1833).

Beasland, Alexander. *See* **Bisley**.

Beauchamp, Abel, of Worcester, who died in Virginia, bachelor. Administration to the brother, Richard Beauchamp. (Dec. 1678).

Beauchamp, John, of St. Giles Cripplegate, London, who had lands in Virginia. Probate to the uncle, James Jauncy, and the brother, William Beauchamp. (Sep. 1668). Wi.

Beaucham, Joseph, formerly of the High Street, Portland Town, St. Marylebone, Middlesex, but late of Fredericksburg, Virginia. Administration to Richard Hewlett, attorney for the relict, Rachel Beaucham, in Fredericksburg. (Oct. 1849).

Beavay, Thomas, of Bristol, whose son, Thomas Beavay, was in Virginia. Probate to the relict, Mary Beavay. (Apr. 1657). Wa.

Beavour, John, of Stepney, Middlesex, master of the merchant ship *Britannia*, who died in Maryland. Administration to the relict, Mary Beavour. (July 1718).

Beckett, Simon, lately in America, bachelor. Administration to the aunt and next-of-kin, Elizabeth Smith. (Mar. 1762).

Becon, John, of Ratcliffe, Stepney, Middlesex, who died in Virginia. Administration to the principal creditor, Giles Shute; the relict, Mary Becon, renouncing. (June 1678).

Bedford, John, of York, Hampton parish, Virginia, but late of Stepney, Middlesex. Probate to the relict, Mary Bedford. (Sep. 1716). Wi.

Bedingfield, Thomas, of Dorking, Surrey, whose nephew, Thomas Bedingfield Hands, was in Maryland. Probate to Ann, wife of James Le Counte, with similar powers reserved to Bedingfield Hands. (Feb. 1743).

Bedon, Stephen, of Charles Town, South Carolina, and of St. Clement Danes and Chelsea, Middlesex, but who died in the City of Bristol.

Bedon, *(contd)* Probate to the cousin german, George Bedon with similar powers reserved to the relict, Ruth Bedon, and to Henry and Benjamin Bedon and Isaac Nicholls. (Feb. 1752).

Bee, Henry, of Deptford, Kent, who died on the merchant ship *South River* in Virginia. Administration to the relict, Jane Bee. (Nov. 1708).

Beekman, Gerard, of Mount Pleasant, Westchester County, New York. Administration with will to Gabriel Shaw, attorney for the relict, Cornelia Beekman, Pierre Van Cortlandt, the son, Stephen D. Beekman, and Robert G.S. De Freyster, in the United States of America. (Nov. 1823).

Beekman, Gerard G., of Mount Pleasant, Westchester County, New York, widower. Administration to Gabriel Shaw, administrator with will of the only child, Gerard Beekman deceased, and attorney for his executors. (Nov. 1823).

Bere, Theodore, of Topsham, Devon, who died in Virginia, widower. Administration to the son, George Bere. (Dec. 1757).

Beer, Thomas, of Virginia. Administration to the mother, Elizabeth Beer, widow. (July 1700).

Beesley, Samuel, of Bristol, who died in Virginia. Probate to William Beesley. (Sep. 1727).

Beetham, William, of St. Mary le Bow, Middlesex, who died in South Carolina. Probate to the father and surviving executor, Thomas Beetham. (Mar. 1783).

Beheathland, John, of St. Endellion, Cornwall, who died abroad (bound for Virginia), bachelor. Administration with will to Charles Beheathland; no executor having been named. (Oct. 1639). Sh.Wi.

Belbin, Edward, of Romsey, Hampshire, who died in South Carolina, bachelor. Administration to the cousin german, Richard Belbin. (Feb. 1734).

Belcher, John, boatswain of the merchant ship *Timothy and Jacob*, who died in Virginia, bachelor. Administration to the principal creditor, James Powers. (Jan. 1740). Revoked and granted by decree to the father, James Belcher. (May 1740).

Belin, Elizabeth, of Brewood, Staffordshire, but late of Charles Town, South Carolina. Administration to the husband, Peter Belin. (Feb. 1785).

Belin, Peter, formerly of Knightsbridge, St. George Hanover Square, Middlesex, and afterwards of Birmingham, Warwickshire, but who died at sea on passage to South Carolina, widower. Administration to Francis Cope, administrator of the creditor, Thomas Salt the elder, deceased. (June 1842).

Belisario, Henry Mendes, of Baltimore, North America. Probate to the uncle, Charles Mendes Da Costa, and to Jacob Mendes Da Costa, with similar powers reserved to Benjamin Mendes Da Costa and Isaac Pretto. (June 1855).

Bell, David, of St. Giles in the Fields, Middlesex, who died in Albany Fort, America. Probate to the relict, Elizabeth Bell. (Jan. 1713). Eliza alias Elizabeth, formerly Eliza Webb, of Mobile, Alabama. Administration

Bell, *(contd)*
to the husband, William Bell. (Sep. 1827).

Bell, John, of Newport, Rhode Island, purser of H.M. ship *Apollo*. Administration with will to William Roberts, attorney for the relict, Mary Bell, in Newport. (Feb. 1780).

Bell, John, of Vera Cruz, Mexico, who died in Charleston, United States of America, bachelor. Administration to the brother, Robert Bell. (Aug 1853).

Bell, John, of St. Louis, United States of America, surgeon and bachelor. Administration to the brother and sister and only next-of-kin, Edward Bell and Catherine Meredith, widow. (Oct. 1853).

Bell, Robert, of Deptford, Kent, whose cousin, Anne Bickley, was in Virginia. Probate to Richard Chapman. (Feb. 1657). Wi.

Bell, Susan, of All Hallows Barking, London, widow, who made a bequest to Anne, wife of John Elliott, of New England. Probate to the son, Thomas Bell. (Mar. 1673). Wa.

Bell, Thomas the elder, of All Hallows Barking, London, whose nephew, Thomas Makins, was in New England. Probate to the relict, Susan Bell. (May 1672). Wa.

Bell, William, formerly of Burr Street, St. Botolph Aldgate, London, but late of Norfolk, Virginia. Probate to the relict, Rebecca Bell, and the brother, Henry Bell. (Mar. 1795).

Bell, William, formerly of Princes Street, Edinburgh, but late of South Carolina. Probate to the nephew, Alexander Morton, and James Kilgour, Robert Saunders, and William Young. (May 1827).

Beman, Thomas, of Petersham, Worcester County, Massachusetts. Administration with will to Samuel Rogers, attorney for the relict, Elizabeth Beman, and for the sons, Ebenezer and Joseph Beman; the executors, Abijah Willard and Josiah Edson, having died. (June 1791).

Benack, William. *See* **Barrack**.

Benbowe, Thomas, of the ship *St. Andrew*. Administration to Joanna, wife of the principal creditor, Roger Frost, in Virginia; the relict, Catherine Benbowe, renouncing. (Jan. 1673).

Bendelow, William, formerly of Putneyvill, Wayne County, but late of Williamson, New York. Administration to Thomas Bendelow, attorney for the relict, Jane Bendelow, in Williamson. (July 1857).

Bengough, John Sowerby, formerly of Austin Friars, London, afterwards of Mazatlin, Mexico, but late of New York. Probate to John Francis Bacon with similar powers reserved to Joseph Javier de Lizardi. (June 1856).

Bennett, Edmond, of Boston, New England, pensioner of the Chatham Chest. Probate to Edward Westall. (Oct. 1743).

Bennet, Elisha, of Rumney Marsh, Suffolk County, New England. Administration with will to Henry Palmer, attorney for the relict and principal legatee, Dorothy Bennet, in Rumney Marsh; no executor having been named. (May 1727). Revoked on the death of Dorothy Bennet and granted to the son, John Bennet. (Jan. 1733).

Bennett, Ellen C.. *See* **Green.**

Bennet, James, of the merchant ship *James*, who died in New York Hospital, bachelor. Probate to John Oswald. (Apr. 1761).

Bennett, John, of St. Gabriel, Fenchurch Street, London, who had lands in Maryland. Probate to Margery Jones. (May 1698).

Bennett, John, of Boston, New England, who died on H.M. ship *New Norwich*. Administration to the relict, Aphram Bennett. (Sep. 1695) Revoked and granted to the daughter, Sarah, wife of Richard Deane. (Aug. 1709).

Bennett, John Morris, formerly of Brosely, Shropshire, but late of Baltimore, North America. Administration to the son, Morris Bennett; the relict, Margaret Bennett, having been cited but not having appeared. (May 1831).

Bennett, Joseph, of New York, who died in New Orleans, bachelor. Administration to the brother, John Morris Bennett. (Mar. 1834).

Bennett, Reuben, of Manlius, New York, widower. Administration to Ann Church, spinster, attorney for the only children, Albertus Reuben, Jamaes Azariah, and Oscar Bennett, in Manlius. (Dec. 1832).

Benet, Richard, of St. Bartholomew by the Exchange, London, but who died in Virginia. Administration to the brother, Edward Benet; the relict, Judith Benet, renouncing. (June 1627).

Bennett, Richard, of Nansemond River, Virginia. Probate to James Joffey with similar powers reserved to Thomas Hodges, Edmund Belson and Robert Peelle. (Aug. 1676). Wa.

Bennett, Richard, of Queen Anne's County, Maryland. Administration with will to John Hanbury and William Anderson, attornies for Edward Lloyd in Maryland. (Aug. 1750).

Bennett, Robert, of Charleston, South Carolina. Probate to Benjamin Burton Johnson with similar powers reserved to Robert Downie, Henry Brimar, John Coburn, Edgar Corrie, and Thomas Corrie. (May 1817).

Bennett, Samuel, of St. Andrew, Holborn, Middlesex, who died in South Carolina, bachelor. Administration by decree to the brother and next-of-kin, William Bennett. (Apr. 1722).

Bennington, Richard, carpenter of the ship *Unicorn* bound to Virginia, who died overseas. Probate to Robert Arnold. (Feb. 1612). Sh.

Benskin, Francis, of St. Martin in the Fields, Middlesex, whose son, Henry Benskin, was in Virginia. Probate to the children, Thomas and Frances Benskin. (Jan. 1692). Wa.

Benskin, Henry, formerly of St. Martin in the Fields, Middlesex, but late of Virginia. Probate to Alexander Roberts and Thomas Whitfield. (Oct. 1692). Wa.

Benskin, Thomas, of Bethlehem, Ohio, widower. Administration to the son, William Benskin. (Apr. 1854).

Benson, Hanns, of Wapping, Middlesex, who died on the merchant ship *Henry* in Virginia, bachelor. Administration to the principal creditor, John Worme. (July 1703).

Benson, Henry, of New York City, who died on H.M. ship *Princess Mary*.

Benson, *(contd)*
Administration to William Bryant, attorney for the relict, Judith Benson, in New York. (Mar. 1747).

Benson, Hugh, of New York, who died on H.M. ship *Princess Mary*. Administration as above. (Mar. 1750).

Benson, William George, of Perth Amboy, New Jersey, bachelor. Administration to the mother, Elizabeth Benson, widow. (Feb. 1811).

Benson, William John Chapman, of Quebec, Canada, who died in Whitehall, New York, merchant. Probate to the brother, Thomas Benson, and William Robert Chapman, with similar powers reserved to Christopher Richardson. (Jan. 1851).

Bentley, Susannah. *See* **Rabbeth**.

Bere. *See* **Beer**.

Berjeu, John, of New York, bachelor. Administration to the father, Samuel Barjeu *(sic)*. (Dec. 1783).

Berkeley, Sir William, Governor of Virginia, who died in Twickenham, Middlesex. Administration to Alexander Culpeper, brother of the relict, Lady Frances Berkeley, during her absence. (July 1677).

Berry, George Charles Bradbury, of New York, bachelor. Administration to the father, John Robert Berry. (Sep. 1850).

Berry, John, of New York City. Probate to the surviving executor, Edward Cox. (June 1795). Revoked on his death and administration granted to the nephew, John Berry. (June 1802).

Bertie, Hon. Peregrine, of Philadelphia, bachelor. Administration to the brother and next-of-kin, Hon. & Rev. Frederick Bertie. (Jan. 1850).

Best, Eliza, of Washington, Pennsylvania, spinster. Administration to George Cox, attorney for the father, John Best the elder, in Washington. (July 1840).

Best, George, of Newark, New Jersey. Probate to the relict, Mary Best, and Thomas Colpitts Granger. (May 1842). Further grant made in July 1872.

Best, Isabella, of Washington, Pennsylvania. Administration to George Cox, attorney for the husband, John Best the elder, in Washington. (July 1840).

Best, Nicholas, of Stratford by Bow, Middlesex, who died in Maryland, widower. Administration to the daughter, Rebecca, wife of Aaron Hawkins. (Sep. 1686).

Besuchet, Francois, of New Orleans, Louisiana. Administration with will to Philip Walther and Auguste de Vos, attornies for the relict, Fredericke Besuchet nee Heinert, in Pesnetz near Desan in the Principality of Anhalt, Germany. (Sep. 1849).

Beswicke, Charles, of South Carolina, bachelor. Administration to the brother, John Beswicke. (Apr. 1734).

Beswicke, Mary, formerly Mary Hill, of Charles Town, South Carolina. Administration to the husband, John Beswicke. (July 1749).

Beswicke, Silence, of Charles Town, South Carolina. Administration to Thomas Fludyer, attorney for the husband, John Beswicke, in South

Beswicke, *(contd)*
Carolina. (Sep. 1740).

Bethune, Benjamin Faneuil, of Cambridge, Massachusetts, bachelor. Administration to Samuel Prince, attorney for the mother, Mary Bethune, in Cambridge. (Jan. 1796).

Bethune, George, of Cambridge, Middlesex County, North America. Probate to the nephew, Samuel Prince, with similar powers reserved to the relict, Mary Bethune, and the son, Nathaniel Bethune. (July 1785).

Beton, John, of Ratcliffe, Stepney, Middlesex, who died in Virginia. Administration to the principal creditor, Giles Shute; the relict, Mary Beton, renouncing. (June 1678).

Bettris, Edward, of Oxford, surgeon, who had lands in Pennsylvania. Probate to the relict, Anne Bettris. (Feb. 1685). Wa.

Betty, Robert Bell, of Philadelphia, bachelor. Administration to James Watson, attorney for the mother and next-of-kin, Mary Betty, widow, in Ithaca, America. (Apr. 1840).

Bevian, Mary, of George Town, South Carolina, widow. Administration to the brother and next-of-kin, Christopher Brocklebank. (Mar. 1785).

Bevis, William, of Topsham, Devon, master of the merchant ship *Hope*, who died in Virginia. Probate to the relict, Margaret Bevis. (Mar. 1717).

Bew, Rigoult, of Virginia, who died in St. Giles Cripplegate, London, bachelor. Limited administration to Micajah Perry of London, merchant, attorney for the sister, Mary Thurston, and for Elizabeth Iremonger and Sarah Dawson. (Sep. 1697). Revoked on production of a will and probate granted to Samuel Dawson with similar powers reserved to Elizabeth Ironmonger and Robert Thurston. (July 1698).

Bexfield, Joseph, formerly of Richmond Terrace, Dalston, Middlesex, but late of Cabell County, Virginia. Probate to the son, Stephen Bexfield, with similar powers reserved to the daughter, Mariana Bexfield. (July 1850).

Bibby, Margaret Johnson, formerly Margaret Johnson McEvers, of New York City. Administration to Gabriel Shaw, attorney for the husband, Thomas Bibby, in New York City. (May 1823).

Bibby, Thomas, of New York, Captain on half pay of the 7th Regiment of Foot. Administration to James Tidbury, attorney for the relict, Rebecca Bibby, in New York. (June 1830).

Bickerton, John, of New York City, bachelor. Administration to the sister, Mary, wife of Jonathan Watmough; the mother and next-of-kin, Martha Bickerton, widow, having died. (May 1854).

Bickerton, Martha, of Constantia, Oswego County, New York, widow. Administration to the daughter, Mary, wife of Jonathan Watmough. (May 1854).

Bicknell, Dorcas, formerly of Coleman Street, London, but late of New York City, who died in Peckham, Surrey. Limited administration with will to the husband, David Bicknell. (Mar. 1856).

Bicknell, Mary, of Philadelphia. Administration to John Bainbridge the

Bicknell, *(contd)* younger, attorney for the daughter, Elizabeth Bicknell, in Philadelphia; the husband, Peter Bicknell, having died. (July 1812).

Bicknell, William, of Annapolis, Maryland, who died on H.M. ship *Richmond*, seaman. Probate to the brother, Andrew Bicknell. (June 1764).

Bidmead, Samuel, of Bristol, Illinois, bachelor. Administration to the father, James Bidmead. (Jan. 1847).

Bigge, John, of Whitechapel, Middlesex, who made a bequest to Frances Rogers of Virginia, spinster. Probate to the relict, Joan Bigge. (Sep. 1636). Wa.

Bigg, John, of Maidstone, Kent, whose mother, brother, and sister were in New England. Probate to Andrew Broughton. (Feb. 1743). Wa.

Bigg, Samuel, of Maryland, who died at sea, bachelor. Administration to the sister, Hannah, wife of Thomas Fox. (May 1703).

Biggs, Richard, of West Sherley Hundred, Virginia. Administration with will to the relict, Sarah Biggs; no executor having been named. (Aug. 1626). Sh.Wi.

Biggs, Richard, of New York, bachelor. Administration to the father, Joseph Biggs. (Dec. 1794).

Biles, Thomas, of New York. Administration to the son, Thomas Biles. (Feb. 1702).

Billing, Eliza, of Williams Town, Oswego County, New York. Administration to John Chalk, attorney for the husband, James Billing, in Williams Town. (May 1854).

Billings, William, surgeon of H.M. ship *Eolus*, who died in Pensacola, West Florida. Probate to the uncle, George Billings. (June 1767).

Billop, Christopher, of the Fleet Prison, London, who had lands in New York. Probate to James Fitter alias Fittar and Thomas Billop. (Apr. 1725).

Billopp, Joseph, of New York, widower. Administration to the brother and principal creditor, Christopher Billopp; the only child, Middleton Billopp, being incapable. (Nov. 1712).

Binding, Sarah, of Chertsey, Surrey, widow, whose daughter, Sarah, wife of Richard Buckley, was in Boston, New England. Probate to Jeremiah Dyke and Abigail Dyke. (Sep. 1687). Wa.

Binsteed, Henry, wheelwright in General Burgoyne's Army, bachelor. Administration to the father, Henry Binsteed. (Nov. 1778).

Birch, Chamberlain, formerly of St. Bride's, London, afterwards of Augustine, Georgia, but who died in New York. Limited administration with will to the relict, Elizabeth Birch. (Jan. 1799).

Birch, Edward, of New York. Administration to the relict, Sarah Birch. (Apr. 1826).

Birch, Elizabeth, of Pennsylvania. Probate to the daughter, Alice Birch. (Jan. 1701).

Birch, Matthew, of Newcastle, Pennsylvania. Administration to the daughter, Alice Birch; the relict, Elizabeth Birch, renouncing. (Feb. 1701).

Bird, John, of St. Sepulchre, London, who died in Virginia. Administration to Robert Bernard. (Feb. 1674).

Bird, John, Lieutenant-Colonel of the 15th Regiment of Foot, who died in Philadelphia. Probate to Lough Carleton. (May 1778).

Bird, John, of Allen Town, Northampton County, Pennsylvania. Limited probate to the sister, Mary Shrigley, widow. (Mar. 1802).

Byrd, Mary, of Westover, Virginia, widow. Administration with will to Walter Stirling, attorney for the surviving executor, William Byrd Page, in Frederick County, Virginia. (Sep. 1819).

Bird, Thomas, formerly of Finsbury Terrace, London, but late of New York City, who died at sea. Administration with will to the father, William Bird; the relict, Anne Bird, renouncing. (Oct. 1808).

Byrd, William, of Westover, Charles City County, Virginia. Probate to the relict, Mary Byrd. (Oct. 1806).

Birkett, Henry, of Albion, Edwards County, Illinois. Limited administration with will to the brother, John Birkett; the relict, Sarah Birkett, renouncing. (Mar. 1826).

Birt, Thomas, of Hershey, Gloucestershire, who died in Boston, New England, bachelor. Administration to the brother, Giles Birt. (Oct, 1670).

Bisaker, Ambrose, corporal in Captain Farmer's Company of the 22nd Regiment of Foot , who died in West Florida, bachelor. Probate to William Chipman. (June 1766).

Bisdee, Edwin, of Lysander, Onandaga County, New York, bachelor. Administration to William Millett Beauchamp, attorney for the father, John Bisdee, in Waterloo, New York. (Dec. 1848).

Bishop, Joseph, of New York City, master's mate of H.M. ship *St. Albans* and afterwards first Lieutenant of the private warship *Experiment*. Administration with will to the relict, Elizabeth Bishop, formerly Elizabeth Groshon; the executors, James and John Le Couteur, having been cited but not having appeared. (Dec. 1784).

Bishop, Nathaniel, master of the ship *Princess Wales Fort*, who died in Hudson's Bay. Probate to Thomas Bird. (Oct. 1723).

Bishop, Richard, of Potz Ville, North America. Administration to George Bishop, attorney for the relict, Eleanor Ann Bishop, in Potz Ville. (Feb. 1837).

Bisland alias Beasland alias Bisley, Alexander, of H.M. ship *Shoreham*, who died in New York. Administration to the principal creditor, Charles Lodwick, in New York. (Jan. 1714).

Bisset, George, Rector of St. John's, New Brunswick, who died in Rhode Island. Administration to the relict, Penelope Bisset. (Aug. 1791).

Bissill, William, of St. Margaret, Westminster, Middlesex, who died in Virginia. Probate to the relict, Anne Bissill. (Sep. 1713).

Bittle, Richard, mariner under Captain John Williams, who died in Annapolis Royal. Administration to the principal creditor, John Irving. (Sep. 1719).

Bize, Hercules Daniel, of Newark, New Jersey. Probate to Anthony Bordenave with similar powers reserved to the daughters, Ursula

Bize, *(contd)*
Elizabeth, wife of —— Roberti, Elizabeth, wife of John Tavel, and to John Woddrop, James Crawford, Thomas Bibby, and Nicholas Gouvernour. (May & June 1800).

Blaau, Eleanor, of New York City, widow. Administration to Jonathan Poot the younger, attorney for the daughter, Cornelia Blaau, in New York. (July 1803).

Blaau, Waldron, of New York City. Administration with will to Charles Cooke, attorney for the relict, Eleanor Blaau, and for the son, Uriah Blaau, in New York. (Nov. 1787).

Black, James, formerly of Philadelphia, afterwards of St. Cuthbert Street, but late of East Claremont Street, Edinburgh, merchant. Probate to Alexander Merton and Thomas Leburn, with similar powwers reserved to George Morris, John McAllister, and Quinton Campbell. (Apr. 1843).

Black, Richard, Controller of Customs in Port Royal, South Carolina, bachelor. Administration to the principal creditor, Edmund Smith. (Jan. 1768).

Blackalar, Philip, of New England, mariner. Probate to Margaret Allsell of Wapping, Middlesex. (Feb. 1709).

Blackall, Abraham, of North Carolina, bachelor. Administration to Mary Harris alias Blackall, the relict and executrix of the brother, Thomas Blackall, who died before administering. (Jan. 1749).

Blackett, William, Captain of the 14th Regiment of Foot, who died in Virginia, bachelor. Administration to the brother, John Blackett. (June 1777).

Blackler, Joas, of the Tower of London, who died in Virginia, bachelor. Administration to the brother, John Blackler. (Jan. 1699).

Blacklock, Christopher, of Boston, New England, and of H.M. ship *Mermaid*. Administration with will to John Coles, attorney for the relict, Ruth Blacklock, in Boston. (Dec. 1750).

Blackman, Anthony, of Shadwell, Middlesex, who died in Spotswood, Virginia. Administration to Anne Munk, attorney for the principal creditor, Daniel Munt, now at sea; the relict, Dorothy Blackman, renouncing. (June 1728).

Blackmore, Arthur, of St. Gregory, London, whose daughter, Susan, wife of William Corker, was in Virginia. Probate to the relict, Elizabeth Blackmore. (Mar. 1664). NGSQ 67/215.

Blackwell, Monro, formerly of Somers Town Terrace, Middlesex, but late of New York City, surgeon on half pay of the Royal Artillery, bachelor. Administration to the brother, Alexander Blackwell. (Mar. 1839).

Bladen, William, of Maryland. Administration to the son, Thomas Bladen, attorney for the relict, Anne Bladen, in Maryland. (Dec. 1718). Revoked and granted to the relict, Anne Bladen. (Sep. 1720).

Blagborne, Rev. William, formerly of Brooklyn, New York, but late of Bermondsey, Surrey, widower. Administration to the daughter, Elizabeth Blagborne. (Mar. 1816). Revoked on production of a will and administration granted to the daughter, Elizabeth Blagborne; the

Blagborne, *(contd)* surviving executors, Rowles Scudamore and Thomas Holy, renouncing. (Dec. 1817).

Blagdon, Sweeting, of North Carolina, bachelor. Administration to the sister and next-of-kin, Susanna, wife of Edward Kershaw. (Sep. 1761).

Blagge, Edward, of Plymouth, Devon, who died in Virginia. Administration to the relict, Patience Blagge. (Mar. 1693).

Blagrave, Edward, of St. Margaret, Westminster, Middlesex, who died in Virginia, bachelor. Administration to the brother and next-of-kin, Walter Blagrave. (Nov. 1678).

Blagrave, Thomas, of Westminster, Middlesex, whose kinswoman, Anne Williams, was in Virginia. Probate to the relict, Margaret Blagrave. (Dec. 1688). Wi.

Blague, Newcombe, of New England, master of the merchant ship *Victory*. Limited administration with will to the son and executor, Newcombe Blague. (Oct. 1718).

Blake, Charles, of Maryland. Probate to the son, Philemon Blake, with similar powers reserved to the son, John Blake. (Jan. 1734).

Blake, John, of Minehead, Somerset, who died in Virginia. Administration to the nephew, Hugh Saffin. (May 1663).

Blake, John Sayer, of Queen Anne County, Maryland. Administration to William Anderson, attorney for the son, John Sayer Blake, in Maryland. (Jan. 1760).

Blake, Joseph, of South Carolina, who died on the merchant ship *Wilmington*, widower. Administration to John Nicholson, guardian of the sons, Daniel and William Blake. (Sep. 1751). Revoked and administration with will granted to the son, Daniel Blake, with similar powers reserved to Ralph and Rebecca Izard. (Feb. 1752).

Blake, Philemon Charles, of Queen Anne County, Maryland. Administration with will to William Anderson, attorney for the relict, Sarah Blake, now in Queen Anne County. (May 1766).

Blanchard, William, of Louisville, Kentucky, widower. Administration with will to the son, George Blanchard. (Aug. 1840).

Blanchflower, Benjamin, of Fitzhead, Somerset, who died in Virginia. Probate to the brother, Alexander Blanchflower. (May 1685). Wi.

Bland, Edward, of Virginia, bachelor. Administration to the brother, John Bland. (July 1652).

Bland, Elias, formerly of All Hallows Barking, London, but late of New York. Administration to the relict, Hannah Bland. (Oct. 1781).

Bland, John, of St. Olave Hart Street, London, whose wife, Sarah Bland, was in Virginia. Probate to Thomas Povey with similar powers reserved to the relict, Sarah Bland. (June 1680). Wa.

Bland, Thomas, of London, who had a plantation in Anne Arundell County, Maryland. Probate to Laurence Pendrill and his wife, Sarah Pendrill. (Jan. 1701).

Blane, Charles Collins, of Richmond, Virginia, unattached Lieutenant-Colonel and Brevet Colonel of H.M. Army, bachelor. Administration

Blane, *(contd)* to the brother and only next-of-kin, Sir Hugh Seymour Blane. (Apr. 1855).

Blaydes, Samuel, of Virginia, bachelor. Administration to the principal creditor, Richard Booth. (June 1683).

Blennerhasset, James, of Virginia, bachelor. Administration to the mother and next-of-kin, Ann Blennerhasset, widow. (Apr. 1848).

Bliss alias Hide, Jean, formerly of London, but late of Philadelphia, spinster. Administration to the brother and only next-of-kin, James Bliss. (May 1820).

Blisse, Mary, of Virginia. Administration to the sister, Martha, wife of John Ward. (Nov. 1655).

Blogg, Anna Maria, of Savannah, America, spinster. Administration to Charles Robert Simpson, attorney for the mother, Mary Blogg, widow, in Savannah. (Jan. 1821).

Bludder, Thomas, of Clewer, Berkshire, who had kinsmen in Virginia. Probate to the relict, Emma Bludder. (Mar. 1654).

Blunt, John, of Shadwell, Middlesex, who died in New England on the ship *Samuel*. Probate to Amy Blunt, the mother and executrix of the named executrix, Amy Blunt, who died before administering. (Feb. 1712).

Blunt, Margaret, of St. Thomas, Southwark, Surrey, widow, whose sister, Mary Welch, was in Martin's Hundred, Virginia. Probate to Sibella Levitt. (Sep. 1659).

Bly, John, who died in Virginia. Probate to the brother, Giles Bly. (May 1664). Wi.

Boddily, Benjamin Peach, of Newbury Port, Essex County, Massachusetts. Limited administration to Petty Vaughan, attorney for Caleb Cushing, the guardian during their minority of the only children, Mary Cushing Boddily and Benjamin Cushing Boddily, in the United States of America; the relict, Ann Mary Boddily, renouncing. (Mar. 1827)

Boddy, John, of Stepney, Middlesex, who died in Maryland. Administration to the relict, Camelia Boddy. (June 1683).

Boggas, John, Lieutenant of an Independent Company in Carolina, bachelor. Administration to the brother, George Boggas. (Dec. 1762).

Boldry, Philip, of the merchant ship *Patsey*, who died in Virginia, bachelor. Probate to William Green. (Sep. 1731).

Bolles, John, of Clerkenwell, Middlesex, whose brother, Joseph Bolles, was in New England. Probate to John Sparrow and Joseph Clarke. (May 1666). Wa.

Bolton, Philip, of St. Leonard Eastcheap, London, who died in Virginia. Administration to the brother, Thomas Bolton. (June 1673). Inventory at PROB 4/9998.

Bolton, William, of Harrow on the Hill, Middlesex, clerk, whose brother, Henry Bolton, was in Virginia. Probate to Robert Payne with similar powers reserved to Thomas Robinson. (Feb. 1692). Wa.

Bond, Barnet, formerly of Maryland but late of Limehouse, Middlesex. Probate to the relict, Alice, now wife of William Grimes. (Apr. 1749).

Bond, Richard, of Bristol, who died in Virginia or overseas. Administration to Margaret Bird, aunt and guardian of the children, William, George, Richard and Mary Bond, during their minority. (Aug. 1652). NGSQ 62/203.

Bonnifield, Abraham, of Reading, Berkshire, who had lands in Pennsylvania. Probate by his solemn affirmation to the son, Abraham Bonnifield. (Apr. 1702).

Bonthron, John, of Capitol Hill, Washington, America, stonecutter. Administration to George Cox, attorney for the relict, Grace Bonthron, in Washington. (Aug. 1840).

Bonus, William. *See* **Bownass**.

Boorman, John, formerly of Hollingbourne, Kent, but late of New York. Probate to David Colgate with similar powers reserved to Benjamin Boorman. (Dec. 1796).

Booteflower, John, of Stepney, Middlesex, who died in Virginia. Administration to the principal creditor, Edmund Bugden; the relict, Margaret Booteflower, renouncing. (Apr. 1663).

Booth, John, of Stepney, Middlesex, who died on the ship *Industry* in Virginia. Probate to the relict, Sarah Booth. (Apr. 1694).

Booth, Sarah, of Richmond, Virginia, widow. Administration to James Dunlop, attorney for the only child, Sarah Bateman Boyce, widow, in Virginia. (Nov. 1827).

Booth, William, of Wapping, Stepney, Middlesex, who died in Virginia, bachelor. Administration to the father, William Booth. (Jan. 1676).

Booth, William, formerly of Chatham, Kent, but late of Philadelphia. Administration to the daughter, Mary, wife of William Belk; the relict, Elizabeth Booth, having been cited but not having appeared. (Jan. 1817).

Bordley, Thomas, of Annapolis, Maryland, who died in Greenwich, Kent. Probate to Martin Smith. (Sep. 1747).

Bordman, Amos, of Reading, Massachusetts, bachelor. Administration to Asbury Dickins, attorney for the father, Amos Bordman, in Massachusetts. (May 1812).

Bordwine, Charles, formerly of the Naval Yard in New York, afterwards of St. Martin in the Fields, Middlesex, but late of Montreal, Canada. Limited administration with will to Joseph Bordwine; the relict, Hannah Bordwine, having died. (Aug. 1826)

Boreman, Thomas, of Virginia, bachelor. Administration to the uncle, Sir William Boreman. (Jan. 1679).

Borland, Francis, of Boston, Massachusetts. Administration with will to William Mills, Edward Brice and Edward Wheeler, attornies for the son, John Borland, and the relict, Phebe Borland, in Boston. (Oct. 1768).

Borland, John, of Boston, Massachusetts. Probate to the relict, Ann Borland. (Feb. 1779).

Borre, John, of Boston, New England. Administration to the relict, Elizabeth Borre. (Sep. 1701).

Boss, Ann, of New York, spinster. Probate to Edward Baker. (June 1779).

Bossinger, Thomas, of New England, who died on the ship *Elizabeth*. Administration to Edward Hull, attorney for the relict, Mary Bossinger, during her absence. (June 1698).

Bostock, Wilcock, of Virginia. Administration to the principal creditor, Amor Blythman. (Jan. 1709).

Botson, Elizabeth. *See* **Davis**.

Botetourt, Lord Norborne, of Virginia. Probate to the nephew, Henry, Duke of Beaufort. (Jan. 1771).

Botson, Mary, of Pringo, North Carolina, spinster. Administration to John Smith Davis, the son and administrator of the sister, Elizabeth, wife of David Davis, deceased; the mother, Mary Botson, having also died. (Dec. 1818).

Bouchier, Edward Bass, sergeant of the Portsmouth Division of Marines, who died in New York. Probate to the sister, Ann Bouchier. (May 1783).

Bough, Thomas. *See* **Baugh**.

Boughton, Robert, of New England, bachelor. Administration to the father, Robert Boughton. (Jan. 1656).

Bouquet, Henry, Brigadier-General of H.M. Forces and Lieutenant-Colonel of the Royal American Regiment, who died in North America. Probate to Frederick Haldimand. (Nov. 1766).

Bourdillon, Jane, of St. Paul Covent Garden, Middlesex, relict of Rev. Benedict Bourdillon of Baltimore, Maryland. Probate to the sons, William Benedict Bourdillon and Thomas Bourdillon. (Jan. 1792).

Bourdillon, Rev. Peter, Minister of a church in Charleston, South Carolina. Administration to the relict, Helena Bourdillon. (Feb. 1801).

Bourne, George Stuart, Captain of the Coldstream Regiment of Foot Guards, who died in New York City. Probate to Goalston Bruere with similar powers reserved to Elizabeth Edgeley Hewer, widow, and Charles Spooner. (Jan. 1777). Further grant to Mark Stuart Harris, son of Sophia Stuart Brown (formerly Harris), the relict of Charles Brown. (Apr. 1793). Further grant 1863.

Bourne, Thomas, citizen and tobacconist of London, who died in Maryland. Probate to Benjamin Bourne, attorney for Richard Johns of Maryland, the executor of the relict and named executrix, Mary Bourne deceased. (Nov. 1711).

Bourne, Thomas, of Fredonia, New York. Probate to the relict, Huldah Ann Bourne. (Jan. 1841).

Boustead, James, of Philadelphia, tanner and currier. Probate to the son, John Boustead, with similar powers reserved to Joseph Snowdon. (Mar. 1852).

Bowdoin, Hon. James, of Boston, Massachusetts. Limited administration with will to Thomas Dickason the elder. (Dec. 1791). Revoked and limited administration granted to George Lee, George Ewing, and Thomas Latham. (May 1803).

Bowen, Charles, of the merchant ship *Catherine*, who died in New York, bachelor. Administration to the sisters, Jane and Margaret Bowen. (Oct. 1777).

Bowen, Goodin, of Mount Pleasant, North Carolina. Probate to John Younger. (Nov. 1799).

Bowen, Sarah, of Bladon County, North Carolina, widow. Administration with will to the son, Goodin Bowen; the surviving executor, Richard Watt, renouncing. (Feb. 1793).

Bowen, Thomas, formerly of Bristol, but late of Charles Town, America, bachelor. Administration to the brother, Henry Edward Bowen; the mother, Ann Bowen, having died. (Feb. 1813).

Bower, Thomas, of Dover, Kent, who died in New England, bachelor. Administration to the brother, William Bower. (Jan. 1659).

Bowerbank, Edward, formerly of Lothbury, London, but late of New York, merchant. Administration to the brother, John Bowerbank. (Oct. 1844). Revoked on his death and granted to the brother, William Bowerbank. (Oct. 1854).

Bowker, James, of St. Peter's parish, New Kent, Virginia. Probate to the brother, Ralph Bowker. (Nov. 1704).

Bowles, James, of Maryland. Probate to the relict, Rebecca Bowles. (June 1729).

Bowles, John, of Poole, Dorset, Captain of the merchant ship *Prince*, who died in Carolina, bachelor. Administration to the brother, Samuel Bowles. (Dec. 1739).

Bowles, Tobias, of London, merchant whose niece, Thomazine Bowles, was in Virginia. Probate to Henry Alexander Primrose and John Underdowne with similar powers reserved to James Bowles. (July 1727). Double probate to James Bowles. (Aug. 1727). *See* NGSQ 62/36.

Bowles, Tobias, of St. Philip's parish, South Carolina. Administration with will to John Stevens, attorney for Rebecca Drayton, widow, and Thomas Winstanley, in St. Philip's. (Oct. 1811).

Bowman, John, of Stepney, Middlesex, who died in Virginia. Limited administration to the principal creditor, Richard Cox of London, merchant, with the consent of the relict, Sarah Bowman. (Dec. 1691).

Bowman, Thomas, of Stepney, Middlesex, who died on the ship *Henry* in Virginia. Administration to the relict, Joanne Bowman. (June 1694).

Bown, Robert Tytherleigh, of Mobile, Alabama, journeyman baker and acting steward on the steam vessel *Palmyra*, bachelor. Administration to the father, Robert Bown. (Dec. 1848).

Bown, Samuel Hasel, of Chicago, America, bachelor. Administration to the sister, Susanna Elizabeth, wife of Robert William Smith; the mother, Mary Bown, wife of Robert Bown, and formerly Mary Bown, widow, having died. (Aug. 1856).

Bowness, George, of Virginia, bachelor. Administration to the brother, Rev. Francis Bowness; the mother, Ann Bowness, renouncing. (Dec. 1787). ALC.

Bownass alias Bonus, William, of New York. Probate to the relict, Martha Bownass, with similar powers reserved to John Cockburn. (Apr. 1784).

Bowring, Charles, of Norfolk, Virginia. Inventory 1824. [*Administration Act not found*].

Bowring, Mary Kelsey, of North Carolina, who died at sea. Administration to the husband, James Bowring. (Jan. 1824).

Bowyer, William, of Jamaica, who died in New York, merchant. Probate to William Turner with similar powers reserved to David Jamison and Richard Mills. (May 1707).

Boxe, Tobias, bound on a voyage to St. Christopher's, who had tobacco in Virginia from George Ayers. Probate to Annis Barber of London, spinster. (Dec. 1629). Wi.

Boyd, Alexander, formerly of South Leith, Edinburgh, but late of Savannah, Georgia, bachelor. Administration to the father, William Boyd. (Dec. 1804).

Boyd, George, formerly of Portsmouth, New Hampshire, and late of Low Layton, Essex, who died as a passenger on the merchant ship *Kitty*. Probate to Thomas Fraser and John Elliott with similar powers reserved to the relict, Jane Boyd, Supply Clapp, Joseph Champney and John Lane, and to the son, William Boyd, when he comes of age. (Dec. 1787). Double probate to John Lane and to the son, William Boyd, with similar powers reserved to Joseph Champney. (Mar. 1804).

Boyd, William, of Charleston, North America. Administration to Edward Boyd, the uncle and guardian during his minority of the only child, Maitland Boyd; the relict, Isabel Susan Boyd, having died. (July 1817).

Boylan, Patrick, Captain's clerk of H.M. ship *Jamaica*, who died in Charles Town, South Carolina. Administration to a creditor, Robert Field, the relict and others having been cited but not having appeared. (Sep. 1767).

Boyle, Catherine, of New York City. Administration to Joseph Boyle, attorney for the husband, John Thomas Boyle, in New York City. (Oct. 1851). Revoked on the death of Joseph Boyle and granted to Alexander Boyle as attorney. (July 1855).

Boyles, Philip, of New York, who died on H.M. ship *Ludlow Castle*. Administration to William Bryant, attorney for the relict, Catherine Boyles, in New York. (Feb. 1744).

Boylston, John, formerly of Boston, Massachusetts, but late of Bath, Somerset. Limited administration with will to Harry Daniel Mander. (May 1795).

Boylston, Thomas, formerly of Boston, Massachusetts, but late of St. Martin Vintry, London. Administration with will to the nephew, Ward Nicholas Boylston; the executors, Thomas Woodroffe Smith, Thomas Coles and Robert Slade, having been cited but not having appeared. (Apr. 1799).

Boylston, Ward Nicholas, of Princeton, Worcester, and late of Roxbury, Massachusetts. Limited administration with will to Petty Vaughan, attorney for John Quincy Adams, President of the United States of America, and for Nathaniel Custis and Alicia Broughton, widow, in the U.S.A. (July 1828). Copy of probate act issued in Dedham, Massachusetts, in February 1828 at PROB 20/1742/400 with further London probate to the nephews and niece, Abram Barber, Ann Hart and John Barber Tuck.

Boys, John, who died abroad, (bound for Virginia). Probate to the uncle, —— Boys, and Thomas Major. (May 1650). Wa.

Boyse, John, of South River, Virginia, bachelor. Administration to the principal creditor, Edmund Hunt. (Jan. 1710).

Boys, Thomas, of Patochnick River, Virginia, widower. Administration to the son, Thomas Boys. (Aug. 1676).

Boys, William, of Cranbrook, Kent, whose kinsmen, Thomas and John Stow, were in New England. Probate to the relict, Joane Boys. (Feb. 1657).

Bracegirdle, John, of London, who died in Virginia, bachelor. Administration to the brother, Joseph Bracegirdle. (Nov. 1673).

Bradburne, Richard, of the merchant ship *Susanna*, who died in Boston, New England. Administration to the father, Joseph Bradburne. (Apr. 1740).

Braddock, Edward, Major-General of H.M. Forces in America. Probate to John Calcraft with similar powers reserved to Mary, wife of John Yorke. (Sep. 1755).

Braddock, Nathaniel, formerly of Norwich, who died abroad (bound for Virginia). Administration to the brother, John Braddock. (Mar. 1636). Revoked on production of a will and probate granted to the brother-in-law, John Rooke. (May 1636). Wa.Wi.

Bradford, Thomas, of Batcombe, Somerset, who died in Virginia, bachelor. Administration to the principal creditor, John Boreman. (Nov. 1671).

Brading, Nathaniel, who died abroad (bound to the East Indies), whose uncle, Richard Kent, was in Newberry, New England. Probate to the father, William Brading, in Godshill, Isle of Wight. (July 1648). Sh.Wa.

Bradley, Anna alias Ann, of Wilmington, North Carolina, spinster. Administration to Hagger Allis, attorney for the mother, Elizabeth Bradley, in Wilmington. (Nov. 1789). Revoked on the death of the mother and granted to the brother, John Bradley. (Aug. 1802).

Bradley, Daniel, of Gosport, Hampshire, who died in Virginia. Administration to the relict, Margery Bradley. (Dec. 1669).

Bradley, Edward, of Philadelphia. Special administration with will to Edward Shepherd. (Nov. 1746).

Bradley, Lewis, of H.M. ship *Happy*, who died in South Carolina. Probate to John Bryan and Paul Debell, attornies for John Owen and William Mallard in South Carolina. (Aug. 1735).

Bradshaw, Robert, formerly of Hungerford, Berkshire, but late of the United States of America. Administration to the relict, Elizabeth Bradshaw. (Aug. 1825).

Bradshaw, Thomas the younger, formerly of Coventry Street, Haymarket, Middlesex, but late of Somerset, Maryland, bachelor. Administration to the father, Thomas Bradshaw. (Aug. 1814).

Bradstreet, Simon, of Portsmouth, New Hampshire, bachelor. Administration to the father, Lyonel Bradstreet. (Apr. 1783).

Brailsford, Edward, of South Carolina. Administration with will to Samuel

Brailsford, *(contd)*
Wragg, attorney for Arthur and Sarah Middleton in South Carolina. (Apr. 1733). Further grant to Samuel Brailsford, attorney for the surviving executor, Sarah Middleton, widow; the other executor, Arthur Middleton, and the attorney, Samuel Wragg, having died. (May 1762).

Brailsford, Samuel, of New York City. Administration to the relict, now Mary Evans. (May 1819). Further grant made in September 1861.

Braine, John, of Wapping, Middlesex, who had lands in New Jersey. Probate to the relict, Margaret Braine, the brother, James Braine, and to Roger Newham. (Jan. 1700).

Brand, John, of the ship *Prince*, who died in Virginia, bachelor. Administration by decree to the principal creditor, Patrick Hopbourne, during the absence of the father, Alexander Brand. (July 1676).

Brand, Jonathan, of Philadelphia, widower. Administration to the son, Thomas Brand. (Feb. 1749).

Branwood, John, of the merchant ship *Providence*, who died in Carolina, bachelor. Administration to the brother, Abraham Branwood. (Dec. 1706).

Brasseur alias Splatt, Ann, of South Carolina, widow. Administration to Johanna, wife of William Cripps, the aunt and guardian of the daughters, Mary Splatt and Ann Brasseur. (Nov. 1742).

Brathwaite, John, of South Carolina. Probate to the relict, Silvia Brathwaite, and to Elizabeth Tichborne, spinster, with similar powers reserved to Margaret Pultney, widow, and Thomas Revell. (Aug. 1740).

Bratt, Esther, of Lost Creek, Terra Hanto, Vigo County, Indiana, widow. Probate to Enoch Pearson with similar powers reserved to William Hartill Bayliss. (Oct. 1842).

Bray, Richard, of Rappahannock River, Virginia. Administration to the sister, Elianor Daniell. (Nov. 1691).

Bray, Thomas, of Bristol, who died in New England. Administration to the father, Henry Bray. (Nov. 1726).

Brayfield, John, formerly of Newington, Surrey, but late of Philadelphia, bachelor. Administration to the sister and next-of-kin, Hester Brayfield. (Sep. 1789).

Brazier, John, of New York City. Administration to William Vaughan, attorney for the relict, Rebecca Brazier, in New York. (Jan. 1810).

Breedon, Zaccheus, who died at sea or abroad (bound for Carolina or Maryland). Probate to Laurence Stevenson. (Sep. 1686). Wa.

Brent, Edward, who died overseas, having goods in Virginia. Probate to Edward Willett, attorney for the brother, Giles Brent, with similar powers reserved to the brother. John Brent. (Aug. 1625). Wa.

Brentnall, Catherine, of Newark. New Jersey, widow. Administration to the son, Amos Brentnall. (Feb. 1856).

Bressey, John, of St. Clement Danes. Middlesex, who died in Maryland, bachelor. Probate to Eleanor Lloyd. (Apr. 1723).

Bretland, Elizabeth, of Barbados, widow, whose brother, Adam Coulson, was of New England. Probate to Edward Munday and John Mortimer. (Dec. 1690). Wa.

Brett, Sir Edward, of Bexley, Kent, who died in St. Margaret, Westminster, Middlesex, and whose nephew, Henry Isham, was of Virginia. Probate to Stephen Beckingham and Richard Watson. (Mar. 1684). Wa.

Brett, Elizabeth, nee Elizabeth Jenkins, formerly of Rotherhithe, Surrey, but late of Savannah, North America. Administration to the husband, John Brett. (June 1832).

Brett, John, of St. Andrew Undershaft, London, who had lands in New England. Probate to the son, John Brett. (Jan. 1686). Wa.

Brett, Robert, of Pennsylvania. Administration to the brother, Roger Brett, attorney for the relict, Mary Tudor alias Brett, in New York. (Sep. 1701).

Brew, Arthur, formerly of St. Sepulchre, London, afterwards of Philadelphia, but who died in Jamaica. Probate to the sister, Jane Brew, with similar powers reserved to the sister, Ann, wife of John Teir. (Feb. 1788).

Brewen, Hubbard, of Maryland. Probate to John Philpot. (July 1756).

Brewer, John, citizen and grocer of London, who died in Virginia. Administration with will to the relict, Mary Brewer alias Butler, during the minority of the children, John, Roger and Margaret Brewer. (May 1636). Sh.Wa.

Brewer, William, formerly of Boston, New England, but late of Titchfield, Hampshire, mariner. Probate to Clement Walcot. (Mar. 1747).

Brewton, Miles, of Charles Town, South Carolina. Limited administration by decree to the creditor, Joseph Nutt, until the will is brought in. (Apr. 1785).

Bridge alias Bridges, John, of Virginia. Administration to a kinsman, George Warren. (Mar. 1637).

Bridgen, Thomas, of Sussex County, New Jersey. Administration with will to Edward Winwood, attorney for the son, Thomas Bridgen, in Albany, North America; the executors, Sanders Lausing and John Vander Spegle, having been cited but not having appeared. (May 1817).

Bridges, Francis, of Clapham, Surrey, who made bequests to friends in Virginia. Probate to the relict, Sarah Bridges. (June 1642). Sh.

Bridges, John, of New York. Administration to the principal creditor, Godfrey Lee, attorney for the relict, Anne Bridges, and the daughter, Elizabeth Bridges, during their absence. (July 1712).

Briggs, Richard, of the City of Northampton, who died at sea on a merchant ship returning from Virginia, widower. Administration to the sister, Elizabeth, wife of Christopher Oliver. (June 1701).

Brighouse, James, of Virginia, bachelor. Administration to the mother, Elizabeth Brighouse. (June 1683).

Brightwell, Charles, of Virginia, bachelor. Administration to the principal creditor, Thomas Darling. (Aug. 1660).

Brinkley, William, of H.M. ship *Sultan*, who died in Rhode Island Hospital, widower. Administration to John Day, attorney for the brother, John Brinkley, in Manningtree, Essex. (Apr. 1781).

Brinley, Elizabeth, formerly of Boston, Massachusetts, but late of Edgware Road, St. Marylebone, Middlesex, widow. Probate to George Lyde and the nephew, Wentworth Brinley. (Apr. 1793).

Brinley, Francis, of Boston, New England. Probate to the grandson, Francis Brinley, with similar powers reserved to William Hutchinson. (July 1721).

Brinley, Thomas, of Datchet, Buckinghamshire, whose daughter, Grissell, was wife of Nathaniel Silvester of New England. Probate to the relict, Anne Brinley. (Dec. 1661). Wa.

Briscoe, John, of H.M. ship *Success*, who died in Virginia, bachelor. Administration to the father, John Briscoe. (Sep. 1716).

Bristol, Joseph, of the transport ship *Marlborough*, who died in New York, bachelor. Administration to Ann Fernley, widow; the father and others having been cited but not having appeared. (Feb. 1764).

Bristow, Robert, of Virginia, bachelor. Administration to the sister, Rachel Bristow; the father, James Bristow, renouncing. (Oct. 1755).

Bristow, Robert, of Micheldever, Hampshire, [who had lands in Virginia]. Probate to the relict, Mary Bristow, and to John Arkell Bucknall and Richard Phillipson. (Dec. 1776). ALC.

Britten, John, of Hadleigh, Suffolk, adventurer to Virginia. Probate to the son, Laurence Britten. (Feb. 1637). Wi.

Broadbent, Edward, of New Orleans, widower. Administration to the daughter, Sarah Broadbent. (Feb. 1851).

Broadhurst, Dorothy, formerly of Philadelphia but late of Charleston, North America, spinster. Administration to the mother, Dorothy Broadhurst, widow. (Nov. 1806).

Broadhurst, Hugh, who died in Virginia, bachelor. Administration to the brother, John Broadhurst. (June 1659).

Broadhurst, John, of Virginia. Probate to the relict, Elizabeth Broadhurst. (Dec. 1701).

Broadribb, John, of Chester River, Talbot County, Maryland. Administration to Charles Cottle, the father of the next-of-kin, John Cottle, the nephew by a sister, during his minority. (July 1687).

Brocas, Richard, of Wilmington, North America, bachelor. Administration to the sister, Elizabeth Brocas. (May 1788).

Brocas, Thomas, of Littleton, New England, bachelor. Probate to Christopher Kilby. (July 1751).

Brockhall, John, of South Carolina, bachelor. Administration to the brother, Joseph Brockhall. (May 1742).

Brockwell, Nathaniel, corporal of the 20th Regiment of Foot, who died in Pennsylvania, bachelor. Limited administration with will to John Noseworthy. (Nov. 1783).

Bromfield, James, of Shadwell, Middlesex, who died on H.M. ship *Somerset* in Boston, New England. Administration to the principal creditor, Richard Merry; the relict, Sarah Bromfield, renouncing. (Feb. 1724).

Bromfield, Thomas, of Boston, Massachusetts. Administration with will to Gilbert Harrison, John Ansley and George Bainbridge, attornies for

Bromfield, *(contd)* William Phillips in Boston. (Sep. 1787). Revoked on the death of William Phillips and administration granted to Henry Bromfield the younger, attorney for Henry Bromfield, the son of a cousin, Edward Bromfield, now in Harvard, Massachusetts. (Sep. 1804).

Bromfield, William, of Stepney, Middlesex, who died on the ship *London Merchant* in Virginia. Administration to the relict, Frances Bromfield. (Oct. 1702).

Bromley, Henry, Captain of a Company under Sir Peter Hulkett, who died in America, bachelor. Administration to the father, William Bromley. (Dec. 1756).

Brooke, Henry, of Port Lewes, Pennsylvania, bachelor. Limited administration with will to John Plumtree. (Dec. 1737).

Brooke, Paulin, of York River, Virginia, bachelor. Special grant of administration with will to William Watts. (Feb. 1748).

Brooke, Ricey, master of the merchant ship *Neptune*, who died in Virginia, bachelor. Administration to the sister, Deborah Brooke; the mother, Margaret Brooke, renouncing. (Apr. 1740).

Brooker, Joanna, of Boston, New England, widow. Special limited administration with will to Edward Pearson, attorney for Silvester Gardiner, Joshua Henshaw and John Winslow in Boston. (Aug. 1763).

Brooks, John, of Stepney, Middlesex, who died in Virginia. Administration to the relict, Mary Brooks. (July 1684).

Brookes, Mildred, of Gloucester County, Virginia, spinster. Administration to the brother, Thomas Brookes. (Nov. 1748).

Brooks, Philip, soldier of the 22nd Regiment of Foot, who died in Mobile, West Florida, bachelor. Administration with will to Jane, wife of John Drummon, (formerly Jane Irvine), administratrix to the universal legatee, Robert Carson, who died before administering. (Apr. 1766).

Brookes, Samuel, of Dorchester, Massachusetts. Limited administration with will to Henry Norris. (Oct. 1758).

Brooks, Thomas, of Plaistow, Essex, whose sister, Ann, wife of Benjamin Dawson, was in Virginia. Probate to Sir Robert Willimott. (Jan. 1746). Wi.

Brookesbancke, Isaac, of the ship *Anne*, who died at sea or abroad (bound for Maryland). Probate to the brother, William Brookesbancke. (Aug. 1675).

Broome, Thomas, of H.M. ship *Dunkirk* (bound from the Leeward Islands to Boston), bachelor. Administration with will to John Aldred, attorney for the executor, Francis Ward, now in distant parts. (June 1695).

Broughton, Edmund, formerly of Crewkerne, Somerset, but late of Charles Town, South Carolina, currier, widower. Administration to the sister and next-of-kin, Margaret Broughton. (May 1813).

Broughton, John, of Lambeth, Surrey, whose nephews by a sister, William and George Roberts, were in Maryland. Administration with will to the great niece and next-of-kin, Catherine, wife of Roger Monk, after

Broughton, *(contd)* sentence for the validity of the will. (July 1789). *See* NGSQ 59/290.

Browne, Benjamin, of Salem, Essex County, New England. Administration with will to John Ive, attorney for the nephews, Samuel and John Browne, in New England. (Jan. 1712).

Brown, Charles, of Williamsburgh, Virginia, bachelor. Administration to the brother, Robert Brown. (June 1741).

Brown, Francis, of Madeira, who died in Philadelphia, bachelor. Administration with will to the creditor, Robert French; the father, Andrew Brown, the brother, Andrew Brown, and the sister, Mary Brown, having been cited but not having appeared, and the executor, Robert Kirwan, having died. (Mar. 1738).

Browne, Isaac, chaplain of the New York Volunteers, who died in Windsor, Nova Scotia. Administration with will to David Thomas, attorney for Daniel Isaac Browne in Annapolis Royal. (Sep. 1789).

Brown, Isabel, of Cincinnati, United States of America, widow. Administration with will to the children, Eliza Liddell Brown, Jane Spears Brown, and Isabella Livingstone Brown. (June 1851).

Brown, James, of Wapping, Stepney, Middlesex, then of Rotherhithe, Surrey, but who died on the merchant ship *Champion* in Maryland. Probate to the relict, Abigail Brown. (Sep. 1725).

Brown, James, of the ship *Priscilla*, who died in Philadelphia. Administration to the relict, Rachel Brown. (Sep. 1725).

Browne, James, of Philadelphia. Administration with will to William Lea, administrator to the relict, Sarah Lea deceased. (Oct. 1749).

Brown, James, Lieutenant of the First Connecticut Regiment of Foot, who died in Havana, bachelor. Administration to Phineas Lyman, attorney for the father, Nathaniel Brown, in Preston, New London County, Connecticut. (Nov. 1764).

Browne, John, of St. Michael Bassishaw, London, who died in Virginia. Administration to the relict, Susan Parrott alias Browne. (Oct. 1668).

Browne, John, of Whitechapel, Middlesex, master of the ship *Happy Union*, who died in Maryland. Administration to the father, John Browne. (Mar. 1700).

Browne, Jonathan, of Philadelphia. Probate to the relict, Elizabeth Browne. (Oct. 1784).

Browne, Moses, of St. Margaret Lothbury, London, whose sister, Sarah Noyse, was in New England. Probate to Benjamin Wilkes, Richard Browne, and Richard Ventham. (June 1688). Wa.

Browne, Peregrine, of Maryland, bachelor. Administration to the father, Peregrine Browne. (Sep. 1712). Revoked on his death and granted to his relict and executrix, Margaret Browne. (Oct. 1713).

Brown, Peter, formerly of East Florida but late of New Providence. Administration to James Phyn, attorney for the relict, Sarah Brown, in New Providence. (May 1791).

Brown, Richard, of H.M. ship *Hector*, who died in Virginia, bachelor. Administration to Elizabeth Brown, attorney for the brother, John

Brown, *(contd)* Brown; the mother, Marjery Brown, widow, having died before administering. (Dec. 1740).

Brown, Robert, of Savannah, Georgia, bachelor. Administration to the brother, Richard Brown; the father, Richard Brown, renouncing. (Jan. 1798).

Browne, Sarah, of Gloucester, widow, whose grandchild Sarah, wife of William Barnes, was in New England. Probate to Gregory Wilshire. Wa. NGSQ 61/115.

Browne, Sarah. *See* **Lea**.

Browne, Thomas, of Plymouth, Devon, who had goods in New England. Administration with will to the relict, Priscilla Browne; no executor having been named. (July 1663). Wa.

Browne, Thomas, of the fireship *Hart*, who died in New England, bachelor. Administration to the mother, Margaret Browne. (Oct. 1693). Revoked and probate granted to the brother, George Browne, with similar powers reserved to Theophilus Rabneere, John Dagger and Joseph Store. (Nov. 1693).

Brown, Thomas, of New York City, who died in St. Sepulchre, London. Probate to William Hardwick with similar powers reserved to Elias Desbrosses and Richard Light. (July 1769). Revoked and administration granted to William Browning, attorney for Edward Laight in New York; the executors William Hardwick and Elias Desbrosses having died. (Apr. 1779).

Browne, William, of Ratcliffe, Middlesex, who died in Virginia. Administration to the relict, Anne Browne. (May 1657).

Browne, William, of Plymouth, Devon, who died in Virginia, widower. Administration to the principal creditor, William Clarke. (June 1668).

Brown, William, of Lyonsburg and Richmond, Virginia. Limited administration with will to the parents, James and Margaret Brown. (Feb. 1815).

Brown, William, of 24 East Lane, Bermondsey, Surrey, mariner, who died as a passenger on the ship *Charles Bartlett*, bound to New York. Administration to the relict, Susan Brown. (Aug. 1849).

Brown, William Hugh, of Sportsman's Hall Estate, Trelawney, Cornwall County, Jamaica, but who died in New York. Probate to William Dawson with similar powers reserved to John Brown. (Apr. 1835).

Browning, John, of the ship *Old Pendennis*, who died in New England. Administration to the principal creditor, Jane Hilling, widow. (Feb. 1702).

Browninge, William, of Virginia. Administration to the uncle, John Browninge. (Sep. 1651).

Brownejohn, Mary, of New York City, widow. Administration to Robert Richard Randall, attorney for the son, Samuel Brownejohn, in Flushing, Queen's County, North America. (May 1786).

Brownjohn, William, of New York City. Administration with will to Robert Richard Randall, attorney for the relict, Mary Brownjohn, in New

Brownjohn, *(contd)* York; the executors, Gabriel William Ludlow, Cornelius Clopper, James Beckman and Henry Remsen, having been cited but not having appeared. (June 1785).

Brownrigg, Henry, of New Orleans, bachelor without parent. Administration to the sister, Ann Brownrigg. (May 1828).

Brownsford, James, of Virginia. Administration to the principal creditor, Tristram Bartlett; the brother and sister, John and Susan Brownsford, renouncing. (Aug. 1684).

Bruce, Charles Key, formerly of Calcutta in the East Indies but late of Richmond, New York. Probate to James McKillop and Joseph Boulderson with similar powers reserved to John Shoolbred, M.D. (Apr. 1827).

Bruce, Frances, of New York City, widow. Administration with will to John Chambers White and John Scott, attornies for Peter Jay Munro in New York. (Sep. 1821).

Brumpsted, Rose, of St. Martin in the Fields, Middlesex, spinster, whose kinsman, Thomas Breedon, was in New England. Administration with will to Thomas Brumpsted, the father of the principal legatees, Thomas and Charles Brumpsted; the executors, John Bredon, Edward Edgins and Edward Noell, renouncing. (July 1666). Wa.

Bryan, Richard, of Milford, New England. Administration to the grandson, Alexander Bryan; the relict, Elizabeth Bryan, having died before administering. (July 1720).

Bryant, Alexander Drake, of Cincinnati. Administration to John Gribble, attorney for the relict, Frances Ann Drake Bryant, in Louisville, Kentucky. (Nov. 1836).

Bryant, Samuel Drake the younger, of Cincinnati, Ohio. Administration to John Gribble, attorney for the father, Samuel Drake Bryant, in Cincinnati; the relict, Ann Drake Bryant, having died. (May 1837).

Bubb, Arthur and Mary Jane, formerly of Bourton on the Water, Gloucestershire, but late of New York. Administration to the father, Charles Bubb the younger. (Aug. 1854).

Buchanan, Archibald, of Baltimore, Maryland. Administration to the principal creditor, Joshua Johnson; the relict, Sarah Buchanan, and the brothers and sisters, George, Andrew, William, Elizabeth wife of James Gittins, and Elizabeth *(sic)* Brocall, widow, having been cited but not having appeared. (Feb. 1786).

Buckland, David, of New York, soap boiler. Administration to the relict, Sarah Buckland. (July 1837).

Buckley, Michael, of New York City. Probate to Jeremiah Shine with similar powers reserved to Very Rev. John Power and John Williams. (Aug. 1840).

Buckmaster, Christopher, of Ohio City. Administration to Richard Price, attorney for the relict Louisa, now wife of James Bradley, in Ohio City. (Aug. 1853).

Buckner, Archibald, of Baltimore, Maryland. Inventory 1786. [*Administration Act not found*].

Buckoll, William, of New York City, bachelor. Administration to the brother, Henry Buckoll; the mother, Sarah Buckoll, having died. (July 1829).

Bugge, Rev. Nathaniel, of Brandeston, Suffolk, whose kinsman, Thomas Bugge, was in Virginia. Probate to the brother, Joseph Bugge. (Apr. 1656). Wi.

Bulfinch, Hannah, of Boston, Massachusetts. Administration to the husband, Charles Bulfinch. (Aug. 1842). Further grant made in December 1874.

Bulkeley, Arthur, of London, merchant, (bound for Virginia). Probate to the brother, Thomas Bulkeley. (Nov. 1645). Sh.Wi.

Bulkeley, John, of St. Katherine by the Tower, London, whose brother, Thomas Bulkeley, was in New England. Probate to Edward and Avis Bulkeley and Elizabeth Faulkener. (Jan. 1690). Wa.

Bulkley, Peter, of Boston, New England, bachelor. Administration to the creditor, John Baynham. (Mar. 1761).

Bull, Absalom, of Savannah, Georgia. Administration with will to Effingham Lawrence, attorney for Thomas Bull, late of New York but now in Ulster County. (July 1797).

Bull, Jonathan, of Boston, New England. Probate to the relict, Elizabeth Bull; Samuel Greenleaf renouncing. (Jan. 1729).

Bullen, Thomas, of Virginia, bachelor. Administration to the brother, Arthur Bullen. (May 1690).

Bullin, Thomas, of Boston, New England, bachelor. Administration to the brother and next-of-kin, John Bullin. (Oct. 1717).

Bullocke, Hugh, of All Hallows Barking, London, whose son, William Bullocke, was in Virginia. Administration with will to the principal creditor, Samuel Burrell; the executor, John Limbry, having died. (Nov. 1650). Wi.

Bullocke, William, of Barking, Essex, (bound for Virginia). Probate to the relict, Elizabeth Bullocke. (May 1650). Sh.Wi.

Burbridge alias Burges alias Church, Elizabeth, of St. Giles in the Fields, Middlesex, widow. Administration to Charles Raven, husband of the sister, Mary Nicholas alias Raven, in New England. (Nov. 1687). Revoked and granted to Anne Yeates, widow, guardian of the nephews and nieces by a brother, Sarah, Samuel and John Church, during the absence of Mary Nicholas alias Raven. (Dec. 1687).

Burchett, Arthur Tertius Nicholas, of Hubbard Street, Chicago, Illinois, bachelor. Administration to the brother, George Martindale Burchett. (Dec. 1855).

Burchett, Frances Anne, of Clark Street, Chicago, Illinois, spinster. Administration to the brother, George Martindale Burchett. (Dec. 1855).

Burger, Peter, of H.M. ship *Worcester*. Administration to Joseph Mico, attorney for the relict, Elizabeth Burger, in New York. (Aug. 1750).

Burges, Elizabeth. *See* **Burbridge**.

Burges, John the elder, of Westley, Devon, (lying sick in New England). Probate to the relict, Joanna Burges alias Bray. (May 1628). Sh.Wa.

Burgis, John, of Virginia, widower. Administration to the son, William Burgis. (July 1712).

Burges, Joseph, of Marlborough, Wiltshire, but late of Maryland, who died in the City of London, merchant. Probate to John Keynes. (Nov. 1672). Wa.

Burgis, Joseph, of St. Giles in the Fields, Middlesex, who died in Virginia, bachelor. Administration to the brother and next-of-kin, Richard Burgis. (Aug. 1749). Revoked and granted by decree to Thomas Card, guardian of the only child, Joseph Burgis. (Aug. 1752).

Burges, William, of South River, Anne Arundell County, Maryland. Administration with will to Micajah Perry, attorney for the relict, Ursula, now wife of Mordecai Moore, in Anne Arundell County. (July 1689). Wa.

Burke, Redmond, of Philadelphia, bachelor. Administration to the brother and next-of-kin, Myles Burke. (Sep. 1814).

Burley, Susannah. *See* **Kearny**.

Burley, William, of New York and H.M. ships *Torbay*, *Tartan* and *Kent*. Probate to Peter Seignoret and Marc Anthony Ravaud. (Aug. 1727).

Burling, Samuel, of Shelburne, Nova Scotia, bachelor. Administration to the sister, Hannah Smith. (Sep. 1799). Revoked and granted by decree to John Fry, attorney for the sister, Hannah Smith, formerly Burling, widow, in Burlington, New Jersey. (Apr. 1803).

Burn, James, formerly of Upper Berkeley Street, Norton Street and Upper Norton Street, Middlesex, but late of Frankford, Pennsylvania. Probate to Joel Roberts Poinsett with similar powers reserved to Richard Willing. (Aug. 1831).

Burnapp, John, of Aston, Hertfordshire, whose son, Thomas Burnapp, was in New England. Probate to the son, John Burnapp. (Mar. 1654). Wa.

Burnell, Robert, formerly of Newton Nottage, Glamorgan, but late of South Carolina. Probate to one of the six children surviving at the date of the will of Mary Davies, widow, with similar powers reserved to the relict, Elizabeth Burnell, and to the children, Ann, wife of David Thomas, and Margaret, wife of Rees Rees. (Apr. 1856).

Burnell, Thomas, citizen and clothworker of London, whose nephew, John Morley, was in New England. Probate to the relict, Hester Burnell. (Oct. 1661). Wa.

Burnell, Thomas, formerly of Whitehaven, Cumberland, mariner, afterwards of Montego Bay, Jamaica, but late of New York. Limited probate to Richard Gordon and Henry Sands with similar powers reserved to John Wallas and Christian Archer. (June 1833).

Burnett, Charlotte, of New York, widow. Administration to Arthur Edward Francis, attorney for the only child, Ward Benjamin Burnett, in New York. (July 1856).

Burnett, John, of New England, who died abroad or at sea. Probate to Thomas Amiger. (Jan. 1716).

Burnett, Thomas, of New York, bachelor. Administration to Arthur Edward Francis, attorney for the brother, Ward Benjamin Burnett, in New

Burnett, *(contd)*
York; the mother, Charlotte Burnett, having died. (July 1856).

Burnett, Hon. William, Governor of New York and New Jersey. Probate to Abraham and Mary Vanhorn. (July 1730).

Burnley, John, of York River, Hanover County, Virginia. Probate to the brother, Hardin Burnley, with similar powers reserved to the brother, Richard Burnley. (Feb. 1780).

Burnside, James, of Calcutta in the East Indies, who died in Norfolk, United States of America. Administration of the estate unadministered by the brother, Anthony Austin Burnside deceased, to the brother, Richard Henry Burnside. (Feb. 1829).

Burr, Emma, of New England, widow. Administration to Benjamin Franklin, attorney for the son, Daniel Burr, in New England. (May 1701).

Burrell, Edward, of Wapping, Middlesex, who died in Virginia on the merchant ship *John*. Administration to the relict Abigael Burrell. (Aug. 1701).

Burrell, William, of Virginia. Probate to the brother-in-law, Richard Kelley. (Aug. 1648). Sh.Wa.Wi.

Burrell, William, of Stepney, Middlesex, who died in Virginia on the ship *Mary*. Administration to the relict, Hannah Burrell. (Jan. 1692).

Burridge, Robert, boatswain of H.M. ship *Launceston*, who died in Virginia. Probate to the relict, Sarah Burridge. (July 1769).

Burrington, John, of St. George Hanover Square, Middlesex, who had lands on Cape Fear River, North Carolina. Probate to Esquire Cary. (Dec. 1747). *See* NGSQ 64/289.

Burrington, Thomas, of Newton Abbott, Devon, who had lands in Georgia and South Carolina. Administration with will to Rev. Gilbert Burrington, sole executor of the uncle and surviving executor, Gilbert Burrington deceased. (June 1792).

Burrough, Nathaniel, of Limehouse, Stepney, Middlesex, whose son, George Burrough, was in New England. Probate to Anne Wheeler. (Mar. 1683). Wa.

Burrowes, John, of Bristol, who died in Virginia. Administration to the principal creditrix, Frances Hobbs; the relict, Deborah Burrowes, having renounced. (Feb. 1691).

Burrows, John, of Williamsburgh, Virginia, bachelor. Administration to the sister, Mary, wife of John Burrows. (June 1785).

Burrowes, William, of Maryland. Administration to the brother, Thomas Burrowes, attorney for the relict, Anne Burrowes, in Maryland. (Feb. 1707).

Burt, Benjamin, of East New Jersey, bachelor. Administration to the brother, Maynard Burt. (Feb. 1733).

Burt, George, of New Barbadoes, Bergen County, New Jersey. Probate to the relict, Harriet Burt, and to John Andrew Zobriskie. (Mar. 1849).

Burton, George, who died overseas (bound to New England), bachelor. Administration with will to the brother John Burton, and to John Ellis, both of St. Clement Danes, Middlesex. (Feb. 1637). Sh.

Burton, Isaac, of Charles Town, South Carolina, who died in Granada in the West Indies. Administration to the brother, George Burton; the relict, Ann Burton, having died before administering. (Apr. 1788).

Burton,John, formerly of Birmingham, Warwickshire, but late of Port Caddo, Texas. Administration to the relict, Eliza Burton. (Apr. 1851). Revoked on her death and granted to Thomas Smith Jones, attorney for Anne Burton, widow, guardian of the only children, George, Eliza, Hannah Sarah, Caroline Ruth, and Louisa Burton, in Texas. (July 1852 & Nov. 1853).

Burton, Richard, of Virginia, bachelor. Administration to the sisters, Elizabeth Vaughan alias Cooke, wife of Hugh Vaughan, and Martha Cooke, spinster. (Oct. 1656).

Burton, Richard, of Virginia. Administration to the daughter, Anne, wife of George Coombe. (Dec. 1656).

Burton, Richard, master of the merchant ship *Richard and Ann*, who died in Charles Town, South Carolina, bachelor. Administration to George Burton, attorney for the father, Richard Burton, in Staiths, Yorkshire. (Oct. 1763).

Burton, Thomas, of New England, who died on the ship *Quaker Ketch*. Administration to the father, Abraham Burton, during the absence in New England of the relict, Susan Burton. (Feb. 1689).

Busby, James, of Over Norton, Oxfordshire, who died in Maryland, bachelor. Administration to the brother, William Busby. (July 1709).

Bushe, Elizabeth. *See* **Noel**.

Bussa, Alexander Placide, of Richmond, Virginia, Professor of Music, bachelor. Administration to William Frederick Collard, attorney for the brother, Henry Placide Bussa, in New York. (Apr. 1837).

Butcher, James, of Maryland, bachelor. Administration to the brother, Francis Butcher. (July 1733).

Butcher, Thomas, of Wadhurst, Sussex, whose kinswoman, Margaret, wife of Thomas Swanne, was in Virginia. Probate to the relict Mary Butcher. (Sep. 1646). Revoked on her death and administration granted to her husband, Henry Dyke. (Nov. 1651). Wi.

Butler, Elizabeth, of Cincinnati, Hamilton County, Ohio, wife of Edmund Butler. Limited administration with will to Edmund Butler the younger, attorney for Francis Miller in Cincinnati. (June 1847).

Butler, George, of Maryland. Administration to the principal creditrix, Jane Cooper; the relict, Margaret Butler, renouncing. (Oct. 1698).

Butler, Henry, of Montgomery, Maryland. Administration to the relict, Mary Butler. (Dec. 1789).

Butler, John the elder, of Connecticut, New England. Administration to the principal creditor, Phillip Frensh; the relict, Mary Butler, and the children, John, William and Alexander Butler, renouncing. (Dec. 1698 & Jan. 1699).

Butler, Mary. *See* **Bagg**.

Butler, Stephen, of New England, who died on the ship *John* of London in Sierra Leone, Gambia. Administration to Benjamin Burges of

Butler, *(contd)*
Stepney, Middlesex, shipwright, the cousin and only next-of-kin in England of the relict, Tabitha Butler. (Nov. 1694).

Butler, Thomas, Minister of God's word, who died overseas (expecting tobacco from Virginia). Probate to the relict, Mary Butler. (July 1637). Wi.

Butlin, Ann and Martha, of Amherst Plato, Lorraine, Ohio, spinsters. Administration to the sister, Mary, wife of Nathaniel Buswell; the mother and next-of-kin, Martha Butlin, having died. (Feb. 1854).

Butt, John, of New York. Administration to the creditor, Amos Butt; the relict, Alice Butt, and the only children, George Amos, Mary Anne, Isabella, wife of —— Lord, Matilda Diana, Frederick, and John Felix Butt, having been cited but not having appeared. (Mar. 1829).

Butt, John Yenn, of Cincinnati, United States of America. Administration to the relict, Cynthia Butt. (Apr. 1852).

Buttall, Mary, of Exeter, Devon, widow, who had lands in Carolina. Probate to the daughter, Mary Hodges, with similar powers reserved to the other children, John Buttall, Charles Buttall, Sarah Wiggington and Elizabeth Wells. (Feb. 1731). NGSQ 63/294.

Buxton, Cornelia, of New York City. Administration to the husband, Charles Buxton, Doctor of Physic. (June 1819).

Buxton, John, of New York City. Limited administration with will to Robert Rolleston, attorney for the relict, Ann Buxton, in New York City. (Apr. 1795).

Buy, John, of Reading, Berkshire, who had lands in Pennsylvania. Probate by their solemn affirmation to the sons, John and William Buy, with similar powers reserved to the relict, Mary Buy. (Aug. 1713).

Buy, Mary, of Reading, Berkshire, widow, who had lands in Ridley, Pennsylvania, and made a bequest to William Passmore, formerly of Philadelphia but late of Hurst, Wiltshire. Probate by his solemn affirmation to John Buy. (June 1719).

Byrd. *See* **Bird**.

Byrn, Barnaby, of Jamaica, Long Island, New York. Limited administration with will to James Rivington, attorney for William and Robert Bayard and for Terence Kerin. (May 1776).

C

Cade, Andrew, of East Betchworth, Surrey, whose cousin, Henry Cade, was in Virginia. Probate to the relict, Magdalen Cade. (Oct. 1662). Wi.

Cadwallader, Thomas, of Martinsbury, Bedford County, Pennsylvania. Probate to Isaac Ironside. (Oct. 1842).

Caffinch, John, formerly of Tenterden, Kent, but late of New Haven in New England. Probate to Samuel Caffinch. (Jan. 1659). Wa.

Cage, Gilbert, of the ship *Hopewell*, who died in Virginia. Administration to Sarah, wife of the principal creditor, Andrew Boswell, during his absence overseas; the relict, Mary Cage, renouncing. (July 1680).

Cahill, Bryan, who died as a passenger on the American steam vessel *Panama*, bachelor. Administration to the sister, Mary Foran, widow. (Nov. 1850).

Cairnes, Alexander, of Islington, Middlesex, who died in Virginia, widower. Probate to John Lidderdale. (Feb. 1761).

Caldwell, Thomas, of Maryland, bachelor. Administration to the sister, Mary Caldwell. (July 1703).

Cailloyell, Isaac, of Boston, New England. Administration to the relict, Rebecca Cailloyell. (Mar. 1721).

Caldwell, James. *See* **Calwell**.

Callaghan, David, of Philadelphia. Administration to William Farquhar, attorney for the relict, Elizabeth Callaghan, in [blank]. (Jan. 1807).

Callanan, Michael, of Philadelphia. Administration with will to Robert Barclay, attorney for Benjamin Wilson and Thomas Park in Philadelphia. (Oct. 1807).

Callaway, Thomas, formerly of Maidstone, Kent, but late of New York City. Administration to the creditor, John Durrant; the relict, Elizabeth Callaway, and the only children, Elizabeth, wife of William Leaycraft, Thomas Christopher, and George Callaway, having been cited but not having appeared. (May 1846).

Calvert, Benedict Leonard, of Epsom, Surrey, bachelor. Limited administration with will to Hon. Cornelius Calvert. (Aug. 1733).

Calvert, Edward Henry, of Annapolis, Maryland. Probate to the relict, Margaret Calvert. (Nov. 1730).

Calvert, George, of St. Mary's, Maryland, who died overseas. Probate to William Peasely with similar powers reserved to the brother, Leonard Calvert. (Jan. 1635). Sh.

Calvet, Peter, of Charles Town, South Carolina, widower. Administration to the brother and next-of-kin, Raimond Calvet. (May 1765).

Calvert, Reynard alias Raymond, of South Carolina. Probate to Emanuel Reller. (Aug. 1767).

Calwell alias Caldwell, James, seaman of H.M. ship *Captain*, who died in Boston Hospital. Probate to Andrew Rice, attorney for the relict, Agnes Calwell, in Falkirk, Scotland. (Sep. 1774).

Cameron, Abigail, of New York City, widow of Alexander Cameron, Lieutenant of the Royal Navy. Administration to Leonard Streate

Cameron, *(contd.)* Coxe, attorney for the son, William H. Cameron, in New York. (Jan. 1808).

Cameron, Alexander, of Savannah, Georgia. Probate to William Ogilvy with similar powers reserved to Donald Cameron. (Feb. 1784).

Cameron, Alexander, Lieutenant of H.M. ship *Roebuck*. Administration to Daniel Coxe, attorney for the relict, Abigail Cameron, in New York City. (Jan. 1802).

Cameron, Allan, corporal of the Second Regiment of Foot, who died in New Jersey, bachelor. Special limited administration to the cousin german, Colin Cameron, pending his production of the will. (June 1765).

Cameron, Charles, Captain of the 71st Regiment, who died in Savannah, Georgia, bachelor. Administration to the father, Donald Cameron, in Kilmally, Scotland. (Jan. 1782).

Cameron, Mary Ann, formerly of Philadelphia, but late of Everton near Liverpool, Lancashire, widow. Limited probate to Samuel Moon and William Cameron Moore. (Aug. 1848).

Cammel, Philipp, of H.M. ship *Jersey*, who died in New York. Administration to the relict, Rose Cammel. (May 1703).

Campbell, Archibald, Captain of Marines, who died in Boston, bachelor. Administration to Neil Malcolm, attorney for the father, Colin Campbell, in Roseneath, Dumbartonshire, Scotland. (Dec. 1775).

Campbell, Archibald, of Fredericksburgh, New York, Captain of the New York Company of Volunteers, who died in Long Island, bachelor. Administration with will to the brothers, Duncan and John Campbell. (Aug. 1781).

Campbell, Collin, of Charles Town, South Carolina. Probate to the brother, Hugh Campbell, and to Daniel Campbell, with similar powers reserved to Hugh Mackay. (Jan. 1783).

Campbell, Collin, of Charles Town, South Carolina. Administration with will to Charles Vicaris Hunter, attorney for the sister, Elizabeth Campbell, in Straban, Argyleshire, Scotland; Hugh Mackay renouncing. (June 1794).

Campbell, Duncan, of Louisville, Kentucky, bachelor. Administration to the sister, Elizabeth Campbell. (Dec. 1841).

Campbell, Edward, formerly of Charing Cross, St. Martin in the Fields, Middlesex, but late of New York City, M.D. Probate to Alexander Campbell with similar powers reserved to Henry Remsen and John B. Yates. (Dec. 1822).

Campbell, Hugh, of St. Helena, Granville County, South Carolina, but late of North Carolina. Administration to Abraham Le Mesurier, attorney for the relict, Katherine Campbell, in St. Helena. (May 1770).

Campbell, James, surgeon's mate of a hospital under the late General Braddock in America, bachelor. Administration to the mother, Dorothy Campbell, widow. (June 1757).

Campbell, James, master of the ship *Maria*, who died in Charles Town, South Carolina, widower. Administration to the creditors, Dr. John Hall and Thomas Emerson Headlam; the sister and only next-of-kin,

Campbell, *(contd.)*
Agnes Campbell, renouncing. (Aug. 1780).

Campbell, Patrick, of New York City, Major of the 71st Regiment. Limited probate to the father, Duncan Campbell, and the brother, Alexander Campbell, with similar powers reserved to the brother, Collin Campbell. (June 1784).

Campbell, William, of Wapping, Middlesex, who died on the ship *Anne* in Virginia. Probate to David Watson after sentence against the validity of a nuncupative will. (Nov. 1693).

Campbell, William, of Glasgow, Scotland, who died in a merchant ship off Maryland, bachelor. Administration to Hugh Campbell, attorney for the mother, Elizabeth Adair, in Scotland. (Sep. 1718).

Campbell, William, formerly master of the brig *Helen* of Pontaferry, Ireland, but late of New York, bachelor. Administration to the mother and next-of-kin, Grace Campbell, widow. (Feb. 1845).

Candler, Anne, of Virginia, spinster. Administration to the brother, John Candler. (Dec. 1733).

Caner, Rev. Henry, of Boston, New England, who died in Long Ashton, Somerset. Probate to the surviving executor, William Bacon. (Jan. 1793).

Cantell, Isaac, formerly of Eynsham, Oxfordshire, but late of Texas. Probate to the brother, John Cantell; the executor, John Brend, renouncing. (Aug. 1847).

Cappel, George Lewis, of Westminster, Middlesex, who died in Virginia, bachelor. Administration to the aunt and only next-of-kin, Mary, wife of George Mullins. (Nov. 1768).

Capper, Henry, of Philadelphia. Administration to the brother and next-of-kin, John Capper; the relict, Hannah Capper, having been cited but not having appeared. (Nov. 1794).

Carbonell, Thomas, Ensign and Quartermaster of the 46th Regiment of Foot under Lieutenant-General Thomas Murray, who died in North America, bachelor. Administration to the father, Stephen Carbonell. (Mar. 1759).

Carew, Nicholas, of St. Martin in the Fields, Middlesex, who had lands in Maryland. Probate to the brother, Swithin Carew. (Oct. 1670). Wa.

Carleton, Arthur, of Maryland, widower. Administration to the brother, Matthew Carleton, the mother, Margaret Carleton, renouncing. (July 1681).

Carnes, Burrell, formerly of Boston, North America, but late of Essequibo, South America. Probate to the brother, Joseph Carnes. (Nov. 1805).

Carpender, Francis, formerly of the City of London but late of Hereford, whose cousin, Simon Carpender, was in Virginia. Probate to the relict, Hellen Carpender. (May 1662).

Carpenter, Bushrod, formerly of Launceston, Cornwall, but late of Virginia, bachelor, who died in 1794. Limited administration to Samuel Steward. (Nov. 1840).

Carpenter, John, of Annapolis, Maryland. Limited administration with will to William Hunt, attorney for the relict, Elizabeth Carpenter. (Feb. 1749).

Carpenter, Nathaniel, of King and Queen County, Virginia. Administration to the son, William Fauntleroy Carpenter; the relict, Ann Bushrod Carpenter, having died. (Mar. 1796). *See* NGSQ 70/115, 73/208.

Carpenter, Thomas, of Rhode Island, who died at sea on a merchant ship, bachelor. Administration to the sisters and next-of-kin, Anne, wife of Henry Atwells, and Mary, wife of Francis Seburt, in the City of Canterbury, Kent. (Aug. 1715).

Carpenter, Thomas, of Laminburgh, United States of America, adjutant on half pay of De Lancey's Regiment. Administration with will to James Tidbury, attorney for John Taylor and Andrew Thompson in America. (May 1832).

Carpenter, William, of St. George, Southwark, Surrey, who died in New York on H.M. ship *Richmond*. Probate to the relict, Elizabeth Carpenter. (July 1695).

Carr, Ralph, of Great Bridge, Virginia, bachelor. Administration to the brother and next-of-kin, Henry Carr. (May 1772).

Carr, Sir Robert, of Carr Island, New England, but who died in Bristol. Administration with will to the son, William Carr; no executor having been named. (July 1667). Wa.

Carr, Simeon, formerly of Chesterfield, Derbyshire, miller, but late of Beardstown, Morgan County, Illinois. Probate to the brother, Robert Carr, with similar powers reserved to John Roebuck. (Mar. 1839).

Carr alias Kerr, Thomas, of Portsmouth, Hampshire, who died in New York. Probate to the relict, Jane Carr. (Apr. 1730).

Carroll, Dorothy, of Maryland. Administration to William Anderson, attorney for the son, Charles Carroll, in Maryland; the husband having died. (Jan. 1760).

Carroll, Edward, Lieutenant of the 16th Regiment, who died in Pensacola, bachelor. Administration to the brother, James Carroll. (June 1787).

Carsan, James, formerly of Charles Town, South Carolina, but late of Troquire, Scotland. Administration to the relict, Agnes Carsan. (Sep. 1787).

Carson, Patrick, of Baltimore, United States of America, bachelor. Administration to the sister and next-of-kin, Rosanna, wife of William Corbett. (Sep. 1822).

Carson, Robert, sergeant of the 22nd Regiment of Foot, who died in Mobile, West Florida, bachelor. Administration with will to Jane, wife of John Drummon, formerly Jane Irvine, administratrix to the sole executor, Jerret Irvine, now deceased. (Apr. 1766).

Carter, Anne. *See* **Ludlam**.

Carter, Edward, of Edmonton, Middlesex, who had lands in Virginia. Probate to the relict, Elizabeth Carter. (Nov. 1682). Wa.

Carter, Elizabeth. *See* **Lloyd**.

Carter, Evans, of the ship *Rose*, who died in Boston, New England, bachelor. Administration to the principal creditor, Phillip Martin. (Feb. 1691).

Carter, George, of the Middle Temple, London, whose father was Robert Carter of Virginia deceased. Probate to John Mann. (Jan. 1742). Wi.

Carter, James, of Whitechapel, Middlesex, who had lands in Virginia. Probate to the relict, Susan Carter. (Apr. 1627). Wa.

Carter, James, [*John* in Probate Act Book], of Hinderclay, Suffolk, whose son, Thomas Carter, was in New England. Administration with will to the relict, Mary Carter. (Oct. 1655). Wa.

Carter, John, of Whitechapel, Middlesex, whose brother, Robert Skelton, was in New York. Probate to Samuel Sheppard and Samuel Perry. (June 1692). Wa.

Carter, John James, formerly of Liverpool, Lancashire, but late of Fearing, Washington County, Ohio, who died in Cincinnati. Administration to the relict, Margaret, now wife of Edward William Jones. (May 1839).

Carter, Richard, of Maryland. Administration to Micajah Perry, attorney for the relict, Elizabeth Carter. (Dec. 1708).

Carteret, Sir George, Vice-Chamberlain of the Royal Household, who had lands in New Jersey. Probate to the relict, Dame Elizabeth Carteret. (Feb. 1680). Wa.

Cartwright, Timothy, of Boston, New England, seaman of H.M. ship *Renown*. Administration with will to Richard Prowse, attorney for the relict, Sarah Cartwright, in Halifax, North America. (Nov. 1787).

Carwithen, David, of Boston, New England, who died on H.M. ship *Coronation*. Administration to William Dibbs, attorney for the relict, Elizabeth Carwithen, in Boston. Marked "pauper." (Jan. 1695).

Carwithen, Digery, of New England. Administration to the relict, Eleanor Carwithen. (July 1653).

Cary, Alice, of Shadwell, Stepney, Middlesex, spinster, whose uncle, Miles Cary, was in Virginia. Probate to Richard and Dorothy Cary. (Nov. 1660). Wa.

Cary, Richard, of Barbados, merchant, who had goods in New York. Probate to Samuel and William Cary and to Damaris Berriff. (Aug. 1685). Wa.

Cary, Richard, of Bristol, who died in Virginia, bachelor. Probate to the niece by a brother and next-of-kin, Jane Cary; the sole executor having died in the testator's lifetime. (Nov. 1730).

Cary, Samuel, of Chelsea, Suffolk County, Massachusetts. Administration with will by his solemn affirmation to Abraham Dettorne, attorney for Richard and Nathaniel Cary in Massachusetts. (Nov. 1770).

Casey, Michael alias Mick, a private soldier in the United States Army of Florida, bachelor. Administration to the brother, Timothy Casey. (Feb. 1843).

Cass, Jane. *See* **Truefitt**.

Castles alias Castle, William, of H.M. ship *Bedford*, who died in Long Island, bachelor. Administration to Abraham Harman, attorney for the sister and only next-of-kin, Nelly Castle, in Scotland. (Oct. 1780).

Caswall, Henry, of Boston, New England. Probate to the sister, Susanna, wife of Thomas Allison, and the cousin, John Caswall, with similar powers reserved to Charles Shearman. (June 1748).

Caswall, Kezia, formerly of Boston, New England, and of London, but late of Camberwell, Surrey, widow, whose son, John Caswall, was in New England. Probate to John Caswall with similar powers reserved to Thomas Lane. (Dec. 1740).

Catherwood, Robert, of St. Augustine, East Florida. Probate to the relict, Jane Catherwood, with similar powers reserved to Hon. John Moultrie, John Adam, Frederick Hesse, and William Colville. (Sep. 1787). Administration of goods not administered by Jane Catherwood, now deceased, to Jane Ann, wife of Richard Draper, the daughter of Lucy Caldewood deceased, who was a sister of the testator; John Adam and Frederick Hesse having died, and Hon. John Moultrie having renounced. (June 1797).

Cato, John, a negro slave of H.M. ships *Launceston* and *Superbe*, bachelor. Administration to Lawrence Reade, son and attorney of the proprietor, Joseph Reade, in New York. (Oct. 1749).

Causton, Thomas, of Savannah, Georgia, who died on the merchant ship *Loyal Judith*, widower. Administration to the principal creditor, William Williamson. (June 1746).

Cavallier, John, surgeon of Livingstone's Hospital on Long Island. Probate to Fergus Forster. (Oct. 1783).

Cawood, Elizabeth, of Boston, New England, widow. Administration to the daughter, Mary, wife of John Smith. (July 1693).

Cay, David, of Philadelphia, merchant. Probate to William Cramond, John Leeming and Hugh Holmes. (May 1797).

Cay, David, of Philadelphia, merchant. Probate to the relict, Ann Colrain, widow. (May 1797).

Cay, Rev. Jonathan, Rector of Christ Church, Calvert County, Maryland. Probate to the relict, Dorothy Cay. (Oct. 1738).

Chabert, Anthony, of Baltimore, North America. Administration with will to David Maitland, attorney for the relict, Renie Charlotte Chabert, in New York City. (Jan. 1797).

Chadwick, Richard, of Nantucket, Massachusetts. Administration to Paul Pease, attorney for the relict, Mary Chadwick, in Nantucket. (June 1811).

Chalfont, Margaret, of St. Sepulchre, London, widow, whose sister, Susanna Harris, was in New England. Probate to the surviving executor, Sarah Norris. (Oct. 1678). Wa.

Chalk, John Self, of Buffalo, United States of America, widower. Administration to the only child, George Henry Chalk. (Aug. 1851).

Chamberlayne, Esther, formerly of Bath, Somerset, but late of Charlestown, North America. Probate to the sister, Patience, wife of Joseph Cook. (Aug. 1808).

Chambrelan, Peter the elder, of St. Dionis Backchurch, London, surgeon, who made a bequest to Robert Smith in Virginia. Probate to Abraham Chambrelan with similar powers reserved to Richard Legge. (Dec. 1631). Wi.

Chamberlin, William, of the General Hospital, Boston, United States of America, bachelor. Administration to the brother, Charles

Chamberlin, *(contd.)* Chamberlin; the mother, Ann Chamberlin, widow, having died. (July 1846).

Chambers, Elizabeth. *See* **Park**.

Chambers, Joseph, of Charles Town, South Carolina, widower. Administration to the brother, Chadwick Chambers. (May 1737).

Chambers, Joseph, of Lucas County, Ohio, widower. Administration to James Percival, attorney for the son, Joseph Chambers, in Toledo, Lucas County, Ohio. (Dec. 1843).

Chambers, Richard, of Maryland. Probate to the mother, Mary Chambers. (July 1701).

Chambers, William, of Virginia, bachelor. Administration to the father, George Chambers. (Apr. 1670).

Chambers, William, of Stepney, Middlesex, who died in Carolina. Administration to the relict, Susan Chambers. (Apr. 1683).

Chamier, Daniel, of Baltimore, Maryland. Limited administration with will to the brother, Anthony Chamier. (Oct. 1780).

Champion, Richard, formerly of Bristol but late of Rocky Branch, South Carolina, widower. Administration to the son, George Lloyd Champion. (Dec. 1800).

Chance, Thomas, soldier of the 31st Regiment of Foot, who died in St. Augustine, East Florida, bachelor. Administration to the brother and next-of-kin, Joseph Chance. (May 1771).

Chandler, Charlotte, formerly of Russell Place, Fitzroy Square, Middlesex, but late of New York City, spinster. Administration to the sister, Mary Ann, wife of Richard Money. (Mar. 1853).

Chandler, Edward, of Ware, Hertfordshire, whose children, Daniel and Sarah Chandler, were in Virginia. Probate to the relict, Elizabeth Chandler, and the son, Edward Chandler. (Apr. 1651). Sh.Wi.

Chandler, Henry Whateley, of New Orleans. Administration to the relict, Mary Carolina Chandler. (Apr. 1854).

Chandler, Nathaniel, of Worcester, Massachusetts. Administration with will to Samuel Paine, attorney for the brother, Thomas Greene Chandler. (Aug. 1801).

Chandler, Richard, of Portobacco Creek, Maryland. Probate to Ralph Pigott. (Oct. 1714).

Chandler, Robert, of New London, Connecticut, seaman of H.M. ship *Penelope*. Administration with will to William Compton, attorney for the relict, Lucy Chandler, in New London. (Mar. 1801).

Chandler, William, formerly of St. Marylebone, Middlesex, but late a Captain in the North Carolina Volunteers, bachelor. Administration to Charles Cooke, attorney for the father, Thomas Bradbury Chandler, now at sea. (May 1785).

Chandler, William, of New Haven, North America, bachelor. Administration to Charles Cooke, attorney for Thomas Chandler in Westmoreland, North America, a son of the intestate's father, Joshua Chandler, who died before administering. (Aug. 1790).

Chandliss, Charles, Captain in the Portsmouth Division of Marines, who

Chandliss, *(contd.)* died in Boston, bachelor. Administration to the half-sister, Mary Monckton, spinster. (Dec. 1775).

Channing, John, of Bedford Square, Middlesex, who had lands in New Jersey. Probate to the relict, Charlotte Channing, and to Rev. William Jarvis Abdy and Samuel Foyster with similar powers reserved to James Alexander Wright. (Apr. 1792).

Chaplin, Clement, of Thetford, Norfolk, clerk, who had lands in New England. Probate to the relict, Sarah Chaplin. (Sep. 1656). Wa.

Chapline, Elizabeth, formerly Elizabeth Nourse, formerly of Brook, Virginia, but late of Clark County, Missouri, widow. Probate to Jesse Sisson. (July 1847).

Chaplin, Harriet. *See* **Newens**.

Chaplen, Moses, of St. Mary's, Guildford, Surrey, whose cousin, Ester Pierce the elder, was in New England. Probate to the parents, Moses and Collett Chaplen. (Aug. 1669). Revoked on their death and administration granted to the brother, William Chaplen. (Jan. 1671). Wa.

Chapman, Anne, of Virginia. Administration to John Weeton, attorney for the son, John Chapman, in Virginia. (Aug. 1716).

Chapman, Mary, of Philadelphia, widow. Administration to the son, James Chapman. (July 1839).

Chappell, Christopher, of Williamsburgh, United States of America, bachelor. Administration to the Rev. Thomas Westlake Blackmore, executor of the father, William Chappell, deceased. (May 1855).

Chapell, William, of Stepney, Middlesex, who died in Virginia. Administration to the relict, Uritha Chapell. (Nov. 1682).

Chardon, Henry, of Charles Town, South Carolina, bachelor. Administration to the sister, Mary Ann Mareschal, widow. (May 1739).

Charles, Peter, of Virginia, mariner of H.M. ship *Shoreham*. Probate to Hendrick Cloyson. (Oct. 1701).

Charlett, Richard, of Calvert County, Maryland, who died at sea or abroad. Probate to Richard Kings. (Apr. 1694). Wa.

Charlton, Daniel, of H.M. ship *Garland*, who died in Maryland. Probate to Elizabeth, wife of Richard Dawley, formerly Elizabeth Libbard. (Dec. 1757).

Charlton, Emily, formerly Emily Waters, of Savannah, Georgia. Administration to John Grierson, attorney for the husband, Thomas Usker Charlton, in Savannah. (Sep. 1821).

Charlton, Robert, of Liverpool, Lancashire, master of the American-owned ship, *The Sisters*. Limited administration to James Lowe pending the outcome of the suit Lees v. Goodrich. (Jan. 1804).

Charter, Andrew, of Wapping, Middlesex, who died on the ship *Edward and Francis* in Virginia, bachelor. Administration to the father, Richard Charter. (Apr. 1694).

Chauncy, Judith, of Yardley, Hertfordshire, spinster, whose brother, Charles Chauncy, was in New England. Probate to Henry Chauncy

Chauncy, *(contd.)* and Montague Lane. (Mar. 1658). Sh.Wa.

Cheesman, John, of Virginia. Administration to the father, John Cheesman, during the minority of the daughters, Margaret and Anne Cheesman. (Sep. 1661).

Cheeseman, John, of Bermondsey, Surrey, who had lands in Virginia. Probate to the relict, Margaret Cheeseman. (May 1665). Sh.Wi.

Cheesman, Joseph, master of H.M. ship *Galatea*, who died in St. Augustine, East Florida. Probate to John Huntingdon. (Dec. 1778).

Cheeseman, Margaret, of Bermondsey, Surrey, widow, whose kinsmen, Lemuel Mason, Elizabeth Theleball and John Matthews, were in Virginia. Probate to Margaret Mason. (July 1680). Wa.

Cheltnam, John, of Norfolk, Virginia. Administration to the relict, Sarah Cheltnam. (Apr. 1800).

Cherry, Robert, of St. Thomas the Apostle, London, whose daughter, Mary, wife of Daniel England, was in Pennsylvania. Probate by his solemn affirmation to Richard Beckett with similar powers reserved to Mary England. (Jan. 1705).

Chesley, Phillip, of York County, Virginia. Probate to the relict, Margaret Chesley. (May 1675). Wi.

Cheston, Francina Augustina, of Kent County, Maryland, widow. Probate to the son, William Stephenson. (Feb. 1767).

Chetwood, Jane, of West Felton, Shropshire, whose sister, Grace, wife of Peter Bulkley, was in New England. Probate to the sister, Abigail Chetwood, with similar powers reserved to Edward Jones and ---- Powell. (Dec. 1648). Wa.

Cheyne, William, of New York, M.D. Administration to the relict, Laura Matilda Cheyne. (Oct. 1842).

Cheyney, Anne, of St. Katherine Creechurch, London, whose cousin, Anne Roe, was in Virginia. Probate to John Gray. (Oct. 1667). Wi.

Chichester, Ellen. *See* **Downeman** and **Robertson**.

Chichester, John, of Virginia. Probate to the brother, Richard Chichester, with similar powers reserved to James Ball the younger. (May 1763). Administration of estate unadministered by Richard Chichester deceased to his administrator with will, William Murdoch, attorney for the relict, Sarah Chichester, in Fairfax, [Virginia]. (June 1803).

Chichester, Mary. *See* **Ball**.

Chichester, Richard, of Virginia. Administration with will to John Tucker and Richard Tucker, attornies for the mother, Ellen Chichester, widow, guardian of the minor son, John Chichester; the relict, Ellen Chichester, renouncing. (Mar. 1746). Revoked and granted to Richard Chichester, brother and executor of John Chichester deceased, the son of the testator. (May 1763). Wi.

Chichester, Richard, of Fairfax, Virginia. Administration with will to William Murdoch, attorney for the relict, Sarah Chichester, in Fairfax. (June 1803).

Chichester, Richard, of Virginia. Administration with will of estate unadministered by the grandson, Richard Chichester deceased,

Chichester, *(contd.)* executor of the son, John Chichester deceased, to William Murdoch, administrator with will to the said John Chichester and attorney for Sarah Chichester, relict of the said Richard Chichester, now in Fairfax, Virginia. (June 1803).

Chiene, Margaret, of Philadelphia, widow. Probate to Peter A. Browne with similar powers reserved to Charles G. Paleske. (Nov. 1834).

Child, Margaret, of Boston, New England. Administration by decree to the husband, Thomas Child. (May 1721).

Child, Mary. *See* **Morse**.

Child, Richard, formerly of Lambeth, Surrey, but late in America, bachelor. Administration to Henry Hughes, father of the nephews and niece, Richard, Henry and Mary Hughes, during their minority. (June 1822).

Child, Richard, formerly of Castle Street, Piccadilly, Middlesex, currier, but late of Newhaven, Connecticut. Limited administration to Robert Hume and Joseph Abbott. (Dec. 1824).

Child, Sarah, of Cincinnati, Ohio, widow. Administration to John Collins, attorney for the son, John Abbott Child, in Medicine, Indiana. (July 1857).

Chollet, Abraham Louis, of Charleston, United States of America, bachelor. Administration to Henry Chollet, attorney for the brother, Isaac Henry Chollet, in Maudon, Switzerland. (Mar. 1821).

Chrisolme, John, of Carolina, bachelor. Administration to John Ord, attorney for the brother and next-of-kin, Kenneth Chrisolme, in Balintrade, Scotland. (Mar. 1801).

Chrystie, John, of the merchant ship *Rumsey*, who died at York River, Virginia, bachelor. Probate to Elizabeth Grimes alias Cheshire, wife of William Grimes. (Nov. 1718).

Christie, William, of Charleston, South Carolina. Administration to the children, William and Maxwell Christie; the relict, Ann Christie, having died. (Jan. 1838).

Chubb, Lydia, of New York, spinster. Administration to William Phillips Parker, attorney for the father, William Chubb, in New York. (Jan. 1851).

Church, Elizabeth. *See* **Burbridge**.

Church, George, of H.M. ship *Hawk*. Administration to John Bradford, attorney for the relict, Mary Church, in New Hampshire. (Jan. 1746).

Churton, Sarah, of Vernon, Oneida County, New York. Administration to the husband, Thomas Churton. (Apr. 1843).

Claiborne, William, of Virginia, who died in Hackney, Middlesex. Limited probate of a codicil to John Hanbury. (July 1746).

Clancy alias Clansie, William, formerly of Bache's Row, Hoxton, Middlesex, but late of New York, who died at sea, bachelor. Administration to the niece and nephews and next-of-kin, Mary, wife of Thomas Clancy, Patrick Curran, and John Curran. (Apr. 1828).

Clare, Alfred, formerly principal clerk of the Will Office of the Bank of England, formerly of Pittsburg but late of Philadelphia. Probate to the

Clare, *(contd.)*
nephew, George Thatcher. (May 1835).

Clare, Charlotte S. *See* **Warren.**

Clare, Joseph, of South Carolina. Administration to the principal creditor, William Adye, other interested parties having been cited but not having appeared. (Jult 1731).

Clarke, Agnes, of Ashill, Somerset, widow, whose kinsman, William Harvey, was in New England. Probate to a kinsman, Richard Harvey. (May 1648). Sh.Wa.

Clarke, Andrew, of St. Sepulchre, London, who died in Maryland. Administration with will to the brother, Andrew *[sic]* Clarke, the named executor, Robert Johnson, renouncing. (Apr. 1691).

Clark, Daniel, of Augusta, Georgia, bachelor. Administration to William Hanson, attorney for the brother and sister, Alexander Clark and Elizabeth, wife of Donald Fraser, in Perth, Scotland. (Aug. 1757).

Clarke, Elizabeth, of Allet's Cove, Long Island, New York. Administration to the husband, Richard Clarke. (July 1845).

Clarke, Frederick, of Carolina, who died in Barbados, bachelor. Administration with will to John Trott, attorney for Robert Stevens alias Stephens in Carolina. (Aug. 1700).

Clarke, George, of Milford, New England. Administration to Daniel Clarke, attorney for Abigail Peirson in New England. (Apr. 1700).

Clark, George, of Brandy Wine Hundred, Newcastle County, Delaware, Captain on half pay of the New Jersey Volunteers. Administration with will to Thomas Courtney, attorney for the relict, Ann Clark, and for John Tally in America. (Oct. 1812).

Clarke, George, of Springfield, New York, and of Hyde, Cheshire. Probate to the son, George Rochfort Clarke. (Aug. 1838).

Clark, Henry, of Shadwell, Middlesex, who died in Pennsylvania. Probate to Elizabeth Clark. (Mar. 1727).

Clarke, Hutchinson, of North Kingstown, King's County, Rhode Island, late of Captain Thomas Fry's Company in the Rhode Island Regiment of Foot, who died in Havana, bachelor. Administration by his solemn declaration to Joseph Sherwood, attorney for the brother and next-of-kin, Joseph Clarke, in North Kingstown. (Dec. 1765).

Clarke, James, of Little Town, Virginia, bachelor. Administration to the brother and sister, John Clarke and Elizabeth, wife of Richard Warner, pending production of a will. (Sep. 1658).

Clark, James formerly of Great Hermitage Street, Wapping, Middlesex, but late of Peoria County, Illinois. Probate to James Balfour with similar powers reserved to the relict, Isabella Clark. (Feb. 1842).

Clark, James Alderson, of Savannah, Georgia. Administration to the relict, Elizabeth Ann Clark. (Mar. 1829).

Clarke, James Henry, of New Orleans. Probate to the sister, Mary Clarke. (Oct. 1831).

Clarke alias Kingman, John, of Wells, Somerset, whose son, James Clarke, was in New England. Probate to the son, Samuel Clarke alias Kingman. (Sep. 1641). Wa.

Clarke, John, of Great Yarmouth, Norfolk, mariner, master of the ship *Unity*, who died in Virginia. Probate to William Clarke. (May 1665). NGSQ 66/3.

Clarke, John, of the ship *Maryland Factor*, who died in Virginia, bachelor. Administration to William Harbottle, surgeon of Galeside near Newcastle-upon-Tyne, attorney for the sister, Abigael Harbottle. (Jan. 1710).

Clarke, John, formerly of London but late of Gloucester County, Virginia, bachelor. Probate to the father, John Clarke. (Nov. 1757).

Clarke, John, of Albion, Edwards County, Illinois. Administration to the relict, Lucy Clarke. (Dec. 1842).

Clark, John, of Delaware, Pennsylvania. Administration to the relict, Mary Clark. (Feb. 1846).

Clarke, Joseph, of Mile End, Stepney, Middlesex, who died in Virginia, bachelor. Administration to the sisters, Mary Whistler, widow, and Anne, wife of Henry Lee. (May 1738).

Clark, Joseph, of New York, bachelor. Administration to the mother, Elizabeth, relict and executrix of George Clark deceased. (July 1766).

Clarke, Joseph, formerly of Leicester but late of Brooklyn, King's County, United States of America. Probate to the brother, John Pretty Clarke. (June 1844).

Clark, Joseph George, formerly of Adam Street, Adelphi, Middlesex, but late of Thompson, New York, widower. Administration to Alexander Massey, attorney for the children, Ann, wife of Josiah Henderson Watts, and Mary Williams, wife of Joseph Plummer, in New York City. (Oct. 1845).

Clarke, Richard, formerly of Boston, New England, but late of St. George, Hanover Square, Middlesex. Probate to John Singleton Copley with similar powers reserved to the son, Isaac Winslow Clarke, and to Henry Bromfield. (June 1795). Double probate in May 1797.

Clarke, Robert, of Rotherhithe, Surrey, and of New England, who died abroad. Administration with will to Walter Rogers, guardian of the son, John Clarke, during his minority. (Mar. 1663). [Marginal note: *Revoked on death of Walter Rogers, March 1663.*].

Clarke, Robert, of St. Giles Cripplegate, London, but late of Maryland. Probate to John Clarke with similar powers reserved to Jane Clarke. (Dec. 1689).

Clark, Sarah, of Clark's Mills, Leeds, Fauquier County, Virginia, widow. Administration with will to John Birkett, attorney for Peter Adams in Fauquier County. (Feb. 1835).

Clarke, Thomas, of York, Virginia. Probate to Peter Temple. (May 1670). Wi.

Clarke, Thomas, of East Sheen, Surrey, who died in Maryland. Administration to the sister, Joane, wife of Edward Absey. (June 1709).

Clarke, William, of the ship *Kings Fisher*, who died in Boston, New England. Administration to the principal creditor, Thomas Long. (Nov. 1687).

Clarke, William, of St. Bride's, London, mariner of the ship *George* of Lyn, who died in Virginia. Administration to the principal creditor, Rubart Vincksteijn. (Aug. 1701).

Clark, William, of Pennsylvania, sergeant of the 20th Regiment. Administration with will to the residual legatee, Henry Rowland; no executor having been named. (Nov. 1783).

Clark, William, of Burnt Prairie, Edwards County, Illinois. Limited administration with will to Charles Clark, attorney for the sons, David and Joseph Clark, in Edwards County. (Oct. 1842).

Clarvise alias Clarvis, Robert, of H.M. ship *Bedford*, who died in Long Island Hospital, bachelor. Administration to Nathaniel Betton, attorney for the father, Thomas Clarvise, in Normanby, Lincolnshire. (Feb. 1780).

Clay, Stephen, of the merchant ship *Anne*, who died in Virginia, bachelor. Probate to William Norwood. (Oct. 1734).

Clayton, John, of Ware, Virginia. Probate to the son, William Clayton. (Apr. 1791).

Cleare, Ambrose, of Great Stratton, New Kent County, Virginia. Administration with will to Richard Parke, merchant, attorney for the relict Anne, now wife of Thomas Tea, in Virginia. (Nov. 1697).

Clegg, James Wilson, formerly of St. Thomas, Southwark, Surrey, but late of Georgia, bachelor. Administration to the sister and only next-of-kin, Mary, wife of Edmund Beck. (Nov. 1796).

Cleghorn, John, of Frederick County, Maryland. Administration with will to John Rothery, attorney for the brother, Alexander Cleghorn, in Jamaica; the sole executor, John Creagh, having been cited but not having appeared. (May 1824).

Clements, James, of New York City. Limited administration with will to John Baring, attorney for the relict, Harriet Clements, and for William Giffing, Timothy Hutton and William Mandeville in New York. (Jan. 1831).

Clendinen, Elizabeth Ann, formerly Elizabeth Ann Stewart, formerly of Blizzard Street, Greenwich, Kent, but late of Baltimore, United States of America. Administration to Thomas Aspinwall, attorney for the husband, Alexander Clendinen, in Baltimore. (Aug. 1836)

Clephan, George, of H.M. ship *Asia*, who died in New York, bachelor. Administration to Henry Creed, attorney for the brother, James Clephan, in New York. (Oct. 1777).

Clephan, James, physician of the Royal Hospital in New York. Probate to William Marsh and Henry Creed with similar powers reserved to John Hills. (Apr. 1783).

Clever, Thomas, of Virginia, bachelor. Probate to the sister, Mary Clever. (July 1700).

Clifford, Peter, of Whitechapel, Middlesex, who died in Annapolis in the West Indies *(sic)*. Probate to the relict, Mary Clifford. (July 1715).

Clifton, Benjamin, of Philadelphia, Inspector-General of Hospitals in Martinique, Guadaloupe and St. Lucia. Administration to the creditor, John Jaffray; the relict and the children having been cited but

Clifton, *(contd.)* not having appeared. (July 1814).

Clifton, William, Chief Justice of West Florida. Administration to the niece and next-of-kin, Ann Raincock. (Mar. 1783).

Clinton, Anne, of New York, spinster. Administration to Maynard Guerin, attorney for the father, Hon. George Clinton, in New York. (Feb. 1746). Revoked on the death of Maynard Guerin and granted to John Catherwood as attorney. (June 1751).

Clowes, John, of Long Island, North America, bachelor. Administration to David Thomas, attorney for the brother and next-of-kin, Gerhardus Clowes, in St. John's, New Brunswick. (Aug. 1795)

Clymer alias Ennis, Anne, of Maryland. Administration to the cousin and next-of-kin, Christopher Rayner. (Apr. 1691).

Coates, Alfred, of Whuling, Virginia, bachelor. Administration to the father, William Coates. (Nov. 1841).

Coates, Fanny, formerly Fanny Dean, of Boston, United States of America. Administration to the sister, Elizabeth, wife of William Withers; the husband, Joshua Coates, having died. (Aug. 1830).

Coates, Sarah, of Baltimore, Maryland, spinster. Administration to the father, Francis Peachey Coates. (Mar. 1772).

Cobb, Arthur, of London, (bound for Syranum in America). Probate to the brother, James Cobb. (Apr. 1666).

Cobb, Woolley, of Virginia. Administration to the father, John Cobb. (Dec. 1732).

Cochet, Robert, of Mickleover, Derbyshire, whose sister, Dorothy, wife of John Joyce, was in New England. Probate to the relict, Anne Cochet. (Apr. 1658).

Cochran, James, steward of H.M. transport ship *Betsey*, who died in Savannah, Georgia, bachelor. Administration to Thomas Gibson, attorney for the mother, Isabell Gairn, in Errol, Scotland. (Jan. 1781).

Cock, Austin, who died in Virginia. Inventory 1772. [*Administration Act not found*].

Cocke, Catesby, of Prince William County, Virginia. Administration with will to William Perkins and William Brown, attornies for the sons, William and John Catesby Cocke, in Virginia; the executors, William Henry Lee, Richard Lee, Thomas Everard and Thomas Jett, renouncing. (Mar. 1773).

Cocke, Christopher, of New York. Administration to the brother, John Cocke. (Oct. 1714).

Cocke, Thomas, of Virginia, bachelor. Administration to the father, John Cocke. (Feb. 1712).

Cockburn, John, of All Hallows the Great, London, who died in New England. Limited administration with will to the relict, Mary Cockburn. (Dec. 1700).

Cockburne, Thomas, of Pennsylvania, who died on the merchant ship *Newberry*, bachelor. Probate to John Cockburne. (Jan. 1725).

Cockin, Stephen, of St. George, Southwark, Surrey, who died on the

Cockin, *(contd.)* merchant frigate *Bibins* in Boston, New England. Administration to the relict, Anne Cockin. (Oct. 1701).

Cockshutt, Geoffrey, of Virginia, bachelor. Probate to the brother, Thomas Cockshutt. (Jan. 1710).

Codenham, Robert, of Shadwell, Middlesex, who died in New York. Administration with will to John Chapman, guardian of the children, Jane, Robert and William Codenham; the executor, Richard Jones, having died. (Feb. 1700).

Codner, William, of Crutched Friars, London, whose father, William Codner deceased, was of Boston, Massachusetts. Probate to the relict, Mary Codner, and to James Colquhoun and Theophilus Hearsey. (Mar. 1792).

Coffin, Gregory, of Stepney, Middlesex, (bound for New England). Probate to John Earle. (Aug. 1662). Wa.

Coffin, Thomas Aston, of Westminster, Middlesex, Commissary-General of the Army, whose sister, Ann Smith, widow of Oliver Smith, was in Boston, Massachusetts; sister, Mary, wife of Shirley Irvine, was in Portsmouth, Massachusetts; and sister, Nooksby, wife of Abel Harris, was in Portsmouth, New Hampshire. Probate to John Turner and Thomas Rowleigh. (June 1810).

Cogell, William, of New York, bachelor. Administration to the sister and only next-of-kin, Ann, wife of David Mackintosh. (Jan. 1792).

Coggeshall, Anne, of Castle Hedingham, Essex, widow, whose son, John Coggeshall, was in New England. Probate to the granddaughter, Anne Raymond. (Nov. 1648). Wa.

Coggeshall, Giles, of Portsmouth, Newport County, Rhode Island, sergeant in Lieutenant-Colonel Christopher Hargill's Company of the Rhode Island Regiment of Foot, who died in Havana, bachelor. Administration by his solemn declaration to Joseph Sherwood, attorney for the brother and next-of-kin, Baulston Coggeshall, in Portsmouth. (Dec. 1765).

Coggeshall, James, formerly of Newport, Rhode Island, but late of Brunswick, Nova Scotia, bachelor. Administration to John Andrews, attorney for the mother, Lucy Ann Coggeshall, in Newport. (Sep. 1790).

Cogswell, Nathaniel, of New York City. Probate to the brother, Jonathan Cogswell, and the sister, Lois Cogswell. (May 1834).

Cohen, Jacob Aron, formerly of Jermyn Street, St. James, Westminster, Middlesex, but late of South Carolina. Probate to John Bulow. (June 1813).

Coke, John, of Dorchester, who had goods in New England. Probate to Gilbert Ironside, clerk, Edward Bragg, and Richard Scovile, with similar powers reserved to Thomas Gollopp and James Gould. (Oct. 1641). Wa.

Coker, William Lawrence, Captain of the 38th Regiment of Foot, who died in Boston, bachelor. Administration to the brother, Robert Coker; the mother, Susanna Coker, having died before administering. (Sep. 1777).

Colchester, Thomas, of H.M. ship *Southampton*, who died in Virginia, bachelor. Administration to the principal creditrix, Mary Starland, widow. (June 1703).

Colcutt, William, of the ship *Planter*, who died in Virginia, widower. Administration with nuncupative will to Anne West, aunt and guardian of the cousin, Patience Dand; no executor having been named. (Aug. 1659).

Colden, Alexander, of New York City. Probate to the brother, John Antill. (Aug. 1784).

Coldstream, William, master of the transport ship *Friendship*, who died in Savannah, Georgia, widower. Administration to the son, Charles Coldstream. (Mar. 1781).

Cole, Charles, of Annapolis, Maryland, bachelor. Administration to the creditrix, Amey Yarp, widow. (Feb. 1759).

Cole, Edward, of East Bergholt, Suffolk, whose grandchildren were in New England. Probate to the daughters, Sarah and Mary Cole. (May 1652). Wa.

Cole, George, of Dorchester, who had lands in New England. Probate to the relict, Ann Cole, and the son, John Cole. (May 1659). Wa.

Cole, John, of Weymouth and Melcombe Regis, Dorset, merchant, who had lands in New England. Probate to James Gold with similar powers reserved to Benjamin Speering. (Oct. 1672). Wa.

Cole, John, of Exeter, Devon, who died in Pennsylvania. Probate to James Kearle. (Oct. 1693).

Cole, Jone, of Exeter, Devon, spinster (*sic*), whose husband, John Cole, was intended for Philadelphia. Probate to James Kearle. (Feb. 1694). Wa.

Cole, Michael, of Stepney, Middlesex, mariner, a creditor of Colonel William Rhett in South Carolina. Probate to Samuel Vans and Jonathan Shakespear with similar powers reserved to George Mainwaring. (Aug. 1719).

Cole, Simon, of Boston, New England, who died at sea, bachelor. Administration to the sister, Mary Mervin. (Nov. 1674).

Cole, Walter, of Lavenham, Suffolk, whose daughter, Elizabeth, wife of John Fuller, was in New England. Probate to the relict, Susan Cole. (Sep. 1653). Wa.

Coleman, Bailey, formerly of Lakenheath, Suffolk, but late of Massillon, Stark County, Ohio. Administration to William Bailey Coleman, attorney for the husband, William Coleman, in Massillon. (Jan. 1854).

Coleman, Christopher, formerly of Woolwich, Kent, but late of the United States of America. Administration to the only child, John Christopher Coleman; the relict, Sarah Coleman, having died. (Apr. 1823).

Coleman, Obed Mitchell, of Saratoga Springs, Saratoga County, New York, bachelor. Administration to Ezra Coleman, attorney for the father, John Coleman, in Saratoga Springs. (Feb. 1846).

Coleman, Peter, of Marblehead, Massachusetts, seaman of H.M. ship *Worcester*. Administration to John Traill, attorney for the relict, Ann Coleman. (June 1800).

Coleman, Sarah, formerly Sarah Stickney, of Newbury, Massachusetts. Administration to the son, John Stickney; the husband, Benjamin Coleman, having died. (Dec. 1801).

Coles, John, of New London, United States of America. Administration to the daughter, Lydia, wife of Richard Langslow; the relict, Ann Coles, having died. (Sep. 1827).

Collart, William, of H.M. ship *Otter*, who died in Norfolk, Virginia. Probate to the mother, Rebecca Collart, widow. (Dec. 1776).

Colles, Thomas, of Deptford, Kent, who died on the ship *Nicholson* in Virginia. Probate to the relict, Mary Colles. (Feb. 1706).

Collet, John, of Washington County, District of Columbia. Limited administration with will to Thomas Wilson, attorney for the relict, Ann Collet, and the son, Thomas Collet, in America. (July 1822).

Colleton, John, of Fairlawns, St. John's, Berkeley County, South Carolina. Probate to the father and surviving executor, Sir John Colleton. (Apr. 1751). Administration with will and two codicils of goods unadministered by Sir John Colleton deceased to his executor, Robert Colleton; the other executors, Susannah, the relict of the testator, and Peter Colleton, his son, having died. (Nov. 1754). Administration of goods unadministered to William Field, guardian of the children, Sir John, Elizabeth, Mary Ann, and Susanna Snell Colleton; Ann Collins, the surviving executor of Sir John Colleton, renouncing; Peter Colleton, the testator's son, having died without issue; and with the consent of the cousins and other relations. (Mar. 1756).

Colleton, Sir John, of St. John's, South Carolina. Probate to Elizabeth Janverin, spinster, during the minority of the daughter, Louisa Carolina Colleton, with similar powers reserved to James Parsons. (Dec. 1779). Revoked and granted to Louisa Carolina Colleton on her coming of age. (Apr. 1785).

Colleton, Margaret, of St. George Hanover Square, Middlesex, relict of John Colleton, who had estate in South Carolina. Probate to Thomas Lloyd and Allen Swainston with similar powers reserved to William Masterman. (Nov. 1779).

Colleton, Sir Peter, of St. James, Westminster, Middlesex, who had lands in Carolina. Probate to the daughter, Catherine Colleton, with similar powers reserved to William Thornburgh; the executor, Colonel John Leslie, having died overseas. (Apr. 1694).

Colleton, Peter, of Fairlawns, St. John's, Berkeley County, South Carolina, who died at sea. Probate to the brother and surviving executor, Robert Colleton. (Nov. 1754).

Colleton, Peter, of Fairlawns, South Carolina. Administration to William Field, administrator with will to the father, John Colleton deceased, for the benefit of the minor children, Sir John, Elizabeth, Mary Ann, and Susanna Snell Colleton. (Mar. 1756).

Collier, Alexander, of H.M. ship *Wolf*, who died in Virginia, bachelor. Probate to William Culling. (Nov. 1739).

Collier, Daniel, of H.M. ship *Devonshire*, who died in New York, bachelor. Probate to Susannah Long, spinster. (June 1763).

Collyer, James, of Coolspring, Mercer County, Pennsylvania. Administration with will to John Goodman, attorney for the daughter, Jane Collyer, in Coolspring; the relict, Mary Collyer, having died. (July 1844).

Collyer, Joseph the elder, of St.Saviour, Southwark, Surrey, whose sister, Mary Browninge, was in New England. Probate to the sons, Benjamin and Joseph Collyer. (Sep. 1649). Wa.

Collier, Joseph, of South Carolina, bachelor. Administration to the mother, Rebecca Collier, widow. (July 1730).

Collyer, Samuel Charles, formerly of Kendall Place, Vassall Road, Brixton, Surrey, but late of Market Street, New York. Administration to the relict, Margaret Eliza Collyer. (Mar. 1837).

Collier, Thomas, of New York, sergeant of Marines on H.M. ship *Coventry*. Administration to the relict, Joanna Collier. (Oct. 1766).

Collington, Edward, of St. Saviour, Southwark, Surrey, joiner, whose daughter, Isabell, was in New England. Probate to the relict, Perrin Collington. (July 1660). Wa.

Collingwood, Gerard, of the merchant ship *Three Brothers*, who died in Virginia, bachelor. Probate to Eleanor Slater, widow. (Oct. 1732).

Collins, John, of New York Province. Administration to Samuel Beven, attorney for the relict, Margaret Collins. (Nov. 1729).

Collins, John, of Cape Fear, North Carolina, bachelor. Administration to the creditor, James Rae. (July 1753).

Collins, Palfrey, of Boston, Massachusetts, seaman of H.M. ship *Liverpool*. Administration to John Callahan, attorney for the relict, Alice Collins, in Boston. (Dec. 1787).

Collins, Richard, of Bristol, who died in Virginia, bachelor. Administration to the principal creditor, Walter Stephens. (Aug. 1667).

Collins, Thomas, citizen and barber-surgeon of London, whose sister, Anne Collins alias Seaward, was in Virginia. Probate to the son, Phillip Collins. (Oct. 1657). Wi.

Collins, Thomas, of Lynsted, Kent, who died in Maryland, bachelor. Administration to the father, Christopher Collins. (July 1725). Revoked on his death and granted to the sisters, Anne and Mary Collins. (Nov. 1726).

Collins, Thomas, of St. Martin in the Fields, Middlesex, who died in Virginia, bachelor. Inventory 1772. [*Administration Act not found*].

Collyer. *See* **Collier**.

Colson, Elizabeth, of Bethnal Green, Middlesex, who died in Charles Town, South Carolina, widow. Probate to James Crockatt, attorney for William Roper in Charles Town. (Aug. 1751).

Colston, Rawleigh, of Berkeley County, Virginia. Limited administration with will to John Dunlop, attorney for the son, Edward Colston, in Berkeley County. (Mar. 1827).

Colsworthy, George, of Maryland, bachelor. Administration to the father, John Colsworthy. (Oct. 1704).

Coltman, Anna, of Christchurch, Newgate, London, whose son was in New England. Probate to Ralph Canninge. (Aug. 1623). Wa.

Coltman, William, of Virginia [but shown as of Wapping, Middlesex, in

Coltman, *(contd.)*
Caveat Book]. Probate to the mother, Alice Coltman. (Nov. 1666).

Colvill, John, of Cranbrook, Kent, whose nephew, John Colvill, was in New England. Probate to the relict, Susan Colvill. (July 1695).

Colvill, Matthew alias Maturin, of Cape Fear, North America, bachelor. Administration to the sister, Mary, wife of Rev. Isaac Patrick. (Aug. 1790).

Comer, Charles, of Stepney, Middlesex, who died in New York. Administration to the relict, Anne Comer. (May 1687).

Comer, John, of New York, bachelor. Administration to the brother, Walter Comer. (Apr. 1736).

Comerford, John Francis, formerly of Corunna, Spain, but who died in America in 1794, bachelor. Limited special probate to the sister, Frances Jane Comerford. (Feb. 1805). Revoked on her death and granted to her husband, Francis, Count de Bryas; the sole executor, Diego Joseph Borrers, renouncing. (Aug. 1816).

Comrin, John, of Boston, New England, master of the merchant ship *Princessa*. Limited administration to William Green of Grosvenor Square, Middlesex, haberdasher; the relict, Sarah Comrin, and the only child, Sarah, wife of James Lloyd, renouncing. (Oct. 1765).

Comyn, Frederick Duke, of West Florida, bachelor. Administration to the father, Thomas Comyn. (Apr. 1778).

Comyn, Phillips, formerly of Pensacola but late of the River Mississippi, West Florida, merchant. Copy will of 16 October 1775 appointing his brother, Frederick Duke Comyn, and Thomas Bowker as executors. (PROB 20/575).

Comyn, Valence Stephen, of West Florida. Administration to the father, Thomas Comyn; the relict, Mary Comyn, and the children, Thomas and Samuel Comyn, renouncing. (Apr. 1778).

Con, Thomas, of Scarborough, Yorkshire, seaman of H.M. ship *Eagle*, who died in New York. Administration to the relict, Mary Con. (May 1779).

Concannon, James, of St. Magnus, London, who died in Virginia, widower. Administration to Christopher Hooke, attorney for the sister, Elinor, wife of John Grant, in Back Lane, Dublin, Ireland. (Sep. 1764).

Connell, John, of Youghall, Ireland, who died in Virginia, bachelor. Administration to Anne, wife of the principal creditor, William Peeters, now at sea. (July 1675).

Conners, John, who died at sea, having assets in Virginia. Probate to the relict, Susannah Conners. (May 1654). Sh.Wa.

Connington, William, of Baltimore County, Maryland, bachelor. Administration to the brother, Walter Connington. (July 1676).

Connop, John, of the merchant ship *Olive Tree*, who died in Virginia. Probate to Edmund Castle. (Dec. 1706)

Connor, John, formerly surgeon of H.M. ship *Cygnet*, but late of Charles Town, South Carolina, bachelor. Administration to the mother, Jane Connor, widow. (May 1768).

Constable, Alexander, of Charles Town, South Carolina. Probate to

Constable, *(contd.)* William Redmon and the relict, Jane Constable. (Mar. 1781).

Constable, John, of St. Christopher's, who died in Philadelphia, bachelor. Administration to the sister, Helen, wife of Rev. William Moir. (Mar. 1791).

Constant, Thomas, of H.M. ship *Apollo*, who died in New York Hospital, bachelor. Administration to the father, William Constant. (Mar. 1779).

Conquest, George, of New York City. Administration with will to the brother, John Fricker Conquest, M.D.; the executors, John Staple and Richard Spaw, and the mother, Ruth Conquest, widow, having died. (Aug. 1835).

Conyers, Richard, of Boston, New England. Administration to John Howes, guardian of the son, James Conyers; the relict, Mary Conyers, renouncing. (Sep. 1709).

Cook, Andrew, of St. Giles in the Fields, Middlesex, who had lands in Dorchester County, Maryland. Probate to the children, Ebenezer and Anne Cook. (Jan. 1712).

Cook, Edmund, of Norwich, Norfolk, who died in St. John's, St. Mary County, Maryland, bachelor. Probate to Charles Martin with similar powers reserved to his wife, Susanna Martin. (May 1747).

Cook, Ellis, of Chatham, Morris County, New Jersey, widower. Administration to Charles James Partington, attorney for the son, James Cook, in Brandon, Vermont. (July 1855).

Cooke, George, of South Carolina, bachelor. Administration to Elizabeth Cooke, spinster, attorney for the sister, Rebecca Cooke, in South Carolina. (Feb. 1755).

Cook, Isabel, of Hanover, Morris County, New Jersey. Administration to Charles James Partington, administrator to the husband, Ellis Cook deceased, attorney for the son, James Cook, in Vermont. (July 1855).

Cooke, James, of Virginia, bachelor. Administration to the sisters, Elizabeth, wife of Hugh Vaughan, and Martha Cooke. (Oct. 1656).

Cooke, John, of Sprowston, Norfolk, who made a bequest to Anne, wife of Edmund Pitts, in New England. Probate to the relict, Elizabeth Cooke. (Nov. 1654). Wa.

Cooke, John, of St. James Santee, Craven County, South Carolina. Administration with will to Elizabeth Cooke, spinster, ttorney for the daughter, Rebecca Cooke, in South Carolina; the executor, James Maxwell having been cited but not having appeared, and the other executor, the son, George Cooke, having died. (June 1755).

Cooke, John the younger, of the 20th Regiment of Foot, who died in Stillwater, North America, bachelor. Administration to the father, John Cooke. (Apr. 1778).

Cook, John, formerly of Ninety Six but late of Richmond District, Quebec, Canada. Administration to James Phyn, attorney for the relict, Elizabeth Cook, in Mecklenberg, Quebec. (Nov. 1790).

Cooke, Nicholas, of St. Botolph Aldgate, London, who died on the

Cooke, *(contd.)* merchant ship *Perry and Lane* in Virginia. Administration to the relict, Margaret Cooke. (Apr. 1700).

Cooke, Samuel, of Dublin, Ireland. Probate to the brother, Erasmus Cooke, and to Thomas Cooke of London, goldsmith, with similar powers reserved to the kinsman, Clement Chaplyn of New England, and to Tobias Norris. (Sep. 1642). Sh.

Cooke, Samuel, of Rotherhithe, Surrey, who died in Virginia, bachelor. Administration to Dorothy Cooke, attorney for the brother, Miles Cooke, now overseas. (Oct. 1686).

Cooke, Sarah, of New York City. Administration to Quintin Dick, attorney for the husband, Edward Cooke, in Tortola. (Dec. 1797).

Cook, William, seaman of the merchant ship *Greenock*, who died in Wilmington, United States of America, bachelor. Administration to the mother, Ann Cook, widow. (Mar. 1824).

Cook, William, formerly of Folkestone, Kent, but late of New York, baker, widower. Administration to Robert Cook, the son and surviving executor of the father, Thomas Cook deceased. (Aug. 1838).

Cookson, George, of St. Augustine, East Florida. Administration with will to Thomas Harrison, attorney for the brother, John Cookson, in East Florida. (Feb. 1777). Revoked and probate granted to the said John Cookson. (Feb. 1786).

Coombes, Nathaniel, Ensign on half pay of the New Jersey Volunteers, who died in Allentown, New Jersey. Administration to James Tidbury, attorney for the relict, Alice Coombes, in Allentown. (Dec. 1822).

Cooper, Edward, of Boston, Massachusetts. Probate to the brother, George Cooper. (Aug. 1809).

Cooper, Elizabeth S. *See* **Lewer**.

Cooper, James, of H.M. ship *Boyne*. Administration to Thomas Lui, attorney for the relict, Susan Cooper, in New England. (Jan. 1705).

Cooper, John, of Weston Hall, Warwickshire, whose brother, Timothy Cooper, was in New England. Probate to the relict, Elizabeth Cooper. (Oct. 1665). Sh.Wa.

Cooper, Justinian, of Virginia. Administration to the uncle, William Cooper. (Sep. 1655).

Cooper, Mary, formerly of Charles Town, South Carolina, but late of Bristol, widow. Probate to John Page and Elias Vanderhorst with similar powers reserved to Arnoldus Vanderhorst. (May 1797).

Cooper, Thomas, formerly of Canterbury, Kent, but late of Philadelphia, bachelor. Administration to the brother, James Cooper. (Aug. 1806).

Cope, Henry, of New York, Lieutenant-Colonel of the American Regiment. Administration with will to Richard Jeneway, attorney for Stephen Byard in New York. (Feb. 1744).

Cope, John, of Maryland, bachelor. Administration to the mother, Blanch Hulen alias Whittington alias Cope, widow of John Hulen alias Whittington, now in Brevell, Gloucestershire. (Apr. 1724).

Copp, Anthony, of Honeley, Warwickshire, whose brother, William Copp,

Copp, *(contd.)* was in New England. Probate to the brother, Walter Copp. (June 1654). Wa.

Copson alias Weaver, John, of St. Paul, Bedford, who died in Maryland. Administration to the only child, Mary, wife of Rev. Jacob Rogers. (Dec. 1740).

Corbisley, Samuel, of Liverpool, Lancashire, who died in Maryland or Virginia, bachelor. Administration to the brother, George Corbisley. (Mar. 1720).

Corderoy, William, of Virginia, bachelor. Probate to the brother, Jasper Corderoy. (Oct. 1667).

Cordis, Hannah, formerly of Boston, New England, but late of St. Andrew by the Wardrobe, London, widow. Limited probate to Thomas Fraser. (Dec. 1779).

Corfield, Richard, of Charleston, South Carolina, bachelor. Administration to the sister, Elizabeth, wife of George Williams. (Jan. 1807).

Corker, Thomas, of Charles Town, South Carolina. Administration with will to James Poyas, attorney for Josiah Smith the younger in Charles Town. (Aug. 1772).

Cormity, Adam. *See* **Cromartie**.

Corneforth, Leonard, of Stepney, Middlesex, who died in Virginia. Administration to Elizabeth, wife of the principal creditor, John Marsingham, during his absence abroad; the relict, Catherine Corneforth, renouncing. (May 1681).

Cornelison, Hanse alias John, of Virginia, bachelor. Administration to the principal creditor, Andrew Anderson. (Nov. 1682).

Cornell, Samuel, formerly of New Bern, North Carolina, but late of New York. Probate to the daughter, Susanna, wife of Henry Chads; the surviving executor, William Low, renouncing, and the other surviving executor, Jacob Blount, having been cited but not having appeared. (May 1787).

Cornish, Henry, of Athol, Warren County, New York. Administration to James Charles Calver, attorney for the relict, Mary Ann Cornish, in Athol. (Apr. 1847).

Cornish, John, of Ottery St. Mary, Devon, who died in New England, bachelor. Administration to the principal creditor, Henry Marker. (Feb. 1695).

Cornock, Samuel, master of the ship *Molly*, who died in South Carolina, bachelor. Probate by his solemn affirmation to Thomas Plumstead. (Aug. 1733).

Cornwall, Alexander, of the ship *Maryland Factor*, who died in Maryland. Probate to William Finlason. (Aug. 1704).

Cornwell, Thomas, of London, who died in Maryland, bachelor. Administration with will to the brother, Anthony Cornwell, the named executor, John Turner, renouncing. (Dec. 1695).

Corran, James, of New York, master of the American ship *Factor*, who died at sea. Probate to John Younger. (Feb. 1821).

Corre, Helene Florentine, of Charleston, South Carolina, spinster.

Corre, *(contd.)*
Administration to the sister, Carolina Renata Corre. (Oct. 1805).

Cosby, Henry, commander of H.M. ship *Centaur*, who died in New York. Probate to the mother, Hon. Grace Cosby, widow. (Aug. 1754).

Cosgrave, John Mahon, of Columbia, Texas, who died at sea on the steamer *Sarah Barnes*. Administration to the relict, Eliza Cosgrave. (Oct. 1844).

Cotchett, Robert, of Mickleover, Derbyshire, whose sister, Dorothy, wife of John Joyce, was in New England. Probate to the relict, Anne Cotchett. (Apr. 1658). Sh.

Cotton, Rev. Nathaniel, formerly of New Inn, Middlesex, but late chaplain of H.M. Garrison in Pensacola, bachelor. Administration to Elizabeth Hendy, relict and administratrix of the creditor, Samuel Hendy deceased; others concerned having been cited but not having appeared. (Jan. 1789).

Cotton, Richard, Captain of the 33rd Regiment, who died in Camden, North America. Probate to the brother, Henry Calveley Cotton, with similar powers reserved to the brother, Thomas Cotton, and to Sir Robert Cotton. (May 1789).

Couch, Charles, formerly of Cow Lane, St. Sepulchre, London, but late of Baltimore, Maryland, bachelor. Administration to Sophia Couch, relict and administratrix of the cousin german, Christopher Couch deceased; the cousin german, Elizabeth, wife of John Parlby, having also died. (Aug. 1802).

Couch, Ralph, of Stepney, Middlesex, who died in Virginia. Administration to the principal creditor, Benjamin Dennis. (Sep. 1676).

Courtenay, Charles Edward Foster, of Pleasant Retreat, Lumpkin County, Georgia. Administration to the relict, Nancey Carey, now wife of John Archibald Moodey, M.D. (June 1854).

Couttes, Henry, of the City of London, merchant, who died in Newcastle, Pennsylvania. Probate to the brother, James Couttes. (Aug. 1709).

Couzens, John, of Oswego, New York, Ensign in Sir William Pepperel's Regiment of Foot, bachelor. Administration with will to Henry Kidgell, attorney for the father, Samuel Couzens, in Dublin, Ireland; the executrix, Anne Hopper, now wife of Edward Barron, renouncing. (Jan. 1757).

Coventry, George, of Fairhill, Hamilton, Lanarkshire, Scotland, Captain of a New York Independent Company. Administration with will to John Bryson, guardian of the children, Alexander, Elizabeth and James Coventry. (Aug. 1777).

Cowan, Joseph, formerly of New York but late of Prosperous near Dublin, Ireland. Probate to the relict, Jane Cowan. (Nov. 1791) Revoked on the death of the relict, Jane, wife of Thomas Davies, and administration granted to her administrator, Samuel Stephenson. (Feb. 1814).

Cowand, John, of Edenton, North Carolina, bachelor. Administration to the brother and next-of-kin, James Cowand. (Oct. 1772).

Coward, William, of Boston, New England, who died in the King's service on the ship *Neptune*. Administration with will to the relict, Christine

Coward, *(contd.)*
Coward, no executor having been named. (Oct. 1691).

Cowden, John, of Frederick County, Virginia, bachelor. Administration to the sister, Mary, wife of George Garrard; the mother, Elizabeth Cowden, widow, having died before administering. (Aug. 1777).

Cowell, Elizabeth, of Greenwich, Kent, who died in Charles Town, South Carolina, spinster. Administration to the father, Martin Cowell. (May 1797).

Cowman, John, of New York City. Probate to James Hay and Daniel Lord the younger with similar powers reserved to David Rogers. (May 1833).

Cowper, Mary, of Savannah, Georgia, widow. Limited administration with will to Charles Shaw, attorney for the daughters and only next-of-kin, Mary Anne Cowper and Margaret, wife of John McQueen, in Savannah. (Aug. 1822).

Cox, Andrew, of Suffolk, Nansemond County, Virginia, who died on the merchant ship *Happy Return*. Probate to Peter Hodgson, attorney for William Shepherd and James Holt in Virginia. (Feb. 1764). Wi.

Cox, Henry, formerly of Sheffield, Yorkshire, but late of New York. Administration to Thomas Champion, attorney for the relict, Caroline Cox, in Boston, North America. (Nov. 1818).

Cox, Isaac, of Philadelphia. Probate to the son, Isaac Cox, and to Isaac Wickoff, with similar powers reserved to Peter Wickoff; the other surviving executor, John Cox, renouncing. (July 1784).

Cox, James, of Bristol, who died in Maryland, bachelor. Administration to the father, Christopher Cox. (Feb. 1680).

Cox, John, of Whitechapel, Middlesex, who died in Maryland. Administration to the relict, Mary Cox. (Nov. 1702).

Cox, John, of St. Thomas the Apostle, London, Ensign of the 17th Regiment of Foot, who died on the River Elk in North America, bachelor. Administration to the father, Rev. Hadley Cox. (May 1778).

Cox, Margery, of Deptford, Kent, widow, whose brother, Giles Webb, was in Virginia. Probate to Mary Waight with similar powers reserved to Elizabeth Waight. (June 1656). Wa.

Cox, Hon. Samuel, of Barbados who died in Maryland. Administration with will to Henry Palmer, attorney for the relict, Elizabeth Cox, in Barbados. (June 1726).

Cox, Sem, of St. Mary's, Richmond, Virginia. Probate to Benjamin Doverill with similar powers reserved to George Downing. (Oct. 1711).

Cox, Thomas, of Nansemum, Virginia, bachelor. Administration to the father, Richard Cox. (June 1697). Revoked on his death and granted to the sister, Mary Tinkerson alias Cox. (Mar. 1698).

Cox, Thomas, citizen and vintner of London, who had lands in Philadelphia. Probate by her solemn affirmation to the relict, Anne Cox, with similar powers reserved to John Antrim. (Mar. 1712).

Cox, William, of Holborn, Middlesex, who died in Georgia.

Cox, *(contd.)*
Administration to the relict, Frances Watt alias Cox. (Jan. 1735).

Crabbe, Osmond, of Brislington, Somerset, whose brother, John Crabbe, was in Virginia. Administration with will to the sister, Alice Vaughan; the executors, Sir William Hayman and William Swimmer, renouncing. (Apr. 1695). Wi.

Crabb, Samuel, of New England, who died in Stepney, Middlesex, bachelor. Administration with nuncupative will to William Marsh; no executor having been named. (Sep. 1694).

Cracklow, January, of Lambeth, Surrey, who died in Pennsylvania, bachelor. Administration to the mother, Mary Cracklow. (Apr. 1727).

Cradock, Mathew, of St. Swithin, London, who had goods in New England. Probate to the relict, Rebecca Cradock. (June 1641). Sh.

Cradock, Sarah, formerly of Edgware Road, Middlesex, but late of Boston, Massachusetts. Administration with will to George Brinley, attorney for Edward Brinley in Boston. (Feb. 1799).

Craig, Archibald Cummings, of Philadelphia, who died in Bedminster, Somerset County, New Jersey. Administration with will to the Rev. Joseph Anderson; no executor having been named, and the half-brother and only next-of-kin, William Currie, having been cited but not having appeared. (Nov. 1802).

Craig, Eleanor, formerly of Donegal, Ireland, who died at sea as a passenger on the merchant steamship *Arctic*. Administration to William Patterson, attorney for the only child, Eliza Jane Patterson, in Penn Township, Butler County, Pennsylvania. (Aug. 1855).

Craig, John, of Philadelphia. Administration with will to James Mackenzie, attorney for the relict, Margaret Craig, the son, James Craig, and Robert Oliver, John Oliver, David Lenox, and William Miller, all in North America. (Jan. 1810).

Craig, John, of Albany, North America, bachelor. Administration to the mother and next-of-kin, Hellen Craig, widow. (Apr. 1833).

Crain, Jotham, of H.M. ship *Duke*, bachelor. Administration to William Bryant, attorney for the father, Robert Crain, in East New Jersey. (Mar. 1747).

Cram, Dorothy, of Philadelphia, widow. Administration to the son, John Cram. (Apr. 1837).

Cramond, James, formerly of Philadelphia but late of New York City. Probate to Joshua Smith and Simmons Smith with similar powers reserved to the relict, Ann Cramond, and the brother, William Cramond. (Nov. 1799).

Crane, Robert, of Great Coggeshall, Essex, whose daughter was wife of Nathaniel Rogers in New England. Probate to Samuel Crane. (Mar. 1659). Wa.

Crane, Robert, of Hadleigh, Suffolk, whose aunt, ——— Rogers, was in New England. Probate to the sister, Mary, wife of Lawrence Stisted. (May 1669). Wa.

Crane, Samuel, of Great Coggeshall, Essex, whose cousin, John Rogers,

Crane, *(contd.)* was in New England. Probate to William Cox the elder and Isaac Hubberd. (Aug. 1670). Wa.

Crane, Thomas, of Kelvedon, Essex, whose sister, Margaret, wife of Nathaniel Rogers, was in New England. Probate to Robert Crane and Henry Whiteing, guardians of the children, Robert and Mary Crane, during their minority. (Mar. 1655). Wa.

Craske, John, of St. Giles Cripplegate, London, who died on a merchant ship in Virginia. Administration to the brother, Andrew Craske; the father, Andrew Craske, renouncing. (May 1705).

Crate, Joseph Henshaw, of Middleton, Carroll County, Mississippi. Probate to Sarah Micoll, spinster, and James Abbott. (June 1856).

Craufurd, James, formerly of Park Lane, Middlesex, but late of New York City. Administration to the brother, John Craufurd; the relict, Alice Craufurd, having been cited but not having appeared. (May 1812).

Craven, John, of Philadelphia, widower. Administration to Edward Ridsdale, guardian of the grandchildren and next-of-kin, Mary, Jane and William Inman; the granddaughter, Dorothy Inman, renouncing. (Feb. 1705).

Craven, Sarah, of New York City. Administration to the husband, Joseph Craven. (July 1851).

Craven, Lawrence, of H.M. ship *York*, who died in Baltimore, Maryland, bachelor. Administration to the brother, Thomas Craven. (Jan. 1772). Revoked on his death and granted to the brother, John Craven. (Mar. 1778).

Crawley, Jacob, formerly of Fulham, Middlesex, mariner, but late of New York City, bachelor. Administration to the brother and sister, John Crawley and Rebekah Jones, widow. (Feb. 1837).

Crawley, John, formerly of Bristol but late of New Jersey, widower. Administration with will to Peter Barlow, attorney for the son, John Crawley, in New Jersey; the executors, Thomas Griffith, M.D., having died, the wife, Catherine Crawley, having died in her husband's lifetime, and Elisha Boudinet having renounced. (Nov. 1800).

Crawley, Mary. *See* **Morrell**.

Creake, Samuel, of Stepney, Middlesex, master of the ship *Britannia*, who died in Maryland. Probate to the relict, Mary Creake. (Oct. 1716).

Crease, Alfred, formerly of Canalside, Camberwell, Surrey, but late of the Northern Liberties of Philadelphia, manufacturing chemist. Administration with will to Orlando Crease, attorney for the relict, Ann Constant Crease, in Philadelphia. (Jan. 1836).

Creed, John, of Martyn's Hundred, Virginia. Administration with will to Anne, wife of Thomas Faussett, during his absence in Virginia. (Apr. 1635). Sh.Wi.

Crego, Stephen, of New York, who died on H.M. ship *Archangel*. Administration to John Corbett, attorney for the relict, Margery Crego, in New York. (May 1692).

Creighton, John, formerly of Dudley, Worcestershire, but late of the Poor House, Oswego, New York. Probate to Jesse Wright with similar

Creighton, *(contd.)* powers reserved to Edward Crockett. (Dec. 1846).

Cresfield, Edward the younger, who died at sea, merchant, and whose daughter-in-law, Lucy, was wife of Thomas Reed of Gloucester, Virginia. Probate to Philip Richards with similar powers reserved to Benjamin Clements. (Dec. 1694). Wi.

Cressey, John, formerly of Christ Church, Surrey, but late of North America, bachelor. Administration to the brother, William Henry Cressey. (May 1812).

Cresswell, Estcourt, of Camden, New Jersey, bachelor. Administration to the brother, Joseph Cresswell, the mother and next-of-kin, Sarah Cresswell, renouncing. (Nov. 1843).

Creswell, Frederick, of Baltimore, United States of America, bachelor. Administration to the half-sister and only next-of-kin, Mary Ninde Columbia, wife of John Savadge Davenhill. (Mar. 1857).

Creswell, George, formerly of New York, afterwards of Barnsley Hall, Bromsgrove, Worcestershire, but late seaman of the merchant ship *Nottingham*, who died at sea. Administration with will to the half-sister, Mary Ninde Columbia, wife of John Savadge Davenhill; the executors, Joseph Creswell having died and John Creswell renouncing. (Jan. 1854).

Cresswell, Joseph, formerly of Box, Wiltshire, but late of Holmesbury near Philadelphia. Probate to the surviving executor, John Gibbs. (Mar. 1856). Further grant made in January 1868.

Crewes, James, of Virginia, widower. Administration to the daughter, Sarah Whittingham. (Sep. 1677).

Crispe, Jemima Humphreys, of Buffalo, New York, spinster. Administration to William Baxter the younger, administrator with will to the father, John Crispe deceased, and attorney for his executor, John Bowles, in Hamilton County, Ohio. (Jan. 1840).

Crispe, John, of Buffalo, New York. Administration with will to William Baxter the younger, attorney for John Bowles in Hamilton County, Ohio. (Jan. 1840).

Crispe, Thomas, of the ship *Isaac and Sarah*, who died in Virginia, bachelor. Administration to the brother, Henry Crispe, clerk. (Nov. 1704).

Critchell, Michael, of Perry County, Ohio. Probate to Charles Carter with similar powers reserved to the relict Ann, now wife of Mathias D. Stotlar. (Dec. 1851).

Crockett, William, of H.M. ship *Alborough*, who died in Providence Island, South Carolina, bachelor. Probate to Thomas Vinter. (June 1730).

Crofts, Henry, of Boston, New England. Administration to the brother, James Crofts, attorney for the mother, Elianor Crofts alias South, in Ireland. (Mar. 1703).

Crokatt, John, formerly of Charles Town, South Carolina, merchant, but late in Lisbon, Portugal. Probate to the father, Charles Crokatt, with similar powers reserved to Alexander Robertson. (June 1740).

Croke, Paulus Ambrosius, of Hasleigh, Essex, (intending for Virginia). Probate to the uncle, John Nevell. (Aug. 1652). Wa.

Cromartie alias Cormity, Adam, of H.M. ship *Colchester*, who died in Virginia. Probate to Elizabeth, wife of John Crafts, with similar powers reserved to the said John Crafts. (Jan. 1741).

Crommelin, Charles, of New York. Probate to the son, Daniel Cox, with similar powers reserved to Samuel Butler, John Read and Joseph Read. (Apr. 1740).

Cronen, Eleanor, formerly of Bristol but late of Philadelphia, spinster. Administration with will to George Haslewood, attorney for Mary Foulke, widow, in Philadelphia. (Aug. 1816).

Crook, Edward, formerly of Heddington, Wiltshire, but late of South Carolina. Probate to George Lockey. (Oct. 1803).

Crooke, Thomas the younger, of London, who died abroad (bound for Virginia). Probate to the father, Thomas Crooke. (June 1681). Wi.

Crosby, William, superintendent of an armed ship, who died in New York. Probate to Edward Ommanney. (Dec. 1780).

Croskey, Alfred, of Philadelphia. Administration to the relict, Elizabeth Croskey. (Aug. 1842).

Cross, Margaret, formerly of Bradford Township, afterwards of Huntingdon County, but late of Clearfield County, Pennsylvania, spinster. Administration to Richard Smith, attorney for the father, Henry Cross, in Clearfield County. (Mar. 1836).

Crosse, Samuel, of St. Saviour, Southwark, Surrey, who had assets in Boston, New England. Probate to the relict, Mary Crosse. (June 1667).

Crosse, William, of Blandford, Dorset, who died in Maryland, widower. Administration to the principal creditor, Richard Draper. (Mar. 1683).

Crossley, Leonard, Lieutenant in Colonel Burton's Regiment in America, bachelor. Administration to the sister, Ann, wife of John Cory; the mother, Elizabeth Crossley, having died. (Oct. 1773).

Crossley, William, of New York, widower. Administration to the nephew and next-of-kin, Nicholas Datton. (Sep. 1788).

Crouch, Richard, of St. Giles Cripplegate, London, whose brother, William Crouch, was in New England. Probate to the relict, Anne Crouch. (Nov. 1660). Wa.

Crouch, Thomas, of Philadelphia. Administration to the relict, Elizabeth Ann Crouch. (Apr. 1779).

Croucher, Henry, of New York City, sailmaker of H.M. ship *Coventry*. Administration to William Sawer alias Sawyer, attorney for the relict, Ann Croucher, in New York. (Feb. 1768). New grant to the same. (Apr. 1768).

Crow, John, of the merchant ship *Providence*, who died in Virginia. Probate to Thomas Jackson. (Jan. 1710).

Crozier, Samuel, of Staten Island, New York, master mariner, who died in Petersburgh, Virginia, bachelor. Administration to the mother, Margaret Robinson, formerly Margaret Crozier, widow. (Feb. 1801).

Cruden, Rev. Alexander, formerly Rector of Farnham, Virginia, but late of Aberdeen, Scotland. Probate to Rev. Roderick MacLeod with similar

Cruden, *(contd.)* powers reserved to Alexander Leslie. (June 1792).

Cruger, Catharine, of New York City, wife of Bertram Peter Cruger. Limited probate to the son, John Church Cruger. (Apr. 1840).

Cruger, Henry the elder, formerly of New York City but late of Bristol. Limited probate to Thomas Hayes and Jeremiah Osborne. (Mar. 1780).

Cruger, John, of New York. Probate to the relict, Martha Cruger. (Mar. 1825).

Cruger, Nicholas, of New York City. Probate to the relict, Ann, now wife of William Rogers, with similar powers reserved to Robert Watts, John Watts, Cornelius Stevenson and William Henry Krause. (Jan. 1805).

Crumpe, Mary. *See* **Harris**.

Crutchfield, John, Lieutenant of the 35th Regiment of Foot, who died in Pensacola, widower. Administration to William Sawtrey, guardian of the only child, Mary Crutchfield. (Apr. 1766).

Cubitt, Robert, of Virginia, bachelor. Administration to the sister, Sarah Cubitt. (Feb. 1675).

Cudlipp, Jonathan, of New York. Administration to the relict, Lucy Cudlipp. (June 1849).

Cully, Abraham, of Stafford County, Virginia, bachelor. Limited administration with will to the brother, John Cully. (Apr. 1694).

Cuming, Alexander, of New England, who died on H.M. ship *Greenwich* in Guinea, surgeon. Administration to the principal creditor, Edward Jasper; the relict, Ann Cuming, the sons, John and Witter (*sic*) Cuming, and the daughters, Frances, wife of Rev. Thomas Thompson, and [blank] Cuming, having been cited but not having appeared. (Dec. 1738).

Cuming, Rev. Robert, of South Carolina, bachelor. Administration to the creditrix, Isabella Campbell, widow; the brothers and sisters, Patrick, Walter, and William Cuming, Janett, wife of Thomas Donald, and Christopher, wife of John Ritchie, having been cited but but not having appeared. (Feb. 1754).

Cummings, Archibald, of Philadelphia, clerk. Limited administration with will to Thomas Moore. (Aug. 1741).

Cummings, Elizabeth Peach, of Newbury Port, Massachusetts, widow. Limited administration to Petty Vaughan, attorney for the only children, Elizabeth Maria and Sarah Ann Cummings. (Mar. 1827).

Cundy, William, formerly of Queen Anne Street, Cavendish Square, Middlesex, but late of Kent Settlement, Kimbles Bend, Texas, civil engineer. Administration to the relict, Mary Charlotte Cundy. (Nov. 1852).

Cunningham, Charles, formerly of New Providence but late of Jefferson County, United States of America. Limited administration to Robert Eve Cunningham, attorney for the relict, Ann Pritchard Cunningham, in the United States of America. (Sep. 1826).

Cunningham, James, Lieutenant of the Royal North British Fusiliers, who died in Florida, bachelor. Administration to James Russell, attorney

Cunningham, *(contd.)* for the mother, Ann Cunningham, widow, in Carrickfergus, County Antrim, Ireland. (Feb. 1679).

Cuninghame, William, formerly surgeon of H.M. ship *Windsor*, but late of New York City. Administration with will to Thomas Maude, attorney for the relict, Margaret Cuninghame, in New York. (May 1789).

Cunningham, William, formerly of St. Augustine, East Florida, but late of Nassau, Bahamas. Administration to Charles Edwards, attorney for the relict, Mary Cunningham, in New Providence. (Sep. 1791).

Cure, Charles, of Rotherhithe, Surrey, who died in Rappahannock, Virginia, widower. Administration to the son, Charles Cure. (Jan. 1734).

Curran, Lucy alias Lucinda Marcella, of Buffalo, North America. Administration to the husband, Michael Curran. (Jan. 1851).

Currie, Ebenezer, of Pennsylvania. Probate to John Sexton with similar powers reserved to Samuel McAll the elder. (Dec. 1747).

Curry, John, of Pennsylvania, bachelor. Administration to the principal creditor, John Adams. (May 1703).

Curry, Samuel, of St. Martin in the Fields, Middlesex, who died in Boston, New England. Probate to the sister, Ester, wife of Henry Herbert; the executor, John Le Sage, renouncing. (Jan. 1737).

Curson, Richard, of Baltimore, North America. Administration to the relict, Elizabeth Curson. (June 1809).

Curtis, Betsey, of Halifax, Nova Scotia. Administration to Thomas Aspinwall, attorney for the husband, Henry Curtis, in Roxburgh, Norfolk County, Massachusetts. (Feb. 1851).

Curtyce, John, of Burghfield, Berkshire, whose sister, Jane, wife of Thomas Collyer, was in New England. Probate to John Curtis of Tilehurst, Berkshire, John Curtis of Tadley, Hampshire, John Go—— of London, merchant, and James Maynard of Reading, Berkshire, wool drawer. (Oct. 1660).

Curtis, John, of Virginia, bachelor. Administration to the brother, Alexander Curtis. (Aug. 1684).

Curtis, John, of Boston, New England, who died on H.M. ship *English Tyger*, bachelor. Probate to Robert Chipchase. (Dec. 1680). Wa.

Curtis, Uriah, of Thedford, Gloucester County, New York. Administration to James Phyn, attorney for the relict, Abigail Curtis, in Quebec. (Dec. 1790).

Curwen, Edward, formerly of London but late of Dubuque City, Iowa. Administration with will to the relict, Eliza Susannah Curwen. (Mar. 1857).

Custis, Daniel Parke, of New Kent County, Virginia. Limited administration to John Morrey. (June 1758). Revoked and granted to the relict, Martha, now wife of George Washington. (July 1774).

Custis, Hon. John, of Williamsburgh, James City County, Virginia. Probate to the son, Daniel Parke Custis. (Nov. 1753). Revoked on his death and administration granted to Wakelin Welch, attorney for Martha, wife of Hon. George Washington, the relict of the said Daniel Parke Custis. (July 1774).

Custis, Joseph, of Kingston-upon-Hull, Yorkshire, who died in Accomack, Virginia. Administration by decree to the principal creditor, Edward Miles. (Feb. 1656). Revoked and granted to the son, Zachary Custis. (July 1685).

Cuthbertson, John, of St. Botolph Aldgate, London, who died on the ship *Sea Horse* in Virginia, bachelor. Administration to the mother, Margaret Bromwich, widow. (Feb. 1727).

Cuthbertson, William, of the ship *Elizabeth and Catherine*, who died in Virginia, bachelor. Administration to the nephew, William Cuthbertson. (June 1678).

Cutmore, Ann Cole, formerly Ann Cole Reddicliffe, formerly of South Brent, Devon, but late of Laselle, Illinois. Administration to John Thomas Savery, attorney for the husband, George Cutmore, in Laselle. (July 1853).

Cutt, Richard, of Portsmouth in Piscataqua in parts overseas. Probate to the relict, Elianor Cutt, and the daughters, Margaret, wife of William Vaughan, and Bridget, wife of Thomas Daniel. (July 1682). Wa.

Cuyler, Abraham, Mayor of Albany, United States of America, who died in Montreal, Canada. Probate to the relict, Jane Cuyler, with similar powers reserved to the son, Jacob Cuyler. (Dec. 1816). Revoked and granted to Archibald Campbell, attorney for the son and surviving executor, Jacob Glen [in the will written as Jacob Cuyler], in Uitehage, Cape of Good Hope. (Apr. 1829).

Cuyler, Henry, of Greenbush, Rensselaer County, New York, Commissary on half pay of the Staff of Martinico. Administration with will to John Thompson, attorney for the relict, Catherine Cuyler, and for William Howe Cuyler and Ralph Barton Cuyler in Greenbush. (July 1806).

D

Dacres, Robert, of Carolina, bachelor. Administration to Robert Johnson, attorney for the principal creditor, Thomas Broughton, Deputy Governor of Carolina; the mother, Lady Mary Dacres, renouncing. (Apr. 1707).

Daft, Thomas, of New York City. Administration to the relict, Elizabeth, now wife of James Williams. (May 1792).

Dagley, Elizabeth, of Charleston, South Carolina, spinster. Administration to the brother, William Thomas Dagley. (June 1856).

Dagworthy, Ely, of Trenton, New Jersey, Captain of the 48th Regiment of Foot. Limited administration with will to Robert Barclay, attorney for John and Sarah De Hart in Elizabeth Town, New Jersey. (June 1780).

Dale, Dame Elizabeth, of Westminster, Middlesex, widow, who had lands in Virginia. Probate to Richard Hamby and William Shrimpton. (Dec. 1640). Wa.

Dallett, Judith, of Philadelphia, widow. Probate to the son, Gillies Dallett, with similar powers reserved to the son, Elijah Dallett. (July 1854).

Dalrumple alias Dalrumble alias Dalrymple, Alexander, formerly of Salem, New England, but late of H.M. ship *Woolwich*, bachelor. Probate to Paul Moor with similar powers reserved to Mary Moor. (Feb. 1747).

Dalrymple, John, of Brunswick County, North Carolina, reduced Captain of Sir William Pepperel's Regiment of Foot. Limited administration with will to Alexander Duncan of Wilmington, North Carolina. (Oct. 1767).

Dalrymple, Martha, of Brunswick County, North Carolina, widow. Administration with will to the residuary legatee, Elizabeth Dalrymple alias Hamilton Macgill, widow; the brother, Samuel Watters, the sister, Sarah, wife of Alexander Lillington, the said Alexander Lillington, and John Rutherford, having all died, and Joseph Watters, executor of the said Samuel Watters, having been cited but not having appeared. (Dec. 1787).

Dalton, Henry, formerly of Sligo, Ireland, but late of New York City. Probate to Rev. Patrick Burke. (May 1825).

Dalton, Joseph, of Virginia, bachelor. Administration to the brother and next-of-kin, Benjamin Dalton. (July 1720).

Daly, John. *See* **Dayly**.

Dandridge, Francis, of St. George the Martyr, Middlesex, but late lodging near Buckingham, whose nephew, William Dandridge, son of the brother, Bartholomew Dandridge, was in Virginia. Probate to James and George Mares with similar powers reserved to the mother, Elizabeth Dandridge, widow. (Nov. 1765). Wi.

Daniel, Henry, formerly of St. Botolph Bishopsgate, London, but late of New York, widower. Administration to the brother, Alexander Daniel. (June 1800).

Daniel, James, of Jersey Hospital and Jersey Prison Ships in New York,

Daniel, *(contd.)*
seaman. Probate to the sister, Jane Daniel. (Sep. 1782).

Daniell, Nicholas, of Stepney, Middlesex, Captain of the ship *Hampshire*, who died in Virginia. Administration to the relict, Mary Daniell. (Mar. 1694).

Danson, Barbara, of Holborn, Middlesex, spinster, who had a plantation in North Carolina. Probate by his solemn affirmation to Daniel Dolley with similar powers reserved to Margaret Mollison. (Apr. 1726).

Darby, Agnes, of Bisley, Surrey, widow, whose kinsman, Edward Darby, was in New England. Probate to Henry Collier. (June 1650). Sh.Wa.

Darby, Josiah, of St. Stephen Coleman Street, London, who died in South Carolina. Administration to the relict, Hannah Darby. (May 1715).

Darch, Thomas, formerly of Taunton, Somerset, but late of Pinchill, Kentucky. Administration to the son, Thomas Darch; the relict, Joan Darch, having been cited but not having appeared. (Apr. 1801).

Dash, John Balthazar, of New York City, widower. Administration to the son, Daniel Bowie Dash. (May 1830).

Daubuz, Henry James, formerly of George Town, South Carolina, but late of Falmouth, Cornwall. Probate to the relict, Christiana Daubuz. (May 1777).

Daulby, William, formerly of Liverpool, Lancashire, but late of New York City. Probate to Ambrose Lace with similar powers reserved to Henry Roscoe. (Dec. 1827).

Dauncey, Joseph, chaplain of the ship *Falcon*. Administration to Samuel Wallin, father of the relict Anne Myles alias Dauncey, in New England. (Jan. 1699).

Davenport, Addington, of Boston, New England, clerk. Administration with will to William Baker, Alderman of London, attorney for Joseph Dowse and William Price in Boston. (Aug. 1747). Revoked and probate granted to the son, Addington Davenport, on his coming of age. (Mar. 1756).

Davenport, Ann, of Boston, Massachusetts. Administration to the husband, Addington Davenport, clerk. (Aug. 1745).

Davenport, Thomas, of New York. Probate to William Horspoole. (Aug. 1716).

Davenport, Thomas Donald, formerly of Marlborough Cottages, College Street, Chelsea, Middlesex, but late of Cincinnati. Probate to the relict, Sophia Donald Davenport alias Danby, the daughter, Margaret Donald Davenport, and to Henry Rance, with similar powers reserved to John Holland and William Stevenson Fitch. (Sep. 1852).

Davenport, William. of Williamsburgh, Virginia, bachelor. Administration by his solemn affirmation to Sampson Hanbury, attorney for the aunts, Mary Davenport, and Peachey, wife of Elias Wills, of Williamsburgh. (Jan. 1796).

Davers, Henry, Lieutenant of H.M. ship *Neptune*, who died in America, bachelor. Probate to Thomas Bilcliffe. (Sep. 1759).

Davers, Jermyn, formerly of Rushbrooke, Suffolk, then of Virginia, who died at sea, bachelor. Probate to the mother, Lady Margaretta Davers, widow. (Mar. 1751).

Davy, John, of Maidstone, Kent, who died in London, and whose nephew, John Davy, was in Virginia. Probate to the daughters, Mary Wall and Elizabeth Andrewes. (June 1649). Wa.

Davey, Thomas Henry, formerly of Montpellier Farm, Bristol, farmer, but late of Memphis, United States of America. Administration to the relict, Ellen Davey. (Apr. 1855).

David, Ezekiel, of Charles Town, South Carolina. Probate to Edward Brice with similar powers reserved to Francis Magnus. (Feb. 1679).

Davis, Elizabeth, wife of David Davis, formerly Elizabeth Botson, of Pringo, North Carolina. Administration to the son, John Smith Davis. (Dec. 1818).

Davis, George, of Philadelphia. Probate to John Wood Nelson and Benjamin Adam with similar powers reserved to Ebenezer Duncan, doctor of physic, and Philip McKenna. (Sep. 1822).

Davies, Isaack, of Virginia, bachelor. Administration to the father, Thomas Davies. (Dec. 1658).

Davies, James, of Yarpole, Herefordshire, who died in New York, bachelor. Administration to the cousin german and next-of-kin, John Nash. (Nov. 1773).

Davis, John, of H.M. ship *Sea Horse*, who died in Boston, New England. Probate to Evan Jones with similar powers reserved to his wife, Mary Jones. (Feb. 1725).

Davis, John, of Philadelphia, mariner of H.M. ship *Roebuck*, bachelor. Administration to the father, John Davis. (Jan. 1779).

Davies, John, of H.M. ships *Rainbow* and *Culloden*, who died on Gardener's Island, New York. Probate to James Mathews. (Apr. 1783).

Davis, John, of Nantucket, Massachusetts. Administration to Thomas Banner, attorney for the children, Obed, William and James Davis, in Boston, America; the relict, Susanna Davis, having died. (Mar. 1843).

Davis, Jonathan, of Barne Elms, Surrey, who died in Virginia. Administration to the son, Jonathan Davis; the relict, Mary Davis, renouncing. (Mar 1684). Revoked on his death and granted to the relict, Mary Davis. (Oct. 1697).

Davis, Lewis, of H.M. ship *Advice*, who died in New England. Probate to the relict, Hannah Davis. (Dec. 1702).

Davies, Richard, of Virginia. Probate to the relict, Joanne Davies. (July 1661). Wi.

Davies, Richard, formerly Lieutenant in the 44th Regiment of Foot, who died in New Orleans. Administration to Hickman Rose, attorney for the father, Simon Davies, in Cork, Ireland. (Aug. 1818).

Davis alias Davies, Richard, of St. Louis, Missouri. Administration with will to John Bryan the elder, grandfather and guardian of the son, Richard Davis, during his minority; the sole executor, James Nolan, having been cited but not having appeared. (Feb. 1853). Revoked on the death of John Bryan and granted to Lemuel Davies, uncle and guardian of the son, Richard Davis. (May 1854).

Davies, Stephen, of St. Saviour, Southwark, Surrey, who died on the

Davies, *(contd.)*
merchant ship *Mermaid* in Virginia. Administration to the relict, Anne Davies. (Dec. 1704).

Davies, Thomas, of North Carolina. Administration to the daughter, Sarah Davies; the relict, Rebecca Davies, having died before administering. (Sep. 1707).

Davies, Thomas, of Bermondsey, Surrey, who died on H.M. ship *Winchelsea* in Virginia, bachelor. Administration to the principal creditrix, Joyce Drake. (Feb. 1735).

Davis, Wells, of Blisland, New Kent County, Virginia, bachelor. Administration to Phillip Jones, attorney for the mother, Temperance Gillmett alias Davis, wife of Richard Gillmett, now in Virginia. (Nov. 1732).

Davis, William, of New York, who died on the ketch *Aldborough*. Probate to the relict, Elianor Davis. (Aug. 1694).

Davies, William, of King George County, Virginia, who died on the merchant ship *Jett* in the River Thames, bachelor. Probate to John Hopkins. (Oct. 1775).

Davies, William, formerly of Newport, Monmouth, who died in America, bachelor. Administration to the brother and next-of-kin, Thomas Davies. (Jan. 1802).

Davis, William, of New Orleans, planter. Administration to Mary Davis, daughter and executrix of the creditrix, Mary Davis, widow deceased; the relict, now Maria Holliday, widow, and the only surviving children, Eliza and Mary Davis, being next-of-kin of William Beaumont Davis, minor deceased, having been cited but not having appeared. (July 1828).

Davison, William, Captain of the 52nd Regiment of Foot, who died in Boston. Administration with will to Robert Douglas, attorney for the sister, Lily Braidfitt, widow, in Biggar, Peeblesshire, Scotland, no executor having been named. (July 1776).

Davy. *See* **Davey**.

Dawkins, Simon, of Petsworth, Hampshire, who died in Long Island in New England, bachelor. Administration to the brother and next-of-kin, John Dawkins. (June 1675).

Dawney, Bryan, who died in Virginia, widower. Administration by decree to the son, John Dawney. (Jan. 1722).

Dawson, Eleanor, of Baltimore, United States of America, who died in Brighton, Sussex, widow. Administration to the son, William Dawson. (Aug. 1834).

Dawson, Patrick, formerly of Bermondsey, Surrey, but late of Philadelphia. Administration with will to the nephew, Patrick Dawson; the sisters and executors in trust, Jane and Ann Dawson, having died in the testator's lifetime. (June 1785).

Dawson, William, formerly of Wakefield, Yorkshire, but late H.M. Consul for Maryland. Probate to the relict, Eleanor Dawson. (June 1822).

Dawson, William, formerly of Wakefield, Yorkshire, but late of Baltimore, North America, M.D. Limited administration to Henry Willoughby

Dawson, *(contd.)* Rooke. (Jan. 1828).

Day, Benjamin, formerly of Norwich, Norfolk, but late of York Town, Pennsylvania, widower. Administration to the son, Jeremiah Ives Day. (Oct. 1805).

Day, John, of Rotherhithe, Surrey, who died overseas, having goods in Virginia. Administration to the relict, Anne Day. (Apr. 1672).

Day, John, of New York and Liverpool, Lancashire, merchant, bachelor. Administration to the sister, Sarah, wife of William Stewart Lodington. (Dec. 1852).

Day, Mary. *See* **Gledhill**.

Day, Thomas, of the merchant ship *Dove*, who died in Maryland, bachelor. Administration to the principal creditor, Colonel Thomas Lascelles; the father, John Day, renouncing. (Oct. 1728).

Day, Thomas, of Charles Town, South Carolina, bachelor. Administration to the brother, James Day; the mother, Elizabeth Day, widow, renouncing. (Mar. 1765).

Day, William, of the City of Oxford, who died in New Jersey. Administration to John Cross, the nephew by a sister; the sister and next-of-kin, Jane, wife of Thomas Shreeve, renouncing. (May 1706).

Dayly alias Daly, John, of H.M. ship *Sardoine*, who died in Charles Town, South Carolina. Administration with will to William Ellis, executor to the named executor, Domnick Copinger deceased. (Mar. 1768).

Dayrell, Paul, of Brooklyn, New York. Administration with will to Robert Miller, attorney for the relict, Mary Dayrell, and for Caleb Shrive, in Brooklyn. (June 1805).

Deacon, Thomas, of St. Saviour, Southwark, Surrey, whose cousin, Thomas Deacon, was in Virginia. Probate to the relict, Margaret Deacon. (Oct. 1652). Wi.

Dean, Fanny. *See* **Coates**.

Deane, George, of New England, who died on the ship *Princess Anne* in Barbados, bachelor. Administration with will to Henry Wilke; no executor having been named. (Dec. 1693). Wa.

Deane, Thomas, of Freefolk, Hampshire, but formerly of Boston, New England. Probate to the brother, John Deane, with similar powers reserved to William Browne. (May 1686). Revoked on the death of John Deane and administration granted to his son, Thomas Deane; William Browne renouncing. (Apr. 1695). Wa.

De Beaufain, Hector Beringer, of Charles Town, South Carolina. Limited probate to George Schutz. (Feb. 1767).

de Begnis, Giuseppe, of New York, professor of music. Administration to the relict, Josephine Ronzi de Begnis. (Nov. 1849). Revoked on her death and granted to Robert Wynne Williams, attorney for the daughter, Clotilde, wife of Gaetano Fraschini, in Naples. (Sep. 1854).

Debuke, Thomas, of Boston, New England. Administration to the son, Thomas Debuke; the relict, Jamima Debuke, having died. (Dec. 1748).

De Butts, Mary, formerly of Prince George's County, Maryland, but late of Alexandria County, District of Columbia, widow. Probate to John Peyton Dulany with similar powers reserved to the son, John Henry De Butts. (June 1831).

De Butts, Samuel, of Prince George's County, America. Probate to Richard Earl Welby with similar powers reserved to the relict, Mary De Butts. (Apr. 1816).

De Cevallos alias Ceballos, Don Ciracio, of New Orleans, Louisiana. Probate to Pedro Marin Argote and Thomas Urquhart. (Aug. 1819).

De Conty, Esther, of New York, widow. Administration to the nephew, Rev. William Dupre, attorney for the only sister, Elizabeth Harrison, during her idiotry. (Aug. 1819).

Dedicott, John, of South Carolina, bachelor. Administration to the mother, Elizabeth Dedicott, widow. (Apr. 1718).

Degen, Elizabeth, of New Orleans, widow. Administration to James Graves Russell, attorney for the son, Charles Russell Degen, in Mobile, North America. (Sep. 1825).

De Gerstner, Francis Anthony Chevalier, formerly of Prague in Austria, but late of Philadelphia. Administration to the relict, Clara Elisabetha Louisa De Gerstner. (June 1840).

Delafield, Charles, of Milwaukee, Wisconsin, merchant. Administration to John Teesdale, attorney for the relict, Louisa Maria Delafield, in Milwaukee. (Jan. 1844). Revoked on his death and granted to Horatio Nelson Fisher as attorney. (Mar. 1854).

Delagal, John, of South Carolina, bachelor. Administration to Abraham Le Mesurier, attorney for the brother and next-of-kin, Philip Delagal, in North America. (Feb. 1769).

Delagal, Philip, formerly of Guernsey but late a Captain in General Parsons' Regiment of Invalids. Administration with will to Abraham Le Mesurier, attorney for the relict, Eleanor Delagal, and the son, Philip Delagal, in Georgia. (Sep. 1764).

De La March, John, of the merchant ship *Prince Royal*, who died in Virginia, bachelor. Administration to Charles De La March, attorney for the father, Daniel De La March. (Sep. 1723).

De Lancey, Oliver, of New York City but late of Beverley, Yorkshire. Probate to the son, Stephen De Lancey, with similar powers reserved to the relict, Phila De Lancey, the son, Oliver De Lancey, and to Ann, wife of John Harris Cruger, and Charlotte De Lancey. (Jan. 1786). Revoked and probate granted to the son, Oliver De Lancey, with similar powers reserved to the relict, Phila De Lancey, and to Ann, wife of John Cruger, and Lady Charlotte Dundas (formerly De Lancey), wife of Sir David Dundas. (Nov. 1809).

De Lanne alias De Laune, John, of South Carolina, who died in Stepney, Middlesex. Probate to Robert Aubert alias Auber and Anne De Laune, spinster. (May 1728).

De Lavall, Thomas, of New York City. Administration with will to Thomas Landon, attorney for the son, John De Lavall, now overseas. (Feb. 1683).

Delawne, Gideon, of Blackfriars, London, who had lands in Virginia. Probate to the relict, Jane Delawne. (Jan. 1659). Wa.

Del Castillo, Dom Manuel Samaniego, of New Orleans, Lieutenant on half pay in Mexican service. Limited administration with will to Anselmo de Arrogave, attorney for Dom Andres Antonio de la Leata in Soto de la Marina, Mexico. (Dec. 1833).

Del Corral, Stanasio Gutienez, of New Orleans, Louisiana. Administration to the relict, Maria Josefe Arrieta. (Jan. 1834).

Deledicq, Lawrence, of the ship *Bever*, bound for New York, who died overseas. Probate to Paul Ray. (Oct. 1691).

Delke alias Kenythorpe, Elizabeth, who died in Virginia, widow. Administration to the sister, Catherine Kenythorpe. (June 1629).

de Mazas, Francisco, formerly of Tampico but late of Philadelphia. Administration to Robert Grant, attorney for the relict, Mary Ann de Mazas, in Philadelphia. (Nov. 1831).

Demere, Paul, Captain of an Independent Company of Foot, who died in Fort Laudon in South Carolina, bachelor. Administration to the creditor, Dr. David Nisbett; the brother and only next-of-kin, Raymond Demere, having been cited but not having appeared. (Nov. 1765).

Dendy, Samuel, formerly of Theobalds Road, Red Lion Square, Middlesex, but late of North America. Administration to the father, John Dendy; the relict, Sarah Dendy, having died. (Apr. 1808).

Neufville, Edward, formerly of Bristol, afterwards of South Carolina, but late of St. Stephen Coleman Street, London. Inventory 1790. [*Administration Act not found*].

De Neufville, John, formerly of Amsterdam but late of Cambridge, Massachusetts. Administration with will to Samuel Williams, attorney for the relict, Anna Margaret, now wife of John Stoughton, in Boston, Massachusetts. (Apr. 1801).

Dennis, William, of Colonel Holt's Regiment, bachelor. Administration by decree to the principal creditrix, Elizabeth Jennings, widow. (July 1722).

Denny, Alexander, of Charles Town, South Carolina, who died in Stepney, Middlesex. Probate to the relict, Lucy Denny; the named executor, John Brome, renouncing. (Aug. 1730).

Denoon, David, of Charleston, South Carolina. Administration with will to Thomas Crokate, attorney for the relict, Margaret Denoon, in Charleston. (July 1823).

Densley, Edith, formerly of St. James, Westminster, Middlesex, but late of Alexandria, Virginia. Administration to Joseph Hume, attorney for the husband, John Bogue (*sic*). (Mar. 1800).

Dent, Elizabeth, of Manchester Square, Middlesex, whose sister-in-law, Anna Travers, widow, was in Philadelphia. Administration with will to Sir William Gibbons, uncle and guardian of the great-nephews and nieces, Frederick, Emily, Robert and Barton Gibbons. (Mar. 1809). Revoked and granted to the great-niece, Caroline Gibbons. (Jan. 1816).

Dent, George, formerly of Bristol but late of Bunkers Hill, North America, bachelor. Administration to the cousin german once removed and only next-of-kin, Jane, wife of Thomas Tyas. (Apr. 1791).

Dent, John, formerly of Bristol but late of Bunkers Hill, North America, bachelor. Administration to Jane, wife of Thomas Tyas, administratrix to the brother and only next-of-kin, George Dent deceased. (Apr. 1791).

Denwood, Mary, of Somerset County, Maryland. Administration to Anthony Bacon, attorney for the husband, Thomas Denwood, in Maryland. (Apr. 1753).

De Olazabal, Jose Javier, of New Orleans. Limited administration with will to Pedro de la Quintana, attorney for the relict, Maria Nicolasa Migoni de Olazabal, in New York. (Dec. 1833).

De Peyster, Frederick, of New York City, Captain on half pay of the New York Regiment of Volunteers. Administration to Charles Downes, attorney for the son, Frederic De Peyster, in New York; the relict, Ann De Peyster, renouncing. (Sep. 1836).

Depont, James, of New York, bachelor. Administration to the principal creditor, Robert Myre; the aunt and next-of-kin, Ester Bernon, renouncing. (July 1706).

Derickson, George, of Shadwell, Middlesex, who died on the ship *Unicorne* in Virginia, bachelor. Administration with will to Anne, wife and attorney of Thomas Anderson, now overseas. (June 1685).

Derickson, Harman, of Virginia, bachelor. Administration to Barbara, wife and attorney of the principal creditor, Stephen Johnson, during his absence. (July 1676).

Derkheim, Moses Myer, of Norfolk, Virginia. Probate to the relict, Elizabeth Derkheim, and to John Busher and Richard Adams. (Feb. 1817).

De Rossett, Lewis Henry, formerly of North Carolina but late of Holborn, Middlesex. Administration with will to Thomas Younger, attorney for James Walker Armand, and for the nephews, John De Rossett and John Armand Du Bois, in Wilmington, North Carolina. (Nov. 1787).

Derrick, Henry, of St. Stephen, Bristol, who died in Virginia. Probate to the relict, Sarah Derrick. (Oct. 1677). Wi.

Des Bouttels, Claude Francois Jean Bellanger, formerly of Paris, France, but late of New Orleans, widower, a native subject of France. Limited administration to Henry Trappes, attorney for Jean Emmanuel Albert Gustave de Bellanger, the only child of the nephew, Alexander Marie Odillon de Bellanger, and for Daniel Ferdinand Osterwald, now in Paris. (May 1837).

Desbrisay, Albert, Captain in General Oglethorpe's Regiment in Georgia, bachelor. Administration to the creditor, George Simpson. (Dec. 1751).

Desbrosses, James, of New York City, widower. Limited administration to Henry Waddington, attorney for the daughters and only next-of-kin, Charlotte Magdalene, wife of Henry Overing, and Elizabeth, wife of

Desbrosses, *(contd.)* John Hunter, in New York City. (June 1808).

Desbrosses, Magdalen, of New York City. Administration with will to William Thwaytes, attorney for James Desbrosses in New York City; the executors, James Desbrosses the younger and David Clarkson, having died, and Samuel Jones having renounced. (June 1796).

Descury, Simon, Captain in General Pepperell's Regiment of Foot, who died at the Ohio in America. Administration to the creditor, Christopher Baron; the mother, Elizabeth Descury, and the brother, Henry Descury, renouncing. (June 1763).

De Silvie, Manuel, of New York City who died on H.M. ship *Gaspie*. Administration to the relict, Jane De Silvie. (Oct. 1771).

Desombrages, Marie Joseph Adine Vezien, of New Orleans, widow. Administration to the daughter, Marie Augustine Elisabeth Sophie Richard, wife of Jean Baptiste Louis Augustine Cauderon. (June 1833).

D'Espinose, Jerome Francois, of Savannah, Georgia. Administration to the relict, Claire Adelaide Armagnac D'Espinose. (Oct. 1830)

De Touchelonge, Paul, of Philadelphia, vintner. Inventory 1794. [*Administration Act not found*].

Deupie, Sarah, of Carolina. Administration to the sister, Catharine Coatsworth, widow. (Aug. 1715).

Deveaux, Andrew, of Red Hook Township, Duchess County, New York. Administration to Daniel Davies, attorney for the relict, Anne Maria Deveaux, in New York. (June 1813).

Deverall alias Deverell, Benjamin, formerly of Bristol but late of Virginia. Probate to the relict, Rachel Deverall, and to Jeremy Deverall, with similar powers reserved to the other executors. (Feb. 1720). Revoked and administration granted to the daughter, Rachel, wife of John Russell, with similar powers reserved to William Bronough and Samuel Matthews. (Aug. 1730). Copy of will at PROB 20/2896 with deposition by the nephew, William Morgan of Bristol.

Devereux, Olivia Camilla, of Port Augusta, America, spinster. Administration to the mother, Sarah Devereux. (Dec. 1804).

Devine alias Devin, Magdalen, formerly of Philadelphia but late of Holborn, Middlesex, relict of George Devine. Sentence for validity of the will and probate granted to the sister, Elizabeth Wade, spinster. (Nov. 1785).

Devisme, Peter, of New York City, bachelor. Administration to the sister, Elizabeth Beaufile Duval; the mother, Ann Devisme, having been cited but not having appeared. (Apr. 1781).

Devonald, Thomas, of Philadelphia. Probate to William Rees and John Napier with similar powers reserved to the brother, George Devonald. (Feb. 1794).

Devonshire, William, Earl of, of St. Botolph Bishopsgate, London, who had shares in Virginia. Probate to the relict, Christian, Duchess of Devonshire. (July 1628).

Dewar, John, of St. Michael Crooked Lane, London, who died in Quitto,

Dewar, *(contd.)*
Virginia, bachelor. Administration to the principal creditor, Raphael Whistler. (June 1686).

Dewell, Edward, of Warwick Squeak, Virginia, who died overseas. Administration to the brother, Humphrey Dewell. (June 1637). Revoked on production of a will and probate granted to Simon Curnocke. (Nov. 1640). Sh.Wi.

Dewin, Richard, of St. Botolph Aldgate, London, whose kinswoman, Sarah Cowley, was in Virginia. Probate to the relict, Alice Dewin. (Sep. 1647). Wi.

Dick, Alexander, of South Carolina, widower. Administration to George Mackenzie, attorney for the father, George Dick, in Airth, Stirling, Scotland. (Jan. 1742).

Dick, Mathew, of Stepney, Middlesex, who died in Virginia. Administration to the relict, Mary Dick. (Nov. 1726).

Dickenson, Michael, of Altrincham, Cheshire, whose nephew, James Talier, was in Virginia. Probate to Michael Colley with similar powers reserved to Hugh Colley. (May 1698).

Dickins, Grace. *See* **Tunstall.**

Dickinson, Francis, of Northam, Devon, mariner, (bound to Virginia). Administration with will to Richard Draper, uncle and guardian during their minority of Laurence and Philip Dickinson. (Sep. 1630).

Dickinson, Nathaniel, formerly of Deerfield, Massachusetts, but late of King's County, New Brunswick. Limited administration with will to Robert Shedden, attorney for Benjamin Minison Woolsey and the relict, Hannah Dickinson. (July 1789).

Dickson. *See* **Dixon.**

Diggs, Edward, of Virginia. Probate to the relict, Elizabeth Diggs. (June 1686). Wi.

Dinwiddie, Robert, formerly of Virginia but late of the City of Bath. Probate to John Hyndman and John Hunter with similar powers reserved to Robert Scott. (Oct. 1770). Wi.

Dison *See* **Dyson.**

Dittrich, Rudolph Moritz, of Tampico, Mexico, and of New Orleans, merchant. Administration to the relict, Jane Louisa Dittrich. (Mar. 1851).

Dickeson, Andrew, of St. Mary Magdalene, Bermondsey, Surrey, who died in Virginia, bachelor. Administration to the principal creditor, Mary Willys. (Aug. 1681).

Dixon, John, of Bristol, whose son, Rev. John Dixon, was Minister of Kingston parish, Gloucester County, Virginia. Probate to the relict, Ann Dixon, with similar powers reserved to the sons, John Dixon and Lionel Dixon. (Dec. 1758). Revoked and granted to the surviving executor, John Dixon. (Apr. 1772). Wi.

Dixon, Jonas, of the ship *Preservation*, who died in Virginia. Probate to Sarah Yates with similar powers reserved to Richard Yates. (Mar. 1699).

Dixon, Miles, of Virginia. Administration to the brother, Robert Dixon. (July 1660).

Dickson, Nicholas, formerly of York Town, Virginia, but late of Bristol. Administration to the relict, Charlotte Dickson. (Apr. 1770).

Dixon, Richard, of Potoxon, Virginia, merchant, bachelor. Probate to the younger brother, William Dixon. (Jan. 1711).

Dixon, Roger, of Bristol, accountant and victualler, who had estate in Virginia. Probate to the relict, Ann Dixon. (Mar. 1747). Wi.

Dickson, Thomas, of Boston, New England, mariner of H.M. ships *Worcester*, *Gibraltar* and *Hawk*. Inventory 1751. [*Administration Act not found*].

Dixon, Thomas, formerly of the Orphan House, Christ Church parish, Georgia, but late of St. Botolph Aldgate, London, widower. Probate to the sister and only next-of-kin, Ann Adams, widow; the wife, Mary Dixon, having died in the testator's lifetime. (Oct. 1773).

Dickson, William, of Virginia, bachelor. Administration to the brother, Robert Dickson. (Oct. 1686).

Dickson, William, of Norfolk, Virginia. Probate to the relict, Angeline Mallory Dickson, the brother, Thomas Southgate, and to John Southgate. (July 1823).

Dobbie, George, of London, mariner, who had lands in Halifax County, Virginia. Probate to Thomas Main and Robert Howden with similar powers reserved to John Hyndman, Edward Staple, Robert Shedden and John Brockenburgh. (Apr. 1776). Wi.

Dobbs, Arthur, Governor of North Carolina. Probate to the son, Conway Richard Dobbs, with similar powers reserved to the relict, Justina Dobbs, and the son, Edward Brice Dobbs. (June 1766).

Dobbyn, Richard, of Carrick, County Tipperary, Ireland, who died in Savannah, Georgia. Administration with will to the relict, Anastasia Dobbyn; the named executor, Edward Somerville, having died. (May 1770).

Dobridge, Robert, of Orange, New Jersey, widower. Administration to James Hoppe, attorney for the daughter, Sarah Ann Dobridge, in Orange. (June 1846).

Dobson, Samuel, of New England, who died in Holborn, Middlesex, bachelor. Administration to the principal creditor, John Stevens. (Apr. 1690).

Docker, Elizabeth Smith, nee Elizabeth Smith Shakspear, formerly of Fillongley and afterwards of Birmingham, Warwickshire, but late of Commerce, Scott County, Missouri. Limited administration with will to William Wilmot, attorney for the husband, William Docker, in Missouri. (Dec. 1855).

Docker, Timothy Strickland, formerly of Birmingham, Warwickshire, but late of New Orleans, bachelor. Administration to the brother, William Docker. (Apr. 1839).

Docker, William, of Commerce, Scott County, Missouri, widower. Administration to the nephew, William Alcock. (Nov. 1857).

Dodd, James, master of the merchant ships *Nancy* and *Holbeach*, and late of

Dodd, *(contd.)* Boston, North America, widower. Administration to Robert Wild, administrator to the father, William Dodd deceased, and attorney for the mother, Margaret Dodd, in Berwick-upon-Tweed. (Mar. 1774).

Dodsworth, Sarah Mary, of Marietta, Washington County, United States of America. Administration to the husband, Thomas Dodsworth. (Oct. 1854).

Doherty, Constantine, of New York, surgeon on half pay of Major Gorman's Regiment of Rangers, bachelor. Administration to the mother, Mary Doherty, widow. (Dec. 1766).

Dolbeare, Grizzle, of Boston, Massachusetts, spinster. Administration to the niece, Hannah Rebecca Dolbeare. (Sep. 1828).

Dolbery, Andrew, of New England, who died in France, widower. Administration to Avis Coombes, spinster, the niece by a sister. (Aug. 1694).

Dolding, Richard, of H.M. ship *Monmouth*, who died in Boston, New England. Administration to the sister and next-of-kin, Africa Chare, widow. (July 1712).

Dolphin, John, of Frederick, Georgia, bachelor. Probate to Martha, wife of Alexander Heron. (Aug. 1745).

Domelaw, Richard, who died overseas having goods in Virginia. Administration with will to the brother, John Domelaw, bachelor of theology; no executor having been named. (Sep. 1624). Sh.

Doncett, John, of Annapolis Royal, America, widower. Administration to Frances Weedon, widow, guardian of the children, Henry, Mary, John, Hugh, and Frances Doncett. (Apr. 1727).

Donkester, William, of the merchant ship *Henrietta*, who died in Boston, New England, bachelor. Probate to Judith, wife of William Cooke. (Dec. 1730).

Donning, William, of Lidney, Gloucestershire, whose cousin, William Donning, was in South Carolina. Probate to the relict, Joanna Donning. (Feb. 1744). *See* NGSQ 65/136.

Douglass, John, formerly of St. Augustine, East Florida, but late of Crooked Island, Bahamas. Administration with will to John Malleson, attorney for the brother, Benjamin Douglass, in Providence Island; the brother, David Douglass, the sisters, Ann Douglass and Katherine Smith, and John Graham having died. (June 1820).

Douglas alias Hamilton, Joseph, of St. Paul's parish, Baltimore, Maryland. Administration to Rachel Crispin, widow, attorney for the relict, Rachel Douglas alias Reachel Dugles, in Baltimore County. (Mar. 1774). Revoked and granted by his solemn affirmation to John Blake, attorney for the only child, George Crispin Douglas, in Maryland. (Nov. 1791).

Douglass, Samuel, formerly of Savannah, Georgia, but late of Jamaica. Limited probate to William Douglass, Samuel McClymont and Hugh McClymont, with similar powers reserved to Samuel Douglass, James Gordon and Alexander Gordon. (Dec. 1800). Revoked and granted to Rev. James Black, Minister of Penningham, Wigtownshire, Rev. John

Douglass, *(contd.)* Sibbald, Minister of Kirmabreck, Kirkudbright, and William McCullock. (Apr. 1823).

Douglas, Sholto, of the merchant ship *St. George*, who died in North America. Administration with will to Robert Mackoun, attorney for John Daiglish in New York. (Apr. 1759).

Douglas, Susanna. *See* **Allman**.

Douglas, William, of Boston, New England, doctor of physick, bachelor. Administration to the sister, Catherine Kerr. (Apr. 1753).

Dover, John, of St. Olave, Southwark, Surrey, who died in New England. Administration to the relict, Hannah Dover. Marked "pauper." (Feb. 1718).

Dover, William, of the merchant ship *Old Neptune*, who died in Virginia, bachelor. Probate to the sister, Anne Dover; the father, Thomas Dover, having died. (Dec. 1706).

Dow, Alexander, of Plymouth, Massachusetts, who died on H.M. ship *Montague*. Administration to William Fletcher, attorney for the relict, Sarah Dow, in Plymouth. (Mar. 1750).

Downe, Abraham, formerly of Wimbish, Essex, but late of Maryland. Probate to the relict, Elizabeth Downe. (Apr. 1734).

Downe, Nicholas, of St. Margaret, Westminster, Middlesex, whose niece, Joane Downe, was in Virginia. Probate to the relict, Ann Downe. (May 1653). Sh.Wi.

Downe, William, of Boston, New England. Administration to Thomas Downe, attorney for the relict, Sarah Downe, in Boston. (Sep. 1753).

Downey, Margaret and Mary, formerly of 6 Torr's Terrace, Rotherhithe, Surrey, spinsters, who died on passage to New York in the American ship *Charles Bartlett*. Limited administration to the cousin german once removed, Justin McCartley. (Sep. 1849).

Downing, John, of St. Clement Danes, Middlesex, whose daughter, Abigail, might go to Virginia. Probate to the sons, Richard and Francis Downing. (July 1623). Wa.

Downman, Ellen, formerly Ellen Chichester, of Lancaster County, Virginia. Administration to the husband, William Downman. (Nov. 1763).

Downman, Frances, of Lancaster County, Virginia, widow. Administration to the son, Joseph Ball Downman. (Sep. 1782).

Downman, Rawleigh, of Christ Church, Lancaster County, Virginia. Limited probate to the son, Joseph Ball Downman. (Sep. 1782).

Dowsing, Ann, formerly of New Broad Street, London, but late of New York, spinster. Administration to the niece and next-of-kin, Elizabeth Kirby, spinster. (Feb. 1825).

Doyley, Cope the elder, of Virginia, widower. Administration to Robert Doyley, guardian of the sons, Charles and Cope Doyley. (Jan. 1706). Revoked and granted to the son, Charles Doyley. (June 1713).

Doyley, Cope the younger, of Virginia, bachelor. Administration to the brother, Charles Doyley. (June 1713). Revoked on his death and granted to the uncle and next-of-kin, Sekeford Cage. (Nov. 1714).

Drake, Francis, of Esher, Surrey, whose cousin, John Drake, was to be sent to New England. Probate to the son, Francis Drake, with similar powers reserved to John White. (May 1634). Wa.

Draper, Elizabeth, of St. Clement Eastcheap, London, widow, whose son-in-law, Abraham Peirsey, was in Virginia. Probate to Thomas Guye, attorney for Richard Berisford and Michael Warryner. (Sep. 1625). Wi.

Drew, James, of New York City, Captain in the Royal Navy. Administration with will to the principal creditor, Stephen Drew. (Aug. 1802). Revoked by decree and granted to Rev. Lucius Coglan and Benjamin Samuel Judah, attornies for Lydia Beckman alias Drew, wife of James Beckman, in New York City; the executors Charles Watkins having died and Samuel Watkins renouncing. (June 1803).

Drexhagen, Jane, formerly Jane Medland, widow, formerly of Holsworthy, Devon, but late of New York City. Administration with will to Henry Henrichsen, attorney for the husband, Arend alias Aaron Drexhagen, in New York City. (Aug. 1856).

Driffill, John, of Pon Pon, South Carolina. Administration with will to Moyer Thomas, attorney for Sarah Ross, a child of the sister, Elizabeth, wife of George Burks, in Hull, Yorkshire; the executors, Lewis Morris and Henry Mulholland, having been cited but not having appeared. (June 1797).

Dring, Stephen, of Deptford, Kent, who died in Virginia. Administration to the relict, Patience Dring. (Mar. 1675).

Driver, Thomas, of Salem, Massachusetts, seaman of H.M. ship *Goliath*. Administration to George Bainbridge, attorney for the relict, Rebecca Driver, in Salem. (Oct. 1800).

Driver, William, of Virginia, bachelor. Administration to the father, Edward Driver. (Apr. 1681).

Drummond, Robert, of New York. Administration to the relict, Elizabeth Drummond. (Feb. 1718).

Drumond, William, of Virginia. Administration to the relict, Sarah Drumond. (Oct. 1677).

Drumont, James, of Virginia, bachelor. Probate to Christian Mustard. (Feb. 1667).

Drury, Edward, Captain of the 63rd Regiment of Foot, who died in Philadelphia, bachelor. Administration with will to James Callaghan, attorney for the brother, James Drury, in New York. (Jan. 1779).

Drysdale, Hon. Hugh, Lieutenant-Governor of Virginia, who died in Virginia. Probate to the relict, Hester Drysdale. (Dec. 1726).

Drysdall, William, of Boston, New England, and seaman of H.M. ships *Rye* and *Stafford*. Administration to Robert Hewes, attorney for the relict, Eleanor Drysdall, in Boston. (July 1750).

Duane, Dennis, of St. Benet Fink, London, who died in Maryland. Administration to the relict, Winifred Duane. (Nov. 1739).

Du Bois, Walter, of New York. Administration with will to William Jackson and Henry Jackson, attornies for the nephew and niece, Gualtherus Du Bois and Margaret, wife of John Du Bois, in New York City. (Apr. 1793).

Duche, Jacob, formerly of Philadelphia but late of Lambeth, Surrey. Probate to the son, Rev. Jacob Duche, and the grandson, Thomas Spence Duche, with similar powers reserved to Andrew Doz, Joseph Swift and Myers Fisher. (Oct. 1788).

Ducheman, Francis Christopher Ambrose, of Baltimore County, Maryland. Probate to the relict, Margaret Moujent Ducheman, and the daughter, Frances Susanna, wife of Jacob Crawford. (July 1826).

Duck, Thomas, clerk of H.M. Stores in New York. Probate to the surviving executor, Duncan Drummond. (Feb. 1778)

Dudgeon, Patrick. *See* **Townsend**.

Dudley, Charles, formerly of Charlestown, South Carolina, afterwards of Newport, Rhode Island, but late of Christ Church, Surrey. Administration to the brother and creditor, Thomas Dudley; the relict, Catherine Dudley, and the only children, Charles Edward Dudley and Mary Ann Dudley, having been cited but not having appeared. (Aug. 1790).

Dudley, Mary Ann Sarah, of 398 Pearl Street, New York City. Administration to the husband, Ellis William Dudley. (June 1854).

Dudley, Thomas, of New England, bachelor. Administration to the father, Joseph Dudley. (Nov. 1696).

Duffy, Francis Thomas, of New York City, bachelor. Administration to Peter Franklin Duffy, son and administrator of the father, Peter Duffy. (Sep. 1841).

Duffy, Peter, of New York City, widower. Administration to the son, Peter Franklin Duffy. (Sep. 1841).

Dugdale, John, of Boston, New England, bachelor. Administration to the brother, Thomas Dugdale. (Feb. 1702).

Dulany, Rebecca, of Newport, Rhode Island, widow. Administration with will to Ann Dulany, executrix of the son, Daniel Dulany deceased. (May 1826).

Dummer, Elizabeth, of Littleton, New England, spinster. Administration to Thomas Hutchinson, attorney for the mother, Elizabeth, wife of Rev. Daniel Rogers, in New England. (Aug. 1741).

Dummer, Jeremiah, agent for Massachusetts and Connecticut, who made a bequest to Elizabeth Burr in Charlestown, Massachusetts. Probate to Francis Wicks and Samuel Storke. (June 1739). *See* NGSQ 64/218.

Dummer, Thomas, of North Stoneham, Hampshire, whose daughter, Margaret Clements, was in New England. Probate to the kinsmen, John and Stephen Dummer, with similar powers reserved to Stephen Penton. (Nov. 1650). Wa.

Dumotier, James, of London, merchant, whose nephew, —— Gardon, was in Carolina. Probate to the relict, Judith Dumotier, with similar powers reserved to Theodore Marnasse and John Raynold. (Feb. 1715). Revoked and granted to James Dumotier of St. Paul Covent Garden, Middlesex. (Nov. 1722).

Du Moulin, James, of Baltimore, Maryland. Limited probate to the brother, Andrew Joseph Aloysius Du Moulin. (Dec. 1821).

Dunant, George John, of New York, bachelor. Administration to the

Dunant, *(contd.)* creditor, Charles Robert Sparrow; the father, James Dunant, renouncing. (Dec. 1821).

Dunbar, George, of Queen's County, New York, Captain on half pay of the First Batallion of Brigadier-General De Lancey's Provincials. Administration to David Davies, attorney for the relict, Elizabeth Dunbar, in Queen's County. (Dec. 1807).

Dunbar, James, Captain of the Third Batallion of the Royal Regiment of Artillery, who died in New York. Probate to the brother, William Dunbar. (Oct. 1783).

Dunbar, Tryphene. *See* **Morel.**

Duncan, George, of Charles Town, South Carolina, bachelor. Administration to the creditor, Robert Steell; the mother, Mary Duncan, widow, and the sister, Margaret Bradly, widow, renouncing. (May 1784).

Dunkan, John, of the merchant ship *Society*, who died in Virginia. Probate to Elizabeth, wife of David Browne. (Aug. 1714).

Duncombe, Susanna. *See* **Johnson.**

Dunkin, Anthony Parker and Henry, formerly of Bermondsey, Surrey, afterwards of Morganfield, Kentucky, but late of Philadelphia, bachelors. Administration to the brother, Zebedee Dunkin. (June 1826).

Dunkin, John, formerly of Aldersgate Street, London, but late of New York and Philadelphia. Administration to the son, John Dunkin; the relict, Mary Dunkin, having died. (Nov. 1840).

Dunkin, Roberts, of Philadelphia, Lieutenant of H.M. ship *Milford*. Administration to the relict, Ann Dunkin. (Dec. 1784).

Dunkley, Carleton, of Charleston, America, bachelor. Administration to the sister, Mary, wife of John Rudd. (Oct. 1817).

Dunn, Charles, of Captain John Williams' Independent Company, who died in Annapolis Royal. Administration by decree to the principal creditor, Richard Roberts. (Feb. 1722).

Dunn, John, of the ship *Resolution*, who died at sea, bachelor. Administration to the principal creditrix, Margaret, wife of Edward Pratt in New England. (Sep. 1686).

Dunn, Joseph, of St. Olave, Southwark, Surrey, who died in Maryland. Probate to the relict, Elizabeth Dunn. (Apr. 1718).

Dunn, Nathan, of Philadelphia and Mount Holly, New Jersey, who died in Vevay, Switzerland. Limited probate to Samuel Gurney the younger. (May 1845).

Dunn, Walter, of Middlesex, Virginia. Limited administration to the father, William Dunn. (Apr. 1820).

Dunn, William, formerly of Bristol, mason, but late of New York. Probate to the sister, Jane, wife of William Muggleworth, formerly Jane Locoak, widow. (Apr. 1842).

Dunster, Charles, of New Jersey, bachelor. Probate to John MacCulloch alias Maculah and John Boughton, with similar powers reserved to James Alexander and Michael Kearney. (Apr. 1732).

Dunton, John, formerly of New England but late of Stepney, Middlesex, citizen and stationer of London. Probate to Richard Rowland. (Mar. 1733). Revoked on his death and administration granted to the creditor, Thomas Danack. (June 1744).

Dunton, Thomas, of Boston, New England, seaman. Probate to James Downing. (Nov. 1707).

Dupee, Elias, of Boston, New England, shipwright of the ship *Adventure*. Copy of will dated 30 August 1752 appointing his father, Daniel Dupee and brother, Benjamin Dupee, as executors. (PROB 20/816).

Dupont, Gideon, of Charles Town, South Carolina, widower. Administration to the daughter and next-of-kin, Mary, wife of John Collett. (Sep. 1788).

Durant, Thomas, of Captain Richard Bradshaigh's Company of Marines commanded by Colonel Cornwall, and late of H.M. ship *Rye*, who died in South Carolina, bachelor. Administration to the brother, Anthony Durant. (Apr. 1744).

Durford, William, of St. Saviour, Southwark, Surrey, who died in Virginia. Administration to the relict, Elizabeth Durford. (Sep. 1646).

Durly, William, of Nansemond, Virginia, who died in St. Martin in the Fields, Middlesex. Administration to William Parker, attorney for the relict, Mary Durly, in Nansemond. (Nov. 1741). Revoked on his death and granted to James Stockdale as attorney. (Dec. 1753).

Durrance, John, of St. Anne's, Westminster, Middlesex, surgeon on a merchant ship, who died in Virginia. Administration to the principal creditrix, Sarah Landman; the relict, Mary Durrance, renouncing. (Jan. 1705).

Durston, Elizabeth. formerly of Catcott, Somerset, but late of Palmyra, Jefferson County, Wisconsin. Administration to Joseph Ruscombe Poole, attorney for the husband, Edmund Durston, in Palmyra. (Dec. 1856).

Dyer, Robert, of Mock Jack Bay, Virginia, bachelor. Administration to the sister and next-of-kin, Sarah, wife of John Mercer. (Sep. 1718).

Dyre, William, of Sussex County, Pennsylvania. Probate to the son, William Dyre, with similar powers reserved to the relict, Mary Dyre. (Sep. 1690). Wa.

Dyson, Charles, mariner of H.M. ship *Hastings*, but late in hospital in Rochester, Kent, whose brother, Philip Dyson, was in Virginia. Probate to John Dyson. (Jan. 1746).

Dyson, Rev. Edward, late Fellow of Peterhouse College, Cambridge, who died in Savannah, Georgia, bachelor. Administration to the brother, John Dyson. (July 1740).

Dison, John, of St. Ann, Middlesex, whose cousins, Philip and Francis Dison, were in Norfolk, Virginia. Probate to the relict, Priscilla Dison, and to Joseph Besse and Silvanus Greville. (Nov. 1747). *See* NGSQ 64/285.

E

Eackman, Martin, of H.M. ship *Bredah*, bachelor. Administration to Elizabeth, wife of the principal creditor in Virginia, Peter Rowlandson. (Dec. 1704).

Eades, John, of New England. Probate to George Hallam with similar powers reserved to Winifred Hall. (Sep. 1698).

Earle, Joseph, formerly midshipman of H.M. sloop *Swift*, afterwards Ensign of the 44th Regiment of Foot, who died in New York, bachelor. Administration to Thomas Courtney, attorney for the creditor, James Courtney, in Shelburne, Nova Scotia; the sister and only next-of-kin, Mary Earle, renouncing. (Oct. 1785 & May 1786).

Eastall, William, of Virginia, who died at sea. Administration to the relict, Anne Mayo alias Eastall. (Jan. 1668).

Easton, Peter, of Nantucket, Massachusetts. Probate to the relict, Janice Easton. (Sep. 1819).

Eaton, Benony, of Bermondsey, Surrey, who had lands in Virginia. Probate to the relict, Deborah Eaton. (May 1677). Wi.

Eaves, Thomas, of Philadelphia, widower. Administration to the daughter, Ann, wife of Henry Smith. (Aug. 1709).

Eckley, John, of Philadelphia. Administration with will to James Lewis, Peregrine Musgrave and Richard Stafford, executors of the relict, Sarah Eckley deceased. (Feb. 1699).

Eckley, Sarah, of Philadelphia. Probate to James Lewis, Peregrine Musgrave and Richard Stafford. (Dec. 1698).

Edds, William, of Colonel Holt's Regiment, bachelor. Administration by decree to the principal creditor, Robert Hood. Marked "pauper." (July 1722).

Eddy, Caspar Wistar, of New York. Limited administration with will to Joseph Jackson Lister, attorney for the relict, Cornelia Eddy, and for Benjamin Roosevelt Kissam and Richard Vanck Kissam, in New York. (Nov. 1838).

Ede, John, of North Carolina, who died in Cork, Ireland. Administration with will to the creditor, Paul Henry Robinson; the brother, Richard Ede, renouncing. (Sep. 1760).

Eden, Thomas, of H.M. ship *Stork*, who died in West Florida, bachelor. Administration to Samuel Inman, attorney for the sister and next-of-kin, Elizabeth, wife of John Stovey, in Acklam, Yorkshire. (July 1788).

Edgar, John, of Maryland. Administration to John Eglesham, attorney for the relict, Mary, now wife of John Hampton. (Jan. 1711).

Edge, John, of Holborn, Middlesex, who died in Boston, New England. Probate to the sister, Martha Darby alias Comby. (Feb. 1724).

Edie, George, of Virginia, Ensign on half pay of the 96th Regiment of Foot, widower. Administration to the brother, John Edie. (May 1781).

Edmonds, Benjamin the younger, of Boston, Massachusetts. Probate to Albert Dennie, attorney for the relict, Rebecca, now wife of Moses

Edmonds, *(contd.)* Penniman, in Braintree, New England. (June 1741).

Edmonds, James, of Boston, New England, bachelor. Administration to the father, Edward Edmonds. (June 1677).

Edmonds, John, formerly of Collingbourne Abbots, Wiltshire, but who died in Virginia, bachelor. Probate to George Blanchard. (July 1672).

Edmonds, John, of Philadelphia, bachelor. Administration to the brother, Joseph Edmonds. (Jan. 1776).

Edwards, Ann, of Charles Town, South Carolina, spinster. Administration to the brother and next-of-kin, Alexander Edwards. (July 1789).

Edwards, David, of Boston, New England. Probate to Edward Hill, attorney for the relict, Mary Edwards, in Boston. (July 1698).

Edwards, Henry, of the ship *Dove*, who died in Virginia. Administration to the cousin german and next-of-kin, Christopher Goulding. (June 1656).

Edwards, John, of London, who died in Virginia. Probate to Spencer Piggott. (Nov. 1668). Wi.

Edwards, Richard, formerly of Bradforton, Worcestershire, but late of Eaton Town [?Edenton], North Carolina. Probate to Henry Murcott with similar powers reserved to William Daniel. (Dec. 1757).

Edwards, Sweet, of New England, who died at sea, bachelor. Administration to Thomas Blettso, attorney for the mother, Mary Edwards, in New England. (Oct. 1705).

Eells, Hannah, of Hanover, Massachusetts, widow. Administration to Joseph Paice, attorney for the sons, Robert Lenthall Eells and William Witherall Eells, in Hanover. (June 1792).

Eeles, Nathaniel, of Harpenden, Hertfordshire, whose son, John Eeles, was in Virginia. Probate to the relict, Sarah Eeles. (Feb. 1678). Wa.

Efford, Peter, of Newington, Surrey, who had lands in Virginia. Probate by decree to Rev. John Weldon and Albert Skinner. (Oct. 1665). Wi.

Egan, Stephen, formerly of St. John's River, East Florida, but late of Dominica, widower. Administration to Robert Payne, attorney for the son, Stephen Egan, in Dominica. (Aug. 1789).

Eggleston, Hezekiah, of Boston, New England, widower. Administration to the son, Samuel Eggleston. (Aug. 1744).

Eilbeck, John, a partner in Eilbeck, Chambre, Ross & Co. of Whitehaven, Cumberland, who had personal estate in America. Limited administration with will to the only surviving child, Mary Eilbeck. (July 1821).

Eilbeck, Jonathan, formerly a partner in Eilbeck, Chambre, Ross & Co. of Whitehaven, Cumberland, but late of Norfolk, Virginia. Limited probate to Peter Hodgson with similar powers reserved to the nephew, Rev. Jonathan Benson. (July 1821).

Eisdell, Thomas, formerly of Cornwall Road, Lambeth, Surrey, but late of Lasalle, Illinois, bachelor. Administration to the brother, Robert Eisdell. (Aug. 1842).

Elam, Joseph, of Philadelphia, bachelor. Administration to the brother

Elam, *(contd.)* and only next-of-kin, Emanuel Elam. (Jan. 1794).

Elam, Samuel, formerly of Leeds, Yorkshire, merchant, but late of Rhode Island. Administration with will to the brothers, Gervas and Robert Elam. (Feb. 1815).

Elbridge, John, of Bristol, merchant, who had goods in New England. Probate to Nathaniel Cale with similar powers reserved to the brother, Thomas Elbridge. (Oct. 1646). Sh.Wa.

Elbridge, John, of Bristol whose sisters, Rebecca Sanders and Elizabeth Russell, were in New England. Probate to Hon. John Scrope, John Cosens and Samuel Creswicke. (Mar. 1739). *See* NGSQ 60/185.

Elbrow, John. of Maryland, who died on the merchant ship *Dover*. Administration to the relict, Anne, now wife of Richmond Eaton. (Dec. 1709).

Eldred, William, of Bermondsey, Surrey, who died in Virginia. Administration to the relict, Ruth Eldred. (Mar. 1660). Revoked on her death and granted to the daughter, Sarah, wife of Iziaker Daldy, now overseas. (Feb. 1683).

Elkin, Elizabeth, of Barbados, who died in Virginia, spinster. Administration to the brother, John Elkin. (Aug. 1752).

Ellaway, Edward, formerly of Surinam but late of New York. Administration with will to the sister, Philly Maria, wife of John McCall; the executor, Jonathan Rudge, having died. (Jan. 1816).

Ellens, Sarah Elizabeth, of Pass Christian, Louisiana, widow. Administration to the sister and only next-of-kin, Emm, wife of John Hester. (June 1845).

Ellerston, James. *See* **Elliott**.

Elletson, Goodin, of North Carolina. Probate to Edward Fuhr and George Hibbert with similar powers reserved to Thomas Hibbert. (Mar. 1790).

Ellice, George. *See* **Ellis**.

Elliott, Andrew, formerly of Senegambia, Africa, but late of Savannah, Georgia. Probate to John Ross and Thomas Davies. (Jan. 1775).

Elliot, Andrew, Major of Marines, who died in Rhode Island, bachelor. Administration to the brother, Gavin Elliot; the mother, Katharine Elliot, renouncing. (Sep. 1778).

Elliot, George, who died overseas, mariner, (bound for Virginia in the ship *Accomack*). Probate to Elizabeth Corbin. (July 1665).

Elliott, Gray, formerly of Georgia but late of St. Margaret, Westminster, Middlesex. Probate to the relict, Mary Elliott. (July 1787).

Elliott alias Ellerston, James, of H.M. ship *Russell*, bachelor. Administration to Jane, wife and attorney of the brother, Niels Ellerston, in Philadelphia. (Apr. 1754).

Elliott, John, of North Carolina. Administration to the son, Bartholomew Elliott. (June 1738).

Eliot, John, Governor of West Florida, bachelor. Administration to the brother and next-of-kin, Edward Eliot. (July 1769).

Elliott, William, of St. James, Westminster, Middlesex, who died at

Elliott, *(contd.)*
Annapolis Royal. Administration to the relict, Mary Elliott. (Mar. 1712).

Ellice, George, of Philadelphia, bachelor. Administration to John Black, clerk, attorney for the brother, William Ellice, in Scotland. (Jan. 1753).

Ellis, Griffith, of Clynnog, Caernarvon, who died in America, bachelor. Administration to John Owen, guardian of the nephew, Thomas Ellis. (Jan. 1732).

Ellis, James, Lieutenant in General Francis Nicholson's Regiment, formerly of St. Margaret, Westminster, Middlesex, who died near New York. Administration to the relict, Anne Ellis. (Jan. 1717).

Ellis, John, of Virginia. Probate to William Jordan with the consent of the brother, Henry Ellis, and with similar powers reserved to Liveing Denwood, Richard Bayley and Stephen Horsey. (June 1659).

Ellis, John, paymaster-sergeant of the 10th Regiment, who died at Bunkers Hill, North America, bachelor. Administration to the sister and next-of-kin, Margaret Ellis. (Jan. 1785).

Ellison, Ellen, formerly of New York City but late of Williamsburgh, New York. Administration with will to John Frederick Isaacson, attorney for the nephew, Joseph Ellison Palmer, in Williamsburgh. (Nov. 1852).

Ellison, Robert, Lieutenant-Colonel of a Regiment of Foot, who died in Albany, North America. Probate to the brother, Hon. Major-General Cuthbert Ellison, with similar powers reserved to the brother, Henry Ellison. (June 1756).

Elliston, Robert, Controller of Customs in New York Province. Administration to Abraham Maddock, clerk, attorney for the relict, Mary Elliston, in New York. (Apr. 1759).

Ellixon. *See* **Alexon.**

Elsam, Dorothy, of New England, spinster. Administration to the sister and next-of-kin, Elizabeth, wife of Henry Bannister. (Jan. 1684).

Elsey, Nicholas, of Merstham, Surrey, whose brother, Nicholas (*sic*), was in New England. Probate to Michael Anscombe. (June 1649). Sh.

Elson, Samuel, of H.M. ship *Greyhound*, who died at Black Point, New England. Probate to Robert Harding. (Sep. 1707).

Elston, David, formerly of Carshalton, Surrey, but late of Morris, New Jersey. Probate to the son, David Elston, with similar powers reserved to William Britton and James Wood. (Oct. 1857).

Elwyn, Thomas Langdon, of Portsmouth, New Hampshire. Probate to the brother, William Brame Elwyn, with similar powers reserved to Samuel Pickering Gardner and to the relict, Elizabeth Langdon Elwyn. (Mar. 1818).

Emerson, Mary, of Bristol, Rhode Island, widow. Probate by his solemn declaration to Richard Partridge with similar powers reserved to Mary Vonheinen, widow. (Nov. 1748).

Emery, Ann, of Wappelow, Louisa County, Iowa, spinster. Administration to the brother, John Emery. (Feb. 1856).

Endicott, John, of Salem, New England. Probate to the relict, Anne Endicott. (Mar. 1695). Wa.

England, John, of Maryland. Probate by their solemn declaration to the sons, Allen and Joseph England. (Mar. 1739).

English, William Molesworth, formerly of Boston, North America, but late of Manchester, Lancashire, merchant. Limited administration with will to Richard Foster Breed with similar powers reserved to Aaron Stone. (Oct. 1816).

Ennis, Anne. *See* **Clymer**.

Ensigne, Thomas, of Cranbrooke, Kent, whose father, Thomas Ensigne, and brothers and sisters were in New England. Probate to the cousin, John Austen. (Mar. 1658). Sh.

Enton, John, of Virginia. Administration with will to John Smith; no executor having been named. (Jan. 1691).

Epes, Francis the elder, of Virginia. Administration to Micajah Perry, attorney for the son, Francis Epes, during his absence. (Oct. 1688).

Erving, George, formerly of Boston, New England, but late of St. George Hanover Square, Middlesex. Probate to the son and sole executor, George William Erving. (Mar. 1806).

Erving, John, of Boston, Massachusetts. Probate pending the production of the original will to the sons, John and George Erving, with similar powers reserved to James Bowdoin and Oliver Wendell alias Wardell. (Mar. 1787). ALC.

Erving, Mary Mackintosh, wife of George Erving, formerly of Boston, New England, but late of Froyle, Hampshire. Probate to the husband, George Erving, with similar powers reserved to Thomas Palmer. (Mar. 1787).

Escott, Gabriel, of St. Katherine Coleman Street, London, who died in South Carolina, widower. Administration to the aunt, Anna Loyd, widow. (Aug. 1741).

Ettricke, John, of Charles Town, Jamaica (*sic*). Administration to the mother, Isabella Ettricke. (Feb. 1766). Declared void and probate granted to the sister, Rachael Ettricke. (Feb. 1767).

Eva, Hannah, of Charles Town, South Carolina, spinster. Administration to the mother and next-of-kin, Mary Eva, widow. (Oct. 1771).

Evans, Anne, of St. Bartholomew, London, who died in Virginia or at sea, spinster. Administration to the cousin and next-of-kin, Norton Westrow. (June 1681).

Evans, Evan, of Satterton, Lincolnshire, who died in Maryland. Probate to John Brace. (Aug. 1727).

Evans, Joseph, of Salina, Onandaga County, New York, bachelor. Administration to the nephew, John Evans. (Feb. 1839).

Evans, Laurence, of St. Benet Fink, London, who died overseas having goods in Virginia. Administration to the principal creditor, Humphrey Streete; the relict, Rebecca Evans, renouncing. (Sep. 1642). Revoked on his death and granted to the relict, Rebecca Evans. (Aug. 1645).

Evans, Mary, of Bertie County, North Carolina, spinster. Administration to the brother, John Evans. (May 1794)

Evans, Phineas, of South Weald, Essex, whose cousin, Edward Collins, was in Virginia. Probate to Daniel Fox with similar powers reserved to Anna Taylor, spinster. (Mar. 1760). *See* NGSQ 64/213.

Evans, Richard, of Virginia. Administration to the relict, Sarah Evans. (Nov. 1673).

Evans, William, formerly of London, Canada, but late of Springfield, Ohio, widower. Administration to John Wickham Flower, attorney for the son, Robert Evans, in Paris, Canada. (June 1853).

Evans, William Henry, of Charleston, South Carolina, steam engineer. Administration to the relict, Eliza Ann Evans. (June 1833).

Eveleigh, Samuel, formerly of Charles Town, South Carolina, but late of Bristol. Administration with will to the son, Nicholas Eveleigh; the executors, Sir William Baker, George Austin, Benjamin Stead and George Eveleigh, renouncing. (Oct. 1766).

Evelyn, Martha B. *See* **Vincent**.

Everest alias Everist, Richard, of Georgia. Administration to the relict, Sarah, now wife of Laurence Dolan. (Feb. 1789).

Everigin, Catherine, of Virginia, spinster. Administration by his solemn affirmation to the brother, William Everigin. (Nov. 1698).

Evett alias Evit, Mary, of Boston, New England, widow. Administration to Joseph Jekyll, attorney for the mother, Joanna, wife of John Cutler, in New England. (Mar. 1744).

Evetts, James, of New York. Administration to the son, Nathaniel Evetts. (Apr. 1707).

Evill, Luke, formerly of Bath, Somerset, but late of Wilmington, Dearborn, North America. Limited administration to Henry Nethersole. (Jan. 1849).

Ewart, John, formerly of Berwick-upon-Tweed, but late of Albany, North America, bachelor. Administration to the sister, Elizabeth, wife of Bartholomew Mitchelson; the mother, Isabella Lanford, formerly Ewart, widow, having died. (May 1825).

Ewens, Edwin Erastus, of New York City, bachelor. Administration to the brother, John Samuel Ewens; the father, Daniel Ewens, renouncing. (Mar. 1846).

Ewens, William, of Greenwich, Kent, mariner, who had lands in Virginia. Probate to the relict, Mary Ewens, with similar powers reserved to the daughter, Mary Ewens, and to Thomas Stevens and Arnold Browne. (Aug. 1650). Sh.Wi.

Ewer, Mary. *See* **Parsons**.

Exter, John and Julia Margaret, of New York City, bachelor and spinster. Administration to the mother and next-of-kin, Dolores Soto de Beales, wife of John Charles de Beales, formerly Exter, widow. (Aug. 1852).

Eyres, Richard, of Bermondsey, Surrey, who made a bequest to Sarah Clapham in Virginia. Probate to the relict, Alice Eyres. (Feb. 1648). Wi.

F

Faber, Conrad William, of New York. Probate to Thomas Achelis with similar powers reserved to the relict, Emilia Faber, and to Christian H. Sands. (Aug. 1855).

Fabian, Edmund, of Holborn, Middlesex, whose son, Simon Fabian, was in Virginia. Probate to the son, Simon Fabian, and to Theophilus Smith and Christopher Pitt. (Aug. 1668). Wi.

Faesh, John, Captain of the 60th or Royal American Regiment. Administration to James Schweighauser, attorney for the relict, Elizabeth Faesh, in New York. (July 1767).

Fagg, Francis, of Philadelphia. Administration with will to the relict, Martha Fagg; the sole executor, James Sibborn, having died. (Dec. 1829).

Fairfax, Catherine, Lady, of Cameron, Scotland, who had lands in Virginia. Probate to William Cage. (June 1719).

Fairfax, George William, formerly of Truro, Fairfax County, Virginia, but late of Bath, Somerset. Special probate to the relict, Sarah Fairfax, and to Samuel Athewes, Robert Burton, John Maud, Joseph Beevers and Martin Bladen, Lord Hawke. (July 1787).

Falcon, Thomas, of Roxbury, Massachusetts. Limited administration with will to George Frazar with the consent of the relict, Bridget Falcon. (Sep. 1856).

Fawkner, Elizabeth, of Epsom, Surrey, whose uncles, Edward, Peter and Gersham Bulkley, were in New England. Probate to Stanley West and William Harris. (July 1720).

Fawconer, Francis, of Kingsclere, Hampshire, whose brother, Edward Fawconer, was in Virginia. Probate to Mathew Webber. (May 1663). Wa.

Falconer, Thomas, of Philadelphia, Captain of the 44th Regiment of Foot. Administration to William Neate, attorney for the relict, Sarah Falconer, in Philadelphia. (June 1767).

Faldo, Charles, of Yateley, Hampshire, who died in Carolina. Probate to William Palmer; the wife, Mary Faldo, having died in the testator's lifetime. (Apr. 1729).

Fananbrouse, John, of H.M. ship *Pembroke*, bachelor. Administration with will to Joseph Argent, attorney for Elizabeth Partridge in Boston, New England. (May 1750).

Fane, George, Captain of H.M. ship *Lowestoft*, who died in New York. Limited probate to the brother, Charles Fane. (Oct. 1709).

Faneuil, Andrew, of Boston, New England. Probate to the nephew, Peter Faneuil. (Sep. 1738).

Fanneuil, Benjamin, formerly of Boston, New England, but late of Bristol. Probate to Brook Watson and Robert Bashleigh. (May 1787).

Faneuil, Peter, of Boston, New England, bachelor. Administration to the brother, Benjamin Faneuil. (Dec. 1743).

Fanning, Robert, of [All Hallows] Barking, London, whose kinsman, John

Fanning, *(contd.)* Fanning, was in Virginia. Probate to John Burges. (July 1672). Wi.

Fargusion, Robert, of Kenton, Northumberland, and of the ship *Falkland*, who died in New England. Probate to George Wallis. (Feb. 1698).

Farley, Sarah, formerly of Edinburgh, Scotland, but late of Savannah, Georgia, spinster. Administration with will to Robert Cooper, attorney for the aunts, Sarah Drysdale, widow, Elizabeth Irvine, widow, and Rachel Johnston, spinster, in Savannah. (Oct. 1814).

Farley, Susanna, of St. Stephen Coleman Street, London, widow, whose daughter, Susanna, was wife of Charles Gregory of Virginia. Probate to John Shippey. (Apr. 1656). Wi.

Farmer, Jasper, formerly of New Jersey, afterwards of Barbados, but late of New York, Captain of the 21st Regiment of Foot. Administration to Effingham Lawrence, attorney for the relict, Susan Farmer, in New Jersey. (Mar. 1801).

Farmer, Richard, of Virginia, who died on the ship *Quaker Ketch* at sea, bachelor. Administration to the principal creditor, Daniel Porter. (May 1689).

Farmar, Robert, of Mobile, West Florida. Limited administration with will to the mother, Mary Farmar, widow, guardian of the children, Elizabeth Mary, Catharine Louisa, and John Theodore Farmar. (Aug. 1784).

Farmar, Samuel, of Norfolk, Virginia. Limited administration to William Innes, attorney for the relict, Susanna Farmar, in Norfolk. (Apr. 1791).

Farmar, Susan Ravand, of New York City, widow. Administration with will to Francis Martin, attorney for John Warren and Edward Martin in New York City. (Oct. 1841).

Farmer, William, of Lambeth, Surrey, who died on H.M. ship *Seaford* in South Carolina. Administration to the relict, Elizabeth Farmer. (Sep. 1739).

Farquharson, John, formerly of Charles Town, South Carolina, afterwards of Broad Street Buildings, London, but late of Aberdeen, Scotland, doctor of physick. Probate to the nephew, John Brown, and to Robert Irvine. (Jan. 1791).

Farr, Robert, of New Orleans, merchant, widower. Administration to the only child, Augustus Farr. (Jan. 1857).

Farr, Sarah. *See* **Scott**.

Farrant, Charlotte Caroline, of Belleville, New Jersey. Administration to the husband, Thomas Farrant. (May 1837).

Farrant, Henry, formerly of Lanton, Northumberland, but late of Schenectady, Albany County, New York, Lieutenant of a New York Independent Company under Captain John Gordon. Probate to John Steel with similar powers reserved to John Sanders. (July 1768).

Farrant, Thomas, of Skaneateles, Onadaga County, New York. Probate to the brother, William Farrant, with similar powers reserved to the relict, Mary Farrant. (Oct. 1855).

Farrell, Kennedy, barrack master for the Forts of Detroit and

Farrell, *(contd.)* Machillimachinac in North America, widower. Administration to the son, John Farrell, in Schenectady. (May 1771).

Farrell, Patrick, of H.M. ship *Jupiter*, who died in Long Island Hospital. Probate to James Mountgaritt. (Oct. 1783).

Farrer, Jane, of Doncaster, Yorkshire, widow, whose uncle, Richard Beale, was in Rhode Island. Probate to the uncle, George Beale, with similar powers reserved to the uncle, Samuel Beale, and the aunt, Alice Brown, widow. (May 1797).

Farrington, Charles, formerly of 8 Union Street, Kingsland Road, Middlesex, but late of the American brig *Herald*, who died in the Isle of France in 1817, bachelor. Limited administration to John Farrington, attorney for Joseph Farrington at 24 Rue de Villiers, Meuilly, France. (Mar. 1844).

Farrow, Benjamin, of London, whose daughter, Elizabeth Russell, was in Williamsburgh, Virginia. Probate to the relict, Elizabeth Farrow. (Apr. 1793).

Farrow, James, of St. Botolph Bishopsgate, London, a recruit for General Oglethorpe's Regiment of Foot in Georgia. Administration to the brother, William Farrow. (May 1748).

Farvacks, Daniel, of St. Giles Cripplegate, London, widower, who had assets in Virginia. Administration to the son, John Farvacks. (Oct. 1669).

Fary, Joseph, of Maryland, who died on the ship *James* in Virginia. Probate to the mother, Mary Fary, widow. (Nov. 1695).

Fassaker, Richard, of Stafford County, Virginia, who died on the ship *Rappahannock Merchant* at sea. Limited administration with will to Samuel Phillipps. (July 1676). Wi.

Fauquier, Hon. Francis, Lieutenant-Governor of Virginia. Limited probate to the son, Francis Fauquier. (Dec. 1771).

Fawconer. *See* **Falconer**.

Fawne, Luke, of St. Augustine, London, whose niece, Elizabeth Clement, daughter of his brother, John Fawne, was in New England. Probate to John Cresset with similar powers reserved to John Macock. (Mar. 1666). Wa.

Fawne, Thomas, [of Lincolnshire], who died abroad having goods in Virginia. Probate to John Young with similar powers reserved to John Stone. (Aug. 1652). Sh.Wa.Wi.

Fay, Julia Margaret, of New York City, spinster. Probate to Arthur Tracy Jones. (Apr. 1843).

Fear, Thomas, of H.M. ships *Sultan* and *Renown*, who died in Rhode Island Hospital. Administration with will to John Broom, administrator to the mother, Mary Brown deceased. (Mar. 1781).

Fearnley, Anthony, of Grenville's Camp, Ottoway River, United States of America, bachelor. Administration to the brother and only next-of-kin, John Fearnley. (Mar. 1848).

Fell, James, of the merchant ship *Dolphin*, who died in Virginia, bachelor. Administration to Mary Williams, wife and attorney of the principal

Fell, *(contd.)* creditor, Griffith Williams. (Aug. 1704).

Fellgate, Tobias, of Westover, Virginia. Probate to the relict, Sarah Fellgate. (Apr. 1635). Sh.Wa.

Fellowes, William, of St. Martin Vintry, London, who died in Virginia. Administration to the son, William Fellowes. (Apr. 1682).

Fenn, Benjamin, of New England, who died in Milford, Connecticut. Probate to the relict, Susan Fenn. (Feb. 1675). Wa.

Fenn, James, formerly of the Isle of Thanet, Kent, but late of Norfolk, Virginia, bachelor. Administration to the father, James Fenn. (Aug. 1794).

Fenn, Robert, of Wapping, Middlesex, mariner, whose wife was in New England. Probate to Thomas Bell and Mary Fenn. (Jan. 1656). Wa.

Fennell, James, formerly of New York but late of Philadelphia, comedian. Administration to the relict, Barbara Harriet Fennell. (Nov. 1817). Revoked on her death and granted to the daughter, Caroline Maria Fennell. (Oct. 1826).

Fenner, Ann, nee Ann Reeve, of Baltimore, United States of America. Administration to Alexander Cavell, attorney for the husband, Richard Sankey Fenner, in Baltimore. (Aug. 1848).

Fenner, Margaret, of Rochester, United States of America. Administration to the husband, John Fenner. (May 1854).

Fenninge, William, of St. Botolph Aldgate, London, (bound to Virginia). Probate to the relict, Margaret Fenninge. (July 1623). Wa.

Fenwick, George, of Warminghurst, Sussex, who had lands in New England. Probate to the daughter, Elizabeth Fenwick. (Apr. 1657). Wa.

Fenwicke, John, formerly of South Carolina but late of St. George Hanover Square, Middlesex. Probate to the daughter, Dowager Countess Delaraine, with similar powers reserved to Isaac Whittington and Edward Fenwicke. (July 1747).

Fenwick, Robert, Captain-Lieutenant of the Royal Regiment of Artillery, who died in New York. Administration with will to the relict, Ann Fenwick; the executors, Erasmus John Philipps and Robert George Bruce, having died before executing. (Mar. 1780). Revoked and administration granted to Robert Douglas, guardian of the only children, Robert George, William, and Thomas Howard Fenwick. (Jan. 1786).

Fenwick, William, of Boston, New England. Probate to the brother and surviving executor, Michael Fenwick. (May 1763).

Ferguson, Adam, of Newport, Rhode Island. Administration with will to James Cockburn, administrator of the daughter, Isabella Ambrose deceased, wife of Robert M. Ambrose, and attorney for the said Ambrose in Newport. (Feb. 1802).

Ferguson, Patrick, formerly Captain of the 17th Regiment, but late Major of the 71st Regiment, who died in Carolina. Probate to the brother, George Ferguson. (Aug. 1782)

Fernald, John, of New England, shipwright. Probate to George Rowe with similar powers reserved to Phoebe Rowe. (Oct. 1701).

Ferne, John, of St. Vedast Foster Lane, London, who had lands in Virginia. Probate to the son, Daniel Ferne. (Jan. 1620). Sh.Wa.

Ferne, John, of the ship *Catherine*, who died in Virginia, bachelor. Administration to Anne Allen, relict of the principal creditor, John Allen deceased. (Mar. 1680).

Fernsley, John, of H.M. ships *Lowestoft* and *Worcester*, who died in Boston Hospital, New England, bachelor. Probate to the sisters, Sarah Fernsley and Mary Crouchefer, widow. (Jan. 1749).

Ferrers, John, of New York City, merchant. Administration with will to James Stachan Glennie, attorney for Cadwallader D. Colden, Charles Wilkes, and the relict, Jane Anne Ferrers, in New York. (Apr. 1815).

Ferris, Samuel the younger, formerly of St. Thomas the Apostle, Devon, but late of Yazoo Valley, Mississippi, surgeon and apothecary. Probate to John Stogdon with similar powers reserved to William Cann and James Cook Cann. (Aug. 1841).

Fidler, James, of Stepney, Middlesex, who died on the ship *Dispatch* in Pennsylvania. Administration with will to the principal creditor, Thomas Coutts; the relict, Deborah Fidler, renouncing. (Jan. 1700).

Field, Elizabeth Truelock, of New York City, widow. Administration to the son, John Field. (Oct. 1851).

Field, Tabitha, of Petersburg, Virginia. Administration to the husband, Thomas Field. (Oct. 1806).

Fielding, Ambrose, of Virginia. Probate to Edward Fielding with similar powers reserved to the other named executors. (July 1675).

Fielding, Cornelius, of the 20th Regiment, who died at Lancaster, Maryland. Administration with will to James Tidswell; no executor having been named. (Oct. 1783).

Fielding, Henry, of King and Queen County, Virginia. Probate to Francis Thompson with similar powers reserved to Gawin Corbin and John Story. (Nov. 1712).

Fielding, John, formerly of Butterworth, Rochdale, Lancashire, woollen carder, but late of Cass County, Illinois. Probate to Isaac Platt and Robert Brearley. (Aug. 1845).

Filbrigg, Robert, of St. Dunstan in the East, London, whose brother, John Filbrigg, was in Virginia. Probate to the brother, William Filbrigg. (July 1638). Wi.

Filbrick, Robert, who died in New England. Administration to the father, Robert Filbrick. (May 1649).

Files, John, of St. Augustine, East Florida, Lieutenant of the armed ship *Lord George Germaine*, bachelor. Administration to the brother and next-of-kin, Stephen Files. (Feb. 1780).

Filleter, William, of Southampton, whose daughter, Anne, was in Virginia. Probate to the relict, Anne Filleter. (Feb. 1659). Wi.

Filmer, Samuel, formerly of Virginia, and late of East Sutton, Kent, who died in Westminster, Middlesex, and whose cousin, Frances, wife of Samuel Stephens, was in Virginia. Administration with will to Warham Horsmonden, father of the relict, Mary Filmer alias Horsmonden, during her absence in Virginia. (May 1670). Revoked

Filmer, *(contd.)* and granted to the said Mary Filmer. (Apr. 1671).

Finch, Anne, of East Looe, Cornwall, whose husband, Philip Finch, was resident in Virginia. Limited administration pending a suit in the Exchequer to Charles Norris of Staple Inn, London. (May 1734). Wi.

Finch, Hon. John, formerly of Grosvenor Square, Middlesex, but late of New York, bachelor. Administration to the brothers, Hon. Charles and Edward Finch. (Apr. 1810).

Finnie, William, Lieutenant of the 61st Company of the Second Division of Marines, who died in Boston. Administration with will to John Ogilvie, attorney for George Skene at Rubislaw, Aberdeen, Scotland. (Nov. 1775).

Fish, Augustine, of Bowden, Leicestershire, whose kinsman, William Fish, was in New England. Probate to the relict, Christian Fish. (Sep. 1647). Wa.

Fisher, Edward, of Euhaws St. Luke, Granville County, South Carolina, widower. Administration to the son, Robert Scrooby Fisher. (Sep. 1783).

Fisher, Giles, formerly of Corn Street, St. James, Bath, Somerset, but late of Savannah, North America, bachelor. Administration to the brother, Henry Fisher. (Dec. 1845).

Fisher, James, seaman of the schooner *Revenue* in the service of the United States of America, bachelor. Administration to the sister, Sarah Fisher. (Mar. 1847).

Fisher, John, of Virginia, widower. Administration to the daughter, Mary Fisher. (Oct. 1654).

Fisher, John, of Conhow, Lorton, Cumberland, who died in Virginia, bachelor. Administration to Richard Barnes, attorney for the sister, Anne Langton, widow, in Cockermouth, Cumberland. (Nov. 1723).

Fisher, Joseph, formerly of Holborn Hill, London, but late of North America. Limited administration to Timothy Fisher. (July 1839).

Fisher, Miers the younger, of Philadelphia who died in the City of Petersburgh. Administration with will to John Bainbridge the younger, attorney for the brother, Redwood Fisher, in Philadelphia. (Feb. 1815).

Fisher, William, formerly of Sweetings Alley, London, but late of Philadelphia. Administration to John Pasley, attorney for the only child, Mary, wife of Thomas Ruston, in Philadelphia. (June 1791).

Fitch, Patrick, of New York Province, who died on H.M. ship *Launceston*. Probate to John Dupre, attorney for the relict, Abigal Fitch, in New York. (Dec. 1751).

Fitch, Thomas, of Boston, New England. Administration with will to Thomas Gainsborough, attorney for the relict, Abiel Fitch, and for Andrew Oliver and James Allen, in Boston. (Sep. 1737).

Fitzer, John, of Maryland, bachelor. Administration to the father, Maurice Fitzer. (Sep. 1683).

Fitzpen alias Phippen, George, clerk, whose brother, David Phippen, was in New England. Probate to the relict, Mary Phippen. (Mar. 1652). Sh.Wa.

Fleet, William, formerly of Martin Worthy, Hampshire, and late of Chopthank, Talbot County, Maryland, who died at sea on the ship *Peach Blossom*, bachelor. Probate to Mary Tanner alias Fleet, wife of Robert Tanner. (Apr. 1733).

Fleetwood, Edward, of London, who had lands in Virginia. Probate to Sir William Fleetwood. (Dec. 1609). Wi.

Fleming, John, of Water Town, New England. Administration to the children, Thomas Fleming, and Mary, wife of John Rathery. (Feb. 1659).

Fleming, Rev. John, formerly of Higley, Shropshire, but late chaplain of H.M. ship *Ajax*, who died in New York, widower. Administration to the only child, Mary, wife of Zachariah Slaney. (Feb. 1829).

Fletcher, Reuben, formerly of Doctors Commons, London, but late of Napoleon, Ripley County, Indiana. Limited probate to George Fletcher Walker. (Nov. 1856).

Fletcher, William, of Stepney, Middlesex, who died on the ship *Elizabeth and Mary* on passage to Virginia. Administration to the principal creditor, Eleazar Bevens. (June 1659).

Fletcher, William, of Boston, New England, late Commander of H.M. armed vessel *Boston Packet*. Administration to William Bollay, attorney for the relict, Margaret Fletcher, in Boston. (Aug. 1746).

Fleete, Deborah, of Westminster, Middlesex, widow, whose son, Henry Fleete, was in Virginia. Probate to the cousin, Robert Filmer, with similar powers reserved to the cousin, Sir Edward Filmer. (Jan. 1652). Wi.

Flint, Thomas, of New England, who died on H.M. ship *Severn*, bachelor. Administration with will to Elizabeth King, widow, administratrix to the named executor, William King deceased. (Feb. 1706).

Flower, Daniel, of London, scissormaker, who had lands in Virginia. Administration to Alexander Martin. (May 1670). Revoked on production of a will and probate by decree granted to Richard Ellis. (June 1670).

Flower, Elizabeth, of Edwards County, Illinois. Administration with will to Edward Fordham Flower, attorney for the son, George Flower, and for Hugh Ronalds the elder, in Illinois. (July 1847).

Flower, Richard, formerly of Marden, Hertfordshire, but late of Park House near Albion, Edwards County, Illinois. Administration with will to Edward Fordham Flower, attorney for the relict, Elizabeth Flower, at Albion. (May 1830).

Flower, Walter, of Virginia, bachelor. Administration to Noblett Ruddock, attorney for the mother, Lucy Flower, widow, in Ireland. (Feb. 1726).

Fly, John, of Piscataway, New England, who died on H.M. ship *Catherine*, widower. Probate of nuncupative will to William Tavern. (Mar. 1698).

Foissin, John, of Virginia, bachelor. Administration to the cousin, Abraham Palmentier. (Dec. 1694).

Follett, John, of Cape Henry, Virginia, who died on H.M. ship *Deptford*. Probate to Richard Mills. (Jan. 1692).

Foote, Richard, of St. Dunstan in the East, London, who had lands in Virginia. Probate to the relict, Hester Foote, the other executor, the son, Samuel Foote, having died. (Apr. 1697).

Forbes, Ann K. *See* **Issit**.

Forbes, George, of St. Mary's County, Maryland. Administration with will to William Black, attorney for George Gordon and Kenelm Greenfield Jowles in Maryland. (June 1742).

Forbes, James, of H.M. ship *Savage*, who died in Long Island Hospital, bachelor. Administration to the father, James Forbes. (Aug. 1782).

Forbes, John, of Philadelphia, Colonel of the 17th Regiment. Inventory 1760. [*Administration Act not found*].

Forbes, Thomas, of St. James, Westminster, Middlesex, Collector of Customs at Lewis, Pennsylvania. Limited administration to John Keith of St. Margaret Patten, London. (Aug. 1739).

Forby, Felix, of Norwich, hosier, whose son and daughter were in Virginia. Probate to the son-in-law, Richard Coates, and to his wife, Martha Coates. (Jan. 1661). Wi.

Ford, Arthur Perroneau, of Charles Town, South Carolina, bachelor. Administration to the brother and next-of-kin, Frederick Augustus Ford. (Nov. 1849).

Foord, Gabriel, of South Carolina, mariner, bachelor. Administration to the father, Isaac Foord. (Mar. 1719).

Fordyce, Charles, Captain of the 14th Regiment of Foot, who died in Virginia, bachelor. Administration to John Seton, attorney for the brother and sisters, John Fordyce, Allan, wife of Andrew Grant, and Ann, wife of Charles Ferguson, in Edinburgh, Scotland. (Nov. 1777).

Forman, William, Commissary and Paymaster of Artillery in New York. Probate to the brother and surviving executor, Richard Forman. (June 1775).

Forrester, George, of New York, mariner. Probate to William Holt. (Feb. 1751).

Fortee, Henry, of Lambeth, Surrey, who died on the East India ship *Josiah* in Virginia. Limited administration to the brothers, Henry and Charles Fortee. (Nov. 1691).

Forten alias Fortune, Thomas, of North Kingston, Rhode Island, a negro. Administration by his solemn affirmation to Joseph Sherwood, attorney for the negro woman, Abigail Mingo, in North Kingston. (Dec. 1765).

Foster, Elizabeth, of Crutched Friars, London, relict of Henry Foster of Virginia. Probate to the mother, Elizabeth Higginson. (Mar. 1674). Wa.

Foster, Isaac, of Christ Church, Middlesex, who died in Philadelphia. Probate by his solemn affirmation to Simon Bailey. (Mar. 1781).

Foster, James Montague, of Richmond, Virginia, bachelor. Administration to John Henry Foster, executor of the father, John Foster deceased. (Dec. 1826).

Foster, John, of Boston, New England. Administration to Thomas Blettsoe of St. Swithin, London, merchant, attorney for Thomas Hutchinson in Boston. (Aug. 1711).

Foster, John, of Richmond, Virginia. Limited probate to the son, John Henry Foster. (Dec. 1826).

Foster, John, of Leonard Street, New York City, widower. Administration to George Cox, attorney for the daughter, Charlotte, wife of Nicholas Spaulding, in New York City. (Feb. 1844).

Foster, John, of St. Sacramento, California, bachelor. Administration to the brother, Henry Foster; the mother, Sarah Foster, widow, having died. (Apr. 1850).

Foster, Martha, of 184 Franklin Street, New York City, spinster. Administration to George Cox, attorney for the sister, Charlotte, wife of Nicholas Spaulding, in New York City. (Feb. 1844).

Fothergill, Anthony, formerly of Bath, Somerset, afterwards of Philadelphia, but late of St. George's Place, Blackfriars Road, Surrey, M.D. Limited administration with will to Thomas Bainbridge and, by his solemn affirmation, to John Coakley. (Dec. 1813).

Fottrell, Edward, of Baltimore County, Maryland, widower. Administration with will to William Black, attorney for the creditor, William Chapman, in Maryland; the executors, Basil Dorsey and Alexander Lawson, and the only children, Edward, Thomas and Achsah Fottrell, having been cited but not having appeared. (Nov. 1748).

Fouace, Sarah. *See* **Nourse**.

Foulks, John Lawrence, of H.M. ship *Sea Horse*, who died in Virginia, bachelor. Administration to the mother, Elizabeth Foulks, widow. (Feb. 1737).

Foulks, Thomas, of Princess Ann County, Virginia. Probate by decree to John Vicary. (Sep. & Oct. 1692). Wa.

Fountain, John, of Abingdon, Berkshire, whose brother, Roger Fountain, was in Lynn Haven, Virginia. Probate to the relict, Margaret Fountain. (Feb. 1712).

Fountain, Thomas, of Sugar Castle, Walworth County, Wisconsin. Probate to the relict, Sarah Fountain. (Aug. 1857).

Fowl, Peter, of H.M. ship *Shoreham*, who died in Virginia. Administration to the relict, Mary Fowl. (Aug. 1700).

Fowler, James, late of Nansemond County, Virginia, who died at Mile End, Stepney, Middlesex. Probate to John Goodwin with similar powers reserved to the relict, Elizabeth Fowler. (May 1709).

Fowler, Samuel, of New York, bachelor. Administration to the brother, William Fowler. (Apr. 1828).

Fownes, John, of Plymouth, Devon, merchant, an adventurer to Virginia and New England. Administration with will to the brother, Warwick Fownes; the named executor having died. (Feb. 1625). Wa.

Fox, Gilbert, of Charleston, South Carolina, widower. Administration to John Somerville, attorney for the only child, Elizabeth, wife of Edward Veazey, in Lancaster County, Pennsylvania. (Aug. 1829).

Fox, Henry Stephen, formerly British Envoy to the United States of America, late of Washington, U.S.A. Administration to the sister, Caroline, wife of William Francis Patrick Napier. (Dec. 1846).

Fox, James, of Liverpool, Lancashire, who died in Savinilla, America.

Fox, *(contd.)*
Administration to the relict, Mary Fox. (Jan. 1843).

Fox, John, of Virginia, bachelor. Administration to the father, Edward Fox. (Feb. 1668).

Fox, John, of H.M. ship *Chester*, who died in Boston, New England. Probate to Anne Perry. (Jan. 1713).

Fox, Phillips, formerly of Totnes, Devon, but late of North America, bachelor. Administration to the sister and only next-of-kin, Anne, wife of Edward Skinner. (Jan. 1829).

Fox, Stephen, of the ship *Fortune*, who died near New England. Administration with will to the brother, John Fox, no executor having been named. (Oct. 1663). Wa.Wi.

Fox, William, formerly of Bourton on the Water, Gloucestershire, but late of New York, bachelor. Administration to the mother and next-of-kin, Jane Fox, widow. (Aug. 1854). Further grant made in April 1861.

Foxall, Catherine, of George Town, District of Columbia, widow. Administration with will to the sister, Elizabeth Martha, wife of Henry Knight; the surviving executors, Isabella Redin, spinster, Angelletta, wife of Francis Lowndes, and William Smallwood Bullock, renouncing. (Feb. 1848).

Foxcroft, John, formerly of James Street, St. James, Westminster, Middlesex, but late of New York City. Administration to the relict, Judith Foxcroft. (Nov. 1791).

Foxcroft, John, of Cambridge, Massachusetts. Administration with will to John Lovell, attorney for Abraham Biglow in North America. (Mar. 1804).

Foxcroft, Sarah, of Cambridge, Massachusetts. Administration to Samuel Savile and William Bourfield, attornies for the husband, John Foxcroft, in Cambridge. (Feb. 1802). Revoked on the death of the husband and granted to his administrator with will, John Lovell, as attorney for the executor, Abraham Biglow; the sister, Deborah, wife of Gideon White, having been cited but not having appeared. (May 1804).

Foxhall, John, of Westmoreland County, Virginia. Probate to Caleb Butler. (Aug. 1704). Wi.

Foxwell, George, of Virginia, bachelor. Administration to the brother and next-of-kin, Henry Foxwell. (Aug. 1673).

Francis, Anne, of Philadelphia, widow. Administration with will to Walter Stirling, attorney for the surviving executor, William Tilghman, in Philadelphia. (June 1818).

Francis, Tarbutt, of Philadelphia, reduced Lieutenant of the 44th Regiment. Probate to the relict and surviving executrix, Sarah, now wife of John Connelly. (Aug. 1782).

Francis, Thomas, of Middletown, Connecticut, bachelor. Administration to the brother, Abraham Francis. (July 1827).

Francomb, George, of General Holt's Regiment, bachelor. Administration by decree to the principal creditrix, Elizabeth Jennings, widow. (July 1722).

Francklyn, Henry, of Boston, New England. Administration to George Chabot, attorney for the relict, Hannah Francklyn, in Boston. (Nov. 1725).

Francklyn, Jonathan, of Boston, New England, seaman of H.M. ship *Magnanime*. Administration to Nathaniel Green, attorney for the relict, Sarah Francklyn, in Boston. (May 1759).

Franks, David, of Philadelphia. Probate to the son, Jacob Franks, with similar powers reserved to the son, Moses Franks, and to Tench Coxe. (July 1794).

Fraser, Alexander, Lieutenant and Adjutant of the 71st Regiment, who died at Savannah, Georgia, bachelor. Administration with will to Robert Waddell, attorney for the brother, Thomas Fraser, in Dalcaitick, Scotland. (Dec. 1783).

Fraser, Anna Laughton, of Bordenham, New Jersey, widow. Administration to Charles Frederick Tilstone, attorney for the daughter, Eliza Smith Fraser, in Bordentown (*sic*). (Jan. 1841).

Fraser, James, of Charlestown, North America. Administration to the creditor, Patrick Macleod; the relict, Mary Fraser, and the children, Sarah Mary, Richard, Ash, Caroline, George, William, Harriet, John, and Alexander Fraser, having been cited but not having appeared. (Dec. 1807).

Fraser, John, of St. Simon's Island, Georgia, Lieutenant on half pay of the Royal Marines. Administration to Charles Menzies, attorney for the relict, Anne Sarah Fraser, in St. Simon's Island. (Jan. 1841)

Fraser, Patrick, of Long Island, Bahamas (*sic*), bachelor. Administration to David Robertson, attorney for the brother and next-of-kin, John Fraser, in Perth, Scotland. (Mar 1795).

Fraser alias Frazer, Thomas, Lieutenant of the 71st Regiment of Foot, who died in Virginia, bachelor. Administration to the creditor, Alexander Alison; the father, Hugh Fraser, renouncing. (July 1782).

Fraser, Thomas, Captain of the 14th Regiment, who died in Norfolk, Virginia, bachelor. Administration to John Ogilvie, attorney for the father, Simon Fraser, in Fannallan, Scotland. (Jan. 1790).

Fraser, Thomas, formerly of St. Bartholomew, Charleston, South Carolina, a reduced Major of the late South Carolina Regiment of Royalists, but late of Philadelphia. Administration with will to Crawford Davison, attorney for the daughter, Eliza Smith Fraser, in Philadelphia; the relict, Ann Loughton Fraser, and the daughter, Jane Winter Fraser, renouncing. (July 1823).

Fraunces, Edward, formerly of Jamaica but late of London, whose cousins, Elizabeth Jacquelin, wife of Richard Ambler, and Martha Jacquelin, spinster, were in York Town, Virginia, and whose cousin, Mary Jaqcuelin, wife of John Smith, was in Gloucester County, Virginia. Probate to the brother, James Fraunces, with similar powers reserved to Varney Phelp and Moses Kerritt. (Apr. 1741).

Frazier, Edward. *See* **Frizell**.

Frazon, Samuel, of Boston, New England, who died in Barbados, bachelor. Administration to the cousin and next-of-kin, Francis de Caseres.

Frazon, *(contd.)* (Sep. 1705).

Freame, Thomas, of Philadelphia, Captain of a Company in Colonel Gooch's Regiment. Probate by his solemn affirmation to Thomas Penn with similar powers reserved to Margaretta Freame and Richard Hockley. (Sep. 1744).

Frederick, Anthony, Ensign of the 15th Regiment of Foot, who died at German Town near Philadelphia, bachelor. Administration to the father, Felix Frederick. (May 1778).

Freed, Elizabeth, nee Elizabeth Woodgate, of Palermo, Oswego County, New York. Limited administration to Edward Millen, attorney for the husband, Joseph Freed, in Palermo. (Oct. 1844).

Freeman, John, of Cohansey, New Jersey, Pennsylvania. Administration to John Blackwell, guardian of the only child, Anthony Freeman; the relict, Mary Freeman, renouncing. (Jan. 1717).

Freeman, John, of Virginia. bachelor. Administration to the sister, Charity Freeman. (July 1739).

French, John, of Clarke County, Alabama. Administration to Henry John Turner, attorney for the relict, Sarah French, in Clarke County. (July 1846).

French, Thomas, formerly of Holborn, Middlesex, but late Captain of the First Batallion of De Lancey's late Corps, bachelor. Administration to David Thomas, attorney for the brother and only next-of-kin, George French, in George Town, South Carolina. (Aug. 1795).

Freshwater, William, of St. James, Clerkenwell, Middlesex, citizen and haberdasher of London, who died in Virginia. Probate to the relict, Elizabeth Freshwater. (May 1706). Revoked on her death and granted to the sister, Elizabeth, wife of Richard Freshwater. (Apr. 1714).

Friend, Henry, of New Orleans, bachelor. Administration to the brother, Charles Friend; the mother, Ann Friend, widow, renouncing. (May 1857).

Frisby, James, of Cecil County, Maryland. Probate to the son, James Frisby, with similar powers reserved to Thomas and Peregrine Frisby. (Dec. 1703). Double probate to the sons, Thomas and Peregrine Frisby. (Dec. 1706).

Frizell alias Frazier, Edward, of H.M. ships *Boyne* and *Harwich*, bachelor. Administration to Isabel, wife of the nearest kin, Hugh Poulson, in Lincoln, Virginia. (Aug. 1701).

Frost, Augustine, of York Fort, North America. Probate to James Isham. (Jan. 1759).

Frost, John, formerly of Grove Street, Camden Town, Middlesex, but late of New York City, jeweller. Administration to the relict, Maria Frost. (Dec. 1843).

Frwid, James, of Liverpool, Lancashire, who died in Maryland, bachelor. Administration to William Jeffreys, attorney for the father, James Frwid, in Scotland. (Oct. 1725).

Fry, George, formerly of Hackney, Middlesex, but late of Lake County, Indiana. Administration to the relict, Dinah Fry. (May 1846).

Fry, James the younger, of Nottingham, Maryland. Probate to William Molleson and Ninian Pinckney. (Mar. 1771).

Fry, Samuel, of Virginia, bachelor. Administration to the mother, Anne Fry, widow. (Mar. 1656).

Fry, Susannah. *See* **Tooley**.

Fry, Thomas, formerly of Bristol but late of South Carolina. Limited administration to William Woodgate, attorney for William George Cowdry, Thomas Cowdry and Nathaniel Cowdry. (Feb. 1838).

Fryer, Sibell, of New Sarum, Wiltshire, widow, who made a bequest to John Bennett in New England. Probate to the daughters, Margaret Good and Anne Jempson. (Feb. 1636). Wa.

Fulham, John, of Carolina. Probate to the relict, Ursula Fulham. (Sep. 1715).

Fuller, James, formerly of Poplar Cottage, Strouds Vale, Maiden Lane, Islington, Middlesex, carpenter, who died a passenger on the ship *Charles Bartlett* bound for New York, widower. Administration to the son, Frederick Fuller. (Aug. 1849).

Fuller, James Cannings, of Skaneateles, Onandaga County, New York. Probate by her solemn affirmation to the relict, Lydia Fuller. (Dec. 1851).

Fullerton, Alexander, of Maryland, who died on the ship *Elizabeth*, bachelor. Administration to the brother, Isaac Fullerton. (Aug. 1694).

Fullerton, George, of Carolina. Probate to William Rhett with similar powers reserved to Sarah Rhett. (Sep. 1709).

Fullwood, Thomas, of Birmingham, Warwickshire, who died at sea between New England and Carolina. Administration to the relict, Elizabeth Fullwood. (May 1725).

Fulton, Mark, of Philadelphia. Administration to the relict, Sarah Fulton. (Apr. 1822).

Furlong, Joseph, formerly of Woolwich, Kent, but late of Cincinnati. Administration to the relict, Mary Ann Furlong. (Mar. 1854).

Furness, Jacob, of Bermondsey, Surrey, who had lands in New York. Probate to the relict, Elizabeth Furness. (Feb. 1725).

Fuser, Louis Valentine, Lieutenant-Colonel of the 60th or Royal American Regiment, who died in North America. Probate to James Wright with similar powers reserved to Alexander Shaw, George McInzie, Andrew Turnbull, James Penman and Spencer Mann. (Dec. 1783). Revoked on the death of James Wright and administration granted to the daughter, Louisa Dorothy, wife of Thomas Grierson; the executors, William Wulff, Alexander Shaw, George McInzie, Andrew Turnbull and James Penman, having died, and Spencer Mann having been cited but not having appeared. (Feb. 1797).

Futerell, Catherine, formerly of St. Mary Axe, St. Andrew Undershaft, London, but late of Charleston, South Carolina, spinster. Administration to William Williams, attorney for James Ramsay M.D. in Charleston. (May 1832).

G

Gabourel, Joshua, of Cape Fear, North Carolina, bachelor. Probate to the brother, Amos alias Amice Gabourel; the brother, Thomas Gabourel, having died. (Apr. 1737).

Gadsby, Edward, of Stepney, Middlesex, and of the ship *Redbridge*, (bound to Virginia). Probate to John Duffield. (Apr. 1696). Wa.

Gaisford, John, formerly of Beckington, Wiltshire, but late of Charles Town, South Carolina, bachelor. Administration to the sister and next-of-kin, Lydia Gaisford. (June 1796).

Gale, Thomas, of New York City, bachelor. Administration to the father, Richard Gale. (Jan. 1823).

Galey, Thomas, soldier of the 22nd Regiment of Foot, who died in West Florida, bachelor. Administration to the sister and next-of-kin, Jane, wife of Thomas Payne. (Apr. 1766).

Galpin, Joseph, of King Street, Wortchester (*sic*) County, North America, bachelor. Administration to Charles Cooke, attorney for the nephew and next-of-kin, Gabriel Strang, in St. John's, New Brunswick. (July 1790).

Gapper, Susan Maria, formerly of Bristol but late of Philadelphia, widow. Probate to Richard Van Heythusen. (Sep. 1838).

Garden, John, of Philadelphia. Probate to William Blackburn. (Jan. 1801).

Gardiner, John, of Virginia, bachelor. Administration to Phebe Gardiner, spinster, attorney for the brother, Peter Gardiner, in Dundee, Scotland. (Nov. 1816).

Gardiner, Silvester, formerly of Boston, North America, afterwards of Poole, but late of Newport, Rhode Island, doctor of physick. Probate to Robert Hallowell alias Hollowell with similar powers reserved to Oliver Whipple. (Apr. 1787).

Gardiner, Thomas, of Kingston-upon-Hull, Yorkshire, master of the transport ship *Juno*, who died in Boston, New England, bachelor. Administration to Ann Gardiner, widow, mother of the niece and only next-of-kin, Ann Loft. (Dec. 1776).

Gardner, Richard, formerly of Lyme Regis, Dorset, but late of Boston, North America, bachelor. Administration to the brother, George Gardner, and the sister, Mary, wife of Thomas Hodder. (June 1820).

Gardner, Robert, of the merchant ship *Society*, who died in Virginia. Administration to Anne Browne, wife and attorney of the principal creditor, William Browne, of the merchant ship *Robert and John*. (Apr. 1710).

Garnett, Henry, of New Brunswick, New Jersey, bachelor. Administration to the mother, Mary Garnett. (June 1835). Revoked on her death and granted to the sister, Harriet Garnett. (Aug. 1853).

Garnett, John, formerly of Bristol but late of New Brunswick, New Jersey. Administration to the relict, Mary Garnett. (Apr. 1822).

Garrard, Anne, of Up Lambourne, Berkshire, widow, whose grandchild, Anne, was wife of Thomas Hinton, lately gone to Virginia. Probate to Jane Busher. (Feb. 1635).

Garraway, Richard, of New England. Administration to the relict, Anne Garraway. (July 1668).

Garratt, Robert, formerly of Clieves in the parish of Muggington, Derbyshire, but late of Ossigon, New York. Administration with will to Thomas Turton, attorney for the sons, John and William Garratt, in the United States of America. (Feb. 1832).

Garrett, Amos, of Maryland, bachelor. Administration with will to the sisters, Elizabeth Ginn and Mary Woodard, widows. (July 1728). Revoked on the death of Mary Woodard and granted to Elizabeth Ginn. (Jan. 1735). Revoked and granted to William Woodard, the son and executor of Mary Woodard deceased; the mother, Sarah Garrett, having died in the testator's lifetime. (Dec. 1739).

Garrett, George, of St. Botolph Bishopsgate, London, and of the ship *Mermaid*, whose son, John Garrett, was in Virginia. Administration to the relict, Mary Garrett. (Sep. 1674). NGSQ 61/258.

Garrett, George, formerly of Christ Church Spitalfields, Middlesex, but late of Charles Town, South Carolina, bachelor. Administration to the father, William Garrett. (Apr. 1769). Revoked on his death and granted to his relict and executrix, Dorothy Garrett. (May 1771).

Gatehouse, Edward, of New York Province, bachelor. Administration to the nephew, Richard Gatehouse; the brother, John Gatehouse, renouncing. (Feb. 1746).

Gatehouse, Richard, of New York, bachelor. Administration to the father, John Gatehouse. (Apr. 1761).

Gates, Ann, of St. Botolph Bishopsgate, London, whose son, Thomas Gates, was in Virginia. Probate to Ann Andrewes, spinster. (Jan. 1751).

Gates, Thomas, of Charleston, South Carolina. Administration with will to James Alexander Simpson, attorney for Henry Alexander De Sayssure, George Kinloch and Robert William Fisher in Charleston. (Mar. 1853).

Gault alias Gallt, James, of Stepney, Middlesex, who died on a prize of H.M. ship *Dove* in Virginia. Probate to the relict, Alice Gault. (Sep. 1697).

Gaych, James, of Shadwell, Middlesex, who died on the merchant ship *Mary* in Virginia. Administration to the relict, Mary Gaych. (Aug. 1709).

Gaylard, Robert, of Virginia, bachelor. Administration to the mother, Mary Gaylard, widow. (Apr.1657).

Gayner, Henry, of the merchant ship *Dove* and then of H.M. ship *Shoreham*, who died in South Carolina, bachelor. Administration to the principal creditor, Charles Disney. (May 1733).

Gayny, Anne, of Virginia, widow. Administration to the creditor, Edward Hurd. (Jan. 1643)

Geary, John, of Dunsley, Hertfordshire, who had lands in Pennsylvania.

Geary, *(contd.)*
Probate to Henry Geary. (Dec. 1696).

Gee, William, formerly of Stamford, Lincolnshire, but late of Bennington Centre, Wyoming County, New York. Administration to the brother, Edward Gee; the relict, Drusilla Gee, and the mother, Elizabeth Gee, renouncing. (June 1853).

Geekie, Daniel, of St. Martin in the Fields, Middlesex, surgeon of H.M. ship *Phoenix*, who died in South Carolina, bachelor. Administration to Robert Ogilvie, attorney for the father, Alexander Geekie, in Scotland. (July 1740).

Geere, Dennis, of Saugus, Massachusetts, who died overseas. Administration with will to Edward Moncke, maternal uncle of the daughters, Elizabeth and Sarah Geere, during their minority; the relict, Elizabeth Geere, having died. (June 1642). Sh.Wa.

Gellie, George, Ensign of the 46th Regiment, who died in Niagara, bachelor. Administration to the brother, Lewis Gellie. (Apr. 1763).

Gembell, Adam, of St. Martin in the Fields, Middlesex, who died in Carolina, bachelor. Administration to the brother, John Gembell. (Aug. 1696).

Gennins, Anne. *See* **Jennings**.

Geoghegan, William, of Concordia, Louisiana, M.D., bachelor. Limited administration to Thomas Todd, attorney for the brother, Richard Geoghegan, in Concordia. (Sep. 1845).

Gerrard, Henry, of St. Martin Brandon, Charles City County, Virginia. Administration with will to Micajah Perry, attorney for the sons, Ferdinand and Nicholas Gerrard, in Virginia; no executor having been named. (Mar. 1693). Wi.

Gibbins, John, of Newport, Rhode Island, corporal in Lieutenant-Colonel Christopher Hargill's Company of the Rhode Island Regiment of Foot, who died in Havana. Administration by his solemn declaration to Joseph Sherwood, attorney for the relict, Hannah Gibbins, in Newport. (Dec. 1765).

Gibbons, Margaret, of New England, who died in Plymouth, Devon. Administration to the daughter, Jerusha, wife of Captain Thomas Rea. (Feb. 1657).

Gibbs, Philip, of Bristol (bound for Virginia). Administration with will to Anthony Marshall; the named executor, Philip Marshall, having died. (Oct. 1674). Wa.

Gibbs, Richard, of St. Dunstan in the West, London, who died in New York. Administration to the relict, Elizabeth, now wife of Peter Ludgar. (Oct. 1683).

Gibbs, Richard, of Bensalem, Pennsylvania. Limited probate to Richard Lowther with similar powers reserved to Brickwood, Prattle & Co. (Mar. 1804).

Gibbs, Thomas, of H.M. ship *Centurion*, who died in Long Island Hospital, bachelor. Administration to the father, John Gibbs. (Feb. 1784).

Giberson, Gilbert, of Sunbury, Northumberland County, Pennsylvania, widower. Administration to William Taylor, attorney for the son,

Giberson, *(contd.)*
Thomas Giberson, in Pennsylvania. (July 1791).

Gibson, Abraham Priest, of Boston, North America, United States Consul at St. Petersburgh, who died in Holles Street, Cavendish Square, Middlesex. Probate to Thomas Aspinwall. (Dec. 1852).

Gibson, Ann, relict of Daniel Gibson of South Carolina. Probate to Rev. Lawrence Neill. (Jan. 1736).

Gibson, John, of the ship *Assurance*, who died at James River, Virginia. Probate to Edward Kirby. (Oct. 1692).

Gibson, Richard, of Newport, Rhode Island, and of H.M. ship *Maidstone*. Administration with will to James Sykes, attorney for William Parker, now at sea. (May 1782).

Gibson, Use, of St. Anne and St. Agnes, Aldersgate, London, who died in York Town, Virginia. Administration to the relict, Hannah Gibson. (Aug. 1709).

Gibson, William, of St. Edmund the King, London, who had goods in New Jersey and Pennsylvania. Administration with will to Jane Barnes, guardian of the children, John, William, and Patience Gibson, during their minority; the relict, Elizabeth Gibson, renouncing. (Jan. 1685).

Gifford, Wearman, formerly of Cliff's End House, Withycombe Rawleigh, Devon, but late of Houston, Texas. Administration to Charles Gifford, son and executor of the father, Charles Gifford deceased; the relict, Sarah Eliza Gifford, renouncing. (May 1855).

Gilchrist, Adam, of Charleston, South Carolina. Administration to John Hopton, attorney for the son, James Gilchrist, in Charleston; the relict, Elizabeth L. Gilchrist, renouncing. (Feb. 1818).

Gilchrist, Adam the elder, of West Chester, New York, widower. Administration to John Hopton, administrator of the son, Adam Gilchrist the younger deceased, and attorney for James Gilchrist, son of Adam Gilchrist the younger, in Charleston, South Carolina; the son, Robert Gilchrist, having died. (Apr. 1819).

Gilchrist, James, of Waccaumaw near George Town, United States of America, doctor of physic, bachelor. Administration to John Hopton, administrator of the father, Adam Gilchrist the elder deceased, attorney for James Gilchrist in Charleston, South Carolina. (Apr. 1819).

Gilchrist, Robert, of New York City. Administration to John Delafield the younger, attorney for the relict, Elizabeth Gilchrist, in Albany. (June 1819).

Gildart, Francis, of Washington, Mississippi, Captain on half pay in Tarlton's Dragoons. Administration with will to James Tidbury, attorney for the relict, Sophia Gildart, and for Theodore Stark, in Mississippi. (July 1816).

Gildemaster, Christopher, of London, who died in East New Jersey, bachelor. Probate to the brothers, John Frederick and Henry Daniel Gildemaster. (July 1736).

Giles, Eleazar, of Beverley, Massachusetts, master of the merchant ship

Giles, *(contd.)*
Harriot, widower. Administration to the creditor, William Eppes Routh; the only child, Ebenezer Giles, having been cited but not having appeared. (Oct. 1809). Revoked on production of a will and administration granted to Benjamin Giles; the relict, Sarah Giles, having been cited but not having appeared. (Dec. 1812).

Giles, Isaac, of Virginia, bachelor. Administration to the sister and next-of-kin, Rebecca, wife of John Lowe. (Nov. 1730).

Giles, Jean alias Jane, of Charles Town, South Carolina. Administration with will to James Farquhar, attorney for the daughter, Elizabeth Warley, widow, and for James Munro, in Charles Town. (June 1797).

Giles, John, of Charles Town, South Carolina. Administration with will to James Farquhar, attorney for the daughter, Elizabeth Warley, widow, in Charles Town; the relict, Jane Giles, and the son, Othniel Giles, having died before executing. (Nov. 1798).

Giles, Robert, of 22 Dock Street, Philadelphia, seaman of the merchant ship *Carolina*, who died at sea. Administration to Thomas Aspinwall, attorney for the relict, Martha Giles, in Philadelphia. (Mar. 1846).

Giles, William, of New York. Probate to the father, George Giles, and to Roger and Charles Rhodes, with similar powers reserved to John Burroughs. (Jan. 1703).

Gyles, William, of Fredericksburg, Virginia, bachelor. Administration to the sister, Elizabeth, wife of John Adams. (Aug. 1769).

Gill, William, of Stepney, Middlesex, who died in Virginia, widower. Administration to the principal creditor, John Booty. (July 1668).

Gill, William, of London, who had lands in South Carolina. Probate to the sister, Frances Gill. (Aug. 1743).

Gillespie, George, of Tinwall, Dumfriesshire, Scotland, who died in St. Mary's parish, Maryland, merchant, bachelor. Administration to Andrew Drummond, attorney for the sisters and next-of-kin, Janett Haliday, widow, Elizabeth, wife of John Lawson, and Jane, wife of Alexander Ackin. (Mar. 1724).

Gillespie, George, formerly of Jamaica but late of Bristol, Bucks County, Pennsylvania. Limited probate to John Abraham de Normandie. (Mar. 1782).

Gilliard, Andrew, of the ship *King of Poland*, who died in Virginia, bachelor. Administration to the cousin german and next-of-kin, John Pulling. (Apr. 1656).

Gilliat, Thomas, of Richmond, Virginia. Probate to the brother, John Gilliat, with similar powers reserved to Joseph Gallego, Thomas Dent and M.W. Hancock. (Dec. 1810 & Nov. 1812). Revoked on the death of John Gilliat and administration granted to the son, Alfred Gallego Gilliat; the executors, Joseph Gallego and Thomas Dent, having died, and Michael W. Hancock having been cited but not having appeared. (June 1821).

Gilligan, Ferdinand, of Virginia who died in Jamaica, widower. Administration to the brother, Thomas Gilligan. (Apr. 1705).

Gilson, John, of St. Bride, London, who died in South Carolina. Administration to the relict, Joane Gilson. (Aug. 1719).

Girard, Peter, of New York, Chatham pensioner. Administration to Robert Crucifix, attorney for the relict, Jane Girard, in New York. (Jan. 1717).

Gittings, Adam, of Virginia, bachelor. Administration to the sister, Sarah Smith alias Gittings, during the absence overseas of the mother, Elizabeth Gittings. (Sep. 1670).

Glanvell, William, of Virginia. Administration to the relict, Alice Glanvell. (Sep. 1668).

Glascock, Richard, of Richmond, Virginia. Administration with will to William Murdock, attorney for the son, Milton Syms Glascock. (Feb. 1812).

Glass, James William, formerly of Newman Street, Oxford Street, Middlesex, but late of New York. Probate to the mother, Maria Hackley Glass, widow. (June 1856).

Glassford, John, of Susquehannah, North America. Administration to John Inglis, attorney for the relict, Sarah Glassford, in Matilda, Quebec. (Oct. 1790).

Glasson, Hugh Dunstan, of California, bachelor. Administration to the father, Josiah Glasson. (Oct. 1854).

Gledhill, Harriet, of Eagle, Wyoming County, New York, who died in 1849. Limited administration to Thomas Plowman, attorney for the husband, Joseph William Gledhill, in Eagle. (Sep. 1857).

Gledhill alias Day, Mary, of the Isle of Wight, Virginia, widow. Administration with will by decree to Micajah Perry, attorney for James Day and Nathaniel Ridley in Virginia. (June 1721).

Glencross, William, of New York. Probate to Broughton Wright. (Dec. 1713).

Glessing, Henry, of Newburg, United States of America. Administration to the relict, Clara Eliza Glessing. (Feb. 1836).

Glocester alias Warkman, Mark, of St. Mary Magdalen, London, whose brother Robert was in Virginia. Probate to the relict, Elizabeth Glocester alias Warkman. (Apr. 1670). Wi.

Glover, Jose, of London, who died overseas, having lands in New England. Probate to Richard Davies with similar powers reserved to John Harris. (Dec. 1638). Wa.

Glover, Mary, of St. Olave, Silver Street, London, widow, whose daughter, Bennett Glover, was in Virginia. Probate to John Watson. (July 1661). Wa.

Glover, Nathaniel, formerly of Dorchester, New England, but late of Bermondsey, Surrey, tanner. Probate to Jane Davis, widow. (Mar. 1726).

Glover, Nicholas, of Virginia, clerk, bachelor. Administration to the nephew by a sister, John Carter. (Aug. 1612).

Glover, Richard, of Virginia, who died at sea on the ship *Maryland*, widower. Administration to the brother, Charles Glover. (Aug. 1684). Revoked on his death and granted to the nephew, Charles Glover. (Nov. 1684).

Glover, Thomas, of Bermondsey, Surrey, who died in Charles Town, South Carolina. Administration to the relict, Mary Glover. (Oct. 1730).

Glynn, John, steward of the merchant ship *Columbia*, who died at Fort Vancouver, Oregon, North America, bachelor. Administration to the aunt and only next-of-kin, Ellen, wife of James Purcell. (Feb. 1852).

Goddard, Edmund, of Virginia, bachelor. Probate to the sister, Hannah Sheffield alias Goddard. (Dec. 1681).

Goddard, Thomas, of Talbot County, Maryland. Administration to the relict, Grace Brockney alias Goddard. (Nov. 1687).

Goddard, William, of St. Margaret Moses, London, who died in South Carolina. Probate to the aunt, Mary Darby, spinster. (May 1740).

Godden, William. *See* **Leggett**.

Godson, Richard, of Stepney, Middlesex, who died on H.M. ship *Advice* in New York. Administration with will to the principal creditor, Henry Willoughby; the relict, Agnes Godson, renouncing. (Dec. 1702).

Godwyn, Mary, of Lyme Regis, Dorset, widow, whose brother, William Hill, was in New England. Probate to John Farrant, Robert Burridge and William Courtney. (June 1665). Wa.

Goe, William, of Philadelphia. Administration with will to the relict, Mary Goe; the executor, William Brufton, having died in the testator's lifetime. (Aug. 1821).

Goffe. *See* **Gough**.

Gold. *See* **Gould**.

Goldhawk, Mary, of Chertsey, Surrey, widow, whose cousin, Thomas Evance, was in South Carolina. Probate to the nephew, John Hayter. (Feb. 1772).

Goldie, William, of H.M. ship *Rose*, who died in Carolina, bachelor. Administration to Samuel Barlow, attorney for the sisters, Janet and Jean Goldie, in Scotland. (Dec. 1736).

Goldsborough, William, of Talbot County, Maryland. Administration with will to William Anderson, attorney for the relict, Henrietta Maria Goldsborough, in Maryland. (Jan. 1766).

Goldstone, Edward, of Limehouse, Stepney, Middlesex, mariner, who had goods in Virginia. Probate to the relict, Sarah Goldstone, and to Rev. Malachi Harris. (July 1663). Wi.

Goldthwaite, Joseph the elder of New York City. Administration to the son, Philip Goldthwaite; the relict, Martha Goldthwaite, having been cited but not having appeared. (Oct. 1780). Revoked on presentation of a will and probate granted to the same. (Nov. 1780).

Goldthwaite, Joseph the younger, of New York City, bachelor. Administration to Thomas Goldthwaite, attorney for the father, Joseph Goldthwaite, in New York. (Mar. 1780). Revoked and granted to Philip Goldthwaite, son and administrator of Joseph Goldthwaite the elder now deceased. (Oct. 1780). Revoked as the previous grant was made on a false suggestion and administration granted to Samuel Goldthwaite, son and administrator of Joseph Goldthwaite the elder. (Nov. 1780). Revoked and administration with will granted to the son, Samuel Goldthwaite, executor of the grandfather, Joseph Goldthwaite

Goldthwaite, *(contd.)*
the elder, who died before administering, with similar powers reserved to the son, Benjamin Goldthwaite. (Nov. 1780).

Goldworth, James Chapman, formerly of Bungay, Suffolk, farmer, but late of Augusta, Georgia. Administration to George Martin James, attorney for the relict, Frances alias Fanny, now wife of William Frederick Smith, in Augusta. (Mar. 1851).

Golightly, Culchett, of St. Andrew's, Berkeley County, South Carolina. Probate to Charles Pinckney with similar powers reserved to Hon. Edward Fenwicke, George Austin and Landgrave Edmund Bellinger. (Mar. 1756).

Golledge, Thomas, of Chichester, Sussex, who provided for his children to go to New England. Probate to the relict, Mary Golledge. (June 1648). Wa.

Gomme, James, of Charles Town, North America, widower. Administration to the father, John Gomme. (May 1787).

Gondry, William, of London, who died overseas (bound for Virginia). Probate to Thomas Palmer. (Apr. 1638). Double probate to the mother, Anne Preston. (July 1638). Sh.Wi.

Gooch, William the younger, of Virginia. Administration to Robert Cary, attorney for the relict, Eleanor Gooch, in Virginia. (Jan. 1744)

Good, Benjamin, of Virginia, bachelor. Administration to the brother, John Good. (Aug. 1672).

Good, Brent, formerly of Hutton, Somerset, but late of Troy in America. Administration with will to Fanny Good, daughter of the testator by his late wife Harriet; the brother, James Good, Thomas Smith and William Sheppard renouncing, and the residuary legatees, Joseph Edgar and James Partridge Caple, also renouncing. (July 1835).

Goode, Marmaduke, of Upton, Berkshire, clerk, whose brother, John Goode, was in Virginia. Probate to Samuel and Mary Goode. (Feb. 1678). Wa.

Goodall, Elizabeth, of New England. Administration to the son, James Goodall. (June 1651).

Goodeve, John, of New York City. Administration to William Lemmon, executor of the relict, Rebecca Goodeve deceased; the brothers, Joseph and William Goodeve, the nephews and nieces, Ann, wife of John West, John and James Goodeve, Mary, wife of Edward White, Edward and Joseph Goodeve, and Winifred Waldon, wife of Daniel Miall, having all died, the nephew, Benjamin Goodeve, renouncing, and the nephew, William Daniel Goodeve, having been cited but not having appeared. (Mar. 1843).

Goodfellowe, Allin, of St. Lawrence Jewry, London, who died in Virginia. Probate to the brother, Christopher Goodfellowe. (May 1638). Sh.Wi.

Goodman, William, of the ship *Honor's Desire*, who died in Virginia, bachelor. Administration to the principal creditor, Thomas Batson. (July 1662).

Goodrich, Danby and Thomas, of Virginia, infants. Administration to the

Goodrich, *(contd.)* uncle, Sir Abstrupus Danby. (Nov. 1703).

Goodwin, Elizabeth, formerly Elizabeth Harwood, widow, wife of Thomas Goodwin, of Van Dam Street, New York. Limited probate to Daniel Walker. (Oct. 1851).

Goodwin, Thomas Fretwell, of Fat Fields, Hampton, Virginia. Administration with will to the relict, Sarah Ann Goodwin; the executors, Martin Long, Daniel Israel, Abraham Jessie, Parris Simkins and Thomas Robins, renouncing. (May 1849).

Gordon, Alexander, formerly of Norfolk, Virginia, but late of Kensington, Middlesex. Limited administration with will to Lewis Wolfe with similar powers reserved to Peter Elmsly. (Mar. 1799).

Gordon, Ann, of Goochland County, Virginia, widow. Administration with will to William Murdock, attorney for the children, James Harrison Gordon and John Matthews Gordon in North America; the brothers and surviving executors, Philip, Smith, and George Woodson Payne, renouncing, and Robert Payne having died. (Apr. 1808).

Gordon, James, Colonel of the 80th Regiment, who died in New York, bachelor. Administration to the mother, Elizabeth Gordon, widow. (May 1784).

Gordon, James, of Lancaster County, North America. Administration with will to William Murdock, administrator with will of the relict, Ann Gordon deceased, and attorney for the children, James Harrison Gordon and John Matthews Gordon, in North America. (Apr. 1808).

Gordon, Patrick, chaplain of H.M. ship *Lennox*, who died in New York Province. Administration to the brother, James Gordon. (Jan. 1703).

Gore, Charles, of Philadelphia, Captain of the 35th Regiment of Foot under Hon. Lieutenant-General Otway. Limited administration to Thomas Brown, attorney for the relict, Rebecca Gore, in Philadelphia. (June 1764).

Gore, Elizabeth Ann, of Newark, United States of America, widow. Probate to William Gerring and George Crane Ruckel. (Apr. 1851).

Gorges, John, of St. Margaret, Westminster, Middlesex, who had lands in Maine, New England. Probate to Ferdinando Gorges. (June 1657). Sh.

Gorham, John, of Boston, New England, Captain of an Independent Company in Nova Scotia, who died in St. Martin in the Fields, Middlesex. Administration to Jonathan Barnard, attorney for the relict, Elizabeth Gorham in Boston. (July 1752).

Goring, Lovet, of the Inner Temple, London. Probate to Susan, wife of Joshua Lambe of Roxbury, New England, administratrix of the named executor, Lovet Saunders deceased, attorney for Elizabeth Saunders, the mother and next-of-kin of the said Lovet Saunders, in Boston. (Apr. 1710).

Gorstich, Thomas, of New York. Administration to the mother, Jane Gorstich, widow, and the brother, John Gorstich. (Aug. 1714).

Gosnold, Robert, of Earl Soham, Suffolk, whose grandson, Anthony

Gosnold, *(contd.)* Gosnold, was in Virginia. Probate to the son, Anthony Gosnold, with similar powers reserved to Thomas Cornewallis. (Nov. 1615). Wi.

Goswell, John, of Virginia, bachelor. Administration to the sister, Elizabeth Goswell. (Sep. 1734).

Gough, Charles, of Maryland, widower. Administration to Stephen Noguier, guardian of the infant son, Thomas Gough. (July 1699). Revoked and granted to Joshua Noguier as guardian. (Nov. 1700).

Goffe, Daniel, Captain of a Company in H.M. American Regiment commanded by Colonel William Gooch. Administration to Jonathan Barnard, attorney for the relict, Mary Goffe, in New England. (Aug. 1744).

Gough, Harry, of Bel Air, Harford County, Maryland. Administration to William Henry Clapham, attorney for the relict, Martha Hilton, formerly Gough, in Baltimore. (Dec. 1829).

Gough, Harry Dorsey and Perry Hall, of Baltimore, North America. Administration with wills to William Hoffman, attorney for the surviving executor, James Carroll, in North America. (Dec. 1822). Revoked on his death and granted to George Carr as attorney. (May 1829).

Gough, William, of Bristol. Probate to the nephew, Isaac Burges. (July 1750). Revoked on his death and administration granted to Henry Dorsey Gough. (May 1767). Revoked on his death and administration granted to William Hoffman, attorney for James Carroll in North America. (Dec. 1822). Revoked on the death of James Carroll and limited administration granted to Charles Meredith. (Apr. 1833).

Gould, James, of Exeter, Devon, who died in Trenton, New Jersey. Administration to the principal creditrix, Elizabeth Gould, spinster; the relict, Ann Gould, and the minor children, Elizabeth and Francis Gould, having been cited but not having appeared. (Feb. 1742).

Gould, Judith, of Watford, Hertfordshire, widow, whose son, Nathan, was in New England. Probate to the children, Abel, Lydia and Elizabeth Gould. (Sep. 1650). Wa.

Gold, Richard, Lieutenant of the 47th Regiment of Foot, who died in Boston, widower. Administration to Charles Yarburgh, Henry Yarburgh and John Kilvington, guardians of the only children, Charles and Joyce Gold. (Dec. 1777).

Gourlay, John, formerly of Streatham, Surrey, but late of Green Township, Harrison County, Ohio. Administration with will to Richard Cattarne, attorney for the brother, George Gourlay, in Green Township. (Oct. 1857).

Goven, John, of New York, afterwards of H.M. ship *Launceston*, but who died on H.M. ship *Assistance*. Administration to the relict, Elizabeth Goven. (Feb. 1747).

Gowan, Alexander, formerly of Weymouth, Dorset, afterwards of Long Acre, St. Martin in the Fields, Middlesex, but late of New York, bachelor. Administration to the aunt and next-of-kin, Jane Burnett, widow. (Oct. 1800).

Grace, William, master of the merchant ship *Owen*, who died in Boston, New England. Probate to Catherine Hunter, widow. (Sep. 1748).

Gracie, James, Lieutenant in the 21st Regiment of Foot, who died in Baltimore, North America, bachelor. Administration to the mother and next-of-kin, Jean Gracie. (Sep. 1817).

Gradwell, Jacob, who died on the ship *Preston* on Cooper River, South Carolina. Probate to Edward Hoole. (Oct. 1699). NGSQ 64/139).

Grafton, Woodbridge, of Philadelphia, Captain in the American merchant service. Probate to Francis Barault, M.D. (Oct. 1826).

Graham, Anne, of West Hall, Dunsyre, Clydesdale, Scotland, widow. Administration to John Graham, attorney for the only child, Hugh Graham, in Philadelphia. (Aug. 1727).

Graeme, David, of Charles Town, South Carolina. Probate to the relict, Anne Graeme. (Apr. 1778).

Graham, John, of Charles Town, South Carolina, bachelor. Probate to William Littleton. (May 1755).

Graham, Joseph the younger, formerly of Scotby, Wetheral, Cumberland, but late of New Orleans, bachelor. Administration to Mary Wilkinson, widow, administratrix of the father, Joseph Graham deceased. (Aug. 1856).

Graham, Lewis, of Pelham, West Chester, New York. Administration with will to Effingham Lawrence, attorney for Egbert Benson and Thomas Hunt in New York; the executor, John Parkinson, having been cited but not having appeared. (Nov. 1800).

Gramer, Elizabeth, of St. Ann, Westminster, Middlesex, widow, who made a bequest to Mary, wife of Augustine Claiborne, in Virginia. Probate to Samuel Turner, Alderman of London, and Samuel Turner the younger. (Mar. 1773). Wi.

Granger, Robert, of Maryland. Administration to the cousins and next-of-kin, William Granger and Elizabeth Benskin. (Nov. 1690).

Grant, Alexander, sergeant of the Second Batallion of the 42nd or Royal Highland Regiment under Lord John Murray, who died in Havana. Administration to Duncan Campbell, attorney for the relict, Barbara Grant, in New York. (Mar. 1766).

Grant, Jasper, of Stepney, Middlesex, who died in Virginia. Administration to the principal creditor, Edmund Bugden; the relict, Judith Grant, renouncing. (Feb. 1663).

Grant, John, of New York City, who died in Kensington, Middlesex. Probate to Sir James Grant with similar powers reserved to the brother, Alexander Grant, and to Ludovick Grant and James Trasch. (May 1781).

Grant, Neal, of New York, Lieutenant of the 77th Regiment of Foot. Administration to the relict, Hellen Grant. (Aug. 1763).

Grape, James, of New Windsor, Berkshire, whose son, Samuel Grape, was in South Carolina. Probate to the son, Richard Grape. (July 1733).

Grave, Anne, of St. Botolph Aldgate, London, widow, whose kinsman, George Grave, was in Hartford, Connecticut, and kinsman, John Grave, in New Haven, New England. Probate to William Kiffin; James

Grave, *(contd.)*
Orbell renouncing. (Mar. 1677). Revoked on the death of William Kiffin and administration granted to his executors, Joseph and Jonathan Hardey. (Oct. 1688).

Grave, John, of Virginia. Administration with will to Walter Potter, the nephew by a sister, during the absence of the named executor, John Murrey. (Sep. 1692). Sh.

Grave, John, formerly of Dublin, Ireland, but late of Annapolis, Maryland. Probate to the brother, Thomas Grave. (July 1757).

Grave alias Graves, Leonard, of Charles Town, South Carolina. Administration with will to the nephew, Leonard Grave; the brother, William Grave, and William Burrows having died before executing, and the father, Robert Grave, having died in the testator's lifetime. (Dec. 1799). Revoked on the death of Leonard Grave and granted to the nephew, Robert Grave. (Mar. 1819).

Graves, Richard, formerly of Sheffield, Yorkshire, but late of New York City. Administration to the relict, Elizabeth Graves. (Apr. 1836).

Gray, Ellis, of Boston, Massachusetts. Limited probate to Thomas Dolbeare. (Aug. 1782).

Gray, Grace, of Symondsbury, Dorset, widow. Administration to the daughter, Grace, wife of John Kemble in Virginia. (Mar. 1695).

Gray, Harrison, formerly of Boston, Massachusetts, but late of Newman Street, St. Marylebone, Middlesex. Probate to the son, Harrison Gray, with similar powers reserved to the sons, Lewis and John Gray. (Jan. 1795).

Grey, Henry, of St. Botolph Aldgate, London, who died in Virginia. Administration with will to the principal creditor, Richard Banckes; the relict, Elizabeth Kerby alias Grey, renouncing. (June 1675).

Gray, James, surgeon of the 21st Regiment of Foot, who died in Philadelphia. Probate to the father, John Gray. (Dec. 1771).

Gray, John, Captain of an Independent Company and Governor of the Fort in Georgia, bachelor. Administration to Henry Davidson, attorney for the brother and next-of-kin, Robert Gray, in Crich, Scotland. (Aug. 1770).

Gray, Thomas, of Boston, Massachusetts. Limited probate to Thomas Dolbeare. (Aug. 1782).

Grey, William, of London, who died in Hackney, Middlesex, and whose brother, John Grey, was in New England. Probate to the relict, Susan Grey. (Nov. 1663). Wa.

Grayson, John, of Whitehaven, Virginia, and of the merchant ship *Prince Frederick*, bachelor. Administration to Benjamin Grayson, attorney for the mother, Mary Grayson, widow, in St. Bees, Cumberland. (Sep. 1733).

Greaves, Adam, of Charles Town, South Carolina, and of H.M. ship *Rose*, bachelor. Probate to Edward Jasper, attorney for Edward Stevens in South Carolina. (Apr. 1738).

Greene, Edward, of Bristol, who died in Virginia. Probate to the brother, Robert Greene. (Aug. 1698). Wa.

Green, Ellen Charlotte, nee Bennett, of Baltimore, United States of America. Administration to James Samuel Bennett, attorney for the husband, Charles Green, in Baltimore. (May 1828).

Green, John, of Petsoe, Gloucester County, Virginia. Probate to the relict, Anne Green. (Jan. 1694). Wa.

Green, Matthew, of New York City. Administration with will to the relict, Jane Green. (June 1852).

Greene, Peter, of the ship *Charles*, who died in Virginia. Administration to the sister-in-law, Mary, wife of the brother, Edward Greene. (July 1678).

Green, Richard, of Jamaica, who died in New York City. Administration to the brother and next-of-kin, William Green. (May 1794).

Greene, Robert, of Stepney, Middlesex, who made a bequest to Thomas Reynolds in Virginia. Probate to Thomas Snow. (Sep. 1658). Wa.

Green, Thomas, of Strutton Major, King and Queen County, York River, Virginia, widower. Administration to Elizabeth Green, relict and executrix of the nephew and next-of-kin, John Green deceased. (Oct. 1729).

Green, Winifred, of Kingsbury, Middlesex, widow, whose son, John Green, went to Virginia. Probate to the brother, John Finch. (Oct. 1641). *See* NGSQ 69/117.

Greenough, William, of Boston, New England, who died abroad or at sea. Administration to the principal creditor, Benjamin Peake, merchant. (May 1684).

Greenslade, Francis, formerly of Martinhoe, Devon, but late of Independent Grove, Illinois. Administration to the relict, Mary Ann Greenslade. (Nov. 1838).

Greenwood, Isaac. of Boston, New England, who died on the ship *Norwich* in Barbados. Administration to John Grimla, attorney for the relict, Anne Greenwood, in Boston. (July 1700).

Greenwood, Isaac, of H.M. ship *Rose*, widower. Administration to James Crockatt, attorney for the principal creditor, Gideon Norton, in Charles Town, South Carolina. (Nov. 1746).

Gregg, Frederick, [formerly of Wilmington, North Carolina], but late of Londonderry, Ireland. Probate to Edward Price Dobbs and Joseph Curry alias Cory. (June 1789). ALC.

Gregory, George, of Kings Town, United States of America, bachelor. Administration to the sister, Eliza, wife of William Latter. (Oct. 1855). Further grant made in June 1859).

Gregory, John, of H.M. ship *Southampton*, who died in Virginia. Administration to the relict, Margaret Gregory. (Oct. 1702).

Gregory, William, of Nottingham, whose brother, Henry Gregory, was in New England. Probate to the son, John Gregory. (Feb. 1652). Wa.

Gregson, Richard, of St. Augustine by St. Paul, London, whose kinsman, Thomas Gregson, was in New England. Probate to the son, Nicholas Gregson. (Aug. 1640). Wa.

Greig, David, formerly of St. Botolph Aldgate, London, but late of New York, bachelor. Administration to John Claphin, attorney for the

Greig, *(contd.)*
mother, Isabel Murison, widow, in Tearn, Scotland. (Oct.1788).

Greive, George, formerly of Swansfield, Northumberland, but late of Brussels, France, a citizen of the United States of America, bachelor. Administration to the creditor, Richard Wilson; all those entitled to administration having been cited but not having appeared. (Oct. 1809).

Greive, James, mariner, (bound to Virginia in the *Sarah*). Probate to Catherine Scott, widow. (Dec. 1732).

Grendon, Thomas, of Westover, Charles City County, Virginia. Limited probate to Arthur North. (Apr. 1685). Sh.Wa.

Gresham, Otway, of the environs of Boston, New England. Probate to Edward Benskin; the named executor, Frances Benskin, having died. (Nov. 1717).

Gresley, Jeffery, of King William County, Virginia. Administration to the daughter, Jane Grammar Gresley; the relict, Mary, now wife of Robert Gaines, having been cited but not having appeared. (Apr. 1791).

Greves, Adam, of Charles Town, South Carolina, mariner of H.M. ship *Rose*, bachelor. Administration with will to Edward Jasper, attorney for Edward Stephens in South Carolina. (Apr. 1738).

Grew, Elizabeth, of Birmingham, Warwickshire, spinster, whose niece, Mary, wife of Benjamin Green, was in Boston, North America. Probate to Samuel Rogers and Culcope Bond; Thomas Beilby renouncing. (Dec. 1818).

Grey. *See* **Gray**.

Gribb, John, of Stepney, Middlesex, who died in Virginia. Administration to the principal creditor, John Sackell; the relict, Susan Gribb, renouncing. (June 1698).

Grice, Caesar, of Maryland. Administration to the brother, John Grice; the relict having died. (Aug. 1754).

Grice, Peter, formerly of Coalbrook Dale, Shropshire, but late of Rondout, Ulster County, New York, barge builder, widower. Administration to the father, Peter Grice. (Dec. 1853).

Grierson, James, of Augusta, Georgia, Colonel of the Loyal Militia Regiment, who died in St. Paul's, Georgia. Probate to the son, Thomas Grierson, with similar powers reserved to Andrew Johnson and John Glen. (Feb. 1789). ALC.

Griffin, David, of St. Michael Bassishaw, London, whose brother, Samuel Griffin, was in Virginia. Probate to John Hobbs. (Dec. 1679). Wa.

Griffin, Elizabeth, of Virginia, widow. Administration to the niece by a sister and next-of-kin, Lidya, wife of Thomas Tonstall. (Nov. 1689). Wa. Inventory PROB 4/1035.

Griffin, James, Lieutenant of General Shirley's Regiment, who died in Oxford, Massachusetts. Administration with will to Thomas Kast, attorney for the relict, Prudence Griffin, and for William Watson, in Massachusetts. (Sep. 1773).

Griffyn, Joanna, of Virginia. Probate to George Griffyn. (Apr. 1661). Wa.

Griffin, Thomas, of the ship *Hope*, who died in Virginia, widower. Probate to Solomon Amos. (July 1697).

Griffith, Edward, formerly of Charles Town, North America, but late of the City of Chester. Probate to William Greenwood and William Higgins with similar powers reserved to Walter Thomas and Charles Goodwin; the relict, Martha, now having married James McNeill. (Oct. 1785).

Griffiths, Andrew, surgeon of H.M. ships *Proteus* and *Guadeloupe*, who died in New York. Probate to the brother, Richard Griffiths. (Feb. 1782).

Griffiths, James, of Port Royal, Carolina, who died in the Palace of St. James, Westminster, Middlesex. Probate to the father, John Griffiths. (Feb. 1709).

Griffiths, John, of New York City. Administration with will to the daughter, Cornelia, Baroness de Diemar, wife of Frederick, Baron de Diemar; the relict, Jane Griffiths, and the sons, John and Anthony Griffiths, having died before executing. (Dec. 1799).

Grigg, Robert, formerly of Looe, Cornwall, but late of Mobile, North America. Administration to the relict, Mary Grigg. (Apr. 1848).

Griggs, Michael, of Lancaster County, Virginia, but late of St. Botolph Aldgate, London, who died in St. Matthew, Friday Street, London. Probate to the relict, Anne, now wife of Richard Bray. (Sep. 1688). Wa.

Grimditch, Thomas, of New York. Administration to the relict, Eshew Grimditch. (Mar. 1684).

Grimes, Gilbert, of Stepney, Middlesex, who died in Panama or Porto Bello in America. Probate to the relict, Eleanor Grimes. (Dec. 1722).

Grismond, Charles, Ensign at Annapolis Royal in North America, who died in General Evans' Regiment in Scotland. Administration to the relict, Anne Grismond. (Mar. 1723).

Grogen, William, formerly of Exeter, Devon, but late of Charleston, South Carolina. Limited administration with will to Edmund Granger and Robert Tothill. (Feb. 1818).

Gronous, Elizabeth, of St. Clement Danes, Middlesex, spinster, whose cousin, William Probert, was in Worcester County, Virginia. Probate to Edward Barnston and Edward Lewis. (June 1750). Wi.

Groombridge, Walter, of Philadelphia. Administration to John Norton and Henry Daniel, guardians of the only child, Jane Groombridge. (July 1710).

Groom, George, of Boston, United States of America. Administration to the relict, Lydia Groom. (June 1808).

Groome, John, of Strood, Kent, who had goods in New England. Probate to the relict, Venice Groome. (June 1658). Sh.

Groome, Nicholas, who died in Virginia. Probate to the brother [blank] Wall and the brother, Henry Groome. (Apr. 1652). Sh.

Groome, Thomas, of the ship *Falkland* in H.M. service, who died in New England. Administration to the principal creditrix, Anne, wife of John Severne. (Apr. 1698).

Grove, Grey, Captain of the 23rd Regiment of Foot, who died in New York, bachelor. Administration to the sister, Mary, wife of Corbett Hale. (Sep. 1777).

Grove, Samuel, of St. Helena, Granville County, South Carolina. Limited administration with will to the relict, Jane Grove. (May 1777).

Grover, John, of King's College, Cambridge, who died in Georgia, bachelor. Administration to the mother, Carolina, wife of William Kindon, she having retracted a former renunciation. (Nov. 1774).

Grover, Joseph alias Jotham, of the merchant ship *Providence*, bachelor. Administration with will to William Lancaster, attorney for the grandmother in Boston, New England. (May 1710).

Grover, William, formerly of Reading, Berkshire, but late Chief Justice of East Florida, who died at sea. Probate to the son, John Grover. (Jan. 1768).

Groves, Elizabeth, of Charleston, South Carolina. Probate to the sister, Susannah Hawkins, widow, with similar powers reserved to the sisters, Mary Groves, and Ann, wife of John Rous. (June 1810).

Groves, Peter, of New York, bachelor. Administration to the father, Thomas Groves. (Apr. 1847). Further grant made in October 1874.

Gruet, Peggy, of Newark, New Jersey, widow. Administration with will to Thomas Trevor Tatham and Henry Tatham, attornies for the son, Frederick Gruet, in Newark. (Jan. 1838).

Gudgeon, Henry, of New York City, Lieutenant in Sir William Pepperell's Regiment, who died in Oswego. Administration to the relict, Martha Gudgeon. (July 1765).

Guest, John, of Philadelphia, widower. Probate to John Geast. (Apr. 1708).

Guillume, Peter, master of the brigantine *Jane and Margaret*, who died in Virginia, bachelor. Probate to the father, John Guillume. (Feb. 1702).

Gulline, William, Lieutenant of a New York Independent Company of Foot, who died in Havana, bachelor. Administration to John Cuthbert, attorney for the nephew, John Gulline, in Stranraer, Wigtownshire, Scotland. (Dec. 1763).

Gulliver, Elijah, of Milton, Suffolk County, New England, and of H.M. ships *Vigilant* and *Superbe*, bachelor. Administration to Henry Rainsdon, attorney for the brother, Samuel Gulliver, in New England. (July 1754).

Gunnell, George, of Shoreditch, Middlesex, who died in Virginia. Administration to the relict, Rebecca Gunnell. (July 1674).

Gunning, Peter, formerly of London but late of Mead Township, Crawford County, Pennsylvania. Administration with will to John Joseph Field, attorney for the son, William Peter Gunning, in Pittsburg, North America; the daughter, Elizabeth Gunning, renouncing. (Apr. 1850). Revoked on the death of William P. Gunning and granted, after retraction of her renunciation, to the daughter, Elizabeth Gunning. (Aug. 1851).

Gurney, Daniel, of Christ Church, Middlesex, who died in North America, bachelor. Administration to Ann, wife of Joseph Piggot, administratrix of John Kettle deceased, who was the half brother and only next-of-kin. (July 1788).

Gutteridge, Paul, of H.M. ship *Benjamin*. Administration to Thomas Goodrich Barnes, guardian of the minor son, Richard Gutteridge, now in Virginia. (Aug. 1702).

Guy, Edward, of Appleby, Westmorland, who died in Philadelphia. Administration to the son, John Guy. (Apr. 1698).

Guy, Frances, of St. Botolph Bishopsgate, London, widow, whose brother, William Clutterbuck, was in New England. Probate to John Heyth, M.D. (Aug. 1680). Wa.

Guy, William, of St. Mildred, Broad Street, London, whose cousin, John Gate, was in Virginia. Probate to William Allen and Anthony Field. (Nov. 1665). Wi.

Guyon, Stephen, Second Lieutenant of the 23rd Regiment of Royal Welch Fusiliers, who died in George Town, North America, bachelor. Administration to the father, Henry William Guyon. (Aug. 1784).

Gwinnett, Ann, formerly of Wolverhampton, Staffordshire, but late of Georgia. Administration with will to Peter Belin, husband and administrator of the daughter, Elizabeth Belin, formerly Gwinnett, deceased. (May 1785).

Gwinn, James, of Nantucket, Massachusetts. Probate to the relict, Mary Gwinn. (June 1818).

Gwin, John, of James City, Virginia. Administration with will to Thomas Starke, attorney for the executor, Henry Jenkins, in Virginia. (Nov. 1684). Wi.

Gwyn, John, of Charles Town, South Carolina, bachelor. Administration to the creditor, John Owen. (Nov. 1757).

Gyles. *See* **Giles**.

H

Hacker, John, of Limehouse, Stepney, Middlesex, who had lands in Virginia. Probate to the relict, Elizabeth Hacker. (June 1654). Wa.

Hacker, John, of Bermondsey, Surrey, who died in Virginia. Administration to the relict, Joyce Hacker. (Nov. 1690).

Hackett, John, who died on the merchant ship *Oxford* in Maryland. Administration to the principal creditor, Thomas Watson. (Apr. 1729).

Hackett, John, of Pennsylvania, bachelor. Probate by his solemn affirmation to the brother, Thomas Hackett; no executor having been named and the father, John Hackett, having died before administering. (Feb. 1731).

Haddocke, William, of Virginia, who died overseas. Probate to the brother, Richard Haddocke. (Aug. 1649). Sh.Wa.

Hadfield, George, of the City of Washington, North America, bachelor. Administration to the sister, Charlotte Combe, widow. (Aug. 1827).

Hagen, George, of Ferrisburgh, Addison County, Vermont, miller and gardener. Administration with will by his solemn affirmation to Alfred Brown, attorney for Rufus Hazard and Andrew Holmes in Vermont. (Feb. 1854).

Haigh, Samuel, formerly of Cloudesley Square, Islington, Middlesex, but late of New Orleans, bachelor. Administration to the sister, Jane Haigh; the mother, Jane Haigh, having died. (May 1834).

Hailes. *See* **Hales**.

Haines. *See* **Haynes**.

Hainsworth, Francis, of St. Sepulchre, London, who had goods in Virginia. Administration with will to John White; no executor having been named. (Feb. 1657). Wa.Wi.

Hake, Lucy, of Racine, Wisconsin. Administration to the husband, Thomas Gordon Hake. (Mar. 1857).

Hale, Edward, formerly of Highgate, Middlesex, but late of Water Town near Boston, North America. Probate to Sylvanus Hanley, William Robinson and Edward Hale. (June 1811).

Hale, William, formerly of Alton, Hampshire, but late of Philadelphia, bachelor. Administration to the sister and next-of-kin, Ann Seacocke. (Oct. 1832).

Hailes, Elizabeth, of Shadwell, Stepney, Middlesex, whose cousin, William Foster, was in New England. Probate to Thomas Parker and William Bugby. (Sep. 1664). Wa.

Hales, Sarah, of New England. Administration to Walter Hales, attorney for the husband, Richard Hales, in New England. (May 1696).

Halford, John, of St. Katherine Creechurch, London, who died in Virginia, bachelor. Administration to the sister, Dorothy Benson. (May 1690). Revoked on her death and granted to the sister, Alice Crisdell. (Apr. & May 1693).

Hall, Charles, citizen and fishmonger of London, who died in Virginia,

Hall, *(contd.)*
bachelor. Probate to Peter McArtell. (June 1699).

Hall, George, of Norfolk, Virginia, bachelor. Administration to the brother, William Hall, attorney for the mother, Mary Hall, widow, during her lunacy. (Mar. 1828).

Hall, Henry, of Charleston, South Carolina, bachelor. Administration to the brother, Joseph Hall. (Oct. 1804).

Hall, John, of London, (intending a voyage to Virginia). Probate to the mother, Prudence Hall. (Dec. 1705). Wi.

Hall, John, of St. Marylebone, Middlesex, who died in Williamsburg, Virginia, bachelor. Administration to the mother, Ann Hall, widow. (Sep. 1787).

Hall, John, formerly of Poole, Dorset, but late of New York, bachelor. Administration to the father, Charles Hall. (Apr. 1813). Revoked on his death and granted to his daughter and executrix, Catherine Parkhouse, widow. (Apr. 1815).

Hall, Jonathan, Lieutenant of the 34th Regiment of Foot, who died in New York, bachelor and bastard. Administration to Sir Thomas Clavering for the use of the Crown. (Feb. 1768).

Hall, Richard, of London, who died in Virginia, widower. Administration to the son, Richard Hall. (Jan. 1668).

Hall, Robert, of Marlborough, Prince George County, Maryland. Administration with will to Thomas Sprigg, attorney for James Haddock and Nolden Jefferson in Maryland. (May 1720).

Hall, Thomas, of St. Katherine by the Tower, London, whose brother, John Hall, was in New England. Probate to the relict, Judith Hall. (May 1663). Wa. NGSQ 64/137).

Hall, William, of Virginia, bachelor. Administration to the mother, Elizabeth, wife of Richard Fox. (Mar. 1713).

Hall, William, of Mount Facitus, South Carolina, bachelor. Administration to the brother, Robert Hall. (Jan. 1786).

Hallett, Elizabeth, of St. Edmund the King, London, who died in New York, widow. Administration to Henry Barton, guardian of the daughter, Elizabeth Hallett. (July 1723). Revoked and granted to Elizabeth Hallett on her coming of age. (Sep. 1724).

Hallett, Lancelott, of the River Sarifax in Maryland, bachelor. Administration to the brother, Richard Hallett. (July 1671).

Halley, Francis, of All Hallows Staining, London, who died in Virginia. Probate to Edmund Halley and Richard Pyke. (Sep. 1702).

Hallowell, Robert, of Gardiner, Massachusetts, widower. Administration to the son and next-of-kin, Robert Hallowell Gardiner (*sic*). (Dec. 1818).

Halsey, Esau, of Suffolk, New England, bachelor. Administration to John Bynne during the absence of the brother, William Halsey. (Sep. 1677).

Halsted, Abraham, of Rotterdam, whose sister was in New England. Probate to the relict, Dorcas Whitman alias Halsted, with similar powers reserved to William Scapes. (May 1651). Sh.Wa.

Ham, Matthew, formerly of New England, mariner, but late of St. Olave, Southwark, Surrey. Probate to Alice Pomery. (Jan. 1704).

Ham, Samuel, of Portsmouth, New Hampshire. Administration to the creditors, Thomas Wilson and William Rowlett; the relict, Jane Ham, and the only children, Abigail and William Ham, having been cited but not having appeared. (June 1815).

Haman, Richard, of St. Olave, Southwark, Surrey, who died on the merchant ship *New York* in New York. Probate to the relict, Anne Haman. (Feb. 1717).

Hambeton/Hambleton, John. *See* **Hamilton**.

Hamilton, Andrew, of Philadelphia. Administration with will to Ferdinando John Paris, attorney for William Allen, James Hamilton and Andrew Hamilton, in Pennsylvania. (Dec. 1742).

Hamilton, Douglas, of Suffolk, Virginia, bachelor. Administration to the brother, Archibald Hamilton. (July 1783).

Hamilton, Hugh, of Pensacola, Lieutenant in H.M. Forces, bachelor. Administration to the brother and next-of-kin, Andrew Hamilton. (Apr. 1793).

Hamilton, James, of Vienna, Maryland, bachelor. Administration to the sister and next-of-kin, Margaret Howe, widow. (Feb. 1772).

Hamilton alias Hambleton alias Hambeton, John, of H.M. ship *Canterbury*, bachelor. Administration with will to Owen Gray, administrator of the named executor, Thomas McKenly deceased, and attorney for William Gale in New York, the principal creditor of the said McKenly; the legatee, David Chancelor, having died before administering. (Mar. 1750).

Hamilton, John, of Harrisburg, Dauphin County, Pennsylvania. Administration to Michael Smith Parnther, Richard Grose Burfoot and Charles Robert Turner, attornies for the relict, Margaret, now wife of Andrew Mitchell, in America. (June 1823).

Hamilton, Mary, of Philadelphia, widow. Administration with will to Lady Ann Hamilton, attorney for Samuel Duffield in Philadelphia. (Dec. 1794).

Hamilton, Paul, formerly of Charleston, South Carolina, but late of Clerkenwell, Middlesex. Limited probate to Robert Williams and Rev. Alexander Hewat. (Jan. 1798).

Hammand, Thomas, of Newport, North America, widower. Administration to the son, Benjamin Hammand. (July 1786).

Hammell, John, of New York, surgeon of the Third Batallion of the late New Jersey Volunteers. Administration to David Thomas, attorney for the relict, Hannah Hammell, in New York. (Aug. 1797).

Hammer, Martin, of the merchant ship *Pertuxan Merchant*, who died in Virginia, widower. Administration to Gustavus Hammer, guardian of the children, Anne Catherine, Beren and Martin Hammer, now in Scotland or at sea. (Aug. 1704).

Hammerton, Elizabeth, of Charles Town, South Carolina. Administration with will to Nathaniel Hollier; the named executors, Ann de la Brasseur, Joseph Barry, Adam Beauchamp and Thomas Bolton,

Hammerton, *(contd.)*
having been cited but not having appeared, and the son, Hollier Hammerton, having died. (Jan. 1750).

Hamerton, Pinchback, of Virginia, bachelor. Probate to Hannah, wife of Richard Cloke. (Dec. 1729).

Hammet, Frances, wife of John Hammet, formerly Frances Hutchins, formerly of Bandon, Cork County, Ireland, but late of Philadelphia. Administration to Reuben Harvey, attorney for the only surviving children, Emanuel Hammet and Ann, wife of Edward Clayton, in Philadelphia. (Sep. 1819).

Hammond, Abijah, formerly of New York City but late of Westchester, New York, merchant. Administration to George Atkinson, attorney for the son, Charles Henry Hammond, in New York City; the relict, Margaret Hammond, renouncing. (July 1838).

Hammond, James, of Zainsville, Ohio, surgeon of H.M. ship *Osprey*. Administration to Alexander Haldane, attorney for the relict, Elizabeth Hammond, in Zainsville. (May 1834).

Hammond, John, of Warwick, Rhode Island, master mariner. Administration to George William Oleary, attorney for the relict, Sarah Hammond, in Washington, District of Columbia. (Jan. 1844).

Hammond, Samuel, formerly of Birmingham, Warwickshire, but late of Brooklyn, New York. Administration to Isaac Hadley, attorney for the relict, Maria Hammond, in Brooklyn. (Jan. 1852).

Hammond, William, of Stepney, Middlesex, whose uncle, William Clopton, was in Virginia. Probate to Samuel Skinner and Josiah Cole. (July 1732). *See* NGSQ 60/260.

Hampton, John, of Somerset County, Maryland. Limited probate to the brother, Robert Hampton. (Aug. 1722).

Hamson, Daniel, of H.M. ship *Mermaid*, who died on the merchant ship *Hamilton*, bachelor. Administration with will to Thomas Newby, attorney for John Newby in New England. (June 1715).

Hanbury, Edward, of Old Brentford, Ealing, Middlesex, whose son, Peter, was in New England. Probate to the relict, Mary Hanbury. (Apr. 1647). Wa.

Hancock, John, of New Orleans, bachelor. Administration to James Hancock, the son and administrator of the father, Robert Hancock deceased. (May 1836).

Hans alias Hance, Peter, of the merchant ship *Providence*, who died in Virginia. Probate to the relict, Sarah Hans, with similar powers reserved to Robert Townsend. (Nov. 1708).

Hance, Rawleigh, of Shadwell, Middlesex, who died in Virginia, bachelor. Administration to the brother, Edward Wren alias Hance. (Oct. 1673).

Handford, John, of Ludlow, Shropshire, whose kinsman, Tobias Handford, was in Virginia. Probate to the relict, Elinor Handford; Sir Walter Williams and Sir John Winford renouncing. (Jan. 1670). Wi.

Handford, Tobias, formerly of Ware, Gloucester County, Virginia, who died in the parish of St. George Botolph Lane, London. Probate to

Handford, *(contd.)* Elizabeth and John Handford and to William Smith. (Dec. 1677). Wi.

Handy, Charles, of Newport, Rhode Island. Probate to the sons, John and Thomas Handy, and to Stephen Deblois, with similar powers reserved to the sons, Levin and William Handy. (Mar. 1796).

Hanford, Elnathan, of Norwall, Connecticut, seaman of H.M. ship *Weymouth*, who died in Bombay Hospital. Administration to James Perrot, attorney for the relict, Ann Hanford, in Norwall. (Nov. 1769).

Hannam, Minty, formerly of St. John, Southwark, Surrey, but late of Dorchester County, Maryland. Administration to the cousin german, Hester Read; the relict, Mary Holland formerly Hannam, having been cited but not having appeared. (Apr. 1791).

Hannam, William, of New York, bachelor. Administration to the sister, Ann, wife of James May. (May 1806).

Hannyford, Edward, of Virginia. Administration to the relict, Marchebell Hannyford. (June 1656).

Hans. *See* **Hance**.

Hansworth, Francis, of St. Sepulchre, London, who made bequests to Thomas Wilkinson, Elizabeth Camsey and John Creed in Virginia. Administration with will to the principal legatee, John White; no executor having been named. (Feb. 1657). Wi.

Hanton, William, of Ramsgate, Kent, master of the merchant ship *Sarah*. Limited administration to Rodrigo Pachecor to recover debts owed to William Yeomans and Gabriell Escott of South Carolina. (Aug. 1736). Revoked and limited administration granted to the relict, Sarah Hanton. (Jan. 1737).

Hardich, William, of Nominy, Westmoreland County, Virginia, who died in Bristol. Probate to Thomas Burgis and Richard Winston. (Jan. 1669). Wi.

Harding, Richard, formerly of Market Harborough, Leicestershire, wool stapler, but late of Meade County, Kentucky, widower. Administration to the niece, Mary Ann Milner, spinster; the sisters and only next-of-kin, Anne, wife of Thomas Stevenson, and Martha, wife of Benjamin Page, renouncing. (Dec. 1832).

Harding, William, of Virginia, bachelor. Probate to Adriana Dunn alias Oakley, wife of Samuel Dunn. (Nov. 1742). NGSQ 64/288.

Hardwick, Mary A. *See* **Stonier**.

Hardy, John, of West Florida, bachelor. Administration to the father, Rev. Joseph Hardy. (July 1775).

Hare, Margaret, of Pennsylvania, widow. Administration with will to Walter Stirling, attorney for Robert Hare and John Hare Powel in Philadelphia; the other executor, Charles Willing Hare, having been cited but not having appeared. (Dec. 1819).

Harford, Samuel, formerly of Bristol, merchant, but late of New York. Probate by his solemn affirmation to the brother, John Harford. (Jan. 1839).

Harley, John, of H.M. ship *Terrible*, who died in Long Island Hospital. Probate to Elizabeth Halfpenny, spinster. (July 1781).

Harman, John, of Bermondsey, Surrey, who died on the merchant ship *Forward* in Virginia. Probate to the relict, Mary Harman. (Dec. 1728).

Harman, Thomas, of Poplar, Stepney, Middlesex, who died in Virginia, bachelor. Administration to the principal creditrix, Mary Fisher, widow. (Apr. 1701).

Harmer, Charles, of Virginia. Administration to the creditor, Richard Roch. (July 1639).

Harmer, George, formerly of Bristol but late of Albermarle County, North America. Administration with will to John Lambert, no executor having been named. (Apr. 1799).

Harrendon, Tristian, of New England, bachelor. Administration to the cousin and next-of-kin, Philip White. (Sep. 1681).

Harries. *See* **Harris**.

Harriman, William, formerly of Upper Thames Street, London, but late of New York City, merchant. Administration to the daughter, Eliza Harriman; the relict, Frances Harriman, having died. (Apr. 1826).

Harrington, Mary, formerly of Thorncombe, Devon, but late of Pike near the village of Le Raysville, Bradford County, Pennsylvania, widow. Administration with will to the son, William Harrington. (June 1843).

Harris, Benjamin, of Newbury Port, Massachusetts. Administration to the creditor, Joseph Hooper; the relict, Lucy Harris, having died before administering, and the only child, Mary, wife of the said Hooper, having been cited but not having appeared. (Apr. 1779).

Harris, Daniel. *See* **Howard**.

Harris, Edward, of Moorestown, Burlington County, New Jersey. Limited administration with will to the son, Edward Harris. (Aug. 1827).

Harris, George, of Westover, Charles County, Virginia. Administration with nuncupative will to the relict, Sarah Greendon alias Harris; no executor having been named. (Aug. 1674). Wi.

Harris, John, of Hillmarton, Wiltshire, who had lands in Pennsylvania. Probate to the relict, Jane Harris, and the son, Samuel Harris. (June 1693).

Harris, John, of St. Stephen's, Northumberland County, Virginia. Probate to the relict, Hannah, now wife of Thomas Cralle. (Sep. 1723). Wi.

Harris, John, formerly of Dublin, Ireland, but late of Charleston, South Carolina, bachelor. Administration to the sister and only next-of-kin, Elizabeth Patterson, widow. (Sep. 1804).

Harries, John Hill, of Priskilly, Pembrokeshire, Lieutenant of the 33rd Regiment of Foot, who died in Boston, bachelor. Administration to the father, John Harries. (June 1778).

Harris alias Crumpe, Mary, of Virginia. Administration to the daughter, Martha, wife of John Jennings. (June 1656).

Harris, Priscilla, of Northam, Devon, spinster, whose sister, Agnes, was in New England. Probate to the brother, Richard Harris. (Sep. 1651). Sh.Wa.

Harris, Richard, of Pennsylvania, who died at St. Stephen Coleman Street, London. Limited probate to Theodore Eccleston. (Mar. 1701).

Harris, Richard the younger, Lieutenant in Colonel Cane's Regiment, who died in America. Administration by decree to James Rane, executor of the father, Richard Harris deceased. (Feb. 1723). Revoked on the death of James Rane and granted to his executor, Francis Marshall. (Jan. 1726).

Harris, Robert, of H.M. ship *Hampshire*, bachelor. Administration to Margaret, wife of Magnus Alexander, attorney for the sister, Isabel, wife of William Tilley, in New England. (May 1700).

Harris, Robert, of H.M. ship *Essex*'s prize, who died in Virginia. Administration to Susan Biddell, grandmother of the children, Robert, Sarah, Mary, and Elizabeth Harris. (July 1700).

Harris, Samuel, of Boston, New England, who died on the merchant ship *Martha and Hannah*. Probate by decree of nuncupative will to the brother, Amos Harris. (Jan. 1721).

Harris, Stephen, of Norham, Devon County, Virginia or Maryland. Administration to the relict, Margaret Harris. (Aug. 1699).

Harrison, Charles, Captain in the New Jersey Volunteers, who died in Sheffield, New Brunswick. Administration with will to Evan Davies, attorney for the brother, James Harrison, in Sheffield. (Dec. 1803).

Harrison, Denise, of New York, widow. Administration to Rev. William Dupre, attorney for the only child, Esther, wife of Edward Shepherd, in New York. (Aug. 1819).

Harrison, Elizabeth, of New York City, widow. Administration to the nephew, Rev. William Dupre. (Aug. 1821).

Harrison, George, of Philadelphia. Administration to the sister and only next-of-kin, Rachel, wife of Samuel Jones; the relict, Elizabeth Harrison [having died]. (Apr. 1795).

Harrison, Henrick, of the ship *Barnardiston*, who died in Virginia. Probate to Anne Thompson alias Holliday. (Mar. 1694).

Harrison, James, of Sheffield, New Brunswick, a reduced Lieutenant in the Second Batallion of the New Jersey Volunteers. Administration to David Davies, attorney for the relict, Charity Harrison, in Sheffield. (Dec. 1806).

Harrison, John, formerly of Manehack, Louisiana, planter, but late a reduced Major in the South Carolina Royalists, who died in New Orleans. Administration with will to John Bannatyne, attorney for the surviving executor, William Durnford, in New Orleans. (Mar. 1806).

Harrison, Jonas, of Savannah, bachelor. Administration to the father, George Harrison. (July 1822).

Harrison, Lother, of St. Margaret, Westminster, Middlesex, who died on the merchant ship *Mary* in Carolina. Administration to the relict, Catherine Harrison. (Apr. 1720).

Harrison, Margaret, of Battersea, Surrey, widow, who made a bequest to Alice Andrewes in New England. Probate to the son, Thomas Andrewes. (Mar. 1642). Wa.

Harrison, Nicholas, of Virginia, who died in the parish of St. Sepulchre, London, bachelor. Administration with will to the mother, Dorothy Harrison, no executor having been named. (Sep. 1653). Sh.Wa.Wi.

Harrison, Robert, of Augusta, Georgia. Probate to Charles Sumerson and Thomas Nickelson; the relict, Mary Harrison, renouncing. (Feb. 1776).

Harrison, Robert, formerly of Plaistow, Essex, but late of Buffalo in the United States of America. Probate to George Price with similar powers reserved to John William Cundy. (Oct. 1833).

Harrison, Samuel, Lieutenant of the Artillery Train, who died in Albany, North America. Administration to the creditor, James Taylor; the mother and only next-of-kin, Ann Robins, renouncing. (Oct. 1759).

Harrison, Thomas, of Rotherhithe, Surrey, who died in New England, bachelor. Administration to the father, Edmund Harrison. (Dec. 1669).

Harrison, William Cockworthy, formerly of Strensham near Tewkesbury, Gloucestershire, but late of Crocketts, Texas, bachelor. Administration to the creditor, Charles Harrison; the father, George Harrison, renouncing. (Mar. 1853).

Harrold, Alfred, of Philadelphia, merchant. Probate to the brother, Frederick William Harrold, and to Arthur Ryland. (May 1845).

Hart, Andrew, of Wapping, Middlesex, who died on the merchant ship *Amity* in Virginia. Probate to Robert Wilson. (Nov. 1723).

Hart, Charles, of Charles Town, South Carolina, widower. Administration to the sister, Mary, wife of Sidney Harris. (Dec. 1758).

Hart, Charles, formerly of Stafford but late of Philadelphia, bachelor. Administration to Elizabeth, wife of Charles Boult, administratrix with will to the father, John Hart deceased. (Jan. 1853).

Hart, Ephraim, formerly of Mark Lane, London, but late of New York City, who had title in the New Synagogue in Leadenhall Street, London. Limited administration to Louis Lucas and Philip Phillips. (July 1840).

Hart, John, of Cumberland Town, New Kent County, Virginia, bachelor. Administration to James Miller, attorney for the brother and next-of-kin, Patrick Hart, in New York City. (Dec. 1779). Revoked and granted to James Miller as attorney for the mother, Elizabeth Smith, widow. (Dec. 1780).

Hart, John, of H.M. ship *Avenger*, who died in Long Island Hospital, bachelor. Administration to the father, John Hart. (Apr. 1784).

Hart, Samuel, formerly of Russia Row, Moorfields, London, but late of New Orleans, Louisiana, merchant. Limited administration with will to John Hodgson, attorney for James Ramsay in New Orleans. (Mar. 1834).

Hart, Thomas, of New York City. Probate to the relict, Esther Hart. (Jan. 1774).

Hartwell, Henry, of Stepney, Middlesex, who died in Virginia. Probate to Micajah and Richard Perry. (Aug. 1699). Wa.

Harvey, Charles, formerly of Bourton House, Flax Bourton, Somerset, but

Harvey, *(contd.)*
late of Bath, Mason County, Illinois. Probate to the sister, Mary Robinson Palmer, wife of Frederick Palmer. (Apr. 1853).

Harvey, Charles Arbuthnot, of Albany, New York, bachelor. Administration to the mother and next-of-kin, Maria Harvey. (May 1855).

Harvey, Elizabeth, of Upper Canada, New York, spinster. Probate to the father, George Harvey. (Sep. 1807). Revoked on his death and granted to the brother, William Harvey; the mother, Elizabeth Harvey, having died in the testatrix's lifetime. (Feb. 1817).

Harvey, Sir John, of London, who died overseas with interests in Virginia, bachelor. Administration with will to Alice Dixon, relict and administratrix of Thomas Dixon deceased. (July 1650). Sh.

Harvey, John, of Mexico, who died in the Military Service of the United States of America, bachelor. Administration to the sister, Christiana Harvey. (Aug. 1848).

Harvey, Joseph, of Bellevue, Michigan, bachelor. Administration to John Curry and William Curry, administrators of the aunt and only next-of-kin, Hannah Curry deceased. (Feb. 1843).

Harvey, Nicholas, Lieutenant of Captain Clarke's Independent Company of Foot, who died in Albany, New York, bachelor. Administration to the brother, Rev. Peter Harvey; the mother, Jane Harvey, renouncing. (Dec. 1750).

Harvey, Peter, of New England, bachelor. Administration by decree to the principal creditor, Joseph Davis; the sister, Deborah Oakley, widow, renouncing. (Oct. 1719).

Harvey, Robert, of New England, bachelor. Administration to the cousin german and next-of-kin, Margaret, wife of John Dorrell now on a voyage. (May 1655).

Harvey, Stephen, of Saratoga, North America, Lieutenant of the 62nd Regiment of Foot, bachelor. Administration to the brother, Eliab Harvey. (Dec. 1782).

Harvey, Thomas, of H.M. ship *Deptford*, bachelor. Administration to Rebecca, wife and attorney of Abraham Allaway in Boston, New England. (Aug. 1707). Revoked and granted to the sister, Elizabeth, wife of Thomas Sly. (Sep. 1707).

Harwar, Thomas, of Essex County, Virginia, widower. Limited administration to the son, Thomas Harwar. (Nov. 1704).

Harwood, Anthony, of Virginia. Administration to Edmond Pike, guardian of the children, Sarah, Margaret and James Harwood, during their minority. (Aug. 1659).

Harwood, Arthur, formerly of Virginia but late of St. Peter ad Vincula, London, who died overseas. Probate to Alexander Harwood. (Dec. 1642). Sh.Wi.

Harwood, Elizabeth, of Bethnal Green, Middlesex, widow, whose brother, Hezekiah Usher, was in New England. Probate to James Harwood. (Apr. 1687). Wa.

Harwood, Elizabeth. *See* **Goodwin**.

Harwood, John, of St. Leonard, Shoreditch, Middlesex, whose brother,

Harwood, *(contd.)*
Thomas Harwood, daughter, Elizabeth Sedgwick, and other kin were in New England. Probate to the relict, Elizabeth Harwood. (June 1685). Wa.

Harwood, Thomas, of Streatley, Berkshire, who had lands in Maryland. Probate to Rev. Thomas Harwood. (Mar. 1713).

Haslehurst, Mary, of Philadelphia, who died at sea, widow. Administration to the mother, Mary Abraham, widow. (Jan. 1736).

Haslewood, William, Lieutenant in the Royal American Regiment, who died in North America, bachelor. Administration with will to the father, Edward Haslewood; no executor having been named. (May 1759).

Hassock, George Fisher, formerly of Wimblington, Isle of Ely, but afterwards of Rockford, Illinois, who died as a passenger on the steamship *Sarah Sands*, bachelor. Administration to the father, Christopher Hassock. (Oct. 1850).

Hasted, Thomas, of Stepney, Middlesex, who died on the ship *Bristow* in Virginia, widower. Administration to Thomas Wych, guardian of the children, Judith Reynolds and Thomas Hasted, during their minority. (Feb. 1699). Revoked on his death and granted to John Hogg the younger as guardian of the children. (Feb. 1704). Revoked and granted to Mary Hone, widow, guardian of the son, Thomas Hasted. (Apr. 1706).

Hastings, John, master of the ship *James*, who died in Virginia. Administration with will to William Finlason, attorney for the only sister, Janette Hastings, in Preston Pans, Scotland; the executor, William Brock, renouncing. (Sep. 1707).

Haswell, John, of Stepney, Middlesex, who died in Virginia. Administration to the relict, Sarah Haswell. (July 1682).

Haswell, Sarah, of Watervliet, Albany County, New York, widow. Administration to the son, John Haswell. (Oct. 1829).

Hatch, Matthew, of St. Leonard Eastcheap, London, who died in Georgia, bachelor. Administration with will to Thomas Gorst; no executor having been named (Mar. 1765).

Hatton, John, of Virginia. Probate to the brother, Thomas Hatton, the other executor, Robert Lewellin, having died. (July 1663).

Haviland, Margaret, of New York City. Administration to the husband, Joseph Haviland. (June 1768).

Haviland, Matthew, of Shoreditch, Middlesex, clerk, whose sister, Jane, was wife of William Torry of New England. Probate to the relict, Constance Haviland. (Feb. 1671). Wa.

Hawes, William, of Virginia, bachelor. Administration to the brother, Henry Hawes. (May 1735).

Hawker, George, of St. Martin Ludgate, London, whose brother, Edward Hawker, was in Virginia. Probate to the relict, Martha Hawker. (Jan, 1658). Sh.Wi.

Hawker, Humphrey, of St. Mary le Bow, London, whose daughter, Dorothy, was in Virginia. Probate to John Oresbie with similar powers reserved

Hawker, *(contd.)* to Henry Hodges. (Nov. 1647). Wi.

Hawkes, John, formerly of Whitechapel, Middlesex, but late of Norfolk, Virginia, bachelor. Administration to the brother, William Hawkes. (Jan. 1790).

Hawkins, Anne, of Virginia. Administration to the brother, Matthew Hawkins. (July 1654).

Hawkins, John, of Queen Anne County, Maryland. Probate to the son, Ernault Hawkins. (Nov. 1719).

Hawkins, John, of H.M. ship *Essex* but late of H.M. ship *Juno*, who died in New York Hospital. Probate to Elizabeth Yarworth. (June 1767).

Hawkins, Mary, of Boston, New England, widow. Probate to Randolph Hopley the younger with similar powers reserved to Randolph Hopley the elder. (Feb. 1721).

Hawkins, Philip, formerly of South Carolina and Islington, Middlesex, but late of St. Croix in the West Indies. Probate to the brother, John Hawkins, with similar powers reserved to John Lewis Jervies, George Cook and John Owen. (Feb. 1782).

Hawkins, William, of Kingston-on-Thames, Surrey, who died in New England. Probate to the sister, Rachel Wade alias Sudell, wife of Christopher Wade, with similar powers reserved to Frances Blanch. (July 1686). NGSQ 65/219.

Hawkins, William, of Boston, New England. Sentence against the validity of the will and administration granted to the relict, Dorothy Hawkins. (Nov. 1700).

Hawkins, William, of Boston, New England, surgeon. Probate to the relict, Dorothy Hawkins. (Apr. 1702).

Hawksley, Alfred, formerly of 10 Sidmouth Street, Grays Inn Road, Middlesex, who died as a passenger on the ship *Charles Bartlett* bound for New York, bachelor. Administration to the father, Thomas Hawksley. (Aug. 1849).

Hawley, Jeremiah, of Maryland. Administration to the principal creditor, Thomas Cornwallis. (Jan. 1651).

Haxby alias Axby alias Hicksby, Thomas, of New York, flax dresser and rope maker. Administration to the mother, Sarah Haxby. (July 1842).

Hay, Alexander, of Charles Town, South Carolina. Probate to Francis Mercer. (July 1776).

Hay, Charles, of H.M. ship *Tamer*, who died in Boston, New England, widower. Administration to the only children, Eleanor and Anna Maria Hay. (June 1773).

Hey, Eleanor, of East Greenwich, Kent. Administration to John Grant of East Greenwich, glover, attorney for the husband, James Hey, now in New England. (Apr. 1695).

Hay, James, of Cloughton near Scarborough, Yorkshire, who died in Virginia. Administration to the relict, Priscilla Hay. (Oct. 1678).

Hay, John, of New York, carpenter of the merchant ship *Bolivar*. Administration to the only child, Christian Hay, spinster; the relict, Christian Hay alias Browne, widow, having died. (Feb. 1845).

Hayden, Jemima, of Castine, Hancock County, United States of America, widow. Administration to Henry Frederick Edward Downes, attorney for the only child, John Hayden, in Castine. (Nov. 1836).

Hayden, Samuel, Captain on half pay of the late Lieutenant-Colonel Rogers' Regiment, who died in Castine, Hancock County, United States of America. Administration to Henry Frederick Edward Downes, attorney for the only child, John Hayden, in Castine. (Nov. 1836).

Hayes, Frederick, of Saratoga Springs, Saratoga County, New York, bachelor. Administration to the brother, Edward Hayes; the mother and next-of-kin, Frances Hayes, renouncing. (Dec. 1855).

Hey. *See* **Hay**.

Heyes, Hugh, of Presbury, Cheshire, whose cousin, William Stone, was in Virginia. Probate to the brother-in-law, Benjamin Bannester. (May 1637). Wi.

Haighes, John, who died in Virginia, bachelor. Administration to the brother, Edward Haighes. (Jan. 1628).

Hayes, Joseph, of Ware, Gloucester County, Virginia. Probate by decree to Anne Hayes with similar powers reserved to the son, William Hayes. (June 1678). Wi.

Hayes, Rebecca, of Carolina, spinster. Administration to the third cousin and next-of-kin, Richard Hayes. (Jan. 1736).

Hayes, Thomas, Ensign in General Delancey's Corps of Infantry in North America, who died in Georgia, bachelor. Administration to David Thomas, surviving executor of the brother, Robert Hayes deceased; the mother, Sarah Hayes, widow, having died. (July 1818).

Hayne, William, formerly of Exeter, Devon, grocer, but late of New York. Administration to the relict, Louisa Hayne. (Sep. 1846).

Haines, Anna Maria, formerly of Great Russell Street, Covent Garden, Middlesex, but late of Marmion, Virginia, spinster. Administration to the brother, Thomas Haines. (Oct. 1797).

Haynes, George, of St. George, Southwark, Surrey, whose relict, Elizabeth, was formerly wife of Thomas Adams of New England. Probate to the relict, Elizabeth Haynes, the brother, William Haynes, and the nephew, William Haynes. (Jan. 1763).

Haynes, Herbert, of Abingdon, Gloucester County, Virginia, who died in St. Peter Cornhill, London. Probate to Job Wilkes, attorney for the relict, Sarah Haynes, and the father, Thomas Haynes, in Virginia. (Dec. 1737).

Haynes, John, of Philadelphia, bachelor. Administration to the sister, Mary, wife of Hugh McBride. (Oct. 1806).

Haynes, Thomas, of Warwick County, Virginia. Administration with will to James Wilkes, attorney for Andrew Haynes in Virginia. (Sep. 1746).

Hayt, James, of Bridgeport, Connecticut, Quartermaster on half pay of the Prince of Wales' American Regiment. Administration to David Davies, attorney for the relict, Mercy Hayt, in Bridgeport. (Apr. 1807).

Hayt, Monson, of New York City, Lieutenant on half pay of the Prince of

Hayt, *(contd.)*
Wales' American Regiment. Administration to David Davies, attorney for the relict, Lucretia Hayt, in New York City. (Apr. 1807).

Hayward, John, of Rappahannock River, Virginia, bachelor. Administration to the mother, Charity Britton alias Hayward. (Oct. 1698).

Hayward, Margaret. *See* **Agar**.

Hayward, Thomas, of Beverley, New York, who died on H.M. ship *Royal William*. Probate to Margaret Eldridge. (Sep. 1694).

Hayward, Thomas, of Rappahannock River, Virginia, who died at sea on the ship *William and Mary*. Administration to the relict, Charity, now wife of John Britton. (Oct. 1698).

Heywood, Richard, of Stepney, Middlesex, who died in Virginia. Administration to John Hill, the principal creditor and guardian of the children, Richard, Elizabeth and Rebecca Heywood; the relict, Elizabeth Heywood, renouncing. (Aug. 1695).

Hazleton, William. *See* **Heselton**.

Heacock, Peter, of Middletown, Delaware County, Pennsylvania, widower. Administration with will by her solemn affirmation to the daughter, Elizabeth, wife of James Bottomley; the executors, Thomas Dutton and James Young, renouncing. (June 1837).

Head, George, of Philadelphia, who died in Charles Town, South Carolina, bachelor. Administration to the brother, Thomas Head; the father, Rowland Head, renouncing. (Nov. 1734).

Head, William, marine of H.M. ship *Andromache*. Administration to Thomas Head, attorney for the relict, Barbara Austin, formerly Head, in Pennsylvania. (Jan. 1834).

Heal, Charles, formerly of Bridgwater, Somerset, but late of Illinois. Administration to Frederick Charles Foster, attorney for the relict, Betsey Heal, in Illinois. (Apr. 1854).

Heale, George, of Lancaster City, Rappahannock, Virginia. Administration with will to Arthur Bayly, attorney for the son, George Heale, in Virginia. (Mar. 1709). Wi.

Hele, Warwick, of Pennsylvania, widower. Administration to the principal creditor, Michael Hammond. (Mar. 1711).

Heal, William, formerly of Church Street, Hackney, Middlesex, but late of Baltimore in North America. Administration to the relict, Elizabeth Heal. (Feb. 1833).

Healy, John, of Albany, New York, bachelor. Administration to the brother, Michael Healy. (Nov. 1831).

Healy, William, of H.M. ships *Boreas* and *Alcide*, who died in hospital in Governor's Island, New York. Probate to Thomas Healy. (July 1783).

Heapy, John, of Philadelphia, who died in 1809. Limited administration to Charles Rowland Packer of Greenwich, Kent, attorney for Abraham Nettlefold and James Cronk. (July 1822).

Hearne. *See* **Herne**.

Hearsum, Elizabeth, of Albion, Illinois. Administration to the husband, David Hearsum. (Apr. 1844).

Hearsum, Mary, of Albion, Illinois. Administration to the husband, David Hearsum (*sic*). (Apr. 1844).

Heath, Henry, of Fredericksburg, Virginia. Administration to the relict, Susanna Heath. (Sep. 1772).

Heath, Joseph Thomas, formerly of Millend Farm, Buckinghamshire, but late of Steilcoom, Oregon. Probate to the brother, Thomas Mason Heath, with similar powers reserved to William Fraser Tolmie. (Feb. 1851).

Heath, William, formerly of Topsham, Devon, but late of New York City. Administration to the brother and next-of-kin, David Heath; the relict, Sarah Heath, renouncing. (Feb. 1789).

Heathcote, Elizabeth, of New York Province. Administration to Samuel Baker, attorney for the mother, Martha Heathcote, widow, in New York. (Feb. 1736).

Heathcote, Gilbert, of New York Province. Administration to Samuel Baker, attorney for the mother, Martha Heathcote, widow, in New York. (July 1731).

Heathcote, John, formerly of Love Lane, Aldermanbury, London, but late of Baltimore, United States of America. Limited administration with will to Thomas Edwards, Enoch Durant and George Elwall. (July 1814).

Heathcote, Mary, of New York Province. Administration to Samuel Baker, attorney for the mother, Martha Heathcote, widow, in New York. (July 1731).

Heathcote, Nathaniel, of Anne Arundell County, Maryland. Administration to the grandson, Samuel Heathcote. (July 1682).

Heathcote, William, of New York Province, bachelor. Administration to the mother, Martha Heathcote, widow. (Jan. 1723). Revoked and granted to to Samuel Baker, attorney for the mother, Martha Heathcote, widow, in New York. (Feb. 1736).

Hedges, Thomas, of Wilmington, North Carolina, widower. Administration to the brother, Joseph Hedges. (Dec. 1769).

Heighway, John, of New Orleans, bachelor. Administration to the brother and only next-of-kin, Richard Husband Heighway. (May 1851).

Helcott, Matthew, of H.M. ship *Robust*, who died in New York. Administration to the sister, Anne, wife of Benjamin Cole. (Jan. 1683).

Hele. *See* **Heal**.

Hemard, Peter, of Stepney, Middlesex, who died in Virginia. Probate to the relict, Elizabeth Hemard. (Mar. 1719).

Hemming, George, formerly of Hampstead Marshall near Newbury, Berkshire, but late of Lockport, North America, bachelor. Administration to the brother, William Hemming; the mother, Priscilla Kimber, formerly Hemming, widow, having died. (Feb. 1853).

Hemsley, William, of Baltimore, North America, millwright and widower. Administration to the son, Thomas Hemsley. (Dec. 1834).

Henderson, Henry, of York River, Virginia, who died in Clerkenwell,

Henderson, *(contd.)*
Middlesex. Probate to Richard Stone. (Nov. 1674). Wi.

Henderson, Henry, of H.M. ship *Culloden*, who died in Long Island Hospital, bachelor. Administration to the cousin german, William Gunn. (Apr. 1782).

Henderson, James, of New York City. Probate to the relict, Tessia Henderson, and the daughter, Margaret, wife of Joseph Haviland. (Feb. 1760).

Henderson, James, Lieutenant of the 78th Regiment, who died in New York. Administration to John Ogilvie, attorney for the relict, Elizabeth Henderson, in New York. (Oct. 1770).

Henderson, James, surgeon of the Royal Artillery, who died in New York, bachelor. Administration to the sister, Margaret, wife of Robert Marshall. (Apr. 1781).

Hendrie, James, of Mobile, Florida, widower. Administration to the sisters, Jean and Marian Hendrie; the mother, Jean Hendrie, widow, having died. (Aug. 1808).

Henly, Henry, of Virginia, who died at sea. Administration to the brother, John Henly. (Mar. 1700).

Henley, Peter, Chief Justice of North Carolina, widower. Administration to Charles Frederick Henley, administrator of the only child, John Henley deceased. (Feb. 1825).

Hennessey, Mary Frank, formerly of 33 Baker Street, Portman Square, Middlesex, and afterwards of Philadelphia, who died in St. Croix in the West Indies, widow. Administration to the sister, Ann Akers Price, wife of John Price. (Nov. 1836).

Henry, John, of Richmond, Virginia. Probate to the brother, James Henry, with similar powers reserved to Conway Whittle. (Dec. 1809).

Henshaw, Sarah Richards, of New York City, spinster. Administration to Percival White, attorney for the mother and next-of-kin, Sarah Richards Henshaw, in New York City. (Feb. 1811).

Herault, Elizabeth, of Sherman, Fairfield County, Connecticut, widow. Administration to George Goryer, attorney for the natural child, Hannah Hubbell, in Queensbury, Washington County, New York. (Oct. 1804).

Herault, John, of Charles Town, South Carolina, bachelor. Administration to the second cousin and next-of-kin, Henry Ayme. (Mar. 1705).

Herbert, William, of Scarborough, Yorkshire, who died in Philadelphia. Probate to William Herbert. (May 1778).

Hearn, Anthony, of Penn Township, Philadelphia County, Pennsylvania. Probate to Redmond Byrne, John Carroll and Joseph Smyde. (Apr. 1818).

Herne, Sir Nathaniel, alderman of London, whose niece, ——- Whitlock, was in Virginia. Probate to Joseph Herne with similar powers reserved to Sir John Frederick, William Wheatley and John Banckes. (Aug. 1679). Revoked and administration granted to the son, Nathaniel Herne; Sir John Frederick and William Wheatley having died and John Banks having been cited but not having appeared. (Dec. 1694). Wi.

Heyrne alias Iron, Nicholas, who died on the ship *James Town* coming from Virginia, bachelor. Administration to the brother, William Heyrne alias Iron. (Dec. 1659).

Hearne, Peter, of Carolina, who died on H.M. ship *Monmouth*. Administration to the relict, Joan Hearne. (Jan. 1696).

Heron, Andrew, of Augusta, Georgia, bachelor. Administration to the brother, Peter Heron. (Feb. 1817).

Heron, Benjamin, of New Hanover County, North Carolina. Probate to the relict, Alice Heron, with similar powers reserved to Lewis De Rosser, Frederick Fones and Samuel Swann the younger. (July 1770).

Heron, Margaret. *See* **Moncrieffe**.

Herring, Arthur, of Maryland. Administration to the sister, Mary Herring. (Sep. 1691).

Herring, James, of New York. Probate to the relict, Mary Herring, with similar powers reserved to the son, James Herring. (Aug. 1830).

Herring, William Edward, formerly of St. Marylebone, Middlesex, but late of Charleston, South Carolina, widower. Administration to the brother and only next-of-kin, Sampson George Herring. (May 1789).

Heselton alias Hazleton, William, of Virginia, mate of the merchant ship *Resolution*. Administration to the relict, Hannah Heselton. (Jan. 1766).

Hesketh, Henry, of Sacramento, California, bachelor. Administration to the brother and only next-of-kin, Robert Hesketh. (Dec. 1856).

Hesletine, James, of St. Mary le Bow, Durham, widower. Administration to Thomas Philpot, attorney for the nephew and niece, Charles Hesletine and Catherine, wife of James Fraizier, in Maryland. (June 1765).

Hewetson, James, of New York State, bachelor. Administration to the brother and next-of-kin, Benjamin Hewetson. (July 1813).

Hewetson, Thomas Wallis, Lieutenant of Marines, who died in Boston. Administration to James Fitter, attorney for the brother, Boyle Hewetson, in Kilkenny, Ireland. (May 1777).

Hewet, Sir Thomas, of St. Martin in the Fields, Middlesex, and of Old Jewry, London, adventurer to Virginia. Probate to the brother, Sir William Hewet. (Feb. 1624). Wi.

Hewett, William, surgeon and Ensign of the 28th Regiment of Foot, who died in Charles Town, South Carolina, bachelor. Administration with will to John Cole, attorney for the brother and next-of-kin, Thomas Hewett, in Cork, Ireland; the executors, Arthur Price and Lionel Chalmer, doctor of physick, renouncing. (Dec. 1766).

Hewgill, Henry, master of the merchant ship *Lord Middleton*, who died in Savannah, Georgia. Administration with will to the sister, Cordelia, wife of Daniel Kitchen; the executor, Sir Thomas Coxhead, renouncing. (Apr. 1798).

Hewson, Mary, of Pennsylvania, widow. Limited probate to James Blunt with similar powers reserved to Miles Satterthwaite. (Apr. 1796).

Hewson, Thomas, formerly of College Street, Westminster, Middlesex, but late of Charlestown in America, bachelor. Administration to the sister,

Hewson, *(contd.)*
Maria Catherine, wife of James Sanders; the mother and next-of-kin, Fanny Hewson, widow, having died. (July 1836).

Hext, Edward, of Charles Town, South Carolina. Probate to David Hext and John McCall with similar powers reserved to Thomas Hext, John Bee the younger, Jonathan Bryan and Philip Prisleau. (Dec. 1742).

Hey. *See* **Hay**.

Heyes. *See* **Hayes**.

Heyrne. *See* **Herne**.

Heywood. *See* **Haywood**.

Hiatt, James, of Point Township, Northumberland County, Pennsylvania, purser in the Royal Navy. Administration with will to James Park, attorney for James Hepburn in Northumberland County. (Feb. 1814).

Hibbard, Eliphaz, late of Picton, Nova Scotia, who died in New Orleans. Administration to the relict, now Ann Jones. (Aug. 1838).

Hichens, Thomas, Captain of the 93rd Regiment of Foot, who died in New Orleans. Probate to the brother and sole heir, Richard Hichens. (Feb. 1816).

Hickman, John, of Columbia, Caldwell County, Louisiana. Administration to the brother, Charles Randall Hickman; the relict, Eliza Hickman, having been cited but not having appeared. (June 1847). Revoked on his death and granted to the sister, Harriet, wife of Francis Arthur. (May 1850).

Hickman, William, of St. Swithin, London, whose kinsman, Joseph Hickman, was in Virginia. Probate to the relict, Margaret Hickman. (Sep. 1672). Wa.

Hicks, Jacob, of Portsmouth, Newport County, Rhode Island, a private in Lieutenant-Colonel Hargill's Company, who died in Havana, an apprentice to Robert Burrington the younger in Portsmouth. Limited administration to Joseph Sherwood of Throckmorton Street, London, attorney for the said Burrington. (Dec. 1765).

Hicksby, Thomas. *See* **Haxby**.

Hide. *See* **Hyde**.

Higgins alias Higgons, John, of H.M. ship *Dunkirk*, who died in New England, bachelor. Administration to the sister and next-of-kin, Elizabeth, wife of Thomas Pattison. (Oct. 1711).

Higgins, Nathaniel, of Cape Cod, New England, formerly mariner of H.M. ship *Torbay* but late of H.M. ship *Hornet*, bachelor. Administration with will to Sarah Browne, wife and attorney of Thomas Browne now on H.M. ship *Nottingham*. (Dec.1746). *See* NGSQ 64/290.

Higgins, Robert Harpur, Lieutenant of the 52nd Regiment of Foot, who died in Boston. Administration to the mother, Mary, wife of James Robinson. (Apr. 1776).

Higginson, Humphrey, of Ratcliffe, Stepney, Middlesex, whose brother, Christopher Higginson, was in Virginia. Probate to the relict, Elizabeth Higginson. (Mar. 1666). Wa.

Higginson, John, of Maryland, bachelor. Administration to the brother,

Higginson, *(contd.)*
Robert Higginson. (Jan. 1746).

Higgs, William, of Pennsylvania, bachelor. Administration to the brother, John Higgs. (Oct. 1709).

Highlord, Katherine, of St. Stephen, Coleman Street, London, widow, whose cousins, Robert and Richard Wilson, were in Virginia. Probate to Robert Wilson. (July 1648). Wa.

Hildyard, William, of New Providence, America, late Lieutenant in Governor Tinker's Company. Administration to the grandmother, Elizabeth Hildyard, guardian of the only child, Hannah Hildyard; the relict, Hannah Hildyard, having died. (July 1756).

Hill, Adam, of Talbot County, Maryland. Probate to William Campbell with similar powers reserved to Ebenezer Mackie and Robert Campbell. (Mar. 1768).

Hill, Allen, of Bermondsey, Surrey, who died in Virginia. Administration to the relict, Mary Hill. (Dec. 1726).

Hill, James, formerly of Tipton, Staffordshire, but late of Chicago, Illinois. Administration to John Richardson, attorney for the relict, Jane Elizabeth Hill, in Chicago. (June 1853).

Hill, James Spackman, formerly of Twickenham, Middlesex, and afterwards of Old Hall near Ware, Hertfordshire, but late of Cincinnati. Probate to Marlow John Francis Sidney. (Dec. 1830).

Hill, John, of St. Olave Hart Street, London, merchant, whose brother, Valentine Hill, was in New England. Probate to the relict, Sarah Hill. (Feb. 1688). Wa.

Hill, Littleton, Lieutenant of H.M. ship *Scorpio*, who died in South Carolina, widower. Administration to George Hill, uncle and guardian of the only child, Littleton Hill. (May 1752).

Hill, Martha, formerly of St. Saviour, Southwark, Surrey, but late of Virginia, spinster. Administration to the brother, Thomas Hill. (Dec. 1778).

Hill, Mary. *See* **Beswicke** and **Lanfear**.

Hill, Richard, of Cookham, Berkshire, (bound for New England). who died overseas, bachelor. Probate to Nicholas Greene. (Sep. 1635).

Hill, Samuel, of Virginia, bachelor. Probate to the father, Edward Hill. (Aug. 1695).

Hill, Samuel, of Charles Town, South Carolina. Probate to James Alexander with similar powers reserved to James Dawson. (Aug. 1787).

Hill, William, of H.M. ship *Lynn*, bachelor. Administration to John Bradford, attorney for the half brother, William Abraham, in Charlestown, New England. (Jan. 1750).

Hill, William, Controller of Customs at Sydney, Cape Breton Island. Administration to Alexander Harper, attorney for the relict, Rebecca Hill, in Boston, Massachusetts. (June 1804).

Hill, Willoughby, of the ship *India King*, who died in Virginia. Probate to the relict, Joane Hill. (May 1703).

Hilson, George, master of the ship *Friends Increase*, who died in Virginia.

Hilson, *(contd.)*
Administration to the principal creditor, Anthony Phillips; the relict, Anne Hilson, renouncing. (May 1679).

Hilton, Benjamin, of New York City, widower. Administration with will to James Tidbury, attorney for the children, Edward Hilton, John Hilton, and Ann Benjamin Halsted, widow, in New York. (Mar. 1834).

Hilton, Nowell, of Charles Town, Middlesex County, New England, mariner. Administration with will to Nathaniel Cutler, no executor having been named. (Sep. 1689). Wa.

Hilton, Robert, formerly of New England, but late of London. Probate to Samuel Lilly; Alexander Holmes renouncing. (Mar. 1717). *See* NGSQ 69/196.

Hinchman, John, of Burlington, New Jersey. Administration with will to James Bell, attorney for John Hinchman Stokes, Joseph Atkinson alias Hatkinson, and Hinchman Bispham, in Burlington. (June 1790).

Hinckley, William, of Joseph, Calhan County, Florida, gardener. Administration to the brother, James Hinckley; the relict, Ann Hinckley, having died. (Nov. 1850).

Hind, William, of Virginia, widower. Administration to the son, William Hind. (Mar 1673).

Hine, Thomas, of New Orleans. Administration with will to the brother, Michael George Hine. (May 1845).

Hines, Richard Johnston, of New Orleans, bachelor. Administration to the mother and next-of-kin, Marrian Hines, widow. (Dec. 1850).

Hiorns, William, formerly of Philadelphia but late of Natchez, West Florida. Probate to the brother, Francis Hiorns. (June 1781).

Hipkins, Paris, of Galveston, Texas. Administration to the daughter, Maryann, wife of John Bush; the relict, Maryann Hipkins, having died. (Aug. 1855).

Hitch, Mildred, of St. John the Evangelist, London, widow, whose kinswoman, Mary Johnson formerly Hazard, was in New England. Probate to Robert Hitch. (Mar. 1658). Sh.Wa.

Hitchcock, Elizabeth, nee Elizabeth Wigmore, formerly of Woolwich, Kent, but late of New York City. Administration to Ann, wife of Thomas Bond, attorney for the husband, William George Hitchcock, in New York. (Feb. 1840).

Hitchins, Samuel, of All Hallows Barking, London, whose nephews, Daniel and Joseph Hitchins, were in New England. Probate to Daniel Morse and Nicholas Morse; Robert Hitchins renouncing. (Dec. 1679). Sh.

Hitchins, Thomas, Ensign in Colonel Venderduson's Independent Company, who died in South Carolina, bachelor. Administration to the principal creditor, George Daniel. (Oct. 1749).

Hobbs, Joseph, of Crewkerne, Somerset, who died in New England, bachelor. Administration to the sister, Margaret Hobbs. (June 1697).

Hobbs, Dr. Thomas, of St. Clement Danes, Middlesex, whose sister,

Hobbs, *(contd.)*
Elizabeth, was wife of Francis Weekes in Middlesex County, Virginia. Probate to Sir John Hawles, John Lilly, and the relict, Catherine Hobbs, with similar powers reserved to Sir John Somers. (Oct. 1698). NGSQ 62/38.

Hobby, Sir Charles, formerly of Boston, New England, but late of St. James, Westminster, Middlesex. Limited administration to Stephen Mason of Islington, Middlesex, merchant. (June 1715).

Hobkirk, John, of New York City. Administration to the relict, Hannah Hobkirk. (Jan. 1780).

Hockenhull, Richard, of South Carolina, widower. Administration to the creditor, Austin Ashby; the brother, George Hockenhull, and John Howe, guardian of the nephew, Chadwell Hockenhull, renouncing. (May 1733).

Hocking, John, formerly of Camborne, Cornwall, but late of Rockland, Ontario County, United States of America. Administration to the relict, Margaret Hocking. (July 1855).

Hockley, Thomas, of Philadelphia. Probate to Samuel Smith with similar powers reserved to Jacob Duche, James Reynolds and William Garriques. (Dec. 1781).

Hockley, William Branson, of Philadelphia, bachelor. Administration to the nephew, Richard Hockley Wilcocks. (Jan. 1796).

Hodd, Thomas, of Virginia, bachelor. Administration to Lucy Swinhoe, spinster, executrix of the mother and next-of-kin, Hannah Hodd, widow deceased. (Nov. 1797).

Hodge, Robert Bickford, formerly of Exeter, Devon, but late of Camden, New Jersey, bachelor. Administration to the brother and sister, Coplestone Edward Hodge and Betsy Damerell Bickford Hodge. (Sep. 1845).

Hodges, Frederick Downer, formerly of Victoria Cottage, Farleigh Down near Hastings, Sussex, but late of New York City. Probate to the relict, Elizabeth Hodges. (Nov. 1845).

Hodges, Nathaniel, of Gravesend, Kent, who died in Providence Island, bachelor. Administration to the brother, George Hodges; the mother, Mary Hodges, having died. (July 1748).

Hodges, Peter, of East West Jersey who died in Bermondsey, Surrey. Probate to Elizabeth Willis. (Dec. 1697). Wa.

Hodgskinson, Christopher, of Virginia. Administration to the sister and next-of-kin, Anne, wife of Richard Walley. (Apr. 1718).

Hogan, Michael, of New York State. Administration to the relict, Frances Hogan. (May 1835).

Hogarth, George, formerly of the Middle Temple, London, but late of Baltimore in North America. Limited administration to Henry Farnell. (Apr. 1844).

Hogg, William, formerly of London, jeweller, but late of the United States of America, bachelor. Administration to the nephew and only next-of-kin, Abraham Hogg. (Apr. 1809).

Holcombe, John, of Virginia, bachelor. Administration to the principal

Holcombe, *(contd.)* creditor, John Wilcox. (May 1670).

Holcroft, George, of Virginia, bachelor. Administration to the father, Michael Holcroft. (Dec. 1666).

Holding, Edward, master of the merchant ship *Friends Goodwill*, who died in Boston, New England, bachelor. Probate to Mary Pomfrett, widow. (Feb. 1751).

Holding, Peter, of the ship *Resolution*, who died in New England, widower. Administration to the daughter, Elizabeth Holding. (Dec. 1693).

Holditch, James, of Carolina. Administration to Richard Boys, attorney and father of Susan Holditch in Carolina. (Mar. 1702).

Holiday, William, of Goose Creek, South Carolina, planter. Administration with will to William Lee, attorney for Joan Carlyle alias Bell, wife of Walter Bell, the administratrix with will of the cousin, Jean alias Jane Bell deceased, in Nether Albie, Dumfries, Scotland; the executors, Charles Johnson, John Simpson, Jacob Valk, Ziphaniah Kinsley, William Edwards and the relict, Sarah Holiday, having died; the sister, Sarah Paisley Jane Carlyle, wife of John Carlyle, and the legatees, Jane Bell and Elizabeth Groves, having also died; and the surviving legatee, William Blacklock, having been cited but not having appeared. (May 1810).

Hollamby, James, of New York City. Administration with will to Alexander Goudge, attorney for Luke Bird and Thomas Goudge in New York. (Apr. 1780).

Holland, Joseph, of St. Sepulchre, citizen and clothworker of London, whose daughter, Elizabeth, was wife of Richard Bessy in Virginia, and whose son, Samuel Holland, was in Virginia. Probate to John White. (Jan. 1658). Wa.

Holland, Joshua, of Shadwell, Middlesex, whose daughter, Elizabeth, was in Pennsylvania. Probate to the son, Thanks Holland, with similar powers reserved to Frances Jackson. (May 1690).

Hollis, Thomas Frederick, of Dominica in the West Indies, bachelor. Administration to the mother, Lucinda Hollis, widow; the father, Thomas Pelham Hollis, having died. (Feb. 1834).

Hollis, Thomas Pelham, of New York. Administration to the relict, Lucinda Hollis. (Feb. 1834).

Hollister, George, of Boston, New England, who died on H.M. fireship *Hawk*, bachelor. Administration to the heir, Prospero Winchester of Pandon Magna. (Dec. 1693).

Hollowell, John, of Philadelphia. Administration to Elizabeth Linch, widow, attorney for the relict, Mary Hollowell, in Philadelphia. (Feb. 1779).

Holman, Mary. *See* **Sellens**.

Holmes, James, of H.M. ships *Prince George* and *Lowestoft*, but who died on H.M. ship *Oxford* in Virginia. Administration to the relict, Mary Holmes. (Mar. 1709).

Holmes, William, who died overseas, leaving a bequest for his two children to be sent to Virginia. Probate to the nephews, Oliver Holmes and

Holmes, *(contd.)*
Richard Graby. (Feb. 1649). Sh.Wi.

Holt, Elizabeth, of Washington, North America. Administration to John Hay, attorney for the husband, Theophilus Holt, in Washington. (Aug. 1809).

Holton, John, of H.M. ship *Greenwich*, who died in Maryland, bachelor. Administration to the father, Thomas Holton. (July 1697).

Home, Charles, of New York. Probate to William Home with similar powers reserved to William Jameson, James Henderson and James Rochead. (Feb. 1748).

Homfray, Jeston, formerly of Oldswinford, Worcestershire, but late of Spottswood, New Jersey, widower. Administration to the only child, Francis Homfray. (May 1803).

Honywood, John, of London who died in America, bachelor. Probate to Thomas Denne. (Jan. 1639). Sh.

Hood, William, formerly of Bristol but late of Charleston, United States of America. Administration with will to the relict, Sarah Hood; the executor, John Acraman, having died in the testator's lifetime, and the executor, Robert Jenkins, after his death. (Sep. 1837).

Hookamer, Jacob. *See* **Vandrez**.

Hooker, Col. Edward, of St. Mary at Hill, London, whose sister, Mary Hooker, was in New England. Probate to the son, Cornelius Hooker; the relict, Elizabeth Hooker, renouncing. (July 1651).

Hooker, John, of Marefield, Leicestershire, whose cousin, Samuel Hooker, was in New England. Probate to William Jennings. (Nov. 1655). Wa.

Hooker, Mary, of Virginia, spinster. Administration to the cousin and next-of-kin, Oliver Gregory. (Oct. 1682).

Hooker, Peter, of London, who died overseas (bound to Virginia), bachelor. Probate to the brother, Edward Hooker. (Nov. 1639). Sh.Wi.

Hooker, Ralph, of Barbados who died overseas and whose cousin, Richard Bennett, was in New England. Probate to John Hooker. (May 1665). Wa.

Hooker, William, formerly of H.M. ships *Advice*, *Lynn* and *Suffolk*, but late of New York City, who died on H.M. ship *St. George*. Administration to William Bryant, attorney for the relict, Cloe Hooker, in New York. (Feb. 1749).

Hooker, William, Captain of the 31st Regiment of Foot, who died in Pensacola, West Florida, widower. Administration to the creditor, James Gibson; others with any title having been cited but not having appeared. (July 1767).

Hooton, George, of Sullivan Street, New York. Administration to the son, William Henry Hooton; the relict, Rachel Hooton, having died. (Sep. 1851).

Hooton, John, of Gloucester County, New Jersey, Captain of the late Batallion of West Jersey Volunteers. Administration to Leonard Streate Coxe, attorney for the relict, Rachel Hooton, in Gloucester

Hooton, *(contd.)* County. (Mar. 1805).

Hope, Henry, of North Carolina, who died in Liverpool, Lancashire, widower. Administration to the brother, John Hope, attorney for the father, Archibald Hope. (Nov. 1738).

Hopkins, Edward, of St. Olave, Hart Street, London, who had goods in New England. Probate to the nephew, Henry Dalley. (Apr. 1657). Sh.

Hopkins, John, of Philadelphia. Probate to Samuel Fatin with similar powers reserved to Samuel Griffiths. (Aug. 1850).

Hopkins, William, of Virginia, who died in St. Dunstan in the West, London, bachelor. Administration to the brother, James Hopkins, pending production of a will; the mother, Ruth Hopkins, renouncing. (Feb. 1735).

Hopkinson, Daniel, who died overseas having goods in Virginia. Probate to the brother, Joseph Clifton. (Apr. 1637). Sh.Wi.

Hopper, Thomas, of Lyons, Wayne County, New York. Administration to the relict, Mary Hopper. (May 1851).

Hopton, John, formerly of Charleston, South Carolina, but late of Islington, Middlesex. Probate to John Hopton Russell Chichester with similar powers reserved to Robert William Powell, Robert Williams and Robert William Chichester. (June 1832). *See* NGSQ 65/135.

Hopton, William, of Charles Town, South Carolina. Administration with will to John Hopton, attorney for the daughters, Mary Christiana Hopton and Sarah Hopton, the relict, Sarah Hopton, and for Nathaniel Russell and Samuel Legare, all in South Carolina. (Aug. 1788).

Hopwood, Jemima. *See* **Rolph**.

Horley, John, formerly of Croydon, Surrey, but late of Charles Town, South Carolina, bachelor. Probate to the mother, Mary White, widow. (May 1804).

Horley, William, formerly of Croydon, Surrey, but late of Charles Town, South Carolina, bachelor. Probate to the mother, Mary White, widow. (May 1804).

Horlock, Joseph, formerly of Southwark, Surrey, but late of Charleston, South Carolina. Administration to the relict, Dorothy Horlock. (Aug. 1803).

Hornbe, Robert, of the ship *Benjamin*, who died in Virginia. Probate to the relict, Elizabeth Hornbe. (Aug. 1704).

Horrell, Thomas Armstrong, of Texas, North America, widower. Administration to the daughter, Mary Ann Horrell. (July 1841).

Horrocks, Rev. James, formerly of Bruton Parish, Williamsburg, Virginia, but late of St. Olave Hart Street, London, who died in Oporto, Portugal. Administration to the relict, Frances Horrocks. (May 1772).

Horsmanden, Daniel, of New York City. Probate to Miles Sherbrooke with similar powers reserved to Thomas Hayes. (Apr. 1786).

Horwood, Joel, of Boston, New England, seaman of H.M. ship *Sheerness*. Probate to the brother, Henry Horwood. (Aug. 1697).

Hosier, William, formerly of Laverton, Suffolk, farmer, but late of

Hosier, *(contd.)* Milwankel, Wisconsin, bachelor. Administration to the brother and next-of-kin, Joshua Hosier. (Sep. 1857).

Hoskins, Mary, of Richmond, Surrey, widow, whose brother, John Githins, was in Maryland. Probate to the brother, William Githins. (Feb. 1678). Wa.

Hoskins, Richard, formerly of Pennsylvania but late of St. Stephen Coleman Street, London. Limited probate to Theodore Eccleston with similar powers reserved to Philip Collins and John Groves. (Mar. 1701).

Hoskins, William, formerly of Rood, Somerset, then of Westbury, Wiltshire, who died in Westchester, North America. Inventory 1808. [*Administration Act not found*].

Hough, Francis, of St. Peter le Poor, London, whose son, William Hough, was to be sent to Virginia. Administration with will to Anne Cooke, grandmother of the children, William, John, Jane, and Ann Hough, during their minority. (July 1648). Revoked on her death and granted to the children, John Hough, Jane Andrewes and Ann Tirrick, who have come of age. (Sep. 1667). Wi.

Houghton, Jane, of Fulton Street, Brooklyn, New York, widow. Administration to Jonathan Stevens, attorney for the daughter, Mary Jane Smith, widow, in New York. (Dec. 1854).

Houghton, John, of Charles Town, South Carolina. Probate to the surviving executor, John Owen. (Apr. 1751).

Houghton, Robert, of St. Olave, Southwark, Surrey, whose sister, Mary, was wife of Francis Norton in New England. Probate to the relict, Mary Houghton. (Jan. 1653). Wa.

Houldsworth, Michael, of Jamaica, who died in New York. Administration to the relict, Mary, now wife of Thomas Nuttall. (Jan. 1706).

Hounslow alias Hunt, Mary Ann, formerly of Exeter Change, Middlesex, but late of Philadelphia County, Pennsylvania, spinster. Probate to Henry Hunt with similar powers reserved to Samuel Hunt. (June 1828)

Houseal, Frances, of Prince William Parish, South Carolina, wife of John Bernard Houseal, formerly of Streatham, Surrey, but late of North America. Limited administration to William Marsh and Richard Creed. (July 1810).

Howard, Abigail, of Boston, Massachusetts, widow. Administration with will to Alexander Thomson, attorney for Rev. Samuel Parker D.D. in Boston. (Feb. 1802).

Howard alias Harris, Daniel, formerly of Jamaica but late of Newport, Rhode Island, bachelor. Administration to the father, Thomas Howard. (Apr. 1807).

Howard, Michael, of Talbot County, Maryland. Probate to the brother, Francis Howard, with similar powers reserved to Samuel and Herbert Hyde and to Adam and Michael William Howard. (May 1738). Revoked on the death intestate of Francis Howard and granted to Christopher Plunkett, son of Ann Plunkett, widow; Samuel Hyde renouncing and Herbert Hyde, Adam and Michael William Howard,

Howard, *(contd.)*
Daniel Delany and Walter Carmichael having died. (Aug. 1757).

Howard, Thomas George, of Pulaski, Arkansas, widower. Administration to the mother, Mary Calvert Howard, widow. (Oct. 1847). Revoked on her death and granted to the brother and sisters, Edward John Howard, Harriet Howard and Margaret Howard. (Aug. 1852).

Howe, Elizabeth, of St. Giles Cripplegate, London, widow, whose son-in-law, Edward Hill, was in Virginia. Probate to Edward Hill and Sarah Alcorne. (May. 1677). Wi.

Howell, Edward, of St. Mary Woolnoth, London, who died in Carolina. Administration to the principal creditor, Anthony Church; the relict, Mary Howell, renouncing. (Oct. 1692).

Howell, Henry, formerly of Bath, Somerset, but late of Savannah, bachelor. Administration to the brother and sisters, Williams Howell, Catharine, wife of William Marks, and Elizabeth, wife of John Howell. (Jan. 1818).

Howell, William, of Boston, New England, widower. Administration to the son, Joseph Howell. (May 1727).

Howes, William, of Virginia. Administration to the son, Richard Howes. (May 1694).

Howett, John, of Elizabeth City, Virginia. Probate to Thomas Howett. (July 1659). Wi.

Howson, Thomas, of Maryland. Probate to the mother, Mary Howson. (June 1718).

Hoyle, Samuel, of St. Katherine Creechurch, London, who died in Rappahannock, Virginia, bachelor. Administration to the mother, Anne Atkinson, widow. (Apr. 1708).

Hoyt, Esther, of New York, widow. Administration to James Tidbury, attorney for the son, Stephen Hoyt, in New York. (Oct. 1828).

Hoyt, Stephen, of Poughkeepsie, New York, Captain on half pay of the Prince of Wales' American Regiment. Administration to Daniel Thomas, attorney for the relict, Esther Hoyt, in New York. (July 1810).

Hubbard, Nathaniel, of Newhaven, Connecticut, surgeon's mate of H.M. Regiment of Foot, who died in Havana, bachelor. Administration to Phineas Lyman, attorney for the brother, Leverett Hubbard, in Newhaven. (Dec. 1763).

Hubbard, Thomas, of Virginia, bachelor. Administration to the brother, Edward Hubbard. (Sep. 1697).

Huckstep, Samuel, of King and Queen County, Virginia, and Ewhurst, Sussex. Probate to the relict, Jane Huckstep. (Jan. 1696).

Hudson, Abednego, of New Bern, North Carolina. Administration to Thomas Blount, attorney for the relict, Ann Hill, in New Bern. (July 1787).

Hudson, John, of Boston, New England, and of the ship *Paget*. Probate to Jane, wife of William Jenkinson. (July 1702).

Hudson, John, of Bristol, clothier, whose brother, William Hudson deceased, was in Virginia. Probate to George Martin with similar

Hudson, *(contd.)* powers reserved to Henry Martin. (Oct. 1725). Wi.

Huertis, James. *See* **Hustis.**

Huger, Daniel, of Berkeley County, South Carolina. Limited administration with will to Thomas Corbett, attorney for Francis Lejan the elder and Francis Lejan the younger in South Carolina. (Jan. 1756).

Huggins, Robert, of Carolina, bachelor. Probate to William Peasley. (Nov. 1677).

Hughes, Charles, formerly of Devizes, Wiltshire, afterwards of Chelsham, Surrey, but late of Fairfax Courthouse, Virginia. Administration to the creditor, Richard Miller; the relict, Nancy Hughes, and the children, Elizabeth, Sarah Ann and others, and Thomas Hughes having been cited but not having appeared. (Dec. 1809).

Hughes, David, of Bristol and late of the ship *Lackey*, who died in Pennsylvania. Administration to the brother and next-of-kin, John Hughes. (June 1772).

Hughes, Edward, of Westchester, [New York?], mariner. Probate to Elizabeth Clayton of Stepney, Middlesex, widow. (Dec. 1703).

Hughs, John, of Fort Albany, Hudsons Bay, bachelor. Probate to the brother and next-of-kin, William Hughs. (Nov. 1726).

Hughes, John Stokes, of New Orleans, who died in Messina, Sicily, merchant. Probate to the sister and surviving executor, Elizabeth Mary, wife of Rev. Horatio Moule. (Oct. 1856).

Hughes, Richard, of Georgia, bachelor. Administration to the great aunt, Jemima Elliott, widow, guardian of the nephew and next-of-kin, Philip Hughes. (Mar. 1763). Revoked because issued under false pretences and granted to the cousin and next-of-kin, Richard Hughes. (May 1765).

Hughes, Robert, of Stepney, Middlesex, who died on H.M. ship *Tartar* in Virginia. Probate to the relict, Mary Hughes. (May 1727).

Hughes, William, of Boston, New England, bachelor. Administration to John Carling, attorney for the brother, John Hughes, in Boston. (Mar. 1731).

Huisman, Abraham, of New York City. Limited probate to Joseph Mico of London, merchant. (Dec. 1748).

Huling, John, of H.M. ship *Triton*'s prize, bachelor. Administration to Charles Lodwick, attorney for the brother, Alexander Huling, in New York. (Nov. 1711).

Humble, Edward, of Staten Island, New York, bachelor. Administration to the sisters, Maria, wife of Charles Smith, and Jessie Humble; the mother and next-of-kin, Isabella Humble, having died. (Jan. 1856).

Humble, William, of New York City. Probate to Mary Spark, spinster. (June 1778).

Hummerston, Thomas, formerly of St. Margaret Lothbury, London, but late of North America, bachelor. Administration to the brothers and sisters, James Hummerston, William Dunn Hummerston, and Elizabeth, wife of William Hibbert. (June 1783).

Humphreys, Jane, of Philadelphia, widow. Administration to the only child, Thomas Humphreys. (Aug. 1843).

Humfreys, John, of Honiton, Devon, who died in Virginia, widower. Administration to the brother, Henry Humfreys. (Sep. 1656).

Humphries, Richard, formerly of Cork, Ireland, afterwards of St. John, Southwark, Surrey, but late of New Orleans. Probate to John Burrell and William Hance. (Jan. 1797).

Humphries, Thomas, of Christ Church, Surrey, who died in Maryland. Probate to the relict, Jane Humphries; no executor having been named. (Nov. 1722).

Hunlocke, Martha, of Clapham, Surrey, widow, whose son, Edward Hunlocke, was in New England. Probate to William Hardcastle. (Jan. 1691). Wa.

Hunt, Betty, formerly of Derby but late of New York City, spinster. Administration with will to Edward Leam, attorney for Richard Brown in New York. (Jan. 1847).

Hunt, Charles, formerly of Queen Street, St. Marylebone, Middlesex, but late of Williamsburg, North America. Probate to the surviving executor, Richard Adams. (Dec. 1794).

Hunt, John, of Virginia. Administration to the relict, Thomasine Hunt. (Oct. 1669).

Hunt, John, of Virginia, bachelor. Administration to the sisters and next-of-kin, Mary Hunt and Willielma, wife of Francis Rawlings. (May. 1702).

Hunt, John, of Virginia, widower. Administration to the principal creditor, William Moore; the children having been cited but not having appeared. (Sep. 1718).

Hunt, John, of Taunton, Somerset, who died in Charles Town, South Carolina, widower. Administration to the creditrix, Betty Wansbrough, widow; the only child, John Hunt, renouncing by his uncle and guardian, William Hunt. (Apr. 1760).

Hunt, John, of Newport, Rhode Island, who died on H.M. ship *Valiant*. Administration by his solemn declaration to Joseph Sherwood, attorney for the relict, Carolina Hunt, in Rhode Island. (Sep. 1763).

Hunt, Mary A. *See* **Hounslow**.

Hunt, Nicholas, of Virginia, bachelor. Administration to the sisters and next-of-kin, Mary Hunt and Willielma, wife of Francis Rawlings. (May. 1702).

Hunt, Thomas, of Chalfont St. Giles, Buckinghamshire, who died in Carolina. Probate to the brother, Andrew Hunt; the named executors renouncing. (Aug. 1699).

Hunter, Daniel, of Wilmington, North Carolina. Limited administration with will to Jameson Hunter, attorney for the relict, Sarah J., now wife of Nathaniel Potter, in Wilmington. (Apr. 1831).

Hunter, John, of Norfolk, Virginia, who died in New York City. Probate to Thomas McCulloch with similar powers reserved to James Parker. (Apr. 1783). ALC.

Hunter, John, formerly of Little England, Virginia, but late of Bath,

Hunter, *(contd.)*
Somerset. Probate to Archibald Hamilton and Osgood Hamilton: Benjamin Colborne renouncing. (Apr. 1791).

Hunter, Septimus Hewgill alias Robert Edward, formerly of the High Street, Margate, Kent, but late of New Orleans, surgeon. Administration to the relict, Frances Margaret Hunter. (May 1848).

Hunter, William, formerly of Bristol but late of Philadelphia. Administration with will to Robert Lewis, attorney for the relict, Susanna Hunter, in Philadelphia. (Dec. 1796).

Huntington, Henry, of New York City, bachelor. Administration to the father, Thomas Huntington. (June 1832).

Huntington, Sarah, wife of Hezekiah Huntington, formerly Sarah Morgan, of Hartford, Connecticut. Limited administration to the brother, James Francis Morgan, attorney for the niece, Lucretia Williams Imlay, wife of William Edward Imlay, in Connecticut. (Mar. 1850).

Huntington, Thomas, formerly of Bristol but late of New Rochelle, New York. Probate to Peter Shute and Newberry Davenport with similar powers reserved to Pitcher Huntington. (July 1801). Revoked and granted to the son, James Pitcher Huntington. (July 1817).

Huntley, Richard, formerly of Newcastle-upon-Tyne, Northumberland, but late of Staten Island, New York, merchant. Administration to Michael Clayton, attorney for the relict, Susannah Huntley, in Staten Island. (Apr. 1829).

Hunton, Nathaniel, of East Ham, Essex, whose sister, Elizabeth March, was in New England. Probate to Samuel Hunton. (Aug. 1706). NGSQ 68/115.

Hurry, Samuel, of Philadelphia. Probate to the relict, Elizabeth Ann Hurry, with similar powers reserved to the son, John Hurry. (May 1824).

Husband, Thomas Craskell, formerly of Manchester, Jamaica, but late of Trenton, New Jersey. Administration with will to Edward Husband, attorney for the relict, Adah Ann Husband, and the sister, Caroline Husband, in the United States of America. (Apr. 1838).

Hussey, Amiel, of Nantucket, North America, master of the merchant ship *Britannia* employed in the southern whale fishery. Administration to the creditor, Abraham Lyon Moses; the relict, Anis Hussey, and the only child, Lydia Hussey, having been cited but not having appeared. (Oct. 1808).

Hussey, John, Lieutenant-Colonel of the 47th Regiment of Foot under Lieutenant-General Peregrine Lascelles, who died in North America, bachelor. Administration to the brother, Richard Hussey; the mother, Elizabeth Hussey, widow, renouncing. (Dec. 1760).

Hustis alias Huertis, James, of New York City, Lieutenant of half pay of the Loyal American Chasseurs. Limited administration to James Tidbury, attorney for the relict, Margaret Hustis, in New York. (June 1824).

Hutchin, Frederick, of Deptford, Kent, who died in Virginia on the merchant ship *Forward*. Administration to the principal creditor, John Lutwyche; the relict, Anne Hutchin, renouncing. (July 1727).

Hutchins, Charles, of Maryland. Administration to the relict, Dorothy

Hutchins, *(contd.)*
Hutchins. (Oct. 1701).

Hutchins, Frances. *See* **Hammet.**

Hutchins, John, Quartermaster of the 17th Regiment of Dragoons, who died in New York, bachelor. Administration to the brother, Joseph Hutchins. (July 1777).

Hutchings, Noy Willey, of Charles Town, South Carolina, bachelor. Administration to the mother and only next-of-kin, Sarah Hutchings, widow. (Apr. 1792).

Hutchings, Richard, of Charles Town, South Carolina. Probate to the nephew, William Hutchins. (Feb. 1791).

Hutchinson, Abraham, of Virginia, bachelor. Administration to the brother, John Hutchinson. (May 1687).

Hutchinson, Anthony John, of Helena, Arkansas, bachelor. Administration to the sister, Elizabeth, wife of Joseph Fryer. (Nov. 1850).

Hutchinson, Richard, of Hertford, citizen and ironmonger of London, who had lands in New England. Probate to Edward Hutchinson with similar powers reserved to the other executors. (Apr. 1670). Wa.

Hutchinson, Robert, of Virginia. Administration to the sister, Jane Daberry. (July 1650).

Hutton, Charles, of Ploxen, Virginia, bachelor. Administration to the nephew and next-of-kin, John Hutton; the mother, Jane Hutton, widow, renouncing. (Sep. 1722).

Hutton, Robert, of H.M. ship *Southampton*, who died in Virginia, bachelor. Administration to the principal creditrix, Christiana Thompson. (June 1703).

Hyde, Catherine, of St. Giles in the Fields, Middlesex, spinster. Administration to Henry, Earl of Clarendon, the father and attorney of Edward, Viscount Cornbury, in New York. (June 1708).

Hyde, Charlotte. *See* **Young.**

Hyde, Sir Henry, of London, who had lands in Virginia. Probate to the brothers, Thomas Hyde, doctor of laws, and James Hyde M.D. (June 1660). Sh.Wi.

Hide, Jean. *See* **Bliss.**

I

Imer, Rev. Abraham, of Congrees, South Carolina. Administration to James McKenzie, now husband and attorney of the relict, Ann McKenzie, in South Carolina. (Jan. 1775).

Indian, Thomas, of Bristol Township, New England, who died at Barbados on H.M. ship *Dolphin*, bachelor. Administration to the principal creditor, Thomas Newton. (Apr. 1695).

Ingate, Anne, of 29 Greenwich Avenue, New York City, widow. Administration with will to George Laurence, attorney for the son, James Wright Ingate, in New York City. (June 1847).

Ingersoll, Jared, of Newhaven, Connecticut. Administration with will to Dennis de Berds, attorney for Jared Ingersoll in Philadelphia. (Feb. 1783).

Inglis, Thomas, formerly of Charles Town, South Carolina, but late of Jamaica, bachelor. Administration to the sister, Sarah Inglis; the mother, Mary Inglis, widow, renouncing. (Aug. 1788).

Ingoldsby, Mary. *See* **Langhorne**.

Ingoldsby, Richard, a Captain who died in New York. Administration to the son, George Ingoldsby, attorney for the relict, Mary Ingoldsby, in New York. (July 1719).

Ingraham, George, formerly of New England but late of H.M. ships *Newcastle* and *Grafton*. Probate to Robert Smith. (June 1764).

Ingram, Joseph, who died overseas (bound for Virginia). Probate to the father, Robert Ingram. (Sep. 1653). Sh.Wi.

Ingram, Thomas, of Birmingham, Warwickshire, who died in Maryland. Administration to the principal creditor, Thomas James; the relict, Ann Ingram, renouncing. (July 1717).

Inman, Mary, of Chesterfield, Derbyshire, who died in South Carolina, spinster. Probate to Thomas Pike. (Nov. 1769).

Inman, Robert, of Colonel Burr's Marines of H.M. ship *Windsor*, who died in Boston, New England. Administration to the relict, Elizabeth Inman pending production of a will. (Aug. 1712).

Innerarity, John, formerly of Montpelier Row, Stockwell, Surrey, but late of Savannah, Georgia. Administration to the creditor, Andrew Millar; the relict, Henrietta Innerarity, and the daughter, Henrietta Innerarity, renouncing, they and the sons, James and John Innerarity, being the only persons entitled to administer. (Jan. 1805).

Inwood, John Payne, of Savannah, Georgia, bachelor. Administration to the sister, Sarah Inwood. (Nov. 1847).

Irbie, Edward, of St. Michael Cornhill, London, whose brother-in-law, George Yardley, was in Virginia. Probate to the relict, Catherine Irbie, after sentence for the validity of the will. (Mar. 1617). Wi.

Irby, Walter, of Accomack, Northampton County, Virginia, who died overseas. Probate to the mother, Olive Irby alias Cooper, widow. (July 1652). Sh.Wi.

Ireland, John, of Boston, New England, who died at sea. Administration to John Lane, attorney for the relict, Mary Ireland, in New England. (Jan. 1699).

Irish, Zachary, of Windsor, Berkshire, whose brother, Edward Newman, was in Virginia. Probate to John Weekes and Richard Newman. (July 1672). Wa.

Iron, Nicholas. *See* **Herne**.

Ironmonger, Corderoy, of Virginia, bachelor. Administration to the sister, Elizabeth Everndon alias Ironmonger, wife of Anthony Everndon. (Nov. 1681).

Ironmonger, Martha. *See* **Jones**.

Isham, Henry, of Henrico County, Virginia. Probate to William Randolph. (June 1680). Wa.Wi.

Isham, Thomas, of the Middle Temple, London, whose cousin, Henry Isham, was in Virginia. Probate to Francis Drake. (July 1676). Wi.

Israel, Israel the younger, of Philadelphia, bachelor. Administration to James Mackenzie, attorney for the father, Israel Israel, in Philadelphia. (Mar. 1812).

Issabell, Robert, of Philadelphia, bachelor. Administration to the mother, Ann, wife of William Cock. (Oct. 1781).

Issit, Ann Katherine, formerly Ann Katherine Forbes, of Charleston, South Carolina. Administration to the husband, Charles Gorman Issit. (Apr. 1824).

Ive, John, of Boston, New England. Administration to Benjamin Stow, father of the relict, Sarah Ive, until she comes of age. (Oct. 1698).

Ivy, James, formerly of Shoreditch, Middlesex, but late of New York City, widower. Administration to the daughter, Esther, wife of James Mills. (June 1800).

Izard, Mary, of Carolina. Probate to the husband, Ralph Izard. (July 1700).

Izard, Ralph, of Berkeley County, South Carolina. Administration with will to Ralph Izard, attorney for Daniel Blake, Henry Middleton and Benjamin Smith in South Carolina. (May 1763).

J

Jackman, Joseph John, of Surry County, Virginia, who died in Deal, Kent. Probate to the relict, Mary Jackman. (May 1714).

Jackson, Arthur, of Bristol, who died at Quarry Creek, Potomack River, Stafford County, Virginia, bachelor. Administration to the father, Arthur Jackson. (July 1712). Revoked and administration with will granted to the sisters, Elizabeth, wife of James Kelson, and Rachel, wife of Joseph End; the named executors having died. (Nov. 1713).

Jackson, Edward, of Boston, New England. Administration with will to Nathaniel Paice, attorney for the surviving executors, Daniel Marsh, Samuel Sewall and Thomas Cushing, in Boston; the relict, Dorothy Jackson, having died before executing. (May 1763).

Jackson, George Knowil, of Boston, Massachusetts, doctor of music, widower. Administration to the son, Charles Jackson. (Mar. 1824).

Jackson, Harry, of Philadelphia, Lieutenant in H.M. Forces, bachelor. Administration to David Thomas, attorney for the sister and only next-of-kin, Sarah, wife of Edward Miles, in Liverpool, Lancaster County, North America. (Aug. 1797).

Jackson, Jane, wife of George Knowil Jackson, of Boston, Massachusetts. Administration to the son, Charles Jackson. (Mar. 1824).

Jackson, John, of Boston, Massachusetts, Ensign of the 64th Regiment, bachelor. Administration to Charles Lincoln, attorney for the brother and next-of-kin, Richard Jackson, in Dublin, Ireland. (May 1783).

Jackson, Samuel, of Boston, Lincolnshire, whose sister, Mary Woodward, was in Boston, New England. Administration with will to the brother, Nathaniel Jackson; no executor having been named. (Nov. 1646). Wa.

Jackson, Samuel, of New England, who died on H.M. ship *Windsor Castle*. Probate to Anthony Dowrich. (Feb. 1693). Wa.

Jackson, Theodore, of Boston, Massachusetts, bachelor. Administration to the brother, Charles Jackson, administrator of the father, George Knowil Jackson deceased. (Mar. 1824).

Jackson, William, formerly of Wetherden, Suffolk, but late of Kingston, Luzerne County, Pennsylvania. Administration to Johan Seaman, attorney for the relict, Elizabeth Jackson, in Kingston. (Jan. 1841).

Jacob, Henry, of St. Andrew Hubbard, London, whose children were to go to Virginia. Administration with will to the relict, Sarah Jacob; no executor having been named. (May 1624). (1624).

Jacob, William, of Deptford, Kent, who died in Virginia, bachelor. Administration to the mother, Anne Jacob. (Apr. 1682).

Jacobson, Swansea, of the Naval Asylum in Philadelphia, bachelor. Administration to the brother, John Jacobson. (Sep. 1844).

Jadwyn, Thomas, of St. Michael Paternoster Row, London, who had lands in Virginia. Probate to the relict, Elizabeth Jadwyn. (Mar. 1628). Wa.

Jago, John, a negro of the merchant ship *Humphrey*, who died in Virginia, bachelor. Probate to John Coldham, father and guardian of John

Jago, *(contd.)*
Coldham; no executor having been named. (Dec. 1739).

Jalland, John, formerly of Lutton, Lincolnshire, but late of Baltimore, North America. Administration to Thomas Gaisford, attorney for the brother and next-of-kin, Joseph Jalland, in Coddington, Nottinghamshire; the relict, Ruth Jane Jalland, having been cited but not having appeared. (Aug. 1810).

James, Benjamin, of Frankfort, North America. Administration to the daughter, Elizabeth Amer, widow; the relict, Ursula James, having died. (July 1829).

James, Edward, of Virginia. Administration to the sisters, Margery, wife of Christopher Price, Ellinor, wife of John Richardson, and Mary James. (June 1659).

James, Elisha, of Bristol, who died in Virginia. Administration to the relict, Hester James. (Nov. 1706).

James, Henry, of Bristol, merchant, who had lands in Pennsylvania. Probate to the daughter, Hannah James. (Oct. 1728).

James, Thomas, of Charles Town, South Carolina, bachelor. Administration to the father, John James. (July 1759).

Janson, Mary, relict of Bryan Janson, whose son, George Janson, was in Virginia. Probate to Sir William Janson with similar powers reserved to George Janson; the other executor, John Janson, having died. (May 1695). *See* NGSQ 67/290.

Janson, Thomazine, of St. Dunstan in the West, London, widow, whose kinswomen, Judith Tower and Elizabeth Winthrop, were in New England. Probate to Thomas Easington with similar powers reserved to Thomas Oldfield. (Feb. 1659). Wa.

Jardine, Robert S., of Madison County, Virginia. Limited administration with will to James Ross with similar powers reserved to John Thom and John Mundell. (Dec. 1815).

Jarvis, Edward, of Rhode Island, bachelor. Administration by decree to the sister and next-of-kin, Elizabeth, wife of Edward Sharp. (Jan. 1722).

Jarvis, Elizabeth, of Enfield, Middlesex, widow of James Jarvis, smith, whose sister, Ann Torbet, was in Little Winchester, Frederick County, Maryland. Probate to the sole executor, Robert Norton. (Mar. 1803). *See* NGSQ 63/200.

Jarvis, Thomas, formerly of Virginia but late of St. Olave, Old Jewry, London. Probate to the relict, Elizabeth Jarvis, and to Edmund Foster and George Richards. (Apr. 1684).

Jauncy, James, formerly of New York City but late of St. Marylebone, Middlesex. Probate to the son, William Jauncey with similar powers reserved to the son, Thomas John Jauncey, and the daughter, Mary Jauncey. (July 1790).

Jauncey, Mary, of New York City, spinster. Administration to the brother and next-of-kin, William Jauncey. (Jan. 1822).

Jauncey, William, formerly of Charlotte Street, Portland Place, Middlesex, but late of New York City. Probate to Thomas Barclay and John Rutherford with similar powers reserved to John Chambers. (July 1829).

Jay, Peter, formerly of Rye, Westchester County, but who died in Poughkeepsie, Dutchess County, New York. Administration with will to James Daltera, attorney for the sons, Sir James Jay, John Jay and Frederick Jay, and for Egbert Benson, in North America. (May 1785).

Jeane, John, Collector of Brunswick, North Carolina, widower. Administration to the principal creditor, David Deacon; the sister and only next-of-kin, Jenney, wife of Richard Score, renouncing. (May 1752).

Jeckell. *See* **Jekyll**.

Jeffrey, Joseph, carpenter of H.M. ship *Apollo*, who died in New York. Probate to Edward Trythall. (Feb. 1779).

Jeffries, David, of Taunton, Somerset, whose son, David Jeffries, was in New England. Probate to the relict, Dorothy Jeffries, and the daughters, Sarah and Hester Jeffries. (Jan. 1691). Wa.

Jeffreys, Herbert, Governor of Virginia, who died in Virginia. Administration to Bartholomew Price, attorney for the relict, Susannah Jeffreys, and the son, John Jeffreys. (May 1679). NGSQ 66/118.

Jefferies, John, of H.M. ship *Scorpion*, who died in North Carolina, bachelor. Administration to the mother, Catherine Jefferies, widow. (Jan. 1777).

Jeffreys, Peter, of the merchant ship *Prosperous Ann*, who died in Maryland, bachelor. Probate to the brother, Robert Jeffreys. (Jan. 1733).

Jefferys, William, of the merchant ship *Mary and Francis*, who died in Virginia, bachelor. Probate to John Jefferys. (Jan. 1715).

Jeffs, Charles, of the ship *St. John*, who died in Virginia, bachelor. Administration to the mother, Mary Jeffs, widow. (Apr. 1694).

Jekyll, John, of Boston, New England. Administration to Thomas Sandford, attorney for the relict, Margaret Jekyll, in Boston. (June 1748). Revoked on the deaths of Thomas Sandford and Margaret Jekyll and granted to the son, Rev. John Jekyll. (Nov. 1769).

Jeckell, John, of New York, widower. Administration to the brothers, William and Samuel Jeckell, and the sister, Esther, wife of Robert Almoney. (May 1783).

Jenkins, Elizabeth. *See* **Brett**.

Jenney, John, of St. Mary at Hill, London, who died in Virginia, bachelor. Administration to the brother, Samuel Jenney. (Aug. 1676). Revoked on his death and granted to his executor, Edmund Strudwick; the nieces and next-of-kin, Jane Wyldbore and Mary Formoson, renouncing. (July 1734).

Jennifer, Daniel de St. Thomas, of Patuxen River, Maryland, who died in St. Botolph Bishopsgate, London. Administration to the creditor, Jonathan Forward; the relict, Elizabeth Jennifer, and the daughters, Mary and Elizabeth Jennifer, having been cited but not having appeared. (Apr. 1730).

Jennings alias Gennings, Anne, formerly Anne Radcliffe, of Roxburgh, United States of America. Administration to George Cox, attorney for

Jennings alias Gennings, *(contd.)* the husband, Thomas Jennings, in Pennsylvania. (Nov. 1833).

Jennings, Edmund, of Yorkshire, whose former wife, Ariana, was of Virginia and whose nephew, Edmund Jennings, was in Maryland. Probate to the son, Edmund Jennings, with similar powers reserved to James Buchanan. (Mar. 1756).

Jennings, Samuel, of Wingan, South Carolina, widower. Administration to the son, Samuel Jennings. (Dec. 1745).

Jennings, William, formerly of St. Giles in the Fields, Middlesex, but late of Kildwicke, Yorkshire, who had lands in Virginia. Probate to the relict, Elizabeth Jennings. (Aug. 1711). Wi.

Jenys, Thomas, of Charles Town, South Carolina. Probate to Stephen Bedon with similar powers reserved to Elizabeth Gibbes, Branfill Evance and Paul Jenys. (Oct. 1750).

Jephson, Christopher, Ensign of William Shirley's Regiment of Foot, who died in New England, bachelor. Administration to the mother, Elizabeth Jephson, widow. (Sep. 1750).

Jerningham, Henry, of St. Mary's County, Maryland. Limited administration with will to the daughter, Frances Henrietta Jerningham. (May 1775).

Jerrard, John, formerly of Chideoak, Dorset, but late of Boston, North America. Administration with will to John Perham, husband and administrator of the sister, Joan Perham deceased. (May 1814).

Jesson, James, of St. Andrew Undershaft, London, who had lands in New England. Administration with will to the relict, Mary Jesson; the executor, Richard Lloyd, having died and the surviving executor, George Scott, renouncing. (Aug. 1686). Wa.

Jesson, Robert, of Pennsylvania, widower. Probate to Rebecca, wife of Solomon Goade. (June 1740).

Jimenez, Jose. *See* **Ximenez**.

Jobson, Samuel, of Bermondsey, Surrey, whose son, Michael Jobson, was in Philadelphia. Probate by his solemn affirmation to the son, Samuel Jobson, with similar powers reserved to Joseph Grove and Silvanus Grove. (Nov. 1708).

Joddrell, William, of H.M. ship *Dunbarton*, who died in Virginia, bachelor. Administration to the principal creditor, Thomas Collin. (Apr. 1692).

Johns, John, of St. Botolph Bishopsgate, London, who died in Carolina. Probate to the relict, Frances Johns. (Jan. 1700).

Johnson, Abraham, of St. Dunstan in the East, London, who died in Maryland. Administration to the relict, Mary Johnson. (Aug. 1701).

Johnson, Andrew, of the merchant ship *Sussex*, who died in Virginia, bachelor. Probate to the sister, Martha Tilbury alias Splidt, wife of Thomas Tilbury. (Apr. 1708).

Johnson, Charles, formerly of Calcutta in the East Indies and afterwards of Newcastle, Delaware, who died in Newark, New Jersey, in 1820, bachelor and bastard, whose natural brother, Samuel Johnson, was a naturalised American citizen. Administration to the said Samuel

Johnson, *(contd.)* Johnson for the use of the Crown. (Mar. 1827).

Johnson, Daniel, of Lynn, New England, seaman of H.M. ship *Advice*, who died in St. Thomas's Hospital, Southwark, Surrey. Probate to Patrick Hayes. (Apr. 1696).

Johnson, John, of the ship *Concordat*, who died in Virginia, bachelor. Probate to Jane Cheney with similar powers reserved to Robert Cheney. (July 1682).

Johnson, John, of Virginia, bachelor. Administration to Dorcas, wife of the principal creditor. Gerard Dobson, during his absence. (July & Oct. 1688). Marked "pauper."

Johnson, John, of New London, Chester County, Pennsylvania. Administration to William Lumley, attorney for the relict, Sarah Johnson, in North Milford Hundred, Cecil County, Maryland. (June 1827). Revoked on his death and granted to the relict, Sarah, now wife of Levin Shockley. (Dec. 1834).

Johnson, Joshua, formerly of Coopers Row, St. Botolph Aldgate, London, but late of the City of Washington, North America. Administration to the creditor, William Taylor; the relict, Louisa Johnson, and the only children, Ann Johnson, Louisa, wife of John Quincy Adams, Caroline, Thomas, Harriet, Eliza and Adelaide Johnson, having been cited but not having appeared. (May 1805).

Johnson, Luke, of Virginia. Probate to John Turton and James Cary. (Aug. 1659). Sh.Wi.

Johnson, Nicholas, of Shadwell, Middlesex, who died in Virginia. Administration to the principal creditor, Roger Stackhouse; the relict, Emma Johnson, renouncing. (Apr. 1663).

Johnson, Peter, of the ship *Anne*, who died in Virginia, bachelor. Probate to Gabriel Whitehorne. (Aug. 1693).

Johnson, Robert, Governor of South Carolina. Limited administration with will to the son, Robert Johnson. (Aug. 1735).

Johnson, Sarah, of Charleston, South Carolina, widow. Administration with will to Thomas Crowder, attorney for the sons, Joseph and James Johnson, in Charleston. (July 1838).

Johnson, Simon, of New York City. Administration with will to Gabriel Shaw, administrator of the granddaughter, Margaret Johnson Bibby deceased, formerly McEvers, wife of Thomas Bibby; the relict, Margaret Johnson, and the executors, Robert G. Livingston, Gerrard Beekman the elder and William Neilson, having died. (May 1823).

Johnson alias Duncombe, Susanna, of Virginia. Administration to Gawen Corbin, attorney for the husband, Colonel Richard Johnson, in Virginia. (Oct. 1694).

Johnson, Thomas, of Savannah, North America, bachelor. Administration to the sister and only next-of-kin, Elizabeth Nicholson. (Jan. 1808).

Johnson, Uzal, surgeon on half pay of the New Jersey Volunteers. Administration with will to James Tidbury, attorney for the relict, Jane Johnson, and the son, Isaac Arthur Johnson, in New Jersey. (Apr. 1828).

Johnson, William, Captain of H.M. ship *Lizard*, bachelor. Administration to Fairfax Overton, attorney for the father, Sir Nathaniel Johnson, in Carolina. (Oct. 1701). Revoked on the death of Overton and granted to the son, Robert Johnson, as attorney. (Jan. 1709).

Johnson, Sir William, of Johnson Hall, Tryon County, New York. Administration with will to Samuel Baker, attorney for the son, Sir John Johnson, and for Daniel Claus, Guy Johnson, Robert Adams, Dr. John Dease and Joseph Chew, in America. (Feb. 1776).

Johnsons, George, formerly of Corsham, Wiltshire, but late of Albany, United States of America, widower. Administration to Thomas Branson, attorney for the daughter, Elizabeth Fleet, widow, in America. (Sep. 1817).

Johnston, Francis, Lieutenant of the 38th Regiment of Foot, who died in Philadelphia, bachelor. Administration to the cousin german, Thomas Noble; the sister, Grace Johnston, renouncing. (Dec. 1778).

Johnston, Gabriel, of Edenhouse, North Carolina, Governor of North Carolina. Limited administration with will to Alexander Anderson, attorney for Samuel Johnston in Carolina. (Aug. 1791). Revoked and granted to Alexander McDougall, attorney for Hannah Bruce, formerly Ferrier, wife of Robert Bruce, and Elizabeth Ferrier, both in Edinburgh, the daughters and executrices of Rev. Robert Ferrier deceased, who was the sole executor of Elizabeth Ferrier, the sister of the testator; Samuel Johnston, the relict, Frances Johnston, and Henry Johnston, having died. (Mar. 1795).

Johnston, Johanna, formerly of Woolwich, Kent, and afterwards of Philadelphia, who died as a passenger at sea on the merchant ship *Three Brothers*, widow. Administration to the nephew and next-of-kin, George Boston. (Sep. 1839).

Johnston, Lewis, formerly of Edinburgh, Scotland, but late of Georgia. Probate to the daughters, Elizabeth, Rachel and Ann Johnston, with similar powers reserved to William Johnston, John Wood and James Hume. (Apr. 1798).

Johnston, Robert, formerly of Virginia but late of St. Olave Hart Street, London. Probate to James Russell. (Apr. 1766). Wi.

Johnstone, John, of Fort Vancouver, City of Columbia, United States of America. Probate to the surviving executrix, Isabella Miller alias Moar, wife of Jonathan Moar, formerly wife of James Logie. (June 1856).

Jolland, Charles, of H.M. ships *Grafton* and *Raisonable*, who died in Rhode Island Hospital, bachelor. Administration to the father, Robert Jolland. (Jan. 1780).

Jones, Allen, of Bourbon, Virginia. Administration with will to William Murdock, attorney for William Goosley in York, Virginia. (Oct. 1792).

Jones, Anne, of St. Clement Danes, Middlesex, whose son, Thomas Daniell, was in Virginia. Probate to the said Thomas Daniell. (Feb. 1678). Wa.

Jones, Christopher, formerly of St. Asaph, Flint, but late of New York City,

Jones, *(contd.)*
painter and glazier, bachelor. Administration to the mother and next-of-kin, Elizabeth Jones, widow. (Sep. 1852).

Jones, Eden Henry, formerly of Bristol, chemist, but late of New York. Administration to the relict, Annatilda Juliet, now wife of Joseph Haythorne Latcham. (Mar. 1853).

Jones, George, late of Philadelphia, who died in Worcester. Limited administration with will to Elizabeth Clay. (Feb. 1752).

Jones, Henry, formerly of Throgmorton Street, London, but late of Charleston, South Carolina, merchant. Administration with will to Thomas Crokatt and Charles Alderman, attornies for John McDowall and James Harper in Charleston; William Inglesby renouncing. (June 1815).

Jones, Hugh, Minister of Christ Church, Calvert County, Maryland. Administration with will to Barbara Jones, attorney for Thomas Cockshutt and John Bigger in Maryland. (June 1704).

Jones, Jane. *See* **Vaughan**.

Jones, John, of Pennsylvania. Probate to the relict, Joanne Jones. (Dec. 1723).

Jones, John, of H.M. ship *Mermaid*, who died in South Carolina, bachelor. Administration to the father, John Jones. (May 1754).

Jones, John, formerly of St. Bride, London, but late of New York, bachelor. Administration to the brother and only next-of-kin, Robert Jones. (May 1790).

Jones, John, formerly of Gilfach Wood, Dolgelly, Monmouth, farmer, but late of New York City, widower. Administration to the mother, Catherine Jones, widow. (Aug. 1849).

Jones, John Coffin, of Boston, United States of America. Limited probate to Ebenezer Chadwick with similar powers reserved to Isaac Underhill Coles and Margaret Champlin Coles; the relict, Elizabeth Jones, having died. (Sep. 1838).

Jones, Josias, of Greenwich, Kent, who died in Virginia. Administration to the relict, Hannah Jones. (Sep. 1686).

Jones, Lewis, of St. Helena, South Carolina. Probate to the brother, John Jones, with similar powers reserved to Gabriel Manigault and Charles Purry. (Oct. 1748).

Jones, Livellet alias Elipilor, of Fairfield, New England, seaman of H.M. ship *Suffolk* who died on H.M. ship *Lancaster*. Administration with will to Mary Collins, wife and attorney of the named executor, William Collins, now at sea. (Mar. 1710).

Jones, Losco, formerly of Bethnal Green, Middlesex, but late of California. Probate to Dennis Peele with similar powers reserved to Jane Jones, widow. (Nov. 1829).

Jones, Louisa, formerly of Toronto, Canada, but late of Hamilton County, Ohio. Administration to the husband, John Jones. (Jan. 1852).

Jones alias Ironmonger, Martha, wife of John Jones of Virginia. Administration to Elizabeth Evernden alias Ironmonger, wife of Anthony Evernden, the maternal aunt of the son, John Jones, during

Jones alias Ironmonger, *(contd.)* his absence. (Nov. 1681).

Jones, Mary Ann, of Boston, Massachusetts, widow. Probate to the son, Edward Jones, and to James Hughes. (Nov. 1791).

Jones, Owen, of H.M. ship *Richmond*, who died in New York. Limited probate to George Farewell, attorney for the relict, Elizabeth Jones. (Oct. 1698).

Jones, Richard, of St. Clement Eastcheap, London, who died in Virginia. Administration to the relict, Frances Williams alias Jones. (June 1659).

Jones, Robert, of Henrico, King William County, Virginia, bachelor. Administration to the brother and next-of-kin, Richard Jones. (Aug. 1771).

Jones, Samuel, of Gloucester, New England, and of the ship *Warspight* in the King's service, who died in St. Thomas, Southwark, Surrey. Probate to the sister, Susan Smith. (Oct. 1673).

Jones, Samuel, of the ship *James*, who died on the ship *York* (bound for Virginia), bachelor. Probate to the brother, John Jones. (May 1693).

Jones, Simon, of Maryland, who died at sea, bachelor. Administration to the mother, Margaret, wife of Anthony Royston. (July 1776).

Jones, Thomas, who died in Virginia. Administration to the principal creditor, Rowland Gold. (Apr. 1626).

Jones, Thomas, of H.M. ship *Pembroke*, who died in Virginia. Probate to Elizabeth, wife of Richard Jones, during his absence. (Nov. 1697). Revoked and granted to Dyer Wade. (Oct. 1698).

Jones, Thomas, of Virginia, bachelor. Administration to the father, Richard Jones. (Nov. 1724).

Jones, Thomas, formerly Judge of the Supreme Court of New York but late of Hoddesdon, Broxbourne, Hertfordshire. Probate to the relict, Ann Jones. (Aug. 1792).

Jones, William, of Rotherhithe, Surrey, who died in Virginia. Probate to Thomas May. (Dec. 1718).

Jones, William, of Philadelphia, bachelor. Administration to the sister, Mary Jones. (May 1735).

Jones, William, purser of H.M. ship *Coventry*, who died in New York. Probate to the relict, Rachael Jones. (July 1765).

Jones, William, formerly of Charles Town, South Carolina, but late of St. Martin in the Fields, Middlesex. Probate to the sister, Margaret Jones, with similar powers reserved to Richard Downes and Theodore Gaillard. (May 1774).

Jones, William, formerly of Goodge Street, Tottenham Court Road, Middlesex, but late of Nacogdockes, Texas, merchant, widower. Administration to the sister, Sarah, wife of Edward Davis. (June 1848).

Jope, Priscilla. *See* **Balsley**.

Jope, Sarah. *See* **Williams**.

Jordan, Jane, of Virginia, widow. Administration to the niece and only next-of-kin, Susanna Jane Purdue, formerly Browne, wife of William

Jordan, *(contd.)* Purdue. (Oct. 1792).

Jordan, Robert, formerly of Portland Island but late of St. Giles Cripplegate, London, who died in Virginia. Administration to the relict, Joanne Jordan. (Nov. 1668). Revoked and granted to the son, Thomas Jordan; the relict, Joanna Jordan alias Wyse, having died. (Nov. 1688). Inventory PROB 4/1101.

Jose, John, master of the ship *John Adventure*, who died in Boston, New England. Limited administration to John Ive, attorney for the ship's owners. (Nov. 1706).

Joseph, Benedictus, of New York. Administration to Henry Joseph, attorney for the relict, Jane Joseph, in New York. (Mar. 1851).

Joseph, Eliza, of New York, widow. Administration to the son, John Joseph. (Oct. 1853).

Joseph, Samuel, formerly of Plymouth, Devon, afterwards of Philadelphia, but late of Cincinnati, Ohio. Administration to Nathan Joseph, attorney for the relict, Rebecca Joseph, in Philadelphia. (July 1827).

Jouett, Daniel Troop, of Philadelphia. Administration to Rev. William Parker, attorney for the relict, Margaret Jouett, in Philadelphia. (July 1814).

Jouet, John Troup, of Elizabeth Town, New Jersey, Ensign on half pay of the Third Batallion of New Jersey Volunteers, bachelor. Administration to the creditor, Thomas Courtney; the father, Rev. Cavalier Jouet, renouncing. (July 1794).

Joy, Erasmus, of Plymouth, Devon, who died in Virginia. Administration to the relict, Jane Joy. (Nov. 1682).

Joy, George, of Boston, New England. Administration to Mary, wife and attorney of the principal creditor, Francis Davis, during his absence. (Oct. 1680).

Joyner, Thomas, of Stepney, Middlesex, who died in Virginia. Administration to the principal creditor, Dalby Thomas; the relict, Jane Joyner, renouncing. (July 1675).

Juckes, Edward, of South Carolina. Probate to Dorothy Juckes. (Nov. 1715).

Judd, James, formerly of Wyke Regis, Dorset, but late of Cincinnati, bachelor. Administration to the sisters, Georgiana and Anna Maria Judd; the mother and next-of-kin, Mary Judd, widow, having died. (Apr. 1851).

Julin, Carls, of the ship *Charles Town Packet*, bachelor. Probate to Johannes Scheelhase with similar powers reserved to his wife, Sarah Scheelhase. (Sep. 1760).

Juxon, Thomas, of Mortlake, Surrey, whose cousin, William Juxon, was in Virginia. Probate to the daughter, Elizabeth Juxon. (Dec. 1672). Wa.

K

Kaine, Benjamin, of Glasgow, Scotland, whose father was in Boston, New England. Administration with will to the next-of-kin, Simon Bradstreet. (May 1662). Wa.

Kane, John the elder, of New York City. Administration with will to Gabriel Shaw, administrator of John Kane the younger deceased, who was named as sole executor. (Nov. 1822).

Kane, John the younger, of New York City. Administration to Gabriel Shaw, attorney for the relict, Maria Kane, in New York City. (Nov. 1822).

Kasner, Barnet, of San Francisco, California, bachelor. Administration to the father, Isaac Kasner. (Nov. 1851).

Kearney, Julia L. *See* **Morris**.

Kearny, Philip, of Perth Amboy, New Jersey. Limited administration with will to John Abraham Denormandie, attorney for Isabella Kearny and Andrew Eliot in North America. (Mar. 1783).

Kearny alias Burley alias Ravaud, Susannah, of Perth Amboy, Middlesex County, New Jersey. Administration to Anthony Merle, attorney for the husband, Philip Kearny, in Perth Amboy. (Mar. 1746).

Kearney, Susan alias Susannah, of Newark, New Jersey, widow. Limited administration with will to John James Watts, attorney for the daughter, Eliza Kearney, in New York City. (Aug. 1851).

Kearsley, Margaret, of Philadelphia, widow. Limited administration with will to Phineas Bond. (Aug. 1779).

Kebby, John, of St. Benet Fink, London, whose brother, Henry Kebby, was in New England. Probate to the relict, Joan Kebby. (May 1642). Wa.

Keech, Simon, of Stepney, Middlesex, who died in Virginia, bachelor. Administration with will to Ellis Kelly of St. Michael Cornhill, London, merchant, attorney for the sisters, Mary and Joanna Keech, Elizabeth Woodnett, widow, and Sarah Tilly, widow. (Aug. 1688).

Keech, Thomas, surgeon of the merchant ship *Goodwill*, who died in Maryland. Probate to George Fisher. (Nov. 1717).

Keeling, Charles, of New York City, who died in the Bay of Honduras. Administration to the brother, Anthony Keeling; the relict, Catherine Keeling, having been cited but not having appeared. (July 1787).

Keeling, William, of New York, bachelor. Administration to John Keeling, son and executor of Alice Keeling, the relict and sole executrix of the father, Joseph Keeling deceased. (Aug. 1823).

Keen, Arthur. *See* **Kyne**.

Keen, Mary, formerly of Witney, Oxfordshire, but late of New Orleans. Administration to the husband, Richard Keen. (Apr. 1854).

Keich, Simon, of Virginia. Administration to the relict, Sarah Keich. (Aug. 1655).

Keith, Ann. *See* **McAlister**.

Keith, Charles, of Georgia, America, Lieutenant of the Royal Navy,

Keith, *(contd.)* bachelor. Administration to the father, William Keith. (Mar. 1818).

Keith, Charlotte. *See* **Barron**.

Keith, James, formerly of Charles Town, South Carolina, but late of Blairskinnock, Banff, Scotland. Limited probate to William Irvine, George Gerrard and Robert Falder. (Nov. 1788). Revoked and administration with will of estate unadministered by James Irving alias Irvine deceased to Marion Irving, widow, attorney for the nephew, John Keith, in George Town, South Carolina; the executor, George Gerrard, having died, and the executors, William Irvine and Robert Falder alias Folder, having been cited but not having appeared. (Aug. 1810).

Keith, Mary, of George Town, South Carolina, spinster. Limited administration to John Tunno, attorney for the brother and only next-of-kin, John Keith. (Aug. 1807).

Kellond, John, of Paignsford, Devon, whose son, Thomas Kellond, was in Boston, New England. Probate to the son, John Kellond. (July 1679). Wa.

Kelly, Edmond, of Baltimore, Maryland, widower. Administration to the only child, Frances Kelly. (Nov. 1794).

Kelly, James, of the merchant ship *Friendship*, who died in Rhode Island. Probate to Jane Nance, spinster. (May 1778).

Kelly, Richard, formerly of South Carolina but late of Westminster, Middlesex, widower. Inventory 1786. [*Administration Act not found*].

Kelway, Walter, of Chelmsford, Essex, whose daughters, Margaret Mountague, Melcas Snow and Mary Lane, were in New England. Probate to the relict, Joan Kelway. (Feb. 1651). Sh.Wa.

Kembe, Margaret, of St. Saviour, Southwark, Surrey, widow, whose son, Thomas Kembe, was in Virginia. Probate to Sarah Feake. (Nov. 1665). Wa.

Kemp, George, formerly of East Florida but late of Nassau, doctor of physick, bachelor. Administration to Thomas Finlayson, attorney for the cousin german and only next-of-kin, Agnes Muir alias Ferguson, in Haddington, Scotland. (July 1789).

Kempe, Richard, of Kick Neck, Virginia. Probate to the relict, Elizabeth Lunsford alias Kempe; the other executors, the daughter, Elizabeth Kempe, and Ralph Wormley, having died. (Dec. 1656). Sh.

Kempster, John, of Plaistow, Essex, whose cousin, John Wilkins, was in Boston, New England. Probate to James Whitton with similar powers reserved to Edward Withers, Philip Perry and Thomas Aunger. (June 1687). Wa.

Kenian, Abraham, of Warfield, Berkshire, clerk, who had estate in Virginia. Probate to Jabez Kenian with similar powers reserved to Joseph Kenian. (Jan. 1704).

Kennan, William, of Richmond County, Virginia, bachelor. Administration to Robert Wallace Johnson alias Johnston, doctor of physick, attorney for the sister and next-of-kin, Janet, wife of John Wallace, in Dumfries, Scotland. (Feb. 1765).

Kennedy, Adam, of Antigua (and intending for New York). Probate to William Gordon. (Aug. 1698).

Kennedy, Rev. John, formerly of East Florida but late of Glasgow, Scotland. Probate to Coll McDonald with similar powers reserved to Alexander McDonald and Charles McPherson. (Dec. 1802).

Kent, Elizabeth, of Sonning, Berkshire, widow, whose brother, Carey Latham, was in New England. Probate to Catherine Hunt. (June 1680). Wa.

Kenythorpe, Elizabeth. *See* **Delke**.

Kenyon, Samuel, formerly of Manchester, Lancashire, but late of Boston, New England, mariner. Copy of will probated in Boston to the relict, Elizabeth Kenyon, at PROB 20/2952. (Jan. 1710).

Kerie, Rev. John Julius, formerly of St. Christopher's Island but late of Philadelphia. Administration with will to the son, Julius Samuel Kerie; the brother and surviving executor, Jedediah Kerie, renouncing. (Aug. 1847).

Kerr, Alexander, Lieutenant of the 62nd Regiment, who died in Philadelphia, bachelor. Administration to the mother, Elizabeth Kerr. (May 1802).

Kerr, Thomas. *See* **Carr**.

Kestin, Francis, of St. Olave, Southwark, Surrey, whose brother, Thomas Kestin, was in Virginia. Probate to the relict, Elizabeth Kestin. (Jan. 1667). Wi.

Kettell, John, of H.M. ship *Merlin*, bachelor. Administration to John Coles, attorney for the brother, Jonathan Kettell, in Charles Town, New England. (May 1757).

Key, Isaac, of St. Saviour, Southwark, Surrey, who died in Virginia. Administration to [*Act not completed*]. (May 1680).

Keylock, Anthony, of New England, bachelor. Administration to the cousin and next-of-kin, Frances Smith, widow. (Oct. 1711).

Kibble, Stephen, of New York City. Probate to the surviving executor, William Butler, with similar powers reserved to James Dole and Benjamin James. (Jan. 1782).

Kidby, John, who died on the ship *Providence* coming from Virginia. Administration to the relict, Joane Kidby. (July 1655).

Kidd, Mary Adeline, of Derby, Connecticut. Administration to the husband, Samuel Kidd. (Mar. 1826).

Kidgell, Nicholas, of Stepney, Middlesex, who died in Charles Town, America. Probate to Sarah Kidgell, no executor having been named. (July 1727).

Killick, Sarah, of Ripley Farm, Rochester, New York. Administration to William Stevens, attorney for the husband, Thomas Killick, at Ripley Farm. (July 1838).

Kilpin, William, of Virginia, bachelor. Administration to the brother and next-of-kin, James Kilpin. (Aug. 1716).

Kincaid, George, formerly of Christ Church, Georgia, but late of Exeter, Devon. Probate to the relict, Marion Kincaid, and the brother, Patrick Kincaid, with similar powers reserved to Basil Cowper and Samuel

Kincaid, *(contd.)*
Douglass. (Oct. 1791).

King, Anne, of South Carolina, widow. Administration to the sister, Joanne, wife of William Cripps. (Mar. 1740).

King, Catherine, nee Catherine Albin, of Charleston, South Carolina. Limited administration to the brother-in-law, David Henry King, attorney for the husband, William King, in New York. (Jan. 1854).

King, Daniel, of Annapolis Royal, Arundell County, Maryland, who died at sea on the merchant ship *Content*. Administration to the relict, Anne King. (Nov. 1725).

King, Edward, of Virginia, bachelor. Administration to the sister, Mariane Carlton, widow. (July 1688).

King, Eusebius, of Bristol, Prince George County, Virginia. Administration with will to Isham Randolph, attorney for William Randolph in Henrico County, Virginia. (Sep. 1711). Revoked on the death of William Randolph and granted to Richard Oakly. (Jan. 1713).

King, James, of Glasgow, Scotland, who had property in Virginia. Limited probate to the father, James King, and the mother, Elizabeth King. (Nov. 1788).

King, John, formerly of High Wycombe, Buckinghamshire, but late of Baltimore, Maryland, bachelor. Administration to the father, Edward King. (Mar. 1805). Revoked on his death and granted to one of his executors, Isaac Sheffield. (Feb. 1821).

King, John, formerly of Grays, Essex, and afterwards of Hoxton, Middlesex, but late of Jersey, America. Probate to John Bourne of Crutched Friars, London, and to George Swan with similar powers reserved to Joan Dyer Dommott, spinster. (June 1831).

King, John Curle, formerly of H.M. ships *Port Royal* and *Orford* but late of Virginia, who died in St. Martin in the Fields, Middlesex. Probate to William Boyd with similar powers reserved to James Casey. (Nov. 1763).

King, Nathaniel, of Boston, New England, who died on H.M. ship *York*. Administration with will to Thomas Newman, attorney for the relict, Mary King, in Boston. (Nov. 1747).

King, Peter, of Shaston, Dorset, whose brother, Thomas King, was in New England. Probate to the son, Peter King. (Dec. 1658). Wa.

King, Samuel, of Bristol, who died in Gloucester, Virginia, bachelor. Administration to the brother, John King. (Feb. 1745).

King, Seth, Captain of the First Connecticut Regiment of Foot, who died in Havana, bachelor. Administration to Phineas Lyman, attorney for the father, Josiah King, in Suffield, Connecticut. (Nov. 1764).

King, Thomas the younger, of Charles Town, America, widower. Administration to the brother, William Robert Wale King, administrator of the father, Thomas King deceased. (May 1810).

King, William, of the merchant ship *Cambridge*, who died in or near Maryland, bachelor. Administration to the principal creditor, William Gray. (Dec. 1732).

King, William, formerly of Ipswich, Suffolk, but late of Philadelphia,

King, *(contd.)*
bachelor. Administration to the father, Stephen King. (Oct. 1795).

Kingman, John. *See* **Clarke**.

Kingsbury, Jonathan, of Needham, Massachusetts. Probate to the son, Asa Kingsbury. (Aug. 1807).

Kingswell, Edward, of St. Sepulchre Newgate, London, who had goods in Virginia. Probate to the brother and sister, Roger Wingate and Dorothy his wife. (Apr. 1636). Wi.

Kinnersley, William, of Philadelphia, bachelor. Administration to the nephew, William Kinnersley; the brother and sister and next-of-kin, Richard Kinnersley and Hannah, wife of William Fencott, renouncing. (Apr. 1714).

Kinnicutt, Edward, of Providence, Rhode Island, who died in St. Bartholomew by the Exchange, London. Administration to the creditor, William Stead; the relict, Mary Kinnicutt, and the children, Lydia, Elizabeth and Sarah Kinnicutt, having been cited but not having appeared. (Oct. 1754).

Kinsey, Ralph, of St. Botolph Aldersgate, London, who had lands in Pennsylvania. Probate to William Kinsey and Robert Browne. (June 1682).

Kirby, James, of Richmond, Virginia. Probate to the brother, Robert Kirby, with similar powers reserved to Joseph Gallego. (Apr. 1815).

Kirk, Thomas, of St. James Duke's Place, Middlesex, who died in Virginia. Limited administration to Barbara Kirk pending production of a will. (May 1741).

Kirkland, Moses, formerly of South Carolina but late of St. Andrew, Jamaica. Probate to the relict, Catherine Kirkland, with similar powers reserved to Thomas Edgehill and John Bruce. (July 1789).

Kirkman, Thomas, formerly of Dalkey, Dublin County, Ireland, but late of Nashville, Tennessee. Administration with will to the son, Thomas Kirkman, attorney for the relict, Barbara Carroll Kirkman, in Philadelphia; Ephraim Carroll and Robert Jones renouncing. (June 1815).

Kirkman, Thomas, of Nashville, Davidson County, Tennessee. Probate to the relict, Eleanor Kirkman, with similar powers reserved to Washington Jackson and Bolton Jackson. (Sep. 1828).

Kitts, William, of York River, Gloucester County, Virginia, bachelor. Administration to the sister and next-of-kin, Elizabeth Kitts. (Sep. 1710).

Klingender, Frederick, of New Orleans, bachelor. Administration to Catherine Martha Klingender, the relict and administratrix of the father, Frederick Charles Louis Klingender deceased. (July 1836).

Knapp, Jonathan, of Killingley, Connecticut, a soldier of H.M. Regiment of Foot in Connecticut, who died in Havana. Administration to Phineas Lyman, attorney for the relict, Sarah Knapp, in Killingley. (Dec. 1763).

Knapton, Albin, of Carolina. Administration to James Brent, guardian of the daughter, Margaret Knapton. (Mar. 1708).

Knight, Charles, of Philadelphia. Administration to John Cryder, attorney for the relict, Sarah Knight, in Berwick, Columbia County, United States of America. (July 1839).

Knight, George, of Virginia, bachelor. Administration to the sister, Frances, wife of Charles Bayley. (May 1684).

Knight, Henry, of Maryland. Probate to Robert Day. (Jan. 1675).

Knight, John, of Abington, Montgomery County, Pennsylvania. Administration with will to Abel Evans, attorney for Isaac Knight and Jonathan Tyson in Abington, the executors of Isaac Knight deceased, who was the executor named by the testator. (Apr. 1793).

Knight, Mary, of Virginia, spinster. Administration to the mother, Elizabeth Knight. (June 1685). Revoked on her death and granted to the sister, Catherine, wife of Richard Shaw. (June 1686).

Knight, Nathaniel, of James Town, Virginia. Administration to the brother, Joseph Knight; the father, Samuel Knight, renouncing. (Sep. 1678).

Knight, Richard, of Norfolk, Virginia. Administration to the brother and next-of-kin, Benjamin Knight; the relict having died before administering. (May 1771).

Knight, Toby, of New England, bachelor. Administration to Nicholas Phelps, guardian of the nieces and nephew, Elizabeth, Margaret and John Ellys, and to Alice and John Phelps. (Sep. 1660).

Knight, William, of Williamsburgh, Virginia. Probate to the brother, Robert Knight. (Jan. 1771).

Knighton, John, of Maryland, bachelor. Administration to the mother, Mary, wife of Ellis Farnworth. (Sep. 1720).

Knipe, William, of Portsmouth, New England, and late of H.M. ships *Centurion* and *America*. Probate to Robert Ratsey. (Nov. 1750).

Knolles, John, surgeon's mate of West Florida Hospital. Probate to William Street. (Sep. 1767).

Knolton, Christian David, formerly of New York City but late of New Providence Island. Administration to Jarvis Roebuck, guardian of the only child, Catherine Knolton. (July 1787). Revoked and granted to the same as attorney for Catherine Knolton on her coming of age; the relict, Jennet Arabella Knolton, having died before administyering. (Nov. 1788).

Nott, Edward, Governor-General of Virginia. Probate to Susan Leighton. (Nov. 1706). Wi.

Knott, Elizabeth, of Utica, Oneida County, New York, widow. Administration to Ann Holliday, widow, attorney for the son, Joseph Marshall Knott, in Utica. (Mar. 1854).

Knott, Jeremiah, of Charles Town, South Carolina. Administration to David Lucas, administrator of Sarah Knott deceased, who was the sister and next-of-kin; the relict, Isabella Knott, having also died. (Feb. 1765).

Knott, Jeremiah, of Charles Town, South Carolina, bachelor. Administration to the nephew and next-of-kin, Luke Knott. (Feb. 1773).

Knowles, John, formerly of Philadelphia and afterwards of Trinidad but

Knowles, *(contd.)*
late of Tottenham Court Road, Middlesex, watch and clock maker. Administration to the relict, Sarah Knowles. (May 1810).

Knowles, John, of Bound Brook, North America, bachelor. Administration to the mother, Sarah Knowles, widow. (Nov. 1835).

Knowles, Richard, formerly of Nailstone, Leicestershire, but late of New York City, bachelor. Administration to the brother, Joseph Knowles. (May 1837).

Knowles, Robert, of H.M. Artillery Train, who died in Pennsylvania, bachelor. Administration to the father, John Knowles. (Apr. 1761).

Knox, Frances, formerly of High Park and Levington Park, Westmeath, Ireland, but late of Philadelphia, widow. Administration to Dame Mary Levinge, widow, the relict and executrix of the father, Sir Richard Levinge. (Sep. 1818).

Nox, Thomas, of H.M. ship *Hornet*, who died in Brunswick, North Carolina. Administration with will to Thomas Howard, attorney for Michael Cashio Howard in Douai, Flanders, and for Patrick Howard in Angiers, France. (Mar. 1768).

Kuchental, Henry Philip, of St. Clair, Schuylkill County, Pennsylvania, widower. Administration to Henry Lindsell, attorney for the daughter, Julia, wife of George Sebastian Repplier, in St. Clair. (Feb. 1853).

Kuper, Heinrich George, of Baltimore, United States of America, H.M. Consul there. Administration to the relict, Mary Kuper. (Apr. 1857).

Kyne alas Keen, Arthur, of H.M. ship *Gosport*, bachelor. Administration to Houghan Tober, husband and attorney of the sister, Rachel Tober, in New England. (June 1705). Declared null in May 1709.

L

Lacy, Patrick, of H.M. ship *Essex*'s prize, who died in Virginia, bachelor. Probate to Thomas Conaway. (Aug. 1700).

Ladstone, William, of Shadwell, Middlesex, who died on the merchant ship *Joseph and Thomas* in Virginia. Administration to the relict, Mary Ladstone. (Aug. 1709).

Laffette, Mary, of Port Royal, South Carolina. Administration to the daughter, Jane, wife of Charles Blundy; the husband, Peter Laffette, having died before administering. (Mar. 1752).

Laight, Edward, of Virginia, bachelor. Administration to the mother, Elizabeth Laight. (Aug. 1679).

Lake, Charles, Rector of St. James' parish, Ann Arundell County, Maryland, clerk. Administration with will to Messenger Monsey, doctor of physick, attorney for William Keene and Rev. Samuel Keene in Maryland. (Apr. 1765).

Lake, William Walton, of New York, bachelor. Administration to the father, William Walton Lake. (Aug. 1838).

Lamb, Stephen, mariner of H.M. ship *Tartar*, who died in Long Island Hospital, bachelor. Administration to the father, William Lamb. (Mar. 1778).

Lambert, Jonathan, of Boston, New England. Administration to John Charnock of Whitechapel, Middlesex, mariner, attorney for the relict, Elizabeth Lambert, in Boston. (July 1711).

Lambert, Vincent, of Maryland, who died as a prisoner in France. Probate to the father, Edward Lambert. (July 1703).

Lambert, Walter, of New Orleans, who died on the merchant ship *Sampson* at sea, widower. Administration to John Cropper, guardian of the minor children, Bridget, Michael, Thomas and Eliza Lambert. (July 1821).

Lambert, William, of Boston, New England. Administration with will to Thomas Lane, attorney for the nephew, William Lambert, in Boston. (Mar. 1750).

Lamotte, William Henry, formerly master of the merchant ship *Morayshire* of London but late of Wawarsing, Ulster County, United States of America. Probate to the surviving executor, John Lagier Lamotte. (Mar. 1857).

Lancaster, Elisha, of Bristol, who died in Virginia. Administration to the relict, Elianor Lancaster. (Nov. 1694).

Lancaster, Robert, of Bristol, who died at sea, surgeon, having goods in Virginia. Probate to the mother, Anne Lancaster, widow. (Aug. 1685). Wa.Wi.

Landen, Henry, of Maryland, bachelor. Administration to the sister, Hannah, wife of Thomas Linthall. (Jan. 1737).

Landifield, William, master of the transport ship *Hanger*, who died in Boston, bachelor. Administration to the brother and only next-of-kin, Thomas Landifield. (Mar. 1776).

Lane, John, of North Carolina, bachelor. Administration to the sister, Elizabeth, wife of Rev. Rodney Croxall; the mother, Bridget Lane, widow, renouncing. (Aug. 1748).

Lane, Margaret, of London, widow, whose sister, Martha, wife of William Eaton, was in New England. Administration with will to Elizabeth Jenkins, relict and administratrix with will of the named executor, Daniel Jenkins deceased. (Aug. 1667). Wa.

Lane, Martha, of Blandford, Dorset, who died in North Carolina, spinster. Probate to Thomas Fitzherbert. (Dec. 1756).

Lane, Thomas, of London, who died in Virginia, bachelor. Administration to the brother, William Lane. (July 1677).

Lanfear, Mary, nee Mary Hill, of New Orleans. Administration to Henry Dunkin Francis, attorney for the husband, Ambrose Lanfear, in New Orleans. (Jan. 1842).

Lang, Benjamin, of Portsmouth, New England, who died on H.M. ship *Hind*. Administration to Thomas Adams, attorney for the relict, Elizabeth Lang, in Portsmouth. (Mar. 1750).

Lang, William Giltenan, of Boston, United States of America. Administration with will to John Holmes, attorney for the relict, Elizabeth Frances Lang, in New York City. (June 1856).

Langdon, William, formerly of 19 Penny Fields, Poplar, Middlesex, but late of New York. Administration to the brother, Anthony Langdon. (May 1842).

Langhorne alias Ingoldsby, Mary, of Holborn, Middlesex, who died in Staughton, Huntingdonshire, and whose nephew, Oxenbridge, was in New England. Probate to Sir William Langhorne. (Dec. 1686).

Langhorne, Thomas, of Pennsylvania. Administration to the principal creditor, Seth Flower. (Dec. 1689).

Langhorne, William, of Maryland, bachelor. Administration to the sister and next-of-kin, Elizabeth, wife of John Hall. (May 1716).

Langley, John, of St. Saviour, Southwark, Surrey, doctor of medicine, whose daughter, Margaret Day, was in Maryland. Probate to the relict, Thomazine Langley. (Feb. 1699).

Langston, William, of Virginia. Administration to the brother, Henry Langston, during the minority and absence of the children, Anthony, Judith, Francis and Mary Langston. (Dec. 1659).

Lanman, William, of Boston, New England. Probate to the son, William Lanman. (Sep. 1726).

Larabee, John, of New England. Probate to Elizabeth Crawford. (June 1694). Wa.

Larkins, James, of New York. Administration to Lancaster Symms, now husband and attorney of the relict, Catherine Symms alias Larkins. (Feb. 1697).

Larkins, Thomas, formerly of Old Broad Street, London, and of Layton, Essex, a master in the maritime service of the East India Company, but late of San Francisco, California, merchant. Limited probate to Thomas Brown Horsley, Thomas Collingwood and George John Steer. (Sep. 1850).

Larmount, John, of Boston, New England, bachelor. Administration to the principal creditor, Edward Blackstock; the brother and next-of-kin, Adam Larmount, renouncing. (June 1720).

Larner, Richard, of St. Martin in the Fields, Middlesex, Lieutenant of Major-General Richard O'Farrell's 22nd Regiment of Foot, who died in Albany, North America. Administration pending production of a will to Ann Lynes, wife of Thomas Lynes, the daughter of William and Mary Ashburn of Kersley near Coventry, Warwickshire. (Aug. 1758).

Larrence. *See* **Lawrence**.

Latham, William Henry, of New York, who died at sea, comedian and musical composer. Administration to the relict, Ellen Mary Latham. (Mar. 1844).

Lathbury, John, of London, who died in Virginia. Probate to John Drewry. (July 1655). Sh.Wi.

Laugher, Elizabeth. *See* **Worthington**.

Laundon, Margarett, of Elyria Loraine, Ohio. Administration to William John Woolley, attorney for the husband, Thomas Winkles Laundon, in Elyria Loraine. (Mar. 1855).

Lavington, Stephen, formerly of Arundell Street, St. Clement Danes, Middlesex, but late of South Carolina. Limited administration with will to Edward Codrington, attorney for John Lightfoot and Samuel Redhead in Antigua. (Dec. 1759).

Law, John, of H.M. ship *Pembroke*, bachelor. Administration with will to Joseph Argent, attorney for Elizabeth Partridge in Boston, New England. (May 1750).

Lawford, Susannah Josephine, formerly of Mill Bridge, Birstal, Yorkshire, but late of Amora, Dearborne County, Indiana, widow. Administration to the only child, Frederick Lawford. (Dec. 1850).

Lawne, Christopher, formerly of Blandford, Dorset, but late in Virginia. Administration with will to William Willis during the minority of the sons, Lovewell and Symon Lawne. (June 1620). Sh.

Larrence, Charles, of Boston, New England. Administration to the principal creditor, John Baker. (Feb. 1687).

Laurence, James, of Kingston, Warwickshire, who died in Virginia, bachelor. Administration to the mother, Mary, wife of William Russell. (Dec. 1694).

Lawrence, John, formerly of Buckland, Gloucestershire, afterwards of Liverpool, Lancashire, but late of Norfolk County, Virginia, bachelor who died in December 1814. Administration to the cousins german once removed and next-of-kin, Diana Kemp, widow, Matthew Wilkinson and Benjamin Wilkinson. (May 1828). Revoked and granted to the Treasury Solicitor. (Dec. 1830). Revoked by decree and granted to George Maule as nominee of H.M. the King; all others with an interest having been cited but not having appeared. (Jan. 1833).

Lawrence, John, of Philadelphia. Administration to the relict, Ann Lawrence. (Dec. 1857).

Lawrence, Richard, of H.M. ship *Squirrel*, who died overseas.

Lawrence, *(contd.)*
Administration with will to Peter Warre, attorney for the relict, Mary Lawrence, in Boston, New England. (Jan. 1742).

Lorence, William, of the transport ship *Firm*, who died in Charles Town, South Carolina, bachelor. Administration to the uncle and next-of-kin, Thomas Lorence. (Oct. 1783).

Lawrie, Gawen, Governor of East Jersey. Administration with will to the grandson by a daughter, Obediah Haige; the executrix, Johanna Watt, renouncing. (Sep. 1697).

Lawson, Robert, of Maryland. Administration to the relict, Margaret Lawson. (Oct. 1714). Revoked on her death and granted to Robert White, guardian of the daughter, Margaret Lawson. (Dec. 1715).

Lawton, Joseph, of Charleston, South Carolina, and of Saddleworth, Yorkshire. Administration with will to Francis Frederick Whitehead and John Dicken Whitehead; the executors, William Nayler and William Matthews, renouncing. (Aug. 1855).

Laxon, Thomas, of H.M. ship *Jason*, who died in Long Island Hospital, bachelor. Administration to the son, Matthew Laxon; the other son, John Laxon, having died before administering. (Apr. 1784)

Laxton, Catharine. *See* **White**.

Lay, Benjamin, of Abington, Pennsylvania. Administration with will by his solemn affirmation to Samuel Cook; the wife, Sarah Lay, having died in the testator's lifetime. (July 1760).

Layton, Susannah, of Illinois, widow. Administration to the daughter, Mary, wife of Robert Pantall. (Sep. 1842).

Lea. *See* **Lee**.

Leach, John, of H.M. ship *Nassau*, who died in New England, bachelor. Administration by decree to Mary Lightfoot, wife and attorney of the principal creditor, Matthew Lightfoot, now at sea on H.M. ship *Sheerness*. (Nov. 1722)

Learwood, James, formerly of Esher, Surrey, gardener, but late of New Settlement, Ann Harbour, Michigan. Administration to the relict, Mary Ann Learwood. (Jan. 1836).

Lechmere, Anthony, of Charles Town, South Carolina, bachelor. Administration to the principal creditor, John Lane; the brother, Nicholas Lechmere, renouncing. (Aug. 1783).

Lechmere, Anthony, of Charleston, South Carolina, bachelor. Administration to John Lane, administrator of the father, Nicholas Lechmere deceased, and attorney for his granddaughter, Catherine Lechmere, in America. (June 1823).

Le Cocq, Peter, formerly of Liverpool, Lancashire, but late of Boston, Massachusetts. Probate to the relict, Elizabeth Le Cocq. (Mar. 1799).

Le Cras, Eleanor Treandaphelia Sarah, formerly of Campbell Terrace, St. Helier, Jersey, but late of Buffalo, New York, spinster. Administration to the father, Abraham Jones Le Cras. (Sep. 1841).

Ledain, George, of H.M. ships *Rippon*'s prize and *Cornwall*, bachelor. Administration to Benjamin Hallowell the younger, attorney for the

Ledain, *(contd.)* mother, Mary Ledain, widow, in Boston, New England. (Feb. 1750).

Ledger, John, of Williamsburg, Virginia. Probate to James Minzies. (Apr. 1779).

Ledger, Matthew, of Sonora, California. Administration to the relict, Martha Ledger. (Dec. 1852).

Ledwidge, John, of H.M. ship *Southampton*, who died in Virginia. Administration to the relict, Sarah Ledwidge. (June 1703).

Ley, Aden, of York Town, Virginia, Captain of Colonel Warge's Regiment of Foot, who died in Goree. Administration to the relict, Mary Ley. (May 1712).

Lee, Alice, of Mount Pleasant, Burlington County, New Jersey. Administration to the husband, John Lee. (Mar. 1785).

Lee, Charles, formerly of Westminster, Middlesex, but late of Berkeley County, Virginia, a Major-General in the service of the United States of America. Administration with will to Sir Robert Kerries and Charles Kerries, attornies for Alexander White in Frederick County, Virginia; the other executor, Charles Mym Thurston, having been cited but not having appeared. (June 1785).

Leigh, Humphrey, who died overseas (bound for Virginia), bachelor. Administration with will to the sister, Judith Skinn alias Leigh; no executor having been named. (Mar. 1663).

Lee, Isaac, of Rappahannock River, Virginia, who died in Stepney, Middlesex. Limited administration with will to William Dawkins alias Dawkings. (Nov. 1727).

Lee, James, of Hackensack, Bergen County, New Jersey, widower. Administration to Christopher Benson, attorney for the children, William Lee, John Lee, Tabitha, wife of John Oats, Catherine, wife of John Smith, Justina Ridgeway, widow, Elizabeth, wife of James Van Gelder, and Mary, wife of Christopher Benson, in America. (Mar. 1763).

Lee, John, of Charles Town, New England, who died at sea on the ship *Swallow*. Administration with nuncupative will to Giles Tifield; no executor having been named. (June 1692). Wa.

Lee, John, of Granville Courthouse, South Carolina. Administration to the mother and next-of-kin, Elizabeth Belhaven Lee, widow. (June 1833).

Lee, John, formerly of Birmingham, Warwickshire, but late of Boston, Massachusetts. Probate to the son, John Francis Lee. (Nov. 1840).

Lee, Joseph, of Cambridge, Massachusetts. Administration with will to Thomas Dickason the younger, attorney for the nephews, Thomas Lee and Joseph Lee, in North America. (Apr. 1803).

Ley, Lawrence, of St. Martin Ironmonger Lane, London, who had lands in Virginia. Probate to the relict, Emma Ley. (Apr. 1625). Wa.

Lee, Martha, of Whitechapel, Middlesex, widow, whose son, George Lee, was in Virginia. Probate to Toby Silk and William Wareham. (May 1725). *See* NGSQ 63/131.

Lee, Richard, of Stratford Langton, Essex, who died in Virginia. Probate to

Lee, *(contd.)*
Thomas Griffith and John Lockey with similar powers reserved to John and Richard Lee. (Jan. 1665).

Lee, Richard, of St. Michael Bassishaw, London, who had goods in Virginia. Probate to Samuel Stone and Richard Cock. (Jan. 1667). Wa. NGSQ 62/45,63/42.

Lea, Sarah, formerly Sarah Brown, wife of William Lea of Philadelphia. Administration to the son, William Lea; the husband having died before administering. (Oct. 1749).

Lee, Sarah, of Boston, Massachusetts, spinster. Probate to the brother, John Francis Lee. (Oct. 1850).

Lee, Thomas, bound to Virginia in the ship *Levite*. Probate to the father, Francis Lee. (Jan. 1703). Wi.

Lee, William, of Dartmouth, Devon, master of the merchant ship *Prosperous*, who died in North Carolina, bachelor. Administration to the mother, Elizabeth Lee, widow. (June 1761).

Lee, William, of Philadelphia, bachelor. Administration to the sister, Ann Lee. (Apr. 1778).

Leeds, Rev. John, of Coteau du Lac, Canada, who died in New York, bachelor. Administration to the brother, William Henry Leeds. (Aug. 1854).

Leeth, Thomas, of the merchant ship *Anne and Mary*, who died in Virginia. Probate to Jane Holmes alias Usher, wife of John Holmes. (May 1711).

Leggett alias Godden, William, of Rochester, Massachusetts, who died in Bordeaux, France, master mariner, bachelor. Administration to the father, John Leggett. (July 1817). Revoked because made on false information and granted to John Hambrook, attorney for the relict, Sarah, now wife of Nathaniel Carpenter, in New York. (Dec. 1823). Further grant in May 1871.

Leigh. *See* **Lee**.

Leman, Hickford, of Piscatua, Maryland, bachelor. Probate to Daniel Cooper. (Aug. 1732).

Lemon, Ransom, a coloured man, native of Virginia, late a servant of Lady Augusta Murray, a bachelor who died intestate without any lawful next-of-kin. Administration to Ann Banks, the natural mother of the infant bastard son of the deceased. (Dec. 1807).

Le Neve, Michael, of Maryland, bachelor. Administration to the father, Edward Le Neve. (Sep. 1707).

Lenns, John *See* **Linn**.

Lenthall, Phillip, of Philadelphia. Probate to the son, John Lenthall. (Jan. 1724).

Le Reux, Peeter, of St. Benet Sheerhog, London, who died in Virginia. Administration to the uncle, Phillipp Le Reux. (Jan. 1654).

L'Escott, Frances, of Charles Town, South Carolina, widow. Administration with will to George Chardin, attorney for Zachariah Villepontoux and Isaac Mazyck in South Carolina. (Sep. 1753).

Leslie alias Leslee, John, of Richmond, Virginia. Probate to James Scott

Leslie alias Leslee, *(contd.)* with similar powers reserved to James Caskie and Robert Graham. (Nov. 1820).

Leslie, John, formerly of Wapping, Middlesex, but late of Norfolk, Virginia, who died at sea, mariner, bachelor. Administration to Charles Lever, attorney for the brothers, George and Henry Leslie, in Portsmouth, Norfolk County, Virginia. (Dec. 1831).

Lestourgeon, Susannah. *See* **Shepherd.**

Letchworth, Thomas the younger, citizen and fishmonger of London, who died in Virginia. Probate to the father, Thomas Letchworth. (Mar. 1657).

Levermore, Barbara, of Virginia, who died at sea on the merchant ship *Mary*. Probate to Thomas Richardson. (Sep. 1716). Wi.

Levett, Elizabeth, of Maryland, widow. Probate to James Maddock and Margaret Clarke alias Buchanan, now wife of George Buchanan. (Dec. 1730).

Levett, Francis, of St. Augustine, East Florida. Probate to the relict, Juliana Levett. (Oct. 1786).

Levick, George, formerly of Clayworth, Nottinghamshire, but late of New York, miller, bachelor. Administration to John Levick, son and administrator with will of the father, James Levick deceased. (Jan. 1851).

Levy, Ashur, formerly of Gower Street, Bedford Square, Middlesex, but late of New York City. Probate to Louis Lucas, Philip Lucas and Jacob Aaron Melhado. (June 1846).

Lewer, Elizabeth Susannah, nee Elizabeth S. Cooper, of South Amboy, New York. Administration to the husband, William Lewer. (Mar. 1836).

Lewis, Ann, formerly of St. James, Bristol, but late of New York City, spinster. Administration to the brother and only next-of-kin, John Lewis. (Feb. 1833).

Lewis, Daniel, of Charles Town Hospital, South Carolina, bachelor. Administration to the mother, Martha Lewis, widow. (Aug. 1784).

Lewis, John, marine of Colonel Jefferys' Regiment, formerly of H.M. ship *Launceston* and afterwards of H.M. ships *Vigilant* and *Mermaid*, who died in Hampton Hospital, Virginia, bachelor. Administration to the father, John Lewis. (Nov. 1746).

Lewis, John, of Charles Town, South Carolina, who died in St. Thomas' Hospital, Southwark, Surrey. Probate to John Taylor and Thomas Hardwick with similar powers reserved to the relict, Sarah Lewis. (July 1753).

Lewis, John, of Bluefields, North America, bachelor. Administration to the aunt, Elizabeth Gourley. (July 1794).

Lewis, John, of Boston, United States of America, currier, bachelor. Administration to Mary Lewis, administratrix and daughter of the father, Robert Lewis deceased. (Feb. 1836).

Lewis, John William, formerly of the Stock Exchange in London but late of Baltimore, Maryland, bachelor. Administration to the brother and next-of-kin, David Lewis. (Dec. 1805).

Lewis, Warner the younger, of Virginia. Administration with will to the son, John Lewis; the executors, Philip Ludwell Grymes, William Nelson, Burwell Stark, Mann Page the younger, Matthew Anderson, and the son, Warner Lewis, having died, and the surviving executors, the brothers, Fielding Lewis and John Lewis, the daughter, Mary Chiswell Nelson (formerly wife of Thomas Lewis the younger), and the daughter, Elizabeth, wife of Matthew Whiting Brook, renouncing. (Mar. 1818).

Lewis, William, of Philadelphia. Administration to the relict, Catherine Anne Lewis. (Jan. 1846).

Lewis, William, formerly of Trelleck Grange, Monmouth, but late of Sharon, Hamilton County, Ohio, bachelor. Administration to the brother, John Lewis. (Sep. 1850).

Ley. *See* **Lee**.

Leyburn, George, formerly of Maryland but late of Liverpool, Lancashire, master of the merchant ship *Benedict*. Limited administration pending production of a will to the brother, Peter Leyburn. (Dec. 1782).

Liddell, Archibald, master of the merchant ship *Elliott*, who died in Charles Town, South Carolina. Probate to Archibald Elliott with similar powers reserved to Abraham Cridland alias Creedlan. (June 1748).

Lidget, Charles, formerly of Boston, New England, who died in St. Bride, London. Special administration with will to John Hester with similar powers reserved to the relict, Mary Lidget. (May 1698). Revoked and granted to the relict, Mary Lidget. (Mar. 1701).

Lightfoot, Frances, of Newport, Rhode Island, spinster. Limited probate to Rev. William Lloyd Baker with similar powers reserved to John Bours. (Nov. 1800).

Lilley, Jane. *See* **Smith**.

Lillingstone, Mary Ann, of Maryland. Administration by decree to Robert Myre the younger, attorney for the husband, Carpender Lillingstone, in Maryland. (Dec. 1721).

Lillystone, John, of Holborn, Middlesex, and of Philadelphia, who died on the ship *Rowser*, bachelor. Administration to the mother, Hannah Lillystone. (June 1751).

Linch. *See* **Lynch**.

Lincolne, William, of Bury St. Edmunds, Suffolk, who had lands in Massachusetts. Probate to the son, William Lincolne, and to Robert Dixon. (May 1792). Further grant 1868.

Lindsay, Charles Philip, of Hudson Street, New York City, Post Office agent. Administration to George Nelson Emmet, attorney for the relict, Grace, now wife of Frederick C. Parks, in New York. (Apr. 1855).

Lindesay, John, of New York. Administration to the relict, Penelope Lindesay. (Apr. 1753).

Linn. *See* **Lynn**.

Linton, Ann, formerly of Rotherhithe, Surrey, but late of Philadelphia. Administration to Thomas Gilbert, the surviving executor of the husband, John Linton deceased; the only next-of-kin, the sister, Mary, wife of William Nichols, and the niece, Maria Butcher, spinster, a

Linton, *(contd.)* minor, having been cited but not having appeared. (Nov. 1785).

Linzee, John, formerly a Captain of the Royal Navy but late of Milton, Massachusetts. Administration with will to William Burgess, attorney for Thomas Amory in Boston, Massachusetts. (Apr. 1799).

Lisle, Dame Alicia, of Moyles Court, Hampshire, whose daughter, Bridget, was in New England. Probate to Tarphena Lloyd with similar powers reserved to the other executors. (Nov. 1689). Wa.

Lisle, Margaret Warren, of New Haven, Connecticut, spinster. Probate to the nephew, Lisle Lloyd, with similar powers reserved to George Williams. (Jan. 1827).

Lithgow, Hugh, formerly of the United States of America who died overseas, bachelor and bastard. Administration to George Maule for the use of the Crown. (Aug. 1823).

Lithgow, John, formerly of Woolwich, Kent, who died overseas, bachelor and bastard. Administration to George Maule for the use of the Crown. (Aug. 1823).

Lithgow, William, of Wilmington, North Carolina. Probate to Sir Peter Thompson with similar powers reserved to Job Pearson. (July 1754).

Little, Basill, of London, who died in Virginia, bachelor. Administration to the only sister, Anne Little; the mother, Mary Little, renouncing. (July 1658).

Littleboy, Laurence, of Virginia. Administration by decree, pending a suit between John Allen and Michael Bayley, to the said John Allen of Virginia. (June 1653). NGSQ 61/261.

Littlepage, Edmund, formerly of York River, Virginia, but late of St. Mary Abchurch, London, who died in Enfield, Middlesex, bachelor. Probate to the nephew, Joseph Littlepage. (Aug. 1712).

Littler, William, Captain of the Third Batallion of Royal Americans, who died in Boston, New England, bachelor. Administration to the mother, Dorothy Littler, widow. (Feb. 1765).

Livingston alias Ash, Ann, of Charles Town, South Carolina. Administration by decree to the husband, William Livingston. (Aug. 1721).

Livingston, Gilbert Robert, a reduced Captain of Cavalry in the late American Legion of Schenectady, New York. Limited administration with will to James Tidbury, attorney for the relict, Patty Livingston, in Schenectady. (Jan. 1817).

Livingstone, Henry, Ensign in the British American Forces, who died in New York, bachelor. Administration to Charles Cooke, attorney for the father, John Livingstone, in New York City. (Apr. 1786).

Livingston, John, of New London, Connecticut, who died in St. James, Westminster, Middlesex. Probate to James Douglass with similar powers reserved to Elizabeth Livingston. (May 1720).

Livingston, Mortimer, of New York City. Probate to Charles William Foster and William Sydney Drayton with similar powers reserved to the relict, Sylvia Livingston. (Jan. 1858).

Livingstone, William, formerly a Lieutenant on half pay of an Independent Company of Foot in South Carolina but late of Bodlorme, Linlithgow County, Scotland. Administration to Alexander Small, attorney for the sister and next-of-kin, Grisel, wife of William Nimmo, in Bodlorme; the relict, Helen Livingstone, having died. (June 1770).

Lloyd, Alexander, of Bristol, who died in Virginia. Administration to the brother and next-of-kin, Lewis Lloyd. (Jan. 1679).

Lloyd, Daniel, formerly of Wandsworth, Surrey, but late of Saugherties, Ulster County, New York, widower. Administration to the only child, Daniel Lloyd. (Mar. 1840 & Aug. 1842).

Lloyd, Edward, formerly of Maryland but late of Whitechapel, Middlesex. Probate to the relict, Grace Lloyd. (July 1696).

Lloyd, Elizabeth, of Elizabeth River, Lower Norfolk, Virginia, widow. Probate to the brother-in-law, Thomas Eavans. (June 1657). Sh.Wi.

Lloyd alias Carter, Elizabeth, of Richmond County, Virginia. Administration to the husband, John Lloyd. (Oct. 1694).

Lloyd, Henrietta Maria, of Talbot County, Maryland, widow. Administration to the son, Richard Benett, pending receipt of a copy of the will. (Sep. 1697).

Lloyd, Henry, formerly of Boston, Massachusetts, but late of Bryanston Street, St. Marylebone, Middlesex. Probate to Katharine Lloyd with similar powers reserved to the nephew, Henry Smith. (Apr. 1796).

Lloyd, James, of Boston, New England. Probate to Francis Brinley and John Nelson. (Apr. 1696). Wa.

Lloyde, John, of Virginia. Administration to the daughter, Mary Lloyde. (Aug. 1653). Marked "poor."

Lloyd, John, of Sarphley, St. James, Goose Creek, South Carolina. Administration with will to John Nickelson, administrator of the son, John Lloyd deceased, and attorney for the daughter, Sarah Lloyd, a minor; the relict, Sarah Lloyd, and the executors, Ralph Izard and Benjamin Wareing, having died before executing. (June 1746).

Lloyd, John, of Goose Creek, Berkeley County, South Carolina, a minor. Administration to John Nickelson, guardian of the sister, Sarah Lloyd. (June 1746).

Lloyd, Margaret, of New Orleans State, widow. Administration to the daughter, Harriet Lloyd. (Sep. 1838).

Lloyd, Sarah. *See* **Waring**.

Lloyd, Simon, of Virginia. Probate to Robert Conway. (July 1657).

Lloyd, William, of Redcliffe, Bristol, who had lands in Rhode Island. Probate to the relict, Alice Lloyd. (Feb. 1676). Wa.

Lloyd, William, of Westminster, Middlesex, who died in Virginia, bachelor. Administration to the principal creditor, William Binsley. (May 1678).

Lluellin, Daniel, of Chelmsford, Essex, who had lands in Virginia. Probate to Thomas Vervell, James Jauncy, Giles Sussex and William Walker. (Mar. 1664). Wi.

Lock, John, of the merchant ship *Rappahannock*, bachelor. Administration to the sister, Alexandra Gun. (Sep. 1725).

Locker, James, of Liverpool, Lancashire, who died in Virginia, bachelor. Administration to the sister and next-of-kin, Hannah Locker. (June 1722).

Lockley, William, of Prince George County, Virginia, merchant. Probate to the relict, Margaret Frances Lockley. (June 1745). Wi.

Locky, Edward, of Virginia, planter, who died in St. Katherine Creechurch, London. Limited administration to Richard Walton, scissor merchant. (Oct. 1667).

Loge, Abraham, a private in the Rhode Island Regiment of Foot, who died in Havana. Administration by his solemn declaration to Joseph Sherwood, attorney for the relict, Hannah Loge, in Rhode Island. (Dec. 1765).

Lodge, Edward, of Stepney, Middlesex, who died in Maryland. Administration to the principal creditor, Samson Burrows. (Mar. 1700).

Lofthouse, Alvara, of St. Katherine by the Tower, London, master of the merchant ship *Judith*, who died in St. Augustine, East Florida. Probate to the sister, Mary, wife of William Thomas, with similar powers reserved to Peter Simon. (May. 1778).

Logan, George, of Princess Anne County, Virginia, who died in Glasgow, Scotland. Probate to the relict, Isabella Logan. (Aug. 1781). ALC.

Logan, Margaret, of South Carolina. Administration to the husband, William Logan. (May 1791).

Logan, William, of Philadelphia. Limited administration with will to David Barclay, attorney for the son, George Logan, doctor of physick, in New York; the executors having been cited but not having appeared. (June 1780). *See* NGSQ 69/42.

Logan, William, of Charleston, South Carolina, widower. Limited administration to William Wynch, attorney for the grandson, William Logan, in South Carolina. (Sep. 1802).

Loge. *See* **Lodge**.

Lomas, John, formerly of Annapolis, Maryland, but late of Glasgow, Scotland. Administration with will to John Mill, attorney for James Johnson in Virginia. (Nov. 1757).

Long, Augustine, citizen and wheeler of London, whose granddaughter, Elizabeth Rise, was in Virginia. Probate to the relict, Alice Long. (Apr. 1726).

Long, Elizabeth Burgh, of Culpeper County, Virginia. Administration to John Dunlop, attorney for the husband, Armistead Long, in Culpeper County. (Mar. 1827).

Long, Richard, of the merchant ship *Hope*, who died in South Carolina. Administration to the principal creditor, Jeremy Mackneer, now at sea on H.M. ship *Grafton*. (Jan. 1719).

Long, Robert, formerly of Sutton Veny, Wiltshire, but late of Anuhuac, Galveston Bay, Texas, bachelor. Administration to Alfred Long, son and executor of the father, Stephen Long deceased. (Feb. 1849).

Longland, John, commander of the sloop *Eastmain*, who died in Albany Road, bachelor. Administration to the creditrix, Mary Hallam, widow.

Longland, *(contd.)*
(Dec. 1757). Revoked because made on false pretences and granted to the cousin german and next-of-kin, Elizabeth Thomas, widow. (Feb. 1758). Revoked because made on false pretences and granted to the niece, Lucy Sweet. (June 1758).

Longley, Robert Benjamin, of Boston, Massachusetts, master of the merchant ship *Salue*. Administration with will to the creditor, Francis Henry Christin; the father, Robert Longley, renouncing. (Dec. 1792).

Longman, Richard, of Virginia, bachelor. Administration to the brother, James Longman. (May 1679).

Lord, Thomas, formerly of Bushley, Worcestershire, but late of Gibson's County, Tennessee, who died at sea as a passenger on the American steamship *Colonel Thompson*, bachelor. Administration to John Lord, administrator of the father, William Lord deceased. (Apr. 1856). Revoked on the presentation of a will and probate granted to Daniel Smith and Thomas Farr. (July 1857).

Lorence, William. *See* **Lawrence**.

Loring, William, formerly of Boston, North America, afterwards of Bordeaux, France, but late of Buenos Aires in South America, bachelor. Administration to the creditor, John Ward. (Nov. 1804). Revoked and granted to James Abel, attorney for the creditor, John Ward, in Providence, Rhode Island. (Mar. 1805).

Lormier, Lewis, of South Carolina. Administration to the principal creditor, James Lardant; the relict, Jane Lormier, and the brother and sisters and only next-of-kin, David Lormier, Ann Gueront and Ann Rachel Michel, having been cited but not having appeared. (May 1749).

Loughton, Sarah, of Charles Town, South Carolina, who died in Barbados. Administration to the husband, Edward Loughton. (Mar. 1701)

Love, William, formerly of South Carolina but late of London, whose daughter, Elinor, wife of Horner Powell, was in Ninety Six, South Carolina. Probate to Thomas Shivers. (Aug. 1789). ALC.

Loveless, Thamar, of New York City, spinster. Probate to John Marles with similar powers reserved to Thomas Cox. (Jan. 1856).

Lovell, William King, Second Lieutenant of the Royal Regiment of Artillery, who died in Long Island, New York, bachelor. Probate to the sister, Alisha Skingle Lovell. (Oct. 1776).

Lovett, Thomas, of Belfast, Ireland, and of Virginia, who died at sea on H.M. ship *Falkland*. Administration to the principal creditor, William Browne. (July 1709).

Lowe, Henry, of St. Mary's County, Maryland. Probate to the daughters, Elizabeth, wife of Henry Darnall, and Dorothy, wife of Francis Hall; the sons, Henry Lowe and Bennet Lowe, having died. (Sep. 1731).

Lowe, John, of Hingham, New England, mariner of H.M. ship *Triton*, bachelor. Administration with will to Adam Bird, attorney for William Mason, father and administrator of the named executor, William Mason deceased. (Nov. 1708).

Lowe, Micajah, formerly of Charles City County, Virginia, but late of Carshalton, Surrey, merchant. Probate to the uncle, Micajah Perry, with similar powers reserved to the relict, Sarah Lowe. (Mar. 1704).

Low, Richard, of Virginia, bachelor. Administration to the mother, Jane Allen alias Low. (Sep. 1655).

Lowe, Stead, formerly of Annapolis, Maryland, but late of St. Olave Hart Street, London. Inventory 1790. [*Administration Act not found*].

Lowe, Thomas, of New York City, bachelor. Administration to the sister, Margaret, wife of Richard Linaker. (Apr. 1782).

Lowndes, Roger, Lieutenant of H.M. ship *Happy*, who died in South Carolina, bachelor. Administration to the brother, Robert Lowndes. (Oct. 1735).

Lucas, Bridget, of St. Stephen Coleman Street, London, whose kinswoman, Mary Bishop, was in Virginia. Probate to the son, Ralph Leeke. (Nov. 1657). Sh.Wa.

Lucas, Charles, of the merchant ship *Hopewell*, who died in Maryland. Probate to Edward Poulter. (June 1722).

Lucas, Jonathan, of Charleston, South Carolina, and of Whitehaven, Cumberland. Probate to Richard Sherwin, Peter William Sherwin and Thomas Naylor. (Apr. 1822).

Lucas, Peter, of Chipping Norton, Oxfordshire, who died in Virginia, bachelor. Administration to the brother, David Lucas; the mother, Sarah Lucas alias Bolgye, renouncing. (Mar. 1693).

Lucas, Robert, of Hitchin, Hertfordshire, who had lands in New England. Probate to George Draper and Simon Lucas. (Feb. 1679). Wa.

Lucas, Thomas the younger, of Virginia, bachelor. Administration to the cousin and next-of-kin, John Lucas. (July 1675).

Lucas, William, of H.M. ship *Warwick*, who died on H.M. ship *Sea Horse* in Virginia. Administration to Benjamin Bristowe. (June 1738).

Ludham, Edmund, of Ratcliffe, Middlesex, who died in Virginia. Administration to the relict, Margaret Ludham. (July 1655).

Ludlam alias Carter, Anne, of South Carolina, widow. Administration to the son, Thomas Carter. (Aug. 1729).

Ludlow, Francis, of Horningham, Wiltshire, who died in Virginia. Administration to William Richards, the uncle and guardian of the children, Francis and William Ludlow, until they come of age. (July 1671).

Ludlow, Gabriel Gabriel, President and Commander-in-Chief of New Brunswick. Administration with will to Isaac Minet, attorney for the relict, Ann Ludlow, and the sons, Gulian and Gabriel Ludlow, in New York. (Aug. 1809).

Ludlow, George, of York, Virginia. Administration with will by decree to Roger Ludlow, father of the nephews and nieces, Jonathan, Joseph, Roger, Anne, Mary and Sarah Ludlow, during their minority; no executor having been named. (Aug. 1656). Sh.Wa.Wi.

Ludlowe, George, of Hedingham Sible, Essex, who died in Virginia, bachelor. Administration to the mother, Mary, wife of Peter Temple. (Oct. 1683).

Ludlow, Gulian, of New York. Administration with will to John Stride, attorney for the relict, Maria Ludlow, and for Thomas William Ludlow, in New York. (Mar. 1848).

Ludlow, John, of Virginia, bachelor. Administration to the brother, Francis Ludlow. (Sep. 1664).

Ludwell, Philip, formerly of Virginia but late of St. Martin in the Fields, Middlesex. Limited probate to the daughter, Hannah Philippa Ludwell, with similar powers reserved to the daughters, Frances Ludwell and Lucy Ludwell. (May 1767). Wi.

Ludwell, Thomas, of Bruton, Somerset, who died in Virginia. Probate to John Jeffries, Edward Leman and John Browne. (Jan. 1679). Wa.

Lungley, Thomas, of Makefield, Birmingham County, United States of America, bachelor. Administration to the niece, Elizabeth, wife of John Sibley. (Mar. 1834).

Luscombe, Thomas, of Boston, New England. Administration to Edward Hull, attorney for the principal creditor, Benjamin Mountford, in Boston. (Sep. 1699).

Luscombe, Thomas, of Boston, New England. Administration to the mother, Sarah Luscombe, widow. (Apr. 1700).

Lycett, William, Lieutenant of Marines, who died in New York, bachelor. Administration to Frances Layton, spinster, executrix of the creditrix, Frances Russell deceased; the brother and only next-of-kin, John Lycett, renouncing. (Feb. 1778).

Lyde, Byfield, formerly of Boston, Massachusetts, but late of Halifax, Nova Scotia, widower. Administration to the son, Edward Lyde. (Mar. 1777).

Lymbrie, George, of St. Katherine by the Tower, London, who died in Virginia. Administration to the principal creditor, William Day. (Sep. 1637). *See* NGSQ 67/63.

Lymburner, Matthew, formerly of St. Andrew, New Brunswick, but late of Penobscot, Massachusetts. Administration to Robert Shedden, attorney for the relict, Margaret Lymburner, in St. Andrew. (Mar. 1789).

Lynch, Dominick, formerly of New York but late of Paris. Probate to Nicholas Luguer and the daughter, Jane, wife of Julius Pringle. (Dec. 1840).

Linch, John, of New York City. Administration to the relict, Elizabeth Linch. (Mar. 1778).

Lyndon, Augustine, of Boston, New England, shipwright, who died in Shadwell, Middlesex. Probate to John Johnson. (Aug. 1699). Wa.

Lyne, Joseph, of Blackfriars, London, who died on H.M. ship *Shoreham* in Virginia. Administration to the relict, Abishag Lyne. (May 1700).

Linn alias Lenns, John, formerly of Maryland but late of Bristol, mariner. Probate to Sarah, wife of John Hunphreys. NGSQ 63/130.

Linn, William, of Charles Town, South Carolina, bachelor. Administration to Fergus Baillie, attorney for the sisters and next-of-kin, Janet, wife of Anthony Ellis, Jeane Atkine, widow, and Agnes, wife of William Campbell, in Scotland. (Feb. 1735).

Lyon, George, Colonel of the Royal North Carolina Regiment, formerly of Cape Fear, North America, bachelor. Administration to Walsingham Collins, attorney for the nephews and next-of-kin, John Dunlop and Colin Campbell, in Port Glasgow, Scotland. (Aug. 1790).

Lyon, John, formerly of New England but late of the ship *Elizabeth* in State service. Administration with will to Alice Linsey. (Oct. 1658).

Lyon, John, of Charles Town, South Carolina. Administration with will to Robert Naylor, attorney for the mother, Elizabeth Hill, widow, in Charles Town; the executor, Charles Paxton Butler, having been cited but not having appeared. (May 1802).

Lyon alias Lyons, John, formerly of Hammersmith, Middlesex, but late of Philadelphia, botanist and gardener. Administration with will to James Lee, attorney for Thomas Dobson and David Landreth in the United States of America. (Oct. 1816).

Lyon, Nathan, a soldier in H.M. Regiment of Foot of Connecticut, who died in Havana. Administration to Phineas Lyman, attorney for the father, Ephraim Lyon, in Connecticut. (Dec. 1763).

Lyon, Seth, a soldier in H.M. Regiment of Foot of Connecticut, who died in Havana. Administration to Phineas Lyman, attorney for the father, Jonathan Lyon, in Connecticut. (Dec. 1763).

Lysnar, George, of Brooklyn, New York, goldsmith, widower. Administration to the son, George Lee Lysnar. (Nov. 1856).

M

Macaire, Francis, who died in Charles Town, South Carolina. Probate to Cephas Tutet. (Apr. 1691).

McAlister, Ann, formerly Ann Keith, of Queenborough, Georgia. Limited administration to John Tunno, attorney for the husband, John McAlister. (Aug. 1807).

Macaulay, Daniel, chief mate of the merchant ship *Georgia*, who died in America. Administration to the brother, George Macaulay. (Dec. 1770).

Macaulay, Daniel, formerly of Charleston, South Carolina, merchant, but late of Liverpool, Lancashire. Probate to the relict, Mary Leaycroft Macaulay, and to David Lamb and Duncan Gibb. (Jan. 1856).

McBryde, Thomas, of Charles Town, South Carolina, bachelor. Administration to the father, Edward McBryde. (Sep. 1795).

McCall, Catharine Flood, formerly of Clydeside, Essex County, and of Richmond, Virginia, but late of George Town, District of Columbia, spinster. Limited administration with will to Archibald McCall. (Apr. 1831).

McCartney, Eliza, of Madison County, Alabama. Administration to Josiah Roberts, attorney for the husband, James McCartney, in Alabama. (Dec. 1829).

McClentock, Alexander, of Charles Town, New England, who died on H.M. ship *Otter*, bachelor. Administration to William Lance, attorney for the father, William McClentock, in Charles Town. (Jan. 1753).

McCloud, John, of New York, sergeant of the 42nd Regiment of Foot. Administration to John Small, attorney for the relict, Isabella, now wife of Peter Barclay, in New York. (Mar. 1765).

McClure, Alexander, of Charles Town, South Carolina. Probate to the uncle, Cochrane McClure, with similar powers reserved to the uncle, William McClure, and to William Muir. (Dec. 1812). Revoked on the death of Cochrane McClure and granted to Janet, wife of William McClure, the daughter of the uncle, William McClure. (July 1813).

McCrackan, John, of Old Glenlure, Galloway, Scotland, who died in New Haven, New England. Probate to James McDouall with similar powwers reserved to the father, Andrew McCrackan. (Feb. 1769).

MeCrow, John, of Shadwell, Stepney, Middlesex, who died in Virginia. Administration to the relict, Luce Johnson alias Jonson alias MeCrow. (Mar. 1658).

McCullok, Eleanor, of Rockland, Baltimore County, Maryland. Limited administration with will to John Stuart Roupell; the husband, Samuel McCullok, renouncing. (Nov. 1840).

McCutchon, David, formerly of Dudley, Worcestershire, but late of Davenport, Scott County, Iowa. Limited administration to the creditors, Thomas Hunter and James Perram. (Apr. 1852).

Macdonald, Alexander, late of Kingsburgh in the Isle of Skye, Captain of the late Regiment of North Carolina Volunteers. Administration to

Macdonald, *(contd.)*
Andrew Lawrie, attorney for the relict, Annabella Macdonald, in Mugstole, Isle of Skye. (May 1798).

McDonald, Alexander, of Aberdeen, Scotland, Captain on half pay of the Florida Rangers, widower. Administration to the cousin german, Mary, wife of William Patterson, guardian of the only children, Alexia, James and Margaret McDonald; the aunts, Jane Munro, widow, and Mary MacLain, having renounced guardianship. (Apr. 1805).

McDonald, Ann, of Cumberland County, North Carolina, widow. Administration to Charles Cooke, attorney for the cousin german and next-of-kin, Daniel Monk, in Cumberland County. (Mar. 1803).

MacDonald, Archibald, surgeon in the Regiment of Pioneers during the American Revolutionary War, and late of White Plains, West Chester County, New York. Administration to James Tidbury, attorney for the relict, Flora MacDonald, in New York. (Feb. 1817).

McDonald, Donald, formerly Major and then Lieutenant-Colonel on half pay of the American Provincials in Chatham, but late of Edinburgh, Scotland. Probate to the relict, Jane McDonald. (May 1789).

McDonald, Evan, of Charles Town, South Carolina, widower. Administration to the only child, Katherine Cramond, widow. (Mar. 1764).

Macdonald, James, of Anson County, North Carolina. Administration to the relict, Isabella Macdonald. (Oct. 1784).

McDonaugh, John, formerly of New Orleans, Louisiana, but late of Judd Place, Somer Town, St. Pancras, Middlesex. Probate to John Tate and Martin French with similar powers reserved to James Canick, John Joyce and John Turnbull. (Dec. 1797).

MacDonogh, Thomas, of Charleston, Massachusetts, British Consul for New Hampshire, Massachusetts, Rhode Island and Connecticut. Administration to Thomas Dickason the younger, attorney for the relict, Harriet MacDonogh, in Charleston. (Dec. 1805).

Mace, Sandford, Ensign of General Oglethorpe's Regiment of Foot, who died in Georgia, bachelor. Administration to the brother, James Mace. (Mar. 1745).

McDuell, Ann, of Frederick County, Maryland, widow. Administration to Thomas Aspinwall, attorney for the son, Robert McDuell, in Frederick County. (July 1846).

McEvers, Charles I., of New York, who died on the merchant ship *Mary*, bachelor. Administration to the brother, James McEvers; the mother, Elizabeth Baynard, renouncing. (Dec. 1794).

McEvers, James, of New York City. Administration with will to the daughter, Dame Elizabeth Myers; the relict, Elizabeth, late wife of Robert Baynard, and the executors, Charles Ward Apthorp, and the brother, Charles McEvers, having all died. (July 1811). Revoked on the death of Dame Elizabeth Myers and granted to her sole executrix, Margaret Baynard, spinster; the children, James, John, Charles, Elizabeth, Catherine, wife of Thomas Palmer, and Mary McEvers (afterwards Mary Myers) who was born after the testator's death,

McEvers, *(contd.)* having all died. (June 1823).

McEvers, Margaret J. *See* **Bibby**.

McFadyen, Daniel, formerly of Glasgow, Scotland, but late of New York City. Limited administration with will to Thomas Maude, attorney for the relict, Elizabeth McFadyen, in New York. (June 1781).

McFadyen alias McFadzean, John, of Boston, North America. Administration with will to John Boyd, attorney for Jacob Rhoades in Boston. (Dec. 1805).

McFarlan, James, formerly of Ivy Place, Hoxton, Middlesex, but late of Cheviot near Cincinnati, Hamilton County, Ohio. Administration to Thomas Olney, attorney for the relict, Ann McFarlan, in Cheviot. (Mar. 1850).

McGeorge, Matthew, of Franklinvale near Lyndon, Cattarangus County, New York, hotel keeper. Administration to William Fisher, attorney for the relict, Louisa McGeorge, in Franklinvale. (Nov. 1857).

McGill, Catharine, formerly Catharine Norry alias Norie, of Portsmouth, New England, widow. Administration to John Anderson and Alexander Anderson, attornies for Samuel Bowles, guardian of the only children, Mary, Margaret and Jane Norie, during their minority. (Feb. 1804).

McGillivray, James, formerly of Savannah, Georgia, but late of Inverness, Scotland. Limited probate to the brother, Lachlan McGillivray, with similar powers reserved to Andrew McCudie, William Mein, Robert Mackay and James Mackintosh. (Nov. 1806).

McGown, Lodowick, of the West Indies, Lieutenant in the American Regiment, who died in South Carolina. Inventory 1746. [*Administration Act not found*].

McGreevy, Peter, of New York City, widower. Administration to Francis McEvoy, uncle and guardian of the only child, James McGreevy, during his minority. (Jan. 1852).

McGregor, William, private of the First Batallion of the 42nd or Royal Highland Regiment, who died in Havana. Administration to Duncan Campbell, attorney for the relict, Mary McGregor, in New York. (Mar. 1766).

McGuiry, Laughlin, of New York, who died on the merchant ship *Monmouth*, bachelor. Probate to Thomas Parker. (June 1750).

McIntosh, Alexander, of Charles Town, South Carolina, bachelor. Administration to the brother, William McIntosh; the father, John McIntosh, renouncing. (Apr. 1772).

Mackintosh, Charles, formerly of New York but late of St. Martin in the Fields, Middlesex, who died at sea. Administration to the principal creditor, Alexander Mackintosh; the relict and the children having been cited but not having appeared. (June 1749). Declared null and administration with will granted to John Fell, husband and attorney of the relict, now Susanna Fell, in New York. (June 1750).

Macintosh, Gregor, of New York, sergeant of the 42nd Regiment of Foot, who died in Havana. Administration to Samuel Willis, attorney for the

Macintosh, *(contd.)* relict, Catherine Macintosh, in New York. (June 1765).

Mackintosh, James, formerly of Mobile, West Florida, but late of the Chicksaw Nation in North America. Administration with will to Charles Graham, attorney for the brother, John Mackintosh; the sole executor, Daniel Ward, having been cited but not having appeared. (Apr. 1787).

Mackintosh, Lachlan, of Charleston, South Carolina. Limited probate to Simon Mackintosh. (Oct. 1789).

Mackintosh, Robert, of New York City, who died in Tortola, bachelor. Administration to the brother, Alexander Mackintosh. (Apr. 1782).

McIsaac, Malcolm, of New York, bachelor. Administration to the father, Archibald McIsaac. (Mar. 1781).

McIver, Alexander, of Liberty County, Georgia, planter, widower. Limited administration to Alexander Carruthers Daubeny, attorney for the daughter, Harriette, wife of Samuel Spencer, in Georgia. (Sep. 1837).

McIver, Donald, of Augusta, Georgia, who died on St. Bartholomew Island in the West Indies, bachelor. Administration to the sister, Helen, wife of Colin Leitch. (Feb. 1817).

McIver, John, formerly of Georgia but late of New York City. Administration with will to Charles Everett, attorney for John Taylor in New York City; the other executor, Amasa Jackson, having been cited but not having appeared. (Nov. 1821).

Mackay, Robert, Lieutenant on half pay of the 88th Regiment of Foot, who died in Virginia, bachelor. Administration to John Crocker, attorney for the mother and next-of-kin, Jean Mackay, in Rothesay, Isle of Bute, Scotland. (Sep. 1772).

McKenzie, Alexander, private of the Second Batallion of the 42nd Royal Highland Regiment, who died in Havana. Administration to Duncan Campbell, attorney for the relict, Margaret McKenzie, in New York. (Mar. 1766).

Mackenzie, Duncan, of New York, bachelor. Probate to Alexander Mackenzie. (Apr. 1736).

Mackenzie, Hector, formerly of Bath on Cockerton River, Steuben County, New York, afterwards of Hatton Garden, Middlesex, but late of Trinidad in the West Indies. Probate to Daniel Wilson Davison with similar powers reserved to William McCaa. (July 1808). Revoked on production of a later will and probate granted to Robert Davison, doctor of physic, and William McCaa, with similar powers reserved to George Sheviz. (July 1808).

McKenzie, John, formerly of St. George, Middlesex, who died in Pensacola. Probate to Nicholas Sanders. (Feb. 1782).

Mackenzie, Robert, corporal of the 77th Regiment, who died in Amboy. Probate to Donald Mackenzie; no executor having been named. (May 1764).

Mackethen, Dugald, of Raleigh, North Carolina, Lieutenant of the Royal North Carolina Regiment. Administration to Robert Sheddon,

Mackethen, *(contd.)* attorney for the relict, Martha Mackethen, in America. (June 1805).

Mackey, William, of the transport ship *Tweed*, who died in Savannah, bachelor. Administration to William Thornton, attorney for the father, Robert Mackey, in Woodhaven, Scotland. (May 1781).

McKinley, Duncan, of Wapping, Middlesex, and the merchant ship *Royal Prince*, who died in Southwark, Surrey. Administration to Isabell, wife of William Betts, in Boston, New England, administratrix of the principal creditrix, Margaret Rogers deceased. (Apr. 1725).

McKenley, Thomas, of H.M. ship *Cornwall*, bachelor. Administration to Owen Gray, attorney for the principal creditor, William Gale, in New York. (Mar. 1750).

McKinnon, Donald, formerly of North Uist, Scotland, but late of North Carolina, bachelor. Administration to Charles Cooke, administrator of the sister and only next-of-kin, Ann McDonald, widow, deceased. (Mar. 1803).

Mackinen, Robert, of the 35th Regiment, who died in Pensacola, West Florida, bachelor. Administration to the creditor, Hunt Fitzgerald; the uncle and only next-of-kin, Robert Mackinen, having been cited but not having appeared. (Feb. 1767).

McKinstry, Rev. William, formerly of Goring, Oxfordshire, afterwards of Lingfield, Surrey, but late of Concord, Merrimack County, New Hampshire. Administration with will to William Pulsford, attorney for Samuel Sparhawk; Isaac Winslow and John William Stark renouncing. (Mar. 1824).

McLatchie, Charles, of East Florida. Administration to John McLatchie, uncle and guardian of the children, James and Elizabeth McLatchie. (June 1796).

McLeod, Hector, of Newburgh, Orange County, New York, a master in the Royal Navy, widower. Administration to the son, William McLeod. (Aug. 1822).

Macleod, Mary, of Fayette Ville, North Carolina, spinster. Administration to Hector Mackay, attorney for the brother and next-of-kin, Norman Macleod. (Aug. 1792).

McLeod, Susannah, of Newburgh, Orange County, New York. Administration to the son, William McLeod; the husband, Hector McLeod, having died. (July 1822).

Maclure, William, of New Harmony, Posey County, Indiana. Administration with will to John Christopher Fry, attorney for the surviving executor, Alexander Maclure, in New Harmony. (Sep. 1845).

McMaster, John, of Wiscasset, Lincoln County, Maine. Administration to the brother, Daniel McMaster; the mother, Grizell McMaster, widow, renouncing. (Dec. 1824).

McMaster, William, of Augusta, Kennebee County, Massachusetts. Limited administration with will to Samuel Williams, attorney for the son, Daniel McMaster, in Augusta. (May 1815).

McMillan, Betty, of Horse Shoe Swamp, Bladen County, North Carolina,

McMillan, *(contd.)* spinster. Administration to David Caldwell, attorney for the mother, Jane McMillan, in North Carolina. (Jan. 1818).

McMullin, John, of Calf Pasture, Virginia, cook of H.M. ship *Charlestown*. Administration to the relict, Jane McMullin. (Feb. 1783).

McNab, Archibald, Lieutenant of the 42nd Regiment, who died in New York, bachelor. Administration to Henry Davidson, attorney for the sisters, Catherine, wife of Robert McAlpin, and Ann, wife of Even Cameron, in Scotland. (June 1767).

McNeil, Neil, of Charleston, South Carolina. Administration with will to John Bambridge, attorney for the sole executor, William Smith, in America. (Mar. 1824).

McNeil, Thomas, formerly of South Carolina, but late of New Providence. Administration to Lewis Wolfe, attorney for the relict, Margaret, now wife of Robert Lightfoot, in New Providence. (Mar. 1790).

McNicol, Colin, soldier of the 77th Regiment, who died in Amboy, New Jersey. Limited administration pending production of the will to the cousin german and next-of-kin, Archibald McNicol. (May 1764).

Macombe, James, of Cloak Lane, London, who died in New York. Administration to the relict, Margaret Macombe. (Feb. 1797).

McPhearson, Colin, Quartermaster of the 42nd Regiment, who died in New York, bachelor. Administration to John Small, attorney for the mother, Ann McPhearson, in New York. (Mar. 1765).

McPherson, Mary, formerly of Tryon County, New York, but late of River Raisin, Quebec. Administration to James Phyn, attorney for the son, James McPherson, in River Raisin. (July 1792).

Macpherson, Melville, of New York City. Administration to the relict, Margaret Macpherson. (Feb. 1839).

Maddox, Jonathan, of H.M. ship *Lizard*, who died in New York Hospital, widower. Administration to Elizabeth, wife of William Richards, the aunt and guardian of the children, Martha, Elizabeth and William Maddox. (Mar. 1779).

Madgwick, Martha. *See* **Street**.

Mahier, Richard, of New England, who died in Rotherhithe, Surrey. Limited administration with will to John Lloyd. (Apr. & July 1721).

Maiden, William, of Philadelphia, bachelor. Administration to William Bruce, attorney for the father, John Maiden, in Dundee, Scotland. (Apr. 1756).

Mainwaring, William, Captain of H.M. ship *Arundell*, who died in Virginia, bachelor. Administration to the father, Gilbert Mainwaring. (May 1764).

Maitland, Hon. Richard, of New York City, Deputy Adjutant-General of H.M. Forces. Administration with will to James Syme, attorney for Rev. John Ogilvie, William McAdam, William Bruce and Thomas Montcrieffe, in New York City; the brother, Alexander Maitland, Major-General of H.M. Forces, renouncing. (July 1773).

Major, Jerman, of St. Faith the Virgin, London, whose cousin, Ann Jones, was in New England. Probate to the relict, Deborah Major, and the

Major, *(contd.)*
son, Thomas Major. (Oct. 1661). Wa.

Makins, John, of Chicago, United States of America, widower. Administration to the brother, Jeremiah Makins. (June 1857).

Malcolm, Farquhar, formerly of Georgia but late of Bow Street, St. Margaret, Westminster, Middlesex. Probate to Neill Malcolm. (May 1791).

Malcolm, John, of Norfolk, North America, bachelor. Administration to Mark Noble Daniell, attorney for the mother, Jane alias Jean Malcolm, in Madderly, Scotland. (Dec. 1793).

Mallett alias Wolseley, Winifred, of Maryland, widow. Administration with will to the principal creditor, James Annis; the niece and executrix, Mary Bilookes, having died and the surviving legatee, Helen Spratt, wife of the Bishop of Rochester, renouncing. (Mar. 1697).

Mallortie, David, of Port Royal, South Carolina, Commander of the merchant ship *Susannah*, bachelor. Probate to the father, James Mallortie. (Oct. 1736).

Mallory, Florisabella, of King William County, Virginia, spinster. Probate to William Mallory and Thomas Avora. (Sep. 1769).

Mallory, Phillip, of Virginia, who died in Whitechapel, Middlesex. Probate to John Whitty with similar powers reserved to the nephew, Roger Mallory. (July 1661). Wi.

Mallory, William, of Virginia. Administration with will to the son, William Mallory; the relict, Mary Mallory, having died before executing. (Sep. 1769).

Maltby, Charles, of Philadelphia. Administration to John Bainbridge, attorney for the relict, Sarah Maltby, in Philadelphia. (June 1808).

Maltby, George, formerly of London but late of Baltimore, North America, widower. Administration to the creditor, George Cooke; the minor sons, George Edward Maltby and Thomas William Maltby, having been cited but not having appeared. (Jan. 1808).

Manby, Aaron, of Kingston, Jamaica, who died in Savannah, Georgia. Limited probate to Joseph Lane the younger with similar powers reserved to Edward Manby and Joseph Lane the elder. (Apr. 1780).

Mander, William, of Brooklyn, New York. Administration to the relict, Mary Mander. (Apr. 1849).

Manfield, George, of Virginia, who died overseas, bachelor. Probate to John Beale. (July 1670). Wi.

Manigault, Gabriel, of South Carolina. Probate to the grandson, Joseph Manigault, with similar powers reserved to Bacott Samuel Proleau the younger, Peter Bonnetheare and Gabriel Manigault. (Oct. 1784).

Manley, Henry Chorley, of Charles Town, South Carolina, bachelor. Administration to the father, Rev. Henry Chorley Manley. (June 1800).

Man, Edward, of New York, bachelor. Administration to the sister, Martha Man. (Mar. 1707).

Mann, Mary, of Needham near Boston, North America, widow. Administration to the only child, Mary, wife of Isaac Morrill. (Dec. 1803).

Mann, William, formerly of Jamaica but late of Pensacola, West Florida. Limited administration with will to the sister, Elizabeth, wife of John Walker. (Dec. 1781).

Manning, Francis, formerly of Uley, Gloucestershire, but late of Charles Town, North America, widower. Administration to the nephew, Thomas Smithwick Manning; the brother, Thomas Fielding Manning, having died. (Sep. 1826).

Manning, Jacob, of Salem, New England, mariner of H.M. ship *Romney*. Probate to Warwick Palfray. (Jan. 1709).

Manstidge, Robert, of Taunton, Somerset, who died overseas having goods in Virginia. Probate to the brothers and sister, William, Isaack, Emanuel, and Jone Manstidge. (Feb. 1630).

Maplet, John, of Bath, Somerset, whose sister, Mary Gorton, was in New England. Probate to the relict, Anne Maplet. (Feb. 1671). Wa.

Maplet alias Mayplett, Mary, of St. Giles Cripplegate, London, widow, whose daughter, Mary, wife of Samuel Gorton, was in New England. Probate to the son, John Maplet. (Apr. 1647). Wa.

Maplisden, Joan, of Westminster, Middlesex, whose kinsman, John Lee, was in Virginia. Probate to the husband, Peter Maplisden. (Dec. 1656). Wa.

Mapson, Thomas, of Bethnal Green, Middlesex, whose granddaughter, Susanna Mapson, was feared lost on a voyage to New England. Probate to the relict, Joane Mapson, with similar powers reserved to the son, James Mapson. (July 1660).

Marbin, Thomas, of Stepney, Middlesex, who died in Maryland, master of the ship *Sarah and Hannah*. Probate to the relict, Sarah Marbin. (Feb. 1713).

Marchand, Charles Laurent Marie, of New York, proprietor of St. Domingo, bachelor. Administration to the sister and only next-of-kin, Clotilde Ursule Marchand. (Oct. 1830).

Marke, John, formerly of Rock House near Taunton, Somerset, but late of Houston, Republic of Texas, cow keeper and farmer, bachelor. Administration to the mother and next-of-kin, Elizabeth Marke, widow. (Oct. 1839).

Markham, Ann, of Turtle, Wisconsin. Administration to William Jackson, attorney for the husband, William Markham, in Turtle. (Dec. 1853).

Marks, John James, formerly of Portland, Massachusetts, but late of Bristol, mariner. Inventory 1817. [*Administration Act not found*].

Marlar, John Thomas, formerly of Baltimore, Maryland, but late of Maguire's Bridge, County Fermanagh, Ireland. Probate by decree to Edward Stewart. (Dec. 1804).

Marquois, William, First Lieutenant of the Royal Artillery, who died in South Carolina, bachelor. Administration to the father, Thomas Marquois. (Mar. 1783).

Marr, Andrew, of Charles Town, South Carolina. Limited probate to James Carsan with similar powers reserved to the relict, Ann Marr, and to George Haig and John Fisher. (Sep. 1786).

Marriott, William, of Grays Inn, Middlesex, whose sister, Dorothy, wife of

Marriott, *(contd.)*
William Waters, was in New England. Probate to William Cooper. (Sep. 1719). *See* NGSQ 62/199.

Marsden, William, sergeant of the 64th Regiment, who died in Spiking Devil, North America, bachelor. Administration to the daughter, Betty, wife of Benjamin Bottomley. (Feb. 1785).

Marsh, Joseph, of H.M. ship *Romney*, who died in Boston, New England, bachelor. Probate to Thomas Marston. (Dec. 1770).

Marsh, Joseph, formerly of New Hampshire but late of Fredericksburgh Province, Quebec. Administration to James Phyn, attorney for the relict, Susannah Marsh, in Fredericksburgh. (Nov. 1790).

Marsh, Thomas, of Queen Anne County, Maryland. Administration with will to Joseph Reed, attorney for Ezekiel Forman in Philadelphia; the other surviving executors, James Frisby, John Thompson and Samuel Thompson, renouncing. (Apr. 1784).

Marsh, William, of Charles Town, New England, who died on the ship *Mary* in Stepney, Middlesex. Probate to the principal creditor, John Casey. (Aug. 1695). Revoked and granted to Robert Robinson. (Sep. 1695).

Marshall, Charles Henry, formerly of Cambridge but late of New York, bachelor. Administration to the brother, Newcombe Marshall. (Feb. 1857).

Marshall, George, of the merchant ship *Bayly*, who died in Virginia, bachelor. Probate to Anne, wife of Edward Coggin, with similar powers reserved to the said Edward Coggin. (June 1720). Marked "pauper."

Marshall, Henry, of Boston, New England, bachelor. Administration to the cousin and next-of-kin, Richard Marshall. (Jan. 1733). Revoked and granted by decree to the aunt, Sarah Percival, widow. (Nov. 1733).

Marshall, James, of St. Philip, Charles Town, South Carolina. Administration to John Ritchie, attorney for the brother and next-of-kin, John Marshall, in Aberdeen, Scotland. (June 1767).

Marshall, John, of the merchant ship *Resolution*, who died in Maryland. Probate to the relict, Sarah Marshall. (Dec. 1717).

Marshall, John, formerly of Islington, Middlesex, but late of Virginia, bachelor. Administration to the sister, Frances Peers Smith, wife of Owen Smith; the mother, Ann Marshall, widow, having died. (May 1793).

Marshall, Samuel, of Great Waltham, Essex, who died in New England. Administration to the son, John Marshall. (Feb. 1694).

Marshall, William, of Baton Rouge, River Mississippi. Limited probate to the brother, George Marshall, with similar powers reserved to James Profit, Philip Hicky and Charles Norwood. (Apr. 1804).

Marston, Thomas, of New York City. Probate to Francis Bayard Winthrop with similar powers reserved to William Bayard. (Nov. 1814).

Martin, Henry, of Wapping, Middlesex, mariner, who had lands in New England. Probate to the relict, Margaret Martin. (Feb. 1662). Wa.

Martyn, Henry, of Boston, United States of America. Administration to

Martyn, *(contd.)*
Thomas Aspinwall, attorney for the relict, Mary Ann Martyn, in Boston. (July 1849).

Martin, John, of New England, who died at sea on the ship *Jersey*, bachelor. Administration with will to James Babson; no executor having been named. (Feb. 1674). Wa.

Martin, John, of Stepney, Middlesex, who had lands in Virginia. Probate to Micajah Perry. (Oct. 1684). Wi.

Martin, John, Captain of the Royal North Carolina Regiment. Administration with will to Hector Mackay, attorney for Angus Martin, Donald Martin and Malcolm McLeod in Scotland. (Jan. 1793).

Martin, Joseph, who died in the King's service at sea or in Virginia, bachelor. Administration to the principal creditrix, Avitia Foster. (Aug. 1667).

Martin, Michael, of Boston, New England. Probate to the relict, Sarah Martin. (Mar. 1701).

Martyn, Nicholas, of Ratcliffe, Middlesex, who died coming from Virginia. Administration with nuncupative will to Mary Farthing; no executor having been named. [*in Administration Act Book*]. (Nov. 1656). Sh.

Martin, Richard, of Chatham, Kent, whose son, Richard Martin, was in New England. Probate to the relict, Rose Martin. (June 1659). Wa.

Martin, Richard, of Bristol, who died in Virginia. Probate to Nathaniel Wraxall, Lyonel Lyde and Andrew Pope. (June 1721).

Martyn, Richard, of Portsmouth, New Hampshire, who died on H.M. ship *Princess Amelia* in Lisbon, bachelor. Administration to William Slayton, attorney for the mother, Jane Martyn, in Portsmouth. (Apr. 1737).

Martin, Robert, formerly of Tewkesbury, Gloucestershire, but late of New Orleans, private in the 41st Regiment of Foot, bachelor. Administration to the father, Thomas Martin. (June 1834).

Martin, Robert Anthony, of Louisiana, bachelor. Administration to Mary Ann Bridget Martin, spinster, attorney for Anthony Martin in Geelong, Australia, administrator of the father, Anthony Crosbie Martin deceased. (Sep. 1857).

Martyn, Samuel, of Charles Town, South Carolina. Administration to the relict, Elizabeth Martyn. (Oct. 1734).

Martin, Samuel, of Far Rockaway, Hempstead, Long Island, New York. Probate to the brother, William Martin, with similar powers reserved to Thomas Banister. (July 1806).

Martin, William, of Baltimore, North America, bachelor. Administration to the sister, Mary, wife of Alexander Woodward. (Feb. 1800).

Martindale, Jonathan, of H.M. ship *Europe*, who died in Long Island Hospital, bachelor. Administration to the mother, Mary, wife of John Grave. (July 1782).

Martineau, Matthew, of Philadelphia. Administration to Honorius Combauld, attorney for the relict, Sarah Martineau, in Philadelphia. (Mar. 1799).

Mascal, Giles, of Wartling, Sussex, clerk, whose son, Edward Mascal, was to go to New England, Virginia, or Barbados. Probate to the son, Samuel Mascal. (July 1652). Sh.

Mason, Arthur, of New England, bachelor. Administration to the brother and next-of-kin, Nicholas Mason. (Feb. 1718).

Mason, Caleb, of New York, bachelor. Administration to the father, Thomas Mason. (Aug. 1851).

Mason, Hester, of Water Town, New England. Administration to Benjamin Franklin, attorney for the sons, John and Joseph Mason, in New England. (May. 1702).

Mason, Hugh, of Water Town, New England. Administration to Benjamin Franklin, attorney for the sons, John and Joseph Mason, in New England. (May. 1702).

Mason, John, of Westminster, Middlesex, who had lands in New England. Probate to the relict, Anne Mason. (Dec. 1635). Sh.

Mason, John Baptist, of the ship *South River Merchant*, bachelor. Administration to the principal creditor, John Roberts. (Feb. 1710).

Mason, Peter, of Bristol, who died in Virginia, bachelor. Administration to the sister, Matilda, wife of William Collins; the mother, Matilda Mason, having died. (Jan. 1751).

Mason, Thomas, of Virginia, bachelor. Administration to the sister, Anne, wife of Peter Booker. (Jan. 1675).

Mason, Thomas, of Cecil County, Maryland, who died in Philadelphia, bachelor. Probate to Andrew Duche, husband of the sister, Mary Duche, in Philadelphia; the named executor, John Copson, renouncing. (June 1732).

Massenburgh, John, formerly of Elizabeth City and County, Virginia, but late of St. Katherine by the Tower, London, mariner. Probate to Thomas Turner with similar powers reserved to the brother, Nicholas Massenburgh. (July 1749). Wi.

Master, Robert, of Savannah, Georgia, physician to the British Army at Santo Domingo, bachelor. Administration to the father, Rev. Robert Master. (Apr. 1798).

Masurer, Philip, of Stepney, Middlesex, who died in New York on the merchant ship *Elizabeth* of London. Administration to the relict, Elianor Masurer. (July 1702).

Mather, Gilbert, of Whitechapel, Middlesex, who died in Virginia. Administration to the relict, Mary Mather. (July 1668).

Mather, Richard, Captain of the First Batallion of Royal Americans, who died in Pittsburg, America, bachelor. Probate to the brother, Thomas Mather; no executor having been named. (Apr. 1763).

Mather, Samuel, formerly of Boston but late of Milton, America. Administration with will to John Bainbridge, attorney for the relict, Margaret Mather, in Cambridge, America. (Mar. 1816).

Mather, Thomas, who died at sea (bound for New York), bachelor. Probate to the sister, Martha Coppocke. (Mar. 1687).

Mathers, Joseph, of New York City, merchant. Probate to the surviving executor, Charles Denston. (Jan. 1843).

Mathew, Thomas, of Holborn, Middlesex, whose daughter, Mary, was in Maryland. Probate to the relict, Mary Mathew. (Mar. 1667). Wi.

Matthew, Thomas, formerly of Cherry Point, Bow Tracy, Northumberland County, Virginia. Probate to the sons, John and Thomas Matthew. (Feb. 1707). Wi.

Matthewes, Elizabeth, of St. Mary Woolnoth, London, who died in New England. Probate to Susan Lansdale with similar powers reserved to John Lansdale. (Nov. 1690).

Matthews, Isaac, of St. John, Southwark, Surrey, master of the merchant ship *Joseph and Elizabeth*, who died in New York, widower. Administration to the principal creditor, Robert Wood; the only child, Sarah Matthews, renouncing. (Apr. 1741).

Matthews, John, of H.M. ships *Launceston* and *Mermaid*. Administration to the principal creditor, Israel Harlow the younger. (Apr. 1747). Revoked by Act of Court and granted by his solemn affirmation to Joseph Basherwile, attorney for the relict, Sarah Matthews, in Boston, New England. (Sep. 1749).

Matthews, Lowther, Lieutenant of the 62nd Regiment, who died in Rhode Island, bachelor. Administration to the brother, John Matthews. (Sep. 1781).

Matthews, Mary, formerly of Bishops Waltham, Hampshire, but late of South Carolina, spinster. Administration to James Guillet, surviving executor of the brother and only next-of-kin, Charles Matthews deceased. (Mar. 1799).

Mathews, Stephen, of South Carolina, widower. Administration to the son, Stephen Mathews. (Mar. 1740).

Matthews, Thomas, of Boston, New England, who died on H.M. ship *Eltham*. Probate to Richard Crafts. (Dec. 1746).

Matthews, William, of South Carolina, bachelor. Administration to the mother, Susannah Tabet. (June 1809).

Mattison, Oliver, of H.M. ship *Lyme*. Administration to John Coles, attorney for the relict, Mary Mattison, in Boston, New England. (July 1750).

Mauduit, William, of Maryland. Administration to the creditor, Jasper Mauduit; the relict, Mary Mauduit, and the children, Jasper Mauduit, Elizabeth Lamy, Deborah Jackson and Anne Ruth Mauduit, having been cited but not having appeared, and the only other child, William Issac John Mauduit, having renounced through his guardian, Thomas Wright. (Nov. 1750).

Mauduit, William, of Bladenburgh, Maryland. Administration to the son, William Mauduit; the relict, Mary Mauduit, having died before administering. (Sep. 1786).

Mauger, Isaac. *See* **Moger**.

Mauroumet, John, midshipman of the private warship *Boyne*, and late Lieutenant of the New York Provincials, who died in Havana. Administration with will to James McKenzie, now husband of the relict, Ann, in South Carolina; the executors, Thomas Grollier and John Mairac, having died before executing. (Jan. 1775).

Mavell, Richard, of Hanley Castle, Worcestershire, who died in Virginia, bachelor. Administration to the brother and next-of-kin, Thomas Mavell. (Aug. 1678).

Mawer, George, of the Durham Bishopric, who died in Virginia. Administration to the daughter, Rachael Mawer; the relict, Helen Mawer, renouncing. (Sep. 1682).

Maxfield, Jeremiah, of Bristol, Rhode Island, and Providence Plantations, New England, who died on H.M. ship *Lyon*, bachelor. Administration to Thomas Lane, attorney for the father, Joseph Maxfield, in Bristol. (June 1753)..

May, John, of Coldash, Thatcham, Berkshire, who had lands in Pennsylvania. Probate by her solemn affirmation to the relict, Mary May. (June 1722).

Maye, Joseph, of St. Mary le Strand, Middlesex, whose cousin, Cornelius Maye, was in Virginia. Probate to the brother, Phineas Maye. (Feb. 1636). Wa.Wi.

May, Thomas, of the ship *Hopeful Jacob*, who died in Virginia. Administration to the relict, Martha May. (Jan. 1700).

May, William, of H.M. ship *Rose*, who died in South Carolina. Administration to George Ryall, guardian of the son, William May; the relict, Mary May, having died before administering. (Aug. 1739).

Maybank, David, of Christ Church, Berkeley County, South Carolina. Administration with will to Samuel Wragg, attorney for Susan Bond alias Maybank, wife of James Bond, and for Thomas Barton, in South Carolina. (Feb. 1725).

Maybank, Susan, of Christ Church, Berkeley County, South Carolina. Administration with will to Samuel Wragg, attorney for Susan Bond alias Maybank, wife of James Bond, and for Thomas Barton, in South Carolina. (Feb. 1725).

Maybery, Charles, of Warren County, Tennessee, widower. Administration to Henry Maybery, attorney for the son, Thomas Maybery, in Warren County. (June 1843).

Maynard, Henry, of Dublin, Ireland, who died in Virginia. Probate to the relict, Henrietta Maynard. (Oct. 1727).

Maynard, John, of King Street, Wapping, Middlesex, who died in Virginia. Administration to the relict, Mary Maynard. (Mar. 1660).

Maynard, William, Lieutenant of the Second Regiment of Foot Guards, who died in North Carolina. Administration with will to the brother, Henry Maynard. (June 1781).

Mayow, John, of Bath, Somerset, who died in St. Paul Covent Garden, Middlesex, doctor of laws, whose daughter, Mary Slater, was in New York. Administration with will to the relict, Alice Mayow; the executor, Thomas Mayow, having died. (June 1680). *See* NGSQ 64/48.

Mayplett. *See* **Maplet**.

Mayrick. *See* **Merrick**.

Mead, John, of Wapping, Whitechapel, Middlesex, who had goods in Maryland. Limited administration to Peter Renou, owner of the ship

Mead, *(contd.)*
Samuel and Henry, formerly the *Europe*. (Oct. 1694).

Mears, John, of Pittsburgh, who died on the island of St. Domingo in the West Indies. Administration to the son, John Mears; the relict, Esther Mears, having died. (June 1818).

Meeres, Stephen, of Boston, New England, who died on H.M. ship *Warspite*, bachelor. Administration to the principal creditor, John Cockburne. (Oct. 1689).

Mears, Walter Hunter, of East Baton Rouge, Louisiana. Administration to the relict, Augustine Verret Mears. (Jan. 1839).

Mears, William, of Pittsburgh, Pennsylvania, who died in Cincinnati, Ohio, bachelor. Administration to John Mears, son and administrator of the father, John Mears deceased. (June 1828).

Mease. *See* **Meese**.

Medhurst, Thomas, of Virginia. Administration to the relict, Anne Medhurst. (Sep. 1713).

Medland, Jane. *See* **Drexhagen**.

Medlicott, Edmund, of Charles Town, South Carolina, bachelor. Administration to the sister, Mary, wife of John Andrews. (May 1717).

Mee, Edward James, formerly of Ludlow, Shropshire, veterinary surgeon, afterwards of Down House near Bromyard, Herefordshire, veterinary surgeon and farmer, but late of Philadelphia and New York. Administration to the relict, Sarah Mee. (Apr. 1848).

Meeres. *See* **Mears**.

Mease, Edward, of Pensacola, West Florida, bachelor. Administration to the cousin german and next-of-kin, Michael Driver Mease. (Mar. 1781).

Meese, Henry, of St. Katherine Creechurch, London, who had lands in Virginia. Probate to the relict, Anne Meese. (Apr. 1682).

Meier, John Hardenbergh, of Schenectady, New York. Administration with will to Edward Ellice, attorney for the surviving executors, Sanders Lansing and Gerrit Lansing. (Dec. 1820).

Meier, Rachel, formerly of Clermont, Columbia County, but late of New Palz, Ulster County, New York, widow. Administration with will to Edward Ellice, attorney for the surviving executrix, Rebecca Romeyn, widow. (Dec. 1820).

Mendes, Isaac, of Pensacola, West Florida. Probate to William Barrow with similar powers reserved to William Aird, Arthur Neil and Alexander Solomons. (July 1769).

Menefie, George, of Buckland, Virginia. Probate to the relict, Mary Menefie. (Feb. 1647). Sh.Wi.

Menzies, Sarah, of New York, widow. Administration to the son, Gilbert Lester Menzies. (Feb. 1818).

Mercer, James, Captain of General Webb's Regiment of Foot, who died in Albany, North America, bachelor. Probate to the uncle, Robert Fenton. (Feb. 1759).

Mercer, James Francis, Lieutenant-Colonel of Sir William Pepperell's late

Mercer, *(contd.)* regiment, who died in Oswego, North America, bachelor. Administration to Andrew Douglas, attorney for the brother, William Mercer, in Perth, Scotland. (July 1760).

Mercer, Richard, of Charles Town, South Carolina. Probate to the relict, Grace Mercer, with similar powers reserved to John McCall the younger. (Apr. 1788).

Mercer, William, citizen and haberdasher of London, whose brother, Burrandine Mercer, was in Virginia. Probate to the brother, Walter Mercer. (Mar. 1654). Wi.

Merchant, William, of Boston, New England, who died in Barbados. Administration to the creditor, James Johnson; the relict and child or children and any others interested having been cited but not having appeared. (Apr. 1756).

Mercier, Thomas, Lieutenant of General Lacelles' Regiment of Foot, who died in Louisburgh, bachelor. Administration to the father, Philip Mercier. (July 1759).

Meriton, Joshua, of Virginia. Administration to the relict, Mary Meriton. (Oct. 1674).

Merriken, Hugh, of Maryland. Administration to the relict, Anne Merriken. (Feb. 1698).

Merrick, Dennis, of the Hokills, Pennsylvania. Administration to the principal creditor, Richard Chope. (Nov. 1702).

Mayrick, Walter, of the merchant ship *Providence*, who died in Virginia, bachelor. Administration to the principal creditor, Dennis Fox. (Oct. 1703).

Merriman, George, citizen and cooper of London, whose son was in New England. Probate to the son, John Merriman. (May 1656). Sh.Wa.

Merryman, John, of Christ Church, Spitalfields, Middlesex, whose son, John Merryman, was in Philadelphia. Probate to John Johnson and Thomas Homewood. (Apr. 1821).

Merritt, Richard, of Stepney, Middlesex, who died in Virginia. Administration to the principal creditor, Benjamin Andrews. (Jan. 1692).

Merryfield [Merefield], Edward, of German Town, Pennsylvania. Probate to the son, Vernon Merryfield, with similar powers reserved to Benjamin Condy. (July 1768).

Merryman. *See* **Merriman**.

Mesick, Mary, of Hudson, New York. Administration to Robert Samuel Palmer, administrator of the husband, Peter Henry Mesick deceased, and attorney for the only child, Catharine Mary, wife of Richard Ramsay Jones, in New York State. (Aug. 1836).

Mesick, Peter Henry, of Hudson, New York, merchant, widower. Administration to Robert Samuel Palmer, attorney for the only child, Catharine Mary Jones, in New York State. (Aug. 1836).

Messenger, James, formerly of West Street, North Bermondsey, Surrey, carpenter and builder, but late of Goochland County, Virginia, Deputy Superintendent of the Waller Mines. Probate to the relict,

Messenger, *(contd.)* Maria Messenger, with similar powers reserved to Charles Eustace Goldring. (Jan. 1857). Further grant in July 1889.

Metcalfe, John, of King and Queen County, Virginia, who died at sea, bachelor. Probate to Thomas Metcalfe with similar powers reserved to Samuel Metcalfe, John Craven and Daniel Ker. (Mar. 1762).

Metcalfe, Richard, of Lewis, Pennsylvania, widower. Administration to the daughter, Elizabeth Metcalfe. (July 1763).

Metcalfe, Simon, formerly of Prattsburgh, Charlotte County, New York, but late of Albany, New York. Administration with will to Alexander Ellice, attorney for the relict, Catherine Metcalfe. (Feb. 1797).

Mew, Noel, of Newport, Rhode Island, and Providence Plantation, New England. Administration with will to Thomas Zachary, attorney for the relict, Mary Mew, in Newport. (Apr. 1700).

Mew, Samuel, of St. Mildred Poultry, London, whose brother, Ellis Mew, and sister, Sarah Cowper, were in New England. Probate to Edward Bilton and Thomas Lambe. (May. 1671).

Michell. *See* **Mitchell.**

Middleton, Arthur, of St. James, Goose Creek, South Carolina. Administration with will to William Middleton, attorney for Sarah Middleton, widow, in South Carolina; the other executor, Henry Harwood, having died. (Aug. 1740).

Middleton, James, of Philadelphia, Lieutenant of H.M. ship *Launceston*. Administration by his solemn declaration to David Barclay, attorney for the relict, Mary Middleton, in Philadelphia. (Aug. 1746).

Middleton, Mary Helen, of Philadelphia, widow. Administration to the son, Henry Middleton. (May 1857).

Middleton, Philip, of St. Olave, Southwark, Surrey, whose daughter, Hannah, wife of Edward Pomfast, was in New England. Probate to the daughter, Mary, wife of George Seale. (Dec. 1650). Wa.

Middleton, Robert, of Virginia, bachelor. Administration with will to Thomas Babb during the absence of the brother, William Middleton; no executor having been named. (July 1627). Sh.Wa.Wi.

Middleton, Thomas, of London, who had lands in New England. Probate to the son, Benjamin Middleton. (Dec. 1672).

Middleton, Thomas, of Charles Town, South Carolina. Administration with will to John Shoolbred, attorney for the daughter, Mary alias Polly Shoolbred, wife of James Shoolbred, in Charles Town; the brother, Henry Middleton, renouncing, and Ralph Izard, John Deas, Robert Gibbes, and the relict, Elizabeth Middleton, having been cited but not having appeared. (Mar. 1799). Limited administration of goods in Little Chelsea, Middlesex, granted to William Williams as attorney for Mary Shoolbred in Charleston. (Aug. 1803). Former grants revoked and administration with will granted to William Williams as attorney for Mary alias Polly Shoolbred in Charleston; John Shoolbred having died, the brother, Henry Middleton, renouncing, and the surviving executors having been cited but not having appeared. (July 1806). Further grant of limited administration made in September 1820.

Middleton, William Thomas, formerly of Findsbury near Rochester, Kent, but late of Cincinnati, North America. Administration to the relict, Elizabeth Middleton. (Nov. 1839).

Midford, John, of St. Dunstan in the East, London, merchant, widower. Limited administration to Brian Philpott to recover debts in Virginia and Maryland. (Mar. 1735). Further grant to the same. (June 1742).

Midford, William, of the Inner Temple, London, who died in Charles Town, South Carolina, bachelor. Administration to the sister, Frances Burton, widow. (Aug. 1746).

Milam. *See* **Mylam**.

Miles, Harriet L. *See* **Squire**.

Mill, Matthew, formerly of Lower Shadwell, Middlesex, but late of Philadelphia. Probate to the sister, Sarah Mill the younger, with similar powers reserved to Robert Wright. (May 1830). Revoked on the death of Sarah Mill and granted to Ann, wife of James Broadbridge, formerly Ann Hutchings; the mother, Sarah Mill, widow, having died. (Feb. 1854).

Millechamp, Timothy, rector of Colesborne, Gloucestershire, who had lands in South Carolina. Probate to William Veel. (May 1780).

Miller, Henry, of H.M. ship *Pembroke*, who died in Long Island Hospital. Administration with will to Samuel Davis and Jacob Aaron, attornies for Jane Donaldson of Plymouth, Hampshire [*sic*]. (July 1783).

Miller, John, of New Providence, who died in New York. Probate to the relict, Mary Miller, with similar powers reserved to Lawrence Brickwood, John Brickwood, Robert Thompson, Abraham Eve and John Stevens. (July 1816).

Miller, Margaret, of Halifax, Nova Scotia, the relict of Tobias Miller, Ensign in the Regiment of South Carolina Loyalists. Limited administration to Andrew Belcher, attorney for the only child, Tobias Emanuel Miller, in Nova Scotia. (Dec. 1823).

Milligan, William, of Charlestown, South Carolina, merchant. Probate to Alexander Anderson with similar powers reserved to John Black, William Birnie, William Drayton, Charles Edmonstone, William Thompson, Robert Sturgeon, John Sutherland, Benjamin Moodie, William Blacklock and Archibald MacLachlan. (June 1811).

Millington, Mary, of Hempstead Branch, Queen's County, New York. Administration to Frederick Millington, attorney for the husband, Matthew Millington, in Hempstead. (Apr. 1856).

Mills, Andrew, of New York, purser of H.M. ship *Greyhound*. Probate to the relict, Eleanor Mills. (Feb. 1750).

Mills, George, of the merchant ship *Betty*, who died in Virginia, bachelor. Administration to the principal creditrix, Jane Sutherland. (Dec. 1712).

Mills, John, of Alexandria, Virginia, widower. Administration to the nephew and next-of-kin, John James Harrop. (Jan. 1786).

Mills, John, of Alexandria, North America, bachelor. Administration to the cousin german, John Mills. (Mar. 1847).

Mills, Thomas, of Exeter, Devon, whose son, William Mills, was in

Mills, *(contd.)*
Virginia. Probate to the relict, Honor Mills. (Sep. 1653).

Mills, William Henry, formerly of South Carolina, afterwards of Nassau, but late of the City of Chester. Limited probate to John Simpson with similar powers reserved to Thomas Moss, William Moss and James Hepburn. (Aug. 1790).

Milne, James, Lieutenant and surgeon of the Second Batallion of Royal Americans and surgeon of the hospital of Fort Pitt, bachelor. Administration to the brother and next-of-kin, Robert Milne. (Jan. 1765).

Milner, William, of H.M. ship *Enterprise*, Lieutenant in Colonel Churchill's Regiment of Marines, who died in Boston, New England, bachelor. Administration to the mother, Anne Milner, widow. Nov. 1713).

Milward, Robert, of Yanoak near Swinnards Bay, James River, Virginia, bachelor. Administration by decree to the principal creditor, Marmaduke Carver the younger; the sisters and next-of-kin, Mary, wife of John Dudley, and Anne, wife of William Gilbert, renouncing. (July 1718).

Minnick, Christian, of Bristol, Bucks County, Pennsylvania. Probate to Joseph Plant with similar powers reserved to the son, John Minnick, and to Seymour Hart and William McIlwaine. (July 1786).

Minott, Theophilus, of Boston, seaman of H.M. ships *Gloucester* and *Windsor*, bachelor. Administration to William Walford, attorney for the sister, Mechetabel Cooper, widow, in Boston, New England. (Nov. 1705).

Mynterne, John, of Manigo, Virginia. Administration with will to the relict, Alice Mynterne; no executor having been named. (Jan. 1619).

Mitchell, Benjamin, of Niagara, North America, bachelor. Administration to the father, William Mitchell. (Dec. 1761).

Mitchell, James, quarter gunner of H.M. ship *Renown*, who died in Rhode Island Hospital, bachelor. Administration to the mother, Elizabeth Mitchell, widow, in Montrose, Scotland. (Apr. 1781).

Michell alias Townsend, Joane, of Virginia. Administration to Isaac Plavier, father and guardian of the nephew and nieces, James, Judith and Anne Plavier. (Sep. 1661).

Mitchell, Joseph, of the merchant ships *Oxford* and *Essex Loan*, who died in Virginia. Administration to the relict, Rebecca Mitchell. (Nov. 1710).

Mitchell, Robert, of Savannah, Georgia. Administration with will to Eliza, wife of Hector Turnbull, the daughter of the brother, John Mitchell; the executors, Peter Mitchell and James Marshall, having died, and Norman Wallace renouncing. (Oct. 1846).

Mitchelson, John, formerly of Virginia, merchant, but late in London. Probate to the brother, James Mitchelson, with similar powers reserved to William Bowden, William Nelson and Richard Ambler. (Aug. 1750). Wi.

Moffatt, Thomas, formerly of Rhode Island but late of Westminster, Middlesex, doctor of physic. Probate to Rev. Samuel Peters. (Mar.

Moffatt, *(contd.)* 1787). *See* NGSQ 60/258.

Moger alias Mauger, Isaac, formerly of Fairfield, Connecticut, but late of Williamstown, Berkshire County, Massachusetts, widower. Administration to George Gouger, attorney for the daughter, Elizabeth Herault Moger, in Lebanon, New York. (Apr. 1807).

Mogridge, Alexander Augustus Perry, of New Orleans, widower. Administration to the son, Richard Perry Mogridge. (Aug. 1856).

Molloy, John, of the merchant ship *Offer*, who died in Virginia, bachelor. Administration by decree to the father, Daniel Molloy. (Feb. 1722).

Molyneux, Anthony Lancaster, British Consul in Georgia. Administration with will to the brother, William Hargraves Molyneux; the surviving executor, Anthony Barclay, renouncing. (June 1852).

Moncrieff, Isabella, of Pembroke, who died in St. Augustine, East Florida, widow. Probate to the daughter, Christiana, wife of Jacob Vanbraam, formerly Christiana Scott. (Oct. 1779).

Moncrieffe, Margaret, formerly Margaret Heron, of New York. Administration to Charles Gould, attorney for the husband, Thomas Moncrieffe, in New York. (Dec. 1764).

Moncrieffe, Thomas, of New York, Major in H.M. service, widower. Administration to Thomas Vaughan, attorney for the son, Edward Cornwallis Moncrieffe, in Dungannon, Ireland. (July 1792).

Moncrief, William, Captain of the Queen's Rangers, who died in New York, bachelor. Administration to the father, James Moncrief. (Feb. 1790).

Money, John, Lieutenant of the 63rd Regiment, who died in North Carolina, bachelor. Administration to the father, Rev. Thomas Money. (May 1781). Revoked on his death and granted to the mother, Margaret Money, widow. (Oct. 1793).

Monck, Edward, of South Carolina, bachelor. Administration to the mother, Joan Monck, widow. (July 1713).

Monk, John, of Charles Town, South Carolina. Limited probate to William Monk and James Horsnell. (Oct. 1789).

Monk, Samuel, formerly of Ilford, Essex, but late of the Northern Hotel, New York City, bachelor. Administration to the sister, Ann Monk. (Mar. 1839).

Montague, George, formerly of Phillack, Cornwall, but late of New Orleans. Administration to the relict, Phillis Montague. (Mar. 1849).

Montgomerie, John, Governor of New York, widower. Administration to Robert Dalrymple, attorney for the principal creditor, Sir John Anstruther, in Scotland; the sister and next-of-kin, Elizabeth, wife of Patrick Ogilvy, renouncing. (Mar. 1732).

Montgomrey, Malcolm, formerly of Brentford, Middlesex, but late of Syracuse, New York. Probate to the relict, Anna Rosina Montgomrey, with similar powers reserved to William Kelly and John Charles Heath. (July 1856).

Montgomery, Samuel the elder, of Savannah, Georgia, widower.

Montgomery, *(contd.)*
Administration to John Simpson and Crawford Davison, attornies for the only children, Samuel, William and Jane Montgomery, and Mary, wife of John Wilson, in Savannah. (June 1797).

Monylockes, Jacob, of Ratcliffe, Stepney, Middlesex, who died in Virginia. Administration to the relict, Alice Monylockes. (Apr. 1668).

Moody, Ann, of York County, Virginia. Administration to the husband, Mathew Moody. (Feb. 1760).

Moodie, Benjamin, of Charleston, North America, British Consul. Probate to the relict, Caroline Moodie, with similar powers reserved to Adam Tunno, William Birnie and Charles Edmondstone. (Nov. 1825).

Moodie, Caroline, formerly of Liverpool, Lancashire, but late of Charlestown, South Carolina, widow. Administration to the son, James Gairdner Moodie. (Nov. 1844),

Moody, John, of Virginia. Administration to Susan Poynts, the sister of the relict, Rebecca Moody, during her absence. (Sep. 1681).

Moone, George, of Fremington, Devon, who died in Virginia, mariner. Probate to the relict, Alice Moone. (Nov. 1680). *See* NGSQ 69/199.

Moon, James Lawson, formerly of Brotherton near Ferrybridge, Yorkshire, but late of Princton, Gibson County, Indiana. Probate to Robert Henry Anderson. (May 1841).

Moon, John Radwell, formerly of Orange Street, Bloomsbury Square, Middlesex, but late of Mechanics' Farm, Milwaukee County, Wisconsin, bachelor. Administration to the sister, Marianne Moon. (Sep. 1846).

Moone, Patrick, of Shadwell, Middlesex, who died in Virginia. Administration to the relict, Joanna Moone. (Dec. 1679).

Moore, Alexander, of Boston, Massachusetts, who died at sea. Probate to John Lane. (Feb. 1794).

Moore, Catharine Charles, of Holmesburg, Philadelphia County, North America, widow. Administration with will to Alfred Alexander Julius, attorney for the daughters, Jane Moore and Catharine Mary Moore. (Dec. 1837).

Moore, Elizabeth. *See* **Quigly**.

Moor, Ferguson, of Philadelphia, seaman of H.M. ship *Argonaut*. Administration to William Coningham, attorney for the relict, Jane Moor, in Philadelphia. (Oct. 1798).

Moore, Sir Henry, Governor of New York. Probate to the relict, Dame Catharine Maria Moore. (June 1770).

Moore, Jane, of Holmesburg near Philadelphia, spinster. Administration with will to Alfred Alexander Julius, attorney for the sister, Catharine Mary Moore, in Holmesburg. (Dec. 1846).

Moore, John, of Russelville, Kentucky, widower. Administration to Cameron Eneas Quilter, attorney for the only child, Caroline Balfour Wood, wife of Thomas Wood, in Nelson County, Kentucky. (Mar. 1852).

Moore, Lambert, of Brooklyn, New York. Administration with will to John Mackenzie, attorney for John. H. Moore and Adam Tredwell in New York. (May 1808).

More, Mary, of Kennington, Surrey, whose son, Samuel Hardy, was in New England. Probate to Edward Palmer and Isaac Gildersleeve. (Oct. 1678). Wa.

Moore, Mary, of New York. Administration to the husband, William Moore. (Apr. 1784).

Moore, Maurice alias Morice, formerly of 13 Upper Fitzroy Place, New Road, St. Pancras, Middlesex, papier mache maker, who died as a passenger on the American ship *Charles Bartlett* bound for New York with his wife, Julia, and six children, Mary, Margaret, Julia, Maurice, John, and Bridget Moore. Limited administration to Owen McCarthy the elder, guardian of the only surviving child, Catherine, wife of Owen McCarthy the younger, during her minority. (Sep. 1849 & Aug. 1853).

Moorland, Joseph, formerly of Stroudwater, Gloucestershire, but late of Boston, North America, bachelor. Administration to the sisters and only next-of-kin, Susanna Bamford, widow, and Sarah Ford, widow. (Feb. 1816).

Morcombe, Johnson, of Bideford, Devon, who died in Virginia. Administration to the relict, Dorcas Morcombe. (May 1680).

Mordant, George, of Felmingham, Norfolk, an adventurer to Virginia. Probate to the nephew, Henry Mordant, and to Talbot Pepys, with similar powers reserved to Ralph Ward and Thomas Utbert. (Nov. 1633). Sh.Wi.

Mordoch. *See* **Murdoch**.

More. *See* **Moore**.

Morecroft, Edmund, of Virginia. Probate to the sister, Elizabeth Morecroft, with similar powers reserved to the sister, Mary Morecroft. (June 1639). Sh.Wi.

Morehouse, Ann. *See* **Wadup**.

Moreton. *See* **Morton**.

Morgan, Ann, formerly of Galway, Herefordshire, but late of Illinois, spinster. Administration to the brother, Walter Prosser Morgan; the mother, Mary Morgan, widow, having died. (Oct. 1847).

Morgan, Anne, of Stockbridge, Berkshire County, Massachusetts, widow. Administration to George Hurrey, attorney for the granddaughter, Mary Elizabeth, wife of William Burke Skinner, in Hudson, North America; the son, Edmund Cobb Morgan, having died, and the only other next-of-kin, the son, Richard Morgan, having been cited but not having appeared. (Feb. 1849).

Morgan, Christopher, of Bromley by Bow, Middlesex, bachelor, who had assets in Virginia. Administration with will to the brother, John Morgan: no executor having been named. (Feb. 1706).

Morgan, Francis, of New London, Connecticut. Administration with will to James Francis Morgan, attorney for the brothers, James Morgan in New York City, and John Morgan in New London. (Nov. 1849).

Morgan, George, who died at sea or in Virginia, bachelor. Probate to Richard Knewstubb. (Apr. 1669).

Morgan, George Cadogan, of Stockbridge, Berkshire County, Massachusetts,

Morgan, *(contd.)* widower. Administration to George Hurrey, attorney for the daughter, Mary Elizabeth, wife of William Burke Skinner, in Hudson, Columbia County, New York. (Apr. 1848).

Morgan, Harriet, of New London, Connecticut, spinster. Administration to the father, William Morgan. (Oct. 1839).

Morgan, John Sextus, of Stockbridge, Massachusetts, bachelor. Administration to George Hurrey, attorney for the niece, Grace Ashburner, spinster, in Stockbridge; the mother, Ann Morgan, widow, having died. (July 1848).

Morgan, Luke Ashburner, of Stockbridge, Massachusetts, bachelor. Administration to George Hurrey, attorney for the niece, Grace Ashburner, spinster, in Stockbridge; the mother, Ann Morgan, widow, having died. (July 1848).

Morgan, Patrick, formerly of the Crescent, Minories, London, afterwards of Bernard Street, Russell Square, Middlesex, but late of New Orleans, Louisiana. Probate to the relict, Mary Morgan. (May 1806).

Morgan, Richard, of Islington, Middlesex. Administration to George Smith, attorney for the only child, Jude Morgan, in Virginia. (June 1661).

Morgan, Sarah. *See* **Huntington**.

Morgan, Thomas, formerly of Red Cross Street, London, but late of New York, widower. Administration to the only child, William Morgan. Mar. 1836).

Morgan, Thomas, of Upwood near Chicago, Illinois. Probate to the son, James Morgan, with similar powers reserved to the relict, Anna Maria Morgan, and the sons, Charles Morgan, Thomas Charles Morgan, William Morgan, Francis Morgan, and John Robert Morgan. (July 1851).

Morison. *See* **Morrison**.

Morley, David, of Brompton, North Carolina, bachelor. Administration to the brother, Philip Morley. (Jan. 1752).

Morrant, John, of H.M. ship *Perseus*, who died in Long Island Hospital, bachelor. Administration to Jane Dalton, spinster, attorney for the mother, Mary Morrant, widow, in Hartsbourne, Northamptonshire. (Jan. 1780).

Morrell, John, of Newark, New Jersey, bachelor. Administration to Peter Barlow, attorney for the father, Stephen Haddon Morrell in St. Nicholas Island, Cape Verde. (July 1823).

Morrell, Mary, formerly Mary Crawley, of Newark, New Jersey. Administration to Peter Barlow, attorney for the husband, Stephen Haddon Morrell, in St. Nicholas Island, Cape Verde. (July 1823).

Morel, Tryphena, formerly Tryphena Dunbar, of Savannah, Georgia. Administration to Alexander Mein, attorney for the husband, Peter Henry Morel, in Savannah. (Aug. 1810).

Morrey, Anne, of Philadelphia. Administration by his solemn affirmation to the husband, Richard Morrey. (Mar. 1749).

Morrey, Richard, of Philadelphia. Administration with will to John Sprettell, attorney for

Morrey, *(contd.)* the surviving executor, John Bazelee, in Philadelphia; the relict, Sarah Morrey, having died before executing. (Nov. 1756).

Morrey, Sarah, of Philadelphia, widow. Administration to John Sprettell, attorney for the son, Stephen Williams, in Philadelphia. (Nov. 1756).

Morris, Anna, wife of Cadwallader Morris of Philadelphia, who died in 1792. Limited administration with will to John Brickwood, attorney for Frances Morris, wife of Benjamin Morris, (formerly Frances Stretter or Strettle), in Pennsylvania. (Jan. 1801).

Morris, John, of St. George Hanover Square, Middlesex, Controller of Customs in Charles Town, South Carolina, who died in Kingston, Jamaica. Probate to the relict, Elizabeth Morris. (Mar. 1778).

Morris, John, Lieutenant-Colonel of H.M. Corps of New Jersey Volunteers. Administration to John Turner and William Goodall, attornies for the relict, Sarah Morris, in Montreal. (Jan. 1797).

Morris, Joseph Handford, formerly of Buffalo, Erie County, New York, afterwards of Letchurch Lodge, Derbyshire, but late of Cleveland, Ohio. Probate to the brother, William Morris, with similar powers reserved to the brother, John Morris. (June 1849).

Morris, Judith, of Dedham, Essex, widow, whose kinsman, Stephen Hart, was in New England. Probate to John Morris with similar powers reserved to Clement Fenne. (Mar. 1646). Wa.

Morris, Julia Louisa, nee Julia Louisa Kearney, of Auburn, Cayuga County, New York. Limited administration to William Phillipps, attorney for the husband, Joseph Marcus Morris, in Auburn. (Apr. 1857).

Morris, Rachel. *See* **Weems**.

Morris, Richard, of Richmond, Virginia. Administration to the brother and only next-of-kin, Henry John Morris. (July 1809).

Morris, Thomas, of Shadwell, Middlesex, who died on the ship *Dunbarton* in Virginia. Administration to the principal creditor, Humphrey Cock; the relict, Margaret Morris, renouncing. (June 1687).

Morris, Thomas, of East Florida. Administration with will to William Murdock and Horatio Clagett, administrators of the daughter, Rachel, relict of William Weems, and attornies for the said William Weems in Arundell County, Maryland; the executors, James Penman, Robert Payne, Peter Gimel and John Martin, having died. (June 1797).

Morris, William, of Anne Arundell County, Maryland, bachelor. Administration to the sister and only next-of-kin, Rachel, wife of William Weems. (Apr. 1793). Revoked on her death and granted to her administrators, William Murdock and Horatio Clagett, attornies for her husband, William Weems, in Anne Arundell County. (June 1797).

Morrisey, John, of H.M. ship *Greyhound*, who died in New York, bachelor. Administration to the brother, Thomas Morrisey. (Apr. 1752).

Morison, John, formerly of Jamaica but late of Mount Vernon, Ohio, Upper Canada, practitioner of physick and surgery. Probate to William Pirrie

Morison, *(contd.)* with similar powers reserved to Gray Rutherford, Charles Nockells and James Matthew Whyte. (Aug. 1840).

Morison, Malcolm, formerly of Fredericksburgh, Dutchess County, North America, but late of Annapolis, Nova Scotia, who died in Quebec. Administration to the son, Archibald Morison; the relict, Mary Morison, having been cited but not having appeared. (Jan. 1790).

Morse, Henry, of Williamsburg, Virginia. Probate to Thomas Woodall with similar powers reserved to Benjamin Waller and Robert Prentis. (Dec. 1775).

Morse, Mary, nee Mary Child, of Zanesville, Ohio. Limited administration to William Henry King pending the Chancery suit of King v. Cockill. (Oct. 1829).

Mortier, Abraham, of New York City. Probate to the brother, David Mortier, with similar powers reserved to the relict, Martha Mortier, and to Goldsbrow Banyar. (Jan. 1785).

Moreton, Anthony, Lieutenant in General Oglethorpe's Regiment of Foot, who died in Frederica, Georgia, bachelor. Probate to Niel alias Neal Holland with similar powers reserved to Thomas Bosom. (July 1749).

Morton, John, who died in Carolina. Probate to Robert Cuthbert the younger. (May 1699). Revoked on his death and granted to the relict, Anne, now wife of Thomas Wills; the mother of the executor, Elinor Cuthbert, renouncing. (Mar. 1706).

Morton, Joseph the elder, of Carolina, widower. Probate to the daughter-in-law, Anne, now wife of Thomas Wills. (Mar. 1706).

Morton, Richard, of Virginia, bachelor. Administration to the principal creditrix, Alice Usher. (May 1663).

Morton, Thomas, of Clifford Inn, London, who died overseas and who had lands in New England. Probate to the niece, Sarah Wilson alias Bruce. (Aug. 1660). Sh.

Morton, William, formerly of Limehouse, Middlesex, but late of New York, bachelor. Administration to Joseph Ashby, administrator with will of the half-brother, Samuel Carter deceased; the mother, Jane, wife of Elijah Carter, and the half-brothers and half-sisters, Joshua Carter, Ann Isaacs, widow, Mary, wife of John Passey, and Elijah Carter, having died. (Feb. 1857).

Moses, Joseph, formerly of Gun Square, Houndsditch, London, but late of Charlestown, United States of America. Administration to the relict, Sarah Moses. (July 1803).

Mott, Edmund, of New York, bachelor. Administration to the principal creditor, Joseph Bentham; the sisters, Bridget and Elizabeth Mott, renouncing. (Feb. 1705).

Motteux, Benjamin, of South Carolina, bachelor. Probate to the brother, John Anthony Motteux. (Dec. 1725).

Moulson, Peter, of St. Bartholomew the Less, London, whose brother, Foulke Moulson, was in Virginia. Probate to Margaret Blague. (June 1674).

Moult, William, of London, who died in Accawacke, Virginia. Administration with will to the brother, Francis Moult; no executor having been named. (June 1657).

Moulton, Foulk, of Westover, Virginia. Administration to the niece by a brother, Mary, wife of Daniel Kerye. (Nov. 1679).

Moultrie, Cecilia, of St. Augustine, East Florida, widow. Administration to the son, James Moultrie. (Mar. 1781).

Mountcastle, John, of Talmadge, Portage County, Ohio, tinman and brazier. Administration to the relict, Mary Mountcastle. (Apr. 1833).

Mountgomery, James, of James River, Virginia, who died in St. Katherine Creechurch, London. Probate to William Wilson with similar powers reserved to Robert Wilson. (Dec. 1697). Wa.

Mowate, Alexander, of H.M. ship *Chatham*, who died on the merchant ship *Tyger* in Philadelphia, bachelor. Administration to the father, Roger Mowate. (Mar. 1717).

Moxon, Martha, of Greece, Monroe County, New York. Limited administration with will to the husband, John Moxon. (Aug. 1831).

Muire, James, of Virginia. Administration to the principal creditor, William Jefferys. (July 1689).

Muller, Albert, of Bristol, who died in South Carolina, bachelor. Administration with will to the nephew, Walter Lougher, guardian of Lyder Muller. (Jan. 1729). Revoked on the death of Lyder Muller and granted to his administrator, Walter Lougher. (Jan. 1738).

Mullins, William, of Dorking, Surrey, who died in Virginia. Administration with will to the daughter, Sarah Blunden alias Mullins; no executor having been named. (July 1621). Wa.

Mullony, John, of Philadelphia, widower. Administration to Charles Cooke, attorney for the only child, John Mullony. (Dec. 1800).

Mumford, Brenton, of New Bedford, Rhode Island, bachelor. Administration to the sister, Frances Augusta, wife of William Henry Yarnold. (Nov. 1817).

Munday, Joseph, of Deptford, Kent, who died on the merchant ship *Nicholson* in Virginia. Administration to the relict, Susan Munday. (Apr. 1702).

Munday, Richard, of Stepney, Middlesex, master of the merchant ship *Europa*, who died in Virginia, bachelor. Probate to Samuel Bonham. (Aug. 1738).

Mundell, John, of Newcastle, Pennsylvania, who died in Boston, merchant. Probate to the brother and surviving executor, William Mundell. (Apr. 1697).

Mundy, Ann, formerly of Bradford, Wiltshire, but late of Long Island, New York, widow. Administration to Samuel Bowyer, attorney for the son, William Mundy, in Saugerties, New York. (Jan. 1851).

Munford, William, of Virginia, who died in London, bachelor. Administration to the brother, John Munford. (Sep. 1678).

Munn, William, of 62 Grove Street, New York. Administration to Lewis Munn, attorney for the relict, Louisa Munn, in New York. (Oct. 1841).

Munn, *(contd.)*
Revoked on her death and granted to the son, George Duncan Munn. (June 1852).

Munnings, George Garnett Husk, formerly of Thorpe le Soken, Essex, but late of New York, master mariner, bachelor. Administration to Caroline Munnings, daughter and administratrix of the father, George Garnett Husk Munnings deceased. (Feb. 1855).

Munro, Daniel, of H.M. ship *Carisfoot*, who died in Long Island Hospital. Inventory 1784. [*Administration Act not found*].

Munro, Malcolm, sergeant in Captain John McNeill's Company of the First Batallion of the Highland Regiment, who died in Long Island, New York, bachelor. Administration to the cousin german and only next-of-kin, Hugh Ross. (May 1766).

Murdock, Andrew, of New York, master of the merchant ship *Jane*, who died at sea. Administration to the relict, Eliza Murdock. (Feb. 1812).

Mordoch, David, of New York. Administration to the sister, Jane Mordoch, during the absence of the relict, Mary Mordoch. (Nov. 1687).

Murdoch alias Murdock, Robert, of Trenton, North America. Probate to Rev. Hugh Dixon and James Riddle. (July 1759).

Murray, Rev. Alexander, of Philadelphia. Limited probate to Rev. John Chalmers and Roderick McLeod. (Dec. 1795).

Murray, Capt. Charles, who died in America. Administration to the principal creditor, Theophilus Rabiniere. (June 1700).

Murray, John, Captain-Lieutenant of the 55th Regiment of Foot, who died in North America, bachelor. Administration to Henry Davidson, attorney for the brothers, Duncan and Evan Murray, in Edinburgh, Scotland. (May 1759).

Murray, James, of Newark, New Jersey. Administration with will to William Taylor, attorney for William Murray and Edward Blackford in Newark. (July 1810).

Murray, John, formerly of Rutland, Massachusetts, afterwards of Cowbridge, Glamorgan, but late of New Brunswick. Probate to the relict, Deborah Murray, and the children, Deborah and Thomas Murray. (Oct. 1795).

Murray, John, sergeant in the First Batallion of Royals, who died in Buffalo, America. Administration to the relict, Ann, now wife of Patrick Collins. (July 1817).

Murray, John William Boyles, of New York, who died at sea, doctor of physic, bachelor. Administration to Christ Knight Murray, attorney for the father, George William Murray, in New York. (July 1817).

Muschamp, George, of Potoxen, Maryland, bachelor. Administration to the sister and next-of-kin, Elizabeth Muschamp. (Aug. 1713).

Musgrave, Michael, of Virginia, who died in St. Sepulchre, London. Probate to Thomas Musgrave with similar powers reserved to William Newton. (Jan. 1698). Wi.

Musgrove, Robert, carpenter of the merchant brig *Jarrow* of Liverpool, who died in New York, bachelor. Administration to the mother, Margaret

Musgrove, *(contd.)*
Musgrove, widow. (Aug. 1838).

Myatt, Joseph, of Albany Fort, America, widower. Probate to Thomas Bird and Richard Staunton. (Nov. 1730).

Myers, Arthur, of Bristol, who died in Boston, Massachusetts, bachelor. Administration to the cousins german and next-of-kin, Jane, wife of Bashan Carter, John Robinson and William Robinson. (Jan. 1787).

Milam, John, of Bristol, who died in Virginia. Administration to Dorothy, wife of Richard Dyer, aunt and guardian of the children, John and Elizabeth Milam. (Dec. 1701).

Mynterne. *See* **Minterne**.

N

Nall, William, of Boston, New England, who died on the ship *Greenwich*, bachelor. Probate to Henry Causton. (Jan. 1696).

Nancolas, Anthony, of Iowa County, Wisconsin. Limited administration to Henry Ford, attorney for the relict, Anna Nancolas, in Iowa County. (May 1856).

Nanfan, John, Deputy Governor of New York. Administration to Middleton Chamberlain, attorney for the relict, Elizabeth Nanfan, in Barbados. (Feb. 1708).

Nash, Alexander, formerly of Edmonton, Middlesex, but late of Flatbush, New York. Probate to the brothers, William and Henry Nash. (Aug. 1845).

Nash, Paul, of Petersburgh, Virginia, merchant. Inventory 1823. [*Administration Act not found*].

Neufville. *See* **De Neufville**.

Naters, Thomas, formerly of Liverpool, Lancashire, ship master and owner, afterwards of Quebec, Canada, then of Newtown, Long Island, New York, but late of Goldenburg near Winterthur, Switzerland. Probate to William Mather. (Nov. 1836).

Neale alias Oneale, John, of Stepney, Middlesex, who died in Virginia. Administration to the principal creditor, Richard Rawlins; the relict, Elizabeth Neale, renouncing. (Sep. 1682).

Neill, Samuel, of Natchez, Mississippi, merchant. Administration to George Greene, attorney for the relict, Mary Neill, in New York City. (Feb. 1809).

Neale, Thomas, of Maryland. Administration to the brother, John Neale. (Aug. 1675).

Nedham, James, of Virginia, bachelor. Administration to the mother, Barbara Nedham. (Feb. 1677). Revoked on her death and granted to the brother and next-of-kin, George Nedham. (Jan. 1678).

Needham, William, of Montgomery County, Maryland. Administration with will to James Oswald, attorney for John Laird in George Town, North America; the son, William Abington Needham, having died intestate and the nephew and only next-of-kin, Thomas Marshall McCubbin, renouncing. (July 1826).

Neeve, Mary, of Virginia, spinster. Probate to the sister, Sarah Lewis. (Jan. 1674).

Neve, Timothy, of Ludlow, Shropshire, who died in Annapolis, Maryland, bachelor. Administration to Thomas Hughes, attorney for the father, William Neve, in Ludlow. (Nov. 1746).

Neill. *See* **Neal**.

Neilson, Richard, of Brigadier Guise's Regiment of Foot, who died in Carolina, bachelor. Probate to William Chancellor. (Feb. 1743).

Nelson, Elizabeth, nee Elizabeth Smith, of Newark, New Jersey, widow. Administration to John Stables, attorney for the only surviving child, Sophia Augusta Preintall, in Newark. (Aug. 1848).

Nelson, James, formerly of Little Hampstone, Devon, but late of Philadelphia, bachelor. Administration to the father, William Nelson. (Aug. 1813).

Nelson, Paschall, formerly of Boston, New England, but late of St. Margaret, Westminster, Middlesex. Probate to the nephew, John Temple, with similar powers reserved to the nephew, John Nelson. (Sep. 1760).

Nelson, Robert, of Carolina, bachelor. Probate to Dorcas Wellin with similar powers reserved to Thomas Wellin. (Jan. 1683).

Nelson, Thomas, of Rowhay, Essex County, New England. Probate to the wife's uncle, Richard Dummer, with similar powers reserved to Richard Bellingham. (Feb. 1651). Sh.Wa.

Nelson, William, formerly of Little Hampstone, Devon, but late a prisoner in France. Administration to the father, William Nelson. (Aug. 1813).

Ness, William, of New York, bachelor. Administration to the brother, Richard Ness. (May 1820).

Nevett, Hugh, of Virginia, bachelor. Administration with will to the nephew and next-of-kin, John Nevett; the executors, George Seaton and John Throckmorton, having died. (Oct. 1680).

Nevett, Samuel, of London, who died in Virginia, bachelor. Administration to the brother and sister, John Nevett and Alice Nevett. (Aug. 1680).

Nevill, John, of St. Margaret, Westminster, Middlesex, who died in Virginia, Vice-Admiral. Probate to the relict, Mary Nevill. (Nov. 1697).

Neville, Thomas, of Washington Street, New York. Administration to the relict, Catherine Maxted Neville. (July 1847).

Nevin, James, of New Hampshire. Probate to Thomas Lane with similar powers reserved to James Cummins, Theodore Atkinson, and the relict, Isabella Nevin. (June 1769).

Nevins, John, formerly of Aldermanbury, London, but late of East Port, Maine. Probate to the nephew, Samuel Gatliff, with similar powers reserved to the brother, Thomas Nevins. (Oct. 1829).

New, Thomas, of Bristol, who died in Pennsylvania. Limited administration with will to the relict, Elizabeth, now wife of Joseph Reynolds. (Jan. 1732).

Newall, John, of Bath Town, North Carolina, bachelor. Administration to the brother, James Newall; the father, James Newall, renouncing. (Nov. 1772).

Newberry, Roger, of Windsor, New England, Captain in the American Regiment, who died in the West Indies. Administration with will to Christopher Kilby, attorney for the relict, Elizabeth Newberry, and for Roger Wolcott. (Aug. 1744).

Newberry, Walter, of Gracechurch Street, London, whose sister, Sarah Parson, was in South Carolina; brother-in-law, John Cranston, and sister, Elizabeth Bordon, were in Newport, Rhode Island; sister, Martha, wife of Nathan Allen, was in New Jersey; and sister, Mary, wife of Jeremiah Williams, was in Long Island. Probate by their

Newberry, *(contd.)* solemn affirmation to Thomas Plumsted and Margaret Wyeth. (Mar. 1737).

Newcombe, Richard, formerly of Devonport, Devon, but late of Bermuda, stone mason. Administration with will to Benjamin Charles Thomas Gray, attorney for the relict, Sarah Jane Pepper, in Bermuda. (Mar. 1848). Revoked on his death and granted to Charles William Gray and Benjamin Gerrish Gray as attornies for the relict, Sarah Jane, now wife of John Joseph Coakley, in New York. (Aug. 1854).

Newcomen, Samuel, of Charles Town, South Carolina, bachelor. Administration to the mother, Hannah Newcomen, widow. (Dec. 1792).

Newdigate alias Newgate, Nathaniel, of Greenwich, Kent, whose brother-in-law, Edward Jackson, was in New England. Probate to the relict, Isabel Newdigate. (Sep. 1668). Wa.

Newdigate, Nathaniel, of Warwick, Rhode Island, widower. Administration to Thomas Sandford, attorney for the daughter, Sarah Mumford, widow. Revoked on his death and granted to William Stead as attorney for Sarah Mumford in Newport. (Sep. 1756).

Newell, Andrew, formerly of Massachusetts but late of Rotherhithe, Surrey, mariner. Probate by his solemn declaration to Henton Brown with similar powers reserved to John Owen. (Dec. 1741).

Newell, John, of Holborn, Middlesex, who died in New York. Administration to the relict, Catherine Newell. (May 1729).

Newell, Jonathan, of Virginia. Administration to the principal creditor, John Randall. (Mar. 1675).

Newens alias Chaplin, Harriet, of Castleton, Richmond County, New York, spinster. Probate to William Chaplin with similar powers reserved to William Henry Pillow. (Sep. 1846).

Newgate, Nathaniel. *See* **Newdigate**.

Newman, Francis, formerly of Headley Park, Hampshire, and Cadbury Castle, Somerset, but late of Grange, Charles County, Maryland. Limited probate to the daughter, Frances Charlotte, wife of Robert Albion Cox; the surviving executor, James Meadowcroft, and the relict, Frances Newman, having been cited but not having appeared. (Sep. 1820). Revoked by decree on the production of a new will and administration granted to Robert Trower and Francis Smedley, attornies for the relict, Elizabeth Hannah Friers alias Newman, in Charles County. (Aug. 1822).

Newman, John, of New England, who died on H.M. ship *Spence*, bachelor. Administration to the brother, Thomas Newman. (Feb. 1739).

Newman, John, of New York, bachelor. Administration to the brother, Thomas Newman; the father, John Newman, renouncing. (Dec. 1744).

Newman, Robert, of New York, seaman of H.M. ship *Pandora*. Probate to the relict, Mary Newman. (Oct. 1783).

Newman, Roger, of Baltimore County, Maryland. Administration with will to the sister, Susan, wife of Caleb Coatsworth, attorney for Charles

Newman, *(contd.)* Greenberry in Maryland. (Dec. 1704).

Newman, Samuel, of Boston, New England, who died in Barbados. Administration to the creditors, John Newman and Thomas Dodge. (Dec. 1696).

Newton, Ambrose, of Pitsburgh, America, bachelor. Administration to the brother and next-of-kin, Isaac Newton. (July 1772).

Newton, Edward, of Maryland, bachelor. Administration to the father, James Newton. (Nov. 1725).

Newton, Elizabeth, formerly of Colchester, Essex, but late of New Orleans. Administration to the husband, James Newton. (Dec. 1853).

Newton, Francis, of London, grocer, (bound for New England). Probate to Anthony Stanford with similar powers reserved to John Berry and Joseph Wilson. (Jan. 1662). Wa.Wi. *See* NGSQ 69/200.

Newton, John, of Colyton, Devon, whose children, Anthony and Joane, were in New England. Probate to the daughter, Mary, wife of Thomas Stocker. (Apr. 1647). Wa.

Newton, Joseph, of the ship *Dreadnaught* (bound for Virginia). Probate to Richard Martin. (Oct. 1694).

Newton, William, formerly of New York City but late of Dacre Street, St. Margaret, Westminster, Middlesex. Probate to the relict, Mary Newton, with similar powers reserved to Dennis Carleton. (Mar. 1790).

Nicholas, William, of H.M. ship *Winchelsea*, who died in Virginia, bachelor. Probate to Thomas Page. (Oct. 1734).

Nicoll, Andrew, Captain-Lieutenant of Captain Hubert Marshall's Company, who died in New York City. Probate to Rev. James Orem with similar powers reserved to Richard Nicholls and George Burnet. (Feb. 1749).

Nicoll, John, late Controller of Customs in Rhode Island, who died in Long Island. Administration to the relict, Penelope Nicoll. (Aug. 1782).

Nicholl, William, of Charles Town, North America, bachelor. Administration to the brother, Robert Nicholl; the mother, Mary Heane, widow, having died before administering. (Nov. 1787).

Nickolls, James Bruce, of Alexandria, District of Columbia. Probate to Rev. William Jackson and, by his solemn affirmation, to Phineas Janney. (May 1832).

Nicholls, John, of Philadelphia, who died at sea on the merchant ship *Dorothy*. Probate to Charles Willing. (Mar. 1751).

Nickols, Randolph, of Charlestown, Massachusetts, mariner. Probate to the relict, Sarah Nickols. (Dec. 1707).

Nicholls, Richard, of St. Olave, Southwark, Surrey, who died on the ship *Susanna* in Virginia. Administration to the relict, Tabitha Nicholls. (May 1692).

Nicholls, Richard, of New York City. Administration with will to Francis Donaldson, attorney for the surviving executor, Richard Harrison, in New York City. (Oct. 1783).

Nicholls, Stephen, of Salem, New England, mariner of H.M. ship *Lyon*,

Nicholls, *(contd.)* bachelor. Administration with will to Hannah Gobell, wife and attorney of John Gobell now on board H.M. ship *Lichfield.* (Aug. 1740).

Nichols, Stephen, of Newport, Rhode Island, and of H.M. ship *Vigilant*, who died in Louisburg, bachelor. Administration with will to Benjamin Wickham, attorney for Samuel Pool in Newport; no executor having been named. (July 1751).

Nicholls, William, of Kent County, Pennsylvania. Probate to William Nicholls. (Mar. 1700).

Nicholson, Hon. Francis, Governor of South Carolina, who died in St. George Hanover Square, Middlesex. Probate to Kingsmyll Eyre. (Mar. 1728).

Nicholson, George, of Boston, New England, who died in Virginia. Administration to the brother, Edward Nicholson, during the absence in New England of the relict, Hannah Nicholson. (July 1692).

Nicholson, Henry, Lieutenant in General Amherst's Regiment of Foot, who died in Louisburgh, bachelor. Administration with will to Sampson Barber, attorney for Richard Burton in Germany. (Oct. 1758).

Nicholson, John, of Maryland, who died on the ship *Anne*. Probate to the relict, Catherine Nicholson. (Aug. 1693).

Nicholson, Joseph, formerly of Charles Town, South Carolina, but late of Hackney, Middlesex. Administration with will to the son, Samuel Nicholson; the executors, Robert Raper, Richard Downes and Aaron Loocock, having been cited but not having appeared, and William Greenwood renouncing. (June 1783).

Nicholson, Richard, Ensign in the 8th or King's Own Regiment, who died in Chippawa, North America, bachelor. Administration to John Nicholson, son and executor of the father, Richard Nicholson deceased. (June 1820).

Nicholson, Robert, of London, merchant, who died overseas, and to be buried in Barbados or Virginia. Administration with will to the father, Francis Nicholson; John Corbin and John Young renouncing. (Aug. 1652). Sh.Wa.

Nicholson, Thomas, of Marblehead, New England. Administration to Thomas Newton, attorney for the relict, Elizabeth, now wife of Richard Crafts, during her absence. (Jan. 1697).

Nicholson, William, of Anne Arundell County, Maryland, merchant. Limited administration with will to William Hunt with similar powers reserved to Elianor Foster, Anne Nicholson and Elizabeth Nicholson. (Feb. & July 1720).

Nickson, Henrietta, of Ithaca, Tompkins County, United States of America. Administration to William Walker, administrator of the husband, William Nickson deceased, and attorney for the children, Jamima, wife of William Turnbull Reid, and Richard Nickson, in New York City. (Dec. 1852).

Nickson, William, of Ithaca, United States of America, butcher, widower. Administration to William Walker, attorney for the only children,

Nickson, *(contd.)*
Jamima Reid and Richard Nickson, in New York City. (Dec. 1852).

Nisbit, Elizabeth. *See* **Wallace**.

Niven, John, of Patterson, Passaic County, New Jersey. Administration to the sister, Marion Dunlop, widow; the relict, Jane Niven, renouncing. (June 1843).

Noble, Nevill, of New York. Administration to the creditors, Richard Clay and Hilton Wray; the relict Samuel (*sic*) Noble, and the children, Charles and Mark Noble, having been cited but not having appeared. (July 1787).

Nockold, Samuel, of New York, widower. Administration by decree to the brother and next-of-kin, Robert Nockold. (June 1719).

Noel. *See* **Nowell**.

Noke, William, of Annapolis Royal, Maryland. Administration to the sister, Elizabeth, wife of Joseph Sandell; the relict, Ann Noke, having died before administering, and the mother, Elizabeth, wife of John Stone, renouncing. (Feb. 1783).

Noore, John, of Stepney, Middlesex, (bound for Virginia). Probate to the relict, Anne Noore. (July 1693).

Norcross, Jeremiah, of Walsingham, Norfolk, who had goods in New England. Probate to the son, Nathaniel Norcross. (Apr. 1658). Sh.

Norcrosse, Rev. Nathaniel, of St. Dunstan in the East, London, who had goods in New England. Probate to the relict, Mary Norcrosse; Thomas Brookes and Edward Henninge renouncing. (Oct. 1662). Wa

Norie, Catharine. *See* **McGill**.

Norman, John the younger of Charles Town, North America, who died at sea, bachelor. Administration to the sister, Ann, wife of Timothy Roper, administratrix of the father, John Norman deceased. (June 1813).

Norrington, William, master of the frigate ?*Leart*, who died in Virginia. Administration to the relict, Rebecca Norrington. (July 1697).

Norris, Andrew, formerly of the merchant ship *Friendship* and of H.M. ship *Bideford*, but late of Boston, New England, widower. Administration to the brother, Richard Norris. (June 1753).

Norris, Isaac, of Philadelphia, widower. Administration by their solemn declarations to the daughters, Mary and Sarah Norris. (Aug. 1767).

Norry, Catharine. *See* **McGill**.

North, Stephen, of Boston, New England, who died in St. Botolph Aldgate, London. Probate to Francis North. (Jan. 1723).

Northcote, Catherine, of Hoxton, Middlesex, widow, whose kinswoman, Joane Poole, and her son, Theophilus Poole, were in Boston, New England. Probate to Thomas Rowe with similar powers reserved to John Rowe and William Rowe. (Aug. 1685). Wa.

Norton, James, of H.M. ship *Ardent*, who died in New York Hospital, bachelor. Administration to the father, John Norton. (Jan. 1780).

Norton, Martha, of New York City, widow. Administration to the son, John Leake Norton. (Feb. 1815).

Norton, Samuel, formerly of North Yarmouth, Norfolk, but late of New

Norton, *(contd.)* York City. Probate to the relict, Martha Norton. (Dec. 1791). Revoked on her death and administration granted to the son, John Leake Norton. (Feb. 1815).

Norton, Tobias, of Virginia. Administration to the relict, Joane Norton. (Dec. 1658).

Norwood, Thomas, of Virginia, widower. Administration to the son, Wolstenholme Norwood. (Nov. 1679). Marked "pauper."

Nourse, Elizabeth. *See* **Chapline**.

Nourse, Sarah, formerly Sarah Fouace, of Philadelphia. Administration to the son, Joseph Nourse; the husband, James Nourse, having died before administering. (June 1785).

Nott. *See* **Knott**.

Nowell, Christopher, of Leeds, Yorkshire, who had lands in New England. Probate to Margaret Nowell. (Sep. 1657). Wa.

Nowell, Edward, of Virginia, bachelor. Administration to Elizabeth Quint, attorney for the father, Edward Nowell, in Cornwall. (July 1689).

Noel alias Bushe, Elizabeth, formerly of New York City but late of Edinburgh, Scotland, widow. Probate to the mother, Elizabeth Harriet Hellyer. (June 1846).

Nowell, Henry Cradock, of Plantersville, Lowndes County, Alabama, bachelor. Administration to the mother, Rosamira Nowell, widow. (Apr. 1837).

Nowell, Thomas, of St. Dunstan in the West, London. Administration with will to Martha, wife of John Marshall, in New England; the named executor, Alexander Nisbett, renouncing. (May 1713).

Nox. *See* **Knox**.

Noye, Philip, formerly of St. Buryan but late of St. Just, Cornwall, adventurer to Virginia. Probate to the mother, Sarah Noye. (June 1650). Wi.

Noyes, Anne, of Cholderton, Wiltshire, widow, whose sons, James and Nicholas Noyes, were in New England. Probate to Robert Rede. (Apr. 1658). Sh.Wa.

Noyes, Peter, of Sudbury, New England. Probate to William and John Crouch, attornies for the sisters, Mary Mountjoy, Dorothy, wife of Samuel Parris, Sarah, wife of Thomas Frinck, and Ester Noyes, all in New England. (Sep. 1699).

Nugent, Thomas, formerly of St. Croix in the West Indies, afterwards of New York City, but late of Dorset Street, Dublin, Ireland. Probate to the sister, Eliza Skelly, widow, with similar powers reserved to David Rogers and Samuel David Rogers, merchants in New York City, and to the nephew, William Skelly. (Dec. 1833).

Nugent, Walter, Lieutenant of the Second Batallion of Marines, who died in Long Island. Administration to the relict, Rebecca Nugent. (Jan. 1777).

Nunez, Aaron, of Cincinnati, Ohio. Administration to the relict, Julia Nunez. (Nov. 1854).

O

Oakley, William Smith, formerly of Southwark, Surrey, wool stapler, but late of Morganfield, Union County, Kentucky. Administration to Jacob Mould, attorney for the relict, Susan Oakley, in New York City. (Nov. 1725).

O'Beirne, Rebecca, formerly of Philadelphia but late of Dinant, France, widow. Probate to Joseph Tilstone. (May 1842).

Odeway, Isaac, of Christ Church, Middlesex, who died in Maryland, widower. Administration to the only child, Elizabeth, wife of William Herrick. (Feb. 1779).

Ogden, David, formerly of Rathbone Place, Middlesex, afterwards of Newark, New Jersey, but late of Flushing, New York. Probate to the son, Nicholas Ogden, with similar powers reserved to Aaron Burr, Richard Varrick, Peter Kemble and Richard Stockton. (Oct. 1799).

Ogden, Nicholas, formerly of Shelburne, Nova Scotia, but late of New York City. Administration with will to Gabriel Shaw, attorney for the daughter, Alida Ogden, in New York City; Thomas Barclay and Edward Brindley and the nephews, David and Thomas Ogden, having been cited but not having appeared, and the relict, Hannah Ogden, having died. (Mar. 1823).

Ogden, Thomas, master of the ship *Thomas and Elizabeth*, who died in Virginia. Probate to the relict, Alice Ogden. (Aug. 1704).

Ogilvie, Alexander, of Virginia, bachelor. Administration to the mother and next-of-kin, Margaret Ogilvie, widow. (Feb. 1843).

Ogilvie, George, of Virginia. Administration to the relict, Helen Ogilvie. (Feb. 1843).

Ogilvie, Henry, of Dundee, Scotland, who died in Pensacola. Administration to the relict, Hannah, now wife of David Scott. (Feb. 1785).

Ogilvie, Rev. John, of New York City. Administration with will to Frederick Philipse, attorney for the surviving executor, Margaret Ogilvie, widow, in New York. (May 1786).

Ogilvie, Patrick, of Boston, New England, widower. Administration to John Lloyd, guardian of the only child, Margaret Ogilvie. (Nov. 1718).

Ogilvie, William, Captain of an Independent Company, who died in New York, bachelor. Administration to Joseph Mico, attorney for the brother, Rev. John Ogilvie, in Montreal. (Aug. 1763).

Ogle, Samuel, Lieutenant Governor of Maryland. Probate to Benjamin Tasker and Colonel Benjamin Tasker. (Sep. 1755).

O'Gorman, George, formerly of 39 Dorset Street, Portman Square, Middlesex, but late of Galveston, Texas. Administration with will to Elizabeth Isabel O'Gorman, widow, attorney for the son, George Charles Richard O'Gorman, in Serajgunge in the East Indies; the nephew and sole executor, Edmond Anthony O'Gorman, renouncing. (Apr. 1855).

Oker, Abraham, of the ship *Lord Salisbury*, who died at sea on the ship *Bendish* (bound for Virginia), bachelor. Administration with will to the principal creditrix, Elianor Hitchcock; the executor, James Farthing, renouncing. (Aug. 1667).

Oldmixon, Dame Mary, of Philadelphia, widow. Administration to the son, William Henry Oldmixon. (Jan. 1838).

Oliver, John, formerly of St. Martin's, Hereford, who died on passage from Cuba to New Orleans, bachelor. Administration to the father, Thomas Oliver. (Nov. 1854). Revoked on his death and granted to his relict and administratrix, Elizabeth Oliver. (May 1855).

Oliver, Joseph, of Virginia, bachelor. Administration to the principal creditor, James Emerson. (Sep. 1688).

Ollier, Jane, of Charles Town, South Carolina. Administration to Thomas Elliot, attorney for the mother, Mary Satur, widow, in South Carolina. (Nov. 1737).

Ollier, Ponz, of Charles Town, South Carolina. Administration to Thomas Elliot, attorney for the mother, Mary Satur, widow, in South Carolina. (Nov. 1737).

Oneale, John. *See* **Neale**.

O'Neill, John, Lieutenant of the Prince of Wales' American Regiment. Administration to David Thomas, attorney for the relict, Margaret O'Neill, in Philadelphia. (May 1792).

Onions, John, formerly of Birmingham, Warwickshire, but late of New York, bachelor. Administration to Charles James, administrator of the sister, Catherina James deceased; the mother, Mary Onions, and the other sisters, Sarah, wife of William Grove, Mary, wife of Joshua Taylor, and Elizabeth Onions, having also died. (Feb. 1816).

Onwin, Richard, formerly of Mary Street, Hampstead, Middlesex, but late of Harlem near New York, cabinet maker. Administration to the relict, Amalia Sophia Onwin. (July 1840).

Opie, Thomas, of Bristol, who died in Virginia, mariner. Probate of will (requesting his tombstone to be sent to Virginia) to the sister, Susan Cole. (July 1703).

Orange, Thomas, of New York City. Probate to the surviving executor, Henry Kermit. (Nov. 1824).

Orange, William, formerly of Norfolk, Virginia, but late of Liverpool, Lancashire. Probate to John Sparling, William Bolden, Richard Kent and William Charles Lake. (June 1789).

Oreck, William, of the ship *Arseller*, who died in Virginia, bachelor. Administration to Catherine, wife and attorney of the principal creditor, Simon Symondson, now at sea on the ship *Speedwell*. (Dec. 1706).

Orlton, Griffith, of New York. Administration to the brother, John Orlton; the relict, Jane Orlton, having died. (Dec. 1816).

Ormandey, John, of Maryland and of the ship *Anne and Mary*, who died overseas, bachelor. Probate to Arthur Holme. (Aug. 1700).

Ormsby, Eubule, Lieutenant of the 35th Regiment, who died in West Florida. Probate to the sister, Mary Ormsby. (June 1768).

Orne, Susannah, of Marblehead, North America. Administration to Samuel Williams, attorney for the daughter, Annis Orne, in Salem, North America; the husband, Joshua Orne, having died. (Feb. 1818).

Orpwood, Mary, of St. Margaret, Westminster, Middlesex, spinster, whose grandfather was Edmond Orpwood deceased of Philadelphia. Administration with will to William Collins, father of the sole executrix, Mary Collins, spinster, a minor, until she is 17. (Dec. 1747).

Orrery, Charles, Earl of, who made a bequest to William Bird in Virginia. Probate to Henry, Earl of Uxbridge. (Sep. 1731). Declared invalid and administration with will granted to the son, John, Earl of Orrery. (Sep. 1732).

Osborn, Joseph, of New York City. Probate to the son, William Osborn, with similar powers reserved to the relict, Judith Osborn. (June 1830).

Osborne, Samuel, of St. Olave, Southwark, Surrey, who died in Carolina. Administration to the principal creditor, Chaning Radcliffe; the relict, Sarah Osborne, renouncing. (Apr. 1683).

Osgood, John, of Leytonstone, Essex, who had lands in New Jersey. Probate to the son, Salem Osgood, and to Theodore Ecclestone and John Hall. (June 1694). NGSQ 63/135.

Osgood, Salem, of London, merchant, who had lands in West Jersey. Probate by her solemn affirmation to the relict, Anne Osgood. (Feb. 1706).

O'Sullivan, Caroline, of New York City. Administration to Jonathan Outram, attorney for the husband, Jeremiah O'Sullivan, in New York. (Apr. 1855).

O'Sullivan, John, of New York, who died at sea aboard the merchant ship *Dick*. Administration to the relict, Mary O'Sullivan. (Aug. 1825).

Oswin, Thomas, of the merchant ship *Essex*, who died in York River, Virginia. Probate to the father, Christopher Oswin. Marked "pauper." (Dec. 1721).

Otterton, John, of Nansemum, Virginia. Administration to the relict, Mary Otterton. (June 1654).

Ottway, John, of Hersom [*sic*], Surrey, who died overseas (bound for New England), bachelor. Administration with will to Elizabeth, wife of Thomas Ernall. (Mar. 1670).

Overing, Henry John, of Newport, Rhode Island, and Providence Plantation. Administration to Henry Overing, attorney for the relict, Mary Overing, at Newport. (Aug. 1784).

Overington, John, formerly of Belmont Place, Lambeth, Surrey, but late of Oxford Township, Philadelphia County, Pennsylvania. Probate to the relict, Sarah Overington. (Dec. 1810). Revoked on her death and administration granted to James Sowton, attorney for the son, William Overington, in Oxford Township. (Oct. 1836).

Owen, Edward, of Philadelphia. Administration to the brother, Wyriotte Owen; the relict, Esther Owen, having died. (Dec. 1821).

Owen, Joseph, of St. Botolph Bishopsgate, London, who died in Virginia.

Owen, *(contd.)*
Administration to the brother, Benjamin Owen. (Oct. 1709).

Owen, Thomas, of Granville County, South Carolina. Probate to the brother, Jeremiah Owen, with similar powers reserved to Joseph Wragg and William Yeomans. (July 1738).

Owen, William, of Limehouse, Middlesex, who died in Virginia. Administration to Anne Bascombe, guardian of the only child, William Owen, during his minority. (Oct. 1655).

Owen, William, of Carolina. Administration to the brother, Henry Owen. (Dec. 1690).

Owen, William, of Bath, North Carolina, bachelor. Administration to the uncle and principal creditor, Thomas Walker; the sister and next-of-kin, Elizabeth Owen, renouncing. (Jan. 1735).

Owen, William, of Adelaide, South Australia, who died in Stockton, Upper California, bachelor. Administration to the mother and next-of-kin, Grace, wife of Richard Thomas. (Nov. 1850).

Oxenbridge, William, of St. Alban Wood Street, London, who left a bequest for the Indians in New England. Probate to the son, Clement Oxenbridge; the son, John Oxenbridge, renouncing. (Nov. 1651). Wa.

Oyles, Phillip, of Maryland, bachelor. Probate by his solemn declaration to the brother, Thomas Oyles. (Nov. 1710).

P

Packharness alias Peckharness, John, of New York City. Pobate to Richard Packharness with similar powers reserved to the brother and sister, Richard and Deborah Packharness. (Nov. 1796).

Paddock, Adino, of Boston, North America, an Army Captain who died in New Jersey. Probate to James South, James Simpson and William Forman. (Aug. 1804).

Page, John, of Gloucester County, Virginia, who died in Bethnal Green, Middlesex, merchant. Probate to the son, John Page. (Jan. 1719).

Paine. *See* **Payne**.

Palairet, Mary Ann, formerly of Mount Clements near Stanmore, Middlesex, but late of Philadelphia. Limited administration with will to Rev. Richard Thomas Palairet, brother and executor of the husband, Septimus Henry Palairet deceased. (Apr. 1856).

Palmer, Anthony, Lieutenant in Lieutenant-General Dalzel's Regiment in the Leeward Islands, who died in Philadelphia. Probate to Robert Lowe with similar powers reserved to the relict, Elizabeth Palmer. (May 1749). Revoked and granted to the said Elizabeth Palmer. (July 1750).

Palmer, Edward, of Leamington, Gloucestershire, who died in London having lands in Virginia and New England. Probate to the son, Giles Palmer. (Dec. 1624). Wa.

Palmer, Eliakim, of St. Peter le Poer, London, who had estate in Boston, New England. Limited probate to Beeston Long, Henry Norris and William Palmer. (May 1749).

Palmer, Giles, of Bridgenorth, Shropshire, who had lands in Virginia. Probate to Edward Palmer. (June 1637). Wi.

Palmer, John Temple, of Boston, United States of America, bachelor. Administration to the father, William Lamb Palmer. (Dec. 1822).

Palmer, Peregrine, formerly of Barnard's Inn, afterwards of Fetter Lane, London, but late of New York. Administration with will to Richard Alexander Price, attorney for the daughter, Ann, wife of Hugh McGregor, in Greenock, Scotland. (Mar. 1832).

Palmer, Thomas, of Virginia. Probate to Nicholas Palmer with similar powers reserved to the relict, Mary Palmer. (Nov. 1768).

Panton, Rev. George, formerly of Shelburne, Nova Scotia, and of New York, afterwards of Kelso, Scotland, but late of Edinburgh. Administration to the relict, Jeane Panton. (Oct. 1810).

Panton, William, of Pensacola, West Florida, who died at sea. Limited probate to John Forbes and Adam Gordon with similar powers reserved to John Panton, Thomas Forbes, John Innerarity and others. (Dec. 1804).

Paradise, Lucy, of Williamsburg, Virginia, widow. Administration to the grandson, Count Giovanni Alvise Barziza. (Oct. 1815).

Pargiter, John, of St. Martin in the Fields, Middlesex, whose cousin, Sarah Lovell, was in Virginia. Probate to the sons, John and Samuel Pargiter. (Feb. 1688).

Parham, Joseph. *See* **Parrum**.

Parish, George, of Ogdensburgh, New York. Probate to Joseph Russell. (Aug. 1839).

Parke, Cuthbert, of Philadelphia. Administration to John Charles Laycock, attorney for John Bradley, the guardian appointed by the Philadelphia Orphans' Court to the only children, Ellen and William Parke; the relict, Martha Ann Parke, having died. (June 1847).

Parke, Daniel, of London, who died in Virginia. Special administration with will to the son, Daniel Parke, with similar powers reserved to James Bray and Robert Cobb; the executor, Edward Carter, renouncing. (Sep. 1679). Wi.

Parke, Daniel, Governor of the Leeward Islands, who had estate in Virginia. Probate to Micajah Perry and Richard Perry. (May 1711). Wi.

Park, Elizabeth, widow, formerly Elizabeth Chambers, widow, formerly Elizabeth Watson, spinster, of Bury St. Edmunds, Suffolk, who died in Savannah, Georgia. Administration to the sister, Sarah Elliott, widow. (July 1770).

Parke, Graves, of Virginia, master of the merchant ship *Gooch*. Probate to Edward Randolph with similar powers reserved to John Randolph. (Aug. 1731).

Parke, Thomas, of H.M. ship *Peach*, who died in New York, bachelor. Administration to the sisters, Grace Parke and Mary, wife of John Sowerby. (Nov. 1780).

Parke, William, who died overseas leaving a bequest to Adam Thorowgood in Virginia. Administration with will to the relict, Sarah Parke, during the minority of the son, William Parke. (Aug. 1634). Sh.Wi.

Parker, Alexander, of St. Edmund Lombard Street, London, who had lands in Pennsylvania. Probate to Mary Parker and Prudence Wager. (Apr. 1689).

Parker, Benjamin, of Boston, New England, bachelor. Limited administration to John Hiller of Bread Street, London, attorney pending a lawsuit. (Dec. 1772).

Parker, Dorothy, of Mildenhall, Wiltshire, whose son, Thomas Parker, was in New England. Probate to Benjamin Woodbridge with similar powers reserved to the daughter, Sarah Bayly. (Apr. 1650). Sh.Wa.

Parker, John, of Virginia. Administration with will to John Purvis, attorney for William Colsen in Virginia. (Aug. 1701). Wi.

Parker, John, of Morton, Thornbury, Gloucestershire, who died in Pennsylvania, bachelor. Administration with will to the cousin german and next-of-kin, Isaac Reach; the executors in trust, William Gregory and Thomas Allway, and the brother, William Parker, having died. (Apr. 1750).

Parker, John, formerly of Enfield, Middlesex, but late of Annapolis, Maryland, widower. Administration to the son and next-of-kin, George Parker. (May 1799).

Parker, Joseph, of St. Pancras Soper Lane, London, whose brother, James Parker, was in New England. Probate to the relict, Anne Parker, with similar powers reserved to the daughter, Elizabeth Parker. (Dec. 1644). Wa.

Parker, Joseph, of Charles Town, South Carolina, bachelor. Administration to the brother, George Parker, of Lambs Conduit Street, St. George the Martyr; the mother, Katherine Parker, renouncing. (July 1785).

Parker, Josiah, of Charles Town, North America, Lieutenant on half pay of the late Regiment of New Jersey Volunteers. Administration to David Thomas, attorney for the relict, Levina Parker, in Charles Town. (Nov. 1796).

Parker, Judith, of New England, widow. Probate to Robert Manning of Ipswich, Suffolk. (May 1649). Sh.Wa.

Parker, Robert, of Bosham, Sussex, who had lands in Virginia. Probate to the son, George Parker. (Apr. 1673). Wi.

Parker, William, of Stepney, Middlesex, who had goods in Maryland. Probate to the relict, Grace Parker. (July 1673).

Parker, William, of Staten Island, New York, bachelor. Administration to the mother and next-of-kin, Elizabeth, wife of Abraham Filewood. (Aug. 1855).

Parkes. *See* **Parks**.

Parkhurst, George, of Ipswich, Suffolk, (bound for Virginia). Administration with will to the relict, Elizabeth Parkhurst; no executor having been named. (Oct. 1635).

Parkin alias Perkins, John, seaman of H.M. ship *Eagle*, who died in New York, bachelor. Probate to the brother, Henry Parkin. (Apr. 1777).

Parkin, Thomas, of New York City. Limited administration with will to the nephew, Thomas Parkin. (May 1795).

Parkins, Joseph Wilfred, formerly of London and of Essex Street, Strand, Middlesex, afterwards of New York City, but late of Newark, New Jersey. Administration with will to Thomas Colpitts Granger, executor to the executor, George Best deceased, after sentence for the validity of the will. (Dec. 1843). Revoked on his death and granted to Mary, the relict of George Best and now the wife of William Simpson. (Feb. 1853).

Parkes, Andrew, of London, haberdasher, who died overseas and whose brother, John Parkes, was in Virginia. Probate to the aunt, Ellen Warden, of Christ's Hospital, London, widow. (Feb. 1630).

Parks, Edward, of St. Matthew Friday Street, London, who had lands in New England. Probate to Thomas Plampin and John Bagnall. (Jan. 1651). Revoked on their death and administration granted to the son, John Parks. (Mar. 1673). Revoked on his death and granted to the relict, Mary Cawley alias Parks. (Nov. 1681). Sh.

Parks, Roland, Cornet on half pay of the King's American Dragoons, who died in Westfield, Hampden County, Massachusetts. Administration to James Tidbury, attorney for the relict, Sarah Parks, in Westfield. (June 1830).

Parnel, James, of Pennsylvania. Probate to Ambrose Stevenson. (Oct. 1725).

Parnell, Moses, of Southampton, Long Island, New York, widower. Administration to the son, Moses Parnell. (July 1756).

Parr, Henry, of Boston, New England, bachelor. Administration to the

Parr, *(contd.)* father, Richard Parr. (Aug. 1753).

Parrum alias Parham, Joseph, of Stepney, Middlesex, who died in Boston, New England. Administration to Jane Parrum. (Aug. 1701).

Parry, John, of Virginia, who died overseas, bachelor. Administration with nuncupative will to the brother, William Parry; no executor having been named. (July 1638). Sh.Wi.

Parslow, John, of New Orleans, bachelor. Administration to the brother, Edward Parslow; the mother, Elizabeth Parslow, widow, having died. (Apr. 1845). Further grants of administration made in the same month in repect of the intestate's brothers: Daniel Parslow, Lieutenant of the 6th Regiment of Native Infantry in Bombay; Thomas Parslow, naval storekeeper in Barbados; and James Sharpe Parslow of Kentish Town, Middlesex, midshipman of H.M. ship *Laurel*.

Parsons, Edward Lambert, of James Town, Virginia, who died as a passenger on the merchant ship *Warwick*, Mr. Charles Lasker, bachelor. Administration to the cousin german and only next-of-kin, John Lambert, administrator of the brother and only next-of-kin, John Temple Parsons, who died before administering. (May 1778).

Parsons, John Temple, of Chester Town, Maryland, bachelor. Administration to the cousin german and only next-of-kin, John Lambert. (May 1778).

Parsons, Mary, formerly Mary Ewer, formerly of Charles Street, Grosvenor Square, Middlesex, but late of Boston, North America. Administration to the husband, Thomas Parsons. (Feb. 1818).

Parsons, Robert, of the frigate *James*, who died in Virginia, bachelor. Administration by decree to the mother, Sarah Butler alias Parsons. (June 1655).

Parsons, William, of Newcastle-upon-Tyne, Northumberland, bachelor. Administration to Samuel Sheafe, attorney for the brothers, Humphrey and Joseph Parsons, in Boston, New England. (Mar. 1696).

Parton, Francis, formerly of Queen Anne Street, St. Marylebone, Middlesex, but late of Grand Bank, Newfoundland, and Salem, Massachusetts. Administration to William Matthews, attorney for the relict, Lydia Parton, in Salem. (Apr. 1811).

Partridge, John, formerly of Philadelphia but late of New York City, plasterer. Probate to John Liptrott Graves after retraction of his renunciation. (Aug. 1827).

Partridge, Samuel, of Rappahannock, Virginia. Administration to the sister, Sarah Partridge alias Wilson. (July 1676). Revoked on her death and granted to her her husband, Richard Wilson. (Jan. 1690).

Passapae, John Davis, formerly of Baltimore, North America, but late of Valparaiso, South America, bachelor. Administration to the sister, Mary Ann Hilditch. (June 1853).

Passapae, Joseph, formerly of Baltimore, Maryland, but late of Callao in Peru, widower. Administration to the daughter, Mary Ann Hilditch. (Apr. 1849).

Passey, Samuel A. *See* **Plummer**.

Paston, John, of Old Stratford, Warwickshire, who died in America. Probate to the mother, Elizabeth Paston. (June 1711).

Paston, Robert, Captain of H.M. ship *Feversham*. Administration with will to Thomas Sandford, attorney for Adolph Philips in New York. (July 1712). Revoked and Benjamin Edmonds appointed as attorney. (Jan. 1713).

Pastree, George, of Boston, New England, who died on the armed vessel *Boston Packet*, bachelor. Administration by his solemn affirmation to Anthony Hodgson, attorney for the grandmother, Margaret Pastree, in Boston. (Aug. 1751).

Pate, John, of Virginia, bachelor. Administration to the brother, Edward Pate. (Mar. 1673).

Pate, Richard, of Virginia. Administration to the nephew, John Pate. (Oct. 1657).

Pateshall, Robert, of Boston, Massachusetts, Captain of the 40th Regiment of Foot, bachelor. Administration to Dennys de Berdt, attorney for the brother and only next-of-kin, Richard Pateshall, in Boston. (Aug. 1763).

Patrick, Edward, alias Smith, John Edward, formerly of Petersfield, Hampshire, but late of Southampton, Suffolk County, North America, rigger. Probate to James Harlow Payne and the brother, James Patrick, with similar powers reserved to Henry P. Hedges. (Oct. 1855).

Patten alias Potten, John, Lieutenant of the 48th Regiment of Foot, who died in Havana. Administration to John Pritchard, attorney for the relict, Mary Patten, in Trinity Parish, New York. (Jan. 1765).

Patten, Mary, of Washington County, New York, widow. Administration to David Davies, attorney for the son, Edward Patten, in Washington County. (Nov. 1811).

Patterson, John, of Farmington, Connecticut, Captain of the First Connecticut Regiment of Foot, who died in Havana. Administration with will to Phineas Lyman, attorney for the relict, Ruth Patterson, in Connecticut. (Jan. 1765).

Paterson, Ronert, Lieutenant of the 17th Regiment of Light Dragoons, who died in Charles Town, South Carolina. Probate to John Wilson with similar powers reserved to the brother, William Paterson. (July 1781).

Pattinger, John. *See* **Pettinger**.

Pattishall, Thomas, of Bombay, merchant, whose brother, William Pattishall, was in Virginia. Probate to the brother, William Pattishall. (Oct. 1717). Wi.

Pattison, George, of the merchant ship *Betty*, who died in Virginia, bachelor. Probate to the mother, Jane Pattison, widow. (Jan. 1722)

Pattison, John, of South Carolina, who died on H.M. ship *Windsor*. Probate to the daughter, Isabella, wife of George West. (Feb. 1742).

Pattle, Eliza Henrietta, formerly of Golden Square, Middlesex, but late of Brooklyn, New York, spinster. Administration with will to Edward Beldam, attorney for William Edward Custis in New York. (Feb. 1854).

Patton, Mary, formerly Mary Petifer, of Savannah, Georgia. Administration to John Patton, attorney for the husband, John Patton, in Savannah. (Jan. 1775).

Patyn, Wilhelmina, relict of Justus Everhard Louis Clotterbook Patyn, of Middleburgh, United States of America. Inventory 1834. [*Administration Act not found*].

Paul, Stephen, of New England, who died on the ship *New Castle Merchant*. Administration to the principal creditor, Samuel Hockaday. (May 1696).

Pawlett, William, of Bicton, Hampshire, who died in Maryland. Probate to the relict, Martha Pawlett. (Mar. 1695). *See* NGSQ 68/118.

Paxton, Charles, formerly of Boston, New England, but late of St. James, Westminster, Middlesex. Probate to William Burch and Thomas Palmer. (Feb. 1788).

Paxton, Wentworth, formerly of Rotherhithe, Surrey, but late of Boston, New England. Administration to the son, Charles Paxton; the relict, Faith Paxton, having died. (Feb. 1751).

Payne, Edmund, of Stepney, Middlesex, who died in Maryland. Probate to Catherine Payne. (July 1708).

Paine, Elizabeth, of Evansville, Indiana, spinster. Administration to William Millard, attorney for the father, John Paine, in Evansville. (July 1852).

Pain, James, of H.M. ship *Tartar*, who died in Long Island Hospital. Probate to Jane Cotterell, spinster. (Aug. 1778).

Payne, Jean, of Goochland County, Virginia, widow. Administration with will to William Murdock, attorney for the son, George Woodson Payne, in Goochland County. (June 1808).

Payne, Mathew, of Pennsylvania, widower. Administration to the son, Edmund Payne. (Oct. 1686).

Paine, Samuel, of Worcester, Massachusetts, bachelor. Administration to Harrison Gray, attorney for the brother, William Paine M.D., in Worcester. (Apr. 1808).

Paine, William, of the ship *Charles*, who died in Virginia. Probate to the relict, Susan Paine. (Nov. 1710).

Paynter, Lovell, of the merchant ship *Loyal Judith*, who died in Philadelphia, bachelor. Administration to the creditor, John Lemon; the great-uncle and next-of-kin, John Paynter, renouncing. (Aug. 1741).

Paynter, Nicholas, of Anne Arundell County, Maryland. Probate to Henry Bray. (Oct. 1685).

Payton, Sir Henry, of London, member of the Virginia Company, who died overseas. Administration with will to the creditor, Sir John Payton the younger; the brother and executor, Thomas Payton, having died. (Feb. 1624). Wi.

Payton, John, of Portbury, Somerset, who had assets in Virginia and Maryland. Probate to the relict, Jone Payton. (Aug. 1699). Wi.

Peachy, Mary, of St. Stephen's parish, King and Queen County, Virginia. Probate to Thomas Walker with similar powers reserved to Susan

Peachy, *(contd.)*
Walker. (Jan. 1717). Wi.

Peake, Christopher, of Deptford, Kent, who died on the merchant ship *Mary* in Virginia. Administration to the relict, Anne Peake. (Dec. 1726).

Peake, Sir Robert, of Richmond, Surrey, whose cousin, George Lyddall, was in Virginia. Probate to Gregory Peake and Benjamin Peake. (July 1667). Wa.

Peak, Samuel, of Boston, New England, master of H.M. ship *Lowestoft*. Administration to Samuel Partridge, attorney for the relict, Elizabeth, now wife of Edward Marshall, in Boston. (Feb. 1753).

Peers, Joseph, of H.M. ship *Princess*, who died in Long Island Hospital. Probate to Henry Gillis. (Aug. 1783).

Pierce, Mark, formerly of London but late of New England, who died in Ireland. Probate to William Viner and Robert Newman. (June 1656). Sh.Wa.

Peirce, Tobias, formerly of New England but late of London, mariner. Probate to Sarah Burrows with similar powers reserved to John Burrows. (Jan. 1746).*See* NGSQ 64/289.

Pearne, George, formerly of Dover, Kent, but late of Blackwall, Poplar, Middlesex, engineer of the merchant steam vessel *Great Western*, who died in New York, bachelor. Probate to William Crandall. (July 1838).

Pearle, Richard, of Virginia, bachelor. Administration to the father and principal creditor, Thomas Pearle. (Oct. 1668).

Pearman, Ann, of Annapolis, Maryland, spinster. Administration to Zachariah Hood, attorney for the uncle and next-of-kin, Thomas Hyde, in Annapolis. (Jan. 1785).

Pearson, John, of Mount Airy, Richmond County, Virginia, widower. Administration to the son, John Pearson. (July 1766).

Pearson, Joseph, of Shadwell, Middlesex, master of the merchant ship *Providence*, who died in Maryland. Administration to the relict Elianor Pearson. (Jan. 1726).

Pearson, Richard, seaman of H.M. ship *Shoreham*, who died in New York, bachelor. Administration to the principal creditor, Samuel Wood. (Sep. 1730).

Peck, Edward, sergeant at law of the Inner Temple, London, whose son, Edward [Peck], was in New England. Probate to the son, William Peck. (June 1676). Wa.

Pecke, Robert, of Hingham, Norfolk, clerk, whose daughter, Anne, wife of Captain John Mason, was in New England . Probate to Samuel Pecke. (Apr. 1658). Sh.Wa.

Peckharness. *See* **Packharness**.

Pecknell, Elizabeth, of New York City. Probate to William Orcher Huddlestone and to the daughter, Rebecca, his wife. (Nov. 1786).

Peele, Elizabeth, of Maryland, spinster. Administration to the father, Bartholomew Peele. (Aug. 1685).

Peel, John, of New York City, widower. Administration to the sister and

Peel, *(contd.)*
only next-of-kin, Ann, wife of Francis Graham. (Sep. 1800).

Peele, Robert, of Maryland, bachelor. Administration to the brother, John Peele. (Jan. 1734).

Peele, Samuel, of Maryland, bachelor. Administration to the brother, John Peele. (Aug. 1733).

Peer, Thomas, of St. Mary Magdalene, Bermondsey, Surrey, who died in Smith's Creek, St. Mary's County, Virginia. Administration to the principal creditor, Ralph Norton; the relict Joane Peer, renouncing. (Nov. 1670).

Peers. *See* **Pearce**.

Peet, Joseph, formerly of St. Mary's, Nottingham, but late of Philadelphia, widower. Administration to the sister and next-of-kin, Abigail, wife of James Newton. (Feb. & Mar. 1797).

Pelham, Penelope, of Boston, New England, spinster. Administration to William Pelham, attorney for the half-brother and next-of-kin, Peter Pelham, in Grenville County, Virginia. (Feb. 1790).

Pelham, William, of Boston, New England, bachelor. Administration to William Pelham, attorney for the brother, Peter Pelham, in Grenville County, Virginia. (Feb. 1790).

Pelley, James, of Hoboken, New Jersey, bachelor. Administration to the brother and next-of-kin, William Pelley. (June 1825).

Pemerton, John, of Lawford, Essex, whose daughter-in-law, Deborah Goffe, was in New England. Probate to John Beeston. (Mar. 1654). Wa.

Pendergrass, Thomas, of Stepney, Middlesex, who died in Virginia. Administration to the relict, Elizabeth Pendergrass. (Apr. 1699).

Penman, James, formerly of Charles Town, South Carolina, but late of St. Paul Covent Garden, Middlesex. Probate to William Drummond and Thomas Young with similar powers reserved to Sir William Forbes and Spencer Man. (Nov. 1789 & Jan. 1794).

Penn, John, of Philadelphia. Probate to the relict, Anne Penn, with similar powers reserved to John Fishbourne Mifflin. (Jan. 1796).

Penn, Richard, of St. Marylebone, Middlesex, who had estate in America. Limited probate to the relict, Hannah Penn. (Mar. 1771).

Penn, William, of Patuxent River, Maryland. Probate to the relict, Elizabeth Penn. (Nov. 1697).

Pennington, James, of St. Bartholomew by the Exchange, London, who died in Maryland. Administration to the principal creditor, Mathew Travers; the relict, Sarah Pennington, renouncing. (Feb. 1679).

Pennoyer, William, of London, whose kinsman, Robert Pennoyer, was in New England. Probate to Richard Loton and Michael Dewison. (Feb. 1671). Wa. *See* NGSQ 60/244.

Penny, John, of H.M. ship *Roebuck*, who died in Philadelphia, bachelor. Administration to the mother, Elizabeth, wife of Peter Sawrey. (Feb. 1779).

Penney, William Honeycombe, of New York, seaman on the steam vessel *Oscela*, bachelor. Administration to the father, John Penney. (Nov. 1840).

Pepperell, Andrew, formerly of Portsmouth, New Hampshire, but late of St. Marylebone, Middlesex. Probate to Sir William Pepperell with similar powers reserved to George Atkinson. (July 1783).

Pepperell, Sir William, late of Kittery, York County, Massachusetts. Probate to the grandson, William Pepperell, formerly William Pepperell Sparhawk, with similar powers reserved to the relict, Dame Mary Pepperell, and the grandson, Nathaniel Sparhawk. (Nov. 1768).

Percey. *See* **Persey**.

Percivall, Andrew, of St. Margaret, Westminster, Middlesex, who had lands in Carolina. Probate to the relict, Essex Percivall. (Mar. 1696). Revoked on her death and administration granted to her administrator, Andrew Percivall. (June 1730).

Perdrian, Lewis, of Carolina who died in Barbados. Probate to the sister, Judith, wife of Paul Faneuil; no executor having been named. (July 1697).

Perdrian, Peter, of Carolina, bachelor. Administration to the brother, Daniel Perdrian. (Apr. 1693).

Perira, Emanuel, of New York and the transport ship *Juliana*. Probate to Emanuel Bandira. (Apr. 1780).

Perkins, Catherine, of Charles Town, South Carolina. Administration to William Perkins, attorney for the husband, Samuel Perkins, in Charles Town. (July 1746).

Perkins, Christopher, formerly of Norfolk, Virginia, but late of St. Andrew, Holborn, Middlesex, merchant. Probate to the brother, Hutton Perkins. (Dec. 1765). Wi.

Perkins, John. *See* **Parkin**.

Perkins, Nathaniel, carpenter of H.M. ship *Ardent*, who died in New York Hospital. Probate to John Taplin. (Nov. 1779).

Perman, John, of Charleston, South Carolina, merchant. Administration to Rev. Thomas Evans, attorney for the relict, Isabella Perman, in Charleston. (Dec. 1847).

Perrin, Edward, of Bristol, merchant, who had lands in Virginia, Maryland and Pennsylvania. Probate to the son, Thomas Perrin. (Dec. 1709). Wi.

Perroneau, Alexander, of Charles Town, South Carolina. Limited administration with will to Robert Wells and Aaron Loocock. (Sep. 1781).

Perroneau, Ann. *See* **Petrie**.

Perroneau, Henry, of Charles Town, South Carolina. Limited administration with will to James Crockatt of London, merchant, attorney for Benjamin D'Harriette, Henry Perroneau, Alexander Perroneau and Arthur Perroneau, in South Carolina. (Aug. 1755).

Perroneau, Henry, formerly of Charles Town, South Carolina, then of Stepney, Middlesex, afterwards of St. Pancras, Middlesex, but late of Ramsgate, Kent. Probate to the nephew, Robert Cooper, and to William Powell and Benjamin Savage, with similar powers reserved to Dr. Alexander Garden, John Hopton, John Savage, Hon. Rawlin Lowndes, Isaac Motte and Edward Penman. (Nov. 1786).

Perroneau, Mary Coffin, of Charleston, South Carolina, spinster. Probate to William Henry Perroneau. (Nov. 1849).

Perry, John, of St. Antholin, London, who died in James City, Virginia. Probate to the brother, Richard Perry. (Apr. 1629). Sh.

Perry, Robert, of Bristol, clerk, whose nephew, Robert Perry, was in Virginia. Probate to the relict, Elizabeth Perry. (July 1652). Sh.Wa.Wi.

Perry, Robert, formerly of Birmingham, Warwickshire, but late of New York, merchant. Probate to Thomas Lamb with similar powers reserved to William Shakespear, Henry Pope and William J. Bradford. (July 1827).

Perry, Thomas, of Virginia. Administration to the sister, Margaret, wife of Bartholomew Terrett. (July 1670).

Perryman, Thomas, formerly of Tottenham Court Road, St. Pancras, Middlesex, but late of Fernton near Philadelphia. Probate to the sister, Sarah Perryman. (Apr. 1807).

Persey, Abraham, of Persey's Hundred, Virginia. Administration with will to the daughter, Mary Hill; the relict, Frances Persey, having died. (May 1633). Sh.Wi.

Percey, Richard, of the ship *Two Brothers*, (sick in Virginia). Probate to the relict, Annis Percey. (Mar. 1654). Sh.

Peter, William, of Philadelphia. Administration with will to John Thomas Henry Peter, attorney for the relict, Sarah Peter, in Philadelphia. (July 1853). New grant made in March 1894.

Peters, Edward, of Bristol, mariner, who had lands in Pennsylvania. Probate to the mother and surviving executor, Elizabeth Peters. (Feb. 1735).

Peters, John, of York County, Virginia, bachelor. Administration to William Evans, attorney for the mother, Mary, wife of John Evans, in York County. (Oct. 1759).

Peters, John, of Vermont, New York, Colonel of the Queen's Rangers, who died in Canada. Administration to the relict, Ann Peters. (May 1790).

Peterson alias Petterson, Gilbert, who died on the merchant ship *Prince Royal* in Virginia, bachelor. Probate to James Carrack. (Jan. 1724).

Petifer, Mary. *See* **Patton**.

Petrie, Ann, formerly Ann Perroneau, of Charles Town, South Carolina. Administration to Robert Williams, attorney for the husband, Edmund Petrie, in Charles Town. (June 1787).

Petrie, Frederick Henry, of Union, Monroe County, Virginia. Administration with will to John Miller, attorney for Elizabeth Clara, wife of Addison Dunlap, in Union. (July 1846).

Pettengell, Frederick, of South Carolina, bachelor. Administration to the sister, Ann, wife of Edward William Turner; the mother, Sarah Pettengell, having died. (Oct. 1843).

Pettengell, William Henn, of South Carolina. Administration to the relict, Ann Pettengell. (Oct. 1843).

Petterson. *See* **Peterson**.

Pettinger, John. *See* **Pottinger**.

Petty, Francis, of the ship *Hope*, (bound for New England). Probate to the relict, Sarah Petty. (Sep. 1693).

Pewsey, George, of Limehouse, Middlesex, master of the *Marmaduke* and trader to Virginia. Administration with will to the relict, Rebecca Pewsey. (Jan. 1637). *See* NGSQ 68/116).

Pfeffel, Peter Carl, formerly of Frankfurt am Main but late of New York, merchant, bachelor, who died at sea as a passenger on the steamship *President*. Administration to Adolphus Bach, attorney for the father, Carl Friederich Pfeffel, in Frankfurt. (Apr. 1842).

Pheasant, Rachel. *See* **Bartlett**.

Phelps, Edward, of Virginia, bachelor. Administration to the sister, Mary, wife of Jonathan Davis. (May 1678).

Phelps, Edwin, formerly of Hartpury, Gloucestershire, yeoman, but late of Limaville, Ohio. Administration to Henry Pritchard, attorney for the relict, Jane Phelps, in Limaville. (Aug. 1854).

Phillips, Ann, formerly of Wapping High Street, Wapping, Middlesex, but late of New York, widow. Administration to the brother, John Bluck. (July 1811).

Philipps, Erasmus John, Captain of the 35th Regiment of Foot, who died in New York. Administration with will to the daughter, Ann Fenwick, widow, administratrix of the mother, Ann Philipps deceased. (Sep. 1780).

Philipps, Caleb, of New England, who died on H.M. ship *Expedition*. Administration with will to James Harris of Bermondsey, Surrey, attorney for the relict, Elizabeth Philipps. (Jan. 1693).

Philips, Frederick, formerly of New York but late of Chester. Administration to the son, Frederick Philips; the relict, Elizabeth Philips, renouncing. (Oct. 1785). Revoked on his death and granted to the daughter, Eliza Ann Philips; the relict, Elizabeth Philips, still renouncing. (Feb. 1822).

Philips, Frederick, of Philipstown, Putnam County, New York. Administration to Frederick Codd, attorney for the only child, Mary, wife of Samuel Gouvernour, in New York City; the relict, Maria Philips, renouncing. (Feb. 1831).

Phillipps, Giles, formerly of Ipswich, Suffolk, but late of Pensacola, West Florida. Probate to the relict, Elizabeth Phillipps. (Jan. 1766).

Phillips, Gillam, of Boston, Massachusetts. Administration with will to Samuel Prince, administrator with will of the relict, Mary Phillips, who died without executing. (Aug. 1782).

Phillips, Grace Amos, of Cincinnati, United States of America. Administration to Joseph Isaac, attorney for the husband, Isaac Phillips, in Pleasant Hill, Missouri. (Oct. 1857).

Phillips, Henry, of Boston, New England, who died in Rochelle, France. Administration to the mother, Hannah Phillips, widow. (July 1729).

Phillips, Henry, of Exeter, New Hampshire. Probate to the relict, Elizabeth Phillips. (Aug. 1813).

Philips, John, of Pennsylvania, widower. Administration to James Philips,

Philips, *(contd.)* son and executor of the nephew and only next-of-kin, William Philips, who died before executing. (June 1775).

Phillips, John, of H.M. ship *Sultana*, who died in Virginia. Administration to the brother, Thomas Phillips; the relict, Elizabeth Phillips, having been cited but not having appeared. (July 1779).

Phillips, Lewis, of Huntingdon, whose cousin, John Throckmorton, was in Virginia. Probate to William Hally. (Mar. 1670).

Phillips, Mary, of Boston, Massachusetts, widow. Limited administration with will to Samuel Prince, attorney for Benjamin Faneuil and George Bethune. (Aug. 1782).

Philips, Nasel, of the merchant ship *Brunswick*, who died in Boston, New England. Probate to William Thompson with similar powers reserved to his wife, Joanna Thompson. (Feb. 1739).

Phillips, Patrick, formerly of Hungerford Market, Strand, Middlesex, but late of Bath Town, Virginia. Administration to the brother, Michael Phillips. (Nov. 1827). Revoked on his death and granted to the brother, William Phillips. (Mar. 1829). Revoked because grants were made on the false suggestion that the deceased was a childless widower, and now granted to the only child, Patrick Phillips; the relict, Susannah Morgan formerly Phillips, renouncing. (Aug. 1837).

Phillips, Thomas, of Maryland, clerk, bachelor. Administration to the sister, Elizabeth, wife of Lewis Lloyd. (Sep. 1739).

Philips, Thomas, of Boston, New England, Captain in Colonel Gooch's American Regiment, who died in Jamaica, widower. Administration to Robert Farmar, attorney for the only children, spinsters; all others with an interest having been cited but not having appeared. (Dec. 1747).

Philipps, William, of Boston, New England. Probate to John Lovelock. (Dec. 1727).

Phillips, William, of Stepney, Middlesex, who died on the merchant ship *Alexander* in Virginia, bachelor. Administration to the principal creditor, Dugall Ferguson. (Aug. 1728).

Phillips, William, Major-General of H.M. Forces, who died in New York City. Administration with will to the legatee in trust, William Collier; no executor having been named and Elizabeth Macaulay, formerly Browne, now the wife of Rev. Angus Macaulay, renouncing. (Apr. 1783). Revoked on the death of William Collier and granted to Thomas Forsyth. (Nov. 1797).

Philpott, Thomas, of Boston, North America, widower. Administration to the son, Henry Philpott. (Mar. 1833).

Phippen, George. *See* **Fitzpen**.

Phipping, William, of Wedmore, Somerset, whose daughter, Judah, was in New England. Probate to the daughter, Elizabeth, wife of John Addams. (Nov. 1650). Sh.

Phipps, John, of London, whose son, Henry Phipps, was in Maryland. Probate to the son, Henry Phipps. (Oct. 1673). Sh.

Phipps alias Sergeant, Lady Mary, of Boston, New England. Administration

Phipps alias Sergeant, *(contd.)* with will to John Metcalfe, attorney for Spencer Phipps alias Bennett. (Jan. 1707).

Phipps, Sir William, Governor of New England, who died in London. Probate to the relict, Lady Mary Phipps. (Jan. 1697). Sm.Wa.

Pierce. *See* **Pearce**.

Piggott, Rev. George, chaplain in Colonel John Wynyard's Regiment of Marines, who died in Jamaica. Administration to the son, Rev. George Piggott, attorney for the relict, Sarah Piggott, in New England. (June 1743).

Pyke, John, of Philadelphia, bachelor. Administration to the mother, Margaret Pyke, widow. (Apr. 1704).

Pike, John, formerly clerk of H.M. ships *Resolution*, *Iris* and *Jersey*, but late of New York City. Probate to Jane, wife of Thomas Griffin, formery Jane North. (Apr. 1793).

Pike, Richard, of Stoke Newington, Middlesex, who had lands in Pennsylvania. Probate by their solemn affirmation to Samuel Hoare and Nathaniel Newberry. (Apr. 1755). *See* NGSQ 61/34.

Pilkington, William, of Virginia. Administration to the brother, Sir Arthur Pilkington. (Oct. 1641).

Pinckney, Charles, of Charles Town, South Carolina. Probate to the son, Charles Cotesworth Pinckney, with similar powers reserved to the relict, Elizabeth Pinckney, and the son, Thomas Pinckney. (Mar. 1769).

Pinckney, Charles Cotesworth, of Charleston, South Carolina, General in the United States' Army. Administration with will to Benjamin Stead, attorney for the daughters, Maria Henrietta Pinckney, Harriott Pinckney, and Eliza Lucas Izard, widow, formerly wife of Ralph D. Izard, in Charleston; the wife, Mary Pinckney, having died in the testator's lifetime, and the sister, Harriott Horry, widow, and the brother, Thomas Pinckney, renouncing. (Apr. 1827).

Pindar, William, Rector of Mottisfount, Hampshire, clerk, whose kinsman, Thomas Shingleton alias Lea, was in Virginia. Administration with will by decree to Sarah Pindar, mother of the grandson, Samuel Pindar, during his minority; no executor having been named. (Feb. 1627). Wa.

Pinder, Mathew, of Virginia, bachelor. Administration to the brother, William Pinder. (June 1675).

Pine, Robert Edge, of Philadelphia. Probate to the relict, Mary Pine. (Dec. 1789).

Pine, Stephen, formerly of Ulster, New York, but late of King's County, North America, widower. Administration to Samuel Waddington, substitute attorney for the only child, Alpheus Pine, in King's County. (May 1789).

Pinhorne, John, of Halifax, Nova Scotia, Lieutenant of the 45th Regiment of Foot under Hugh Warburton, bachelor. Administration to Joseph Mico, attorney for the sister and next-of-kin, Mary Pinhorne, in New York. (Mar. 1765).

Pinhorne, Mary, of New York City, widow. Administration to George Streetfield, attorney for the son, John Pinhorne, in New York. (May 1740).

Pirsson, Joseph Poole, of New York City, counsellor at law. Administration with will to William Warren Hastings, attorney for the relict, Mary Chapman Pirsson, in New York. (Jan. 1848).

Pitcher, James, of New York City. Probate to the sister, Grace Pitcher, with similar powers reserved to William Porter and Cornelius Clopper. (May 1783). Revoked on her death and granted to the niece, Ann, wife of Thomas Broadbear, executrix of Grace Pitcher now deceased; the other executors, William Porter and Cornelius Clopper, having also died. (Mar. 1800).

Pitkin, James, Lieutenant of the First Connecticut Regiment of Foot, who died in Havana, bachelor. Administration with will to Phineas Lyman, attorney for the brother, Daniel Pitkin, in Hartford, Connecticut. (Jan. 1765).

Pitman, Henry, of Limehouse, Stepney, Middlesex, who died in Carolina. Administration to the relict, Elizabeth Pitman. (May 1701).

Pitt, Samuel Grove, of Ionia County, Michigan, bachelor. Administration to the brother, Peter Pitt; the father, William Pitt, renouncing. (Nov. 1854).

Plaisted. *See* **Playsted**.

Planck, John, of Serjeant's Inn, Fleet Street, London, who died in Wilmington, North America, bachelor. Administration to the creditor, Peter Planck; the sisters, Mary and Sarah Planck, renouncing. (Dec. 1795).

Platas, Antonio, of Baton Rouge, Louisiana, widower. Administration to the daughter, Maria Merced Platas. (June 1831).

Platts, Christopher, of King and Queen County, Maryland, who died in Holborn, Middlesex, clerk. Administration to the sister, Christiana Topham alias Platts, widow. (Nov. 1700).

Plaxton, George, of Barbados, who died in Salem, New England. Administration to the brother, William Plaxton. (Apr. 1736).

Playsted, Edward, of H.M. ship *Shoreham*, who died in Virginia, bachelor. Administration to the father, James Playsted. (May 1701).

Plaisted, Francis, of Boston, New England, who died at sea. Administration to the principal creditrix, Judith Butler, widow; the relict, Hester, now wife of James Gooch the younger, and the children having been cited but not having appeared. (Jan. 1733).

Pleasants, James, formerly of Richmond, United States of America, but late of Masanzas, Cuba, bachelor. Administration to Robert Auld, attorney for the creditor, James Ross; all others with an interest having been cited but not having appeared. (Apr. 1821).

Plenderleath, Gabriel George, of New York, bachelor and bastard. Administration to George Maule for the use of the Crown. (Jan. 1827).

Plesto, Edward, of Maryland, bachelor. Probate to the niece and next-of-kin, Mary, wife of Charles Boardman, administratrix of the sister,

Plesto, *(contd.)*
Catherine Eates alias Yeats deceased; the executors, Thomas Smith and William Thomas, renouncing. (Aug. 1727). Revoked and granted to William Yeates, son of Catherine Eates alias Yeates deceased; Mary Boardman, Thomas Smith and William Thomas having died. (Dec. 1735).

Plowden, Catherine, of Carolina, spinster. Administration to the sister, Anne Queladur alias Plowden, wife of Yves Queladur. (Feb. 1718).

Plowden, Sir Edmund, of Wanstead, Hampshire, Captain-General of New Albion, America. Probate to Henry Sharpe. (July 1659). Sh.

Plowden, Florence, of Havre de Grace, France, spinster. Administration to the sister, Anne Queladur alias Plowden, wife of Yves Queladur. (Feb. 1718).

Plowden, Frances, of Carolina, widow. Administration to the daughter, Anne, wife of Yves Queladur. (Apr. 1717).

Plowden, Thomas, of Lasham, Hampshire, who had lands in Virginia. Probate to the relict, Thomasine Plowden. (Sep. 1698).

Plumbe, Frances Margaretta, of Dubuque, Iowa, widow. Administration to the son, Richard Plumbe. (Oct. 1857).

Plummer, Benjamin, of Portsmouth, New Hampshire. Probate to Thomas Plummer with similar powers reserved to Theodore Atkinson. (Mar. 1741).

Plummer alias Passey, Samuel Aggs, of Philadelphia. Limited probate to the cousin, Francis Gardner. (Aug. 1829).

Plunket, David, of Baltimore, Maryland, merchant. Administration with will to Hon. William Conyngham Plunket. (Aug. 1818).

Pocock, Joseph, of Rochester, New York, widower. Administration to Charles Pocock, son and administrator of the father, Thomas Bartholomew Pocock deceased. (Dec. 1856).

Pocock, Sarah, of Rochester, New York. Administration to Charles Pocock, administrator of the husband, Joseph Pocock deceased. (Dec. 1856).

Pogson, Rev. George, of Charles Town, North America, bachelor and bastard. Administration to Rev. Thomas Preston for the use of the Crown. (Oct. 1789). Revoked on his death and granted to the natural brother, Thomas Pogson of Kingrave House, Suffolk, for the use of the Crown. (Nov. 1816).

Poinsett, Fanny alias Frances, formerly of Freshford, Somerset, but late of Charleston, South Carolina, widow. Limited administration with will to Joel Richards Poinsett, attorney for the daughter, Frances Poinsett, in Charleston. (Aug. 1806).

Poitevin alias Potovin, Sebastian, of Dartmouth, Devon, master of the *Pelican* of Dartmouth, who died in or near New England, bachelor. Administration to the brother and next-of-kin, Raymond Poitevin. (Jan. 1716).

Poizer, Thomas, soldier of the 22nd Regiment of Foot, who died in Captain Campbell's Company in Mobile, West Florida, bachelor. Probate to Elizabeth, wife of William Chipman. (June 1767).

Pollard, Edward, of Nashua, Hillsborough County, New Hampshire. Administration to Matthew Forster, attorney for the father, Cumings Pollard, in Nashua. (Aug. 1841).

Pollard, Francis, of Grenada and Martinique, who died in Boston, New England. Probate to James Inglis with similar powers reserved to John Inglis. (July 1800).

Pollard, John, formerly of Carey Street, St. Clement Danes, Middlesex, but late of Philadelphia. Administration to the sister and next-of-kin, Sarah, wife of Charles Price; the relict, Mary Pollard, having been cited but not having appeared. (Oct. 1809).

Pollock, Thomas, of Paisley, Scotland, merchant, widower. Administration to William Swainson, attorney for the sons, George and Thomas Pollock, in Boston, North America. (Nov. 1838).

Pomeroy, Robert, seaman of H.M. ships *Vigilant* and *Vindictive*, who died in Philadelphia. Probate to the relict, Ann, now wife of Robert Hunter. (Mar. 1790).

Pond, Samuel, of Virginia. Limited administration to Micajah Perry of St. Katherine Creechurch, London, merchant, attorney for the relict, Rebecca, now wife of Thomas Mountfort. (July 1698).

Ponsonby, Richard, formerly of Whitehaven, Cumberland, but late of Maryland, bachelor. Administration to the niece, Elizabeth, wife of Isaac Nicholson; the sisters and only next-of-kin, Elizabeth, wife of Isaac Brown, Jane Nicholson, widow, Mary, wife of Richard Clark, Bridget Topping, widow, and Dinah McDougal, widow, having died. (Feb. 1837).

Poole, Elizabeth. *See* **Rolfe**.

Poole, Richard, formerly of East Florida but late of Roseau, Dominica. Administration to Robert Payne, attorney for the relict, Hannah Poole, in Roseau. (Sep. 1790).

Poole, Thomas, physician of Lord Howe's fleet, who died in Long Island, bachelor. Administration to the brother, Edward Poole. (Sep. 1778).

Pope, Alexander, of Jamaica, who died in Philadelphia, bachelor. Administration to the brother, Thomas Pope. (Mar. 1787).

Pope, Charles, formerly of Bishopstone, Wiltshire, farmer, but late of Newgarden, United States of America. Administration to the sister and only next-of-kin, Elizabeth, wife of Isaac Archer; the relict, Susannah Pope, renouncing. (Dec. 1830).

Pope, Francis, formerly of Bristol but late of Rhode Island. Probate by his solemn declaration to John Harford with similar powers reserved to Thomas Powell. (July 1788).

Pope, Mary, of Newport, Rhode Island, spinster. Administration to James Davenant, attorney for the father, Francis Pope, in Newport. (Aug. 1749).

Pope, Thomas, of St. Philip and James, Bristol, merchant, who had lands in Virginia. Probate to Richard Gotley with similar powers reserved to Charles Jones. (Oct. 1685).

Poppleton, William, of St. Giles Cripplegate, London, who had lands in Virginia. Probate to William Emerson with similar powers reserved to

Poppleton, *(contd.)*
William Thorowgood and Richard Buffington. (July 1632). Wi.

Porcher, James, of St. Peter's parish, South Carolina. Administration to the relict, Mary J. Porcher. (Oct. 1824).

Pordage, Joshua, of St. Botolph Bishopsgate, London, whose son, George Pordage, was in Boston, New England. Probate to Thomas Major. (June 1691). Wa.

Porter, Frederick, of Boston, New England, Captain of the Third Batallion of the Royal American Regiment. Administration with will to William Hodshon, attorney for Metatiah Brown, James Bowdoin, and the relict, Mahettable Porter, in Boston. (Feb. 1762).

Porter, Thomas, of New York. Probate to George Streatfield, attorney for John Fred in New York. (July 1724).

Porteus, Edward, of Gloucester County, Virginia. Limited administration with will to Geoffrey Jeffreys, attorney for the relict, Margaret Porteus, in Virginia. (Oct. 1700). Wi.

Portman, Robert, who died overseas having goods in Virginia. Probate to the sister, Margaret Portman. (Aug. 1654). Sh.

Postlethwaite, George, of New York City, bachelor. Administration to the father, Richard Postlethwaite. (July 1803).

Potovin. *See* **Potevin.**

Potten, John. *See* **Patten.**

Pottinger, James, Lieutenant of Major Rogers' Company of Rangers, who died in Ticonderoga, bachelor. Administration to the mother, Agnes Pottinger. (Feb. 1764).

Pottinger alias Pettinger alias Pattinger, John, formerly of New York City but late boatswain of H.M. ship *Caroline*. Administration to John Fallowfield Scott, attorney for the mother, Ruth Pettinger, in New York. (July 1820).

Potts, Joseph, of Philadelphia, Lieutenant of half pay of the Royal Navy. Administration with will to Oliver Toulmin, attorney for the relict, Miriam Potts, in Philadelphia. (Sep. 1773).

Potts, Joseph, of Maryland. Probate to the brother, Selby Potts. (Apr. 1777).

Potts, Theophilus, of Virginia, bachelor. Administration to the sister, Sarah, wife of Edward Huit. (July 1678).

Pouls alias Poulson, Paul, of Virginia, bachelor. Administration to the principal creditor, Andrew Anderson. (May 1684).

Poulter, Hannah. *See* **Wallin.**

Pountes, John, citizen and clothworker of London, who supervised the Virginia fisheries. Probate to Sir Thomas Merry. (June 1624). Wa.

Powell, Howell, of New York City, widower. Administration to the daughter, Margaret, wife of Griffith Edwards. (Jan. 1842).

Powell, Hugh, of Bridgenorth, Shropshire, who died in Philadelphia, bachelor. Administration to the sister, Jane Powell. (Dec. 1771).

Powell, James, of [Abbey] Dore, Herefordshire, who died in Maryland, bachelor. Administration to the brother and next-of-kin, William Powell. (Apr. 1747). Revoked on his death and granted to Edward

Powell, *(contd.)* Westmore, attorney for the brother, Hugh Powell, in [Abbey] Dore. (Feb. 1755).

Powell, John, of St. Michael Crooked Lane, London, whose cousin was in Virginia. Probate to the relict, Ann Powell. (Dec. 1624). Wi.

Powell, John, of New England, who died at sea on the frigate *Moncke*, bachelor. Administration to the principal creditor, Thomas Raye. (Feb. 1673).

Powell, John, formerly of Boston, New England, but late of Ludlow, Shropshire. Probate to Grant Allan and the daughter, Jane Powell. (June 1799).

Powell, John Parry, formerly of Moor Park, Brecon, but late of St. Louis, Missouri, widower. Administration to the son, William John Powell. (Dec. 1841).

Powell, Joseph, formerly of Leominster, Herefordshire, but late of New York, plumber and glazier. Probate to Thomas Brayer the younger. (Apr. 1833).

Powell, Richard, of Virginia. Administration to the uncle and next-of-kin, William Powell. (Nov. 1654).

Powell, William the elder, of Virginia. Administration to the brother, William Powell (*sic*). (Aug. 1651).

Power, Emily, of Youghall, Cork County, Ireland, who died in Utica, New York, spinster. Administration to the brother, George Farmer Power; the mother and next-of-kin, Emily Bromfield Power, having died. (Nov. 1856).

Power, Lucy, of King William County, Virginia, widower. Administration to the son, Jack Power. (Sep. 1769).

Power, Thomas, of St. Margaret Lothbury, London, who died in Virginia. Administration to the son, Benjamin Power. (July 1686).

Powles, Thomas, of Ohio, bachelor. Administration to the brother, James Powles; the father, James Powles, renouncing. (Aug. 1856).

Powling, Benjamin, of Illinois. Administration to the relict, Elizabeth Powling. (May 1855).

Powys, Thomas, of London, who died in Boston, New England, bachelor. Administration to the brother, Richard Powys. (Sep. 1684).

Poyntell, William, of Philadelphia. Administration with will to the son, George Poyntell; the executor, Paul Beck, Robert Alexander Caldcleugh, and the son, William Poyntell, having been cited but not having appeared. (Mar. 1812). Revoked on the death of George Poyntell and granted to William Taylor, attorney for Robert A. Caldcleugh, Paul Beck and the son, William Poyntell, in Philadelphia. (Oct. 1812).

Poynton, Thomas, of Shrewsbury, Shropshire. Administration with will to Lewis Deblois, attorney for the relict, Hannah Poynton, in Salem, Massachusetts, after evidence that she and the testator were married in St. Peter's, Salem, in 1743. (Mar. 1792).

Pratt, Caleb, of H.M. ship *York*, bachelor. Administration to Daniel Ballard, attorney for the father, Caleb Pratt, in Boston, New England. (Jan. 1748).

Pratt, Horace Southworth, of Tuskaloosa, Alabama. Administration to James Bullock Dunwody, attorney for the relict, Isabel Ann Pratt, in Tuskaloosa. (May 1843).

Pratt, Jane Farley, of Tuskaloosa, Alabama. Administration to James Bullock Dunwody, administrator of Horace S. Pratt deceased, and attorney for his relict, Isabel Ann Pratt, in Tuskaloosa. (June 1843).

Pratt, John, formerly of Virginia, merchant, but late of Chelsea, Middlesex. Probate to Joseph Windham, Roger Tubley and Phillip Perry with similar powers reserved to William Hunt. (July 1731).

Pratt, Josiah, of Boston, New England, bachelor. Administration to the brother and nect-of-kin, James Pratt. (July 1767).

Pratt, Samuel, of Boston, New England, bachelor. Administration to the brother and next-of-kin, James Pratt. (July 1767).

Predix, Gabriel, of Virginia. Administration with will to the principal creditor, Peter Senth; the relict, Susanna Predix, renouncing. (July 1697).

Preece, Henry, of California, America, who died at sea, bachelor. Administration to the mother and next-of-kin, Martha, wife of John James Catton. (Dec. 1850).

Prentis, Alice, of New England, widow. Administration to Joseph Marion, attorney for the son, John Prentis, in New England. (May 1701).

Prentis, John, formerly of New London, Connecticut, afterwards of St. Martin in the Fields, Middlesex, but late commander of H.M. ship *Defence*. Limited probate to William Bowdoin. (Aug. 1746).

Preston, Richard, of Patuxent, Maryland. Administration with will to the son, John Preston, during the absence overseas of the executors, Peter Sharpe, Thomas Taylor, William Berry and John Meares. (Aug. 1670).

Preswick, Mary, of Mount Pleasant, New York, widow. Administration to William Maryan, attorney for the son, Christopher Preswick, now at sea. (Aug. 1815).

Prevost, William, of Cincinnati, Ohio. Probate to Thomas James. (Jan. 1830). Further grant in November 1859.

Prewitt, Robert, of New England, who died on H.M. ship *Devonshire*. Administration to the son, Robert Prewitt. (May 1697).

Pryce, Charles, of Savannah, Georgia. Probate to the father, Charles Pryce, with similar powers reserved to William Stephens and James Habersham. (July 1780).

Price, Edward, of Somerset County, Maryland, bachelor. Administration to the brother, William Price. (Nov. 1714).

Price, Francis, of Maryland, bachelor. Administration to the cousin and next-of-kin, Richard Price. (Feb. 1714).

Price, Hopkin, formerly of Stepney, Middlesex, but late of Rappahannock River, Middlesex County, Virginia. Probate to Thurston Withnall. (Nov. 1679). Wi.

Price, John, of the Precinct of the Tower, London, who died in Virginia. Administration to the relict, Anne Price. (May 1668).

Prise, John, of Shadwell, Middlesex, who died overseas (bound for

Prise, *(contd.)*
Virginia). Probate to the relict, Joanne Prise. (Sep. 1677).

Price, John, of H.M. ship *Mermaid*, who died in South Carolina, bachelor. Probate to Mary Rea. (July 1753).

Price, Richard, of St. Margaret, Westminster, Middlesex, citizen and vintner of London and adventurer to Virginia. Probate to the relict, Margaret Price. (Nov. 1630).

Price, Roger, of Virginia. Probate to the son, Richard Price, with similar powers reserved to William Price. (May 1672).

Price, William, formerly of Beckett, Berkshire, but late of New York, bachelor. Administration to the father, Barrington Price. (Apr. 1818).

Prickett, Miles, of St. Cross near Canterbury, Kent, adventurer to Virginia. Probate to the brother, John Prickett. (June 1627). Wa.

Priest, Henry, of New York City, widower. Limited administration to George Dollond, attorney for the sons, William Henry Priest, Frederic Dollond Priest, and Edward Carleton Priest, in New York. (Dec. 1815).

Prime, Richard Airey, of New Orleans. Probate to the sisters, Mary Airey Prime and Cornelia Airey Prime. (Apr. 1818).

Primerose, Catherine, of Charleston, South Carolina, widow. Probate to Christopher Gadsden Morris with similar powers reserved to Hugh Perroneau Dawes. (Aug. 1841).

Primerose, Robert, of Charleston, South Carolina. Probate to Christopher Gadsden and Hugh Perroneau with similar powers reserved to Adam Tunno and James Lamb. (Aug. 1825).

Primus, John, of H.M. ship *St. Albans'* prize, who died in Virginia, bachelor. Probate to Prudence Poulsen, widow. (Oct. 1697).

Prinn, Nicholas, of Stepney, Middlesex, who died in Virginia. Probate to the relict, Dorothy Prinn. (May 1684).

Prior, James, of Newport, Rhode Island, who died on H.M. ship *Hussar*. Administration to William Maude, attorney for the relict, Lydia Prior, in Newport. (June 1769).

Pryor, William, who died overseas having lands in Virginia. Administration with will to Jasper Clayton and Thomas Harrison during the minority of the daughters, Margaret and Mary Pryor. (Apr. 1647). Revoked and granted to the daughter, Mary Pryor, on her coming of age. (Nov. 1660). Sh.Wi.

Prise. *See* **Price**.

Pritchard, Hesther, of Holborn, Middlesex, widow, whose granddaughter, Elizabeth, daughter of Robert Pritchard, was in Virginia. Probate to Richard Shute with similar powers reserved to Anne Turner. (July 1691). Wi.

Prichard, James, of Hyde Park, Dutchess County, New York. Administration with will to James Prichard, attorney for Peter Schryver in Hyde Park. (May 1840).

Prichard, John, of Bell Town, Maryland. Probate to Anthony Donne. (Jan. 1742).

Pritts, Benedict, of the ship *Merchant's Delight*, who died in Virginia, bachelor. Administration to the principal creditrix, Hester Gateley alias Getley, widow. (Sep. 1681).

Proberts, John, of Philadelphia and of the merchant ship *Alexander*, who died in St. Thomas's Hospital, Southwark, Surrey. Administration to William Playter, attorney for the relict, Grace Proberts, in Philadelphia. (Nov. 1742).

Proctor, Thomas, of Stepney, Middlesex, who had goods in Virginia. Probate to the uncle, William Gray. (Nov. 1624). Revoked on his death and administration granted to the relict, Jane Proctor alias Squire, during the minority of the son, Samuel Proctor. (Nov. 1625). Wi.

Prole, George, of Stafford, New York, bachelor. Administration to the niece, Marian Elizabeth Harris; the brothers and only next-of-kin, Frederick and Henry Prole, renouncing. (Jan. 1844).

Prosser, Mathias, of St. Giles Cripplegate, London, who died in Virginia. Administration to the grandmother, Jane Prosser alias Pitt alias Pindar alias Sayward. (Sep. 1667).

Prout, Robert, formerly of Bristol, afterwards of Charles Town, South Carolina, but late of Halifax, Nova Scotia. Probate to the brother, William Prout. (Aug. 1783).

Provoast, Elias, of New York, who died on H.M. ship *Samuel and Henry* in Virginia. Administration with will to John Castle; no executor having been named. (June 1691).

Prowell, Joseph, formerly of Demarara and Berbice, but late of Philadelphia. Probate to Robert Pulsford with similar powers reserved to John Wilson, John Douglas and David Lenox. (Feb. 1806).

Pryce. *See* **Price**.

Pryor. *See* **Prior**.

Puffer, George, of New York, merchant, widower. Administration to the creditor, Peter Puffer; the son, George Shelford Puffer, renouncing for himself and as guardian of the other children, Caroline Augusta, Elizabeth, Charles Drevar, Emily and Joan Parton Puffer. (Aug. 1837).

Puffer, Matilda Brown, of New York, spinster. Administration to the creditor, Peter Puffer; the brothers and sisters renouncing. (Aug. 1837).

Pugh, Eliza, wife of William Pugh, of Philadelphia. Limited administration with will to Samuel James Blacklow and David Morrison. (Nov. 1838).

Punfield, Samuel, formerly of Birmingham, Warwickshire, but late of Baltimore, Maryland, bachelor. Administration to the sister and next-of-kin, Elizabeth Punfield. (Dec. 1801).

Purchase, James, formerly of Haselbury Plucknett, Somerset, but late of Arkansas. Probate to Joseph Purchase and Adam Rendall. (Apr. 1851).

Purdy, David, of New Town, New York, Lieutenant on half pay in General Edmund Fanning's American Regiment. Administration to James Tidbury, attorney for the relict, Maria Purdy, in New Town. (Dec. 1827).

Purdy, Gilbert, of Ulster County, New York, widower. Administration to James Phyn, attorney for the son, David Purdy, at the Bay of Quinty, Quebec. (Dec. 1790).

Purkis, George, of New England, who died in Algiers. Administration to the principal creditor, John Lake. (Apr. 1682).

Putnam, John, soldier of the Connecticut Regiment of Foot, who died in Havana. Administration to Phineas Lyman, attorney for the father, Henry Putnam, in Massachusetts. (Dec. 1763).

Putnam, John Chandler, of Boston, Massachusetts. Limited administration with will to George Pope, attorney for the relict, Abigail Smith Putnam, in Boston. (Nov. 1840).

Putnam, Thomas, aboard the *Increase* bound for Virginia. Administration with will to Thomas Putnam during the absence in Virginia of the relict, Dorothy Putnam, and the son, Thomas Putnam. (May 1659). Wi.

Pye, Edward Henry, of Cornwallis's Neck, Charles County, Maryland. Administration with will to William Barksdale, attorney for the brothers, James B. Pye and Nicholas Stonestreet, in America. (Jan. 1826).

Pyke. *See* **Pike**.

Pynchon, William, of Wraysbury, Buckinghamshire, whose daughter, Margaret Davis, was in Boston, whose sons, John Pynchon and Eliazar Holioke, were also in New England, and who had goods in Virginia. Probate to John Wickens. (Dec. 1662). Wa.

Q

Quarles, Aaron, of King William County, Virginia. Probate to John Quarles the younger with similar powers reserved to Joseph Fox and Bartholomew Dandridge. (Dec. 1771).

Quicke, William, of Christ Church, London, who had lands in Virginia. Probate to the relict, Elizabeth Quicke, with similar powers reserved to Roger Harris. (Jan. 1615). Wa.

Quigly, Elizabeth, formerly Elizabeth Moore, of Virginia. Administration to the husband, James Quigly. (Dec. 1789).

Quiney, Richard, of St. Stephen Wallbrook, London, who had lands in Virginia. Probate to the son, Richard Quiney. (Jan. 1657).

Quinn, Peter, of Springfield, United States of America, bachelor. Administration to the brother, Philip Quinn; the relict, Honora Quinn, renouncing. (Oct. 1847).

R

Rabbeth, Susannah, nee Susannah Bentley, formerly of Clay Bridge, Lincolnshire, but late of New York City. Administration to Frederick Burton, attorney for the husband, James Rabbeth, in New York City. (May 1845).

Rabey, Peter, of the merchant ship *Rainbow*, who died in Virginia, bachelor. Administration to the principal creditor, Paul Boucher. (Mar. 1705).

Rably, William, of Philadelphia, who died at sea. Administration to the principal creditor, Richard Deeble; the brother and sister, John and Mary Rably, renouncing. (Feb. 1731).

Raboteau, Charles the younger, of Philadelphia. Administration to Joseph Reed, attorney for the relict, Mary Raboteau, in Philadelphia. (Mar. 1784).

Radburn, Thomas, formerly of Chipping Norton, Oxfordshire, but late of Charleston, North (*sic*) Carolina, widow. Administration with will to the only child, Elizabeth, wife of William Faulkener; the wife, Mary Radburn, having died in the testator's lifetime. (June 1826).

Radcliffe, Anne. *See* **Jennings**.

Radford, George, of Dartmouth and Lympston, Devon, who died in New York, mariner. Inventory 1759. [*Administration Act not found*].

Rae, James, of Maryland. Probate to John Glissell. (Mar. 1703).

Rae, William Glen, of San Francisco, Upper California. Administration with will to Edward Roberts, attorney for John McLoughlin in Fort Vancouver, Columbia River; Sir George Simpson renouncing. (June 1849). Further grant in April 1863.

Ragg. *See* **Wragg**

Rainborowe, William, of St. Leonard Eastcheap, London, whose daughter, Martha, wife of Thomas Cotymore, was in New England. Probate to the sons, Thomas and William Rainborowe. (Apr. 1642). Wa.

Rainbow, Richard, of H.M. ship *Burford*, who died on H.M. ship *Nonsuch*. Administration to the maternal aunt, Susan, wife of James Scott of the merchant ship *Richard and Sarah*, in New England. (Feb. 1713).

Raitt, Alexander, formerly of Kittery, Maine, who died at sea. Administration to George Muirson Woolsey, attorney for the son, William Raitt, in Eliot, Kittery; the relict, Miriam Raitt, having died. (May 1825).

Ramsay, Charles, of H.M. ship *Harwich*, who died in America, bachelor. Administration with will to Henry Mills, attorney for the brother, John Ramsay, in New York. (Feb. 1761).

Ramsay, James, Captain of an Independent Company of Fusiliers, who died in New York. Administration to Eleanor Ramsay, attorney for the relict, Catharine Ramsay, in New York. (Apr. 1745).

Ramsay, James, of Charles Town, South Carolina, M.D. Administration to Robert Goulding, attorney for the relict, Eleanor Ramsay, in Charles Town. (May 1833).

Rand, James, of St. Mary Colechurch, London, a creditor of William Bancks in Virginia. Probate to Mary Gould, wife of Christopher Gould; the relict, Grace Rand, having died. (May 1686). Wa.

Randall, Richard, of St. Olave, Southwark, Surrey, who died in Virginia. Administration to the relict, Anne Randall. (Jan. 1693).

Randall, Robert, of Virginia, bachelor. Administration to Robert Crosby, attorney for the brother and next-of-kin, George Randall, now overseas. (Nov. 1726).

Randolph, Benjamin, formerly of Bristol but late of Virginia. Administration with will to James Randolph, attorney for the brother, Thomas Eston Randolph, in Albemarle County, Virginia. (Sep. 1818).

Randolph, Brett, formerly of Virginia but late of Dursley, Gloucestershire. Probate to the relict, Mary Randolph, and to John Scott with similar powers reserved to James Murray, Joseph Farrell and John Markham. (Oct. 1759). Wi.

Randolph, Edward, of Acquamat, Virginia. Administration with will to Sarah, wife of John Howard, guardian of the minor daughter, Sarah Randolph. (Nov. 1703).

Randolph, Hon. Peter, of Chatsworth, Henrico County, Virginia, Surveyor-General of Customs for the Middle Western District of America. Administration with will to William Robertson Lidderdale, attorney for Archibald Cary, Richard Randolph and John Wayles, and for Seth Ward in Virginia. (Oct. 1768).

Ranolds. *See* **Reynolds**.

Raper, Robert, of Charles Town, South Carolina. Limited administration with will to William Raper. (Oct. 1789).

Rapp, John, formerly of Holborn, Middlesex, but late of Baltimore, North America, merchant, widower. Administration to the only child, John Rapp. (Nov. 1838).

Ratcliff, James, of the 62nd Regiment of Foot, who died in Boston. Administration to the uncle and next-of-kin, Robert Ratcliff. (Apr. 1781).

Ratcliffe, John. *See* **Sicklemore**.

Ratcliffe, John, of the Emigrant Refuge, Ward Island, New York, bachelor. Administration to the father, Thomas Ratcliffe. (Jan. 1856).

Ravaud, Ferdinand, of New York. Administration to Sampson Broughton, husband and attorney of the relict, Mary Broughton alias Ravaud, and for the only child, Susan Ravaud, in New York. (Sep. 1708). Revoked on the death of Sampson Broughton and granted to Mark Anthony Ravaud as attorney. (May 1714).

Ravaud, Susan. *See* **Kearny**.

Rawlins, Edward, of New York, bachelor. Administration to the principal creditor, Thomas Butler. (Feb. 1678).

Rawlins, George, of Virginia. Administration to the brother, Giles Rawlins. (Jan. 1654).

Rawlins, Joseph, formerly of St. Christopher's but late of Baltimore, Maryland. Probate to the surviving executor, William Manning, with similar powers reserved to John Hutchinson Nallwin and Edward Fleming Akers. (Apr. 1797).

Raydon, William, of Philadelphia. Probate to John Tyzack. (Jan. 1696).

Rayment, George, of Glastonbury, Somerset, whose children, William, John and Elizabeth Rayment, were in New England. Probate to the son, Maurice Rayment. (Oct. 1651). Sh.Wa.

Rayment, John, who died overseas (bound for Virginia on the *Friendship*). Administration with will to the relict, Mary Graves alias Rayment. (Sep. 1630). Sh.Wa.

Rayner, Roger, of Burnham Abbey, Buckinghamshire, whose kinsman, John Rayner, was in New England. Probate to Thomas Rayner. (Oct. 1682). Wa.

Reade, Alexander, of Middlesex County, Virginia. Limited probate to the surviving executor, George Thornburgh. (July 1767).

Reid, Andrew, of Charles Town, South Carolina. Administration with will to John Tunno, attorney for Robert Johnson and John Wagner in Charles Town. (June 1784).

Read, George, of Whitechapel, Middlesex, who died on the ship *Culpepper* in Virginia. Probate to the relict, Margaret Read. (Oct. 1685).

Reade, Hayden, First Lieutenant of Marines on half pay, who died in New York, bachelor. Administration to the mother, Mary Reade, widow. (Dec. 1796).

Reed, Isaac, of Boston, New England, who died on H.M. ship *Tyger*'s prize. Probate to Mark Poyd. (Nov. 1695).

Read, James, of Beaufort, South Carolina. Administration to the relict, Elizabeth, now wife of John Hammond. (July 1791).

Read, John, of Bristol, who died in Virginia. Administration with will to the relict, Mary Read; no executor having been named. (July 1688). Wa.

Reed, Robert, of Southwark, Surrey, mariner of the ship *Baltimore*, bound for Virginia. Probate to the relict, Elizabeth Reed. (Dec. 1705).

Reade, Thomas, of Wickford, Essex, who had lands in New England. Probate to the relict, Priscilla Reade. (Nov. 1662). Wa.

Reade, Thomas, of Colchester, Essex, carpenter, whose son, Thomas Reade, and son-in-law, Daniel Bacon, were in New England. Probate to Isaac Reade and John Clarke. (Mar. 1666).

Reade, Thomas, who died overseas (bound for Virginia). Probate to the brother, William Reade. (June 1663). Wa.

Reed, Thomas, of New York, who died on the island of Goree. Administration to David Knor, attorney for the relict, Euphen Reed, in New York. (May 1802).

Reed, William, of Newcastle-upon-Tyne, whose children, George, Ralph and Abigael Reed, were in New England. Administration with will to the relict, Mabell Reed. (Oct. 1656). Sh.Wa.

Read, William, of New England and of the ship *Granada*, who died in Jamaica. Probate to Elizabeth Harlock with similar powers reserved to John Harlock. (Sep. 1692). Wa.

Reed, William, of H.M. ship *Southampton*, who died on James River, Virginia. Probate to David Cluny. (July 1703).

Reading, Richard, of Aurora, New York. Probate to the nephew, Thomas Reading. (July 1851).

Reddicliffe, Ann C. *See* **Cutmore**.

Redmond, Edward, formerly of Bow Churchyard, afterwards of Milk Street, Cheapside, London, but late of Philadelphia. Probate to Henry Redmond. (June 1804).

Redrup, Abel, formerly of Saunderton, Buckinghamshire, but late of Royalton near Cincinnati, Ohio. Probate to the surviving executor, Joseph Allen. (Apr. 1849).

Redwood, Abraham, recently of Newport, Rhode Island, but late of Mendon, Massachusetts. Probate to the son, Abraham Redwood, with similar powers reserved to Joseph Clarke. (Feb. 1789).

Redwood, Langford, of Flushing, New York. Administration with will to John Coles Symes, James Trecothick and John Henry Roper the younger, attornies for John McCahill and David Maitland in New York City. (Sep. 1844)

Reece, Thomas, of Philadelphia. Administration to the relict, Sarah Reece. (Mar. 1777).

Reeks, Nicholas, of the merchant ship *William and Sarah*, who died in Maryland. Probate to Samuel Spurrier. (Oct. 1734).

Reeve, Ann. *See* **Fenner**.

Reeve, James, of Bristol, who died on passage to Pennsylvania. Administration to the father, Charles Reeve; the relict, Jane Reeve, having gone to Pennsylvania. (Aug. 1714).

Reeve, Stephen, of New York City, widower. Administration to Robert Pears, attorney for the only child, Ann, wife of Richard Sankey Fenner, in New York City. (May 1838). Revoked on her death and granted to her administrator, Alexander Cowell, attorney for Richard Sankey Fenner in Baltimore, North America. (Oct. 1848).

Reeves, Charlotte, of Charles Town, South Carolina. Probate to James Murray and James Freshfield with similar powers reserved to the sister, Ann Elliott, spinster. (Dec. 1789).

Reeves, Elizabeth, of Chester, Delaware County, United States of America, widow. Administration to George White, attorney for the son, Hiram Reeves, in Philadelphia. (May 1854).

Reeves, George, of Virginia, widower. Administration to the brother, Charles Reeves. (Mar. 1689). Revoked on the introduction of a will and probate granted to the same. (Apr. 1689). Wi.

Reid. *See* **Read**.

Reilly, Charles, of Charlestown, North America, merchant. Limited administration to John Hopton. (June 1807).

Remington, Jonathan, of New England, who died on H.M. ship *Pearl*. Administration to Jeremiah Fones, attorney for the relict, Larana Remington, in New England. (Oct. 1751).

Remnant, John, of H.M. ship *Pearl*, who died in Virginia, bachelor. Probate to John Macky. (Feb. 1743).

Remnant, John, formerly of St. Giles in the Fields, Middlesex, but late of Alexandria, North America, bachelor. Administration to the brother and next-of-kin, Richard Remnant. (July 1793).

Remsen, Peter, of New York City. Probate to the son and surviving executor, Simeon Remsen. (July 1792).

Renaud, Charlotte, of Philadelphia, widow. Administration to the only child, Charlotte, wife of Francis Gordon. (Jan. 1804).

Renton, Joseph, of the merchant ship *Rose*, who died in Virginia, bachelor. Probate to Cuthbert Birkley. (July 1742).

Renwick, Robert [*William in the Act*], of New York City. Administration to John Mountgomery, attorney for the relict, Jane Renwick, in New York. (Dec. 1816).

Reynell, Emily, of Louisville, Kentucky, spinster. Administration to the sister, Mary Anne, wife of Elijah Carter; the mother, Lydia Reynell, widow, having died. (Dec. 1845).

Ranolds, Samuel, of H.M. ship *Fox*, who died in South Carolina, bachelor. Probate to Richard Miller. (Aug. 1732).

Reynolds, William, of Philadelphia, widower. Limited administration to Richard Gwynn, attorney for the only child, Herbert Reynolds, in Philadelphia. (Dec. 1853).

Rhodes, Nathaniel, of Virginia, bachelor. Administration by decree to the brother, James Rhodes; the mother, Ester Rhodes, widow, renouncing. (Sep. 1697).

Roades, William, of Maryland, bachelor. Administration to the brother, Thomas Roades. (Jan. 1727).

Rhodes, William, of St. Pancras Soper Lane, London, who died in Philadelphia. Administration to the relict, Isabella Rhodes. (Mar. 1733).

Ricard, Francis, formerly of Jersey but late of the 29th Regiment of Foot, who died in New England, bachelor. Administration to Noah Le Cras, attorney for the father, Edward Ricard, in Jersey. (Mar. 1773).

Rice, David, of Annapolis in America. Probate to the relict, Anne Rice. (Sep. 1724).

Rice, Robert, of Preston, Suffolk, whose brother-in-law, Samuel Appleton, was in New England. Administration to the next-of-kin, William Hobart. (Nov. 1638). Revoked on the introduction of a will and probate granted to Sarah Allen. (Feb. 1639). Wa.

Rich, Jeremiah, of Stepney, Middlesex, who died in Virginia. Administration to the relict, Sarah Rich. (July 1682).

Rich, Sir Nathaniel, of Dalham, Suffolk, who made a bequest to

Rich, *(contd.)* Nathaniel Browne in New England. Probate to Edward, Viscount Mandeville. (Dec. 1636). Wa.

Richards, George, of St. Botolph Aldgate, London, who had goods in Virginia. Probate to the son, Phillip Richards. (Apr. 1694). Revoked on his death and administration granted to his sister and administratrix, Sarah Perry alias Richards. (Apr. 1695). Wi.

Richards, John, of Teston, Kent, who died in Virginia, widower. Administration to the creditor, John Thunder. (Mar. 1745). Revoked on his death and granted to his executor, John Watkins. (Oct. 1765).

Richards, Samuel, of the ship *Elizabeth*, who died in Virginia on the King's service. Administration to the relict, Elizabeth Richards. (Jan. 1668).

Richards, Thomas, of Alverstoke, Hampshire, who died in Virginia. Administration to the relict, Mary Richards. (July 1677).

Richards, William, of St. Martin in the Fields, Middlesex, who died on the merhant ship *Easter* in Carolina. Probate to the relict, Elizabeth Richards. (June 1722).

Richards, William Fayting, of Old Providence, North America, bachelor. Administration to the half-sister, Jane Kirkland, spinster; the mother, Ann Kirkland, widow, renouncing. (Dec. 1843).

Richardson, Anthony, of Limehouse, Middlesex, who died in Virginia. Administration to the relict, Sarah Richardson. (Sep. 1656).

Richardson, Richard, who died in Pennsylvania. Administration to the principal creditor, John Marsden. (June 1700).

Richardson, William, of Maryland, who died in Rotherhithe, Surrey. Probate by his solemn affirmation to Thomas Plumsted. (Mar. 1732).

Richardson, William, formerly of Kensington, Middlesex, but late of Cross Oak, Wiltshire, who died in Pensacola. Administration with will to the sister and next-of-kin, Mary, wife of Rev. William Robinson; the executor, Thomas Athawes, having died, and the other executor, Samuel Commeline, renouncing. (Feb. 1769). Revoked on the death of Mary Robinson and granted to her son, Rev. Matthew Robinson. (Nov. 1794). Revoked and limited administration granted to Dame Mary Brydges. (July 1828).

Richardson, Zachariah, formerly of Bermondsey, Surrey, but late of Philadelphia. Probate by their solemn affirmation to the relict, Rebecca Richardson, and to Thomas Bincks and John Warner. (Feb. 1736). *See* NGSQ 61/3.

Richman, Francis Henry, of Philadelphia. Probate to Emanuel Loury and to the relict, Hannah Richman. (June 1856).

Richmond, George, of Boston, North America, bachelor. Administration to the sister and only next-of-kin, Ord Lind, widow. (Feb. 1819).

Richmond, Richard, of St. Leonard Foster Lane, London, whose sister, Margaret Richmond, was in Virginia. Probate to the relict, Grace Richmond. (Jan. 1685). Wa.

Ricketts, Ann, of St. Helier, Jersey, widow. Administration to James Hampson, attorney for the son, Jervis Ricketts, in Philadelphia. (May 1843).

Ridd, Francis, formerly of Tawstock, Devon, but late of Utica, North America, bachelor. Administration to the father, Thomas Ridd. (Mar. 1833).

Riddell, Susanna, of Williamsburg, Virginia, widow. Probate to Charles Philips with similar powers reserved to Jaquelin Ambler and Robert Andrews. (July 1790).

Riddle, Susanna, of Rolls County, Missouri, widow. Administration to the creditor, Thomas Aspinwall; the only children, James Nourse Riddle, William Nourse Riddle, David Hunter Riddle and Catherine Burton, wife of William Stone, and the nephews and nieces, Martha Susan Riddle, William Tabb Riddle, Catherine Burton Riddle, Joseph Nourse Riddle, Mary Matthews Riddle, Elizabeth Frances Riddle, Lavinia Anderson Riddle and David Hoge Riddle, renouncing. (July 1850).

Ridley, Matthew, formerly of Essex Street, Strand, Middlesex, but late of Baltimore, Maryland. Administration to Samuel Montague Sears, son and administrator of the creditor, Samuel Sears deceased; the relict having been cited but not having appeared and the son having died a bachelor before administering. (May 1806).

Riensset alias Hays, Mary, wife of John Riensset of Bath Town, North Carolina, who died in Cork, Ireland. Administration to the son, John Riensset; the husband, John Riensset, having died. (May 1744).

Riggs, William, of Fairfax, Vermont. Administration to John Stuart, attorney for the relict, Nancy Riggs, in Vermont. (Nov. 1855).

Ryley, John, of H.M. ships *Winchelsea* and *Chester*, who died in Boston, New England. Probate to Bryan Norman with similar powers reserved to Hugh Dyer. (May 1713).

Ryley, William, of New England, bachelor. Administration to the brother and next-of-kin, Ambrose Ryley. (June 1715).

Rimes. *See* **Rymes**.

Rimus, Ann, formerly Ann Barrett, late of Virginia, widow. Administration to the brother, Gerard Barrett. (Feb. 1755).

Ring, James, of New York, bachelor. Administration to Mary Ring, relict and administratrix of the brother and only next-of-kin, Thomas Ring deceased. (Jan. 1818).

Ring, John, who died overseas (bound for Virginia), bachelor. Probate to the brother, Matthias Ring, with similar powers reserved to Richard Atkins. (Apr. 1637). Sh.Wi.

Ring, John, formerly of Bath, [Somerset], but late of New York, bachelor. Administration to the nephew and only next-of-kin, Thomas Ring. (Mar. 1840).

Rioch, Kenneth, of Boston, New England, bachelor. Administration to the sister, Ann Rioch. (Oct. 1802).

Ripley, John, formerly of the Tower of London, who died in Fort

Ripley, *(contd.)*
Augustus, East Florida. Probate to the mother, Judith Ripley. (Sep. 1773).

Ritchie, Peter, of Philadelphia, who died in Havana, Cuba, bachelor. Administration to Juliana, wife and attorney of the brother and next-of-kin, William Ritchie, in Philadelphia. (Mar. 1765).

Rivett, Daniel, of Georgia. Probate to the relict, Barbe Rivett. (May 1739).

Roach, Henry, of Abbots Leigh, [Somerset], mariner, who had lands in Virginia. Probate to the son, John Roach. (Mar. 1678). Wi.

Roades. *See* **Rhodes**.

Roane, Robert, of Chaldon, Surrey, whose son, Charles Roane, was in Virginia. Probate to George Perryer, Roger Lambert and Thomas Landon. (May 1676). Wi.

Robarts, Josiah, of Mile End, Middlesex, whose daughter, Mary, wife of Matthew Randall, was in Philadelphia. Probate to the son, Nathaniel Robarts, and to William Hainworth, with similar powers reserved to John Wilkinson. (Dec. 1796). *See* NGSQ 70/113.

Roberts, Elizabeth, of London, widow, whose daughter, Elizabeth Shrimpton, widow, was in New England. Probate to the daughter, Mary Breedon. (Jan. 1702). Revoked and granted to John Richardson. (Mar. 1702). *See* NGSQ 63/200.

Roberts, Humphrey, of Portsmouth, Virginia. Administration with will to William Roberts, attorney for the son, Edward Roberts, in Portsmouth. (Apr. 1793).

Roberts, Jane, of Rochester, United States of America, widow. Administration to Mary Davies, widow, attorney for the daughter, Mary Roberts, in Oberlin, United States of America. (July 1852).

Roberts, Sophia, of Pennsylvania, spinster. Administration to the sister, Rebecca Roberts; the mother, Anne Roberts, having died before administering. (Nov. 1731).

Robertson, Ellen, formerly Ellen Chichester, of Virginia. Administration to the husband, Andrew Robertson. (Nov. 1763).

Robertson, John, of Charles County, Maryland. Administration with will to John Blair, attorney for the son, John Robertson, in Claiborne County, Mississippi; the executors, Alexander Green and Henry Henley Chapman, having been cited but not having appeared. (Dec. 1824).

Robertson, Moses, of St. Michael, Northumberland County, Virginia. Administration to Newton Keene, attorney for the minor children, John Willoughby Robertson, Moses Roberton and Frances Robertson, in Virginia; the relict, Susannah Robertson, having died before administering. (Apr. 1752).

Robertson, Paul Douglas, Lieutenant of Marines of the Plymouth Division, who died in Rhode Island, bachelor. Administration to the father, Rev. William Robertson. (Mar. 1779).

Robey, Thomas the younger, of Derby, who died in Philadelphia. Probate to Francis Green. (Apr. 1764).

Robins, Clementine, of New York, widow. Administration to Edward Colston Hague, administrator of the only child, Emily Robins deceased. (Sep. 1857).

Robins, Daniel, of New Shoreham, Newport County, Rhode Island, a private in Captain Giles Russell's Company of the Rhode Island Regiment of Foot, who died in Havana, bachelor, apprentice to Abel Franklin of New Shoreham, yeoman. Limited administration by his solemn affirmation to Joseph Sherwood of Throgmorton Street, London, attorney for the said Abel Franklin. (Dec. 1765).

Robyns, Edward, who died in Virginia. Administration to the principal creditor, Francis Burroughes. (Sep. 1647).

Robins, Francis, of Exeter, Devon, whose nephew, Francis Robins, was in Boston, New England. Probate to the relict, Rebecca Robins, with similar powers reserved to Samuel Luscombe, George Wrideat and Samuel Luscombe the younger. (Dec. 1767).

Robins, Jeremy, of St. Martin in the Fields, Middlesex, whose daughter, Rebecca Robins, was in Virginia. Probate to the relict, Sarah Robins. (Oct. 1671). Wi.

Robins, John, of the merchant ship *Britannia*, who died in Virginia, bachelor. Administration to the principal creditor, William Jackson. (Feb. 1720).

Robins, Thomas, of East Linington, Warwickshire, who died in Maryland. Administration to the relict, Jane Robins. (Oct. 1704).

Robinson, George, formerly of Scarborough, Yorkshire, but late of New York City. Probate to the mother, Margaret Robinson. (Mar. 1802).

Robinson, Joseph, master of the merchant ship *Fortitude*, who died in New York, bachelor. Administration to the father, Henry Robinson. (Apr. 1778).

Robinson, Joseph, Quartermaster of the 23rd Regiment, who died in South Carolina. Administration to the son, Phanas Robinson; the relict, Hannah Robinson, having died before administering. (Aug. 1784).

Robinson, Joseph, formerly a Lieutenant in the South Carolina Royalists but late of Charlotte, Prince Edward Island. Administration with will to Goodinch Murray Thompson, attorney for the relict, Lilly alias Lilia Robinson, Robert Hodgson and Ralph Brecken in Prince Edward Island. (Jan. 1808).

Robinson, Margaret. *See* **Taylerson**.

Robinson, Mary, of St. Olave Hart Street, London, widow, who left a bequest for the poor people in Virginia. Probate to Nicholas Farrer and Thomas Smith. (Sep. 1618). Sentence for the validity of the will 1619. Wi.

Robinson, Maximilian, of Rotherhithe, Surrey, who died on the ship *Aurelia* at sea, mariner, and who had lands in Virginia. Probate to Robert Bristow the younger with similar powers reserved to the brother, Heneage Robinson. (Oct. 1695). Wi.

Robinson, Richard, of New England, bachelor. Administration to the sister, Catherine Robinson. (Feb. 1732).

Robinson, Samuel, of Boston, New England, who died overseas. Probate to

Robinson, *(contd.)* John Robinson with similar powers reserved to Thomas Robinson. (Apr. 1664). Wa.

Robinson, Sarah, formerly of Gloucester Place, New Road, Middlesex, but late of Vermillion County, North America. Probate to Henry Callaway. (Dec. 1851).

Robinson, Thomas, formerly of Sussex County, Delaware, but late of Nova Scotia. Administration with will to Charles Cooke, attorney for Peter and Burton Robinson and for the son, Thomas Robinson, in Delaware. (Aug. 1788).

Robinson, William, of Maryland. Probate to William Calvert. (Aug. 1697).

Robinson, William, of Limehouse, Stepney, Middlesex, who died on the merchant ship *Susanna* in South Carolina. Administration to the relict, Grace Robinson. (July 1730).

Robotham. *See* **Rowbotham**

Robson, Isaac, of the merchant ship *Britannia*, who died in Virginia. Probate to the relict, Mary Robson. (Sep. 1710).

Roby, Anthony, of parts overseas who died in Carolina. Administration with will to the brother, Thomas Roby; the executor, Andrew Percivall, now being abroad, and the mother, Early alias Avelyn Roby, having died. (July 1688). Wa.

Roche, James, of Warwicksqueak, Isle of Wight, Virginia. Probate to the brother, Robert Roche. (Sep. 1652). Sh.

Roche, Patrick, of Limerick, Ireland, who died in Sypruss, South Carolina. Administration to the relict, Bridget Roche. (Apr. 1726).

Rockwell, Honor, of Dorchester, who died in Fitzhead, Somerset, widow, and whose grandchildren, Richard, William and John Rockwell, were in New England. Probate to the son, Roger Rockwell. (Jan. 1638). Wa.

Rodaway, Aaron Miller, formerly of Pontypool, Monmouth, but late of Philadelphia, widower. Administration to the brother and next-of-kin, Alfred Biggs Rodaway. (Oct. 1852).

Roddam, Lucy, of New York. Administration to the husband, Robert Roddam. (Nov. 1751).

Rodling, Christiana, of Virginia. Administration to the husband, John Rodling. (Apr. 1676).

Rodman, Thomas Rotch, formerly of New Bedford, Massachusetts, but late of Havana, Cuba. Administration to Thomas Dickason the younger, attorney for the father, Samuel Rodman, in New Bedford. (June 1810).

Roe, John the elder, of Hazlewood in Madison Township, Licking County, Ohio. Probate to the son, Thomas Henry Roe M.D. (Dec. 1849).

Roe, Sarah, of Hazlewood near Newark, Licking County, Ohio. Administration to the husband, John Roe. (July 1847).

Rogers, Ann, of Charleston, South Carolina, widow. Administration to the daughter, Elizabeth, wife of Robert Barlow. (Sep. 1805).

Rogers, Anthony, of New York. Administration to Thomas Parry, guardian

Rogers, *(contd.)* of the daughter, Catherine Rogers; the relict, Catherine Rogers, renouncing. (June 1704).

Rogers, Fanny, of New York, widow. Administration to Richard Rogers, attorney for the son, William Rogers, in New York. (Apr. 1841).

Rodgers, James, of South Carolina. Probate to John Beswicke with similar powers reserved to John Savage and Robert Raper. (June 1763). Double probate to the surviving executor, Robert Raper. (Sep. 1764).

Rogers, John, of H.M. ship *Tartar*, who died on the hospital ship *Jersey* in New York. Probate to the brother, Thomas Rogers. (Dec. 1778).

Rogers, John Morris, of New York City. Administration to Edward Henry Rickards, attorney for the relict, Ann Rogers, in New York. (Jan. 1846).

Rogers, Margaret, of Ipswich, New England, widow. Administration to the principal creditor, William Hubbard. (Mar. 1678).

Rogers, Margaret, of Wapping, Middlesex, widow. Administration to the daughter, Isabella, wife of William Betts, in Boston, New England. (Apr. 1725).

Rogers, Mary. *See* **Stevenson**.

Rogers, Richard, of St. Michael Crooked Lane, London, Controller of H.M. Mint, who had lands in Virginia. Probate to the son, Edward Rogers, and to Jasper Draper, with similar powers reserved to the daughter, Anne Draper. (Sep. 1636).

Rogers, Samuel, formerly of St. Marylebone, Middlesex, but late of Boston, Massachusetts. Administration to the son, John Rogers. (Aug. 1805).

Rogers, Samuel, of Boston, North America, merchant. Administration to Timothy Wiggin, attorney for the relict, Nancy Rogers, in Boston. (Nov. 1833).

Rogers, Theophilus, of Northampton, whose grandson, Richard Rogers, was in Virginia. Probate to Robert Rogers and William Beever with similar powers reserved to Jonathan Warner. (Sep. 1730). *See* NGSQ 62/215.

Rogers, Thomas, formerly Captain and then Lieutenant-Colonel of the Georgia Militia, but late of Rouen, France. Limited probate to Walsingham Collins. (July 1790).

Rogers, William, of Truro, Cornwall, widower. Administration to Isaac Milner, attorney for the only brother and next-of-kin, Robert Rogers, now in Virginia. (Nov. 1733).

Rogers, William, formerly of Bristol but late of New York City. Probate to John Wesley Hall with similar powers reserved to James Maize and Benjamin W. Rogers. (Oct. 1829).

Rolfe, Elizabeth, nee Elizabeth Poole, of Brooklyn, New York. Administration to John Poole, attorney for the husband, John Rolfe, in Brooklyn. (Mar. 1839).

Rolph, Jemima, nee Jemima Hopwood, of Williamsburgh, New York. Administration to William Hopwood, attorney for the husband, John

Rolph, *(contd.)*
Adey Rolph, in New York City. (Nov. 1844).

Rollfe, John, of James City, Virginia. Probate to William Peyrs. (May 1630). Sh.Wa.

Rolles, Francis, of Maryland. Probate to Ernault Hawkins. (Dec. 1724).

Romman, William, of Woodborough, Wiltshire, who died in Philadelphia, bachelor. Probate to Richard Romman. (Mar. 1722).

Rooke, John Bolton, of Charles Town, South Carolina. Probate to the relict, Sarah Rooke, with similar powers reserved to William Palmer. (Mar. 1802).

Rootes, Thomas Reade, of Virginia, who died in St. Faith, London. Probate to John Hyndman. (Mar. 1766). Double probate to John Smith. (Mar. 1767).

Roper, Thomas, who died overseas having goods in Virginia. Administration to Thomas Shepherd, father and guardian during their minority of the brother and sister on the mother's side, John, Elizabeth and Constance Shepherd. (May 1624). Revoked and administration with will granted to the brother, John Roper; no executor having been named. (Feb. 1627). Wa.Wi.

Ropes, Jonathan, of Salem, Essex County, New England, who died on H.M. ship *Rumney Castle*, bachelor. Administration to Bryan and Joanna Woolwik, attornies for the father, William Ropes, in Salem. (May 1715).

Rose, Hugh, of Schenectady, Albany County, New York, Lieutenant of an Independent Company. Administration to Augustine Oldham, attorney for the relict, Anna Rose, in Schenectady. (Sep. 1764).

Rose, John, of Deptford, Kent, who died in Virginia, bachelor. Administration to the principal creditor, Robert Graves. (Nov. 1688).

Rose, John Wallington, of New Orleans, bachelor. Administration to the uncle, Thomas Rose. (Nov. 1851).

Rose, Robert, of Rochester, Kent, whose brothers, Christopher Rose and Henry West, were in Virginia. Probate to the relict, Mary Rose. (Oct. 1670). Wi.

Rose, Thomas, of South Kingstown, King's County, Rhode Island, Lieutenant of Captain Fry's Company of the Rhode Island Regiment of Foot, who died in Havana, bachelor. Administration by his solemn declaration to Joseph Sherwood, attorney for the father, John Rose, in South Kingstown. (Dec. 1765).

Rose, William, formerly of Bromsgrove, Worcestershire, but late of New Brunswick, New Jersey, who died in 1792. Limited administration to John Irvine Glennie. (Sep. 1825).

Rose, William James, of New York City. Administration to the relict, Mary Ann Margaret Rose. (Dec. 1849).

Ross, David, of Richmond, Virginia. Administration with will to John Fallowfield Scott, attorney for Thomas T. Bouldin in the United States of America; the son, Frederick Augustus Ross, and Jacob Myers having been cited but not having appeared. (Apr. 1822).

Ross, Elizabeth, of Virginia, widow. Probate to Anthony Hawkins. (Nov. 1768).

Rosse, Henry, of Potomack River, Virginia, widower. Administration to the sister, Eunice Thistelwheate, widow. (Aug. 1700).

Ross, John, formerly of Wapping, Middlesex, but late of New England. Probate to John Thompson. (Oct. 1770).

Ross, Robert, of New York. Administration to Henry Waddington, attorney for the relict, Deborah Ross, in New York. (Jan. 1792).

Ross, William, of St. Martin in the Fields, Middlesex, who died on H.M. ship *Betty* in Virginia, bachelor. Administration to the mother, Alexandra Ross. (Jan. 1718).

Rossiter, Eliza, of Cleveland, Cuyahogo County, Ohio. Administration to the husband, William Rossiter. (Jan. 1836).

Rossiter, John, of Scranton, Luzerne County, Pennsylvania, labourer, bachelor. Administration to the father, John Rossiter. (Oct. 1852).

Rounde, George, of Virginia, widower. Administration to the only sister, Grissell Willmore alias Rounde. (Sep. 1654).

Round, George, of Mobile, Alabama. Administration to James Flavell, attorney for the relict, Mary Round, in Mobile. (Mar. 1850).

Rousby, Christopher, of Maryland, widower. Administration to the brother, William Rousby. (Jan. 1685).

Route, Robert, of St. Dunstan in the West, London, who died in South Carolina. Administration to the son, Robert Route; the relict, Mary Route, renouncing. (Apr. 1725).

Robotham, George, of Talbot County, Maryland. Limited probate to Mary, wife of John Erp, Anne, wife of John Cooke, and Anne, wife of William Cotton. (Nov. 1698).

Robotham, John, of the ship *Dartmouth*, who died in Virginia, bachelor. Administration to the next heir, Richard Fuller. (Sep. 1677).

Rowbotham, Joseph, formerly of St. Batholomew the Great, London, and late of H.M. ship *Southampton*, who died in Virginia. Administration to the relict, Mary Rowbotham. (June 1703).

Rowe, James, formerly of New Brunswick but late of Whampoa, China, bachelor. Administration to Edmund Clarke, attorney for the mother and next-of-kin, Catherine Rowe, widow, in Boston, North America. (Dec. 1853).

Rowland, John, of New England, who died on passage from France to London, mariner. Administration with will to Francis Cane, attorney for the mother, Abigail Cane, in New England; the executor, Joseph Dearing, renouncing, and Mary Dearing having died in the testator's lifetime. (July 1714).

Rowland, Peter, of Shadwell, Middlesex, who died in Virginia. Administration to the principal creditor, Francis Greene; the relict, Marriane Rowland, renouncing. (Sep. 1674).

Rowland, Thomas, formerly of Salford, Lancashire, but late of Sacramento, California. Administration to William Webb, attorney for the relict, Caroline Rowland, in Sacramento. (Feb. 1853).

Rowley, George, formerly of Staple Inn, London, but late of Philadelphia,

Rowley, *(contd.)* bachelor. Limited administration to Mylam Garling, attorney for Elizabeth, wife of William Garrett. (Mar. 1802).

Rowlson, Matthew, of the ship *Susan* of London, who died in Virginia, bachelor. Administration to the principal creditor, Richard Featherstone. (Aug. 1688).

Rowzee, Lodowick, of Ashford, Kent, who died in Virginia. Administration to John Catlett, half brother of the eldest son, Ralph Rowzee in Virginia, and for the benefit of the other children, Edward and Martha Rowzee, also overseas. (July 1655).

Royall, Joseph, of Boston, New England, who died on H.M. ship *Boyne*. Administration to the cousin, Mary Faucett. (Sep. 1710). Revoked and granted to the relict, Mary Royall. (Jan. 1713).

Royle, William, of Williamsburg, Virginia, widower. Administration to Benjamin Blake, a minor; the brother of the whole blood, Hunter Royle, and the half-brothers and half-sister, Henry St. John Dixon, Mary Dixon and George Washington Dixon, having died. (July 1852).

Royse, John, of London, merchant, who died in Gravesend, Kent, (bound for New York). Probate to the father, Daniel Royse; the executor, James Wancklen, renouncing. (Nov. 1686).

Rudd, Charles, of Piscatua, Maryland, bachelor. Administration to the mother, Ann Rudd, widow. (Sep. 1752).

Ruddy, John, formerly of Killala, Mayo County, Ireland, but late of Springfield, Massachusetts. Administration to the relict, Bridget Ruddy. (Mar. 1856).

Rudge, Jonathan, formerly of Ross, Herefordshire, afterwards of Bristol, but late of New Orleans, bachelor. Administration to the brother, Thomas Rudge. (Mar. 1805).

Ruggle, George, of Lavenham, Suffolk, and the University of Cambridge, who left a bequest for the infidels in Virginia. Probate to Tobias Palavicino. (Nov. 1622). Wi.

Ruggles, Timothy, formerly of Massachusetts but late of Wilmot, Nova Scotia. Administration with will to John Turner, attorney for the sons, Timothy and John Ruggles, in Wilmot. (July 1796).

Rumbold, Thomas, of All Hallows on the Wall, London, who died in Boston, New England. Administration to the relict, Elizabeth Rumbold. (May 1727).

Rumley, Johan, of the transport ship *Nancy*, who died in New York. Probate to Ezre alias Ellicksander Norman. (Apr. 1778).

Rundle, Daniel, of Philadelphia. Limited administration with will to Robert Barclay, attorney for the nephew, Richard Rundle, in Philadelphia. (Sep. 1795).

Rush, John, of New York, hatter. Probate to Edward Daniel. (June 1743).

Rusher, Daniel, of Wapping, Middlesex, who died in Virginia. Administration to the relict, Joane Rusher. (June 1659).

Rusk, Hugh, of Baltimore, Maryland, bachelor. Administration to William

Rusk, *(contd.)*
Brown, attorney for the brother and only next-of-kin, Robert Rusk, in Maryland. (Nov. 1829).

Ruske, Peter, of Virginia, bachelor. Administration to the cousin german and only next-of-kin, Christopher Ruske. (Apr. 1656).

Russell, Elizabeth, of Marblehead, Massachusetts, widow. Probate to the son, Russell Trevett, with similar powers reserved to Daniel Waldo and William Gray. (Jan. 1772). Revoked on the death of Russell Trevett and administration granted to Samuel Russell Trevett and Samuel Hooper; the executor, William Gray, having died, and the executor, Daniel Waldo, renouncing. (Sep. 1803).

Russell, Henry, of H.M. ship *Alborough*, who died in South Carolina, bachelor. Administration with will to John Pick, attorney for William Randall in South Carolina. (Aug. 1734).

Russell, James, of Queen Street, Westminster, Middlesex, Virginia merchant. Probate to the relict, Ann Russell. (Sep. 1788).

Russell, James, of Charleston, North America, widower. Administration to the son, James Russell. (Feb. 1810).

Russell, John, of Brunswick Cape Fear, North Carolina, Commander of H.M. ship *Scorpion*. Probate to the relict, Alice Russell. (July 1753).

Russell, Thomas, of Boston, North America, bachelor. Administration to James Russell, son and administrator of the father, James Russell deceased. (Feb. 1810).

Russell, William, formerly of Savannah, Georgia, but late of Whitechapel, Middlesex. Probate to the relict, Jane Russell, with similar powers reserved to Francis Harris, Henry Yonge, John Smith, Noble Wimberly Jones and Joseph Clay. (Mar. 1769).

Rutherford, John, of Edgerston, New Jersey. Probate to the daughter, Mary Rutherford, with similar powers reserved to Peter Augustus Jay, his wife, Mary Rutherford Jay, Peter Gerard Stuyvesant, his wife, Helen Stuyvesant, the daughter, Louisa Morris Rutherford, the daughter, Anna Watts, widow, the granddaughter, Helen Russell, her husband, Archibald Russell, the son, Robert Walter Rutherford, and the grandson, John Rutherford the younger. (Oct. 1841).

Ruthra, Arthur, of Virginia. Administration to the relict, Anne Ruthra. (Sep. 1667).

Rutledge, Sarah Motte, formerly of Brighton, Sussex, but late of Charleston, South Carolina, widow. Limited administration to Charles Francis Cobb, attorney for the son, John Rutledge, in Charleston. (July 1852).

Ryder, William, Lieutenant of the 9th Regiment of Foot, who died in Florida, bachelor. Administration to the sister and next-of-kin, Mary Browne, widow. (Sep. 1768).

Ryland, George, formerly of St. Clement Danes, Middlesex, who died in New York, bachelor. Administration to the sister and only next-of-kin, Elizabeth, wife of James White. (Jan. 1792).

Ryland, John, formerly of St. Clement Danes, Middlesex, who died in Philadelphia, bachelor. Administration to the sister and only next-of-kin,

Ryland, *(contd.)*
Elizabeth, wife of James White. (Jan. 1793).

Ryley. *See* **Riley**.

Rimes, Edward, of Captain Wemm's Company, who died in New York. Probate to the relict, Elizabeth Rimes. (Feb. 1704).

Rymes, Samuel, master of the ship *Barbados Merchant* of Portsmouth, New England, who died in Kingsale, Ireland. Administration to the relict, Mary Rymes. (Mar. 1709).

S

Sabatier, Richard, formerly of Shepton Mallet, Somerset, but late of Massachusetts, brewer, widower. Administration to Elisha Hayden Collier, attorney for the only children, Sarah Staines, wife of William Gardiner, Anna Maria Housley, divorced wife of William Housley, and Jane Sabatier, in Massachusetts. (Aug. 1819).

Sabine, William, Captain of the First Batallion of Marines, who died in Boston, New England. Probate to the sister, Sarah Sabine. (Mar. 1776).

Sadler, John, of St. Stephen Walbrook, London, who had lands in Virginia. Probate to Anthony Walker with similar powers reserved to John Wilkey. (Jan. 1659). Wa.

Sadleir, John, formerly of London, grocer, but late of Hunsdon, Hertfordshire, who had a plantation in Virginia. Probate to Sir Charles Ingleby. (Nov. 1716).

Sadler, Mary, of Mayfield, Sussex, widow, whose daughter, Mary Sadler, was in New England. Probate to the daughter, Elizabeth James. (Nov. 1647).

Saffin, Thomas, of Boston, New England, who died in Stepney, Middlesex, bachelor. Administration to Edward Hull, attorney for the father, John Saffin, merchant, in Boston. (Feb. 1688).

Sage, Philipp, of Stepney, Middlesex, who died in Virginia. Administration to the relict, Sarah, now wife of John Rumball. (Feb. 1691).

Saintbury alias Sainbry, Rebecca, of St. Olave, Southwark, Surrey, who had kin in Virginia. Probate to John Spicer. (Jan. 1679). Wa.

St. Clair, Sir John, Deputy Quartermaster-General in America, Lieutenant-Colonel of the 28th Regiment of Foot, late of Elizabeth Town, New Jersey. Administration with will to Richard Moland alias Morland, attorney for the relict, Elizabeth, now wife of Dudley Templer, and for Andrew Eliot, in America. (Sep. 1769).

Saker, William, of Lambeth, Surrey, whose servant, Thomas Gregory, was in Virginia. Probate to Sir Thomas Jay and Nathaniel Finch. (Dec. 1627). Wa.Wi.

Sale, Nathaniel, of London, who died in Charles Town, Carolina, merchant, bachelor. Probate to Mary Johnson, widow. (June 1711).

Salisbury, Nicholas, of Boston, New England. Administration with will to Thomas Lane, attorney for the relict, Martha Salisbury, in Boston. (Nov. 1749).

Salkeld, George, formerly of Liverpool, Lancashire, but late of New Orleans, widower. Administration to William Collins, attorney for the son, Frederick Salkeld, now on passage to Peru, South America. (Dec. 1834).

Sallitt, William, of Charles Town, South Carolina, bachelor. Administration to the father, James Sallitt. (Nov. 1784).

Salmon, Michael, of H.M. ship *Chatham*, who died in New York. Administration to Patrick Hart, attorney for the relict, Anotice

(contd.)
Salmon, in Kilkenny, Ireland. (Mar. 1777).

Salmonson, Frederick, of New York. Administration to the relict, Eugenia Salmonson. (May 1854).

Salter, Daniel, of the merchant ship *Seven Sisters*, who died on passage to Virginia. Administration to the sister, Avis, wife of John Nutt. (June 1656).

Salter, George, of Dedham, Essex, whose daughters, Abigail and Hannah, were in New England. Probate to the relict, Mary Salter. (July 1654). Wa.

Salter, James, of Knox County, Ohio, widower. Administration to the son, Samuel Salter. (Aug. 1846).

Saltonstall, Mary, of Haverhill, Essex County, Massachusetts. Administration to Eliakin Palmer, attorney for the husband, Richard Saltonstall, in Massachusetts. (Apr. 1748). Revoked on the death of Eliakin Palmer and granted to Benjamin Pemberton as attorney. (Aug. 1749). Revoked on the death of the husband and granted to the brother, Thomas Jekyll. (Nov. 1769).

Salvador, Joseph, formerly of Jermyn Street, Westminster, Middlesex, but late of Charles Town, South Carolina. Limited probate to the daughters, Abigail, Elizabeth and Susanna Salvador. (Nov. 1788).

Salwey, Anthony, of Ann Arundell County, Maryland. Probate to the brother, Richard Salwey. (Aug. 1672).

Sammes, Edward, of St. Helen the Great, London, whose cousin, ——- Stone, was in New England. Administration with will to the relict, Bennett Sammes; no executor having been named. (Feb. 1636). Sh.Wa.

Sampson, Henry, Captain of the 31st Regiment of Foot, who died in Florida. Probate to the brother, Thomas Sampson. (Dec. 1772).

Sampson, John, of Marysville, Upper California, bachelor. Administration to the sister, Augusta Sampson; the mother, Anna Sampson, widow, renouncing. (Feb. 1851).

Sanckley, Richard, of Virginia, bachelor. Administration to the cousin, George Dare. (Aug. 1675).

Sander, Francis, of Congham, Norfolk, whose kinsman, Henry Spelman, was in Virginia. Probate to Richard Sander. (Aug. 1613). Will confirmed by sentence November 1613. Wi.

Sanders. *See* **Saunders**.

Sandford, John, of Virginia. Administration to William Sandford, guardian of the son, John Sandford. (June 1704).

Sandford, Samuel, of Accomack County, Virginia, who died in St. Mary at Hill, London. Probate to Catherine Sandford. (Apr. 1710). Wi.

Sandford, Thomas James Harris, formerly of Rotherham, Yorkshire, but late of Marietta, Ohio. Probate to the relict, Mary Sandford, the brother, Charles Samuel Roberts Sandford, and the sister, Anna Maria Yonge, widow. (Nov. 1825).

Sanford, Richard, of Virginia, bachelor. Administration to the brother, Francis Sanford. (May 1683).

Sanger, Richard, of Philadelphia, bachelor. Administration to the sister, Deborah, wife of Jonathan Cohner. (May 1737).

Sansom, Joseph, of Philadelphia. Limited administration with will to Richard Van Heythuysen, attorney for the relict, Beulah Sansom, in Philadelphia. (May 1828).

Sargent, John, of Bermondsey, Surrey, weaver, whose daughter, Rebecca, was wife of James Tyre in New Kent, York River, Virginia. Probate to John Rouse and Joseph Rouse. (Oct. 1701). Wi.

Sargeant, John, formerly of Newnham, Gloucestershire, but late of Philadelphia. Probate to the mother, Margaret Sargeant, widow. (Dec. 1822).

Sergeant, Lady Mary. *See* **Phipps**.

Sargent, Stephen, of H.M. ship *Swan*, bachelor. Administration to the sister, Elizabeth, wife of John Davis, attorney for the father, Stephen Sargent, in Boston, New England. (Sep. 1692). Revoked on production of a will and administration granted to Frances Nash, relict and executrix of the universal legatee, Joseph Nash deceased. (Oct. 1692).

Sarti, Antonio, formerly of Spur Street, Leicester Square, Middlesex, but late of Boston, United States of America, modeller. Probate to the surviving executrix, Selina Isabella, wife of Daniel Barker. (Feb. 1851).

Sash, Richard, of H.M. ship *Elephant*, who died on H.M. ship *Suffolk*. Administration to Mary, wife and attorney of the principal creditor, John Stott, in New England. (Dec. 1711).

Satchwell, William, formerly of Bermuda but late of Philadelphia, bachelor. Administration to the cousin german once removed and only next-of-kin, Margaret Redhead, spinster. (Nov. 1786).

Saubere, Samuel, of Philadelphia. Administration with will to Henry Lloyd Magan, attorney for Mary, wife of David Simpson, in Philadelphia; the sole executor, Peter Keller, renouncing. (Apr. 1849).

Sanders, Edward William, formerly of Columbus, Colorado, Texas, but late of Havana, Cuba, bachelor. Administration to the brother, George Lee Sanders. (Sep. 1849).

Saunders, Israel, of the Connecticut Regiment of Foot, who died in Havana, bachelor. Administration to Phineas Lyman, attorney for the father, Peter Saunders. (Dec. 1763).

Sanders, John, of St. James, Goose Creek, South Carolina, bachelor. Administration to James Crockatt, attorney for the uncle and next-of-kin, Joshua Saunders, in South Carolina. (Mar. 1747).

Saunders, Jonathan, Rector of Lenhaven, Princess Anne County, Virginia. Administration to Jonathan Matthews, attorney for the relict, Mary, now wife of Maximilian Boush, in Virginia. (Dec. 1702).

Sanders, Lovett, of Boston, New England, bachelor. Administration to Susan, wife of Joshua Lamb of Roxbury, New England, attorney for the mother, Elizabeth Sanders, in Boston, widow. (Apr. 1710).

Saunders, Thomas, of St. Saviour, Southwark, Surrey, who died in Virginia.

Saunders, *(contd.)*
Administration to the relict, Mary Saunders. (Feb. 1723).

Saunders, Thomas, of Newport, Rhode Island, a soldier of Captain John Whiting's Company of the Rhode Island Regiment of Provincials. Limited administration with will to Jared Ingersoll, attorney for John Whiting in Newport. (Apr. 1765).

Saunders, William, of Poole, Dorset, whose brother, Samuel Saunders, was in Massachusetts. Probate to Robert Harris Cooper, Francis Cooper and Thomas Young Bird with similar powers reserved to the brother, Thomas Saunders. (Apr. 1788).

Saunders, William, of Philadelphia, bachelor. Administration to Moses Delafont, attorney for the mother, Elizabeth, wife of William Purjean, in St. Omer, France. (Aug. 1792).

Savage, Patrick, British Vice-Consul in Norfolk, Virginia. Administration to James Savage, uncle of the only children, John, Emma Ann and Amelia Stewart Savage, during their minority; the mother, Ann Savage, widow, renouncing. (Dec. 1818).

Savage, Perez, of Salem, New England, who died in Haskenesse in Barbary, Africa. Administration with will to the nephew by a sister, Thomas Thatcher; no executor having been named. (May 1702).

Saviche, Matias, of Pueblo de los Angeles, California, who died at sea on the steamship *Orinoco*, widower. Administration to Joseph Rodney Croskey, attorney for Ignacio Franco Coronel in Los Angeles, the grandfather and guardian of the only children, Matias and Francisco Saviche, during their minority. (Feb. 1853).

Saxby, George, [formerly of South Carolina] but late of St. Pancras, Middlesex. Probate to the relict, Elizabeth Saxby. (Nov. 1786). ALC.

Saxon, George, of Annapolis, Maryland, widower. Administration to the daughter and next-of-kin, Elizabeth Saxon. (July 1781).

Sayer, John, of Virginia. Administration to the principal creditor, Thomas Arnall. (Mar. 1686).

Scaife, Elizabeth, of Maryport, Cumberland, who died in New York, spinster. Administration to the mother, Sally Scaife, widow. (Mar. 1844).

Scaife, Sarah Fell, of Maryport, Cumberland, who died in New York, spinster. Administration to the mother, Sally Scaife, widow. (Mar. 1844).

Scandrett, James, of South Carolina, bachelor. Administration to the sister and next-of-kin, Elizabeth, wife of John Fell. (Aug. 1770).

Scantlebury, Joanna. *See* **Barritt**.

Scarth, Isaac, of St. Botolph Aldgate, Middlesex, who died in Virginia. Administration to the father and next-of-kin, Jonathan Scarth; the relict, Ann Scarth, having died. (July 1728).

Schmitz, Franz Jacob, formerly of Keppel and late of Olpe, both in Prussia, who died in San Francisco, California. Administration with will to the daughter, Mathilda Schmitz; the relict, Amelia Schmitz, having died. (Dec. 1853).

Scholes, James, of Brooklyn, New York. Administration with will to William Pike, attorney for the relict, Maria Scholes, in Brooklyn. (July 1850).

Schouborg, Ann, of Yonkers, New York. Administration with will to Joseph Delevaute, attorney for the husband, Anders Jenson Schouborg, in New York City. (Jan. 1857).

Schuyler, John Cortlandt, of Bethlehem, Albany County, North America, Lieutenant of half pay of H.M. marine forces. Administration with will to the brother, William Schuyler; the mother, Barbara Schuyler, widow, having died in the testator's lifetime. (Aug. 1797).

Scott, Alexander, of Lancaster City, Pennsylvania. Administration with will to Charles Robert Turner, attorney for the relict, Mary Snyder, widow, in America. (Mar. 1824).

Scott, Andrew, of the transport ship *Father's Goodwill*, who died in Newport, Rhode Island, bachelor. Administration to the father, Andrew Scott. (Apr. 1779).

Scott, Edward, mariner of H.M. ship *Nightingale*, bachelor, whose will was made in Annapolis, Maryland. Administration with will to the brother, William Scott; the father, James Scott, having died in the testator's lifetime, and the mother, Bridget Scott, widow, renouncing. (Sep. 1716).

Scott, George, of London, son of Edward Scott of Glemsford, Suffolk, who died overseas, merchant, bachelor, and whose brother, Richard Scott, was in New England. Administration with will to the brother, Frederick Scott; the executor, William Ballowe, having died. (Apr. 1642). Wa.

Scott, George, of London, (but asked to be buried in Sevenoaks, Kent), who had lands in Virginia. Probate to a kinsman, Thomas Brace. (Feb. 1649). Wa.

Scott, James, of Bristol, who died in Virginia. Administration to the relict, Dorothy Scott. (Oct. 1698).

Scott, John, of Southampton, York County, Long Island, New England, who died in St. Thomas, Southwark, Surrey. Limited administration with will to William Clapcott. (May 1692). Wa.

Scott, John, of Mattox, Westmoreland County, Virginia. Administration with will to Elizabeth Scott, wife and attorney of Gustavus Scott, now overseas. (Dec. 1702). Probate granted to the brother, Gustavus Scott, with similar rights reserved to the son, John Scott, and to the other executors. (Aug. 1703). Copy of will proved by the relict, Sarah Martin in November 1701 at PROB 20/2298.

Scott, John, of Charles Town, South Carolina. Administration with will to John Shoolbred, attorney for the relict, Sarah Scott, the nephew, Bartlee Smyth, and for Thomas Winstanley, in South Carolina. (Aug. 1791).

Scott, John, of Barboursville, Virginia, Ensign of the 85th Regiment of Foot. Administration to the relict, Janet Scott. (Jan. 1821).

Scott, Mary, of Virginia, spinster. Administration with will to Ann, wife of Robert Anderson. (July 1781).

Scott, Sarah, formerly Sarah Farr, formerly of Hampton Court, Middlesex, then of North Shields, Northumberland, but late of New York, widow. Administration to the brother and only next-of-kin, Edward Farr. (Apr. 1820).

Scott, Walter, formerly of Maryland but late of St. Benet Gracechurch, London. Probate to James Armour and John Stewart. (Mar. 1752).

Scott, William, of Stepney, Middlesex, master of the merchant ship *Eagle*, who died in New England. Administration to the relict, Elizabeth Scott. (Apr. 1724).

Scott, William, of Charles Town, New England. Probate to Philip Hall. (May 1754).

Scottow, Thomas, of Boston, New England, surgeon, who died on the ship *Gerard* of London. Probate to Margaret Softly, widow. (Sep. 1699). Wa.

Skottowe, Thomas, formerly of Charles Town, South Carolina, but late of Kings Langley, Hertfordshire. Probate to the brother, Nicholas Skottowe, with similar powers reserved to Edmund Bellinger the younger. (Dec. 1788). Revoked on the death of Nicholas Skottowe and administration granted to the nephew and residuary legatee, Thomas Britiffe Skottowe; the surviving executor, Edmund Bellinger, renouncing. (Feb. 1801).

Scrimgeour, John, Rector of Nominie, Westmoreland County, Virginia, bachelor. Administration to the only brother, William Scrimgeour. (Jan. 1693).

Scrivener, John, of Williamsburgh, Virginia, bachelor. Administration to the brother, Francis Scrivener. (Sep. 1752).

Scroggs, Anne, of Earls Colne, Essex, spinster, whose cousin, Sarah Simmes, was in New England. Probate to William Harlakenden with similar powers reserved to Stephen Marshall. (Sep. 1641). Wa.

Seaborne, Bartholomew, of H.M. ships *Mermaid* and *Suffolk*, who died in New York. Administration to the relict, Mary Seaborne. (Mar. 1706).

Seager, Stephen, formerly of Birmingham, Warwickshire, but late of Canonsburgh, Washington County, Pennsylvania. Probate to Andrew Munro. (Jan. 1808).

Seager, Rev. William, of Williamsburgh, New York. Administration to the relict, Catherine Seager. (Dec. 1856).

Seaman, George, of Charles Town, South Carolina. Probate to John Deas with similar powers reserved to James Lennox, David Deas and William Lennox. (July 1769).

Seaman, John, of St. Dunstan in the East, London, who died in Maryland. Administration to Richard Bell, guardian of the only child, Elizabeth Seaman; the relict, Elizabeth Seaman, renouncing. (Apr. 1692). Revoked on production of a will and probate granted by decree to the relict, Elizabeth Seaman. (Oct. 1692).

Seamen, Benjamin, of Staten Island, New York. Probate to Richard Seamen and the son, William Seamen. (Oct. 1786).

Seapit, David, of Boston, New England, seaman of H.M. ship *Rippon*.

Seapit, *(contd.)*
Probate to the relict, Sarah Seapit. (Aug. 1783).

Searle, Joane, of Otterton, Devon, widow, whose daughters, Jane Mason and Mary Veren, were in New England. Probate to the son, Richard Connant. (June 1658). Sh.

Searles, William, carpenter's mate of H.M. ship *Niger*, who died in New York Hospital, bachelor. Limited administration to the mother, Elizabeth Searles, pending production of a will. (Mar. 1779).

Sears, Isaac, of New York City. Administration by his solemn declaration to the creditor, Emanuel Elam; the relict and the son, Isaac Sears, having been cited but not having appeared. (Nov. 1787).

Seckamp, Albert, of Baltimore, North America. Administration to Alexander Glennie, attorney for the relict, Sophia Seckamp, in Baltimore. (July 1811).

Sedgewicke, Isaac, of Virginia, who died in St. Katherine Creechurch, London. Administration to the brother, Thomas Sedgewicke. (Mar. 1711).

Sedgwicke, John, of St. Saviour, Southwark, Surrey, whose brother, Robert Sedgwicke, was in New England. Probate to the relict, Martha Sedgwicke. (Dec. 1638). Wa.

Seguin, Arthur Edward Sheldon, formerly of King William Street, Strand, Middlesex, but late of New York. Administration to the relict, Anne Seguin. (Sep. 1853).

Selby, Skeffington, late of New York, who died in Hitcham, Suffolk. Probate to Rev. George Edis Webster, Edward Compton, and the nephew, Robert Johnson. (June 1821).

Selfe, Abraham, formerly of Little St. Thomas the Apostle, London, but late of Sharon Richfield, Washtenow County, Michigan, widower. Administration to the nephew, Thomas Selfe. (Mar. 1857).

Selkirk, Andrew, seaman of H.M. ship *Drake*, bachelor. Administration to James Ferguson, attorney for the mother, Jean Selkirk, widow, in Barnet, Caledonia County, North America. (Jan. 1822).

Sellens, Mary, nee Mary Holman, of Cicero Corners, Onandaga, United States of America. Administration to the husband, John Sellens. (July 1851).

Sellick, David, of New England, merchant. Administration to the relict, Susan Tilghman alias Sellick. (Apr. 1657).

Semple, Robert, of Rupertsland, North America, bachelor. Administration to the father, Robert Semple. (Aug. 1818).

Senior, James, of Kingston-upon-Hull, Yorkshire, who died in Virginia, bachelor. Administration to the mother, Bridget Senior. (Sep. 1678).

Sergeant. *See* **Sargeant**.

Severy, Edward, of the ship *America*, who died in Barbados, and whose brother, Andrew Severy, was in New England. Probate to Christian Peterson. (Oct. 1694). Wa.

Seward, John, of Bristol, merchant, who had lands in the Isle of Wight, Virginia. Probate to the relict, Sarah Seward. (May 1651). Sh.Wi.

Sewell, Adam, of H.M. ship *Phoenix*, who died in Carolina, bachelor.

Sewell, *(contd.)*
Probate to George Powers. (July 1741).

Sewell, Adam, formerly of Milton by Gravesend, Kent, but late of New York City. Administration to Mason Neale, attorney for the relict, Ann Sewell, in New York City. (Apr. 1807).

Sewell, Noah, of New York, ship agent, bachelor, who died in the Minories, London. Inventory 1834. [*Administration Act not found*].

Sexton, Thomas, of Boston, New England, who died in Deal, Kent. Administration to the principal creditor, John Sturt. (June 1680).

Shakespear, Elizabeth S. *See* **Docker**.

Shank, Matthew, Major in the King's service, who died in New York, widower. Administration to the brother and next-of-kin, Moses Shank. (July 1711).

Shapton, Thomas, formerly of Union Row, Pill, Somerset, but late of Staten Island, New York, steward of the merchant ship *J.W. Paine*. Administration to the relict, Rebecca Shapton. (June 1856).

Sharp, Elizabeth, of Tetbury, Gloucestershire, who died in Maryland, widow. Administration to the son, John Sharp. (Feb. 1781).

Sharpe, John, of New England. Administration to the principal creditor, John Dennis. (Apr. 1667).

Sharp, John, of Lichfield, Staffordshire, who died in Hudson's Bay. Administration to the relict, Isabella Sharp. (Feb. 1712).

Sharpe, Robert, of Rappahannock River, Virginia, who died in Stepney, Middlesex. Administration to the brother, Abraham Sharpe. (Oct. 1666).

Sharpe, Simon, of Scartho, Lincolnshire, who died on the frigate *Grantham* in America. Probate by decree to Charles Brundon. (Mar. 1659).

Sharpe, Thomas, of Virginia. Administration to the principal creditor, Hugh Noden. (Mar. 1678). Revoked and granted to the uncle, Edward Hubbert. (Apr. 1679).

Sharp, Thomas, of Philadelphia, bachelor. Probate to John Thomas. (Apr. 1740).

Sharp, William the elder, Lieutenant of the 9th Regiment of Foot, who died in East Florida. Administration to the relict, Dorothea, now wife of John Hawkins. (July 1764).

Sharples, James, of New York City. Probate to the relict, Ellen Sharples. (July 1811).

Sharwin. *See* **Sherwin**.

Shaw, James Southby, of Columbus, Missouri, bachelor. Administration to the brother, Charles Southby Shaw, and the sister, Mary Southby Shaw; the mother, Frances Naomi Shaw, having died. (Dec. 1847).

Shaw, John, of Surbiton, Kingston-on-Thames, Surrey, who had lands in Virginia. Probate to John Heydon. (Mar. 1828). Wa.

Shaw, Lachlan, Lieutenant of an Independent Company, who died in South Carolina. Administration with will to George Urquhart, atorney for the son, Lachlan Shaw, in Scotland; the relict, Mary Shaw, James Parsons and Francis Kinloch having been cited but not having appeared. (Feb. 1765).

Shaw, Richard, of Virginia. Probate to Moses Lacy. (June 1700).

Shaw, Samuel, of Virginia. Administration to the father, John Shaw. (Oct. 1700).

Shawe, William, of Wapping, Middlesex, (intending for Virginia). Probate to the relict, Martha Shawe. (Oct. 1620). Sh.

Shaw, William, of St. Dunstan in the East, London, whose brother, John Shaw, was in New England. Probate to William Shaw and Mary Williams. (May 1693). Wa.

Shaw, William, of Port Royal, South Carolina, bachelor. Administration to the nephew, Alexander Shaw, executor of the father, John Shaw, who died before administering. (May 1774).

Shearer, William, master of the merchant ship *Friendship*, who died in Boston, New England. Probate to John Freeman. (Dec. 1763).

Shedden, William Ralston, of Roughwood, Ayr, Scotland, who died in New York. Administration with will to the son, Patrick Ralston Shedden; the executors, James Farquhar, David Hosack and the nephew, John Patrick, having died. (July 1852).

Sheffield, Thomas, of Virginia. Administration to the nephew, Lawrance Rutt, during the minority of the son, Samuel Sheffield, with the consent of the father, William Sheffield. (Aug. 1622).

Shell, Richard, formerly of Leend (*sic*), Wiltshire, but late of Sullivan, Madison County, New York. Administration to the son, Steven Shell; the relict, Ann Shell, renouncing. (July 1857).

Shemans, Benjamin, of Stepney, Middlesex, who died on H.M. ship *Dolphin* in Carolina. Probate to Mary Jordan, widow. (Aug. 1723).

Shepperd, James Nutley, of Key West, Florida, bachelor. Administration to Sarah Shepperd, widow, administratrix of the father, James Shepperd deceased. (Apr. 1846).

Sheppard, John, of Towcester, Northamptonshire, whose sons, William and Thomas Sheppard, were in Cambridge, New England. Probate to the relict, Frances Sheppard. (June 1646).

Shepherd, Joseph, formerly deputy chaplain of Colonel Morice's Regiment of Foot but late deputy chaplain of the 21st Regiment of Foot, who died in Florida. Probate to Archibald Grant. (July 1769).

Sheppard, Susannah Mary, nee Susannah Mary Lestourgeon, of Kendall County, Illinois. Administration to the husband, David Chever Sheppard. (Sep. 1857).

Sheppard, William, formerly of Old Street Road, Middlesex, tea dealer, but late of New York. Limited administration to Henry Hutchins, attorney for the relict, Mary Ann Sheppard, in New York. (Feb. 1839).

Sherley. *See* **Shirley**.

Sherlock, James, of Virginia. Administration to the relict, Hannah Sherlock. (Jan. 1710).

Sherman, Ester, of Dedham, Essex, widow, whose kinsman, Richard Sherman, was in New England. Probate to Bezaleel Angier. (Sep. 1646). Wa.

Sherman, Samuel, of Dedham, Essex, whose sister, —— Bacon, was in New England. Probate to the relict, Hester Sherman, and the son,

Sherman, *(contd.)*
Samuel Sherman. (Dec. 1644). Wa.

Sherwin, George, Captain of the 67th Regiment of Foot, who died in Boston, bachelor. Administration with will to the brother, John Sherwin; no executor having been named. (Mar. 1777).

Sherwin alias Sharwin, Richard, of New York City. Administration to John McTaggart, attorney for the relict, Ann Sherwin, in New York. (Nov. 1783).

Sherwood, Joseph Thomas, of Portland, Cumberland County, Maine. Probate to the sons, Charles Deering Sherwood, William Richard Sherwood and Edward Preble Sherwood, with similar powers reserved to the relict, Dorcas Sherwood. (Dec. 1849).

Sheward, William, of Ohio Province, bachelor. Administration to the sister, Mary Ann Sheward. (May 1836).

Shield, Benjamin, formerly of Stamford Hill, Middlesex, but late of Baltimore, North America, seaman of the American merchant ship *Two Friends*, bachelor. Administration to the brother, John Shield, and the sisters, Rebecca Robinson, widow, and Mary Watkins, widow. (Apr. 1820).

Shields, Bryan, of H.M. ships *Blond* and *Rose*, who died in Long Island Hospital. Probate to Mary Gamblin, widow. (Mar. 1781).

Shilborne, William, of Virginia, bachelor. Administration to the mother, Mary Shilborne, widow. (Feb. 1658).

Shipley, George, of New York City. Administration with will to William Remington, attorney for the relict, Hannah Shipley, in New York. (May 1804).

Shipman, Joseph, of H.M. ship *Duke*, bachelor. Administration to William Bryant, attorney for the father, David Shipman, in New Jersey. (Feb. 1749).

Shipton, Thomas, of King and Queen County, Virginia, widower. Administration to the niece, Deborah Weaver, spinster; the sister and next-of-kin, Deborah Weaver, widow, renouncing. (July 1766).

Shurley, Ralph, of Whitechapel, Middlesex, who died in Virginia. Administration to the relict, Elizabeth Shurley. (Nov. 1694).

Shirley, Thomas Frederic, formerly of Carlisle Lane, Westminster Road, Surrey, who died with his wife, Hannah, and only children, Emma and Hannah Shirley, as passengers on the American ship *Charles Bartlett* when she was run down on passage to New York by the steamship *Europa*. Limited administration to Joseph Eugene Shirley. (Sep. 1849).

Shirley, William, of Eton, Buckinghamshire, who died on the ship *James* in Virginia. Administration to the relict, Catherine Shirley. (Feb. 1708).

Sherley, William, of Virginia, bachelor. Probate to Edward Bathurst. (July 1750).

Shirley, William, Secretary to General Edward Braddock, who died in America, bachelor. Administration to the father, William Shirley. (Jan. 1757).

Shirley, William, of Boston, Massachusetts, Lieutenant-General in H.M. service, widower. Administration to the daughter, Elizabeth Hutchinson, widow. (July 1788).

Shoolbred, Mary alias Polly, of Charleston, South Carolina. Administration to the husband, James Shoolbred. (Sep. 1820).

Short, James, of Virginia. Probate to Mungo Baikie and Joseph Clarke. (Feb. 1774).

Short, John, formerly of Barnstaple, Devon, ropemaker, but late of Pleasant Grove near Tremont, Fazewell County, Illinois. Probate to William Gribble with similar powers reserved to Richard Tepper. (Aug. 1842).

Short, Mary, of Stafford, Gennessee County, United States of America. Administration to William Gribble, executor of the husband, John Short deceased. (Jan. 1856).

Shortricke, William, of York Old Fields, Virginia. Administration to the relict, Rachael, now wife of Anthony Melton. (June 1669).

Shoveler, Sarah, of Southwark, Philadelphia, widow. Administration with will by his solemn affirmation to Joseph Hancock, attorney for the sister, Mary McNeran, in Philadelphia. (Mar. 1800).

Showell, Arthur, of Carolina. Administration to the principal creditor, John Colborne. Marked "vacat" and the next entry shows a grant of the administration of Arthur Showell of Rotherhithe, Surrey, to his relict, Elizabeth Showell. (Apr. 1683).

Shower, Nathaniel, of Boston, New England, late purser of H.M. ship *Blandford*, widower. Probate to the daughter, Elizabeth Shower; the sole executor, Sir Joseph Hankey, renouncing. (Nov. 1761).

Shrimpton, Edward, of Bethnal Green, Middlesex, merchant, whose children were in Boston, New England. Administration with will to the relict, Elizabeh Shrimpton, during the absence overseas of the brother, Henry Shrimpton. (Nov. 1661). Revoked and granted to the brother, Henry Shrimpton. (Mar. 1663). Wa.

Shrimpton, Samuel, of Boston, New England. Administration with will to Elizabeth Roberts, widow, mother and attorney of the executrix, Elizabeth Shrimpton, in Boston. (June 1700).

Shrubsole, William, of South Carolina, late Lieutenant of an Independent Company in South Carolina. Probate to the relict, Elizabeth Shrubsole. (Mar. 1759).

Shubrick, Richard, of St. Philip's, Charles Town, United States of America, who died in 1777. Limited administration, following the death of the relict, Susannah Shubrick, to Edward Western Wright, attorney for the daughter, Susannah, wife of Roger Pinckney. (Oct. 1841).

Shubrick, Sarah. *See* **Smith**.

Shurley. *See* **Shirley**.

Shurlock, Robert, of Easton, Northampton County, Pennsylvania, physician, bachelor. Administration to James Stuart, attorney for the brother, Samuel Shurlock, in Big Beaver, Pennsylvania. (June 1831). Further grant in December 1878.

Shurt, George, of Bideford, Devon, merchant, whose brother, Abraham

Shurt, *(contd.)*
Shurt, was in New England. Probate to the relict, Margaret Shurt. (June 1658). Sh.Wa.

Shute, Samuel, of St. Peter Cornhill, London, a trader to New York. Probate to the relict, Anne Shute, and the son, Joseph Shute, with similar powers reserved to Thomas Andrews. (Dec. 1685).

Sibbet, Peter, of Haddington, Scotland, who died in Virginia, bachelor. Administration to the principal creditrix, Sibill Gray. (July 1678).

Sibbet, Robert, of St. Luke, Middlesex, and of the merchant ships *Pointz* and *John*, who died in Maryland, bachelor. Probate to Catherine Stringfellow, spinster. (Mar. 1737).

Sicklemore alias Ratcliffe, John, of the ship *Diamond* bound for Virginia, who died overseas. Probate to the relict, Dorothy Sicklemore, with similar powers reserved to Richard Percivall. (Apr. 1611). Sh.Wi.

Silsby, Daniel, native of Massachusetts, formerly of Georgia, afterwards of South Carolina, but who died in Christ Church, Surrey. Probate to William Gontait with similar powers reserved to Paul Hamilton. (Feb. 1791). *See* NGSQ 63/201.

Silvester, Constant, of Brampton, Huntingdonshire, who had lands in New England. Probate to the relict, Grace Silvester. (Oct. 1671). Revoked and administration granted to the daughter, Grace, wife of Sir Henry Pickering. (June 1702). Wa.

Silvester, John, quartermaster-sergeant of the 49th Regiment in New York, who died in Martinico, widower. Administration to the brother, William Silvester. (Mar. 1763).

Silvester, Joseph Hooper, formerly captain of the maintop of H.M. ship *Lily*, but late seaman of the American merchant ship *Massasoit*, who died at sea, bachelor. Administration to the sister, Frances Hannah, wife of William David Charles Read. (Apr. 1846).

Simondson, Peter, of the ship *Merchants Adventure*. Administration to Susan, wife and attorney of the next heir, Michael Deane, in Virginia. (Dec. 1696).

Simpson, Alexander, of Norfolk, Virginia, late master of H.M. ship *Swallow*. Administration with will to John Gathorne, attorney for the relict, Ann, now wife of William George, in Norfolk. (June 1771).

Simpson, Frances, formerly of Whitby, Yorkshire, afterwards of New York, then of Sligo, Ireland, but who died on the ship *Agenoria* at sea. Administration to the nephew and only next-of-kin, Robert Simpson. (Feb. 1838).

Simpson, Frederick Godwin, of 212 Bowery, New York. Administration to William Frederick Simpson, attorney for the relict, Catherine Simpson, at 160 Spring Street, New York. (Mar. 1857).

Simpson, Henry, of All Hallows on the Wall, London, who died on H.M. ship *Eagle* in Virginia. Administration to the relict, Frances Simpson. (Jan. 1704).

Simpson, John, of Stepney, Middlesex, who died in Virginia. Administration to the principal creditor, Abraham Barret; the relict, Elizabeth Simpson, renouncing. (June 1683). Inventory PROB 4/1138.

Simson, John, of Shadwell, Middlesex, who died on the merchant ship *Henry* in Virginia, bachelor. Administration to Susan, wife of Luke Hall, attorney for the principal creditor, Edward Bell. (Feb. 1727).

Simpson, John, of Savannah, North America, who died in Edinburgh, Scotland. Administration to the relict, [Anna] Jean Simpson. (Dec. 1788). ALC.

Simpson, John, of Sunbury, Georgia, bachelor. Administration to the sister, Elizabeth, wife of Robert Hume. (Feb. 1791).

Simpson, Jonathan, formerly of Boston, Massachusetts, but late of Bristol. Limited probate to Richard Lechmere. (Oct. 1795).

Simpson, Martin, of Hackney, Middlesex, whose niece, Hester Simpson, was in New England. Probate to Henry Ashurst, ---- Blackmore and Thomas Gellibrand. (Aug. 1665). Wa.

Simpson, Patrick, of John's Island, South Carolina. Probate to John Simpson with similar powers reserved to John Thomas, Thomas Black, Adam Tunno, James Witters, James Legare and Thomas Hanscome. (Mar. 1792).

Simpson, Samuel, formerly of Lowestoft, Suffolk, but late master of the brig *Ellen*, who died in New York, bachelor. Administration with will to the sister, Delia, wife of William Woods; the executor, William Woods, renouncing. (Jan. 1827).

Simson, Thomas, of New York and Philadelphia, who died in Port Royal, Jamaica. Administration to the relict, Anne Simson. (Mar. 1729). Revoked on production of a will and limited probate granted to the same. (Feb. 1730). Copy of will dated 13 October 1727, with examinations of witnesses, at PROB 20/2357.

Simpson, Thomas, of Lagan County, Ohio. Administration to Robert Abbott, attorney for the relict, Keziah, now wife of Thomas Sullivan, in Washington, America. (Mar. 1854).

Sinclair alias Sinclear, Henry, of the merchant ship *Wentworth*, who died in Boston, widower. Administration to the creditor, William Shaw; the father, Magnus Sinclair, renouncing. (Feb. 1777).

Sinckler, John, of the ship *Owners Adventure*, who died in Virginia, widower. Probate to Anne Hill. (July 1697).

Sisson, William, of Newport, Rhode Island, and of Lieutenant-Colonel Hargill's Company of the Rhode Island Regiment of Foot, who died in Havana, bachelor. Administration by his solemn declaration to Joseph Sherwood, attorney for the mother, Deliverance Sisson, in Portsmouth, Rhode Island. (Dec. 1765).

Skene, Ann, of Annapolis Royal, Nova Scotia, who died in Boston, New England, widow. Administration to the nephew and next-of-kin, John Hamilton. (Apr. 1773).

Skey, George, of the Wilderness near Stockton, California. Administration with will to John William Partridge, attorney for the relict, Myra Skey, near Stockton. (Dec. 1853).

Skilton, Mary, of St. Mary Woolnoth, London, whose sister, Joane, wife of John Wilkinson, was in New England. Probate to the nephew, Isaac Ashe. (Jan. 1654). Wa.

Skinner, Alexander, of St. Augustine, East Florida, Superintendent of Indian Affairs in the Southern District of North America. Administration with will to James Simpson, attorney for the daughter, Margaret, wife of Nathaniel Munro, in New Providence, Bahamas; the executors, Hon. John Moultrie, Rev. John Forbes, William Alexander and Robert Pain alias Payne, having died. (Feb. 1800).

Skinner, Cortlandt, formerly of New Jersey but late of Bristol. Probate to the relict, Elizabeth Skinner. (Apr. 1799).

Skynner, Henry, barrack master of the Artillery Train in St. Augustine, East Florida. Probate to Ann Samuel. (Nov. 1781).

Skinner, Richard, late of the River Mississippi near Mansack, West Florida, bachelor. Administration with will to the brother, Robert Skinner; no executor having been named. (Sep. 1775).

Skinner, Richard, formerly of London but late of New Orleans. Probate to Thomas Wilson. (Nov. 1817).

Skinner, Stephen, of Shelburne, Nova Scotia, a claimant as an American Loyalist. Limited administration with will to Gabriel Shaw, attorney for the relict, Catherine Skinner, and for Thomas Crowell, in Shelburne. (Nov. 1822).

Skinner, Thomas, of London, who died in Maryland. Probate to the brother, John Skinner. (Dec. 1706).

Skinner, William Stephens, of Boston, Massachusetts. Administration to Edward Clarke, attorney for the relict, Sarah Skinner, in Roxbury, Massachusetts. (Oct. 1845).

Skottowe. *See* **Scottow**.

Skull, Sarah, formerly of Lower Homerton, afterwards of Hammersmith, Middlesex, then of Tours, France, but late of New York, who died on the merchant ship *William and Elizabeth*, widow. Administration to the only child, Joseph Skull. (Apr. 1839).

Skull, William, formerly of Bath, Somerset, but late of Baltimore, North America, widower. Administration to Mary Skull, relict and administratrix of the only child, Robert Skull deceased. (Nov. 1788).

Slany, Thomas, of Kings Lynn, Norfolk, whose daughter, Joane Kinge, was in New England. Probate to Thomas Linge and Thomas Moore. (June 1649). Wa.

Slater, Mary, of New York. Administration with will to Charles Lodwick, attorney for Mary Leaver in New York. (Mar. 1705). *See* NGSQ 64/48.

Slatter, William, of Norfolk, Virginia, who died in Kingston, Jamaica, bachelor. Administration to the brother, Rev. Thomas Slatter; the mother, Elizabeth Slatter, widow, renouncing. (May. 1760).

Slaughter, Elizabeth, of the Bristol Diocese, who made reference to Isaac Walker in New England. Administration with will to Robert Culme; no executor having been named. (June 1646). Wa.

Slaughter, Richard Hampton, of Pensacola, Florida, bachelor. Administration to the brother, William Shewen Slaughter; the mother, Sophia Mary Slaughter, having died. (Sep. 1842).

Slaughter, Sophia Mary, of Port Hudson, Louisiana, widow. Administration to the son, William Shewen Slaughter. (Sep. 1842).

Sleigh, Joseph, of Boston, Massachusetts. Administration to Jonathan Bracebridge, attorney for the relict, Anne Sleigh, in Boston. (June 1740).

Sliter, Robert, of Portobello, America. Probate to James Alworth with similar powers reserved to Mary Ruffin and Abigail Sliter. (Dec. 1716).

Slone, James, of Boston, New England. Probate to John Hayes and James Adams. (Aug. 1737).

Slorach, James, formerly of Deptford, Kent, but late of New York. Administration with will to the mother, Esther alias Hester, wife of Samuel Pollard; the executor, John Marlar, renouncing. (May 1782).

Slough, William, of Carolina. Probate to the relict, Mary Slough. (May 1703).

Slough, William, of Bristol, who died in Virginia, bachelor. Administration to the next-of-kin, Mary Slough, spinster. (Dec. 1708).

Smaile, John, of H.M. ship *Greyhound*, who died in New York. Probate to Alexander Bibb. (Jan. 1725).

Small, Daniel, of Charles Town, South Carolina, widower. Administration to the aunt, Sarah Cadman, widow, guardian of the only children, Isaac and Sarah Small. (Feb. 1772).

Smallay, Captain Robert, of Bermuda Hundred, Virginia. Administration with will to the relict, Elizabeth Smallay; the executor, Samuel Argall, renouncing. (Nov. 1621). Sh.Wi.

Smart, John, of St. Saviour, Southwark, Surrey, who died in Maryland. Probate to the relict, Anne Smart. (June 1720).

Smith, Abraham Lynsen, of New York, Cornet on half pay of the British Legion under Brigadier-General Benedict Arnold. Administration to James Tidbury, attorney for the relict, Diana Smith, in New York. (Dec. 1827).

Smith, Alexander, formerly of Friday Street, London, but late of New York City, bachelor. Administration to William Smith and William Allan, attornies for the father, James Smith, in Auldearn, Nairn, Scotland. (Feb. 1799).

Smith, Ann, of Cook County, Illinois. Administration to John Christian Wilson, attorney for the husband, Charles Smith, in Illinois. (Sep. 1852).

Smith, Benjamin, of Charles Town, South Carolina. Limited administration with will to John Simpson, attorney for Isaac Mott in Charles Town. (June 1791). Revoked on the death of Isaac Mott and granted to John Simpson as attorney for the daughter, Mary, wife of John Gibbes, in South Carolina. (June 1797).

Smith, Boyd, of New Orleans, Louisiana. Administration to Boyd Miller, attorney for the relict, Ann Smith, in New Orleans. (Nov. 1844).

Smith, Brooke, formerly of Birmingham, Warwickshire, but late of Philadelphia. Probate to William Russell and to the brother, Joseph Smith. (Mar. 1788).

Smith, Caroline, of Cambridge, Lanawa County, Michigan, spinster. Administration to John Lacey, attorney for the father, Joseph Smith, in Chicago. (Jan. 1847).

Smith, Christopher, of New York, who died in Portmahon, Minorca. Administration to Christopher Smith, guardian of the children, Christopher and Margaret Smith; the relict, Joane Smith, having died before administering. (Mar. 1731).

Smith, Daniel, soldier of Captain McNeal's Company of the 42nd Regiment of Foot, who died in Elizabeth Town near New York, bachelor. Administration to Hannah Smith, widow, mother of the nephew and only next-of-kin, John Smith. (Apr. 1766).

Smith, David, of Norfolk, Virginia, bachelor. Administration to the brother, Elijah Smith; the father, Allison Smith, renouncing. (Jan. 1811).

Smith, Edmond, of Hopkintown, King's County, Rhode Island, and of Captain Giles Russell's Company of the Rhode Island Regiment of Foot, who died in Havana, bachelor. Administration by his solemn declaration to Joseph Sherwood, attorney for the mother, Elizabeth Smith, widow, in America. (Dec. 1765).

Smith, Edward, smith of H.M. Artillery in New York, bachelor. Probate to James Hannam. (July 1758).

Smith, Elizabeth, of Taunton, Somerset, widow, who made a bequest to Jane, wife of William Williams, in New England. Probate to Johan Westoner. (July 1654). Wa.

Smith, Elizabeth, of New York. Administration to the husband, Joshua Hett Smith. (Mar. 1785).

Smith, Elizabeth, of Wethersfield, Connecticut, widow. Limited probate to the brother, John Scott. (Mar. 1786).

Smith, Elizabeth. *See* **Nelson**.

Smith, Frederick, formerly of Cotton Court, Manchester, Lancashire, but late of Charles Town, South Carolina, merhant. Probate to the brother, Thomas Smith, with similar powers reserved to Henry Gourdin and to the brothers, John Benjamin Smith and Joseph Smith. (Oct. 1839).

Smith, George, of Virginia, who died in St. George the Martyr, Middlesex. Probate to Richard and Sarah Taylor. (Jan. 1729).

Smith, George, of the transport ship *Hercules*, who died in New York, bachelor. Probate to Behrond Ehlers with similar powers reserved to George Fisher. (Apr. 1763).

Smith, George Clement Fearn, formerly of 287 Regent Street, Middlesex, engraver, but late of Philadelphia. Administration with will to the relict, Harriot Elizabeth, now wife of William Lake. (Dec. 1844).

Smith, Henry, of London, whose nephew, Henry Mundy, was in New England. Probate to Richard Berridge. (May 1653). Sh.Wa.

Smith, Henry, of Watford, Hetfordshire, whose brother, William Smith, was in Virginia. Probate to the relict, Sarah Smith. (Feb. 1666). Wi.

Smith, Henry, of Wraysbury, Buckinghamshire, whose daughter, Mary Lord, was in New England. Probate to the relict, Anne Smith. (Oct. 1682). Wa.

Smith, Henry, of Pennsylvania, bachelor. Administration to the principal creditor, John Adams. (May 1703).

Smith, James, of Burlington, New Jersey. Probate to Sir Thomas Mackworth. (Feb. 1733 & Apr. 1736).

Smith, James, formerly of Hackney, Middlesex, but late of Virginia, bachelor. Administration to the daughter, Frances Helen Smith, administratrix with will of the father, Rev. James Smith, who died before administering. (May 1785).

Smyth, James, of Beaufort, Carolina, widower. Administration to the only child, James Smyth. (Jan. 1791).

Smith, James, of New York, Lieutenant of the late 79th Regiment. Administration to David Thomas, attorney for the relict, Mary Smith, in New York City. (Sep. 1797).

Smith, James, formerly of Hammersmith, Middlesex, but late of South Carolina, bachelor. Administration with will to the sister and only next-of-kin, Mary Lapworth, widow; the sole executor, Henry Flint, having died. (Feb. 1820).

Smith, Jane, formerly Jane Lilley, of Jamaica, who died in Philadelphia. Administration to the husband, Joseph Smith. (June 1750).

Smith, Jehosaphat, of London, who died in Boston, New England. Probate to the brother, James [or Jacob] Smith. (July 1678).

Smith, John, of Southwold, Suffolk, who had goods in New England. Probate to the relict, Helen Smith. (Feb. 1651). Sh.Wa.

Smith, John, citizen and merchant tailor of St. Sepulchre, London, whose cousin, William Smith, was in New England. Probate to the daughter, Sarah Whiting. (Oct. 1656). Wa.

Smith, John, citizen and cook of London, who made a bequest to Allen Whore in Virginia. Probate to the son, William Smith; the son-in-law, George Pouchin, renouncing. (July 1672). Wi.

Smith, John, of Carolina. Administration to the principal creditor, John Colborne. (Apr. 1683).

Smith, John, of Pennsylvania. Administration to William Wright, attorney for the relict, Jane Smith, in Scotland. (Feb. 1689).

Smith, John, of Boston, New England, who died on the ship *Nonsuch*. Administration to Elisha Cartwright, attorney for the relict, Mary Smith, in New England. (July 1689).

Smith, John, of Maryland. Administration to the relict, Mary Smith. (Aug. 1727).

Smith, John, of Hartford, Connecticut. Probate to David Williams with similar powers reserved to the relict, Anne Smith. (Jan. 1732).

Smith, John the younger, Lieutenant of the First Connecticut Regiment of Foot, who died in Havana, bachelor. Administration to Phineas Lyman, attorney for the father, John Smith, in Volluntown, Wyndham County, Connecticut. (Nov. 1764).

Smith, John, formerly Customs Officer in Philadelphia but late of Musselburgh, Scotland. Administration with will to William Cooke, attorney for the daughter, Margaret Smith, in Musselburgh. (Mar. 1789).

Smith, John, formerly of Sapcote, Leicestershire, framework knitter, but late of 608 North Third Street below Franklin Avenue, Philadelphia. Administration to the daughter, Eliza, wife of Ephraim Morley; the relict, Elizabeth Smith, renouncing. (Dec. 1856).

Smith, John Edward. *See* **Patrick, Edward**.

Smith, John Laxon, formerly of Whittlesey, Cambridgeshire, but late of Lever Street, Lafayette City, Louisiana. Probate to the brother, Simon Smith, the sister, Alice, wife of John Grounds, and to William Searle, with similar powers reserved to the brother, William Edward Steven Smith, and the sister, Janette, wife of Joseph Gibbs. (July 1840).

Smith, Joseph, soldier of the 28th Regiment, who died in Crown Point, America. Administration to the relict, Hannah Smith. (Dec. 1763).

Smith, Joseph, of New York City. Administration with will to Keene Stables, attorney for the relict, Dorothy Smith, and the daughter, Elizabeth Smith, in New York City; the executors, William Frederick Rhinelander and Robert Carter, renouncing. (Sep. 1795). Revoked on the death of Keene Stables and granted to John Stables, attorney for the daughter, Elizabeth, wife of George Nelson, in New York. (Feb. 1822). Revoked on her death and granted to John Stables as attorney for her only surviving child, Sophia Augusta Breintnall, widow, in Newark, New Jersey. (Aug. 1848).

Smith, Martha, of Chicago, Illinois, spinster. Administration to John Lacey, attorney for the father, Joseph Smith, in Chicago. (Jan. 1847).

Smith, Mary M. *See* **Stone**.

Smith, Nathaniel, who died overseas and whose sister, Hannah Mellowes, was in New England. Administration with will to the kinsman, Thomas Edwards, and the cousin, Nathaniel Edwards; no executor having been named. (Feb. 1651). Sh.Wa.

Smith, Nicholas, of Stepney, Middlesex, who died in Virginia. Administration to the relict, Elizabeth Smith. (Nov. 1710).

Smith, Oliver, of Ratcliffe, Stepney, Middlesex, who died on the ship *Susanna* in Virginia. Probate to the relict, Mary Smith. (Oct. 1686).

Smyth, Peter, late of Brentford Butts, Middlesex, chaplain of H.M. ship *Tilbury*, who died in America, widower. Probate to Rev. William Chilcott. (Dec. 1757).

Smith, Phebe, of Virginia, spinster. Administration to the cousin and next-of-kin, Richard Crowder. (Oct. 1676).

Smith, Richard, of the ship *Duke of York*, who died in Virginia or at sea, bachelor. Probate to Elizabeth Davis. (June 1680).

Smith, Richard, of Williamsburg, Virginia, bachelor. Administration to the aunt, Susan, wife of Matthew Lester. (Oct. 1804).

Smith, Robert, of St. Michael Bassishaw, London, who had lands in Virginia. Probate to the relict, Judith Smith. (July 1623). Revoked on her death and administration granted to James Clarke, half-brother of the daughter, Hannah Smith, during her minority. (Feb. 1630). Wa.

Smith, Robert, of Kent Island, Maryland. Administration to the brother and next-of-kin, William Smith. (Oct. 1707).

Smith, Robert, Lieutenant-Captain of the Royal Artillery Train under Lieutenant-General Braddock, who died in America, bachelor. Administration to the mother, Mary Smith. (Sep. 1756).

Smith, Robert, formerly of Savannah, Georgia, but late of Jamaica. Probate to Benjamin Eyre with similar powers reserved to the brother, Thomas Smith. (Apr. 1778).

Smith, Robert, Bishop of South Carolina. Limited administration with will to Edward Western, attorney for the daughter, Sarah Motte Rutledge, and the son, Robert Smith, in Charleston. (Feb. 1842).

Smith, Roger, of Virginia. Administration to the sisters, Gertrude and Audrey James alias Smith. (Oct. 1625).

Smith, Samuel, of George Town, South Carolina, bachelor. Administration to the brother and next-of-kin, Robert Smith. (Mar. 1768).

Smythe, Samuel, formerly of Baltimore, Maryland, afterwards of Queen Street, Brompton, Middlesex, but late of Belfast, Ireland. Probate to the relict, Elizabeth Smythe, and the daughters, Mary and Ellen Smythe. (May 1827).

Smyth, Sarah, wife of James Smyth, of Beaufort, North America. Administration to the only child, James Smyth. (Mar. 1791).

Smith, Sarah, formerly Sarah Shubrick, wife of Rt. Rev. Robert Smith, Bishop of South Carolina. Limited administration to Edward Western, attorney for Sarah Motte Rutledge, widow, and Robert Smith, in Charleston. (Feb. 1842).

Smith, Sarah, of Newport, Rhode Island. Administration to the husband, William Smith. (June 1856).

Smith, Simon, of Stepney, Middlesex, whose granddaughter, Judith, wife of Richard Tozer, was in New England. Probate to Simon Smith. (Jan. 1666). Wa.

Smith, Sir Thomas, of Sutton at Hone, Kent, who had estate in Virginia. Probate to the relict, Dame Sarah Smith, and to John Smith, Richard Smith and Sir David Watkins, with similar powers reserved to Nicholas Crispe. (Oct. 1625). Wi.

Smith, Thomas, of West Clandon, Surrey, whose brother, John Smith, was in New England. Probate to the nephew, Jeremy Smith. (Oct. 1651). Wa.

Smith, Thomas, of Pennsylvania, who died on H.M. ship *Cumberland*. Probate to Samuel Cherry. (June 1763).

Smith, Thomas, of Hebron, Washington County, North America. Administration to George Wildes, attorney for the relict, Jane Smith, in Hebron. (Mar. 1831).

Smith, Thomas, formerly of Woolwich, Kent, but late of Ceres Town, McKean County, Pennsylvania, farmer, widower. Administration to the son, Christopher Hill Smith. (Apr. 1836).

Smith, Thomas, of Pittsburgh, Pennsylvania. Administration to Anne Todhunter, widow, attorney for the relict, Maria Smith, in Pittsburgh. (Nov. 1851).

Smith, Warrin, of Holborn, Middlesex, an adventurer to Virginia. Probate to Dennis Breton. (May 1615). Wi.

Smith, Whitefoord, formerly of Charlestown, South Carolina, but late of Cowper Street, North Leith, Scotland. Probate to Robert Brunton, Charles Spence and Rev. Charles Clowston. (Sep. 1826).

Smith, William, of St. John the Baptist, Bristol, who died in Virginia. Administration to the relict, Margaret Smith. (Nov. 1679).

Smith, William, of Dunbar, Scotland, who died in Virginia. Administration to John Tod, attorney for the relict, Jane Smith alias Bulcraig, in Dunbar. (Jan. 1738).

Smith, William, of Boston, New England, bachelor. Administration to the mother, Elizabeth, wife of Daniel Clay. (Sep. 1743).

Smith, William, formerly of the Royal Irish Regiment of Foot but late of Philadelphia, bachelor. Administration to the brother, John Galt Smith. (May 1774).

Smith, William, formerly of St. Olave Hart Street, London, but late of Charles Town, South Carolina, bachelor. Administration to John Shoolbred, attorney for the mother, Margaret, wife of William Borland, in Kilmarnock, Scotland. (Dec. 1782).

Smith, William, formerly of Bedford but late of Henderson, Kentucky, widower. Administration to the son, Richard Smith. (Dec. 1831).

Smith, William Barlow, of British Hollow near Potosi, Wisconsin, brewer. Administration with will to Edwin Chadwick, attorney for the relict Sarah Chadwick, now wife of George Walker Suttenfield, in California. (Dec. 1856).

Smithett, Robert, formerly of Bermondsey, Surrey, but late of H.M. ships *Humber* and *Newport*, who died in Boston, New England. Probate to the relict, Proteza Smithett. (Oct. 1695).

Smocke, John, of Maryland, widower. Administration to the brother and next-of-kin, Edward Smocke. (Aug. 1711).

Smythies, William, of New York City. Administration to the relict, Margaret Smythies. (Mar. 1785).

Snape, Timothy, of London, son of Rev. Edmund Snape of St. Saviour, Southwark, Surrey, (bound for Virginia), who died overseas, bachelor. Probate to the brother, Samuel Snape, and the sister, Hannah Barker alias Snape. (July 1629). Wa.

Sneath, Jacob, of H.M. ships *Pearl*, *Liberty* and *Amphion*, who died in New York Hospital. Probate to Susanna Sharp, widow. (Aug. 1785).

Snell, Catherine, of St. James, Goose Creek, South Carolina, spinster. Administration with will to James Crockatt and William Roos, attornies for Rev. Timothy Millechamp and Hugh Grange in South Carolina. (Dec. 1743).

Snell, Nathaniel, of Hillingdon, Middlesex, who made a bequest to David Maybanke in Carolina. Probate to the relict, Sarah Snell. (Apr. 1692). Wa.

Snodgrass, Neal, of Norfolk, Virginia, bachelor. Administration to the creditor, Robert Gilmour; the brother and sisters and only next-of-kin, Hugh, Ann and Margaret Snodgrass, having been cited but not having appeared. (Apr. 1785).

Snooke, John, of St. Clement Danes, Middlesex, who had lands in Virginia.

Snooke, *(contd.)*
Probate to Ralph Sedgewicke with similar powers reserved to William Higginson. (Sep. 1665). Wa.

Solomon, Elias, formerly of New England but late of Rotherhithe, Surrey, mariner. Probate to Sarah Pike, widow, with similar powers reserved to Sarah Pike, spinster. (Aug. 1732).

Solomons, Solomon, of Savannah, Georgia, bachelor. Administration to the brother, Levy Solomons; the father, David Solomons, renouncing. (Feb. 1770).

Somers, Charles, of St. Olave, Southwark, Surrey, who died on the merchant ship *Batchelor's Habitation* in Virginia. Administration to the principal creditor, John Whibben, attorney for the relict, Mary Somers. (Jan. 1702).

Somers, Sir George, of Barne [?Arne], Dorset, (bound for Virginia). Probate to the brother, John Somers. (Aug. 1611). Sh.Wa.

Somers, John, of Virginia, bachelor. Administration to the mother, Agnes Somers. (Nov. 1672).

Southcot, Leonard, of the ship *Loyal Rebecca*, who died in Virginia. Probate to Thomas Short. (June 1677).

Southell, Seth, of Virginia. Administration with will to the principal creditor, William Bowtell; the relict, Anne Southell, having died before executing. (Feb. 1697).

Southen, George, of Virginia. Administration to the relict, Elizabeth Southen. (Nov. 1673).

Soumaien, Simson, of Philadelphia, Lieutenant of Captain Horatio Gates' Independent Company, who died in America. Probate to the relict, Aleathea Soumaien. (Dec. 1755).

Souther, Nathaniel, of the ship *Samuel and Henry*, bachelor. Administration to the brother, Samuel Souther, attorney for the father, Joseph Souther, in Boston, New England. (Aug. 1691).

Southgate, Lydia, of Richmond, Virginia, widow. Administration to William Taylor, attorney for the son, James Southgate, in Richmond. (Mar. 1823).

Southwick, Thomas, of Virginia. Probate to Mary, wife of Roger Hare. (Dec. 1743).

Sowers, Thomas, of New York City, Captain and Engineer of H.M. Ordnance. Administration to John Sowers, attorney for the relict, Ann Sowers, in New York City. (Jan. 1775).

Spalding alias Spaulding, John, of Plainfield, Wyndham County, Connecticut, Captain of the First Connecticut Regiment of Foot, who died in Havana. Administration to Phineas Lyman, attorney for the relict, Lucy Spalding, in Plainfield. (Nov. 1764).

Sparhawke, John the elder, of Great Coggeshall, Essex, whose brother, —— Sparhawke, was in New England. Probate to the son, John Sparhawke, and to Christopher Sheriffe. (Sep. 1653). Wa.

Sparhawk, Susannah, of New York City, widow. Administration to William Limbey Grosvenor, attorney for the only child, Elizabeth Sparhawk, in Halifax, Nova Scotia. (Dec. 1800).

Sparke, Michael, of St. Sepulchre without Newgate, London, who had goods in Virginia. Probate to the son-in-law, Humphrey Baskerville, after sentence for the validity of the will. (Mar. 1654). Wi.

Sparkes, William, formerly of Hereford but late of Brooklyn, North America, bachelor. Administration to the father, Thomas Sparkes. (July 1821).

Sparling, John, of Liverpool, Lancashire. Limited administration with will of estate other than that in America to Edward Chaffers and John Bolton. (May 1800).

Sparrow, Edwin, of Burlington, United States of America, blacksmith. Administration to the relict, Elizabeth Sparrow. (Feb. 1857).

Sparrow, Samuel, formerly of Peckham, Surrey, afterwards of the merchant ship *Industry*, but late of Charleston, South Carolina. Administration with will to the sister, Elizabeth Stansbury. (Feb. 1801). Revoked and granted to the relict, Sarah, now wife of John Edward Acres. (Jan. 1804). Revoked on her death and granted to her husband. (Mar. 1804).

Spearing, William, of New York, Lieutenant of an Independent Company, who died in Havana. Administration to the relict, Ann Spearing. (Aug. 1763).

Speed, Charles, of Deptford, Kent, who died in Rhode Island, bachelor. Administration by his solemn declaration to the cousin german and next-of-kin, William West. (June 1759).

Spelman, Thomas, of Truro, Cornwall, and Virginia. Administration with will to the brother, Francis Spelman, during the absence overseas of the relict, Hannah Spelman. (Apr. 1627). Sentence for the validity of the will December 1628. Sh.Wa.

Spence, Patrick, of Copeley, Westmorland County, Virginia, who died in Allington, Dorset. Probate to Daniel Gundry. (May 1710).

Spencer, Anne, of St. Bride, London, widow. Administration to a nephew by a brother, Paul Batchellor; the sister, Margaret Porter, widow, renouncing. (Feb. 1715). Revoked and granted to the daughter, Margaret, wife of Thomas Addison of Virginia, now in London. (July 1715).

Spencer, John, of Savannah, Georgia, bachelor. Administration to the brother and next-of-kin, Henry Spencer. (May 1761).

Spencer, Mottrom, of Nomini, Westmoreland County, Virginia, and of the Earl of Essex's Regiment, who died in St. Giles in the Fields, Middlesex. Administration with will to the brother, William Spencer of Cople, Bedfordshire. (May 1703).

Spencer, Nicholas, of Virginia. Administration with will to John Rust of All Saints Lombard Street, London, silkman, attorney for the sons, Nicholas and John Spencer; the other executor, William Spencer, renouncing. (Jan. 1700).

Spencer, Thomas, of Kingston-on-Thames, Surrey, who had goods in New England. Probate to Nicholas Kidwell. (Aug. 1648). Wa.

Spencer, Thomas, bastard son of John Spencer by an Indian woman, Jane Miller, bachelor. Administration to Henry Spencer for the benefit of

Spencer, *(contd.)*
the Crown. (Dec. 1764).

Spencer, William, of Cople, Bedfordshire, whose brother, Nicholas Spencer, was in Virginia. Probate to John Luke with similar powers reserved to Oliver Luke. (June 1686). Wa.

Spencer, William, of Upper Marlborough, Maryland, bachelor. Administration to the brother and next-of-kin, Joseph Spencer. (Dec. 1768).

Spendelove, Roger, Major of the 43rd Regiment of Foot, who died in Boston. Probate to the relict, Jane Spendelove. (Aug. 1776).

Spendelow, Charles, of H.M. ship *Gibraltar*, Lieutenant Engineer in General Braddock's expedition in Virginia, bachelor. Administration to the principal creditor, William Wilson; the uncle, Rev. Charles Spendelow, renouncing. (Jan. 1756).

Spenlove, Ann, of Mount Pleasant, North America, spinster. Administration to the sister, Elizabeth Davies, widow. (Sep. 1792).

Sperrmaine, Launce, of the ship *Royal William*, who died in Virginia, bachelor. Probate to Elizabeth, wife of David Sperrmaine, with similar powers reserved to the said David. (June 1700).

Speyer, John, formerly of New York but late of Paris, merchant, widower. Administration to George Law, attorney for the mother, and next-of-kin, Amalia Speyer, widow. (Dec. 1816).

Splatt, Ann. *See* **Brasseur**.

Spooner, John, of Boston, Massachusetts. Administration with will to Sir William Baker, attorney for the sons, John and William Spooner, in Boston. (June 1764).

Spooner, John, of Boston, New England. Administration with will to Abraham Dupuis, attorney for Andrew Oliver and Arnold Welles in Boston. (May 1769).

Spotswood, Alexander, of Orange County, Virginia, late Major-General and Colonel of the American Regiment, who died in Annapolis, Maryland. Administration with will to Robert Cary, attorney for Elliott Bengar and Robert Rose in Virginia. (Feb. 1742).

Sprague, John, of Boston, Massachusetts. Administration to the son, Lawrence Sprague; the relict, Esther Sprague, having died before administering. (Nov. 1776).

Spratley, Benjamin, formerly of Winslow, Buckinghamshire, but late of Virginia, bachelor. Administration to the brother, Richard Spratley; the mother, Jane Spratley, renouncing. (Nov. 1783).

Springer, Benjamin, formerly of St. Augustine, North America, but late of St. Luke, Middlesex. Probate to Richard Dabbs. (Dec. 1786).

Sprowle, Andrew, formerly of Milton, Scotland, but late of Gosport, Virginia. Limited administration pending the suit of McCulloch v. Sprowle to Thomas McCulloch. (June 1778). Revoked and probate granted to Thomas McCulloch with similar powers reserved to George Logan, George Surdy and John Hyndman; the executor, John Bun, renouncing. (Mar. 1782). ALC.

Spurzheim, Gaspar, formerly of Gower Street and Highgate, Middlesex,

Spurzheim, *(contd.)* afterwards of Paris, but late of Boston, North America, M.D., widower. Administration with will to Mathias Hermesdorf, attorney for the brother, Earl Theodor Spurzheim, in Vienna. (Feb. 1835).

Squire, Daniel, of New York. Administration with will to George Moor, father and guardian of the executrix, Jane Moor. (Dec. 1786).

Squire, Harriet Louisa, formerly Harriet Louisa Miles, of Philadelphia. Administration to George Squire, attorney for the husband, Henry John Squire, in Philadelphia. (July 1844).

Stacy, Samuel, of H.M. ship *Nightingale*, who died in New England. Probate to John Stacy. (Mar. 1716).

Stacie, Thomas, of Maidstone, Kent, who had lands in Virginia. Probate to Robert Joye. (Sep. 1619). Wi.

Stagg [Stegge], Captain Thomas, of Virginia, who died off the coast there. Probate to the relict, Elizabeth Stagg. (July 1652). Sh.Wa.

Stegge, Thomas, of Virginia. Probate to the relict, Sarah Stegge. (May 1671). Wa.

Stalker, Peter, of South Carolina, bachelor. Administration to the brother, Samuel Stalker; the brother, John Stalker, renouncing. (Feb. 1769).

Stanesby, John, of Maryland, widower. Administration to the brother, William Stanesby. (Jan. 1692).

Stanfield, Thomas of H.M. ship *Tryton*'s prize, who died in New York. Administration to the niece by the mother, Mary Everatt, spinster. (Nov. 1713).

Stanford, Hugh, of Virginia, bachelor. Administration to the brother, Anthony Stanford. (July 1658).

Stanford, Joseph, of Detroit, North America. Administration with will to the brother, John Stanford; the relict, Susan Stanford, and the only child, George Stanford, having been cited but not having appeared. (Feb.1851).

Stanford, Samuel, formerly of Lingfield, Surrey, but late of Fort Leavenworth, who died in Buffalo, North America, bachelor. Administration to the father, John Stanford. (Jan. 1852).

Stanley, Hugh, of Maryland. Administration with will to Elizabeth Stanley, mother of the nephews, John and Edward Stanley, during their minority; the relict, Dorothy Stanley, renouncing. (Dec. 1671).

Stanley, Margaret, of Vauxhall Cottage near Camptown, Essex County, New Jersey, widow. Administration to the brother, John Reynolds. (Aug. 1851).

Stanover alias Stannever, John, of St. Martin in the Fields, Middlesex, late of H.M. ships *Bredah* and *Tryal*, but who died as boatswain of H.M. ship *Alborough* in South Carolina. Administration to the sister, Dorothy Banck. (Nov. 1733). Revoked and granted to the relict, Deborah Stanover. (Sep. 1734).

Stansbury, Samuel, of East Haven, New Haven County, Connecticut. Administration to Samuel Williams, attorney for the relict, Elizabeth Stansbury, in East Haven. (Feb. 1825).

Stanton, George, of Virginia. Administration to Catherine Cooke, widow, grandmother of the children, Joseph and Mary Stanton, during their minority. (Aug. 1698).

Stanton, Jeremiah, of Staten Island, New York. Limited administration with will to Isaac Lascelles Winn of New York City, attorney for the relict, Louisa Teresia Stanton. (July 1772).

Stanton, John, of Groton, Connecticut, Captain of the First Connecticut Regiment of Foot, who died in Havana. Administration with will to Phineas Lyman, attorney for the relict, Prudence Stanton, and the son, Samuel Stanton, in Connecticut. (Jan. 1765).

Stanton, Nicholas, of Ipswich, Suffolk, clerk, whose kinsmen, Judith, wife of Henry Smith, and Joseph Moyse, were in New England. Probate to the relict, Mary Stanton. (Feb. 1650). Wa.

Staple, Peter, of Kittery, York County, Massachusetts, Lieutenant on half pay. Administration to James Fitter, attorney for the son, Peter Staple, in Kittery. (Feb. 1769).

Staples, Amos, of the Connecticut Regiment of Foot, who died in Havana, bachelor. Administration to Phineas Lyman, attorney for the father, Jacob Staples, in Connecticut. (Dec. 1763).

Staples, Isaac, of the Connecticut Regiment of Foot, who died in Havana, bachelor. Administration to Phineas Lyman, attorney for the father, Jacob Staples, in Connecticut. (Dec. 1763).

Staples, Robert, master of the merchant ship *Eagle*, who died in South Carolina, bachelor. Administration to the principal creditors, William Mewse and Thomas Harding; the father, Robert Staples, renouncing. (Dec. 1719).

Staples, William, formerly of Sevenoaks, Kent, but late of Utica, New York. Administration with will to the son, Thomas Staples; the executors, John Barringer and Samuel D. Lamatter, having died. (Jan. 1826).

Stapylton, Francis Samuel, Captain of the 9th Regiment of Foot, who died in Hubberdown, New York. Administration with will to the sister, Ann, wife of Rev. John Bree; no executor having been named. (Nov. 1779).

Stares, Alfred Guildford, formerly of Titchfield, Hampshire, but late of New York, bachelor. Administration to the brother, Thomas Cartwright Stares; the mother, Mary Stares, widow, renouncing. (Apr. 1856).

Starke, Thomas, of London, merchant, who left his estate in Virginia to his son, John Starke. Probate to the sons, John and Thomas Starke. (Mar. 1706). Wi. *See* NGSQ 70/39.

Starr, Anna, of New London, Connecticut. Limited administration to James Morgan, attorney for the husband, Jonathan Starr, in New London. (July 1838).

Stead, Benjamin, formerly of South Carolina but late of St. Marylebone, Middlesex. Probate to the son, Benjamin Stead and the daughter, Mary Stead, with similar powers reserved to the daughter, Elizabeth, wife of Ralph Izard. (June 1776).

Stedman, Robert, of Bow Tracy, Devon, and formerly of London, who died in South Carolina, peruke maker and planter. Administration to the relict, Sarah Stedman. (July 1767).

Stedman, Solomon, of Boston, New England. Administration with will to Henry Cole, trustee for the executor, John Stedman, now overseas. (Dec. 1697). Wa.

Steel, Allen, of Boston, New England, and H.M. ship *Comet Bomb*. Probate to Henry Saunders, attorney for the relict, Deborah Steel, in Boston. (Dec. 1754).

Steele, Edward, of Albion, Illinois. Administration to the son, Arthur Steele; the relict, Sophia Steele, renouncing. (July 1855).

Steele, John, of London, who died in Zeeland on his return from Virginia. Probate to the relict, Amy Steele. (Dec. 1638). Sh.Wi.

Steel, John, of St. Philip's, Charles Town, South Carolina, who died in Plymouth, Devon. Probate to the relict, Mary Steel. June 1745).

Stegge. *See* **Stagg**.

Stehelin, Thomas, Lieutenant of H.M. Artillery Train, who died in Boston, bachelor. Administration to the father, Benjamin Stehelin. (Apr. 1777).

Stent, William, of Portsmouth, Hampshire, who died on the ship *Planters Adventure* in Virginia, bachelor. Administration to the brother, Richard Stent; the mother, Grace Cooke alias Stent, renouncing. (Apr. 1680).

Stephen, Alexander, Lieutenant of Sir Geoffery Amherst's Royal Americans, who died in Virginia. Administration with will to John Russell, attorney for the brother, John Stephen, in Virginia. (June 1770).

Stephens. *See* **Stevens**.

Stephenson. *See* **Stevenson**.

Stepkin, Charles the elder, of London, who died in Virginia. Administration with will to Elizabeth Stepkin, widow, mother of the children, Charles and Theodosia Stepkin, during their minority; the executors, Joseph Lowe and George Richards, renouncing. (July 1689).

Sterry, William, of Bristol, who died in Boston, New England. Administration with will to the principal creditor, Giles Merricke; the executor, Adam Winthrop, in Boston, and the relict, Charity Sterry, renouncing. (Oct. 1685).

Stevens, Charles, formerly of Two Waters Mill, Hemel Hempstead, Hertfordshire, but late of Cumberland Street, Brooklyn, New York. Probate to the sisters, Eliza Ann and Angelina Margaret Stevens. (Nov. 1857).

Stevens, Clement William, of Jefferson, Florida. Administration to John Horsley Palmer, attorney for the relict, Sarah Johnson Stevens, in Pendeton District, Anderson State, South Carolina. (Jan. 1839).

Stevens, Edward, of Bristol, who died in Virginia. Administration to the relict, Grace Stevens. (Apr. 1694).

Stephens, James, Captain of the Royal Regiment of Artillery, who died in

Stephens, *(contd.)* New York, bachelor. Administration to the mother, Ann Stephens, widow. (Nov. 1768). Revoked on the production of a will and administration with will granted to the same; no executor having been named. (May 1769).

Stephens, John, of New York, Captain in Colonel William Gooch's American Regiment, who died in Cuba. Administration to Richard Jenneway, attorney for the relict, Blandina alias Belinda Stephens, in New York. (Apr. 1743).

Stevens, Nathaniel, of St. Merrin, Cornwall, who died on the ship *Margaret* in Virginia. Administration to William Peter, attorney for the relict, Anne Stevens, now in distant parts. (June 1679).

Stephens, Newdigate, of Savannah, Georgia. Administration to the son, William Stephens. (July 1772).

Stevens, Ontario Brook Bridges, formerly of Hamilton, Canada, but late of Keyport, New Jersey, bachelor. Administration to the mother and next-of-kin, Elizabeth Stevens, widow. (Apr. 1852).

Stephens, Richard, of H.M. transport ship *John and Jane*, who died in New York, bachelor. Administration to the mother and next-of-kin, Mary, wife of John Stroud. (Feb. 1781).

Stevens, Robert, of St. James, Goose Creek, South Carolina. Probate to John Vicaridge. (Nov. 1722).

Steevens, Thomas, of New Orleans, mariner. Probate by his solemn declaration to Christopher Young and by his oath to Benjamin Meredith. (July 1823).

Stevens, William, of Virginia. Administration to the principal creditor, Thomas Jauncey. (Sep. 1651).

Stephens, William, of Bristol, who died in Virginia. Administration to the relict, Alice Stephens. (July 1684).

Stevenson, Allen, of Chester, merchant, who had estate in America. Probate to Robert Sparke. (Jan. 1700).

Stevenson, Cornelius, of New York City. Administration with will to Effingham Lawrence, attorney for the nephews and niece and only next-of-kin, Robert Bartow, Anthony Bartow, Thomas Bartow and Charity Wright, spinster, in New York; no executor having been named and the relict, Susannah Stevenson, having died. (Mar. 1806). Revoked on the death of Effingham Lawrence and granted to William Effingham Lawrence as attorney. (Sep. 1806).

Stephenson, Enoch, of New York City. Administration with will to Robert Lindsay, attorney for the relict, Catherine Stephenson, and for Peter Valet and Joseph Robinson; Pennington Stephenson renouncing. (Dec. 1753).

Stevenson, James, of St. Dunstan in the West, London, who died in Salem, New England. Probate to the principal creditor, Jocelyn Dansey; the relict, Elizabeth Stevenson, renouncing. (July 1728).

Stevenson, John, of Albany City, North America. Probate to James Stevenson and Dudley Walsh with similar powers reserved to the relict, Magdalen Stevenson, and the daughters, Sarah, wife of the said

Stevenson, *(contd.)*
Dudley Walsh, and Anne Stevenson. (Dec. 1810).

Stephenson, John, formerly of Hamborough, Yorkshire, but late of Whitesborough, Oneida County, New York. Administration to the relict, Elizabeth Stephenson. (July 1856).

Stevenson, Mary, nee Mary Rogers, formerly of Wadhurst, Sussex, but late of Henrietta, Munro County, New York. Administration to John Rogers, attorney for the husband, Henry Stevenson, in Henrietta. (Apr. 1844).

Steward, William, of Deptford, Kent, who died on H.M. ship *Deptford* in Boston, New England. Administration to the relict, Sarah Steward. (July 1698).

Stewart, Alexander, Lieutenant of General James Oglethorpe's Regiment, who died in Frederica, Georgia. Probate to the brother, James Stewart, with similar powers reserved to Alexander Heron, George Dunbar, Patrick Sutherland, White Outerbridge, Dougal Stewart and Patrick Houston. (Apr. 1748).

Stewart, Alexander, sergeant in Captain Sterling's Company of the First Batallion of the 42nd Regiment, who died in New York. Administration to the brother, William Stewart. (Jan. 1766).

Stewart, Alexander, formerly Major of the New Jersey Volunteers, but late of Stirling, Scotland. Probate to William Stewart with similar powers reserved to John Stewart. (Nov. 1820).

Stewart, Anthony, of London Town, Maryland, widower. Administration to the creditor, Thomas Blane; the children, James, Margaret, Bell, Mary, Jane and Leslie Stewart, having been cited but not having appeared. (Dec. 1791).

Stuart, Charles, of Mobile, West Florida. Probate to Elizabeth Hatfield, widow, with similar powers reserved to Hon. James Bruce, David Hodge and George Troup. (Sep. 1781).

Stuart, Charles, formerly of Gateshead, Durham, but late of Philadelphia, bachelor. Administration to the brother and next-of-kin, Edward Stuart; the mother, Ann Stuart, widow, having died. (June 1809).

Stewart, David, formerly of Doden but late of Ann Arundell County, Maryland. Administration to William Murdoch, attorney for the brothers and next-of-kin, William and James Stewart, in Maryland. (Dec. 1816).

Stewart, Elizabeth A. *See* **Clendinen**.

Stuart, Francis, Captain of the 26th Regiment of Foot, who died in New York. Administration to the relict, Mary Stuart. (May 1779).

Stewart, George, of Boston, New England, Captain in the American Regiment, who died in the West Indies. Administration with will to Christopher Kilby, attorney for Benjamin Faneuil in Boston. (Aug. 1744).

Stuart, Hugh, of Mount Pleasant, West Chester County, North America, Lieutenant of half pay of Donkin's Royal Garrison Batallion. Administration to William Tustin, attorney for the relict, Mary Stuart, in New York City. (Sep. 1812).

Stuart, Isaac, Captain on half pay of Dunlap's Corps of British Provincials in North America, widower. Limited administration to James Tidbury, attorney for the children, Martha, wife of William Kenricks, and Hannah Bown, widow. (Mar. 1821).

Steuart, James, of Woolwich, Kent, who died in Charles Town, South Carolina. Probate to Mungo Murray the younger with similar powers reserved to Mungo Murray the elder. (Oct. 1755).

Stuart, Hon. James, Lieutenant-Colonel of the First Regiment of Guards, who died in Guildford, America, bachelor. Administration to the mother, Lady Margaret Blantyre, widow. (Aug. 1781).

Stewart, James, of New Jersey, Captain on half pay of the New Jersey Volunteers. Administration with will to James Tidbury, attorney for Eleanor Stevens, widow, in New Jersey. (Apr. 1820).

Stuart, John, of Pensacola, West Florida. Probate to the relict, Sarah Stuart, with similar powers reserved to Edward Fenwick, Alexander Rose and William McKinnon. (July 1783).

Stewart, John, Lieutenant in the Regiment of Carolina Highlanders, who died in Woodville near New Orleans, bachelor. Administration to the brother, Alexander Stewart. (Oct. 1827).

Stewart, Kenneth, of Edinburgh, Scotland, Captain in the late North Carolina Highland Regiment. Probate to John Cameron with similar powers reserved to Hector MacLean, Alexander Stewart, Robert Burt, Kenneth McCashill and Donald McCashill. (July 1815).

Stewart, Peter, of Stewart Lodge, Canton, Greene County, New York. Administration with will to Robert Samuel Palmer, attorney for the relict, Catherine Desmont Stewart, on St. Martin's Island in the West Indies. (Aug. 1836).

Stuart, Ruth, of Boston, New England, widow. Probate to the son, Sir John Stuart, with similar powers reserved to Rufus Greene and Mary Johnson, widow. (July 1752).

Stewart, William, of Boston, New England. Administration with will to John Soden, attorney for Thomas Steel in Boston. (Feb. 1729).

Stickney, Caleb, of Newbury Port, Massachusetts. Administration to the relict, Sarah Stickney. (Oct. 1801).

Stickney, Sarah. *See* **Coleman**.

Stickney, William, of Salem, Massachusetts, bachelor. Administration to the father, Samuel Stickney. (June 1835).

Stiebel, Bernhard, of Baltimore, Maryland, bachelor and bastard. Administration to George Maule for the use of the Crown. (Feb. 1848).

Stiffe, William, of Upton, Essex, who died on the ship *Rainbow*, bachelor, a trader to Virginia. Administration to the cousin and next-of-kin, John Digby. (Oct. 1673).

Stirling, George, of Edinburgh, Scotland, Lieutenant of General Oglethorpe's Regiment, who died in Georgia. Administration to Alexander Stirling, attorney for the father, John Stirling, in Glasgow, Scotland. (Jan. 1749).

Stocker, Joseph, of Wiveliscombe, Somerset, whose son, Ephraim Stocker,

Stocker, *(contd.)* went to Virginia. Probate to the relict, Mary Stocker. (May 1679). Revoked on her death and administration granted to Amos Stocker, Robert Hayne, Thomas Grove and Nicholas Marshall, guardians of the minor children, Mary, Ephraim and Obadiah Stocker, in Wiveliscombe. (Feb. 1681). *See* NGSQ 67/212.

Stocking, Francis, of Norfolk, who had a plantation in Pennsylvania. Probate to the nephew, John Stocking. (Feb. 1730).

Stockman, William, of Barford, Wiltshire, whose cousin, Gerret Edington, was in Virginia. Probate to the brother, Joseph Stockman. (Oct. 1658). Wi.

Stockwell, James, formerly of Boston, North America, but late of Madras, East Indies, an officer in the service of Wallajah, the late Nabob of Arcot. Administration to the nephew, Rev. William Batchelder, administrator of the relict, Jane Stockwell deceased; all others with title having been cited but not having appeared. (Feb. 1818).

Stoddard, William, of Boston, New England, Lieutenant of H.M. ship *Antelope*, who died in Flushing, Mylor, Cornwall. Probate to Henry Pascoe and Norris Bawden. (Nov. 1780).

Stodhart, Samuel Lake, of Brunswick, Maine, bachelor. Administration to the sister, Charlotte Stodhart. (Sep. 1851).

Stokes, John, of Ottery St. Mary, Devon, who died in Pennsylvania, bachelor. Administration to the brother and next-of-kin, Thomas Stokes. (Sep. 1717).

Stolpys alias Stolpee, John, of Virginia, who died on the ship *Mary*. Probate to Albert Albertson. (Apr. 1692).

Stolion, Jane, of London, widow, who died overseas having goods in New England. Probate to the son, Abraham Stolion. (May 1647). Sh.Wa.

Stolyon, Thomas, of Warbleton, Sussex, who had goods in New England. Administration with will, after sentence for its validity, to Samuel Spatchurst, John Wood the elder and Samuel Store, attornies for the inhabitants of Warbleton; the executors, Richard Weller and Edward Hawkesworth, renouncing. (Nov. 1680). Wa.

Stone, John, of the merchant ship *Rappahannock*, who died in Virginia, bachelor. Administration to William Morris and Susannah his wife, attornies for the mother, Susannah Stone, in Topsham, Devon. (Dec. 1737).

Stone, Margaret, of St. Peter le Poor, London, widow, whose husband, William Stone, was in Virginia. Probate to Joseph Godwin. (Nov. 1676).

Stone, Mary Maria, nee Mary Maria Smith, of Brooklyn, New York. Administration to Amos Fielding, attorney for the husband, Robert Stone, in Nauvoo, Hancock County, North America. (May 1847).

Stone, William, of Philadelphia. Administration with will to William Vaughan, attorney for Samuel Nicholas and Christopher Kuhler in Philadelphia. (July 1788).

Stonier, Mary Ann, nee Mary Ann Hardwick, of Benton, Yates County, New York. Administration to the husband, Joseph Stonier. (Jan. 1850).

Stooke, Richard, formerly of Exeter, Devon, but late of America, bachelor. Administration to the brother, Pinder Luke Stooke; the mother, Patience Stooke, renouncing. (Jan. 1808).

Story, George, of Stepney, Middlesex, who died in Virginia. Administration to the relict, Elizabeth Story. (Aug. 1675).

Storey, Gorge, chief mate of the merchant ship *Favourite*, who died in Salem, bachelor. Administration to the sister, Mary Storey. (July 1777).

Storey, Ralph, of Wapping, Middlesex, who died in Virginia. Probate to the relict, Avice Storey. (June 1664).

Storrow, Thomas, of Boston, Massachusetts, Lieutenant of the 100th Regiment. Administration to David Thomas, attorney for the relict, Ann Storrow, in Boston. (Aug. 1795).

Stott, Robert, formerly of Charles Town, South Carolina, but late of Manchester, Lancashire. Probate to the sister, Ann Stott. (Nov. 1795).

Stoughton, John, Lieutenant of an Independent Company of Foot, who died in New York City. Administration to Edward Paul, attorney for the relict, Ruth Stoughton, in New York City. (June 1770).

Stowe, Rev. Solon John, formerly of Bermuda but late of Staunton, Virginia. Probate to the niece, Sophia Malvina Cox, spinster; the other executor, William John Cox, renouncing. (Apr. 1856).

Stowers, James, formerly of Bridgenorth, Shropshire, but late of Poughkeepsie, North America, bachelor. Administration to the mother and next-of-kin, Anna Maria Stowers, widow. (Mar. 1837).

Strachan, James, formerly of Montrose, Scotland, afterwards of London, but late of the United States of America, widower. Administration to the son, George Blair Strachan. (June 1844).

Strachey, William, of St. Augustine, London, whose daughter, Arabella, wife of John Waters, was in Virginia. Probate to George Richards. (Mar. 1687).

Stratfold, Thomas, formerly of Bearton, Berkshire, but late of Virginia. Probate to Henry Hinore. (May 1706).

Stratton, Gordon, formerly of Villiers Street, Strand, Middlesex, but late of Charleston, South Carolina. Probate to the relict, Albertina Mary Anna Theresa Maria, now wife of Robert Harrison, with similar powers reserved to William Gordon. (Feb. 1802).

Stratton, John, of James City, Virginia. Administration to the relict, Joanna Stratton. (June 1641).

Strawbridge, William, formerly of Warren Street, Tottenham Court Road, Middlesex, but late of Lower Providence, Montgomery County, Pennsylvania. Limited administration with will to Horatio G. Jones in Roxborough, North America. (Dec. 1830).

Strean, John, surgeon's mate of H.M. ship *Russell*, who died in New York, bachelor. Administration to Robert Boyd and John Bailie, attornies for the brother, Samuel Strean, in Magharafelt, Ireland; the mother, Jean Strean, widow, renouncing. (Aug. 1783).

Streatfield, Louisa Jane, of Varick Street, New York. Administration to

Streatfield, *(contd.)* Edward Hockley, attorney for the husband, William Everest Streatfield, in New York. (July 1851).

Stredwick, Samuel. *See* **Strudwick**.

Street, Martha, formerly Martha Madgwick, of Mount Pleasant, Westchester County, New York. Administration to Elizabeth Sarah, wife of Joshua Gilbert, the daughter and administratrix of the husband, William Street the elder deceased. (Aug. 1839).

Street, William the elder, of New York, widower. Administration to the daughter, [Elizabeth] Sarah Street. (Mar. 1824).

Street, William the younger, of Philadelphia, bachelor. Administration to the sister, Elizabeth Sarah Street. (Mar. 1824).

Streeter, Edward, formerly of Buxted, Sussex, yeoman, but late of Philadelphia, labourer, widower. Administration to Robert Hoffman Faulconer, attorney for the only surviving child, Abel Streeter, in Philadelphia. (Nov. 1839).

Stretton, Henry, formerly of Midland Cottage, Hampshire, afterwards of Mont Cassell in French Flanders, but late of New Orleans. Probate to the surviving executor, Thomas Bourdillon. (July 1853).

Strickland, John, formerly of Camberwell, Surrey, but late of Baltimore, Maryland. Administration to the brother, Charles Strickland; the relict, Ann, now wife of Thomas Shepherd, renouncing. (Jan. 1797).

Stringer, Rowland, of Plymouth, Devon, who died on the ship *Daniel and Elizabeth* in Virginia, bachelor. Administration to the father, Francis Stringer. (Mar. 1690).

Stringer, Samuel, of Epsom, Surrey, whose son [unnamed] was in Maryland. Probate to the relict, Louise Stringer. (July 1738).

Strong, Thomas J., of Baldwin County, Alabama. Administration with will to the creditor, James Jones; the executors, Henry Toulmin and Henry B. Slade, having died, and the executor, James Alexander Torbert, the daughter, Hannah S. Strong, and her mother, Ann Strong, having been cited but not having appeared. (Jan. 1826).

Strong, William, of New York, who died in Savannah, bachelor. Administration to the nephew, James Strong. (Aug. 1828).

Strudwick, Martha, of Orange County, North Carolina, widow. Administration with will to Peter Browne, administrator of the sole executor, William Francis Strudwick deceased, and attorney for the son, Samuel Strudwick, in Orange County. (Sep. 1820).

Strudwick alias Stredwick, Samuel, of Wilmington, North Carolina. Probate to the relict, Martha Strudwick. (Mar. 1797).

Strudwick, William Francis, of Orange County, North Carolina. Administration to Peter Browne, attorney for the son, Samuel Strudwick, in Orange County; the relict, Martha Strudwick, having died. (Sep. 1820).

Stuart. *See* **Stewart**.

Sturdy, Robert, of Virginia, bachelor. Administration to the father, Robert Sturdy. (May 1715).

Sturdy, William, of Stafford County, Virginia. Probate to Robert Sturdy,

Sturdy, *(contd.)* father and administrator of Robert Sturdy deceased; the relict, Margaret Sturdy, having died. (May 1705). Wi.

Sturge, Thomas, formerly of Weston-super-Mare, Somerset, cabinet maker, but late of Mill Farm, Warren County, New York, farmer. Administration by his solemn declaration to the creditor, Thomas Marshall Sturge; the relict, Emma Sophia Sturge, renouncing for herself and for her children, Ellen, Hannah, Thomas Marshall, and Rebecca Sturge. (July 1853).

Sturges, Henry, of the ship *John and Margaret*, who died in Maryland. Administration to the principal creditor, Adam Mason; the relict, Mary Sturges, renouncing. (Aug. 1697).

Sturman, Richard, of Nomini, Westmoreland, Virginia. Probate to Rebecca Frodsham alias Sturman. (Sep. 1672). Wa.

Sturt, Thomas, of Hampton River, Virginia, bachelor. Administration to the sister and next-of-kin, Mary, wife of David Frazier. (Mar. 1765).

Style, John, of Stepney, Middlesex, whose nephew, George Burrough, clerk, was in New England. Probate to William Burrough. (July & Aug. 1686). Wa.

Style, Samuel, of Portugal, whose sister, Elizabeth Style, was in New England. Probate to Henry Boade with similar powers reserved to Simon Smith and John Middleton. (Apr. 1665). Wa.

Suggitt, Jane, of Northampton County, Virginia, widow. Administration to the mother and next-of-kin, Jane Selby, widow. (Oct. 1771).

Suggitt, John, of Newcastle-upon-Tyne but late of Northampton County, Virginia. Administration with will to Jane Selby, widow, mother and administratrix of the relict, Jane Suggitt. (Oct. 1771).

Surman, John, of St. Botolph Bishopsgate, London, who died in Pennsylvania, widower. Administration to the principal creditrix, Ann Thompson. (Feb. 1744).

Susans, John, of H.M. ship *London*, who died in Long Island Hospital. Probate to the brother, William Susans. (Oct. 1783).

Sutherland, Alexander Smith, formerly of New Orleans but late of New York, widower. Administration to Jane Webb, aunt and guardian of the only children, Jane, Ann, William and Mary Sutherland; the grandfather and only next-of-kin of the said children, being an imbecile. (Oct. 1828).

Sutherland, Ebenezer, Lieutenant of Marines, who died in New York, bachelor. Administration to Hector Mackay, attorney for the father, James Sutherland, in Kearquhar, Scotland. (Aug. 1783).

Sutton, Henry, of Stepney, Middlesex, who died on the merchant ship *William and John* in Virginia. Administration to the relict, Elizabeth Sutton. (June 1703).

Sutton, John, of St. Giles Cripplegate, London, who died in Virginia. Administration to the relict, Frances Sutton. (May 1651).

Swan, Thomas, of Southwark, Surrey, who died in Virginia. Administration to Micajah Perry, attorney for the relict, Mary, now wife of Robert Randall, in Virginia. (Oct. 1691).

Swanwick, Mary, of Alexandria, District of Columbia, widow. Administration to George Wharton Marriott, attorney for the only child, Mary, wife of James Bruce Nicholls, in Alexandria. (Dec. 1821).

Swanwick, Thomas, formerly of Chester, tobacconist, but late of Kaskasia, Illinois. Limited administration to Edward Fricker and James Stansfeld. (Jan. 1843).

Swayne, Charles, Ensign of the 33rd Regiment, who died in New York, bachelor. Administration to the mother, Elizabeth Swayne. (Jan. 1785).

Swaine, John, of the ship *New Hopewell*, who died in Virginia. Administration to the creditor, John Neave; the relict, Elizabeth Swaine, renouncing. (Sep. 1700).

Swan, John, who died at sea near New England. Probate to Richard Heading with similar powers reserved to Margaret Heading. (Aug. 1701).

Swan, Mary, of South Carolina. Administration to the husband, Thomas Swan. (May 1784).

Sway, Henry, of New York, mariner of H.M. ship *Star Bomb*. Probate to Morgan Phillips. (Nov. 1712).

Swayne. *See* **Swaine**

Swett, Joseph, of Boston, New England, who died on H.M. ship *Defiant*. Probate to John Gill. (Jan. 1696).

Swift, Benjamin, of Nantucket, North America, mariner. Administration to Paul Pease, attorney for the relict, Elizabeth Swift, in Nantucket. (July 1805).

Swift, James, of St. Mary Abchurch, London, who died in Hackney, Middlesex, having goods in Boston, New England. Probate to the relict, Sarah Swift. (June 1684).

Swift, John the younger, of Philadelphia. Administration to Hannah Wimbolt, widow, sister and attorney of the relict, Elizabeth Swift, in Philadelphia. (Jan. 1714).

Swift, Joseph, a retired Captain of the Pennsylvania Loyalists in North America. Administration to David Davies, attorney for the relict, Ann Swift, in Pennsylvania. (Nov. 1810).

Swift, Thomas, Lieutenant of Colonel Holt's Regiment of Marines, who died in Boston, New England, bachelor. Administration by decree to the principal creditor, Robert Hood. (June 1722).

Swinnerton, Sarah, of 2 Congress Street, Newark, New Jersey, widow. Administration to the only children, George and James Swinnerton. (Feb. 1845).

Sybada, Kempo, of Stepney, Middlesex, mariner, who had lands in New England. Probate to the relict, Mary Sybada. (Apr. 1659).

Sykes, Bernard, of London, who died in Virginia. Administration by decree to George Gay during the absence overseas of the relict, Elizabeth Sykes. (May 1682).

Syme, Andrew, of New Orleans, bachelor. Administration to the brother, Hugh Syme; the mother, Anthony (*sic*) Syme, widow, renouncing. (Jan. 1821).

Symes, Rev. Robert, formerly of Rye, Sussex, but late of America. Administration to the relict, Mary Symes. (May 1813).

Symmes, Ebenezer, of Boston, Massachusetts. Administration to the creditor, John Greenwood; the relict, Ann Symmes, and the only child, Mary Symmes, having been cited but not having appeared. (Dec. 1779).

Symonds, John, of Great Yeldham, Essex, whose cousin, William Symonds, was in New England. Probate to Jane Symonds, John Pepys and Thomazine Pepys. (May 1693). Wa.

Symonds, Ralph, formerly of St. Botolph Aldgate, London, but late of Virginia, surgeon. Caveats by the creditors, William Lake and Thomas Elton. (1666: PROB 40/1).

T

Taber, Gideon, of Rhode Island, who died on H.M. ship *Scarborough*, bachelor. Administration by his solemn declaration to Joseph Sherwood, attorney for the brother and next-of-kin, Stephen Taber, in Tiverton, Rhode Island. (Dec. 1765).

Tait. *See* **Tate**.

Talbot, Henrietta alias Harriet, of Boston, New England, spinster. Administration to the mother and next-of-kin, Mary Talbot, widow. (Apr. 1799).

Talbot, William Henry, Captain of the 17th Regiment of Light Dragoons, who died in New York, bachelor. Administration to the brother, Hon. John Chetwynd, Earl Talbot; the mother, Hon. Catherine Talbot, widow, having died before administering. (Feb. 1785).

Talcott, Noah, of New York. Administration to Frederick Westell, attorney for the relict, Elizabeth Talcott, in New York City. (Apr. 1843).

Tamlyn, George, formerly of Testwood, Eling, Hampshire, but late of Oyster Bay, New York, widower. Administration to the son, Charles Tamlyn. (Jan. 1853).

Tapin, James Alfred, of Pensacola, West Florida, bachelor. Administration to the mother, Theodosia Tapin, widow. (Feb. 1801).

Tappen alias Toppen, David, of Woodbridge, East Jersey, and of H.M. ship *Vigilant*. Administration to William Tappen, attorney for the relict, Mary Tappen, in Woodbridge. (July 1754).

Tapscott, George Loveless, formerly of Minehead, Somerset, afterwards of New York, but late of the Republic of Texas, bachelor. Administration to Amos Greenslade and Thomas Porsford, assignees of the father, John Tapscott, who was cited but did not appear. (Dec. 1840).

Tarry, Samuel, of Mecklenburgh County, Virginia. Limited administration with will to John Tabb of Petersburg, Virginia; the executor, Abraham Green, renouncing, the executors, Edward and Richard Booker, having died, the relict having also died, and the children, Frances, Mary, Rebecca, George and Edward Tarry, having been cited but not having appeared. (Dec. 1768).

Tasker, Benjamin, of Annapolis, Maryland. Limited administration with will to Osgood Hanbury and William Anderson of London, merchants, attornies for the relict, Ann Tasker. (Dec. 1768, Nov. 1770 & Nov. 1772). Wi.

Tait, George, formerly of Wapping High Street, Middlesex, but late of New York City, formerly a merchant but late a master mariner, bachelor. Administration to the brother, Charles Tait. (July 1819).

Tait, James, of H.M. ship *Captain*, who died in Boston Hospital, bachelor. Administration to James Loutted, attorney for the brother, Patrick Tait, in St. Olla, Orkneys. (Aug. 1774).

Tate, John, formerly of the Orkneys but late of Fort Vancouver, Oregon. Probate to Archibald McKinlay and Forbes Barclay. (Jan. 1855).

Tattnall, Edward Fenwick, of Chatham County, Georgia. Administration

Tattnall, *(contd.)*
with will to the brother, Josiah Tattnall; the executor, William Coffee Daniell, renouncing. (Aug. 1846).

Tatnall, Samuel, formerly of London but late of Boston, Massachusetts. Administration to John Sturges, attorney for the relict, Ann Tatnall, in Boston. (Oct. 1830).

Tatton, William, of St. Mary Aldermary, London, who made a bequest to John Machen in Virginia. Probate to the son, William Tatton. (Feb. 1666). Revoked on his death and administration granted to his relict, Anne, now wife of John Cumberlege. (July 1682). Wa.

Taverner, Robert, of Maryland, bachelor. Administration to the brother, Thomas Taverner. (Feb. 1676).

Tavernor, Robert, of London, who died in Virginia, merchant. Probate after sentence for the validity of the will to Bridget Fowlkes. (Jan. 1677).

Tawse, Thomas, Lieutenant of the 71st Regiment of Foot, who died in Savannah, Georgia. Administration with will to Gavin Young, attorney for Janet, wife of John Stewart, for the brother, Charles Tawse, and for Elizabeth, wife of Archibald Jamieson, in Scotland. (July 1781).

Taylerson, Ann, formerly of Sedgefield, Durham, afterwards of London, but who died at sea, spinster. Administration to George Jackson, executor of the brother, Daniel Taylerson deceased; the mother, Margaret Taylerson and the sister, Margaret Taylerson alias Robinson, having also died. (Dec. 1835).

Taylerson alias Robinson, Margaret, formerly of Sedgefield, Durham, but late of the United States of America, spinster. Administration to George Jackson, executor of the brother, Daniel Taylerson deceased; the mother, Margaret Taylerson, widow, having died. (Dec. 1835).

Tayloe, William, of Virginia. Administration to the brother, Thomas Tayloe. (Aug. 1661).

Taylor, Abraham, formerly of Philadelphia but late of Bath, Somerset. Probate to the son, John Taylor. (Mar. 1772).

Taylor, Bryan, of St. Stephen Coleman Street, London, who died in Maryland, bachelor. Probate to the brother, Freeman Taylor; the executor, Philip Smith, having died, and the mother, Mary Taylor, widow, renouncing. (May 1737).

Taylor, Charlotte Anne, of Detroit, Michigan, spinster. Probate to Thomas Bagnall and Thomas Metcalfe. (July 1840).

Taylor, Daniel, of St. Stephen Coleman Street, London, whose brother, Edward Rawson, was in New England. Probate to Mark Hildersley the elder, late Alderman of London. (Apr. 1655). Wa.

Taylor, Daniel, of St. Martin Ludgate, London, who died in Maryland. Administration to the sister and next-of-kin, Anne Yates alias Taylor. (July 1677).

Taylor, Edward the younger, formerly of Charles Town, South Carolina, but late of the River Mississippi, bachelor. Administration to the creditor, John Dolland; the only child, Elizabeth, wife of the said John Dolland, and the only next-of-kin of Edward Taylor the elder, renouncing. (Nov. 1782).

Taylor, George, formerly of New York City but late of Soder Hill, New Jersey, gold beater. Administration to the relict, Sarah Taylor. (June 1836).

Taylor, Henry, of St. Margaret, Westminster, Middlesex, who died in Virginia. Administration to the relict, John (*sic*) Taylor. (May 1677).

Taylor, Humphrey, of Pennsylvania, who died in New York. Probate to the mother, Elizabeth Taylor, widow; the wife, Mary Taylor, having died in the testator's lifetime. (Oct. 1716).

Taylor, Jane, of Red River Settlement, North America, widow. Probate to Sir George Simpson. (Nov. 1845).

Taylor, John, of Whitechapel, Middlesex, who died in Virginia. Administration to Cicely, wife of the principal creditor, Alexander Nash, during his absence. (June 1665).

Taylor, John, of Knightsbridge, Middlesex, whose son, Samuel Taylor, was in Virginia. Probate to Thomas Grover and Nicholas Broadway. (May 1641). Wi.

Taylor, John, of Savannah, Georgia. Probate to the brother, William Taylor. (Oct. 1772).

Taylor, John Chisim, formerly of Crediton, Devon, but late of Shepherdsville, Bullitt County, Kentucky, civil engineer, bachelor. Administration to the father, John Taylor. (May 1854).

Taylor, Joseph, of Potuxon, Maryland. Administration to the son, Benjamin Taylor; the brother, Richard Taylor, renouncing. (Oct. 1709).

Taylor, Robert, of Stepney, Middlesex, who died in Virginia. Administration to the relict, Sarah, now wife of John Bidmore. (Oct. 1656).

Tayler, Thomas, formerly of Clements Inn, Middlesex, but late of Cortlandt Street, New York. Administration to the relict, Sarah Tayler. (Oct. 1852).

Taylor, Thomas Matthew, of Jacksonborough, South Carolina, bachelor. Administration to the father, Christopher Taylor. (Aug. 1807).

Taylor, William, of Perth Amboy, New Jersey. Administration with will to Daniel Coxe, attorney for the relict, Elizabeth Taylor, in Perth Amboy. (July 1808).

Taylor, William, of New York City. Administration to the relict, Hepzibah Elizabeth Taylor. (Nov. 1845).

Taylor, William Blackwell, formerly of Upper Seymour Street, Connaught Square, Middlesex, but late of Dean Street, Brooklyn, New York. Administration to the relict, Emma Taylor. (June 1857).

Taylor, William Swain, formerly of Great Canterbury Buildings, Lambeth, Surrey, afterwards of New York City, but late of Berwick-upon-Tweed, Scotland, who died at sea as a passenger on the merchant ship *Ceres*, widower. Administration to the only child, Mary Taylor. (May 1840).

Tea, Robert, of St. Martin in the Fields, Middlesex, who died in Virginia. Administration to the relict, Thomazine Tea. (Feb. 1709).

Teagle, John, of Clerkenwell, Middlesex, who died in New England.

Teagle, *(contd.)*
Administration to the relict, Deborah Teagle. (Dec. 1711).

Teare, Samuel, of the ship *Anne*, who died in Virginia. Administration to the relict, Mary Teare. (July 1695).

Temple, Dame Elizabeth, of Boston, North America, widow. Probate to Thomas Sendall Winthrop with similar powers reserved to James Bowdoin and James Temple Bowdoin. (May 1816).

Temple, Sir John, Consul-General to the United States of America, who died in New York. Administration with will to Charles Rivington Broughton, attorney for the relict, Lady Elizabeth Temple, in New York City. (Feb. 1799). Revoked and granted to Thomas Sendall Winthrop, executor of the relict, Dame Elizabeth Temple deceased. (May 1816).

Temple, Joseph, of King William County, Virginia. Limited administration with will to the son, William Temple. (Jan. 1762).

Temple, William, of King William County, Virginia. Limited administration with will to John Snow of Bristol, merchant. (May 1767).

Tenant, Rev. James, of Princess Ann County, Virginia. Administration with will to Thomas Sandford, attorney for Elizabeth Conner alias Tenant, wife of Louis Conner and relict of Anthony Walke, and for Charles Sayer, in Virginia. (Dec. 1729).

Terrell, Robert, of London, merchant, who had goods in Virginia. Probate to the cousin, Robert Alpen. (Nov. 1677).

Terron, Samuel, formerly of Christ Church, Middlesex, but late of George Town, North America, bachelor. Administration to the sisters, Esther Gabriel, widow, and Judith Cartwright, widow. (Apr. 1790).

Terry, Zebedee, of Taunton, North America, Captain of the late Royal New England Regiment. Administration to David Thomas, attorney for the relict, Hannah Terry, in Taunton. (Aug. 1795).

Tew, Richard, of Newport, Rhode Island. Probate to the brother, John Tew, with similar powers reserved to the son, Henry Tew. (Mar. 1674). Wa.

Thatcher, Bartholomew, of Hunterdon County, New Jersey. Administration with will to James Tidbury, attorney for Henry Clifton in New Jersey; Hezekiah Waterhouse renouncing. (May 1818).

Thatcher, Peter, of New Sarum, Wiltshire, clerk, whose brother, Anthony Thatcher, was in New England. Probate to the relict, Alice Thatcher. (Aug. 1641). Wa.

Thayer, Arodi, of Dorchester, Norfolk County, United States of America, widower. Administration to Thimothy Wiggin, attorney for the daughter, Charlotte Thayer, in Dorchester. (Mar. 1832).

Thayer, John, of Greenwich, United States of America. Administration to Thomas Holme Bower, attorney for the relict, Achsah Thayer, in Greenwich. (July 1819).

Thelwall, David, Ensign of the 34th Regiment, who died in Fort Chartres in Illinois, bachelor. Administration to the brother, John Thelwall; the mother, Mary Thelwall, renouncing. (Nov. 1767).

Thiring, Anthony, Lieutenant-Paymaster of the 21st Regiment of Foot, who

Thiring, *(contd.)* died in Mobile, West Florida, bachelor. Administration to the creditor, Maria Elizabeth, wife of Richard Spencer; the mother, Anna Thiring, widow, and the brother and sister, Michael Thiring and Juliana, wife of John Frazer, renouncing. (July 1767).

Thomas, Arthur, of New York City, bachelor. Administration to Abraham Pastorius, attorney for the father, Arthur Thomas, in New York. (Feb. 1784).

Thomas, Bartholomew, of Virginia. Administration to the relict, Mary Thomas. (Nov. 1673).

Thomas, David, of Christ Church, London, who died in Carolina. Administration to the sister, Susan, wife of John Staples. (Jan. 1711).

Thomas, Edward, of H.M. ship *Rose*, who died in South Carolina, bachelor. Administration to the creditor, George Jacobs; the brother, John Thomas, renouncing. (May 1738).

Thomas, James, of Philadelphia, who died in St. Margaret Lothbury, London. Administration with will to John Askew, attorney for Samuel Preston in Philadelphia. (Feb. 1712).

Thomas, John, late of Cornwall Road, Lambeth, Surrey, who died as a passenger on the ship *Charles Bartlett* bound for New York, carpenter, bachelor. Administration to the father, Thomas Thomas. (Aug. 1849).

Thomas, Nathaniel Ray, formerly of Marshfield but late of Windsor, Massachusetts. Administration with will to Brook Watson, attorney for the relict, Sarah Thomas, in Windsor. (Oct. 1789).

Thomas, William, of Llantwit Major, Glamorgan, who had lands in America. Probate to the brother, Alexander Thomas. (June 1649).

Thomas, William, of Virginia, who died at sea. Probate to the relict, Judith Thomas. (Oct. 1660). Wi.

Thomlinson. *See* **Tomlinson**.

Thomson, Alexander, of Charles Town, South Carolina, who died in Jamaica. Administration to the relict, Mary Thomson. (Sep. 1783).

Thomson, Alexander, of New York, bachelor. Administration by his solemn affirmation to the brother and only next-of-kin, John Thomson. (Oct. 1798).

Thomson, Andrew, of Elizabeth City and County, Virginia, bachelor. Administration to the brother, Alexander Thomson M.D. (Apr. 1724).

Thomson, Ann, of New Jersey, widow. Administration to the daughter, Anna Maria, wife of Michael Houseal. (Apr. 1801).

Thompson, Anna, of Charleston, South Carolina, widow. Probate to the daughters, Susan Eliza Gaillard, widow, and Sarah Maria Kiddell, widow, and to the son, Robert Thompson. (Aug. 1849).

Thompson, Christopher, of Virginia, widower. Administration to the principal creditor, John Andrewes. (Sep. 1687).

Thompson, David, of Stepney, Middlesex, who died on the ship *Willing Mind* in Virginia. Administration to the creditor, Nicholas Felton; the

Thompson, *(contd.)*
relict, Mary Thompson, renouncing. (June 1679).

Thomson, David, formerly of York Town, Virginia, but late of Carolina. Probate to Joseph Davidson with similar powers reserved to Joseph Anderson. (Dec. 1749).

Thompson, George, of New York City, hatter, bachelor. Administration to the father, Thomas Thompson the elder. (July 1841).

Thompson, Henry, of Boston, New England. Administration to John Sharpe, attorney for the relict, Elizabeth Thompson, in New England. (Dec. 1686).

Thompson, Isaac, Lieutenant of the First Connecticut Regiment of Foot, who died in Havana. Administration with will to Phineas Lyman, attorney for the brother, Samuel Thompson, in New London, Connecticut. (Jan. 1765).

Tompson, Jacob, of Bristol, who died on the ship *Sarah* of Bristol in Virginia. Probate to the relict, Susanna Tompson; no executor having been named. (Aug. 1699).

Thomson, James, of H.M. ship *Rose*, who died in Carolina, bachelor. Probate to William Livingston. (Dec. 1738).

Thompson, John, of Virginia. Probate to Thomas Haistwell with similar powers reserved to Henry Hartwell. (Apr. 1699). Wi.

Thompson, John, of Bermondsey, Surrey, whose cousin, Alexander Thompson, distiller, was in Rhode Island. Probate to the relict, Anne Thompson. (May 1740).

Thompson, John, of Boston, New England, who died on the private warship *Saltash*. Administration to William Ford, attorney for the relict, Mary Thompson, in Boston. (Feb. 1751).

Thompson, Joseph, of Natchez, West Florida. Limited administration with will to John Thompson. (Dec. 1781).

Thompson, Maurice, of Haversham, Buckinghamshire, who had lands in Virginia. Probate to the son, Sir John Thompson. (May 1676). Wa.

Thomson, Robert, of Stoke Newington, Middlesex, who had lands in New England. Probate to the son, Joseph Thomson, with similar powers reserved to the relict, Frances Thomson. (Dec. 1694). Validity of the will confirmed in Trinity Term 1695. Wa.

Thompson, Samuel, of St. Gregory, London, whose nephew, Thomas Thompson, was to go to his mother in New England. Probate to Samuel Gelibrand. (Nov. 1668). Wa.

Thomson, Samuel, of Shadwell, Middlesex, who died in Virginia. Probate to Thomas Anderson. (June 1694).

Thompson, Thomas, of Carolina, bachelor. Administration to the brother, Edward Thompson. (Nov. 1706).

Thomson, Thomas, [of Scotland] bound for Maryland. Probate to the brother, James Thomson. (June 1736).

Thomson, William, Lieutenant of the First Connecticut Regiment of Foot, who died in Havana, bachelor. Administration to Phineas Lyman, attorney for the brother and next-of-kin, Job Thomson, in Windsor, Hartford County, Connecticut. (Nov. 1764).

Thompson, William, formerly of Newbridge, Radnor, but late of Bathurst, New York, bachelor. Administration to the sister, Elizabeth Thompson; the mother and next-of-kin, Ann Thompson, having died. (Feb. 1854).

Thorn, Elizabeth, formerly of Brenchley, Kent, but late of Albany, America, widow. Probate to John Martin with similar powers reserved to John Fuggle. (Oct. 1820).

Thorndike, Herbert, Prebend of Westminster, Middlesex, whose nieces, Alice and Martha Thorndike, were in New England. Probate to Edward Buckley. (July 1672). Wa.

Thornton, George, formerly of Oxford Street, Middlesex, ironmonger, but late of Buffalo, New York. Administration to the relict, Mary Ann Thornton. (July 843).

Thornton, Robert, formerly of Clapham Common, Surrey, but late of New York. Limited administration to John Thornton; the relict, Maria Thornton, renouncing. (Apr. 1839).

Thorowgood, Joseph, of London, who died in Carolina, bachelor. Probate to John Ashby with similar powers reserved to the brother, William Thorowgood. (Jan. 1685). Wa.

Thorogood, Mary. *See* **Wright**.

Thorpe, Catherine, of Middle Plantation, York County, [Virginia], widow. Administration to the father, Francis Seyton. (Nov. 1695).

Thorpe, Henry, formerly of Liverpool, Lancashire, but late of Knowsley, Lancashire, who had lands in Pennsylvania. Probate to the brother, Thomas Thorpe, with similar powers reserved to Elizabeth Smallman. (Jan. 1711). Revoked and granted to William Henderson, husband and administrator of the surviving executor, Elizabeth Henderson alias Smallman deceased. (July 1733).

Thorpe, Otho, of All Hallows on the Wall, London, whose cousin, John Grice, was in Virginia. Probate to the relict, Frances Thorpe. (July 1686). Wi.

Thorpe, Sarah, of Charles Town, South Carolina. Administration to the husband, Robert Thorpe. (Nov. 1737).

Thorpe, Thomas, of Stepney, Middlesex, who died in Virginia. Probate to the relict, Jane Thorpe. (Jan. 1724).

Thorpe, William, of Bangor, Maine, bachelor. Administration to the sister, Catherine Simmons, widow; the mother, Isabella Thorpe, having died. (July 1848).

Thrasher, William, of the ship *Success*, who died at sea, widower. Administration to the sister, Mary Hill, wife of William Thrasher (*sic*), now living in [New] England. (Aug. 1680).

Throckmorton, Raphael, of St. Gregory, London, whose brother-in-law, William Wallthall, was in Virginia. Probate to Edward Throckmorton. (May 1670).

Throckmorton, Richard Samuel, of New York City. Administration to the sister, Catherine, wife of John Wesley Bartleson; the relict, Sarah Jane, now wife of John Wells Littlefield, renouncing. (Apr. 1851).

Throckmorton, Robert, of Paxton Parva, Huntingdonshire, who had lands

Throckmorton, *(contd.)* in Virginia. Probate to Thomas Bromsall and Edward Mason. (May 1699).

Thunell, William, of Newport, Rhode Island, and of Lieutenant-Colonel Christopher Hargill's Company, who died in Havana, bachelor. Administration by his solemn declaration to Joseph Sherwood, attorney for the mother, Elizabeth Thunell, in Bristol County, Rhode Island. (Dec. 1765).

Thurman, Susanna, of New York City, widow. Probate to John Thurman with similar powers reserved to Nicholas Roosvelt and Dirck Shuyler. (Jan. 1760).

Thurmur, John, of Calvert County, Maryland. Administration with will to the principal creditor, Thomas Elwes; no executor having been named. (Feb. 1669).

Thurston, Robert, of St. Sepulchre, London, (bound to Virginia). Probate to the brother-in-law, Thomas Wilde. (Jan. 1678). Wi.

Tice, Susannah, of Cincinnati, Ohio. Administration to the husband, William Tice. (Apr. 1826).

Tice, William, who was born in Motcombe, Dorset, and died overseas, bachelor, whose sister, Anne Tice, was in New England. Probate to Robert Smith with similar powers reserved to John Crouch and William Horder. (Aug. 1649). Sh.Wa.

Tilden, Joseph, citizen and girdler of St. John Walbrook, London, whose nieces were in New England. Administration with will to the brother, Hopestill Tilden, during the absence of the nephew, Joseph Tilden, son of the brother, Nathaniel Tilden. (Mar. 1643).

Tilghman, Richard, of London, (intending a voyage to the East Indies), whose natural daughter, Elizabeth, was in Maryland. Probate to David Godfrey and John Godfrey. (June 1786).

Tilley, James, of Newport, Rhode Island, and of Lieutenant-Colonel Christopher Hargill's Company of the Rhode Island Regiment of Foot, who died in Havana, bachelor. Administration by his solemn declaration to Joseph Sherwood, attorney for the brother and next-of-kin, William Tilley, in Newport. (Dec. 1765).

Tilson, John, of Boston, New England, chief mate of the merchant ship *Blakeney*. Probate to Richard Comport. (Aug. 1757).

Timson, William, of Bruton, York County, Virginia. Administration with will to Neil Buchanan, executor of the brother, John Timson, who died before executing; the mother, Anna Maria Timson, refusing to appear. (June 1736).

Tindall, Ann, of Mansfield, Pennsylvania, widow. Administration to the daughter, Mary Ann, wie of George Snoad. (Apr. 1839).

Tisdale, James, of Boston, North America, who died in 1796. Limited administration to Ebenezer Maitland. (Jan. 1809).

Tobias, Henry, of New York. Administration to the relict, Augusta Tobias. (June 1847).

Todd, Humphrey, of H.M. ship *Deptford*, who died on H.M. ship *Adventure* in Boston, New England. Probate to John Slater with similar powers

Todd, *(contd.)*
reserved to Elianor Slater. (Feb. 1714).

Todd, Samuel, of Londonderry, New Hampshire, commander of the schooner *Rachel*, who died in Jamaica, bachelor. Administration to the sister, Sarah Todd. (Aug. 1755).

Todd, Thomas the elder, of Baltimore, Maryland. Special administration with will to the son, Thomas Todd. (Mar. 1678).

Todhunter, Sarah Anne, of Germanstown, Pennsylvania, widow. Administration to William Hewetson, attorney for Esther, wife of Dundass Taylor, in Philadelphia, aunt and guardian of the children, Mary Elizabeth, Helen and John Todhunter, during their minority. (Jan. 1853).

Tolfrey, Martha, formerly of Portsea, Hampshire, but late of New York City, a minor. Administration to the father, Joseph Tolfrey. (Aug. 1842).

Tolfrey, Sarah Anne, of New York, who died at sea, infant. Administration to the father, Joseph Tolfrey. (Aug. 1842).

Tolfrey, William, of Toronto, Canada, a minor. Administration to the father, Joseph Tolfrey. (Aug. 1842).

Tolmie, Phebe, formerly of Chelsea, Middlesex, but late of New York, widow. Administration with will to Samuel Douglas, attorney for George Douglas the younger and William Beekman the younger in New York City. (Aug. 1796).

Tomlins, James, formerly of Shrewsbury, Shropshire, afterwards of Bath, Somerset, but late of Baltimore, North America. Administration to William Tomlins, attorney for the relict, Ann Tomlins, in Baltimore. (June 1827).

Tomlins, Sarah, of Philadelphia. Probate to Jesse Brush. (July 1856).

Tomlins, Thomas, of St. Bartholomew the Great, London, who had lands in Virginia. Probate to Francis Camfield. (Sep. 1666). Wa.Wi.

Tomlinson, Edward, of Rotherhithe, Surrey, and of the merchant ship *Rappahannock Merchant*, who died in Virginia, widower. Probate to the daughter, Ann Tomlinson. (July 1743).

Tomlinson, John Edge, late of New Bern, North Carolina, but who died in Cardiff, Glamorganshire. Probate to Mary Downs, widow. (May 1793).

Thomlinson, Robert, of Boston, New England, bachelor. Probate to the brother, Richard Thomlinson; no executor having been named. (Jan. 1741).

Tompkins, Russell, of Jamaica, who died in Pennsylvania. Probate to the brother, John Tompkins, with similar powers reserved to George Hind. (Jan. 1750).

Toms, William, of Topsham, Devon, who died in Virginia, bachelor. Administration with will to Elizabeth Evans, wife of the executor, Richard Evans, during his absence overseas. (July 1681).

Tonstall. *See* **Tunstall**.

Tookerman, John, of South Carolina. Probate to Thomas Mathew and Nathaniel Barnardiston. (Apr. 1726).

Tookey, Job, of H.M. ship *Newport*, bachelor. Administration with will to

Tookey, *(contd.)* Henry Fitzhugh, brother and attorney of the executor, Robert Fitzhugh, in Boston, New England. (Dec. 1696).

Tooley, Susannah, nee Susannah Fry, of New York City. Limited administration with will to James Eldridge, attorney for the husband, John Tooley, in New York City. (Aug. 1854).

Topham, Christopher, of South Carolina, bachelor. Administration to the mother, Anne Topham, widow. (Dec. 1737).

Toppen, David. *See* **Tappen**.

Topping, Richard, of Soulbury, Buckinghamshire, whose children were in New England. Probate to the relict, Alice Topping. (Apr. 1658). Sh.Wa.

Topping, Samuel, of Stepney, Middlesex, who had lands in Virginia. Probate to the relict, Hannah Topping. (May 1693).

Topping, William, of the merchant ship *Boughton*, who died on the merchant ship *New York Postilion* in New York. Probate to the relict, Anne Topping. (Jan. 1718).

Torkington, Joseph, of Virginia. Probate to the brother, Samuel Torkington. (Apr. 1653). Sh.Wi.

Toulmin, Harry, of Washington Court House, Washington County, Alabama. Probate to the relict, Martha Toulmin, and the brother, John Butler Toulmin. (Feb. 1825).

Toulson, John, of Accamack, Virginia, bachelor. Administration to the brother, William Toulson. (Sep. 1656).

Tovey, Nicholas, of Maryland. Probate to the relict, Anne Tovey. (June 1675).

Tovey, William, formerly of Rotherhithe, Surrey, but late of New York, bachelor. Administration to the brother and sister and only next-of-kin, George John Tovey and Martha, wife of John Stevens. (Sep. 1800).

Towell, Cornelius, of Shadwell, Middlesex, who died on H.M. ship *Triton*'s prize in New York. Administration to the relict, Margaret Towell. (June 1710).

Towle, George, of the merchant ship *Mary*, who died in New York, bachelor. Probate to Matthew Stamford. (Dec. 1757).

Towell, Joseph, of Colonel Phillips' Regiment, who died in Annapolis Royal, bachelor. Administration to the principal creditor, Richard Roberts alias Hayward. (Aug. 1725).

Townsend, Joane. *See* **Michell**.

Townsend, Mary, of Newton or Higham Ferrers, Northamptonshire, who died in Virginia, widow. Administration to the principal creditors, Walter and John Jeffreys. (Nov. 1694).

Townsend alias Dudgeon, Patrick, of Boston, New England, who died in the West Indies. Probate to William Townsend with similar powers reserved to Hannah, wife of James Green. (July 1702).

Towsey, John, of Boston, New England, bachelor. Administration with will to Benjamin Smith, attorney for the brother, Thomas Towsey. (Sep. 1709).

Tozer, Joseph, soldier of the 40th Regiment, who died in Philadelphia, bachelor. Administration to the father, Henry Tozer. (Feb. 1781).

Traherne, William, of St. Clement Danes, Middlesex, whose brother, Michael Traherne, was in Virginia. Probate to Henry Haisman with similar powers reserved to Ellen Haisman. (June 1658). Sh.Wa.

Traill, George, assistant surgeon of the hospital for sick and wounded soldiers in North America, bachelor. Administration to James Traill, attorney for the father, John Traill, in Edinburgh, Scotland. (Oct. 1759).

Traiell, James, of Shadwell, Middlesex, who died on H.M. ship *Shoreham* in Virginia. Probate to the relict, Margaret Traiell. (June 1718).

Traweek, Robert, of Potomack, Virginia, who died on H.M. ship *Plymouth*, widower. Probate to Thomas Bignall, guardian of the son, George Traweek. (Aug. 1730).

Treat, John, soldier of H.M. Corps of Rangers, who died in Massachusetts. Administration to William Quarrill, attorney for the relict, Abigail Treat, in Boston. (Sep. 1765).

Trench, Alexander, of Granville County, South Carolina. Probate to the surviving executor, Benjamin Whitacre. (Dec. 1733).

Trent, James, of the ship *Charles* in the King's service, who died in Pennsylvania. Probate to Thomas Coutts. (Apr. 1699). Revoked and granted to the brother, William Trent. (Nov. 1699).

Trevethan, Mary. *See* **Wright**.

Trevett, Russell, of Marblehead. Massachusetts. Probate to the son, Russell Trevett, and to Samuel Hooper. (Sep. 1803).

Trevillian, Francis, formerly of Dartmouth, Devon, but late of New York City, widower. Administration to the half-sister, Hannah, wife of Thomas Pering. (Oct. 1778).

Trew, Henry, of Limehouse, Middlesex, who died in Virginia. Administration to the relict, Susanna Trew. (May 1661).

Trickett, Sarah, formerly of Snow Hill, London, but late of New York City, widow. Administration to the sister, Mary Collins, widow. (June 1810).

Trohear, Joseph, formerly of Liverpool, Lancashire, but late of New York, bachelor. Administration to the sister and only next-of-kin, Hannah, wife of James Scott. (Oct. 1781).

Troke, Martha, formerly of Handsworth, Staffordshire, but late of Brooklyn, New York. Administration to Rowland Neate, attorney for the children, Martha Maria, wife of Horatio Shepheard Moate, in Brooklyn, and Mary Eliza Troke in New York. (Feb. 1840).

Tromball. *See* **Trumball**.

Trotman, Throckmorton, of St. Giles Cripplegate, London, whose cousin was in Virginia. Probate to Samuel and Edward Trotman. (Oct. 1664). Wi.

Tromball alias Trombel, Robert, of Boston, New England, who died on the ship *Staple Grove*, bachelor. Administration to the principal creditor, George Darke. (Mar. 1716).

Trumball, Samuel, who died on the ship *Elizabeth* bound for Virginia. Administration to the relict, Elizabeth Trumball. (July 1659).

Truefitt, Jane, formerly Jane Cass, of Philadelphia. Administration to Peter Truefitt, attorney for the husband, Henry Paul Truefitt, in Philadelphia. (June 1832).

Trye, Elianor, of St. Lawrence Jewry, London, spinster, whose nephew, Thomas Buckley, was in New England. Probate to Susan and John Viccaridge. (Mar. 1692). Wa.

Try, Ralph, of York Town, Virginia. Probate to the relict, Frances Try. (May 1701).

Tubervill, Fortescue, of the Middle Temple, London, who died in Carolina, widower. Administration to Elizabeth Tubervill, widow, grandmother and guardian of the daughter, Bridget Tubervill. (Feb. 1711).

Tucker, Edward, formerly of Gosport, Hampshire, but late of New York City. Administration to the sister, Hannah Elizabeth, wife of Richard Lacy. (Sep. 1820).

Tucker, Elizabeth, of Trenton, New Jersey. Limited administration with will to James Allan and Thomas Dickason, attornies for David White in Jamaica and Thomas Murgatroyd in Philadelphia. (Mar. 1790).

Tuite, Robert, of St. Croix in the West Indies, who died in Baltimore, Maryland. Limited administration with will to the nephew, Charles MacCarthy, with similar powers reserved to Joseph Blake Chabert, George B. Kelly and Justin MacCarthy. (Dec. 1813). Further grant made to the creditor, Richard Stephens, in order for him to pursue a claim against the estate in Chancery. (Feb. 1832).

Tull, Richard, of Maryland, bachelor. Administration to the principal creditor, Daniel Biddle. (July 1692). Revoked on production of a will and probate granted to the said Daniel Biddle; the executors, Henry Medlicott, John Ewer and Jane Peck, renouncing. (Oct. 1699).

Tunstall, Grace, formerly Grace Dickins, formerly of St. Dunstan in the East, afterwards of St. Botolph Aldgate, London, but late of Bladenburgh, North America. Administration to James Ayres, attorney for the husband, Henry Tunstall, in Montgomery County, North America. (Oct. 1788).

Tonstall, Robert, of St. Olave, Southwark, Surrey, who died on the ship *Dumbarton* in Virginia, mariner. Administration to the principal creditor, John Jordan. (June 1688).

Tunstall, William, formerly of Leeds, Yorkshire, but late of Mount Sinai near Petersburg, Virginia. Administration to Francis Witham, attorney for the relict, Margaret Tunstall, in Ghent. (Feb. 1823).

Turbill, John, of the Middle Temple, London, who died in Carolina. Administration to the brother, George Turbill; the mother, Hannah Turbill, renouncing. (Jan. 1711).

Turnbull, George, of New York City. Administration with will to David Davies, attorney for Frederick De Peyster in New York; the other executor, Charles Wilkes, renouncing. (Jan. 1812).

Turnbull, George, formerly of New York City but late of New Haven, Connecticut, Commander in the Royal Navy. Probate to the relict, Margaret Turnbull, and to John Day and Henry Wilkes. (July 1826).

Turner, Ann. *See* **Wadup**.

Turner, Barnard, of H.M. ship *Northumberland*, who died in Louisburgh, North America, bachelor. Probate to Elizabeth Greenslade, spinster. (Oct. 1758).

Turner, Hannah, formerly of Croydon, Surrey, but late of Charlestown in America. Probate to Stephen Tapster. (Sep. 1811).

Turner, John, of Whitechapel, Middlesex, who died in Maryland, bachelor. Probate to the brother, Henry Turner. (Nov. 1724). Revoked and granted to Thomas Eycott, father and guardian of the executrix, Rachel Eycott; the testator being now described as late of Badginton, Gloucestershire. (Dec. 1724).

Turner, John, of H.M. ship *Quebec*, who died in New York Hospital. Probate to Elizabeth, wife of John Akhurst, formerly Elizabeth Burges. (Dec. 1783).

Turner, William, formerly of Hounslow, Middlesex, but late of Philadelphia County. Administration to Thomas Bennett, attorney for the relict, Sophia Turner, in Philadelphia County. (July 1852).

Turner, Zachariah, of Harlem, New York, farmer. Administration to the relict, Susanna Turner. (Mar. 1835). Revoked on her death and granted to the daughter, Mary Alicia, wife of James Thorne. (Nov. 1850).

Turpin, James, of Virginia, widower. Probate to John Smith. (May 1678).

Tute, John, of James River, Virginia. Probate to Thomas Parr with similar powers reserved to John Comer. (July 1738).

Tuttie, John, of St. Bartholomew by the Exchange, London, citizen and fruiterer of London, whose sister, Hannah Knight, was in New England. Probate to the relict, Rachel Tuttie. (Oct. 1657).

Tyler, Christopher, of H.M. ships *Namur* and *St. Janeiro* but who died in Boston, New England, on H.M. ship *Modeste*, bachelor. Administration to the sister, Katherine Ochterlony, widow; the mother and next-of-kin, Miriam Tyler, having died. (Feb. 1770).

Tyler, Grace, wife of John Tyler, of Colchester, Essex, whose sister, Elizabeth Brock, was in Dedham, New England. Probate to William Young with similar powers reserved to John Browne. (July 1647). Sh.Wa.

Tyler, Henry, of H.M. ship *Bedford*, who died on Staten Island. Probate to the brother, William Tyler. (Mar. 1781).

Tyler, John, of Philadelphia, bachelor. Administration to the creditors, Joseph Roper and Joseph Townsend; those entitled to the administration having been cited but not having appeared. (Nov. 1804).

Tynte, Edward, Governor of Carolina. Probate to Frances Killner. (Oct. 1710).

U

Underwood, Martha. *See* **Vaughan**.

Upington, Walter, of Bristol, who died in Maryland. Probate to George Tite and Roger Bagg. (Sep. 1692).

Uriell, George, of Maryland, master of the ship *William*. Probate to the sister, Rebecca Iredell, widow. (Dec. 1738).

Usher, Patient, of Philadelphia, widow. Administration by his solemn affirmation to Elias Bland, attorney for the niece and next-of-kin, Margaret, wife of John Kearsley, formerly Margaret Brand, in Pennsylvania. (Apr. 1749).

Utting, Ashby, of South Carolina, commander of H.M. ship *Aldborough*. Probate to the relict, Amy Utting, with similar powers reserved to Thomas Michells. (Jan. 1747).

V

Vaber, Hans, of Colonel Holt's Regiment. Administration by decree to the principal creditor, Robert Hood. (July 1722). Markd "pauper."

Van Alstine, Lambert, of Wyoming, Pennsylvania, widower. Administration to John Inglis, attorney for the son, Isaac Van Alstine, in Fredericksburgh, North America. (Oct. 1790).

Van Camp. Peter, of Half Moon, Albany, North America, widower. Administration to John Inglis, attorney for the son, Jacob Van Camp, in Matilda, North America. (Oct. 1790).

Vanderburgh, Richard, of New Town, Long Island, New York, Captain on half pay of the Emerick Chasseurs. Administration to James Tidbury, attorney for the relict, Sally Vanderburgh, in New York. (Nov. 1829).

Vandrel alias Hookamer, Jacob, of New England, who died in Dover, Kent, bachelor. Administration to the cousin and next-of-kin, Anne Vandrel. (Aug. 1709).

Van Dyke, John, of Somerset County, New Jersey. Limited administration with will to David Davies, attorney for the son, Riclif Van Dyke, and for Abner Houghton and Abraham Van Arsdal. (Jan. 1812).

Vandyne, Douw, formerly of Long Island but late of Queen's County, North America, widower. Administration to Brook Watson, attorney for the son, Cornelis Vandyne, in Queen's County. (Feb. 1789).

Van Horne, Cornelius Garret, of New York City. Administration with will to John Exley, attorney for the son, Augustus Van Horne, in New York; the executors, the relict Judith Van Horne, and the son, Garret Van

Van Horne, *(contd.)* Horne, having died, and Simon Johnson and Peter Jay renouncing. (Mar. 1770).

Vansoldt, Elizabeth, of St. Botolph Bishopsgate, London, widow, whose son, Abraham Vansoldt, was in Virginia. Administration with will to the daughter, Ann White; the executor, James White, having died. (Oct. 1665). Wa.Wi.

Van Swieten, Ouzeel, of New York, bachelor. Limited administration with will to Jacob (*sic*) Minor Cruger, relict and executrix of Valentine Cruger. (Jan. 1703). Revoked and granted to the sister, Beatrice Ouzeel. (July 1705).

Vans, Samuel, of Bermondsey, Surrey, who died in Boston, New England, bachelor. Administration to the father, John Vans. (Feb. 1709).

Van Veghten alias Van Veightin, John, Major of the New York Provincials, who died in Havana. Administration with will to Thomas Harris, attorney for the relict, Ann alias Annatje Veghten, in New York. (Apr. 1764).

Van Wyck, Elizabeth, of Baltimore, North America, widow. Administration with will to Rebecca Hutchinson Thomas, widow, attorney for Richard Cooke Tilghman, John Charles Van Wyck and Louis Barney in North America. (Aug. 1821).

Van Wyck, Elizabeth Linnington, of Baltimore, North America, who died in 1819. Limited administration to Harry Barker pending the Chancery suit of Akers v. Manning. (Mar. 1841).

Vassall, William, of Barbados, who had lands in New England. Probate to the son, John Vassall. (June 1657). Wa.

Vaughan, Charles, of Hallowell, Maine, widower. Administration to the son, Rev. John Apthorp Vaughan. (Aug. 1842). Further grants in August 1874 and February 1879.

Vaughan, Frances Weston, of Hallowell, Maine. Administration to Rev. John Apthorp Vaughan, administrator of the husband, Charles Vaughan deceased. (Aug. 1842). Further grant in March 1879).

Vaughan alias Jones, Jane, of Kent County, Maryland. Administration to the father, Henry Jones, and the husband, Charles Vaughan. (July 1681).

Vaughan, Martha, formerly Martha Underwood, of South Carolina, widow. Administration to the brother, William Underwood. (May 1754).

Vaughan, Petrus W. *See* **Vink**.

Vavasser, Richard, of Philadelphia, bachelor. Administration to the cousin german, Lewis John Cole. (July 1778).

Venables, Thomas, of the Northern Liberties of Philadelphia. Administration with will to Daniel Moore, attorney for the relict, Rebecca Venables, in Philadelphia. (Aug. 1752).

Venner, Samuel, former Secretary to the Board of Customs in America, but late of Rotherham and Sheffield, Yorkshire. Probate to the son, Morris Venner. (July 1802).

Vernon, Christopher, of Maryland, who died in St. Dunstan in the West, London. Probate to Anne Vernon. (Dec. 1724).

Vernon, Margery, of St. Martin Ludgate, London, whose son-in-law, Francis Vernon, was in New England. Probate to Robert Potter and Mary Vernon. (May 1656). Wa.

Vernon, Thomas, of Savannah, Georgia, bachelor. Administration to the brother and next-of-kin, Henry Vernon. (Mar. & Apr. 1784).

Viggory, Thomas, of New England, who died in Deptford, Kent, bachelor. Administration to Elizabeth Jacobson, wife and attorney of John Jacobson, during his absence. (Nov. 1690).

Vincent, Elizabeth, of Holborn, Middlesex, widow, whose kinswoman, Love Meredith, was in Virginia. Probate to Benjamin Wyche. (Nov. 1660). Wi.

Vincent, Martha Boscawen, nee Martha B. Evelyn, of Charlestown, South Carolina, widow. Administration to the creditor, Hugh Evelyn; the children, Hugh and Nicholas Vincent, having been cited but not having appeared. (June 1815). Revoked because obtained under false suggestions and granted to the sons and only next-of-kin, Hugh Edward Vincent and Nicholas William Vincent; the husband, Nicholas Vincent, having died. (Nov. 1818).

Vincent, Nicholas, of Charlestown, South Carolina, widower. Administration to the sons, Hugh Edward Vincent and Nicholas William Vincent. (Nov. 1818).

Vink alias Vaughan, Petrus Wynard, of New York, furrier. Administration to the relict, Sarah Vink. (Oct. 1845).

Vion, Peter, of Stratford, New England, bachelor. Administration to Richard Shuttleworth, guardian of the sisters and only next-of-kin, Mary Ann, Sibell and Christian Vion. (Feb. 1755).

Vizer, Ralph, formerly of Dublin, Ireland, but late of Bristol, whose son, Henry Vizer, was in Virginia. Probate to the relict, Bridget Vizer. (Sep. 1667). Wi.

Volans, William, of Oswegatchie, St. Lawrence County, United States of America, bachelor. Administration to Francis William Calvert, attorney for the mother and next-of-kin, Sarah Volans, in Oswegatchie. (June 1855).

Von Pfister, Francis Joseph, of Hosack, North America. Probate to the relict, Ann, now wife of Thomas Bennett. (Oct. 1786).

Voss, John, master of the merchant ship *John and Mary*, who died in Boston, New England, widower. Administration to Christopher Ford, grandfather and guardian of the children, Susanna and Ford Voss. (June 1740). Revoked on the death of Christopher Ford and granted to his relict, Hannah Ford. (Apr. 1741).

W

Waddington, John, formerly of Leeds, Yorkshire, but late of Philadelphia, merchant. Administration with will to the creditor, John Hain; the relict, Sarah Waddington, renouncing for herself and for the children, Sophia, William Henry, Edward Crosley, and Charles John Waddington; the other children, Lydia Elizabeth Waddington and Robert Waller Waddington, also renouncing. (Dec. 1815).

Wade, Joseph, of Boston, New England, who died on the ship *Mary*. Probate to George Golden with similar powers reserved to Thomas Linch, Valentine Baker and William Barton. (Oct. 1692). Wa.

Wade alias Atkins, Mary, of Maryland. Administration to the sister, Sarah Starkey alias Atkins, wife of John Starkey. (Dec. 1660).

Wade, William, of Westham, Sussex, who died overseas (bound for Pennsylvania), bachelor. Probate to Philip Ford. (Oct. 1682). Wa.

Wadup alias Morehouse, Ann, nee Ann Turner, formerly of Newcastle Court, Strand, Middlesex, but late of Spatenburgh, South Carolina, widow. Administration to the brother and only next-of-kin, William Turner. (Mar. 1817). Revoked on his death and granted to his executor, William Hewitt. (Dec. 1837). Revoked on his death and granted to his surviving executor, Mary Ann Hewitt, widow. (Aug. 1843).

Waghorne, Ann, of New York, who died at sea, widow. Administration to William Nourse, attorney for the brother, Richard Brough, in Nottingham. (Feb. 1751).

Wagstaff, Charles Eden, formerly of Argyle Street, New Road, Middlesex, but late of Boston, Massachusetts, engraver. Probate to the relict, Ann Randall Wagstaff. (Feb. 1853).

Wagstaff, Daniel, formerly of Kidderminster, Worcestershire, but late of Delaware, North America. Administration to the relict, Hannah Housman Wagstaff. (Dec. 1830).

Wayte, John, of Worcester, who had lands in Pennsylvania. Probate to the relict, Elizabeth Wayte. (Nov. 1691).

Waite, William, of Stepney, Middlesex, who died in Virginia. Administration to the principal creditor, Edmund Cussey; the relict, Dorothy Waite, renouncing. (Nov. 1671).

Wake, George Daniel, of Sing Sing near New York City, bachelor. Administration to James Wake, son and executor of the father, Daniel Wake deceased. (Oct. 1857).

Walbank, Edward, of Philadelphia. Probate by her solemn declaration to the relict, Agnes Walbank. (June 1735).

Walbridge, Henry, formerly of Puddletown, Dorset, but late of Baltimore, North America, widower. Administration to the children, Henry William Walbridge and Mary Eliza Walbridge. (Sep. 1825).

Waldo alias Walder, Daniel, of Bombay Island, America. Probate to the sister, Rebecca Hayes, with similar powers reserved to Elizabeth Brock. (Oct. 1713).

Waldo, Francis [Francois], formerly of Falmouth, Massachusetts, but late of

Waldo, *(contd.)*
Brompton, Middlesex. Limited administration with will to George Erving and John Lane, the surviving attornies of the executors, Samuel and Isaac Winslow in Boston. (July 1786).

Waldo, Samuel, of Portland, Massachusetts. Limited administration to George William Erving, attorney for the relict, Sarah Tyng Waldo, in Portland. (June 1803).

Walford, John, formerly of Halford, Warwickshire, but late of the Quarantine Ground, Staten Island, New York, bachelor. Administration to the sister and next-of-kin, Elizabeth, wife of William Fletcher. (Dec. 1844).

Walker, Bartholomew, of the ship *Robert and William*, who died on the King's service in Virginia, bachelor. Administration to the mother, Frances Walker. (Sep. 1678).

Walker, Chapman, of the merchant ship *Burrell*, who died in Virginia, bachelor. Administration to the father, William Walker. (Jan. 1737).

Walker, Daniel, of Woodbridge, Suffolk, who died in Virginia. Administration to the principal creditor, Edward Dakins; the relict, Susan Walker, renouncing. (May 1672). Inventory PROB 4/6669).

Walker, Flower, of Maryland. Probate to Michael Walker with similar powers reserved to Thomas Walker and George Dunn. (Feb. 1709).

Walker, George, of H.M. ship *Pearl*, who died in Virginia. Probate to George Chapman with similar powers reserved to his wife, Hannah Chapman. (Aug. 1719).

Walker, George Henry, of Longford near Holmsburg, Philadelphia. Administration to the daughter, Louisa Letitia Walker; the relict, Marianne Douglass Walker, renouncing. (July 1850).

Walker, Hannah, of St. Giles Cripplegate, London, widow, whose son, Thomas Walker, was in New England. Probate to John Jackson. (Nov. 1675). Revoked on his death and administration granted to the daughter, Hannah Strange, widow. (Dec. 1700). Wa.

Walker, Henry, of Birmingham, Warwickshire, and Philadelphia, merchant, bachelor. Administration to John Walker, son and executor of the father, William Walker deceased. (Aug. 1829).

Walker, John, of Hanover County, Virginia, bachelor. Administration to the brother, James Walker. (May 1772).

Walker, Joseph, of Westminster, Middlesex, who had lands in Virginia. Probate to Mary Snow. (Feb. 1667). Wa.

Walker, Nathan, of Colonel Gooch's late American Regiment, whose cousin, John Gardner, was in Rhode Island. Probate to the surviving executor, Andrew Carre. (Oct. 1746).

Walker, Robert, of H.M. ship *Charon*, who died in Virginia. Probate to Paul Bartrum. (May 1782).

Walker, Samuel, of the merchant ship *Asia*, bachelor. Administration to Joseph Hayward, attorney for the brother and next-of-kin, George Walker, in Portsmouth, New England; the brother, Nicholas Walker, renouncing. (Feb. 1706).

Walker, Thomas, of Boston, Massachusetts, widower. Administration to the

Walker, *(contd.)*
daughter, Ann Walker. (Dec. 1784).

Wall, Bartholomew, of Blakenham on the Waters, Suffolk, whose daughter, Anna Jacob, was in New England. Probate to the daughter, Mary Wall. (Apr. 1673). Wa.

Wall, John, of H.M. ship *Trident*, who died in New York. Probate to the mother, Ann Wall, widow. (Jan. 1779).

Wall, John, formerly of St. Michael Royal, London, but late of Charles Town, South Carolina, bachelor. Administration to the sister, Rebecca, wife of Benjamin Blakesley. (June 1786).

Wall, Joseph, of East Calne, Chester County, Pennsylvania. Administration by decree to the daughter, Hannah, wife of Jonathan Parsons. (Mar. 1752). *Inventory gives name as Joseph Ware.*

Wall, Samuel, formerly of Wetnall, Nottinghamshire, afterwards of Chesterfield, Derbyshire, but late of North America. Probate to Samuel Mettam. (June 1799). Further grant in April 1865.

Wallace, Elizabeth, formerly Elizabeth Nisbit, of South Carolina. Administration to the husband, Thomas Wallace. (Apr. 1762).

Wallace, Hugh, formerly of New York City but late of Waterford, Ireland. Probate to the brother, Alexander Wallace, with similar powers reserved to the relict, Sarah Wallace, the brothers, William and Magill Wallace, and to Robert Paul. (June 1788).

Wallace, James, of Ponds Ponds, Georgia, bachelor. Administration to Ralph Gray, husband and administrator of the niece and only next of kin, Margaret Gray, formerly Wallace, deceased. (Aug. 1798).

Wallace, James, British Consul in Savannah, bachelor. Administration to Charles Robert Simpson, attorney for the brother and next-of-kin, Michael Wallace, in Halifax, Nova Scotia. (Nov. 1829).

Wallace, William, formerly of St. Croix, West Indies, but late of New Haven, North America, merchant. Probate to the relict, Catherine Wallace. (Mar. 1831).

Wallace, William Alexander, of New York City, merchant. Probate to the relict, Susan Wallace. (July 1840).

Wallace, William Oxford, Lieutenant of the Royal Artillery, who died in South Carolina, bachelor. Administration to the mother, Betty Wallace. (Jan. 1790).

Waller, Edmund, of St. John's College, Cambridge University, whose brother, John Waller, was in Virginia. Probate to the nephew, Rev. John Waller. (Jan. 1746). Revoked on his death and administration granted to William Waller. (Jan. 1746). Wi.

Waller, Henry, of Mount Pleasant, West Chester County, New York. Probate to the son, Joseph Fernando Waller, with similar powers reserved to the son, Henry Waller, and to Edward Kemlys. (Mar. 1835).

Walley, Mary, formerly of Williamsburg, Virginia, but late of St. Margaret, Westminster, Middlesex, widow. Probate to Dando Fraunces. (Feb. 1743).

Wallin alias Poulter, Hannah, of St. Andrew Undershaft, London, spinster,

Wallin alias Poulter, *(contd.)* whose kinsman, Thomas Poulter, was in Virginia. Probate to Joseph Alston. (Aug. 1663).

Wallis, Josiah, of H.M. ship *Brune*, who died in New York Hospital. Administration with will to William Marsh and Henry Creed, attornies for George Meuris, now at sea. (Oct. 1779).

Walsh, Richard, of Virginia. Administration to the relict, Mary Walsh. (Apr. 1742).

Walsham, John, of St. Botolph Aldersgate, London, Lieutenant in Colonel Dunbar's Regiment of Foot, who died in Albany, bachelor. Administration to the brother, Robert Walsham; the mother, Elizabeth Walsham, renouncing. (Dec. 1756).

Walter, Eleanor Elizabeth, of Jersey City, New Jersey. Administration to the husband, James Walter. (Sep. 1856).

Walter, John, of New England, bachelor. Administration to the cousin and next-of-kin, William Walter. (Jan. 1697).

Walter, John, of Tooting, Surrey, who had lands in South Carolina. Probate to the son, Abel Walter. (June 1736).

Walter, Richard, of New England. Administration with will to the relict, Sarah Walter; no executor having been named. (Feb. 1654). Revoked on her death and granted to her husband and administrator, Thomas Luck. (Feb. 1661). Sh.

Walter, Rev. William, of Boston, Massachusetts, chaplain of the Second Batallion of New York Volunteers. Administration with will to John Lane, attorney for the sons, Lynde Walter and William Walter, and for Nathaniel Smith, in Massachusetts. (June 1801).

Walters, David, formerly of the hospital ship *Smyrna Factor* but late of Charleston. Probate to Thomas Pyke. (Oct. 1703).

Walters, Emily. *See* **Charlton**.

Walthoe, Nathaniel, of Williamsburg, Virginia. Probate to Thomas Waller with similar powers reserved to Benjamin Waller. (June 1772).

Walton, Mary, wife of Jacob Walton of New York. Administration to the son, Henry Walton; the said husband having died. (June 1793).

Walton, Matilda Carolina, of New York. Administration to the husband, Henry Walton. (Mar. 1825).

Walton alias Wanton, Robert, of Virginia. Administration to the principal creditor, John Tayloe; the relict, Elizabeth Walton alias Wanton, renouncing. (June 1670).

Walton, Walter, son of John Walton of Spofforth, Yorkshire, who had assets in Virginia and Maryland. Probate to Richard Lawson with similar powers reserved to Alexander Ewes. (Aug. 1650). Sh.Wi.

Walton, William the elder, of New York City, merchant, widower. Limited administration to Sir Francis Molyneux Omanney, attorney for James De Lancey Walton in New York. (Aug. 1822).

Wampers, John. *See* **White**.

Wansella alias Wansall, Richard, of H.M. Detachment of Foot Guards in South Carolina, bachelor. Administration to the brother, John Wansall. (Feb. 1783).

Wanton, Robert. *See* **Walton**.

Waple, Thomas, of Maryland, bachelor. Probate to Henry Waple and Jonathan Forward. (Apr. 1715).

Warburton, Rev. Charles, formerly of London but late of Boston, Massachusetts. Probate to Thomas Paul. (Aug. 1815).

Ward, Anthony, of Colonel Holt's Regiment, bachelor. Administration by decree to the principal creditrix, Elizabeth Jennings, widow. (July 1722). Marked "pauper."

Ward, Benjamin, of Peekshill, West Chester County, New York, Lieutenant on half pay of the Royal American Regiment. Administration to James Tidbury, attorney for the relict, Phebe Ward, in New York. (June 1818).

Ward, Henry, of Stepney, Middlesex, who died in Virginia. Administration to the relict, Sarah Ward. (June 1659).

Ward, Henry, Commissary and Paymaster of the English Artillery in Pennsylvania, who died in Fort Bedford, bachelor. Administration to the brother and next-of-kin, Ralph Ward. (June 1771).

Ward, Moses, of New York, Lieutenant on half pay of a Provincial Regiment. Administration to the relict, Abigal Ward. (Oct. 1816).

Ward, Pearson, of Sunderland, Durham, who died in George Town, South Carolina. Probate to the relict, Dorothy Ward. (Nov. 1786).

Ward, Samuel Chandler, formerly of Sise Lane, London, but late of New York. Probate to the sisters, Mary Chandler Ward and Elizabeth Ward. (Dec. 1798).

Ward, Thomas, of New England, mariner of the merchant ship *Industry*, who died in Lisbon, bachelor. Administration with will to Joanna Keast, wife and attorney of John Keast now in Virginia or on the merchant ship *Elizabeth and Martha*. (Jan. 1710).

Warden, William, formerly of Charles Town, South Carolina, but late of Whitechapel, Middlesex. Probate to William Leagoe with similar powers reserved to Stephen Coleman. (Nov. 1746).

Warder, Jeremiah, of Philadelphia, merchant. Administration to Thomas Samuel Girdler, attorney for the relict, Hannah Warder, in Philadelphia. (Jan. 1842).

Wardrop, John, formerly of Calvert County, Maryland, but late of All Hallows Staining, London. Probate to James Russell. (July 1767).

Ware, John, of Boston, New England, who died at sea on the ship *Friendship*. Limited administration to John Hill of St. Katherine Coleman, London, merchant, attorney for the relict, Sarah Ware, in Boston. (July 1694). Revoked and granted to the relict, Sarah Garland alias Ware, now wife of Thomas Garland, in England. (Feb. 1697).

Ware, Joseph. *See* **Wall**.

Ware, Nicholas, of Rappahannock, Virginia. Administration renounced by the relict, Anne Ware. (Aug. 1662). [*Administration Act Book missing for this year*].

Wareham, John, of New York. Administration to the nephew and next-of-kin, Thomas Farmer. (Nov. 1823).

Waring, Ellen, formerly of Royal Row, Lambeth, Surrey, but late of Boston,

Waring, *(contd.)* North America, widow. Administration with will to the sister and next-of-kin, Margaret, wife of Thomas Cruse. (June 1827).

Waring, Sarah, late Sarah Lloyd, of St. James, Goose Creek, South Carolina, widow. Administration with will to Sarah Nickelson, widow, attorney for Benjamin Waring, Elizabeth Akin, Peter Taylor, George Austin and Robert Hume in South Carolina. (July 1760).

Warkman, Mark. *See* **Glocester**.

Warner, Edward, of London, distiller, who had lands in Maryland. Administration with will to the son, Edward Warner; the relict, Mary Warner, renouncing. (Mar. 1724).

Warner, John, of Stepney, Middlesex, mariner, who had goods in Virginia. Administration to the relict, Frances Warner. (Dec. 1677).

Warner, Nathaniel, late of Boston, New England, who died in Stepney, Middlesex. Probate to William Rogers and William Rogers. (Oct. 1746).

Warnett, Thomas, of James City, Virginia, mariner. Probate to the relict, Thomazine Warnett. (Nov. 1630). Sh.Wa.

Warnsley, John, of St. Olave, Southwark, Surrey, (bound for Virginia). Probate to William Glassbrooke. (May 1698). Wi.

Warre, Francis Whitehead, formerly of Rugby, Warwickshire, but late of New York, bachelor. Administration to the sister, Caroline Lucy, wife of Rev. William Harriott. (Feb. 1846).

Warren, Anna, formerly Anna Wignell, of Philadelphia. Administration to John Cole Brooke, attorney for the husband, William Warren, in Philadelphia. (Sep. 1813).

Warren, Charlotte Susannah, nee Charlotte S. Clare, of Galveston, Texas. Administration to Edwin Albery, administrator of the husband, John Warren deceased, and attorney for the daughter, Mary Earnest, wife of William Prewitt Boidstone. (Dec. 1855).

Warren, John, Captain of an Independent Company, who died in Albany, New York. Administration to the relict, Elizabeth Warren. (June 1722).

Warren, John, of Mayoville, De Kalb County, Missouri, farmer and merchant, widower. Administration to Edwin Albery, attorney for the daughter, Mary Earnest, wife of William Prewitt Boidstone, in Mayoville. (Dec. 1855).

Warren, Samuel, of Detroit, Michigan. Probate to Charles Christopher Trowbridge. (Sep. 1850).

Warren, Thomas, formerly of Portsea, Hampshire, but late of Boston, North America. Probate to the son, Thomas Benjamin Warren, with similar powers reserved to the relict, Clarissa Warren. (Oct. 1850).

Washington, Laurence, of Luton, Bedfordshire, who died in Virginia. Administration to the principal creditor, Edmund Jones. (May 1677).

Washington, Laurence, of Washington, Westmoreland County, Virginia. Probate to Mildred Gale alias Washington, wife of George Gale. (Dec. 1700).

Wasson, William, of Dublin, Ireland, who died in Virginia. Administration to the principal creditor, James MacCartney; the relict having been cited but not having appeared. (Apr. 1733).

Waters, Edward, of Elizabeth City, Virginia, who died in Hormead, Hertfordshire. Administration with will to the brother, John Waters, during the minority of the son, William Waters. (Sep. 1630). Sh.

Waters, Emily. *See* **Charlton**.

Waters, Humphrey, formerly of St. Ann, Westminster, Middlesex, but late of New York, bachelor. Administration with will to the nephew, Humphrey Waters; the mother, Mary Waters, and the brother, James Waters, having died in the testator's lifetime, and the sister, Ann, wife of Richard Mawby, renouncing. (Mar. 1809).

Waters, Richard, of Somerset County, Maryland. Administration with will to Jonathan Scarth, attorney for the relict, Elizabeth Waters, and for William Waters, in Maryland. (Nov. 1722).

Waters, Richard, of Maryland, widower. Administration to Anthony Bacon, attorney for the mother, Elizabeth Waters, widow, in Maryland. (Mar. 1748).

Waters, William, of Northampton County, Virginia. Probate to William Waters. (Oct. 1722). Revoked on the death of the relict, ——- Burton, formerly Waters, and administration granted to Anthony Bacon, attorney for the son, William Waters, in Williamsburg, Virginia. (Oct. 1757). Revoked on the death of William Waters and granted to Anthony Bacon, attorney for the grandson, William Waters, in Williamsburg; the daughter and only next-of-kin, Margaret Kincade, formerly Preeson, having died. (Oct. 1757).

Waterson, Catherine, of Newark, New Jersey, widow. Administration to William Parkin, attorney for the only children, Benjamin Joseph Waterson and Elizabeth Catherine Robins, widow, in the United States of America. (Nov. 1857).

Waterton, Anne, formerly of Woodlands, Yorkshire, afterwards of Demarara, West Indies, but late of New York City, widow. Limited administration with will to the son, Edward Birmingham, commonly called Lord Athenry; the executor, John Wright, renouncing, and the other executors, the brother, John Waddell, Sir Richard Bedingfield and James Forrest, having been cited but not having appeared. (Mar. 1834). Further limited administration to James and Thomas Croft. (Aug. 1840). Administration of the estate unadministered by the sons, Francis and Edward Birmingham, granted to the son, Henry Waterton. (Aug. 1845).

Watkin, Gifford, of London, merchant, who died in Virginia, bachelor. Probate to the brother, Arthur Watkin. (June 1637). Sh.

Watkins, Andrew, of Piscataway, New England, Captain in Sir William Pepperell's 51st Regiment of Foot. Administration to the creditrix, Christian Padget. (Sep. 1762).

Watkins, Charles, of South Carolina, who died on the merchant ship *Dolphin* at sea, bachelor. Probate to the brother, William Watkins. (Oct. 1742).

Watkins, Christopher, of St. Botolph Aldersgate, London, whose kinsman, George Watkins, was in Virginia. Administration to the relict, Jane Watkins. (Dec. 1673).

Watkins, Elijah, formerly of Penbiddle, Llanfihangel Crucorney, Monmouth, but late of Cleveland, North America, who died at sea as a passenger on the steamship *City of Glasgow*, bachelor. Administration to the father, James Watkins. (Oct. 1857).

Watkinson, Samuel, formerly of Lavenham, Suffolk, but late of Middletown, Connecticut. Probate to the son, David Watkinson, with similar powers reserved to the sons, John Revel Watkinson and Edward Watkinson. (Nov. 1819).

Watson, Francis, of the merchant ship *Little Betsy*, who died in York River, Virginia, bachelor. Administration to Mary Vaughan alias Watson, wife of John Vaughan. (June 1713).

Watson, Henry, of St. George's, Prince George County, Maryland. Probate to the son, John Watson; the executors, the relict, Lucy Watson, and Peter Wright having died, Peter Sykes renouncing, and John Belt the younger having been cited but not having appeared. (Nov. 1767).

Watson, John, of Shadwell, Middlesex, who died in Virginia, widower. Administration to the principal creditor, Edward Savage. (May 1677).

Watson, John, of Maryland, bachelor. Probate to Christopher Marshall. (June 1746).

Watson, John, of News River, North Carolina, bachelor. Administration to the father, Thomas Watson. (May 1759).

Watson, John, formerly of Rhode Island but late of Fishlake, Yorkshire. Administration to the relict, Ruth, now wife of George Paul. (Apr. 1789).

Watson, John, Lieutenant of the 60th or Royal American Regiment. Probate to Ann Weches, spinster. (May 1789).

Watson, John James, of New York, bachelor. Administration to the brother and next-of-kin, Robert Mackie Watson. (Jan. 1853).

Watson, Nicholas, formerly of Mortlake, Surrey, but late of South Carolina, bachelor. Administration to the sister and next-of-kin, Sarah Hill, widow. (Mar. 1793).

Watson, Philip, of New England, widower. Administration to the son, Elia Watson. (Aug. 1697).

Watson, Richard, of St. Margaret, Westminster, Middlesex, whose stepson, Robert Boodle, was in Virginia. Probate to Bruce Clench. (Jan. 1686). Revoked on his death and limited administration granted to Nathaniel Wilkins Brett, administrator of the residuary legatee, Cecily Brandreth, widow, deceased. (Sep.1733). Limited administration granted to George Hancock in respect of estates in Bexley and Bromley, Kent. (Jan. 1808).

Watson, William, citizen and blacksmith of London, whose daughter, Rebecca, was in New England. Probate to Edward Palmer and Thomas Rollinson. (Oct. 1652). Sh.

Watson, William, who died on the ship *James Town*, bound for Virginia,

Watson, *(contd.)*
mariner. Administration to the relict, Sarah Watson. (Aug. 1659).

Watson, William, of Rotherhithe, Surrey, who died at sea near Carolina. Administration to the principal creditor, Thomas Balden. (Sep. 1686).

Watson, William, of the ship *Rachel* bound to Virginia. Probate to the relict, Katherine Watson of Dover, Kent. (Apr. 1756). Wi.

Watson, William, of Baton Rouge, West Florida. Probate to David Rose and William Watson with similar powers reserved to the brother, Adam Watson. (July 1782).

Watt, John, formerly of Minchinhampton, Gloucestershire, but late of Pittsburgh, Pennsylvania, hawker and peddler. Administration with will to George Cox, attorney for Samuel Trew and John Turbitt. (June 1837).

Watters, David, of Charlestown, New England, mariner. Probate to Thomas Pike, late of Boston, New England. (Oct. 1703).

Watts, Cornelius, of Wells, Somerset, whose kinsman, William Watts, was in Virginia. Probate to the relict, Ann Watts, and the children, Edmund and Ann Watts. (Oct. 1640). Wi.

Watts, Edward, of Stepney, Middlesex, who died in Virginia. Administration to the principal creditor, John Bugbye; the relict, Jane Watts, renouncing. (July 1669).

Watts, Elizabeth, of Maryland, spinster. Administration to the brother, Charles Watts. (Feb. 1708).

Watts, John, of Workington, Cumberland, who died in Maryland. Probate to the brother, Richard Watts, with similar powers reserved to Joseph Milnor. (Oct. 1736).

Watts, John, formerly of New York but late of St. James, Westminster, Middlesex. Limited probate to Edmund Antrobus and John Antrobus with similar powers reserved to Thomas Coutts. (Sep. 1789).

Watts, Mary, of New York, widow. Administration to the daughter, Sarah Maria, wife of Bertram Peter Cruger. (Feb. 1852).

Watts, Robert, of Westchester, New York. Administration with will to Sarah Maria, wife of Bertram Cruger, the administratrix of the relict, Mary Watts deceased. (Feb. 1852).

Waugh, David, of Stafford County, Virginia, who died on the ship *Elizabeth*. Administration with will to Henry Bowen, attorney for the brother, Peter Waugh, now overseas. (Feb. 1694). Wi.

Way, George, of Dorchester, Dorset, who had lands in New England. Probate to the relict, Sarah Way. (Dec. 1641). Wa.

Way, Richard, of New England, who died on H.M. ship *Namur*. Probate to John Nightingal alias Nightingirl. (Mar. 1736).

Wayte. *See* **Waite**.

Weare, Thomas, of Charfield, Gloucestershire, whose brother, Peter Weare, was in York, New England. Probate to the brother, Peter Weare. (Oct. 1685).

Weatherhead, William, of the merchant ship *Boston*, who died in New England, bachelor. Administration to Alice, wife of James Rogerson,

Weatherhead, *(contd.)* now at sea, the guardian of the brother and next-of-kin, Isaac Weatherhead. (May 1710).

Weatherley, Robert, formerly of Newcastle-upon-Tyne but late of Detroit, North America. Limited administration to Edward Gatly. (July 1848).

Weaver, Edward, formerly of Nottingham but late of Philadelphia, merchant. Administration to the daughter, Anne Christian, wife of William Berridge. (Mar. 1824).

Weaver, Job, of West Greenwich, Kent County, Rhode Island, and of Lieutenant-Colonel Christopher Hargill's Company of the Rhode Island Regiment of Foot, who died in Havana, bachelor. Administration by his solemn declaration to Joseph Sherwood, attorney for the father, Harris Weaver, in West Greenwich. (Dec. 1765).

Weaver, John. *See* **Copson**.

Weaver, John, of Bristol, who died in Maryland. Administration with will to the sister, Mary Weaver; the executor, John Pikswort, renouncing. (Nov. 1705).

Webb, Charles, of Henrico County, Virginia. Administration with will to the brother, Thomas Webb. (May 1715).

Webb, Daniel, of Monkton Farley, Wiltshire, whose brother, Isaac Webb, was in New England. Probate to Edward Seymour. (June 1733).

Webb, Edward, formerly of Stoke Bishop, Westbury-on-Trym, Gloucestershire, afterwards of Adwell, Essex, but late of New York. Administration with will to the daughter, Elizabeth Frances Webb; the executors, Sir Berkeley William Guise and John Webb, having died in the testator's lifetime. (Dec. 1839).

Webb, Elizabeth. *See* **Bell**.

Webb, Gilbert, of Cornwall, Orange County, New York. Probate to Peter Roe with similar powers reserved to John Eastmond. (Nov. 1824).

Webb, James, of Fort St. Augustine, Deputy Commissary of Musters to H.M. Forces, who died in Georgia. Administration to the relict, Mary Webb. (Nov. 1780).

Webb, Richard, of St. Anne's, North Jamaica, who died in Boston, New England, bachelor. Administration to the brother, Thomas Webb. (Jan. 1731).

Webb, Robert, of Virginia, bachelor. Administration to the cousin german, William Webb; the uncle, William Webb, renouncing. (Aug. 1659).

Webb, William, of Bristol, who died in Maryland. Probate to the relict, Sarah Webb. (Oct. 1711).

Webb, William, of South Carolina. Administration to the principal creditor, John Owen; the relict, Sarah Webb, having died and the uncle, John Webb, guardian of the children, John and William Webb, renouncing. (Sep. 1751). Revoked on the death of John Owen and granted by his solemn affirmation to his executor, John Strettell. (Sep. 1759).

Webb, William, of New Orleans. Administration to the relict, Margaret Proctor Webb. (Oct. 1848).

Webber, Daniel, of Stepney, Middlesex, (intending a voyage to New England), mariner. Probate to the relict, Susan Webber. (Apr. 1731).

Webber, Stephen, of Penobscot, Hancock County, Massachusetts, seaman of H.M. ship *Leviathan*, bachelor. Administration to Joseph Westcot, attorney for the father, Joseph Webber, in Penobscot. (Sep. 1805).

Webster, David, gunner's mate of H.M. ship *Squirrel*, who died in Virginia, bachelor. Administration to John Beatson, attorney for the sister and next-of-kin, Margaret Webster, in Pinkie near Musselburgh, Scotland. (Feb. 1767).

Webster, James, of Virginia, bachelor. Administration to the father, John Webster. (Nov. 1766).

Webster, John, of Maryland, bachelor. Administration to the brother, Robert Webster. (Nov. 1671).

Weedon, John, of Boston, New England, who died on H.M. ship *Mary*. Administration to Thomas Dummer, attorney for the relict, Ruth Weedon, now overseas. (July 1699).

Weeden, John, of Boston, New England. Sentence pronounced against validity of will. (June 1702).

Weedon, William, of St. Botolph Bishopsgate, London, whose nephew and niece, William and Ann Weedon, were in Maryland. Probate to William Weedon; Anne Weedon having died. (Nov. 1692).

Weems, Rachael, formerly Rachael Morris, of Anne Arundell County, Maryland. Administration to William Murdoch and Horatio Clagett, attornies for the husband, William Weems, in Anne Arundell County. (June 1797).

Welch, Francis, formerly of New York but late of Knightsbridge, Middlesex. Probate to Richard Neave. (Mar. 1775).

Welch, Mary Ann, of Chestertown, Kent County, Maryland. Administration to the husband, John Day Welch. (Feb. 1856).

Welchman, Edward, formerly of Kington, Warwickshire, surgeon, but late of New Albion, North America, widower. Administration to the daughter, Emma Jemima, wife of Barnabas Henry Bartol. (Dec. 1845).

Wells, Francis, of Bermondsey, Surrey, who died in Virginia. Administration to the relict, Mildred Wells. (Nov. 1709).

Wells, Richard, of Ann Arundell County, Maryland. Probate to Richard Wells. (Nov. 1668). Wa.

Welsh, Charlotte, of Philadelphia. Administration to the husband, James Welsh. (Mar. 1842).

Wentworth, John, formerly of Portsmouth, New Hampshire, but late of Paris. Administration to the relict, Martha Wentworth. (May 1833).

West, Francis, of Winchester, Hampshire, who died in Virginia. Probate to the relict, Jane West. (Apr. 1634). Sh.Wi.

West, Hannah, of Chester, Delaware County, Pennsylvania, widow. Administration to Benjamin West the younger, attorney for the son, Samuel West, in Delaware County. (Nov. 1819).

West, John, formerly of New York but late of Boston, New England, who

West, *(contd.)* died in St. Martin Ludgate, London. Probate to the relict, Anne West. (Nov. 1691). Wa.

West, John, of St. Sepulchre, London, whose grandson, John East, and daughter, Hannah Streete, were in Pennsylvania. Probate to the son, Richard West. (July 1699).

West, Silas, of Nantucket, North America, late master of the merchant ship *Indian*, who died at sea, widower. Administration to John Thompson, attorney for the brother and next-of-kin, Paul West. (Oct. 1822).

West, William, of Slinfold, Sussex, (bound for Virginia). Probate to Mary Blount. (June 1616). Sh.Wi.

West, William, of Eton, Buckinghamshire, whose son, William West, was in Virginia. Probate to Thomas West. (June 1687). Wa.

Westhrope, John, of London, merchant, who died in Virginia. Probate to Edward Henshaw and Edmond Beckford. (June 1656). Revoked and granted to the sister, Dorothy Drewers alias Westhrope. (Oct. 1660). Sh. Wi.

Westlake, Edward, of Maryland. Administration to Ellis Asby, brother of the relict, Margery Westlake, in Maryland. (May 1694).

Westland, John, of H.M. ship *Portsmouth*, bachelor. Administration to the principal creditor, Thomas Jordan. (May 1707). Revoked and granted to John Whiting, attorney for the father, Nathaniel Westland, in West Jersey. (Nov. 1710).

Westley, Ambrose, a soldier of the 65th Regiment of Foot, who died in Charles Town, South Carolina, bachelor. Probate to the mother, Mary Westley, widow; no executor having been named. (Oct. 1763).

Weston, Francis Marion, of All Saints, George Town, South Carolina. Administration with will to William John Slade Foster, attorney for the son, Plowden Charles Jennett Weston, and for Rev. Alexander Glennie, in George Town. (Nov. 1855).

Weston, Mildred, formerly Mildred Weston, formerly of Portman Square, Middlesex, but late of South Carolina. Administration to the husband, Francis Marion Weston. (July 1825).

Wethered, Henry, of Boston, New England, widower. Administration to the aunt and next-of-kin, Sophia Lewin, guardian of the children, Sarah and Henry Wethered. (Apr. 1763).

Whalley, John, of Charleston, North America. Administration to the brother, Joseph Wilkinson Whalley; the relict, Mary Whalley, having been cited but not having appeared. (Feb. 1820).

Whaplett, Thomas, who died in Virginia. Probate to the sister, Rebecca Whaplett, with similar powers reserved to John Redman. (July 1636). Revoked on her death and administration granted to Ralph Gregge. (Nov. 1636). Sh.Wi.

Wharton, Edmund, of New England, bachelor. Administration to the brother, George Wharton. (June 1678).

Wharton, Richard, of Boston, New England, merchant. Probate after sentence for the validity of the will to Samuel Read and Nathaniel Whitfield, with similar powers reserved to Waite Winthrop, John

Wharton, *(contd.)*
Eyres, John Higginson and Isaac Addington. (Apr. 1690).

Wharton, Richard, of Williamsburg, Virginia. Probate to the brothers, Thomas and John Wharton; the relict, Ruth Wharton, renouncing. (Apr. 1713).

Whearley, Henry, of Barbados, whose brother, Francis Whearley, was in Pennsylvania. Probate to the brother, Daniel Whearley. (Apr. 1689).

Wheatcroft, William, formerly of Ditchford, Worcestershire, but late of Plymouth, Connecticut. Administration with will to the mother, Anne Wheatcroft, widow; no executor having been named. (Feb. 1825).

Wheaton, Henry, formerly Minister of the United States of America in Berlin, but late of Providence, Rhode Island. Administration to the son, Robert Wheaton; the relict, Catherine Wheaton, renouncing. (Mar. 1849).

Wheeler, Francis, of London, merchant, (bound to Virginia). Probate to the son, Francis Wheeler. (Mar. 1660).

Wheeler, James, of Maryland, bachelor. Administration to the sister, Alice Gutridge alias Wheeler. (Oct. 1674).

Wheeler, Joseph, of North Carolina, bachelor. Administration to the sister and only next-of-kin, Frances Norris, widow. (Sep. 1770). Revoked on her death and granted to her daughter and executrix, Frances Norris. (Mar. 1778).

Wheeler, Richard, of Shoreditch, Middlesex, citizen and innholder of London, whose grandsons, Richard and John Moye, were in Virginia. Probate to George Kelsey. (Jan. 1658). Sh.Wi.

Whilhelme, Christian, of St. Olave, Southwark, Surrey, galley pot maker, adventurer to Virginia. Probate to the daughter, Mary Townsend and her husband, Thomas Townsend. (Apr. 1630). Wi.

Whitborn, John, formerly of West Teignmouth, Devon, afterwards mate of the merchant ship *Brislington*, but late of South Carolina, bachelor. Administration with will to the brother, Peter Whitborn; no executor having been named. (Apr. 1760).

White, Benjamin, of Boston, New England, master in the Royal Navy on half pay. Probate to Henry Cort. (Mar. 1774).

White, Betty, formerly of Huish Champflower, Somerset, but late of Cleveland, Cuyahoga County, Ohio, widow. Administration with will to William Rossiter, husband and administrator of the daughter, Eliza Rossiter deceased. (Jan. 1836).

White, Catherine, formerly Catherine Laxton, of Cincinnati, Ohio, widow. Administration to Sarah Gilford, widow, attorney for the daughter, Elizabeth Attlesey, widow, in Cincinnati. (Dec. 1845).

White, Charles, formerly of Baldock, Hertfordshire, surgeon, but late of Millageville, North America. Administration to the only surviving child, Matilda Freshfield Winkley, wife of John Winkley; the relict, Margaretta White, having died. (Apr. 1840).

White, Daniel, formerly of Blakeney, Gloucestershire, but late of Albany, New York. Administration to the son, James White; the relict, Sarah White, renouncing. (May 1841).

White, Edmund, of St. Giles Cripplegate, London, whose son-in-law, Humphrey Davie, was in Boston, New England. Probate to the son, Edmund White, and to William Coxe. (Dec. 1674). Wa.

White, Elizabeth, wife of Anthony White of New Brunswick, New Jersey. Probate to John Watts. (Dec. 1785).

White, James, of London, adventurer to Virginia. Probate to the sister, Mary White.(Jan. 1611). Wi.

White, James, of Barbados, merchant, who died in Boston, New England. Probate to William White with similar powers reserved to Henry Hawley, Edward Pye, James Beake, William Bate and Jeremy Edgington. (Feb. 1668).

White, James, who died on the ship *Archangel* in Virginia, bachelor. Administration to the principal creditor, John Barnes. (Apr. 1694).

White, James, private of the 64th Regiment, who died in Lancaster, North America, bachelor. Administration to the father, Robert White. (June 1785).

White, John, vicar of Cheriton, Wiltshire, whose nephews were in Virginia. Probate to John Broadhurst and Phillis Broadhurst. (Feb. 1672). Wi.

White alias Wampers, John, of Boston, New England, who died while travelling in Stepney, Middlesex. Probate to John Blake with similar powers reserved to Edward Pratt. (Oct. 1679). Wa.

White, John, of Boston, Massachusetts. Administration with will to Thomas Latham, attorney for Isaac Rand, doctor of physic, in Boston, with similar powers reserved to Greene Amory. (Jan. 1796).

White, John, formerly of Northampton, draper, who died at sea on the steamship *Pacific* while on passage to New York with his wife, Hepzibah, and only child, Elizabeth, when all on board perished. Limited administration to the sister, Emma White. (Mar. 1857).

White, Limpany, Lieutenant in Colonel William Gooch's Regiment of Foot in Cartagena, West Indies, bachelor, who made a bequest to Katherine Duron, widow, in New Jersey. Administration with will to the residual legatee, Martha White; no executor having been named. (Mar. 1747).

White, Marmaduke John Horton, of Franklin Street, New York City, artist. Administration to John Shadwell White, attorney for the relict, Mary White, in New York City. (Apr. 1846). Further grant made in September 1860.

White, Mary, of New York City, spinster. Administration to the sister, Ann Combs, widow; the mother, Mary White, having died before administering. (Dec. 1790).

White, Robert, of New York, bachelor. Probate to the brother, Rev. Nathaniel White. (Nov. 1774).

White, Thomas, of Philadelphia. Administration with will to Richard Peters, attorney for the relict, Esther White, the son, William White, and for Robert Morris, in Philadelphia. (Mar. 1786).

White, Thomas, formerly of Newington, Surrey, but late of Georgia. Probate to the relict, Philipi White, with similar powers reserved to James Benson. (Feb. 1798).

White, Thomas, of New York City. Administration with will to Matthew White, attorney for the relict, Ann White, in New York. (Aug. 1822).

White, William, of London, linen draper, who died overseas and who had lands in Virginia. Probate to the brother, John White. (June 1627). Wa.

White, William, of St. Bride, London, whose brother, John White, was in Virginia. Probate to the children, William White and Elizabeth Saunders. (Dec. 1676). Wi.

White, William, of James City, Virginia. Limited administration to Micajah Perry, attorney for the relict, Jane White, during her absence. (Aug. 1682).

White, William, of H.M. ship *St. Albans*' prize, who was drowned in Virginia. Probate to Edward Daniel. (Sep. 1697).

White, William, of St. Katherine by the Tower, London, who died on the merchant ship *Hope* in New England. Administration to the relict, Anne White. (Aug. 1722).

White, William, of Charles Town, South Carolina. Probate to William Smith with similar powers reserved to Robert Shand and Kenneth Rose. (Jan. 1795).

Whitehaire, Robert, of Willesden, Middlesex, who died in Virginia. Administration to the relict, Elizabeth Whitehaire. (June 1674).

Whitehall, Robert, of Currituck County, North Carolina. Administration to William Broden, attorney for the son, Robert Whitehall, in North Carolina; the relict, Ann Whitehall, renouncing. (Mar. 1769).

Whitehead, Rev. John, of South Carolina. Administration to the relict, Frances Whitehead. (Aug. 1717).

Whitehead, Mary, of Binfield, Berkshire, whose son, Richard Whitehead, was in Virginia. Probate to the daughter, Philadelphia Whitehead. (May 1679).

Whitehead, Richard, of Windsor on the Connecticut River, who died in St. Mary's, Warwick. Probate to John Andrewes with similar powers reserved to Thomas Fish. (June 1645). Sh.Wa.

Whitehorne, George, of Boston, New England. Probate to Benjamin Thorp; the executor, James Warren, having died. (Aug. 1722).

Whitehurst alias Whitehust, Thomas, of Brunswick, North Carolina, bachelor. Probate to the sister, Ann Whitehurst, with similar powers reserved to Jacob Lobb. (Oct. 1766).

Whiteman, John, formerly of Ditchling, Sussex, but late of Troy near Albany, North America. Probate to Peter Rowland. (Jan. 1798).

Whitefield, Rev. George, of St. Luke, Middlesex, who died in Georgia, widower. Limited administration with will to Charles Hardy, Daniel West and Robert Keen. (Feb. 1771).

Whitfield, Thomas, of the transport ship *Hopewell*, who died in York River. Probate to Barbara, wife of James Bonnes, with similar powers reserved to the said James Bonnes. (Sep. 1779).

Whitford, John, of West Greenwich, Kent County, Rhode Island, and of Lieutenant-Colonel Christopher Hargill's Company of the Rhode Island Regiment of Foot, who died in Havana, bachelor.

Whitford, *(contd.)*
Administration by his solemn declaration to Joseph Sherwood, attorney for the uncle and next-of-kin, Edward Casey, in Kent County. (Dec. 1765).

Whiting, John, of Hadleigh, Suffolk, whose brother, Robert Payne, was in New England. Probate to the relict, Judith Whiting. (Jan. 1645). Wa.

Whiting, Simon, of Dedham, Essex, who made a bequest to Richard Sherman in New England. Probate to the relict, Jane Whiting; Clement Fenn renouncing. (June 1637). Wa.

Whitley, Roger, of General Nicholson's Independent Company, who died in Fort King George, South Carolina. Probate to William Livingston, attorney for Alexander Nisbett in Edinburgh, Scotland; no executor having been named. (Dec. 1729).

Whitlock, Thomas, of Virginia, bachelor. Administration to the nephew and next-of-kin, Anthony Whitlock. (July 1680).

Whitmore, Benjamin, of Middletown, New England, who died on H.M. ship *Royal Katherine*. Administration with will to Isabella Edwards, wife of Hugh Edwards, attorney for the executor, Charles Hill. (Sep. 1696).

Whitrowe, Benjamin, of South Carolina, bachelor. Administration to the niece, Rebecca Whitrowe. (Aug. 1726).

Whitaker, Alexander, of Canterbury, Kent, who died on a voyage to Virginia. Administration with will to the sister, Susan Lowthrop alias Whitaker; the named executor, Samuel Whitaker, having died. (Oct. 1617).

Whittacre, George, of London, who died as a passenger from Virginia to London. Probate of nuncupative will to William Scott. (June 1654). Sh.Wa.

Whitaker, Robert, marine of H.M. ship *Chatham*, who died in New York. Administration to the relict, Ann Whitaker. (Nov. 1783).

Whittingham, Heber, of Princess Ann Town, Maryland, widower. Administration to Thomas Thorns, attorney for the son, John Whittingham, in Montpellier Wharf, St. James parish, Jamaica. (Oct. 1801).

Whittingham, William, formerly of Boston, New England, but who died in St. Mary le Savoy, Middlesex. Probate to Nathaniel Hubbard with similar powers reserved to John Lawrence, William Hubbert and John Lewen. (Apr. 1672). Double probate to William Hubbert. (Mar. 1678). Wa.

Whittle, Conway, of Norfolk, Virginia, widower. Administration to the daughter, Mary Neale, widow. (Nov. 1819).

Wickeat, Jacob, born of Indian parents in New England, mariner of H.M. ship *Hampton Court*, bachelor. Administration with will to the legatee, Richard Jefferys; no executor having been named. (Sep. 1741).

Wickes, Robert, of Staines, Middlesex, whose son, John Wickes, was in New England. Probate to the son, Thomas Wickes. (Nov. 1638). Wa.

Wickham, Moses, of Southampton, master of H.M. ship *Soulings*, who died in New York. Probate to Thomas Orr. (Jan. 1715).

Widdop, George, of Dear Island, United States of America. Administration to the relict, Caroline, now wife of Joseph Read the younger. (Aug. 1857).

Wier, Daniel, Commissary-General of the Army in America, who died in New York City. Probate to Jacob Wilkinson with similar powers reserved to Henry White, Gregory Townsend and Thomas Aston Coffin. (Feb. 1782).

Wiggins, Emily, of Bond Street, New York City. Administration to Francis Rivington, attorney for the husband, William Wiggins, in New York. (Aug. 1843).

Wightman, Shardlow, formerly of Aldersgate Street, London, but late of Kentucky, North America, bachelor. Administration to the nephew, Joseph Brownell. (July 1817).

Wigington, Henry, of South Carolina, who died in St. Martin in the Fields, Middlesex. Limited administration with will to Robert Horne. (Dec. 1722).

Wigmore, Elizabeth. *See* **Hitchcock**.

Wignell, Anne. *See* **Warren**.

Wigram, William, seaman of H.M. ship *Thames*, who died in New York Hospital. Administration to the sister and next-of-kin, Betty, wife of William Atherley. (Sep. 1781).

Wigston, William, of 176 Mercer Street, Bleecher Street, Broadway, New York. Administration to the relict, Mary Wigston. (Dec. 1855).

Wilberfoss, William, of Charles Town, South Carolina, bachelor. Administration to the father, Robert Wilberfoss. (Mar. 1753).

Willcox, Elizabeth. *See* **Windeyer**.

Wilcocks, Captain John, of Plymouth, Devon, and Accomack, New England. Probate to the relict, Temperance Wilcocks. (June 1628). Sh.Wa.

Wileman, Henry, of St. Mary Aldermary, London, widower. Administration to Charles Savage, attorney for the children, Elizabeth, wife of Henry Gibbs, Magdalen Wileman in Lisbon, Portugal, and Henry Wileman in New York. (Aug. 1714).

Wilkes, Israel, of New York, widower. Administration to John De Ponthieu, attorney for the only children, John De Ponthieu Wilkes, Charles Wilkes, and Frances, wife of Lewis Simond, in New York. (Sep. 1809).

Wilkes, John De Ponthieu, formerly of London but late of New York City, notary public. Administration with will to Edmund John Scott, attorney for the children, Eliza Henry, widow, Henry Wilkes and Edmund Wilkes, in New York; the brother and executor, Charles Wilkes, having died. (Mar. 1846).

Wilkinson, Henry, of Nottingham, whose cousin, Isabel Blood, was in New England. Administration with will to Richard Hardmett. (Mar. 1646). Wa.

Wilkinson, Joseph, of Calvert County, Maryland. Administration with will

Wilkinson, *(contd.)*
to William Tarver, attorney for the creditor, James Fletcher, in South Carolina. (July 1736).

Wilkinson, Wilfred, Lieutenant of the Third Regiment, who died in Charles Town, South Carolina, bachelor. Administration to the brother, Richard Wilkinson; the mother, Philadelphia Wilkinson, renouncing. (July 1784).

Willard, Abijah, formerly of Lancaster, Massachusetts, but late of St. John's, New Brunswick. Administration to George Erving, son and executor of the creditor, John Erving deceased; the relict, Mary Willard, and the children, Samuel, Elizabeth and Anna Willard, having been cited but not having appeared. (Feb. 1790).

Willdy, Benjamin, of Carolina. Probate to the sister, Martha, wife of Edward Wood; the mother, Martha Doggett, having died in the lifetime of the testator. (Feb. 1697).

Willett, John, formerly of St. Christopher's, afterwards of New York, but late of St. Croix in the West Indies. Probate to the relict, Frances Willett. (Jan. 1767).

Willett, Margaret, of West Chester, New York, widow. Administration with will to Effingham Lawrence, administrator with will of the nephew and surviving executor, Lewis Graham deceased, and attorney for Egbert Benson and Thomas Hart in New York. (Dec. 1800).

Willett, Thomas, of New York City. Probate to the son, John Willett, with similar powers reserved to the relict, Elizabeth Willett, and to Christopher Billop, Thomas Miller and Joseph Royal. (Oct. 1768).

Williams, Arthur, Major of the 52nd Regiment of Foot, who died in Boston, bachelor. Limited administration with will to the brother, Rev. William Williams, sole executor of the father, William Williams deceased. (Aug. 1776).

Williams, Ayliffe, formerly of North Carolina but late of Westminster, Middlesex. Probate to Henry Kean and James Webb. (May 1735).

Williams, Benjamin, of Stoke by Guildford, Surrey, whose cousins, Samuel, Thomas and Benjamin Williams, and Elizabeth Bird, were in New England. Probate to the brother, Nathaniel Williams. (Sep. 1698). Wa.

Williams, Elijah, formerly of St. John's, New Brunswick, but late of Deerfield, Massachusetts. Administration with will to David Thomas, attorney for John Williams and Seth Cathin in St. John's. (Aug. 1795).

Williams, Elizabeth, of Piscataway, New England, widow. Administration to the cousin and next-of-kin, John Atkins. (Apr. 1716).

Williams, Henry, formerly of Shepton Mallet, Somerset, but late of Bedford Township, Nassau Island, New York. Probate to the nephew, John Williams. (Mar. 1784).

Williams, Jane, of Wheatenhurst, Gloucestershire, spinster, whose brother and sister, Richard and Elizabeth Williams, were in New England. Probate to the brother-in-law, John Hall. (June 1655). Wa.

Williams, John, of Deal, Kent, who died on the merchant ship *Robert and*

Williams, *(contd.)*
John in Virginia. Administration to the principal creditor, John Musgrave; the relict, Margaret Williams, renouncing. (Jan. 1714).

Williams, John, formerly of H.M. ship *Nightingale* but late of the privateer *Hornet* of New York, who died in hospital in France, bachelor. Probate to the mother, Ann Williams, widow. (Oct. 1758).

Williams, John, of Newport, Rhode Island, mariner of H.M. ships *Boreas* and *Defiance*. Administration with will to Thomas and William Maude, attornies for the relict, Mary Williams, in Newport. (Jan. 1775).

Williams, Jonathan, of West Chester City, widower. Administration to the nephews and next-of-kin, Robert and Joseph Griffiths. (Mar. 1783).

Williams, Joseph, formerly of New Street, Chelsea, Middlesex, but late of New York, carpenter. Administration to the relict, Mary Ann Williams. (Mar. 1842).

Williams, Margaretta Marian, formerly of Trinity Terrace, Southwark, Surrey, but late of Greenville, Bond County, Illinois, spinster. Probate to Rev. Clement Dawsonne Strong with similar powers reserved to Rev. Paul Hyman Sternchuss. (Oct. 1857).

Williams, Mary, relict of William Williams of West Florida, late of St. Pancras, Middlesex. Administration with will to the residual legatee, Ann, wife of Robert Arch; no executor having been named. (Feb. 1791).

Williams, Richard, of St. Katherine Creechurch, London, bachelor, (bound to Virginia). Probate to Walter Hawkins. (May 1653). Wi.

Williams, Richard, of Limehouse, Middlesex, who died in Virginia, widower. Administration to Susan Stock, aunt and guardian of the children, Richard, Anne, Mary and Stephen Williams, during their minority. (July 1655).

Williams, Richard, of Pensacola, West Florida, sergeant of the 35th Regiment of Foot, who died on H.M. ship *Integrity*. Administration to the relict, Margaret Hannah Williams. (Dec. 1765).

Williams, Samuel, of Finsbury Square, Middlesex, who died in Boston, North America, bachelor. Administration to the brother and next-of-kin, Francis Williams. (Dec. 1841).

Williams, Sarah, nee Sarah Jope, of Pittsburgh, Pennsylvania. Administration to George Cox, attorney for the husband, Rev. John R. Williams, in Pittsburgh. (June 1852).

Williams, Thomas, of Bermondsey, Surrey, who died on H.M. ship *Scarborough* in Carolina. Administration to the relict, Jane Williams, pending the production of a will. (Apr. 1727).

Williams, Thomas Charles, of New York City. Probate to the relict, Sarah Williams, and the brother, John Williams, with similar powers reserved to Samuel Shomacken. (Oct. 1784).

Williams, William, formerly of Wood Street, London, afterwards of New Orleans in Florida, but late of Bath, Somerset. Probate to the relict, Mary Williams, and to John Stephenson and John Miller. (Aug. 1790). Revoked and granted to John Stephenson and John Miller. (Nov. 1792).

Williamson, Richard, of St. Andrew Undershaft, London, citizen and merchant tailor of London, whose brother, Roger Williamson, was in Virginia. Probate to the relict, Mary Williamson. (Dec. 1646). Revoked on her death and administration granted to her sister, Mary Osbolston, during the minority of the niece, Sarah Williamson. (Sep. 1657). Sh.Wi.

Williamson, Richard, formerly of Covington, Kentucky, but late of Mormon Diggings, California. Administration to the relict, Bridget, now wife of Martin Molloy. (Jan. 1856).

Williamson, Thomas, seaman of H.M. ship *Carisfoot*, who died in Charles Town Hospital. Probate to the sister, Hannah, wife of John Wilson, with similar powers reserved to the sister, Ann Williamson, and to Martha Palfrey, spinster. (Dec. 1782).

Williamson, William, of Whitechapel, Middlesex, merchant, who made a bequest to William Welch, natural son of Susannah Welch, in Nansemond County, Virginia, widow. Probate to Robert Cary. (Feb. 1723). Wi.

Williamson, William, of Charles Town, South Carolina. Probate to Robert Halcrow. (Dec. 1770).

Willing, Charles, of Philadelphia. Probate to the relict, Ann Willing, and to Thomas Willing. (Jan. 1756).

Willing, James, of Bristol, soap boiler, whose brother was in Philadelphia. Probate to the brother, Richard Willing. (Dec. 1727).

Willing, James, of Haverford Township, Cleveland, Delaware County, Pennsylvania, bachelor. Administration with will to Walter Stirling, attorney for the brother, Thomas Willing, in Philadelphia; the executors, Richard Willing and Thomas Willing Francis, having died. (Sep. 1819).

Willing, Richard, of Delaware County, Pennsylvania. Administration with will to Walter Stirling, attorney for the surviving executor, Thomas Mayere. (June 1820).

Willington, James, of St. Giles Cripplegate, London, who died on the ship *Burdis Factor* in Virginia. Administration to the relict, Jane Willington. (Oct. 1691).

Willis, Ann Packer, formerly of Grovesend, Alverton, Gloucestershire, but late of Charleston, North America, spinster. Administration with will to the sister, Temperance Jane Willis; the executrix, Diana, wife of Richard Lubbock, renouncing. (Dec. 1808).

Willis, Benjamin Winthorne, formerly of Poole, Dorset, afterwards of Liverpool, Lancashire, but late of North America, merchant seaman, bachelor. Administration to James Revans, administrator of the sister, Martha Revans deceased; the mother, Martha Willis, and the sisters, Eliza, wife of William Dicker Stroud, and Susanna Durell Snock, wife of George Chappel Snock, having also died. (May 1849).

Willis, Eliza, of Santo Domingo. Administration to Anna, wife of James Furber, administratrix of the husband, Robert Willis deceased. (Nov. 1849 & Mar. 1850).

Willis, Francis, of East Greenwich, Kent, and Ware River, Virginia. Probate

Willis, *(contd.)* to William Willis. (Apr. 1691). Wa.

Willys, George, of Hartford, New England. Administration with will to the son, George Willys, during the absence of the relict, Mary Willys. (Feb. 1648). Sh.Wa.

Willis, Robert, formerly of Santo Domingo but late of Newark, New Jersey, widower. Administration to the aunt, Anna, wife of James Furber, guardian of the only child, Robert James Furber Willis, during his minority. (Nov. 1849). Revoked on the death of Robert J.F. Willis and granted to the said Anna Furber. (Mar. 1850).

Willis, Robert James Furber, of Philadelphia, bachelor. Administration to the aunt, Anna, wife of James Furber. (Mar. 1850).

Willison, Robert, formerly of South Carolina but late of St. Saviour, Southwark, Surrey, merchant. Probate by his solemn affirmation to George Oldner; Zaccheus Routh renouncing. (May 1729).

Willoughby, Stephen, of Virginia. Administration to the daughter, Anne Willoughby, attorney for the mother, Grissell Willoughby, during her absence. (July 1677).

Willoughby, Thomas, of Virginia, who died in All Hallows Barking, London. Administration to the nephew, Thomas Midleton, during the minority of the children, Thomas and Elizabeth Willoughby. (Apr. 1657).

Willoughby alias Willobey, Thomas, of the merchant ship *Prince Amelia*, who died on the Potuxon River, America, bachelor. Administration to the principal creditor, John Norwood. (Feb. 1721).

Willabee, William, of the merchant ship *Williamsburg*, who died in Virginia, bachelor. Administration to the sister, Elizabeth Willabee. (Aug. 1723).

Wills, Bartholomew, of New England, bachelor. Administration to the principal creditor, Nathaniel Yems. (Nov. 1688).

Wills, George, of New England, who died on H.M. ship *Dragon*. Administration to Alexander Wath, attorney for the relict, Mary Wills, in New England. (Jan. 1742).

Wills, John, of H.M. ship *Happy*, who died in South Carolina, bachelor. Administration to William Vaughan, attorney for the creditor, James Fletcher, in South Carolina. (June 1734).

Willys. *See* **Willis**.

Wilmer, Jonathan, of Baltimore, North America, widower. Administration to Richard Bell, administrator of the brother, Simon Wilmer deceased, and attorney for Elizabeth Graves Worrell in Chestertown, Maryland; the mother, Mary Wilmer, widow, having also died. (June 1833).

Wilmer, Lambert, of Kent County, North America, bachelor. Administration to Richard Bell, administrator of the brother, Simon Wilmer deceased, and attorney for Elizabeth Graves Worrell, widow, in Chestertown, Maryland; the mother, Mary Wilmer, widow, and the brother, Jonathan Wilmer, having also died. (June 1833).

Wilmer, Simon, of Kent County, North America. Administration to Richard Bell, attorney for the only child, Elizabeth Graves Worrell,

Wilmer, *(contd.)* widow, in Chesterborough, Maryland; the relict, Mary Wilmer, having died. (June 1833).

Wilmot, Henry, of New York, bachelor. Administration to the half-brother, George Wilmot; the mother, Mary Wilmot, widow, renouncing. (Jan. 1777).

Wilmshurst, John, of Charles Town, South Carolina. Probate to the daughter, Elizabeth, wife of John Dugleby. (July 1774).

Wilson, Alexander, formerly of New York City but late of Bombay, who died in the service of the East India Company's Batallion. Administration to the sister and only next-of-kin, Elizabeth, wife of James Boggs, in Stone Araben, New York. (Apr. 1788).

Wilson, Benjamin, of Baltimore, North America, bachelor without parent. Administration to the brother and next-of-kin, Charles Wilson. (May 1828).

Wilson, Daniel, of New York City, mason. Probate to the brother, Charles Thomas Wilson. (June 1849).

Wilson, James the younger, of Alexandria, Virginia. Administration to the creditor, James Wilson the elder; the relict, Elizabeth Wilson, and the children, James, Eliza, William, Maria, Ann, Malvina and Robert Wilson, having been cited but not having appeared. (Jan. 1807).

Wilson, John, of the merchant ship *Olive Branch*, who died in Virginia. Administration to the sister, Elizabeth Hilgrove, widow. (Jan. 1700).

Wilson, John, of South Carolina. Limited administration with will to Thomas Irving, attorney for the daughter, Catherine Martha Wilson. (Mar. 1792).

Wilson, Mary, of Laminburgh, New York, spinster. Administration to the father, John Christian Wilson. (Sep. 1852).

Wilson, Robert, of St. Mary Colechurch, London, whose brother, Richard Wilson, was in New England. Probate to the relict, Katherine Wilson. (Jan. 1640). Wa.

Wilson, Robert, who died in Virginia, bachelor. Administration with will to the mother, Katherine Jacob; no executor having been named. (June 1651). Sm

Wilson, Robert, of Wapping, Middlesex, who died on the ship *James and Elizabeth* in Virginia. Administration to the relict, Elizabeth Wilson. (June 1699).

Wilson, Samuel, of Ledbury, Herefordshire, who died in Virginia. Administration to the principal creditor, George Mason; the relict, Catherine Wilson, renouncing. (Apr. 1677).

Wilson, Samuel, of Nashville, Tennessee, bachelor. Administration to the brother, Richard Wilson; the mother, Jane Wilson, widow, having died. (Dec. 1835).

Wilson, Thomas, of Middlesex, commander of the ship *Charles*, late in the East Indies, whose will was written in Virginia. Probate to the relict, Ellinor Wilson. (Jan. 1655). Sh.

Wilson, Thomas the elder, formerly of London but late of Ryecroft, Rawmarsh, Yorkshire, whose cousin, Thomas Brownall, was in Rhode

Wilson, *(contd.)*
Island. Probate to the son, Thomas Wilson. (Feb. 1659). Wa.

Wilson, Thomas, of H.M. ship *Raisonable*, who died in Rhode Island. Probate to Samuel Farguson. (Jan. 1781).

Winch, Elizabeth, of All Hallows, London, spinster, (bound to Virginia). Probate to the brothers, Richard and John Winch. (May 1661). Wi.

Winch, William, of London, merchant, whose relict, Fanny Parke Winch, was the daughter of John Custis of Virginia. Probate to Francis William Massey with similar powers reserved to Samuel Loaswell, Thomas Brooks and William Hunt. (Feb. 1740). Wi.

Winchelsey, Alexander, of Limehouse, Middlesex, who had tobacco in Virginia. Probate to Thomas Ravenett. (May 1621). Wi.

Windeyer, Elizabeth, nee Elizabeth Willcox, of Muscatine, Iowa. Administration to the husband, Richard Cunningham Windeyer. (June 1856).

Winfield, Thomas, of Virginia. Probate to John Orton. (Mar. 1772).

Wingfield, Edward Maria, [former Governor of Virginia], formerly of Keyston, Huntingdonshire, but who died a prisoner in the Fleet. Administration to the relict, Dorothy Wingfield. (July 1661).

Winne. *See* **Wynne**.

Winniett, Charles, formerly of Lowestoft, Suffolk, but late of New York, who died at sea, bachelor. Administration to the son, Benjamin Winniett, executor of the mother, Elizabeth Winniett deceased. (Nov. 1804).

Winslow, Edward, of London, who made a bequest to the poor in New England. Probate to the son, Josias Winslow. (Oct. 1655). Wa.

Winslow, Hannah, of Rhode Island, spinster. Administration to the sister and next-of-kin, Elizabeth, wife of John Winslow. (Mar. 1797).

Winslow, Isaac, of New York City. Probate to the nephew, Isaac Winslow, with similar powers reserved to the nephews, Jonathan Clarke and Isaac Winslow Clarke. (Oct. 1780).

Winslow, John, of Hingham, Massachusetts, a reduced Captain of Colonel William Shirley's First Regiment of Foot. Administration to Elisha Hutchinson, attorney for the only children, Pelham Winslow and Isaac Winslow, now in Massachusetts or Nova Scotia; the relict renouncing. (June 1776).

Winslow, Joshua, of Boston, Massachusetts. Administration to the relict, Hannah Winslow. (Mar. 1781).

Winslow, Mary, of Boston, Masachusetts, widow. Administration to Jonathan Simpson, attorney for the brother, Jonathan Simpson the younger, in Cambridge, North America. (Sep. 1787).

Winter, John, of Charles Town, South Carolina, Lieutenant on half pay of the Royal Navy, bachelor. Administration to the father, Nathaniel Winter. (June 1781).

Winthrop, Stephen, of James Street, Westminster, Middlesex, whose father and mother were buried in Boston, New England. Probate to the relict, Judith Winthrop, and the brother-in-law, John Chamberlaine, with similar powers reserved to Thomas Plampyon. (Aug. 1658). Wa.

Wise, Edward, of Somerset, Pennsylvania, bachelor. Administration to the sister, Lucy Wise. (June 1853).

Wise, John, of Virginia. Probate to the mother, Anne Miller. (June 1685).

Wise, John, of New York, formerly of H.M. ship *Kingston* but who died on H.M. ship *Elizabeth*. Administration to William Bryant, attorney for the relict, Alice Wise, in New York. (Feb. 1749).

Withall, Samuel, of H.M. ship *Spyboat*, who died in Virginia. Administration to the relict, Jane Withall. (July 1701).

Withers, Hazard, of Oswego Fort, North America. Administration to the sister and next-of-kin, Sarah Williams, widow. (Nov. 1763).

Withers, Henry, of Virginia. Administration to the relict, Joane Withers. (Aug. 1658).

Wythers, Ralph, of Bishops Canning, Wiltshire, who died in Pennsylvania. Administration to John Hall, guardian of the only child, Jason Wythers, during his minority. (Apr. 1691).

Wolseley, Winifred. *See* **Mallett**.

Wood, Edward, of Steubenville, Jefferson County, Ohio. Administration with will to Mary Ann Wood, spinster, attorney for the relict, Susan Wood, in Steubenville. (Sep. 1855).

Wood, James, of Woolwich, Kent, who died in Maryland, bachelor. Probate to the mother, Mary, wife of Thomas Harrell. (Apr. 1750).

Wood, Juliana, of Philadelphia. Administration to Charlotte Howis, widow, attorney for the husband, William Burke Wood, in Philadelphia. (July 1837).

Wood, Richard, of Gloucester, whose kinswoman, Sarah Barnes, was in New England. Probate to the relict, Mary Wood. (Feb. 1652). *See* NGSQ 61/115.

Wood, Thomas, of Brookthorpe, Gloucestershire, who died in Maryland. Administration to the brother and next-of-kin, Rowland Wood. (Jan. 1712). Marked "pauper."

Wood, William, of H.M. ship *Nottingham*, widower. Administration to the daughter, Hannah, wife of John Bemond, in Virginia. (Jan. 1729).

Wood, William, of the merchant ship *Prince George*, who died in James Town, Virginia, bachelor. Administration to the aunt and next-of-kin, Mary Jemmison, widow. (Apr. 1770).

Wood, William, H.M. Consul in Baltimore, North America. Administration to Gabriel Wood the younger, attorney for the father, Gabriel Wood the elder, in Greenock, Scotland. (Aug. 1816).

Woodall, William, of H.M. ship *Beaver*, who died in Boston, New England, bachelor. Administration to the sister and next-of-kin, Olive, wife of James Parker. (Feb. 1772).

Woodbridge, Ruth, of Barbados, who died in Boston, New England, widow. Administration with will to Edward Clark Parish, attorney for Nathaniel Haggatt in Barbados. (Feb. 1750).

Woodbury, John, of New England, who died on the ship *Crown* at sea. Administration with will to Daniel Berry; no executor having been named. (Jan. 1673). Wa.

Woodgate, Elizabeth. *See* **Freed**.

Woodhead, Matthew, of Wapping, Middlesex, who died in New England, bachelor. Administration to the sister and next-of-kin, Anne, wife of John Hopkins. (Jan. 1720).

Woodhouse, Henry, of Linhaven, Norfolk County, Virginia. Probate to the son, Henry Woodhouse. (July 1688). Wa.Wi.

Woodney, James, formerly of Bath, Somerset, but late of New York City, mason, widower. Administration to the daughter, Sarah, wife of Joseph Phillips. (July 1820).

Woodrow, Joseph, of New York, bachelor. Administration to the maternal aunt, Sarah Taunton, widow. (Jan. 1706).

Woods, Joseph, formerly of Philadelphia but late of Washbrook, Suffolk. Probate to the father, John Woods, with similar powers reserved to the brother, John Woods. (July 1793).

Woodside, James, of Pemaquid, Massachusetts, late Lieutenant of Colonel Gooch's Regiment of Foot in the West Indies. Administration to Samuel Wragg, attorney for the relict, Jane Woodside, in Boston. (Apr. 1746).

Woodville, John, of Dominica, who died in Philadelphia. Probate to William Thornton, Henry Poole and Benjamin Eyre. (Apr. 1776).

Woodward, Elizabeth, of Hector, Tompkins County, New York, widow. Administration to the son, William Woodward. (Apr. 1849).

Woodward, John, of New York City. Probate to the son, John Woodward, with similar powers reserved to the son, Charles Woodward. (July 1850). Double probate to the son, Rev. Charles Woodward. (Sep. 1850).

Woodward, Samuel, of Cape Fear, Carolina. Administration to Christopher Nicholson, attorney for the nephew, Benjamin Woodward, in Kells, County Meath, Ireland. (Apr. 1751).

Wooldridge, Maria Henrietta, of St. Augustine, East Florida. Administration to Arthur Gordon, attorney for the husband, Thomas Wooldridge, in St. Augustine. (Apr. 1770).

Wormeley, Ralph Randolph, of Newport, Rhode Island, Rear Admiral in the Royal Navy. Administration to the relict, Caroline Wormeley. (Dec. 1852).

Wormington, John, formerly of Philadelphia but late of New York City. Administration to Benjamin John Johnson, attorney for the relict, Anna Wormington, in New York. (Jan. 1793).

Worth, Obed, of Nantucket, Massachusetts, master of the merchant ship *Brook Watson*. Administration to Andrew Worth, attorney for the relict, Janet Worth, in Nantucket. (Mar. 1816).

Worth, Shubael, of Nantucket, Massachusetts. Administration to Paul Pease, attorney for the relict, Anna Worth, in Natucket. (June 1806).

Worthington, Elizabeth, formerly Elizabeth Laugher, widow, formerly of Stourbridge, Worcestershire, afterwards of Hartford, Connecticut, but late of Altrincham, Cheshire. Administration with will to James Smith Hancox, son of the brother, James Hancox deceased; the executor, Joseph Hancox, and the husband, John Worthington, renouncing. (Nov. 1813).

Worthington, John, of Ann Arundell County, Maryland. Administration with will to James Russell, attorney for the sons, John and Charles Worthington, in Maryland. (June 1769).

Worthington, William, of Ann Arundell County, Maryland. Limited administration with will to Silvanus Grove of London, merchant, attorney for John Davis. (Sep. 1771).

Wortley, John, of Portsmouth, New England, bachelor. Administration to the nephew by a sister and next-of-kin, Peter Birkhead. (Dec. 1712).

Wotton, Anne, of Calvert County, Maryland, spinster. Administration to the mother, Susanna Wotton, widow. (Mar. 1698).

Wotton, Philip, of East Budleigh, Devon, whose daughter-in-law, Jane Bennett, was in New England. Probate to the relict, Joane Wotton. (Feb. 1663). Wa.

Wotton, Simon, of Calvert County, Maryland, who died in Jamaica. Probate to Thomas Wharton. (Dec. 1696).

Wotton, William, of Bristol, bachelor, whose will was made in Virginia. Administration with will to the sister, Mary Meredeth; no executor having been named. (May 1656). Sh.Wi.

Ragg, Andrew, of New York. Administration with will to the grandmother and next-of-kin, Anne Ragg, guardian of the daughter, Anna Ragg; the executor, James Gilchrist, having died. (Sep. 1783).

Wragg, Samuel, formerly of Holborn, Middlesex, but late of Charles Town, South Carolina. Probate to the son, William Wragg, and to Robert Henshaw. (Jan. 1750 & Jan. 1751). Revoked and limited administration with will and codicil granted to the daughters, Mary and Judith Wragg. (July 1754).

Wragg, William, of Charles Town, South Carolina, who died as a passenger on the merchant ship *Caesar*. Limited administration with will to George Curling of Whitechapel, Middlesex, attorney for the relict, Henrietta Wragg, in Charles Town. (Apr. 1779). Revoked and limited administration granted to George Curling as attorney for the sisters, Henrietta, wife of Rev. Milward Pogson, and Charlotte, wife of William Loughton Smith, in Charles Town. (Sep. 1807). Revoked on the death of George Curling and granted to Alexander Simpson as attorney for the sisters, Henrietta Pogson, Elizabeth Wragg and Charlotte Wragg Smith, widow. (July 1826).

Wraxall, Peter, of New York City, Captain of an Independent Company of New York. Probate to the relict, Elizabeth Wraxall. (Feb. 1762).

Wraxhall, William, of London, joiner, who died overseas (bound to Virginia). Probate to the relict, Anne Wraxhall. (June 1630). Sh.Wi.

Wright, Benjamin, of the merchant ship *Levite*, who died in Virginia. Administration with will to John Hunt, attorney for Robert Jones now at sea; no executor having been named. (Jan. 1707).

Wright, Elihu, of Glassenbury, Connecticut. Copy of will proved in Hartford, Connecticut, by Thomas Marley. (Dec. 1762). PROB 20/2060.

Wright, Sir James, formerly Governor of Georgia. Probate to the son, Alexander Wright, and to Archibald Hamilton and William Knox,

Wright, *(contd.)* with similar powers reserved to the son, Sir James Wright. (Apr. 1786). Double probate to Sir James Wright. (Aug. 1787). ALC.

Wright, John, of Maryland, bachelor. Administration to the brother, Thomas Wright. (Jan. 1703).

Wright, John, of St. James, Wasamtam, South Carolina, bachelor. Administration to the cousin german and next-of-kin, William Miles. (July 1791). Revoked on the production of a will and probate granted to the surviving executrix, Keating Simons. (July 1828).

Wright, John Joseph Thomas, formerly of Robleston Farm, Pembrokeshire, but late of New York City, who died at sea. Probate to the father, Joseph Wright. (Oct. 1855).

Wright, Mary, wife of Stephen Wright, formerly Mary Thorogood, formerly Mary Trevethan, of Virginia. Administration to Daniel Highmore, attorney for the son, Stephen Wright, in Virginia. (Aug. 1754).

Wright, Moses, of Boston, New England, who died on H.M. ship *Victory*. Probate to the sister, Ann, wife of ——- Dougless alias Duglass. (Nov. 1744).

Wright, Peter, of New Orleans, Lieutenant in the Royal Engineers Corps, bachelor. Administration with will to the mother, Ann Wright, widow. (Feb. 1816). Revoked on her death and granted to the sister, Martha Wright; James Bogue Lobb, sole excutor of the said Ann Wright deceased, renouncing. (Feb. 1816).

Wright, William, of Boston, New England, who died on H.M. ship *Mermaid*, bachelor. Administration to the father, Henry Wright. (Feb. 1695).

Wright, William, of Annapolis Royal. Probate to the relict, Sarah Wright. (Feb. 1719).

Wrisburg, Daniel, Lieutenant on half pay of the 47th Regiment of Foot, who died in New Jersey, bachelor. Administration to the sister, Johanna Lucia Henriette, wife of Michael Christop Hinrickson. (July 1778).

Wyatt, Thomas, of Boreham, Essex, who died in Maryland. Probate by his solemn affirmation to the brother, Samuel Wyatt. (Nov. 1756).

Wyett, Davey, of St. Gregory Stoke, Somerset, who died in Carolina, bachelor. Probate to the brother, John Wyett. (May 1685).

Wyborne, Thomas, of New England, surgeon, who died at sea, bachelor. Probate to Nathaniel Wickham. (Oct. 1691).

Wyld, Daniel, of Brewerton, York County, Virginia. Probate to Margaret, wife of John Martin, with similar powers reserved to the said John Martin. (Oct. 1676). Revoked on their death and administration granted to their only child, Margaret Martin. (Dec. 1691). Wa.

Wylly, Margaret, of St. Simon's Island, Georgia, widow. Limited administration with will to Charles Robert Simpson, attorney for the son, Alexander William Wylly, and for James Hamilton Couper, in Georgia. (Oct. 1852).

Winne, John, of the merchant ship *Nancy*, who died in Virginia, bachelor. Administration to the brother, William Winne; the mother, Rebecca, wife of James Ryall, renouncing. (Oct. 1753).

Wyn, Owen, [of Hertfordshire], adventurer to Virginia. Probate to Richard

Wyn, *(contd.)*
Hughes. (May 1611). Wi.

Wynne, Robert, of Jordans, Charles City, Virginia. Administration with will to Thomas Crane, attorney for the relict, Mary Wynne, in Virginia. (Aug. 1678).

Wyron, John, of Reading, Berkshire, whose daughter, Grace, wife of William Rackstraw, was in Pennsylvania. Probate to Thomas Smith with similar powers reserved to the relict, Elizabeth Wyron, and the daughter, Mary Moore. (May 1688).

Wythers. *See* **Withers**.

X

Ximenez alias Jimenez, Jose, of Baton Rouge, Louisiana. Administration with will to Jose Ventura de Aquirre Solarte and Cristobal de Murrieta, attornies for Diego Dias in Monte Morelos, Mexico. (June 1832).

Y

Yale, Thomas, of London, merchant, who died in Grone, Denbighshire, and whose uncle, Thomas Yale, was in New England. Administration with will to John Evans and Robert Harbin; no executor having been named. (Jan. 1698).

Yallowley, Joshua, formerly of East Florida but late of New Providence, Bahamas, bachelor. Administration to John Fairlamb, attorney for the mother, Elizabeth Yallowley, in Hexham, Northumberland. (Mar. 1787).

Yardley, Edward, of Virginia, bachelor. Administration to the brother and principal creditor, Thomas Yardley. (Nov. 1676).

Yeardley, Sir George, who died in Virginia. Administration to the brother, Ralph Yeardley, during the absence overseas of the relict, Temperance Yeardley. (Mar. 1629). Sh.Wa.

Yarnold, Benjamin, of Augusta, Georgia, widower. Administration to Ann Faver, widow, administratrix of the only child, Harriot, wife of James Faver, deceased. (July 1847).

Yeamans, William, of St. Giles in the Fields, Middlesex, whose brother,

Yeamans, *(contd.)*
Christopher Yeamans, was in New York. Probate to the relict, Elizabeth Yeamans. (May 1687). Wa.

Yeardley. *See* **Yardley**.

Yeaveley, Thomas, surgeon of the 70th Regiment of Foot, who died in New York, bachelor. Administration to the sister, Susanna Yeaveley. (Apr. 1767).

Yeo, Henry, of Gun Alley, Wapping, Middlesex, who died in Virginia. Administration to the relict, Hannah Yeo. (Aug. 1659).

Yesline, Jonas, of H.M. ship *Seaford*, bachelor. Administration with will to Margaret, wife of John Cudlipp, on H.M. ship *Blandford* in South Carolina, attorney for Mary Scott, widow. (Oct. 1723).

Yonge. *See* **Young**.

Yorston, David, formerly of Well Alley, St. George, Middlesex, but late of Charleston, North America. Administration to the niece and only next-of-kin, Christiana Enson. (May 1791).

Youle, George, carpenter of the merchant ship *Concord* in the transport service at New York. Administration to the sister, Katherine Youle. (Mar. 1778).

Young, Alexander, of Mobile, Alabama, widower. Limited administration to George Young of Pimlico, Middlesex, attorney pending the Chancery suit of Young v. Young. (Dec. 1828). *See* NGSQ 69/279.

Younge, Anthony, of St. Dunstan in the East, London, who died overseas having goods in Virginia. Probate to John Gace with similar powers reserved to the brother, William Younge. (Apr. 1636). Wi.

Young, Benjamin, of Baltimore, Maryland, widower. Administration to the niece by a sister, Henrietta Montgomerie, spinster; the sisters, Ann, wife of James Calder, Laetitia, wife of Stead Lowe, and Mary Young, and the half-brother, Motley Young, having died. (May 1805).

Young, Charlotte, nee Charlotte Hyde, of Baltimore, Maryland. Administration to Henrietta Montgomerie, the niece and administratrix of the husband, Benjamin Young deceased; the mother, Hon. Jane Hyde, having died. (May 1805).

Young, Edward, of the merchant ship *Daniel and Anna*, who died in Maryland, bachelor. Probate to William Speven with similar powers reserved to his wife, Lydia Speven. (July 1734).

Young, Francis, of Stepney, Middlesex, who died in Virginia. Administration to the relict, Elizabeth Young. (July 1678).

Young, George, formerly of Copthall Court, London, but late of New York, merchant. Probate to the brother, John Young, the nephew, James Young, and to Margaret Lyell, widow, with similar powers reserved to the nephew, John Young the younger. (Sep. 1827). *See* NGSQ 69/279.

Young, Henry Blackburn, of Richmond, Virginia, bachelor. Administration to the brother, James Young. (Mar. 1811).

Young, Nathaniel, of Carolina. Probate to Mary Dearing, widow. (Apr. 1706).

Yonge, Philip, formerly Surveyor-General of Georgia, who died in

Yonge, *(contd.)*
Savannah. Administration to William Yonge, attorney for the relict, Christian, now wife of James Fleming, in Wilmington, North Carolina. (Sep. 1793).

Young, Richard, of St. Margaret Steyning, London, who had lands in Virginia. Probate to the son, John Young. (Nov. 1665). Wi.

Young, Samuel, of the merchant ship *Quare*, who died in Virginia. Administration to the relict, Jane Young. (Aug. 1718).

Young, Stephen, of the merchant ship *Dartmouth*, bachelor. Administration to Priscilla, wife and attorney of the brother and next-of-kin, Richard Young, in New England. (Dec. 1714). Marked "pauper."

Young, Theophilus, Lieutenant of the 45th Regiment of Foot, who died in Louisburgh. Probate to the father, Thomas Young. (Dec. 1758).

Younge, William, of Kingsessing, Pennsylvania, botanist to the King. Probate to the relict, Martha Younge, with similar powers reserved to John Leech and Jacob Holman. (Nov. 1787). ALC.

Younie, James, formerly of Theobalds Road, St. George the Martyr, Middlesex, but late of Freedom, Dutchess County, New York. Limited probate to Joshua Needham. (Mar. 1829).

Z

Zaines, John, of Virginia, widower. Administration to the brother, Thomas Zaines. (Sep. 1660).

Zouch, Sir John, who died in Virginia. Administration with will to the son, John Zouch; the executors, Sir Thomas Hutchinson and Gilbert Ward, renouncing. (Dec. 1639). Sh.Wi.

Index of Names

The inclusion of an asterisk after a page number indicates that the name occurs more than once on that page.

Index of Ships

Index of Places

This Index includes place names and locations as described in the original documents: it omits the metropolitan cities of London and New York as well as American colonies and States unless particular localities are mentioned. The inclusion of an asterisk after a page number indicates that the name occurs more than once on that page.

www.ingramcontent.com/pod-product-compliance
Lightning Source LLC
Chambersburg PA
CBHW060131280326
41932CB00012B/1484